The Trickster and the Paranormal

The Trickster
and the Paranormal

George P. Hansen

Copyright 2001 by George P. Hansen.

Library of Congress Number: 2001116933
ISBN#:   Hardcover   1-4010-0081-9
            Softcover   1-4010-0082-7

All rights reserved. No part of this book may be reproduced or transmitted in any form or by any means, electronic or mechanical, including photocopying, recording, or by any information storage and retrieval system, without permission in writing from the copyright owner.

Permission to use material from the following sources is gratefully acknowledged:

Gods in Everyman: A New Psychology of Men's Lives and Loves by Jean Shinoda Bolen, San Francisco: Harper & Row, 1989.

Reprinted with permission from Victor Turner. *The Ritual Process: Structure and Anti-Structure.* (New York: Aldine de Gruyter) Copyright © 1969 by Victor W. Turner, Renewed 1997 by Edith Turner."

This book was printed in the United States of America.

To order additional copies of this book, contact:
Xlibris Corporation
1-888-795-4274
www.Xlibris.com
Orders@Xlibris.com

Contents

Acknowledgements 11
Preface 14
Chapter 1. Introduction 19

Part 1

Overview 33
2. An Overview of Tricksters
    From Mythology, Folklore, and Elsewhere 35
3. Ernest Hartmann's Mental Boundaries 48
4. Victor Turner's Concept of Anti-structure 52

Part 2

Overview 73
5. Mysticism, Holy Madness, and Fools for God 75
6. Shamanism and Its Sham 86

Part 3

Overview 95
7. Michael Winkelman on Magico-religious Practitioners 97
8. Max Weber, Charisma, and the
    Disenchantment of the World 102
9. Cultural Change and the Paranormal 110

Part 4

Overview 117
10. Prominent "Psychics" 119
11. Conjurors and the Paranormal 130
12. CSICOP and the Debunkers 148
13. Small Groups and the Paranormal 162
14. Alternative Religions and Psi 171
15. Institutions and the Paranormal 178
16. Anti-structure and the History of Psychical Research 191
17. Unbounded Conditions 210

18. Government Disinformation 219
19. Hoaxes and the Paranormal 247

Part 5

Overview 273
20. Reflexivity and the Trickster 277
21. Laboratory Research on Psi 309
22. Totemism and the Primitive Mind 344
23. Literary Criticism, Meaning, and the Trickster 368

Part 6

Overview 393
24. The Imagination 395
25. Paranoia 413
26. Conclusions 422

Endnotes 433
References 481
Index 535

To the Memory

of

W. E. Cox

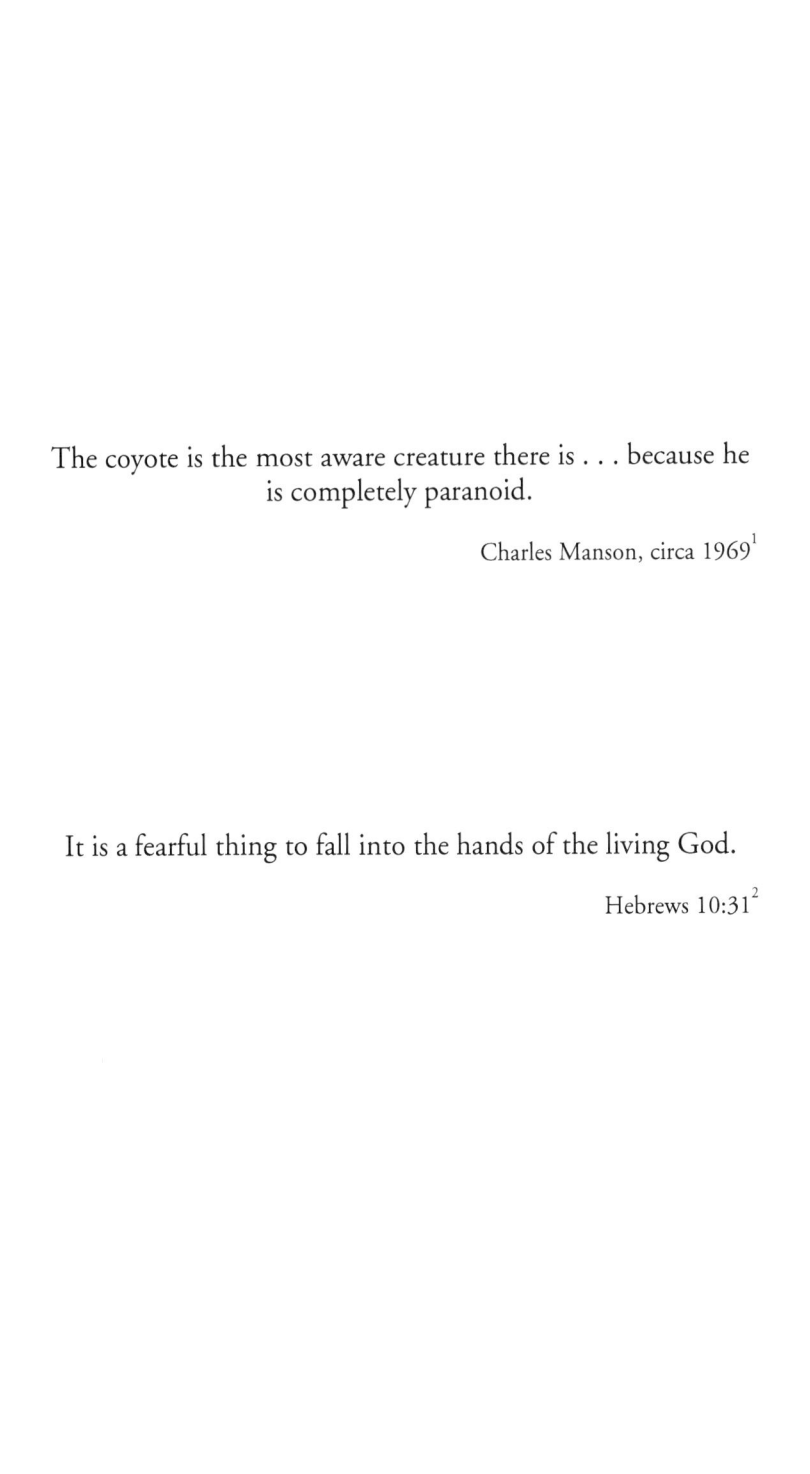

The coyote is the most aware creature there is . . . because he is completely paranoid.

Charles Manson, circa 1969[1]

It is a fearful thing to fall into the hands of the living God.

Hebrews 10:31[2]

ACKNOWLEDGEMENTS

Many people are due thanks for influencing me through their lives, writings, or both. Most of them have had long and direct involvement in the paranormal. Its personalities, concepts, experiences, and controversies form an integral part of their lives.

Dennis Stillings pointed out many aspects of psi that everyone else wanted to ignore, and our discussion of the trickster and Jungian psychology was the single most important factor that lead me to prepare this book. The Reverend Canon William V. Rauscher allowed me frequent use of his library on magic and psychical research; without his help in numerous ways, this volume would not have been written. Magician-sociologist Marcello Truzzi has been a most valuable source of information on magic and the paranormal for me for over 20 years, continuously and longer than anyone else.

John Keel, premier Fortean author, investigator, and organizer of the New York Fortean Society arranged many meetings with a rich variety of perspectives. Participants included: writers Rosemary Guiley, Patrick Huyghe, and Antonio Huneeus; professors Michael Grosso, Kenneth Ring, and Peter Rojcewicz; James W. Moseley editor of the renowned *Saucer Smear*, psychic Ingo Swann who trained remote viewers for U.S. intelligence agencies, Ben Robinson, Andrei Apostol, Ronald Rosenblatt, Michael Lindner, Doug Skinner, William P. La-Parl, Lois Horowitz, Clarence Robbins, Sharon Jarvis, and Sandra Martin. John Keel and Ben Robinson are magicians as well as Forteans, and the examples of their lives, and many discussions with them, have provided much insight.

For years Pat Marcattilio has run a wonderfully diverse UFO study group that has welcomed everyone from rabid secular humanist debunkers, witchcraft high priestesses, those who have had sex with ET aliens in the presence of voyeuristic seven-foot tall praying mantises, to those who regularly report their activities to the CIA. Contributors to the gatherings have included Joseph Stefula, Richard Butler, Vincent Creevy, Art Wagner, Mindy Gerber, Scott Forrest, Hank and Mary Ann Brown, Marge and Roger Testrake, Chelsea Flor, Bob and Frances Eure, Graham Bethune, Pat Stein, John and Paul Nahay, Brian Loomis, Shelby Shellenberger, CIA asset (or liability) Dan T. Smith, Robert Durant, Michael Scott Smith, Alice Haggerty, George Wolkind, Paula Fahsbenner, Maurice Hathaway, Curtis Cooperman, Art Sielicki, Eva Palfalvi, William Muravsky, George Filer, Frank Chille, Richard Benstead, John Pawson, David Lessner, Tom Briggs, George Reynolds, Anna Hayes, Pat Blackwell, Robert Oliveri, Riley Martin, and Alex Fedorov. Tom Benson deserves special mention for many discussions and my use of his extensive UFO library. Mindy Gerber's hospitality provided many occasions for discussions relevant to this book.

David Hufford conducted a discussion group at the Department of Folklore and Folklife at the University of Pennsylvania and provided an early opportunity to present some of my ideas. The comments of Xan Griswold in that group were especially helpful.

I have also benefited from insightful comments of mentalists Max Maven and Ford Kross. Sociologist James McClenon has engaged me in extended discussions on psi in groups. Skeptics Philip J. Klass and Martin Gardner have provided important information.

A number of friends and colleagues have graciously commented on drafts of chapters. These include Ben Robinson, David Ray Griffin, An Trotter, Paul Hansen, Robert Durant, Joanne D. S. McMahon, William P. LaParl, James McClenon, Scott Forrest, Nelson Pacheco, Marcello Truzzi, Wayne Hardy, Simon Pettet, Elliott Madison, Michael Scott Smith, Art Wagner, Maureen Gibbons, and Martin Ebon.

Thanks also go to Joanne D. S. McMahon, William P. LaParl, Martin Kottmeyer, T. Scott Crain, Larry Bryant, Tommy Blann, Nelson Pacheco, Ed Komarek, Bill Ellis, William Clements, Richard Trott, Martin Ebon, and Rhea White for providing materials. The staffs of the Hickory Corner Library and the interlibrary loan department of the Mercer County Library system deserve special thanks for their rapid processing of innumerable interlibrary loan requests over a period of years.

Martin Ebon helped support publication of this book. The efforts of C.G., George Livanos, Maurine Christopher, and David Vine also contributed. The Parapsychology Foundation granted me the D. Scott Rogo award. Karl Petry deserves thanks for providing photographs and Joanne D. S. McMahon for helping with the cover.

In the dark world of government activity in the paranormal, three investigators merit commendation: Martin Cannon, researcher on mind control, and Armen Victorian and W. Todd Zechel, who have made superb use of the Freedom of Information Act.

In their own unique ways, Linda Napolitano, James Randi, Richard C. Doty, and John Thomas Richards have contributed to my understanding of the trickster.

Countless intellectual predecessors have influenced my thinking. The most immediately important are William Braud, Barbara Babcock, and Edmund Leach. Their works deserve greater notice.

Of course none of the above bears any responsibility for my errors, omissions, or misrepresentations. I expect that all of them will grit their teeth at something or other I say in these pages. In fact, I will be disappointed if they don't.

PREFACE

This book was begun with the idea of addressing some fundamental problems in parapsychology, but the scope quickly grew beyond that. Nevertheless, psychic phenomena and parapsychology are central, and because the findings of that field are not well known beyond a small number of researchers it seems wise to include a brief orientation, explain my background, and give some guidance to the reader. The issues covered in this volume are much broader than those typically discussed by parapsychologists, and even readers familiar with their work may find this preface helpful.

Parapsychology is the study of two phenomena, extrasensory perception (ESP) and psychokinesis (PK). ESP is simply the obtaining of information about the external world without the use of any known physical process; correspondingly, PK is the influencing of the external world without using any known physical method.

The term *psychical research* is an older name for parapsychology, and essentially the two are synonymous. Some people prefer to use parapsychology to designate only laboratory research and use psychical research to refer to work outside the lab. General usage does not make that distinction, and neither will I.

For conceptual purposes, ESP is sometimes divided into telepathy (mind to mind communication), clairvoyance (mind's direct perception of an object or event) and precognition (foreseeing the future). PK is divided into micro and macro. Micro-PK refers to events that require statistics to determine whether PK occurred (for instance, someone trying to influence the fall of dice). Poltergeist effects are examples of macro-PK; statistics are not used to determine if such events happen. Collectively, ESP and PK are referred to as psychic phenomena or psi. The subdivisions have been useful for labeling phenomena, but they are not explanations, and it is not clear if the apparently different types of psi involve fundamentally different processes.

Branches of parapsychology address the issue of survival of bodily death by investigating mediumship, near-death experiences, reincarnation, and ghosts. Those phenomena can involve ESP. For instance, mediums have accurately described deceased relatives of clients, even though the mediums knew nothing of the relatives. Someone visiting a home may see a ghost, describe it, and the hosts may recognize the description as fitting a previous occupant. Apparitions are occasionally accompanied by the movement of objects or temperature changes; these are physical effects. Such phenomena are often attributed to deceased entities, but they can be subsumed under the categories of ESP and PK.

Two chapters in this book focus on parapsychology. "Anti-Structure and the History of Psychical Research" gives a sociological and historical overview of the field. "Laboratory Research on Psi" discusses a number of technical matters and theories. The best recent popular book summarizing psi research is *Parapsychology: The Controversial Science* (1991) by Richard Broughton, an active researcher and former Director of the Institute for Parapsychology in Durham, North Carolina.

Parapsychology is a tiny field; in the U.S. fewer than 50 people could be said to be professionally conversant with the scientific findings. Only two laboratories in the U.S. employ more than two full-time researchers, and there are probably no more than 10 full-time professional parapsychologists in the U.S. who conduct research and report it in refereed journals. In addition, a few professors and independent scholars conduct research. Despite the small size, there has been more than a century of continuous, professional, published research on these topics. Two journals have been in publication for more than 60 years, and one for more than a hundred. The highest quality journal is the *Journal of Parapsychology*. Research and theories are summarized in the technical series *Advances in Parapsychological Research* edited by Stanley Krippner (the latest is Volume 8, 1997). Another useful, and superbly documented, book is *The Future of the Body* (1992) by Michael Murphy.

Psi appears to violate conventional scientific expectations of what is possible, and that makes it controversial. Further, it sometimes manifests dramatically in seemingly bizarre circumstances such as with spirit mediums in trance, healers engaging in odd rituals, and saints enduring ascetic practices. Yet according to a number of surveys, over 50% of adults in the U.S. have reported paranormal experiences. Psi is surprisingly common.

Several issues are addressed in this book. One is the ongoing controversy over psi's existence—despite extensive research and a massive amount of published data, the scientific debate has continued for over a hundred years. Another issue concerns the unexpected consequences of direct attempts to elicit psi; these are rarely recognized. A third issue is the paranormal's relationship with institutions.

As for my own background, I was employed full-time in laboratory-based parapsychology for eight years, three at the Institute for Parapsychology in Durham, North Carolina and five at Psychophysical Research Laboratories in Princeton, New Jersey. I have been personally involved with a number of psychic, UFO, and occult subcultures, and I helped start a skeptics group. Compared with other laboratory researchers, I have been relatively active with such groups. Friends of mine practice ritual magic; others are professional mediums; a number tell me that aliens have abducted them, and still others admit to me privately that they are phony psychics.

I hope that there will be diverse readers of this book, including many from non-academic backgrounds. Some may need to be warned that it is not necessary to read from front to back, and the order of presentation certainly does not reflect the origin and development of my ideas. I encourage readers to skip around, perhaps starting with a topic of personal interest.

The peculiarities of psychical research led me to read in anthropology, folklore, sociology, and literary criticism, and I drew upon them in order to understand parapsychological phenomena. Those disciplines have almost completely ignored the reality of the paranormal, and I will explain why.

My central thesis is that psychic phenomena are associated with processes of destructuring. If one keeps this rather abstract formulation in mind, the assortment of seemingly disjointed examples will make a bit more sense. I have included a variety of specific instances in order to demonstrate the generality and consequences of the central idea.

There are six major sections and I will give a brief idea of their coverage.

Part 1 is introductory. The third chapter of Part 1, on Victor Turner's ideas, defines terms that will probably be unfamiliar to those outside anthropology (i.e., anti-structure, liminality, and communitas). It is only necessary to read the first few pages of that chapter to get an initial grasp of the basic ideas.

Part 2 covers shamans and mystics, characters who had strong contact with the supernatural realm but in times that largely pre-date our modern world. Some of these people are truly exotic, and they are striking examples of important, but often neglected, aspects of human existence.

Part 3 discusses the supernatural's relation to culture. Theories from sociology and anthropology explain how recurrent historical patterns continue to manifest in the modern world. The paranormal is frequently marginalized, and this is an important clue to the nature of psi.

Part 4 discusses the material with which I am most familiar; some of it is based on my years of professional work in parapsychology. It presents the data that long puzzled me. The bulk of the material concerns the last few decades, and most of the rest comes from the twentieth century. The modern world is the focus. This section is likely to be the most relevant to readers currently involved with the paranormal.

Part 5 is by far the most theoretical and abstract. Primary topics include reflexivity, parapsychology, totemism and the primitive mind, and literary theory. This Part grapples with paradox, the irrational, and limits of logic. French structuralism and deconstructionism help explain the links among these diverse topics.

Part 6 deals with the imagination, deception, and paranoia, and how they are illuminated by the trickster.

CHAPTER 1

Introduction

This book is about foretelling the future, the occult, magic, telepathy, mind over matter, miracles, power of prayer, UFOs, Bigfoot, clairvoyance, angels, demons, psychokinesis, and spirits of the dead. These all interact with the physical world. This book explains why they are problematical for science.

These topics provoke ambivalent feelings. They hold a strange place in our culture.

Some examples—

- Fortune-telling is often associated with carnivals, gypsies, and fraud. Yet many saints have had the gifts of prophecy and of knowing hearts. Do fraud and sainthood have something in common?
- Why did the teacher of the U.S. government's psychic spies become interested in sightings of the Blessed Virgin Mary?
- The terms "magic" and "conjuring" have two meanings—use of occult powers, and the performance of tricks. The same words are used for both. Why?
- The supernatural features in the world's greatest literature. All major religions have stories of miracles. Over half of the U.S. adult population has had paranormal experiences. Despite all this, there are no university departments of parapsychology. In fact as I write, I can identify only two laboratories in the U.S. devoted to parapsychology that employ two or more full-time scientists who publish in peer-reviewed scientific journals. Why so little research?

- Mediums of dubious reputation have been reported to levitate, but so have religious mystics. What is the connection?
- Innumerable movies have been made about extraterrestrial aliens, some grossing hundreds of millions of dollars. Yet the Mutual UFO Network (MUFON), the largest U.S. organization focused on UFO research, was still headquartered in the home of its founder, 30 years after it began. Why?
- The elite media give the paranormal little serious coverage. The tabloids often put it on the front page. Why?
- In universities one can study literature of the supernatural. Academic psychologists and sociologists willingly investigate belief in the paranormal. However, to attempt direct encounter with the supernatural, or to try eliciting paranormal phenomena in order to observe them directly, brings opposition and hostility. In this scientific age, why isn't such rational inquiry welcomed?
- Why did so many of the U.S. government's psychic spies become interested in UFOs?
- Funding for scientific investigation of the paranormal has come almost entirely from wealthy individuals. Virtually no large philanthropic organizations or government bureaucracies have provided substantial, long-term support for the research. The only exceptions are the intelligence agencies—the only section of government formally allowed to use deception. Why does the money come from these sources?
- Today some liberal Christian Protestant denominations downplay miracles, seeing them as embarrassments, relics from a primitive, superstitious past. Likewise, they view prayer as having only psychological benefits for those who pray, but nothing more. What caused this dramatic shift in beliefs?
- Conservatives still see miracles and answers to prayer as God's intervention in the world. Are these beliefs intellectually backward, superstitious, delusional, and maladapted to the modern world? The conservative denominations are flourishing while the liberal churches decline. Why?

The above points are known to anyone with a moderate familiarity with the paranormal. The questions prove that there is something very odd about it, and similar queries could be generated endlessly. The controversies have swirled for hundreds, even thousands, of years, and they show no sign of being resolved any time soon.

Many of the above questions seem totally unrelated, or at best, only vaguely so. What do the funding sources for psi research have in common with liberal churches downplaying miracles? What is the connection between the MUFON headquarters and mysticism? Why discuss tabloids' front pages along with controversies within religion? These questions seem to be a random hodgepodge, unsuited for any single book or reasonable discussion. It appears preposterous to lump them together. They are out of place, and I will show that this is indeed the nature of the phenomena. They do not fit in our logical world.

The topics of this book resist simple categorization, and there is no way to give a succinct, comprehensive overview. I suspect that virtually all readers will find that substantial portions of the book cover material unfamiliar to them. As such, this introduction will only touch on a few ideas that will give some orientation. Many of the names, terms, and ideas in this introduction are mentioned only briefly and for the benefit of those already knowledgeable in specialized areas. I will fully explain them in later chapters.

In times past, the word "supernatural" designated the phenomena of interest here. That term hints at something ominous, dangerous, and unsettling. More recently the word "paranormal" came into vogue. It suggests that the phenomena are more mundane, odd perhaps, but not worrisome for most people. In the last two decades, a few scientists have begun referring to them as "anomalous," indicating that they are merely minor curiosities, without threat or of much immediate import. The new labeling makes the topic slightly more acceptable in academe, and the term "anomalous" is not incorrect, because the phenomena do not fit within mainstream scientific theories. However, such labeling divorces the phenomena of today from their historical predecessors, and previous knowledge about them is disregarded. In earlier cultures, the supernatural was known to be dangerous and was surrounded by taboos. Today's scientists have no comprehension why, and with their naive terminology, they become vulnerable to the phenomena.

I will use the terms paranormal and supernatural interchangeably. Dictionaries are clear that the two words refer to the same phenomena. I will sometimes use the terms together, although that is redundant. But I wish to emphasize the paranormal's frequent association with religion.

The primary data of this book concern side effects of using psychic abilities and engaging supernatural phenomena. Those effects can be discovered by analyzing the social milieu around the phenomena. Of particular interest are the repercussions to groups and institutions, including families, academe, governments, science, religion, and industry. There is a pattern, and generally the phenomena either provoke or accompany some kind of destructuring—a concept discussed at length in this book. For instance, the phenomena do not flourish within stable institutions, and endless examples illustrate this. Fortunately, two theoretical perspectives are already developed that connect the supernatural to ideas about social order and structure. The first is Victor Turner's work on liminality and anti-structure. The second is Max Weber's theory of rationalization. Both have profound implications for understanding psychic phenomena.

Some of the theoretical models presented here are formulated quite abstractly, and they address psi in relation to the concepts of category, classification, representation, and reflexivity. These are issues important in semiotics, French structuralism, and literary theory, but I am not aware of any prior significant attempt to integrate parapsychology with these topics. The matters concern fundamental limits of logic, rationality, and science. Parapsychology's critics have long decried psi as irrational and have made an important contribution in doing so. The critics are partly right; psi *is* irrational, but it is also real.

The central theme developed in this book is that psi, the paranormal, and the supernatural are fundamentally linked to destructuring, change, transition, disorder, marginality, the ephemeral, fluidity, ambiguity, and blurring of boundaries. In contrast, the phenomena are repressed or excluded with order, structure, routine, stasis, regularity, precision, rigidity, and clear demarcation. I hesitate to offer this very general statement because, by itself, it will almost certainly be misinterpreted; much of the book is devoted to explaining it. I will present some brief examples here.

When entire cultures undergo profound change, there is often an upsurge of interest in the paranormal. During the breakup of the former U.S.S.R. there was an explosion of paranormal activity throughout eastern Europe. Healers and psychics featured prominently in the media. This should not have been a surprise because anthropologists have shown that the supernatural has figured in thousands of cultural revitalization movements.

Numerous mystics have displayed extraordinary paranormal powers, but many of them were outsiders, marginal characters whose lives were exceedingly odd. St. Francis of Assisi performed many miracles, but he was mistrusted by church authorities and caused them many headaches.

Groups that attempt to use paranormal abilities, such as those in modern-day witchcraft and spiritualism, typically have a transitory, ephemeral existence. The few that manage some measure of institutionalizing (with buildings and paid staff) become marginalized, and often are accused of fraud and deception. Likewise psychical research organizations have always had a tenuous existence, and parapsychology has never been truly integrated into the academic establishment.

Magicians (performers of magic tricks) have played central roles in paranormal controversies, not only recently, but for hundreds of years. Magicians on both sides of the dispute have faked psychic phenomena, thereby contributing to the ambiguity surrounding them.

Skeptics understand that frauds and hoaxes plague the paranormal, but parapsychologists naively consider them only a minor problem. Parapsychologists have amassed overwhelming evidence for the reality of psi; skeptics ignore it and even deny that such evidence exists.

Many aspects of the paranormal (e.g., ghosts, UFO abductions, Bigfoot) have temporarily captured intense popular interest, but that has never been translated into financially viable, stable institutions that directly elicit or engage the phenomena. Instead the researchers use their own funds and are given no support from institutions.

In contrast, science has uninhibitedly ventured into virtually all other areas once considered taboo. The study of sexuality, in all its forms, is established in universities and medical schools. Sizeable industries and well-funded research labs are organized around cloning, artificial insemination, and genetic manipulation, despite ethical qualms. The lowly ghost researcher receives only sneers.

Many religions display an ambivalent, wary attitude toward supernatural phenomena. The 1994 *Catechism of the Catholic Church* shows this clearly. It acknowledges that "God can reveal the future to his prophets or to other saints," but in the very next paragraph it states that "interpretation of omens and lots, the phenomena of clairvoyance, and recourse to mediums . . . contradict the honor, respect, and loving fear that we owe to God alone." The following paragraph says "All practices of *magic* or *sorcery*, by which one attempts to tame occult powers . . . even if this were for the sake of restoring health—are gravely contrary to the virtue of religion."[1] Catholicism is not alone in these views, and many other diverse religious and spiritual traditions also acknowledge the existence of such phenomena but warn against seeking that power.

In short, the paranormal and supernatural are ambiguous and marginal in virtually all ways: socially, intellectually, academically, religiously, scientifically, and conceptually. They don't fit in the rational world.

Some may see no pattern to the above examples; they do appear chaotic. But there is a pattern, and it has enormous implications. The theories of anti-structure and rationalization, which will be described later, provide remarkable insight.

One of the implications of the pattern is that there are subtle but pervasive pressures that conspire to keep the paranormal marginalized and scientific investigation at a minimum. This does not require a consciously organized human conspiracy. It is a direct property of the phenomena. Psi interacts with our physical world, with our thoughts, and with our social institutions. Even contemplating certain ideas has consequences. The phenomena are not to be tamed by mere logic and rationality, and attempts to do so are doomed to failure. These notions are undoubtedly anathema to my scientific colleagues in parapsychology. To their chagrin, I will demonstrate that deception and the irrational are keys to understanding psi.

To give some additional orientation, it may help to briefly mention some people whose work I've drawn upon. Psychiatrist Ernest Hartmann is known for his research on mental boundaries. I found many commonalities between his concept of thin boundaries and the Greek trickster Hermes, whose personality has been admirably described by Jean Bolen, a psychiatrist with a Jungian orientation.

In anthropology, Michael Winkelman studied statuses of magico-religious practitioners in conjunction with societal complexity. He demonstrated that as cultures become more complex, there is a decline in status of those who directly engage the supernatural. Sociologist James McClenon surveyed scientists' opinions of psychic phenomena, and he found the lowest level of belief among the highest status scientists. Anthropologist Anthony F. C. Wallace analyzed cultural revitalization movements and demonstrated a clear relationship between societal destructuring and the supernatural.

In the UFO field, John Keel and Jacques Vallee showed the extraordinary prevalence of mythological motifs in that phenomenon, as well as the equally pervasive deception.

In literature, Henry Louis Gates, Jr., chairman of Harvard's Afro-American studies department, developed a theory of literary criticism based on the trickster. African Americans have long been marginalized, and they have an astute perception of what that entails.

Most of the people mentioned above have been active in the last two decades. But there was important earlier work. In fact, the first two decades of the twentieth century were a watershed for theories of the supernatural. Leading figures included: Arnold van Gennep, Emile Durkheim, Marcel Mauss, Max Weber, Lucien Levy-Bruhl, Sigmund Freud, and Rudolf Otto. Linguist Ferdinand de Saussure was also significant. These men's insights on the supernatural have been largely forgotten.

An enormous number of people have influenced my thinking, but three were particularly important: William Braud, Barbara Babcock, and Edmund Leach. Parapsychologist William Braud integrated an enormous range of findings with his model of lability and inertia in psi processes. Barbara Babcock is the most significant interpreter of the trickster figure. She was a student of Victor Turner and extended his work by recognizing the importance of liminality, anti-structure, and reflexivity for the trickster. Her work is frequently cited by women and minority scholars, but the brilliance of her trickster analysis is largely lost on white male academics. British anthropologist Edmund Leach explained and developed structuralism for English-language audiences. He extended the work of Claude Levi-Strauss, but he has not yet received the credit he deserves.

William Braud's lability and inertia model states that labile processes are more susceptible to psychic influence than are ones that are more inert. By lability, Braud referred to systems and processes that are easily varied, more fluid than rigid, more fluctuating than steady, more random than ordered. His theory encompasses a wide range of research. As an example, Braud had people try to use PK to influence a flickering candle and an electrically powered lamp. The subjects were in one room and the light sources were monitored electronically in another. A much stronger PK influence was detected on the candle (the labile system) than the lamp. Another example, explained within Braud's model, is the effect of novelty. Laboratory-based parapsychology studies have found that novelty (a break with previous patterns) facilitates ESP. Research on altered states of consciousness also fits

Braud's model. The cognitive content of many altered states (e.g., dreams) is more fluid, unstable, and quickly varying than in our waking state. Those altered states enhance ESP.

Victor Turner studied the role of ritual in indigenous societies, particularly rites of passage. Those rites signaled periods of transition, as between childhood and adulthood. They were dangerous periods during which previous statuses and relationships were suspended. The "structure" of society was eliminated temporarily, and those periods are labeled liminal or anti-structural. In liminal times supernatural powers manifested. The properties of liminality were not restricted to rites of passage. Turner had a much more encompassing view; persons could be liminal, some even permanently such as monks and mystics.

Because of Turner's writings, the issue of status frequently arises in this book. Statuses define relationships and designate positions in a social structure; they specify required behaviors, expectations, and roles for ourselves and others. Statuses govern a major portion of our lives. The issue of marginality is an issue of status. Periods of liminality and anti-structure are times when statuses are abandoned.

Braud discussed physical systems and individual psyches; Turner addressed social processes. But their ideas were parallel. Both focused on transition, flux, destructuring, and uncertainty, rather than order, structure, stasis, and stability.

Max Weber, the eminent sociologist, wrote about social order, and his work complements Victor Turner's on social transitions. Weber's concept of rationalization has had a substantial impact on sociology and is a core idea in that discipline. Weber pointed out that for several thousand years, there has been a slow, progressive implementation of rational thought and organization of society. Order was first enforced by tribal chiefs with power centered in their persons; later authority was transformed by feudal arrangements where power was more diffuse and distributed. Today bureaucracies hold power that is impersonal and codified by laws, rules, and regulations. Regulations are interpreted and enforced by people who hold a certain office or status in society; power is independent of the actual person. In the last several hundred years the trend to rationalization has accelerated. Weber's phrase "the iron cage of modernity" emphasizes the order, structure, and routinization of everyday modern life.

Charisma is a central concept in Weber's theory of authority. It is an unusual personal power. In fact pure charisma involves supernatural power, a point Weber made explicit. He saw that rationalization entailed "disenchantment" and specifically stated that it required the elimination of magic from the world. For rationalization, charisma had to be channeled and attenuated. Weber's concept of pure charisma is virtually identical to Turner's liminality and anti-structure, and both Weber and Turner used St. Francis of Assisi as an exemplar of the pure forms of charisma and anti-structure, respectively.

Academe is a primary force for rationalization, and it is there that we find the greatest incomprehension of, and antagonism to, the paranormal. Many academics who have written on Weber's concept of charisma seem vaguely puzzled by it, and virtually all have ignored its relation to supernatural phenomena. An amusing, though appalling, example of their incomprehension is that Weber wrote of telepathy as accompanying pure charismatic power; yet I know of no sociologists writing on the paranormal who have ever mentioned this.

Weber slightly misunderstood magic and rationalization. As I will explain, magic is never really eliminated from the world. Rather it is shunted to the margins of society; it is repressed from the conscious awareness of cultural elites, and for them it is relegated to fiction.

The concept of rationalization can also be applied to literary theory because magic is directly tied to meaning. In most rational discourse, and especially in science, the problem of meaning is banished from consciousness. It is assumed that, in principle, there can be a clear, unambiguous connection between a word and its referent, between a signifier and signified. However literary theorists understand that meaning is still problematic. In fact, there are even a few vague allusions in deconstructionist writings that suggest that a satisfactory theory of literature may require a theory of telepathy.

The problem of meaning is central to deconstructionism and other strands of postmodernism. Those movements challenge the notions of rationality and objective reality. The resulting reaction of the establishment is instructive. The furious denunciations of postmodernism in academe by status-conscious, high-verbal, aging white males are exceeded in intensity only by their frantic utterings of rationalistic incantations to ward off the paranormal. Those amusing endeavors provide some of the most important clues to the nature of psi. Both deconstructionism and psi subvert the rational, and there are similar, important consequences to both.

Much of the writing on deconstructionism is opaque, but that is no accident. Some concepts cannot be fully expressed in language. Gerald Vizenor, an American Indian scholar, and Henry Louis Gates, Jr., an African American, have drawn upon deconstructionist ideas in conjunction with the trickster to address problems of ambiguity and interpretation.

Why the Trickster?

Many may wonder what the trickster has to do with any of this. After all, in our society, the trickster figure is simply an odd literary device, a vehicle for amusing and silly stories. It seems preposterous to use him to explain abstruse scientific facts.

But in many less-rationalized societies, trickster tales are not merely literary creations; the tales are sacred; they are descriptions of the world. They bring together many things we consider unconnected, that even appear incoherent and irrational.

Briefly, the trickster is a character type found in mythology, folklore, and literature the world over; tricksters appear as animals, humans, and gods. They have a number of common characteristics, and some of their most salient qualities are disruption, unrestrained sexuality, disorder, and nonconformity to the establishment. They are typically male. Tricksters often deceive larger and more powerful beings who would thwart them; they may be endearingly clever or disgustingly stupid—both cultural heroes and selfish buffoons. Like much of mythology, their stories appear irrational and are difficult to decipher into logical coherence. They have often puzzled scholars. The stories do not follow linear sequences, and their meanings need to be decoded. Fortunately there is a sizeable body of scholarship on the trickster, in a variety of disciplines, and keys to decoding are found in the concepts of liminality and anti-structure.

Carl Jung's idea of archetypes is also helpful in understanding the trickster. The term archetype is often confusing, and there has been much debate over its definition. For purposes of this volume, "archetype" means only a pattern that can manifest at multiple levels. No more is implied, and nothing paranormal is necessarily required to explain it.

The trickster archetype is not designated by immediately observable physical features. Rather it is a more abstract constellation of characteristics that is usually personified (i.e., identified with a person or animal). Individuals, small groups, larger social movements, and even entire cultures can take on this configuration of attributes. It is often sensical to speak of the trickster and his effects in personified form, though this can be jarring for those entrenched in rationalistic modes of thinking. It is helpful to think in terms of constellations of qualities rather than presuming linear cause-and-effect relationships.

When some aspects of a constellation are found in a situation, one should be alert for the others.

Jung's work on archetypes is discussed in this book, but emphasis is on more recent work in anthropology, sociology, folklore, and literary theory. Analyses from these disciplines show the common characteristics of trickster tales. They include: disruption, loss of status, boundary crossing, deception, violation of sexual mores, and supernatural manifestations. Not all tricksters have all characteristics, and like other archetypes, there is ambiguity.

The ground for the trickster is found in neither anthropology, nor folklore, nor sociology, nor religious scholarship, nor psychoanalysis, nor literary criticism. All of these are important; they all aid in explaining, but the trickster cannot be reduced to formulations in any of them. My approach is therefore eclectic, and some may find it disconcerting that I do not stand firmly in one discipline or take just one perspective. I sometimes joltingly skip from one to another. Several commentators have noticed that productions of trickster characters are often something of a bricolage, a French word meaning a product made out of hodgepodge materials at hand. This book is somewhat in that tradition, and the juxtapositions of examples may sometimes strike the reader as odd, if not bizarre. I will draw from mythology, folklore, history, parapsychology, anthropology, psychology, Forteana, religion, and psychiatry. Boundaries must be blurred for the trickster to be seen.

Some may be puzzled why I chose the trickster as a vehicle to explore psychic phenomena. I started this book as an effort to understand why the paranormal is so frequently associated with fraud and deception. Many trickster figures are linked with supernatural powers and with deception, so that is an obvious connection. But as I began reading the scholarly analyses, I saw many other commonalities with the paranormal. Most analysts recognized no more than the link with deceit, but notable exceptions were Allan Combs and Mark Holland's book *Synchronicity: Science, Myth, and the Trickster* (1990) and Lutz Müller's article "Psi and the Archetype of the Trickster" (1981).

ESP and PK are, by definition, boundary crossing. They surmount the barriers between mind and mind (telepathy), mind and matter (clairvoyance and PK), as well as the limitations of time (precognition), and that of life and death (spirit mediumship, ghosts, and reincarnation). Likewise, magic tricks violate our expectations of what is and is not possible, and the relationship between psi and trickery is far deeper than most have assumed. Psi blurs distinctions between imagination and reality, between subjective and objective, between signifier and signified, between internal and external. The same is true in much deception. Studies of animals show that pretense (i.e., pretending) is often required for deceit, and pretense blurs the distinction between imagination and reality. Blurring of fantasy and reality occurs with nonrational beliefs pervasive in religion and myth as well as in good fiction.

Paradoxes of self-reference and reflexivity also blur the subject-object distinction; in fact they subvert it. Paradox challenges the supremacy of the rational, because in paradox logic breaks down. Paradox and reflexivity are important for understanding the trickster and the paranormal and will be discussed at length in the theoretical sections of the book.

Opposites-Boundaries-Structures

The concepts of structure and boundaries, destructuring and boundary crossing pervade this book. Boundaries of all kinds are of interest: geographical, personal, social, moral, psychological, etc. The concept is so broadly useful that it needs to be considered at an abstract level.

The notion of opposites is directly related to boundaries. A boundary creates a distinction. One entity or event is distinguished from another. The two entities are often seen as opposites. Together they form a structure, sometimes sharply demarcated, sometimes less so.

"Distinction" is a central idea. A distinction separates one thing from another. Tricksters are associated with destructuring, boundary crossing, and blurring distinctions.

The theme of opposites is found in a wide range of scholarship, including: the structural anthropology of Claude Levi-Strauss, deconstructionism, Jung's work on alchemy, primitive classification schemes, and Neoplatonic thought, among others. The "coincidence of opposites" is discussed in mystical theology. Some Freudian theory is couched in the language of the male-female opposition.

Many analyses suggest that tricksters are combinations of opposites. Some are both cultural heroes and selfish buffoons. The Spirit Mercurius was associated with gods and with sewers. Wakdjunkaga was able to change from male to female. Some ritual clowns and mystics eat feces, and in so doing they invert the opposites of food and excrement.

Classification schemes in many early societies identified binary oppositions such as God-human, life-death, child-adult, food-excrement, man-woman, heaven-earth, etc. These designated important cultural categories. Anthropologists have shown that these distinctions, and their maintenance, were necessary for stability in society.

Earlier peoples also understood that there was a middle ground, the betwixt and between, which was dangerous and surrounded by taboos. Shamans sometimes served as spirit mediums contacting the other world. They crossed the boundary between life and death (a binary opposition), and shamans were often seen as tricksters. Priests mediated between God and man; they were required to undergo purification rituals. Funerary rites assured that the dead moved to the next world and did not stay to haunt the living. The life-death distinction needed to be strengthened. Crossing from one status to the other (e.g., child to adult, living to dead) required rituals for purification and protection.

The middle area goes by several labels: liminality, interstitiality, transitional space, betwixt and between, anti-structure. These are dangerous positions, situations, and statuses. They break down categories, classifications, and boundaries. Violation of the boundaries was taboo and brought the wrath of the gods. There was a price to be paid. Yet during some liminal periods, taboos were deliberately violated in order to obtain magical power.

Our way of thinking is governed by Aristotelian logic. It too has a binary aspect; something is either A or not-A. In this system, the "law of the excluded middle" specifies that there is no middle ground. The betwixt and between is excluded from thought. Our culture is rationalized; it prefers sharp distinctions and clear boundaries. Even our modern theory of communication is binary, and the term bit is short for binary digit. Bit strings are nothing more than sequences of differences or distinctions (i.e., 0s and 1s).

The trickster is not eliminated simply by making sharp distinctions and clear categories. There is still a realm that lies betwixt and between a signifier and signified, between a word and its referent. Tricksters travel that liminal realm, and ambiguities in communication are their province. In fact the term hermeneutics, the study of interpretation, is derived from Hermes, the trickster of the Greeks. Trickster gods are messengers and communicators; they deal in information, but also in ambiguity.

As mentioned earlier, the issue of status is encountered throughout this volume. Status delineates difference, and thus can be conceived in terms of information. When statuses are abandoned, there is a loss of order, a loss of information. Theorists in many disciplines have viewed status in terms of energy or power relationships. I focus more on information than power or energy, and I have greater concern with the consequences and limitations of information—information in a broad sense.

This book was not written as an exercise in literary theory, anthropology, religion, sociology, or folklore. To the extent that those disciplines ignore or deny the reality of psi, they are seriously flawed. I owe no allegiance to them. This book was produced to address fundamental problems of the paranormal and supernatural. Many peculiar aspects can be understood by recourse to the trickster. He is relevant to everything from random-number-generator (RNG) parapsychology experiments to human sacrifice, from out-of-body experiences to ritual clowns eating excrement. Psi does not merely violate categories; rather subversion of categories is its essence. As such, there are limits as to what can be said about it within our typical logical frameworks.

The themes in this book include uncertainty, ambiguity, instability, the void, and the abyss. These are neither patternless, nor without power. Make no mistake, by using rational means this book endeavors to illuminate the irrational, and to demonstrate the severe limitations of logic and rationality. When the supernatural and irrational are banished from consciousness, they are not destroyed, rather, they become exceedingly dangerous.

Part 1

Overview

The next three chapters introduce the key concepts of liminality, anti-structure, and boundaries. The trickster is best understood in light of them, and this is an over-arching theme of this book. Structure requires boundaries and demarcation. Tricksters are boundary crossers; they destabilize structures. The ramifications of this abstract formulation reach into diverse and unexpected areas including parapsychology and literary theory. Theories of liminality and anti-structure were developed in anthropology. Although they have been adopted in a variety of disciplines, they are not well known outside a limited community of academics. They have made no impact on theories of the paranormal.

The first chapter in this Part describes tricksters. The literature on them is vast, scattered, and has many competing perspectives. The chapter necessarily only summarizes key points, and those will be heavily condensed and telegraphic. I do not even try to present the tales themselves. A bit more space is devoted to their common motifs, themes, and analyses. Later Parts of the book present examples that illustrate the general ideas.

The second chapter in this Part is short. It describes the concept of mental boundaries developed by psychiatrist Ernest Hartmann. His approach has much in common with psychological theories of the trickster. For many people, it is probably easiest to grasp the trickster as a psychological construct, i.e., as it is seen in individuals. However, the trickster is not be limited to the psychology of individuals. Trickster characteristics can manifest with small groups and even entire cultures.

The last chapter is more in-depth, and covers the concepts of liminality and anti-structure, which were developed by Arnold van Gennep, Victor Turner, and Barbara Babcock. Their ideas are used throughout the remainder of the book, and they have an extraordinary number of implications for the paranormal and the irrational.

These chapters are somewhat abstract in places, and readers who get bogged down are encouraged to skip to chapters in Parts 2 and 4, which describe concrete examples.

CHAPTER 2

An Overview of Tricksters From Mythology, Folklore and Elsewhere

The "trickster" is a character type that appears worldwide in folklore and mythology. The term was probably first introduced in this context in 1885 by Daniel G. Brinton.[1] Virtually all cultures have tricksters, and there are innumerable examples; a few include: coyote of North American Indians, Hermes of the Greeks, Eshu-Elegba of West Africa, and Loki of the Norse.[2] There is considerable diversity among them. At one end are primitive buffoons, at the other, gods. Yet they share some common characteristics. The primary purpose of this chapter is to identify attributes that are particularly pertinent to the paranormal.

This is a difficult chapter because I am introducing both the trickster's qualities and neglected characteristics of the paranormal. Neither are particularly well known. To understand how they are related, one needs some familiarity with both. The relevant properties can be perceived only after some acquaintance with a large number of examples. As such, some readers may find it profitable to briefly scan this chapter, read the summary, and go on to chapters with cases that illustrate the ideas.

The idea of "archetype" helps explain the trickster.[3] For purposes here, an archetype is defined as a collection of abstract properties that can manifest on several levels (e.g., within individuals, situations, small groups, entire cultures). The properties are not necessarily related by cause and effect; rather they are a constellation. As more of the properties come together, the archetype strengthens, and others tend to manifest. I often adopt the personified form in speaking of the trickster. Although this is alien to scientific discourse, it is probably the best way to comprehend the concept. In short, the trickster is a personification of a constellation of abstract qualities that can appear in a variety of circumstances.

The trickster unifies major, but seemingly unrelated, themes surrounding the paranormal. For instance, the paranormal is frequently connected with deception, and deceit is second nature to the trickster. Psychic phenomena gain prominence in times of disruption and transition. Tricksters are found in conditions of transition. The paranormal has a peculiar relationship with religion; the trickster was part of many early religions, and he was viewed ambivalently. The statuses of paranormal phenomena are typically uncertain or marginal in a variety of ways. Tricksters' statuses are similar.

When I first began studying the trickster, I found some of the analyses opaque. I did not have any idea what the writers were talking about, and if I did, I could not follow their trains of thought. Because the trickster does not subscribe to Western logic, this introduction to him may seem jumpy, jarring, and not quite coherent. I will only hint at some of the stories' content, allude to major themes, briefly mention the types of analyses, and scan the diversity of implications. These are all lumped together because they cannot be effectively disentangled if one wishes to have a deep understanding.

In some societies, trickster tales are sacred; restrictions and prohibitions surround them. Not just anybody is allowed to tell the stories because they have a power of their own. This assertion seems decidedly irrational in Western thought, but this is the crux of the matter. The trickster shows some fundamental limitations of the Western conceits of logic, objectivity, and rationality.

Mythological tricksters are almost all male. In fact, Lewis Hyde's book *Trickster Makes This World* (1998) includes an entire appendix titled "Trickster and Gender," which begins with the statement "All the standard tricksters are male." Though female mythological characters sometimes engage in deception, rarely are they included under the trickster rubric. Despite all this, women scholars have provided some of the greatest insight. Among the writings I have found of particular value are those of Barbara Babcock, Jean Shinoda Bolen, Joan Wescott, Laura Makarius, Ellen Basso, Enid Welsford, Kimberly Blaeser, Susan Niditch, Kathleen Ashley, Christine Downing, and Claudia Camp. Their work is often unappreciated by males.

In the next several pages, I will introduce several tricksters, who each have an extensive literature. I can only mention a few stories, briefly describe major themes, and draw out common characteristics.

Wakdjunkaga

Wakdjunkaga, the trickster of the Winnebago, became widely known through the writings of anthropologist Paul Radin. His informant Sam Blowsnake collected the tales in 1912, and Radin published them in 1956 in his now-classic *The Trickster*. He provided an extended analysis and included an essay by psychologist Carl Jung. The 1972 edition carried an introduction "Job and the Trickster" by anthropologist Stanley Diamond, which signalled the trickster's importance to theological issues. These commentaries hint at the diverse relevance of trickster tales. They were not just stories to entertain children.

Wakdjunkaga is a relatively primitive being who is sometimes identified with hare (and also with raven, spider, and coyote), but "basically he possesses no well-defined and fixed form."[4] He is usually a selfish buffoon, caring little about his fellows, and he may hurt others and himself with his antics. His tales are full of accounts of eating, release of flatus, excreting, bumbling around exploring, sexual congress with a variety of creatures, temporary transformations into a female in order to give birth, and attempts to use magic, some of which backfire.

In one story, one arm cuts the other during a quarrel between the two. Only after feeling the pain does Trickster start to question what happened and then recognizes his foolishness. His anus and penis can be detached and sent off on various tasks; he gives them orders, and when they disobey, he punishes them, but finally realizes that he hurt himself. Despite his bizarre behavior and blundering about, there are inadvertent benefits for mankind.

Some of the stories are odd and even grotesque. Wakdjunkaga disrupted things and violated taboos. He played tricks, was deceptive and sexually insatiable. Yet like a god, he eventually ascended into the heavens.

There are innumerable perspectives from which to interpret the tales, and it makes no sense to try present them all. Radin's analysis alone spanned many pages. For introductory purposes here, I point out that trickster tales can give some insight into psychology. Wakdjunkaga displays dissociated, autonomous aspects and only limited self-awareness. The tales reflect competing basic life processes. Eating, defecation, and sex are some of the most fundamental requirements for life. Deception and self-concern are necessary for the survival of the organism. A young individual learning about the environment does blunder about, and this exploring and experimenting can be disruptive. Various needs, compulsions, and instincts sometimes compete with each other, and they are often contradictory. The self is not a unified, coherent, logical entity. Paradox, contradiction, and ambiguity abound. This is part of the human condition.

Hermes

Hermes, the trickster of the Greeks, is a god, and he is perhaps better known by his Roman name of Mercury. He is the son of Zeus and Maia. There is a considerable literature on Hermes, and one of the most frequently cited books on him is Norman O. Brown's *Hermes the Thief* (1947). Jungian analysts have provided a number of psychological interpretations. Jean Shinoda Bolen's *Gods in Everyman* (1989) has an accessible chapter, as does Christine Downing's *Gods in Our Midst* (1993). Rafael Lopez-Pedraza's *Hermes and His Children* (1977) gives an extended treatment.

Hermes means "he of the stone heap." In Greece, mounds of stones served as landmarks and property boundaries. Somewhat paradoxically, Hermes is also a boundary-crosser. The themes of boundaries and boundary-crossing arise again and again in interpretations of Hermes, and tricksters generally.

The Greeks recognized that boundaries referred to more than just the physical and geographic kind. Bolen reports that "Hermes is firmly cast in the role of messenger between realms"[5] explaining: "As the traveler between levels, Hermes seeks to understand, integrate, and communicate between the conscious mental world of mind and intellect (Olympus), the realm in which the ego decides and acts (earth), and the collective unconscious (underworld),"[6] and "As Hermes Psychopompos, he accompanied the souls of the dead to the underworld."[7] She cites Jungian analyst Murray Stein, who "calls Hermes the God of Significant Passage. Hermes is the archetype present 'betwixt and between' psychological phases—especially during midlife transitions. He is a liminal god, present in the transitional space (from the Greek word *limen*, the space under the door frame or the threshold)."[8] Boundaries and transitions are explicit here, and these are key themes in this book.

Compared with Wakdjunkaga, Hermes is more refined, more restrained, more considerate and sophisticated. With Wakdjunkaga, the base characteristics are more overt. Hermes displays greater integration of instincts and personality characteristics; he can exist along with and contribute to others in society. He is the friendliest of the gods though a bachelor; whereas Wakdjunkaga is a more solitary figure, almost completely unrestrained by social mores.

Hermes can easily pass unnoticed. His half-brothers, Apollo and Dionysus (all three gods were sons of Zeus), typically receive more attention. Many writers use Apollo and Dionysus to characterize persons, situations, events, and tendencies: Apollo for farsightedness, planning, order and structure; Dionysus for wine, ecstasy, sensuality, and orgiastic excess. Even dictionaries contrast the two. Hermes is betwixt and between them, and is often overlooked. He served as midwife at the birth of Dionysus, and as I will show, this function appears in a number of contexts. Hermes facilitates transitions, as between order (Apollo) and orgiastic excess (Dionysus).

Hermes' links to the paranormal are explicit. In mythology, Apollo gave him the power of prophecy, though not through words but rather interpretation of signs as in divination using dice. We are told that Hermes "is the god of the unexpected, of luck, of coincidences, of synchronicity."[9] Bolen elaborates: "Hermes opens up moments of discovery and synchronistic events—those 'coincidences' that turn out to be meaningful, unforeseen 'accidental' happenings that lead us somewhere we couldn't have known we would go and that yet turn out uncannily right. People miss Hermes if their minds are set on a particular itinerary and schedule, who set out and know ahead of time just what they will see and when. Thus when we go on vacation or even spend an unstructured day on a lark, with an attitude of adventure, not knowing what we will find, letting each day shape itself, we invite Hermes to accompany us—to be part of us."[10] Divination, synchronicity, and foretelling the future all involve psychic phenomena, and they are found in conjunction with other tricksters as well.

Sexuality is salient in the life of Hermes, as it is with many tricksters. Norman Brown notes that Hermes is the patron of trickery in sexual seduction.[11] Lopez-Pedraza gives extended discussion of Hermes' unrestrained sexuality, and Bolen succinctly reports: "Regardless of his sexual orientation, a Hermes man is likely to have a bisexual attitude—isn't judgmental or threatened by any tendencies in himself."[12] This is another instance of boundary blurring.

Deception is a notable quality of Hermes. His deceits are clever, even charming. On the day he was born, he cunningly stole and killed some of Apollo's cattle. When confronted, he denied doing so, with the cute alibi that he was too young and tender to possibly have done the deed. Bolen tells us that: "Hermes as trickster is the archetype embodied as a charming sociopath, who feels no qualms about lying or taking whatever he wants"[13] and that: "As a trickster, he is a 'con artist' who gains the confidence of his victim[s] and then fleeces them, or a selective and imaginative thief, or the imposter. For example, we read of Hermes men who have posed as doctors, fooling hospital staff for a long time before being exposed."[14] Speaking of the Hermes boy, Bolen cautions: "He needs to be caught in the lie or the act and taught the difference between truth and make believe, (because he can move from reality to imagination readily, not examining the boundaries)."[15]

Blurring the boundary between imagination and reality is an important function of Hermes. Both psi and deception blur the same distinction. Others have given brief hints of this. For instance, Norman Brown notes that Hermes' trickery is not simply "a rational device"; it is more subtle than that and is shown "as a manifestation of magical power."[16] Thus Hermes blurs the line between trickery and real magic. This is a confusing and disconcerting idea that is rarely given serious, extended treatment. It is typically regarded as so preposterous as to be beneath consideration, but later chapters will provide a number of examples and extended discussion of it.

Eshu-Elegba

Eshu-Elegba is the trickster god of the Yoruba of West Africa, and he displays remarkable similarities to Hermes. There are variant designations and spellings for this deity, and many distinguish between Eshu (or Esu) and Elegba (or Legba). But the two blend into each other; they are not completely distinct. I will follow Joan Wescott in referring to this deity as Eshu-Elegba because the combination helps emphasize the blurred boundaries that typify trickster gods.

Like Hermes, Eshu-Elegba is associated with boundaries, and his symbol is a mud pillar. Wescott reports: "This symbol, never kept inside houses, is placed instead at doorways, where it serves not only as a protection but also to remind men of boundaries,"[17] and it "is placed wherever trouble may break out ... and also before the divination board to symbolize his presence in all transition states."[18] We are further told that: "As an explorer, and in his concern with transition states, it is fitting that his symbols and also representations of him are present during Ifa divination. In Yoruba cosmology Ifa, the divine oracle, and Elegba are seen as counterparts; both are mediators between gods and men."[19] The connection with magical divination practices is confirmed by Robert Pelton's lengthy study, *The Trickster in West Africa* (1980). Pelton even notes that "Eshu is pure synchronicity."[20] Thus the link with the paranormal is explicit, and these passages contain direct mentions of transition states, divination, synchronicity, and mediation. All are recurring themes in this book.

Sexuality is prominent in the accounts of Eshu-Elegba. Wescott reports: "The most important symbol of Elegba sculpture, however, is the long-tailed hair-dress sometimes carved as a phallus . . . The priests of Eshu wear their hair in this fashion . . . a very high proportion of ethnographic evidence points to an association of long hair with libidinous energy, with power and aggression, with unrestrained sexuality, and with uninhibited instinct. These are indeed all qualities of Elegba,"[21] and she notes "It is in fact Eshu who is held responsible for erotic dreams and for adulterous or other illicit sexual relations."[22]

Disruption is a typical trickster characteristic, and Eshu-Elegba exemplifies it, as Wescott notes: "He is present whenever there is trouble and also wherever there is change and transition,"[23] and "His unscrupulous tricks define him as a creature who has no regard for authority."[24]

Eshu-Elegba, like Hermes, is involved in communication between the divine realm and humanity, but their communication function involves more than that. Foundations of communication are tied to the trickster. In fact hermeneutics is the study of the principles of interpretation, i.e., the determination of meaning. That discipline was named after Hermes.[25] There are parallels with Eshu-Elegba. Henry Louis Gates, Jr., chairman of the Afro-American studies program at Harvard University, developed a theory of literary criticism based upon Eshu-Elegba, focussing on the problems of interpretation. All this brings us rather far afield from what most people might expect in considering trickster stories. In order to better grasp this, some background in semiotics, structuralism, literary theory, and deconstructionism will be needed. They will be presented much later. They are usually seen as having relevance only to analyses of stories and texts. But their implications are far greater.

The Spirit Mercurius

The Spirit Mercurius of alchemy is another trickster figure, and much of what is known about him is due to the explorations of psychologist Carl Jung. Jung began his study of alchemy in mid-life, and his concern was not with precursors to chemistry but rather with transformation, especially in the unconscious. Jung attempted to translate the images, symbols, and concepts of ancient alchemical texts into modern terms and place them in a rational framework. He was fortunate to have had encounters with similar imagery of his own.

Mercurius is closely related to Hermes, and Jung specifically notes that Mercurius is "an evasive trickster"[26] and that "his main characteristic is duplicity."[27] Like Wakdjunkaga, Mercurius has associations with excrement, and Jung reports: "The texts remind us again and again that Mercurius is 'found in the dung-heaps,'"[28] and "Pictures in old manuscripts of excretory acts, including vomiting, likewise belong to this sphere."[29]

Sexuality is prominent, and Jung states: "His lasciviousness is borne out by an illustration in the *Tripus chimicus* of Sendivogius, where he appears on a triumphal chariot drawn by a cock and a hen, and behind him is a naked pair of embracing lovers. In this connection may also be mentioned the numerous somewhat obscene pictures of the coniunctio in old prints, often preserved merely as pornographica."[30]

Like some of the other trickster gods, Jung notes that Mercurius is "a redeeming psychopomp,"[31] i.e., a guide of souls. He is also a link between two worlds, a mediator who dwells in the realm betwixt and between. With Mercurius, transformation is explicit, and Jung notes that: "He is the process by which the lower and material is transformed into the higher and spiritual, and vice versa."[32] Transformation is, of course, nearly synonymous with transition, a recurring theme in trickster literature.

"Opposites" is a common subject in trickster analyses, and a number of Jung's passages reflect the idea, e.g., "Mercurius consists of all conceivable opposites" and "He is the devil . . . and [also] God's reflection in physical nature,"[33] and "He is both material and spiritual,"[34] and "Mercurius truly consists of the most extreme opposites; on the one hand he is undoubtedly akin to the godhead, on the other he is found in sewers."[35] Jung states that: "He is thus quite obviously a duality, but is named a unity in spite of the fact that his innumerable inner contradictions can dramatically fly apart into an equal number of disparate and apparently independent figures."[36] Volume 14 of Jung's collected works is entitled *Mysterium Coniunctionis: An Inquiry into the Separation and Synthesis of Psychic Opposites in Alchemy*. That volume runs to over 700 pages, indicating the importance he gave to opposites. Despite the lengthy exposition, I find it nearly incomprehensible. This notion of opposites can be difficult to grasp because it indicates internal contradictions, and in the forthcoming pages, I will illustrate the idea with a number of specific examples. Other scholars have also addressed the topic, and notable is the work of Claude Levi-Strauss, the French anthropologist who was the premier figure in the French structuralist movement. The coincidence of opposites is also found in discussions of Neoplatonism.

The Spirit Mercurius was associated with both gods and dung heaps. This appears odd, but it is not unique. Abusive language often contains scatological references alongside those to deities. This association signals a primordial nexus of the trickster, communication, and deity, though the link may appear happenstance. It does not seem logical or plausible, but British structural anthropologist Edmund Leach has addressed it, and that will be covered much later in this book when literary theory and taboo are discussed.[37] I inject this example simply to alert the reader that the trickster facilitates unexpected connections, including some that can induce intellectual vertigo.

Biblical Tricksters

Religion professor Susan Niditch analyzed several Biblical characters in her book *Underdogs and Tricksters* (1987). She included the stories of Abram and his wife Sarai (Genesis 12:10–17) and Isaac and his wife Rebekah (Genesis: 26:1–17). In both instances, the families faced famine and were thus forced to flee their homelands. The wives were beautiful, and the husbands worried that foreign peoples would kill them and take their wives. So each husband presented his wife as his sister, and Abram allowed the Pharaoh, and Isaac allowed Abimelech, to take his wife as a sexual partner. Trickster elements are seen in these stories. The wandering (boundary crossing) and deceit, especially in the sexual sphere, are trickster qualities. The forced moves due to famine resulted in a loss of status, and status reduction is often seen in conjunction with tricksters. Additionally, supernatural communication plays a central part in the stories as Yahweh spoke to both Abram and to Abimelech. Niditch acknowledged that the Old Testament Biblical tricksters are relatively sedate versions of the general type, and they do not have the extensive narrative accounts of many tricksters, yet they share qualities with them.

Divine deceit raises problematic theological questions. J. J. M. Roberts of Princeton Theological Seminary published an article entitled "Does God Lie?" (1988). His conclusion was: sometimes, yes.[38] Following that lead, Nancy Bowen, a graduate student at that seminary completed a dissertation entitled "The Role of YHWH as Deceiver in True and False Prophecy (Old Testament)" (1994). She showed that Near Eastern texts from antiquity recognized the untrustworthiness of the gods in divine-human communication. The ancients realized that prophecy and divination were not always reliable. Bowen explicitly drew upon analyses of the trickster, and the abstract of her dissertation states that those ancient writings "share a view that YHWH acts as deceiver in a time of social and historical transition and that YHWH's deception serves as a means to disrupt the present social situation in order to bring about a transformation of the social order."[39]

Other Tricksters

The designation of trickster is not limited to mythology and folklore; some actual persons merit the title. Fools and clowns are subclasses of tricksters and share most essential qualities, including the association with supernatural powers. There is a long history of professional buffoons, known for their wit, gluttony, and sometimes extremely crude jokes, yet honored at the very highest levels of society, and a number of eminent ones were known for their prophecy. Their connection with the paranormal is unmistakable. In fact Enid Welsford's classic *The Fool: His Social and Literary History* (1935) has one chapter entitled "Origins: The Fool as Poet and Clairvoyant." William Willeford's volume *The Fool and His Scepter: A Study in Clowns and Jesters and Their Audience* (1969) demonstrated that fools were associated with chaos, the primitive, and also with the magical and the supernatural. Grete de Francesco in his *The Power of the Charlatan* (1939) noted that charlatans in the Middle Ages and Renaissance often claimed special alchemical knowledge, were wanderers and gluttons, and were considered to possess the power of prophecy. The Harlequin figure is yet another with trickster qualities.[40]

Clowns have many striking trickster characteristics as well as links with shamanism.[41] In earlier cultures clowns were frequently associated with obscene and scatological practices. Ethnographer Adolf Bandelier studied the Pueblo of New Mexico, and he described celebrations where the clowns performed sodomy, coitus and masturbated in front of the entire tribe. His novel *The Delight Makers* (1890) had some influence. Carl Jung began his essay "On the Psychology of the Trickster Figure" mentioning that work. Barbara Babcock, the leading interpreter of the trickster, spent considerable time studying Bandelier's work.[42] John Bourke's 1891 *Scatalogic Rites of All Nations*, a book of over 500 pages, describes other disgusting practices. The subtitle of that book informs us that excrementitious agents were used in religion, divination, witchcraft, and love-philters. The connection between the scatological and the magical should not be overlooked.

The pervasive scatological aspects of clowns, tricksters, and magic cry out for explanation. They evoke a sense of wonder, but also of unease. In our cleaner, more rational world it is easy to ignore these aspects of primitive culture. They challenge our notions not only of propriety, but even of what it means to be human. Extremes tell us far more about ourselves than long lists of average human characteristics. I find it great fun to playfully recount these examples and observe the reactions to them. It is remarkable how few people want to seriously ponder such things, especially professional, academic psychologists and social scientists whose job it is to understand the human condition.

In times past, and in other cultures, clowns, buffoons, and other tricksters were recognized and given their due, sometimes even places of honor. In the modern world, they are mere shadows of their former selves. They are now forced to be more socially respectable, more restrained; today many of their activities are suppressed. We no longer comprehend their messages. This trend has important parallels. Religious mystery and mysticism are likewise largely alien to the elite culture of the present. These all have crucial implications for the paranormal, and they are a direct consequence of rationalization (in Max Weber's sense of the term).

Summary

The above discussion barely skims the literature on the trickster. The body of material is massive, and little more could be attempted. This chapter tries only to point the directions of coming discussions. This is a formidable task because the topics range from the most problematic issues of theology, to fundamental bases of communication, to psychic phenomena, to what it means to be human. Any coverage must be more circumscribed if it is to be manageable and comprehensible. Unifying themes must be found. Fortunately, some basic ideas can be distilled.

The trickster can be thought of as a personification of a constellation of characteristics. The qualities of greatest interest are summarized in the following paragraphs. Many tricksters do not display the complete set (a few are not even known for overt trickery), yet when several of the characteristics appear together, in any context, we should be alert for the others.

Per their name, tricksters typically engage in deceit.

Tricksters often disrupt things. They don't fit in well with the established order.

They violate taboos, sometimes so severely that they are forced to live apart from others.

Sexuality is prominent in their lives. They are uninhibited creatures.

Nearly all the tricksters of myth are involved with magical practices or have direct contact with supernatural beings. Ritual clowns, court jesters, and fools have also been associated with supernatural power.

Many trickster qualities can be understood in terms of boundaries, structures, and transitions. Tricksters are boundary crossers; they destabilize structures; they govern transitions. They also embody paradox, contradiction, and ambiguity.

The topic of marginality can be included here. Tricksters are marginal characters; they live at boundaries, with uncertain, ambiguous statuses. Minority groups often have an affinity for tricksters, and women, American Indians, and African Americans have made particularly valuable contributions to trickster theory. Marginality also characterizes paranormal practitioners and phenomena.

Tricksters are not firmly situated within establishment structures. They typically are not leaders of large groups. They are often unmarried (Hermes is a bachelor god, and in some cults, it is said that "Eshu has no wives."[43]); even the rudimentary institutional structure of marriage is uncongenial. Animals personifying the trickster often have solitary habits.[44] In a multitude of ways, the trickster doesn't quite "fit in."

By his nature, he resists complete and precise definition, and Barbara Babcock and Jay Cox comment that he "eludes and disrupts all orders of things, including the analytic categories of academics."[45] The trickster informs literary criticism, psychic phenomena, and clowns who eat excrement. There are tools to approach such bizarre mixtures, but they are not widely known or understood. In fact they deal with the very notion of category itself. Much later in the book, there is an extended discussion of classification and abstraction, and these are central to understanding the trickster as well as structuralism and deconstructionism.

To reiterate, the trickster characteristics of particular importance include: deception, disruption, reduced sexual inhibitions, and magical (psi, supernatural) practices. In addition, the concept of marginality is significant (i.e., being at the edge or boundary). These qualities seem organically bound together, and in the pages that follow I will address this with recourse to the abstract concepts of "boundary" and "structure."

CHAPTER 3

Ernest Hartmann's Mental Boundaries

The first two chapters have been expansive and diverse in their coverage. It may be helpful to view the trickster in a more restricted context, and psychology is a good place to start. The issue of boundaries is central to understanding the trickster, and psychologists have used the concept in their own research. Ernest Hartmann, a psychiatrist at Tufts University School of Medicine presented an innovative approach in his book *Boundaries in the Mind* (1991). Hartmann's thinking about boundaries has some remarkable parallels with Jean Shinoda Bolen's interpretation of the Greek trickster, Hermes.

Hartmann had a long interest in sleep disorders, particularly nightmares, and during his research, he noticed that nightmare sufferers shared some personality characteristics. They seemed unguarded, and willing to reveal themselves, even their dark secrets; they often had jobs that required creativity. In order to integrate a number of diverse observations, Hartmann utilized the idea of boundaries. The concept covers a wide domain, and thus it escapes a short, concise definition. Briefly, his theory differentiates between "thick" and "thin" boundary types, and it seems easiest to explain the theory by comparing and contrasting the two kinds of personalities. Thick-boundary people strike one as solid, well organized, well defended, and even rigid and armored. Thin-boundary types tend to be open, unguarded, and undefended in several psychological senses. Women tend to have thinner boundaries than men, and children thinner than adults. People with thin boundaries tend to have higher hypnotic ability, greater dream recall, and are more likely to have lucid dreams. People with thick boundaries stay with one thought until its completion; whereas those with thin boundaries show greater fluidity, and their thoughts branch from one to another. People with very thin boundaries report more symptoms of illness; however, compared with thick-boundary types, they are able to exert more control over the autonomic nervous system and can produce greater changes in skin temperature when thinking of hot or cold situations. Thin-boundary persons are more prone to synesthesia, blending of the senses (e.g., seeing colors when certain sounds are heard). Differences are found in occupations as well. Middle managers in large corporations tend to have thick boundaries, and artists, writers and musicians tend to have thinner ones. People with thick boundaries tend to be in stable, long-term marriages; whereas thin types are more likely to be, or have been, divorced or separated.

Hartmann developed the Boundary Questionnaire of 146 items in order to formally define and test the concept. The questionnaire is geared for normal people rather than patients with mental disturbances. It is easy to use, and it is included in the book, along with the scoring method. By the way, the book is very readable and it does not sacrifice scientific sophistication, a rare combination among academic works.

Hartmann separated the questions into 12 categories, with each measuring a different aspect of boundaries. One of the categories, based on 19 items, is "unusual experiences," and thin-boundary people tend to report more of these. After Hartmann collected more than 800 questionnaires, he conducted a factor analysis. This is a common procedure in psychological research that assesses which questions correlate with others. He discovered a number of factors, and nearly all were easily interpreted in terms of thick and thin boundaries. One was labeled "Percipience/Clairvoyance," which included questions about psychic experiences. People who scored high on that factor tended to have thin boundaries; thus the connection between thin boundaries and the paranormal is well supported.

Thin-boundary personality characteristics have much in common with those found in psychological interpretations of the Greek trickster, Hermes, who is also a god of boundaries.

Jean Shinoda Bolen is one of the most accessible writers on Hermes. She is Japanese-American, a professor of psychiatry at the University of California, San Francisco, and is familiar with parapsychology. In the 1970s she wrote for *Psychic* magazine, which her husband edited and published. Her interest in psychic matters is further seen in her book *The Tao of Psychology* (1979), which is subtitled "Synchronicity and the Self."

Hermes' characteristics were discussed in the previous chapter, and I will not cover them in detail here. Instead, I have summarized them in Table 1 along with descriptors of thin-boundary types. Table

1 lists direct quotes from Hartmann and Bolen that demonstrate the clear congruence of their concepts. The similarities are gratifying because the two psychiatrists apparently derived their ideas completely independently, and that makes their convergence of greater significance.

Hartmann	Bolen
Thin boundaries involve easy merging into fantasy or vivid memory, at times not being quite clear what state one is in. (p. 27)	The Hermes boy "can move from reality to imagination readily, not examining the boundaries"(p. 173)
Followed over time, the people with thin boundaries appeared to have intense but often short-lived relationships (p. 139)	He finds new grass always greener, which invites him to flit from one situation or person to another (p. 187)
the person with very thin boundaries is often bisexual, at least potentially. Such a person has fantasies, dreams, and daydreams of having sex with members of both sexes and is willing to consider the possibility of bisexual behavior (p. 42)	he is more likely to have tried (or at least fantasized) sex with a man or men if he is heterosexual, or with women if he is homosexual, than any other type of man. (p. 181)
childhood trauma can be one environmental factor responsible for thin boundaries (p. 119)	I have felt the saving presence of Hermes when my adult patients have spoken of their abusive childhoods (p. 170)
middle managers in large organizations, also tended to be people with thick boundaries (p. 217)	A Hermes man is not likely to be a narrow specialist or a happy cog in a large corporation (p. 177)
The person with thin boundaries will often be seen as a bit unreliable (p. 143)	Hermes can be "unreliable and inconsistent" (p. 188)
Those with thin boundaries are often drawn to occupations that do not require strict schedules and detailed organization (p. 218)	The Hermes man does not "like schedules" (p. 183)
counselors, and therapists also scored quite thin (p. 218)	The Hermes archetype provides qualities that contribute to being a good psychotherapist (p. 178)

Table 1 Thin Boundary Qualities Compared with Hermes' Characteristics

Note: Quotations are from Hartmann's *Boundaries in the Mind* (1991) and Bolen's *Gods in Everyman* (1989).

Hartmann recognized the relationship between paranormal experience and thin boundaries. A few others have understood the significance of that. Martin Kottmeyer, a most perceptive commentator on the UFO phenomena, was one of the first to do so. In a 1988 article in the British magazine *Magonia*, he drew upon Hartmann's earlier book *The Nightmare* (1984) and convincingly showed that persons who had UFO abduction experiences had many similarities to nightmare sufferers, i.e., people with thin boundaries. Kottmeyer has continued to draw upon Hartmann's ideas.

People with thin boundaries are sometimes perceived as less reliable than average, and when they report paranormal experiences, it is easy to dismiss them. For instance, UFO abduction experiences appear to be largely subjective.[1] The experiencers can be viewed as marginal, or worse. However, thin boundaries likely predispose one to experience objective psychic phenomena. Douglas Richards published a paper in the *Journal of Parapsychology* in 1996 reporting a study he had conducted using Hartmann's questionnaire. He confirmed that thin boundaries were related to subjective psychic experiences, but he also reviewed a number of studies on personality factors related to success in psi tasks in the laboratory. Richards noted that characteristics associated with thin boundaries were correlated with objective success. Several examples can be cited. For instance, persons with low perceptual defensiveness tend to score above average on ESP tests,[2] and children seem to be above average ESP subjects.[3] People who have high hypnotic ability seem to do well in ESP performance in the laboratory,[4] and several other psychologists have provided rationales for additional research on the matter.[5]

The concept of boundaries provides a useful framework for understanding personality and its relationship to psychic phenomena. It also helps explain why people who report paranormal experiences are often dismissed as fantasizing even though the events have a basis in reality.

This chapter has been devoted to psychological issues, but I want to caution the reader that the trickster cannot be reduced to the psychology of individuals. That is, personality characteristics of individuals only partly explain trickster manifestations. The issue of boundaries (and psychic phenomena) involves vastly more than that. In the next chapter a more expansive view of boundaries considers theories from anthropology.

CHAPTER 4

Victor Turner's Concept of Anti-Structure

This book is about paranormal phenomena and the conditions surrounding their occurrence. The theories of anthropologists Arnold van Gennep and Victor Turner are especially useful because they address change, transition, and instability—issues central to this book. Their theories have proven their value for understanding religion, literature, folklore, and psychology, but they have rarely been applied to the paranormal.[1]

Van Gennep's book *The Rites of Passage* is a classic; it was first published in 1909 but was not translated into English until 1960.[2] Turner's *The Ritual Process: Structure and Anti-Structure* (1969) substantially extended van Gennep's ideas. As those titles indicate, their primary emphasis was on rites and ritual, but the theories have much wider applicability.

Because I draw so heavily on their work, some biographical material is in order. Van Gennep (1873–1957) was a French scholar who contributed to anthropology, ethnography, and particularly folklore. He was something of an outsider to academe, and he was often at odds with the Durkheim school of sociology. It did not accord him due recognition, and that probably delayed the acceptance of his ideas. Van Gennep never held a university appointment in France, though he did occupy a chair of ethnography for three years in Switzerland.[3] Victor Turner (1920–1983) was a British anthropologist known for his study of ritual. He spent time in Africa studying the Ndembu of Zambia, along with his wife, Edith, who has achieved some note in her own right. Turner taught at several American universities including Cornell, the University of Chicago, and the University of Virginia.[4]

Van Gennep's and Turner's theories diffused into a variety of disciplines, but only limited portions of their work have been effectively integrated. I have encountered a number of people who misapprehended the concepts because of other writers' all-too-brief descriptions, and many have failed to appreciate their generality, diversity, and applicability. As such I will quote both van Gennep and Turner extensively so the readers gain a fuller appreciation of them.

Turner and van Gennep were anthropologists, and I emphasize that discipline for a reason. Anthropologists examine a wide range of cultures, and they observe more of the extremes of the human condition than do practitioners in other fields. Consequently their theories often provide insights unavailable from others. Van Gennep and Turner studied relatively simple societies, but their ideas can be applied to more complex ones, including our own. The complexity of our society makes their relevance a bit difficult to initially perceive, but the ideas directly apply to changes and transitions in our culture.

Van Gennep and Turner had a wide knowledge of many societies. They did not base their ideas on abstract philosophical notions, but rather on concrete examples. They used comparative methods to examine a diversity of phenomena across disciplinary boundaries, and they discovered patterns that others had missed. Comparative methods are a bit alien to other sciences, which tend to emphasize logical cause-effect relationships, narrow focus, and reductionistic thinking. In contrast, the humanities frequently use comparative techniques, and they provide great breadth of insight. Comparative methods encourage interdisciplinary efforts, and they accentuate data rather than imposing spurious cause-effect relationships.

Structure and Status

Through this book we will return repeatedly to the issues of social status and social structure. Social structure has a variety of definitions. Turner adopted the one used by most British anthropologists; that is, society is a system of social positions, and "the units of social structure are relationships between statuses, roles, and offices."[5] Organized culture and civilization *require* differentiation, roles, and structure. Some hunt, others cook, some must raise children. Roles give definition and continuity to a person's life; they designate positions and statuses in the structure of society. By its nature, structure produces social distance and inequality, which often leads to exploitation of people. Some alienation results from all structure; this is part of the human condition.

Social structure and social status are not directly observable. One can see a tree, a forest, a rock, or person. But social structures and statuses are not like that. They are "invisible." In this sense, they are like "spirits" (this comparison is further elaborated in the chapter on totemism). Social structures are very real, and they pervasively influence us, so much so that we typically choose not to acknowledge their effects. We tend to see individuals as having a discrete existence. We think of groups as simply collections of individuals, and assume that the properties of the group can be derived from those of the individuals. This is wrong fundamentally, and to understand why requires a sociological way of thinking.

Liminality

Three concepts are crucial to the work of van Gennep and Turner: liminality, communitas, and anti-structure. The three terms are closely related and are, in some contexts, interchangeable. Van Gennep introduced the term liminality (from "limen", i.e., threshold) in *The Rites of Passage* (1909). In many cultures, elaborate rituals mark important transitions, such as puberty, marriage, change in leadership, and death. These passages involve revisions in roles and statuses, i.e., shifts in structural position; thus the entire group is involved, not just one person. Van Gennep identified three stages of these rites as separation, transition (limen), and incorporation. During the liminal phase of initiatory rites the ritual subjects are often physically separated from the rest of the populace. They may spend long periods in the bush, apart from the tribe. During such transitions, rituals assist the psychological changes of individuals and the group and serve to solidify the new structure. In many societies, these processes are much more intense than in our own.

Describing initiations, van Gennep notes that: "During the entire novitiate, the usual economic and legal ties are modified, sometimes broken altogether. The novices are outside society, and society has no power over them, especially since they are actually sacred and holy, and therefore untouchable and dangerous, just as gods would be."[6] He reports that "although taboos, as negative rites, erect a barrier between the novices and society, the society is defenseless against the novices' undertakings ... During the novitiate, the young people can steal and pillage at will or feed and adorn themselves at the expense of the community."[7] This is a superb example of anti-structure and chaos, and this passage also connects liminality with the sacred and the gods.

Half a century after van Gennep published his book, Turner began to extend the ideas, and in 1964 he presented a paper titled "Betwixt and Between: The Liminal Period in *Rites de Passage*." The phrase "betwixt and between" helped emphasize the liminal period or position as between two stable conditions, and he also used the term "margin" in a similar capacity. He further clarified the ideas in *The Ritual Process: Structure and Anti-Structure* (1969).

The characteristics of liminality can be seen in a welter of contexts involving transitions. Van Gennep's theoretical formulation included matters such as initiations, vision quests, travelers and strangers, retreats into deserts by hermits, sacred contexts, and territorial passage. Turner expanded the realm to include: "subjugated autochthones, small nations, court jesters, holy mendicants, good Samaritans, millenarian movements, 'dharma bums,' ... and monastic orders" explaining that "all have this common characteristic: they are persons or principles that (1) fall in the interstices of social structure, (2) are on its margins, or (3) occupy its lowest rungs."[8] Such a jumble may seem dissonant for many readers and can be problematic because, by their nature, the above items are largely antithetical to structure. This makes them easy to overlook. Yet there are common patterns across them, and this abstract formulation allows us to understand some of the queer aspects of ritual initiation and how they are pertinent to the paranormal and its place in the social order.

Turner reports that: "Ritual symbols of this phase, though some represent inversion of normal reality, characteristically fall into two types: those of effacement and those of ambiguity or paradox ... They [the initiands] are associated with such general oppositions as life and death, male and female, food and excrement, simultaneously, since they are at once dying from or dead to their former status and life, and being born and growing into new ones. Sharp symbolic inversion of social attributes may characterize separation; blurring and merging of distinctions may characterize liminality."[9] He also notes that "liminality is frequently likened to death, to being in the womb, to invisibility, to darkness, to bisexuality, to the wilderness, and to an eclipse of the sun or moon."[10]

Turner later comments: "The novices are, in fact, temporarily undefined, beyond the normative social structure. This weakens them, since they have no rights over others. But it also liberates them from structural obligations. It places them too in a close connection with non-social or asocial powers of life and death. Hence the frequent comparison of novices with, on the one hand, ghosts, gods, or ancestors, and, on the other, with animals or birds . . . In liminality . . . former rights and obligations are suspended, the social order may seem to have been turned upside down, but by way of compensation cosmological systems (as objects of serious study) may become of central importance for the novices."[11] The ritual processes can have great psychological impact, and he goes on to note that "the factors or elements of culture may be recombined in numerous, often grotesque ways, grotesque because they are arrayed in terms of possible or fantasied rather than experienced combinations—thus a monster disguise may combine human, animal, and vegetable features in an 'unnatural' way, while the same features may be differently, but equally 'unnaturally' combined in a painting or described in a tale. In other words, in liminality people 'play' with the elements of the familiar and defamiliarize them. Novelty emerges from unprecedented combinations of familiar objects."[12]

This recombination of elements is a quality also found in altered (i.e., destructured) states of consciousness. Odd assortments of items appear in dreams and in productions of visionary artists. This is perhaps the essence of creativity—producing new patterns, new ways of seeing the world. Turner makes it explicit in relation to liminality: "it is the analysis of culture into factors and their free or 'ludic' recombination in any and every possible pattern, however weird, that is of the essence of liminality, liminality *par excellence*."[13]

Periods of liminality can provoke marked psychological changes. For instance anthropologist Colin Turnbull experienced synesthesia during a liminal period with an African tribe, which he described in his article "Liminality: A Synthesis of Subjective and Objective Experience" (1990). As mentioned in the last chapter, synesthesia is typically associated with thin-boundary personality types. With Turnbull, it manifested during a breakdown of societal boundaries.

The idea of liminality has been adopted in a variety of areas, and it is not possible to review even a representative portion, but a few examples here might help illustrate how the ideas apply. Many more will be presented in forthcoming chapters.

Larry Peters, an anthropologist with an interest in psychotherapy, used the concepts. He pointed out that when shamans are called to their vocation they often undergo a crisis. They may roam forests, fast, see visions, and act in ways that westerners perceive as crazy. Yet by the end of the crisis, the person has new abilities and can become an important member of society.[14]

Peters recognized that the idea of creative illness, advanced by Henri Ellenberger in 1964, can be understood as a liminal process. A number of extraordinarily creative persons underwent a period of withdrawal, marginality, and sometimes even psychosis (e.g., Sigmund Freud, Carl Jung, Friedrich Nietzsche, Max Weber, Kurt Gödel). Several biographies of these figures have lamented the periods of withdrawal and sickness. But they failed to realize that these ultimately led to growth, transformation, intellectual power and leadership. Peters also explored borderline personality disorder. He pointed out that some of the symptoms (e.g., self-mutilation, anorexia) have parallels with shamanistic crisis experiences. The word "borderline" emphasizes the issue of boundaries. He suggested that the prevalence of the disorder today is partly due to lack of effective rites of passage. Our society devalues marginality and withdrawal and stigmatizes them, even though they can be sources of rejuvenation and creativity."[15]

Communitas

"Communitas" is a Latin term meaning feeling of fellowship. Turner adopted it in order to distinguish his concept from that of "community." In communitas, persons drop their normal roles and statuses, and a social leveling occurs. Turner explains that "at certain life crises, such as adolescence, the attainment of elderhood, and death ... the passage from one structural status to another may be accompanied by a strong sentiment of 'humankindness,' a sense of the generic social bond between all members of society ... regardless of their subgroup affiliations or incumbency of structural positions."[16] He notes that "The bonds of communitas are anti-structural in the sense that they are undifferentiated, equalitarian, direct."[17] Such situations can occur spontaneously but can also be organized as in initiations and rites of passage. As an example of spontaneous communitas, Turner mentioned the hippies of Haight-Ashbury in San Francisco in the 1960s. They had strong feelings of equality and sharing, and previous status differences were eliminated. The hippies dressed oddly, signalling their rejection of their prior roles; the work-a-day world was disdained, and any jobs they took were typically temporary and marginal. Drugs facilitated destructuring of consciousness.

Organized communitas occurs in some rites of passage, in which "It is as though they [the initiates] are being reduced or ground down to a uniform condition to be fashioned anew and endowed with additional powers to enable them to cope with their new station in life.

Among themselves, neophytes tend to develop an intense comradeship and egalitarianism."[18] In our culture, Marine Corps basic training (boot camp) is an example. The recruits are put in special quarters and are kept separate from other Marines. Their heads are shaved, and all markings of their former lives are removed. They have the lowest status in the military and are treated as such. They participate in rituals of singing and marching in formation. They become strongly bonded with their buddies and with the Corps generally. If they survive, they emerge transformed, with self-confidence, new abilities, and a new identity.

Communitas is linked with humility and at least interim loss of status; it forces one to realize that one is part of humanity and shares in the human condition. Rituals sometimes incorporate a temporary reversal of status; paupers become kings, and kings paupers. In some rites, a king may be reviled and spat upon—serving to remind him of his humanity, and cautioning him against the abuse of power. Turner likewise notes that "it is the marginal or 'inferior' person or the 'outsider' who often comes to symbolize what David Hume has called 'the sentiment for humanity,' which in its turn relates to the model we have termed 'communitas'."[19]

Turner also comments: "Communitas breaks in through the interstices of structure, in liminality; at the edges of structure, in marginality; and from beneath structure, in inferiority. It is almost everywhere held to be sacred or 'holy,' . . . Instinctual energies are surely liberated by these processes, but I am now inclined to think that communitas is not solely the product of biologically inherited drives released from cultural constraints."[20]

Communitas cannot last for long periods without some containing structure. Love-ins may descend into orgies, and parties into brawls; Dionysian elements can emerge. The great fluidity and chaos can eventually result in a totalitarian structure being rapidly imposed, as with cults and dictatorial regimes. With the potential for disorder, it is not surprising that established structures may be hostile to unregulated communitas. Despite the risks, Turner and van Gennep saw antistructural processes as often positive and crucial for rebirth and regeneration. Turner noted that "man is both a structural and an antistructural entity, who *grows* through anti-structure and *conserves* through structure."[21]

Trickster and Anti-structure

Periods of liminality and communitas disrupt ordinary, everyday activities and at times can completely overwhelm them. Thus the term anti-structure is another appropriate label for those conditions. The term liminality is better known in anthropology and literary studies than is anti-structure, but the word does more to obscure the concept than to explain it. The term anti-structure has distinct advantages. It evokes the idea of disruption, of the border between chaos and order, of being anti-establishment, as well as suggesting a connection with French structuralism and deconstructionism. The term liminal has none of those benefits, and I suspect that the use of that word has delayed the wider application of Turner's ideas. Turner understood the importance of anti-structure, and he used the term in the subtitle of his *The Ritual Process*. He later explicitly stated that "Roughly, the concepts of liminality and communitas define what I mean by anti-structure."[22]

The trickster has essentially the same properties as liminality, anti-structure, and communitas. Just on the face of it, *anti-structure* evokes ideas of disruption, a primary trickster quality, but there are other commonalities as well. Van Gennep's formulations dealt with, among other things, travelers, territorial passages, and boundary crossing. Hermes is a god of travelers and of boundaries. Liminality involves blurring of distinctions and oppositions such as life-death, male-female, and food-excrement. These are also associated with the trickster, and as explained below, the trickster is a mediator between binary oppositions. In relation to liminality, Turner specifically mentioned bisexuality, yet another trickster characteristic. In conjunction with anti-structure, he cited court jesters, and they are a subclass of tricksters. Turner discussed the trickster in his 1968 article "Myth and Symbol," but his later works gave it little or no attention.

Barbara Babcock, a literary theorist (now at the University of Arizona) and former student of Turner, has done more than anyone to explicate the connections between the trickster and liminality. She is the single most insightful commentator on the trickster, but to a large extent, scholars have not appreciated the full depth of her understanding. Her essay "A Tolerated Margin of Mess" was published in 1975 in the *Journal of the Folklore Institute*. In it Babcock identified 16 characteristics of tricksters and explained six functions that trickster tales play in society. Drawing on Turner's ideas of liminality, she suggested that the most important was the reflective-creative function. Trickster tales help us become conscious of aspects of life and culture that might otherwise be neglected. By becoming aware of them, we can rearrange them or see why it is best to leave them as they are.[23]

She addressed the trickster's relevance to creativity, specifically mentioning Arthur Koestler's book *The Act of Creation*, saying: "In contrast to routine thinking, the creative act of thought is always 'double-minded, i.e., a transitory state of unstable equilibrium where the balance of both emotion and thought is disturbed' [quoting Koestler] . . . In his famous essay on laughter, Henri Bergson similarly defined a situation as creative and comic if it belongs simultaneously to two independent series of events and is capable of being interpreted in two entirely different meanings at the same time."[24]

Babcock's essay has several tangential connections with parapsychology, although she was probably unaware of them. The title came from a quote of Aldous Huxley, a British writer who had taken part in telepathy experiments with classicist Gilbert Murray and who had also written about J. B. Rhine. In addition to discussing Bergson and Koestler, she also mentioned William James. Bergson, a Nobel laureate, served as president of the Society for Psychical Research (SPR); James also served as SPR president and helped found the American Society for Psychical Research. Arthur Koestler endowed a chair of parapsychology at the University of Edinburgh.[25]

Babcock noted the connection between creativity and the trickster, and Turner discussed creativity and liminality. Marginality is an aspect of liminality, and it helps foster creativity. Harvard psychologist Howard Gardner reviewed the lives of several highly creative people including Sigmund Freud, T. S. Eliot, Mahatma Gandhi, Pablo Picasso, Igor Stravinsky, Martha Graham, and Albert Einstein. In his book *Creating Minds* (1993) he noted that they typically strived to maintain positions of marginality (i.e., anti-structural or liminal positions). They felt that their creative potential could be stifled if they became too much part of the establishment.

Ellen Basso did extensive work on tricksters in Amazonia, and she recognized some of the same patterns as Babcock. In her book *In Favor of Deceit* (1987) she suggests that in order to understand the trickster: "We might look further, if we could, at Winnebago understandings of creative imagination, of poetic and shamanistic processes, and of dreaming. For example, a most prominent cultural theme involved the development of an adult identity through fasting in puberty, which was connected with quests for visions and protective guardians. The young seeker was forced to live outside the family camp, lonely and fearful ... of sudden encounters with powerful beings. The grandmother (like the grandmother of the Winnebago trickster Hare) seemed to have figured in major ways as a personal guide and guardian during these experiences ... Could there have been expectations that during these crucial life events the world suddenly lost its normal structure, or that a destructured world came into being, and with it the self of the seeker became deconstructed? To what extent were the orgies of self-abandonment connected with war-bundle rituals attempts to reclaim these experiences of a destructured world? If we could answer these questions, we might understand more clearly the various ways personal Winnebago events achieved significance through the sacred trickster narratives."[26]

This is a succinct statement of many crucial points. Unfortunately, Basso did not develop these ideas further, but she certainly recognized the connection between the trickster and anti-structure.

Liminality and communitas typically involve at least a temporary loss of status (i.e., loss of position in the social structure), and status loss can also serve as an impetus in the development of tricksters. This is seen in folklore, as Susan Niditch pointed out in her analysis of Biblical tricksters, but it is not limited to that. The same theme is found in the lives of impostors, which highlight the connection between liminality and deception.[27]

Trickster figures have particular appeal to marginal (low status) groups. In ancient Greece, aristocrats viewed merchants and craftsmen with suspicion and disdain. Norman Brown notes in his *Hermes the Thief* (1947) that "Hermes symbolized the aspirations of the non-aristocratic classes";[28] in fact Hermes was the patron of merchants. A similar situation was seen in the Middle Ages. As feudalism began to crumble, some of the nobility no longer enjoyed the privileges they once did. The merchants' plight improved, but their social position was unsettled, because their status was not bound to the class of their birth. The feudal and church authorities distrusted them, and fittingly, Reynard the Fox, a trickster, was their symbol. All this illustrates the nexus of merchants, liminality, unsettled status, and the trickster, and there was more. Anthropologist James Peacock suggests that monks supported the merchants in their opposition to church authorities.[29] As will be described in the next chapter, monks are permanently liminal persons.

The affinity between the trickster and marginal groups is also found our culture. Jay Edwards in *The Afro-American Trickster Tale* (1978) and John Roberts in *From Trickster to Badman* (1989) discussed the prominence of the trickster in African-American folklore (e.g., Br'er Rabbit). Henry Louis Gates, Jr., director of Harvard University's Afro-American studies program, even developed a theory of African-American literary criticism based on Eshu-Elegba, the Yoruba trickster god. Gerald Vizenor, a writer and professor with a mixed Anishinaabe-French heritage, has drawn attention to the trickster's importance to Native Americans. Gates' and Vizenor's work will be discussed in a later chapter on literary theory.

Structure and Binary Oppositions

"Opposites" is a recurring theme in the literature on the trickster and anti-structure. In periods of liminality, binary oppositions come to the fore, and it is worth repeating Turner's quote that initiates "are associated with such general oppositions as life and death, male and female, food and excrement, simultaneously."[30] As mentioned in the previous chapter, these are also directly associated with the trickster. This is puzzling, and it bespeaks internal contradictions, but this is an important clue to the nature of the trickster.

Scholars from a variety of areas have suggested that human thought is naturally organized in terms of binary oppositions. The oppositions form a kind of structure, parts of a whole; one helps define the other. This idea can be traced at least as far back as the pre-Socratic Greek philosopher Anaximander.

Our current Western worldview is founded upon Aristotelian logic, which is based on dichotomy, a type of binary opposition, i.e., something is either A or not-A. In fact, one of the fundamental laws of logical thought is referred to as "the law of the excluded middle." It allows no betwixt and between. This kind of logic is thus particularly hostile to blurring of distinctions, but tricksters do just that. They are subversive to Western rationality.

Within a binary opposition, one element of the pair is typically privileged (e.g., men having more power than women). When a structure is subverted or deconstructed, there is a reversal of the positions of privilege or a blurring or collapse of the line dividing the pair. When that happens, a liminal condition is established.

Figure 1 illustrates the ideas and gives a glimpse of how they relate to the paranormal.

Anti-Structure

HEAVEN	LIFE	GOD	MALE	FOOD	HUMAN	KING
ANGELS	SPIRITS	PRIESTS	BERDACHE	BIGFOOT		
UFOs	MEDIUMS			WEREWOLF		
	GHOSTS					
	REINCARNATION					
EARTH	DEATH	HUMAN	FEMALE	EXCREMENT	BEAST	PAUPER

(Arrows indicate reversal of status between KING↔PAUPER and FOOD↔EXCREMENT during liminal conditions.)

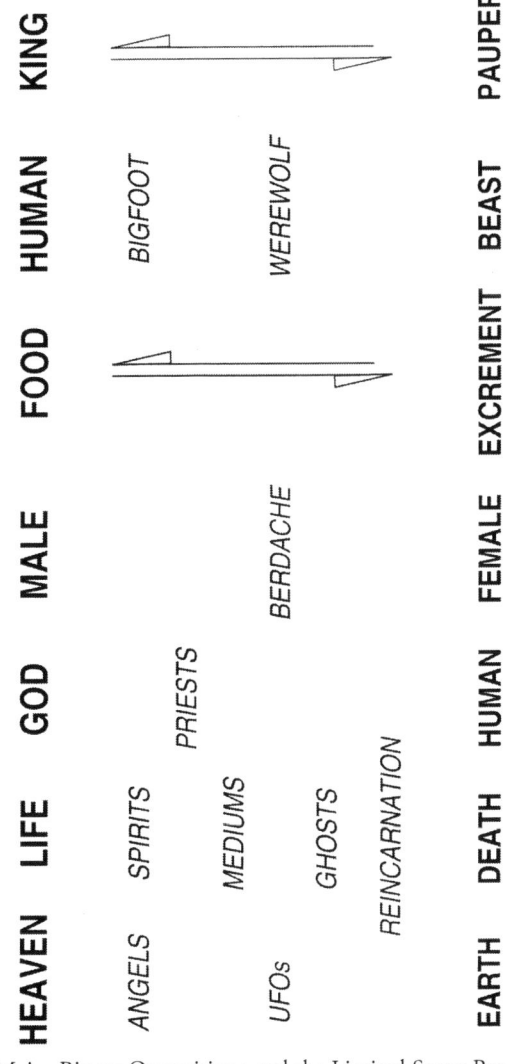

Figure 1 Major Binary Oppositions and the Liminal Space Between Them

Note: The elements in the top row generally have higher status than those in the bottom row. The items between the binary elements blur or mediate them. The arrows indicate a reversal of status during liminal conditions.

Notice that the elements in the top line have the higher status. They are generally viewed as more desirable, as having greater power, prestige, and privilege. Those on the bottom line are relatively inferior and less desirable.

The items between the opposition elements are affiliated with the paranormal or supernatural. Angels and UFOs traverse the realm between the heavens and the earth. Spirits, near-death experiences, reincarnation, and ghosts call into question the boundary between life and death. Priests mediate between gods and humans, and they are ritually protected when doing so. The berdache was a person in some American Indian cultures who took on the role and dress of the opposite sex. The berdache was considered to have supernatural power.

The arrows in Figure 1 indicate reversals. During liminal periods, a pauper may take the role of the king, and vice versa. Ritual clowns may eat excrement in liminal times.

Binary opposition is a significant theme in anthropology. In 1909 Robert Hertz, a student of Emile Durkheim, showed that binary oppositions played important roles in primitive classification schemes.[31] The matter became better known in the 1960s with the study of myth by Claude Levi-Strauss and the short-lived French intellectual movement known as structuralism. Much of Levi-Strauss' analysis involved binary oppositions, and he posited the existence of underlying mental structures that unite social, linguistic and psychological reality. The movement was ultimately unsuccessful in its grand aim, but structuralists introduced a number of seminal ideas that are still influential.

Partly in response to structuralism, the deconstructionist movement arose. Deconstructionism was academically prominent in literary criticism, but its influence is wider and is still causing controversy. Binary oppositions are central to several formulations of it.

Deconstructionists say that oppositions and privileged positions are simply arbitrary human constructions and that any arrangement is as valid as any other. Not surprisingly, those in positions of power are not altogether receptive to such notions. However, the arguments are far deeper than simple disputes between power elites and the disenfranchised. The entire notion of objective reality has been called into question by deconstructionists. Today those advocating deconstructionist ideas have almost no knowledge of their intellectual lineage. Hence important implications are no longer understood by academics. Most of them now think that the area betwixt and between opposition elements is empty. The history of how that happened will be reviewed in a later chapter.

Anti-structure and Danger

Turner notes "that liminal situations and roles are almost everywhere attributed with magico-religious properties . . . [and these are] often . . . regarded as dangerous, inauspicious, or polluting to persons, objects, events, and relationships that have not been ritually incorporated into the liminal context."[32] He explains that: "all sustained manifestations of communitas . . . have to be hedged around with prescriptions, prohibitions, and conditions."[33] The sacred is surrounded by taboos, and there are innumerable examples.

Anthropologist John Middleton investigated binary classification schemes among the Lugbara of Uganda and found that breaches of the schemes are regarded as uncanny and dangerous. He tells us: "The confusion of order and disorder is seen as the confusion of authority (which is moral, responsible, controlled, and predictable) and power (which is amoral, perhaps immoral, irresponsible, uncontrollable, and unpredictable). The people associated with this confusion have in common the characteristic of themselves being incomplete and so representing the essential nature of disorder itself. These people are diviners, prophets, witches, rainmakers."[34] David Hicks reports in his book *Tetum Ghosts and Kin* (1976) that similar patterns were found in Indonesia. Persons ambiguous in binary classification schemes (e.g., hermaphrodites) were viewed as having supernatural power.

Cambridge anthropologist Edmund Leach has given some of the best expositions of the issues. His 1962 essay "Genesis as Myth" notes that God-man is a major opposition, and he explains that "'Mediation' (in this sense) is always achieved by introducing a third category which is 'abnormal' or 'anomalous' in terms of ordinary 'rational' categories. Thus myths are full of fabulous monsters, incarnate gods, virgin mothers. This middle ground is abnormal, non-natural, holy. It is typically the focus of all taboo and ritual observance."[35] This middle ground is the liminal, the interstitial, the betwixt and between, the anti-structural; it provides contact with the supernatural realm.

The same issues are found in religion today, and the writings of German religious scholar Rudolf Otto illuminate these matters. In his seminal work, *The Idea of the Holy* (1917), he explores the concept of the "numinous," a realm peculiar and unique to religion. Otto explains that this domain is an objective reality and not just a subjective feeling, though it has nothing to do with the rational. A primary function of religion is to deal with this aspect of existence. Otto explicitly recognizes that miracles come from the numinous. The numinous evokes an awe and fascination with an extra-rational power, the *mysterium tremendum*. But there is a negative aspect, sometimes referred to as the wrath of God. Otto notes that "this 'wrath' has no concern whatever with moral qualities . . . It is 'incalculable' and 'arbitrary'";[36] it is encountered in the "grisly." There is a duality to the divine.

Otto notes that a much-subdued experience of this wrath is seen in the fear of ghosts. Ghosts are liminal (interstitial) creatures. They exist in the netherworld between life and death, and they challenge the idea that there is a clear separation of the two. The dread evoked by such beings can be profoundly disturbing. Surprisingly, parapsychologists have largely neglected this, but folklorists have drawn attention to it. William Clements' papers "The Interstitial Ogre" (1987) and "Interstitiality in Contemporary Legends" (1991) give a helpful introduction. Linda Degh and Andrew Vazsonyi noted that encounters with such entities raise primal questions such as "Is there anything one can hang onto? Is there a solid basis on which one can base one's trust in this confusing universe . . . ? It is not the individual who is separated from his 'security base' . . . The world itself has lost its protective familiarity."[37] It is precisely this that evokes such intense hostility to claims of the paranormal by some, and extreme anxiety in others, though it is rarely recognized consciously.

British anthropologist Mary Douglas addresses perils of the liminal in her frequently cited book *Purity and Danger* (1966). Speaking of restrictions and taboos, she says "some are intended to protect divinity from profanation, and others to protect the profane from the dangerous intrusion of divinity. Sacred rules are thus merely rules hedging divinity off, and uncleanness is the two-way danger of contact with divinity."[38] The supernatural's intrusion must be limited. Douglas later comments: "Ritual recognizes the potency of disorder. In the disorder of the mind, in dreams, faints and frenzies, ritual expects to find powers and truths which cannot be reached by conscious effort. Energy to command and special powers of healing come to those who can abandon rational control for a time."[39] In disorder, comes power, too, in disorder is danger.

Even though many other scholars could be quoted about the supernatural dangers associated with liminal conditions, scientists today pay them little heed. Such ideas are viewed as quaint superstitions. Any scientist who took them seriously would invite derision, and loss of status. Understandably, parapsychologists rarely discuss these potential risks of their work.

All this is directly applicable to the trickster because he is a denizen of the interstitial realm, and a few analyses of the trickster give clues to the dangers. Laura Makarius' discussions are some of the most disturbing. She called attention to the peculiarities and incongruities so frequently encountered in trickster tales and commented that "they have been introduced for the express purpose of concealing some secret fact striving for expression."[40] Explicit recognition of this is crucial to deciphering the meaning, and she goes on to say: "What that hidden fact is, it is the goal of the student of folklore to discover. But he cannot do so without a knowledge of that deeper contradiction in the behavior of primitive peoples between what they may do and what they may not. The contradiction manifests itself when forbidden acts are committed for the same basic reasons for which they are forbidden. That is why they express themselves only if at the same time they are suppressed . . . The deliberate violation of taboo constitutes one of the deepest contradictions of primitive life. Its purpose is the obtainment of magical power."[41]

Makarius elaborated on the theme in her article "The Magic of Transgression" (1974) and noted that murder and incest are sometimes committed deliberately in order to obtain supernatural benefits. A number of trickster stories involve incest,[42] and cannibalism and human sacrifice have been widely practiced in order to gain magical power.[43] All are extreme violations of taboo—extreme disruptions of moral structure. Occultists such as Aleister Crowley assert that sexual perversion in ritual magic increases its power, and material presented in this book supports that ominous conclusion. These ideas are not limited to primitive cultures and bizarre occultists; I will remind the reader that images of cannibalism and human sacrifice are central to Christianity.

Barre Toelken, the head of the folklore program at Utah State University, has also given warnings about the trickster. Between 1954 and 1994 he carried out extensive fieldwork with the Navajo, preparing scholarly articles on them. All indications are that he was a perceptive and sympathetic investigator and well accepted by the Navajo; in fact he even married the niece of one of his primary informants.[44]

Toelken had a particular interest in coyote stories, and he collected them during his fieldwork. The tales were told only during the winter, and though he tape-recorded them, he agreed to play the tapes only in that season. Further, in his teaching, he presented the stories only during the winter term. Because of his work and sensitivity, he was given the honor of speaking about the trickster to an audience exclusively of Navajos. The talk was greeted favorably, and at the end, a panel of elders made comments. The final commentator praised the talk but said that it would be a good time to discuss "what the Coyote stories are *really* about"[45] and then proceeded to lecture for two hours.

In his analysis, Toelken uncovered several layers of meaning of the stories, and he came to learn how fragments of them might be used in healing ceremonies. Given the elder's comment, he had some glimmer that his own understanding was incomplete. Even though he had heard the stories for almost 30 years, it wasn't until late one night in 1982 that he discovered that he had failed to grasp some substantial implications. As Toelken was interviewing an eminent singer (medicine man) about coyote stories, the singer asked him if he was prepared to lose a member of his family.

The singer explained that though parts of the tales could be used for healing, some could be used for witchcraft. Toelken's analytical dissection of the tales suggested that he intended to use them for that purpose, and losing a family member was the price to be paid for becoming a witch. The singer went on to tell him that even if he had no such intention, his inquiries would lead others to suspect him of being a witch, and to try to kill someone in his family.

Toelken was understandably shocked, and a bit alarmed, and he began to reassess his interpretations. There came to pass several events that gave him pause. His informant's family suffered a series of accidental deaths and other misfortunes. Toelken could not logically link them to the revealing of the tales to outsiders, but he could not dismiss the possible connection either. He considered the risks to his informants and family and eventually decided to halt his inquiries into the coyote tales.

In April 1981, some months before his late-night talk with the singer, Toelken had taken part in a conference that discussed the trickster. It was out of season to tell the stories, so he obtained a special dispensation from a medicine man. Even so, as he was about to leave for the conference, he bent over to pick up his luggage and passed out. He struck his chin and bled profusely; this was followed by other problems and several synchronicities involving coyotes. Those no doubt helped make him receptive to the singer's warning, but he was ambivalent about any "rational" explanation for the events.

Toelken's experiences and discussion raise perplexing questions, not just for the study of the trickster, but for ethnographers and folklorists generally. Even at the basic level of intellectual understanding, an outside investigator may fail to grasp some of the most essential aspects, especially those that do not fit into Western logic. Toelken was very candid about his experiences, but one suspects that many investigators would dismiss similar ones if they occurred to them. They might justifiably fear the ridicule and scorn of their professional colleagues.

But obviously the questions are far deeper, and more disturbing. Probing the religious and supernatural aspects of other cultures may unleash forces alien to Western understanding, even when the information is packaged as humorous stories for children. The very idea that this might be possible goes completely against the ethos of scientific rationalism that decrees that all topics should be open for investigation. Yet close intellectual study and analysis may have unexpected repercussions. Perhaps just possessing certain types of knowledge is dangerous. There are ample examples of Western scientific hubris, and scientific rationalism may be yet another. Toelken's papers should be read by anyone thinking of pursuing fieldwork, especially into the sacred, supernatural, or paranormal.

Psi and Anti-structure

Anti-structure and the paranormal are closely affiliated, and this will be repeatedly illustrated in coming chapters. The next few paragraphs give the reader a brief introduction. Turner made explicit acknowledgement of mystical power in relation to liminality: "In preindustrial and early industrial societies with multiplex social relations, spontaneous communitas appears to be very frequently associated with mystical power and to be regarded as a charism or grace sent by the deities or ancestors . . . by impetrative ritual means, attempts are made, mostly in the phases of liminal seclusion, to cause the deities or ancestors to bring this charism of communitas among men . . . it [is] expected best to arise in the intervals between incumbencies of social positions and statuses, in what used to be known as 'the interstices of the social structure.'"[46]

The direct mention of ghosts, gods, and ancestors in relation to liminality is of particular note because all are sources of supernatural power. They sometimes appear as "hallucinations" and convey verifiable, previously unknown information. The vision quests of shamans and the lives of mystics and mediums are replete with accounts of meetings with supernatural beings and demonstrations of psychic abilities. These people typically cultivate altered states of consciousness

(ASCs), and surveys, case studies, and laboratory experiments all verify that ASCs facilitate the occurrence of psychic phenomena.

Biblical prophets displayed anti-structural characteristics. Abraham Heschel described them in his *The Prophets* (1962). Many were outsiders, and indeed, some appear mad, and Heschel devoted an entire chapter to prophecy and psychosis. Turner similarly noted that: "Prophets and artists tend to be liminal and marginal people, 'edgemen,' who strive with a passionate sincerity to rid themselves of the clichés associated with status incumbency and role-playing and to enter into vital relations with other men in fact or imagination. In their productions we may catch glimpses of that unused evolutionary potential in mankind which has not yet been externalized and fixed in structure."[47]

Turner spoke of the "powers of the weak" and noted the sacred attributes of temporary or permanent low status. He also commented that moral powers reside with them. As I will discuss shortly, mystics often voluntarily take on low status, and mystics have often chastised church authorities (mystics have also displayed some of the most extreme psi functioning ever reported). Turner's allusion to moral powers residing in those with low status pertains to our culture as well. Pollster George H. Gallup, Jr. and Timothy Jones studied saintly people and wrote *The Saints Among Us* in 1992. They found that older, poor black women in the South (the lowest of the low) had an exceptionally high percentage of saintly persons.

Geographic boundary crossing is associated with anti-structure and tricksters. It is also related to psychic functioning. Wanderers and gypsies live outside the larger social structure and its rules and laws. Traditionally they are famous for fortune-telling and clairvoyance, and gypsies also have a reputation for duplicity and thievery.[48] It is no coincidence that Hermes is also the god of thieves. By the way, Victor Turner traveled with a band of gypsies early in his career, and that probably enhanced his appreciation of outsiderhood, marginality, and liminality.

Susan Niditch discussed the association of prophecy with travelers in her *Underdogs and Tricksters*. She noted that biblical tricksters typically were gifted with prophecy but were at times forced to move from their homelands. The geographic boundary crossing idea has wider applicability however, and the relationship can be seen in our society today. Sociologist William Sims Bainbridge found that in metropolitan areas with relatively high mobility (in terms of frequency of change of residence), elevated levels of paranormal experiences were reported.[49] This is just one example how these ideas apply to us.

As will be described, we find openness to the paranormal in marginal, low-status groups and individuals, i.e., those associated with anti-structure. In our own society, paranormal ideas and practices have been kept alive by them. The work of anthropologist Michael Winkelman, covered later, shows that direct, intentional engagement with paranormal practices is associated with low status in a wide range of cultures. This has profound implications for those who wish to study psi scientifically.

To briefly summarize the major points of this chapter, the concepts of anti-structure, liminality, interstitiality, betwixt and between, and marginality are at the core of the trickster and the paranormal. In addition, the matter of binary oppositions is key. These themes will inform the rest of this book. They are all crucial for a theoretical understanding of the trickster as well as many other concepts in the humanities and social sciences. So far they have had virtually no impact on theories of the paranormal.

Part 2

Overview

The next two chapters cover mystics and shamans. They have demonstrated some of the most extraordinary paranormal phenomena ever recorded. They are also prime exemplars of anti-structure, liminality, and the trickster.

I have met a number of people who had limited familiarity with the concept of liminality. They thought that it only referred to rites of passage and transition. They did not realize that individuals can be liminal, some even permanently. This Part focuses on such persons.

Mystics are truly fascinating, and quite exotic. Their trickster and anti-structural qualities are strong, disruptive, even grotesque. I will present a number of bizarre specimens from other cultures. Were they alive now, they would probably be incarcerated. Many are eminently memorable, but most are little known.

Shamans were perhaps the first humans to intentionally wield supernatural power. They have also been observed in trickery. This signals the deep connection between liminality and deception, and highlights the importance of the trickster. Western scholars seem to find shamanic trickery embarrassing, and like the reality of paranormal phenomena, they avoid discussing it.

CHAPTER 5

Mysticism, Holy Madness, And Fools for God

Mysticism is a confusing word. It refers to the belief in, and experience of, a direct, sublime union with the divine. But it also means secret or occult knowledge, or vague and confused speculation. Many saints were mystics, but performers of magic tricks sometimes adopt the label for themselves. The divergent definitions reflect the ambiguous nature of the phenomenon. (I will restrict my usage to the religious sense, but I will not neglect the commonalities with the other types.)

Mystics engage in extended periods of meditation and contemplation and can become detached from the everyday world. They seek to unite with God—obliterating the boundaries between self and divinity.[1] Mysticism is ultimately about boundaries because it inherently challenges the clear separation of God and human, a major binary opposition for all cultures. Mystics can embody liminality.

Victor Turner recognized this saying: "Nowhere has this institutionalization of liminality been more clearly marked and defined than in the monastic and mendicant states in the great world religions."[2] In his essay "Betwixt and Between" Turner noted: "A further structurally negative characteristic of transitional beings is that they *have* nothing. They have no status, property, insignia, secular clothing, rank, kinship position, nothing to demarcate them structurally from their fellows. Their condition is indeed the very prototype of sacred poverty. Rights over property, goods, and services inhere in positions in the politico-jural structure. Since they do not occupy such positions, neophytes exercise no such rights."[3] One could hardly hope to find a better description of the cloistered life. Monks and nuns take vows of poverty and obedience; they are apart from their families and have little or no secular life.

Mystical experiences are ineffable. They cannot be fully described by words. Mysticism is explicitly nonrational, and at times it is greeted with hostility. Academic scientists sometimes use the term as one of disparagement, thereby signalling the unconscious taboos surrounding it. Mysticism has an uneasy position in our culture, even in religion, and many denominations now subtly avoid the topic. It is often connected with the paranormal, but not always comfortably. Some of the most saintly religious mystics have shunned psychic powers while acknowledging their existence.

Mysticism has its disreputable aspects, and many famous mystics and saints were exceedingly disruptive of the social order. They disconcerted people, were persecuted as heretics and often imprisoned or even killed. Many seem decidedly odd and even insane, and there is a long history of "fools for God." This is reflected in book titles such as *Holy Madness* (1991) by Georg Feuerstein and *Perfect Fools* (1980) by John Saward. Mystics have also displayed some of the most extreme manifestations of the trickster. A number of them had ambiguous sexual orientations; some sexually abused their devotees; some simulated paranormal phenomena in order to lure followers. This association between mysticism and deception is long-standing, and many times it is difficult to tell the difference between a holy man and con artist, or even if it is meaningful to speak of any such distinction.

Nevertheless, mystics have fostered important religious traditions. They have also demonstrated some of the most powerful psychic phenomena ever recorded, including instantaneous healings, immunity to fire, and levitation. Herbert Thurston's *The Physical Phenomena of Mysticism* (1952) presents an impressive number of them. (Thurston was a Jesuit, a member of the Society for Psychical Research, and he also helped revise and edit *Butler's Lives of the Saints*. His works are some of the classics of psychical research.)

The examples that follow will illustrate just how odd and grotesque mystics can be. Perhaps understandably, many writers have an aversion to addressing the more unsavory matters. Many try to sanitize the topic and discuss only the respectable features. That is unfortunate because mystics are some of the most extraordinary specimens of humankind, and extreme cases illuminate elemental aspects of human existence.

Some Illustrative Cases

Nityananda of Ganeshpuri (1896?–1961), a renowned Indian teacher and mystic, was especially colorful, and his biographer M. U.

Hatengdi has recounted some of his antics in *Nityananda: The Divine Presence* (1984). During his early years Nityananda walked around naked and greatly embarrassed his devotees. He lived in forests and caves and violated a number of orthodox Hindu laws. Occasionally when a cow would pass by, he would wait for it to defecate and then grab the cowpat and eat it. Nityananda once smeared excrement over his entire body and then sat with large piles of it, offering some to passers-by as a sweet, again mortifying his followers. Yet he was famous for miraculous healings, prophetic powers, and even weather control. Excrement is seen in particularly extreme and primitive manifestations of the trickster and liminality. Nityananda inverted the food-excrement binary opposition. This challenges our current notions of the sacred.

Saint Simeon Salus (d. ca. 590) of the Catholic tradition was another odd character.[4] Simeon was born into a well-to-do family, but in his early twenties, he abandoned his elderly mother and entered a monastery, along with a friend who had abandoned his new wife. The two soon left it for the desert, becoming hermits. After 29 years, Simeon had had enough of the desert and went to the city of Emesa (Homs in modern Syria) where he became known as a fool. Sometimes he simulated madness. For instance he once found a dead dog on a dung heap, tied it to his belt and dragged it along after him. Not surprisingly, he was ridiculed and even beaten for that, but he willingly accepted the consequences. On another occasion he went to church and extinguished the candles, just as the service was beginning. When some of those present tried to remove him, he ran to the pulpit and began throwing nuts at women. He ate sausages on Good Friday, and he was known to run through women's baths. He was notorious for eating beans, which caused him to expel large quantities of gas. He defecated in the marketplace and consorted with prostitutes. Yet St. Simeon possessed miraculous powers. He held hot coals in his hands, predicted the future, and displayed telepathy. He was also known for multiplying food.

Francis of Assisi (1182–1226) is one of the most popular of all saints. His father was a financially successful merchant, but in his early twenties he renounced his inheritance and began associating with lepers and beggars. He stole cloth from his father, sold it, and refused to make any restitution. His father complained to a bishop, who commanded St. Francis to return the money. A large assemblage was present at the time, and upon hearing that command, he took off all his clothes and stood naked. This incident has been immortalized by a number of artists. St. Francis' stigmata included not only bleeding, but also black nail-like protuberances formed from his flesh making it difficult for him to walk.[5] His confessor, Brother Leo, saw him levitate during prayer, sometimes so high that he was not able to touch him. St. Francis was also gifted with prophecy and healing.[6]

Victor Turner discussed St. Francis in his *The Ritual Process* (1969). He mentioned that St. Francis strived to maintain a permanent liminal state. Turner also pointed out that the saint thought in primary, concrete visual images and spoke in parables, rather than abstractions, in order to illustrate his points. St. Francis operated satisfactorily with small groups, but the abstraction required for organizing larger numbers of people was beyond him. He and his followers depended on the church for support, and he insisted that his order own no property or money. This caused the institutional church great difficulties, and the Franciscans were viewed with suspicion. Eventually however, organizational structures were established that contained at least some of the Franciscan ideals. This was partly accomplished through the greater administrative ability of St. Bonaventure, who is considered the second founder of the Franciscan order. (St. Bonaventure was a contemporary of the Dominican, St. Thomas Aquinas, whose writings on theology somewhat eclipsed those of St. Bonaventure. Aquinas is associated more with rationalist and Artistotelian traditions, Bonaventure more with mystical and Neoplatonic traditions, including the concept of the coincidence of opposites.[7])

St. Francis was renowned for his communion with nature, particularly with birds. Tricksters and liminality also share this feature. Barbara Babcock pointed out that the Winnebago trickster was in close contact with nature, and she quoted from Paul Radin's book *The Trickster* that says that the trickster calls "all the objects in the world younger brothers when speaking to them. He and all objects in the world understood one another, understood, indeed, one another's language."[8] This strikingly parallels St. Francis, who in his "Canticle of Brother Sun" refers to Brother Son, Sister Moon, Brother Wind, and others. The similarity to the Winnebago tales powerfully confirms the trickster pattern across cultures. St. Francis' association with birds is very well known, but medieval fools were also frequently connected with birds,[9] as were novices in liminal periods.[10] Religious scholar Mircea Eliade in his book *Shamanism: Archaic Techniques of Ecstasy* (1951) noted that many shamans were reputed to understand animals' language and communicate with them.[11] Classical scholar E. R. Dodds in his *The Greeks and the Irrational* (1951) noted the role of birds in Greek magical practices.[12] Birds can be seen as living between the heavens and the earth and as messengers between the realms. Thus birds have a betwixt and between quality.[13]

Saint Lydwine of Schiedam (1380–1433) was one of the most exotic saints. She was clairvoyant, made prophecies and performed miraculous healings, but her biography is one of the most gruesome ever recorded.[14] Not only was she plagued with stigmata, but she was bedridden for most of her life, and her condition caused much festering. Large worms bred in the putrefaction, and they appeared as if boiling under her skin; over a hundred were taken out at one time. An eminent physician determined that her ills were divinely caused, but in order to ease her suffering, her intestines were removed, separated, cleaned and the fit portion was replaced.[15] Nevertheless, the torment continued, and her belly burst like a ripe fruit, spilling out her entrails, yet she continued to live. Another time, still bedridden, skeptics taunted and ridiculed her, and after accusing her of fraud, they ripped open her abdomen. She was denounced as being in league with the devil, and some church authorities were hostile to her. She rebuked several.

St. Lydwine's life presents us with an impressive collection of liminal and trickster characteristics. Not only did she display psychic powers, but like several of the trickster gods, she made visits to the underworld (purgatory) and also escorted souls to heaven. She spent extended periods in mystical, ecstatic trance (an altered state of consciousness). Her life was characterized by disruption and almost complete dissolution of her body. There were accusations of deception, yet she produced numerous miracles.

St. Joseph of Copertino (1603–1663) was one of the best-attested levitators in history. Eric Dingwall prepared one of the most impressive evaluations of the saint in his book *Some Human Oddities* (1947). Dingwall's assessment merits note as he was a magician, an avowed rationalist, a member of the Committee for the Scientific Investigation of Claims of the Paranormal (CSICOP) and of the Rationalist Press Association (RPA). He was also an exceedingly knowledgeable psychical researcher. The following brief summary is derived from the 39 pages of material he presented.

Joseph of Copertino was a severe ascetic; he wore a prickly hair shirt and bound his loins in chains. To make his food unpalatable, he would put a bitter powder on it. His diet was abominable, and his lack of nutrition and poor hygiene kept him in a ravaged condition. He fastened a metal plate to his body so that it pressed into his sores.

Joseph practiced long hours of contemplation and sometimes spontaneously became entranced. He was often quite useless for any practical work, and in his obliviousness to the world, during his chores he sometimes accidentally broke crockery. Then he would wear the broken pieces around his neck in order to increase his humiliation. This rarely endeared him to his fellows, and St. Joseph was ejected from more than one religious group. Several authorities became suspicious of him, and he was called before the Inquisition but emerged unscathed. His miracles were astounding. He displayed telepathy, clairvoyance, powers of healing, multiplication of food, the ability to find lost objects, in addition to innumerable levitations occurring in good light and confirmed by many observers. The Duke of Brunswick, patron of Leibnitz, was one witness. He was so moved that he converted from Lutheranism after twice seeing Joseph levitate, once for about a quarter of an hour.

Sri Ramakrishna (1836–1886) was one of the greatest saints in India and the spiritual teacher of Vivekananda, who is recognized for bringing Hinduism to the West. In his early days, Ramakrishna sometimes worshiped his own genitals, and he often dressed as a woman.[16] At times he used his hair as a mop to clean the homes of the most wretched poor. He would enter temples, lie down at places reserved for a goddess, and eat the food placed there as an offering for her. During one period he identified with Hanuman, the monkey god. He swung through trees and subsisted on roots and fruits. His coccyx grew, giving him something of a tail, a phenomenon perhaps analogous to the stigmata of Christians. Ramakrishna viewed money and sex as great impediments to the spiritual life. He had precognitive experiences but renounced psychic powers;[17] in fact the well known author and screenwriter Christopher Isherwood quotes Ramakrishna as advising "Shun them, like filthy excrement."[18]

Jansenism produced a number of amazing mystics. It was a loosely organized, somewhat austere and puritanical movement within the Catholic Church in France in the seventeenth and eighteenth centuries. The movement was based on the posthumously published writings of Cornelius Jansen, a bishop who died in 1638. He allotted free will only small role in obtaining salvation, and his writings were condemned as heretical by the Church. The movement attracted a range of people; among the most eminent was Blaise Pascal, the scientist, philosopher and mathematician.

Jansenism had many anti-structural qualities; it had no clearly defined leader nor any uniform, coherent set of beliefs. The Jansenists were disruptive, and both religious and secular authorities persecuted them. History professor B. Robert Kreizer described this in his book *Miracles, Convulsions, and Ecclesiastical Politics in Early Eighteenth-Century Paris* (1978). In 1727 an ascetic Jansenist deacon, Francois de Paris, died and was buried in the cemetery of Saint-Medard. His death attracted great attention, and numerous miracles occurred in association with him and his tomb. Some of the more bizarre are recounted in Dingwall's fascinating work *Some Human Oddities* (1947). Several Jansenists became regular performers at the cemetery and were known as convulsionnaires. Some were immune to fire; others underwent voluntary crucifixions. One of the most wonderful was the Eater of Ordure, a woman who was investigated by Parisian lawyer, M. le Paige. He carefully weighed the amount of fecal matter she ate. At times after eating excrement, she reputedly vomited up fresh milk. This is a wild, graphic reversal of the food-excrement binary opposition. Despite its memorability, I do not recall seeing the case mentioned by anyone but Dingwall.

The milieu of the Jansenists merits comment, especially in light of the numerous miracles. The Jansenists did not trust the ecclesiastical or the political authorities, and the Church and state took a similar view of them. The movement was widespread, but it had no clear focal leadership nor codified belief system. There was little containing structure, and thus it was particularly unbounded. The term anti-structure is especially applicable. In a later chapter on unbounded conditions, I will describe how those situations are especially rife with trickster phenomena.

Anti-structural And Trickster Aspects Of Mysticism

The saints, mystics, and gurus described above are a miniscule fraction of the examples that could be cited. Georg Feuerstein's book *Holy Madness* (1991) provides a superb summary of the lives of many exotic mystics from a variety of religious traditions, and he gives a sophisticated discussion of tricksters and clowns. Feuerstein did not cite Victor Turner nor the concept of anti-structure, but he certainly recognized the pattern when he described holy fools saying: "their folly was clearly not merely passive. First, their spiritual fervor and extreme asceticism could not help but make an impact on their communities, if only by provoking disapproval and mockery. Second, their behavior, which they considered spiritually superior to that of ordinary worldlings, was an implicit criticism of the secular life-style. Third, their folly at times involved offensive acts that were designed to shock and provoke a reaction."[19] In addition, their miraculous phenomena were looked upon as signs of grace from God; the miracles gave them legitimacy, and the authority of the established religious hierarchy was thereby called into question.

The monastic life provides no immunity against deception in the paranormal realm, and it may even stimulate it. Ian Wilson's book *Stigmata* (1989) provides a detailed consideration of problems of fraud attending that phenomenon. Dingwall's *Very Peculiar People* and *Some Human Oddities* report on a number of tricksters among monks and nuns. Jerome Oetgen, the biographer of Boniface Wimmer, head of a Benedictine abbey, tells of the particularly informative case of Paul Keck. Keck was a professional actor, but in 1859 at age 23 he entered Wimmer's abbey in Latrobe, Pennsylvania. Shortly thereafter, he had a vision of a monk who had died 77 years previously and who asked for prayers. There was an investigation, and at least some evidence was found that such a monk had indeed existed. Keck later made prophecies, some of which came true, further enhancing his reputation. Soon he was embroiled in political battles over the direction of the abbey, with his faction wanting a more rigorous observance of monasticism and less involvement with the outside world. Keck's charisma made him persuasive, and he was given a large hand in running the monastery. Skeptical monks had doubts about his holiness, and on a trip away from the abbey, Keck took part in a raucous party and tried to seduce another monk. Additional questions were raised about his honesty. Eventually the Office of the Inquisition reviewed the case and concluded that his visions deserved no credence.[20]

I was alerted to the Keck case by a paper by Van A. Reidhead, an anthropologist at the University of Missouri-St. Louis. Reidhead made an extensive study of the Benedictine tradition, and his article "Structure and Anti-Structure in Monasticism and Anthropology" (1993) provides an excellent discussion of Turner's ideas in relation to monasticism. It helps explain how the highly structured social and physical environment of the monastery can contain the liminality of mystical practices. Liminality is of particular relevance to the Benedictines because they often serve as guides for people undergoing visionary and paranormal experiences (guides through liminality).

I have a debt of gratitude to Reidhead because he explicitly used the term anti-structure in the title of his paper. That attracted my attention. Even though I was completely unfamiliar with the term and knew nothing of Turner's work, I knew that there was a strong relationship between processes of destructuring and psi. When I read his discussion of Keck, I realized that there was also a connection between anti-structure and the trickster, and that led me to study Turner. Reidhead's article was a key link for me.

The nefarious behaviors of monks are relatively little known, and perhaps many would prefer it that way. The cloistered life provides some containing structure for liminality and limits its intrusion, including the trickery, into the larger world. In spite of the problems that accompany mystical practices, Reidhead points out that certain monastic orders are some of the longest-lived institutions in the world. They have much to teach us about structure and anti-structure.

Psychological and Other Aspects Of Mysticism

Mysticism has not only social effects but also profound psychological ones. St. Francis' style of thought is an example. Turner noted that: "This concrete, personal, imagist mode of thinking is highly characteristic of those in love with existential communitas, with the direct relation between man and man, and man and nature. Abstractions appear as hostile to live contact. William Blake, for example, a great literary exponent of communitas in his *Prophetic Books*, wrote that 'he [who] would do good to others must do it in Minute Particulars; General Good is the plea of the Hypocrite and Scoundrel.'"[21]

A few comments should be made about Turner's passage because the large issue of abstraction will continue to be important in this book. As mentioned previously, St. Francis' low level of abstract thinking made it impossible for him to care for large groups, and that is one important effect. However, abstraction is also relevant to understanding theoretical issues in areas as diverse as magic tricks and ethnomethodology, which will be covered later. Turner also alluded to imagery, and that too will be raised in coming chapters, including its use in magic and modern-day witchcraft.

Stigmata is another phenomenon of mysticism related to boundary blurring and liminality. In Catholicism, the pervasive imagery of the crucified Christ affected mystics who strived to identify with him. A number of them displayed the wounds of Christ on their bodies, and this suggests blurring of the usual boundaries between mind and body. Ian Wilson notes that historically, there have been seven women stigmatists for every man. This is consistent with Ernest Hartmann's finding that women have thinner boundaries than men and that thinner boundary people demonstrate greater volitional control over physiological processes.

Mystics sometimes speak of divine marriage, and they often forego the usual earthly unions. Turner noted that in situations of extended communitas, within some constraining structure such as monasteries or utopian societies, either celibacy or group marriage is mandated. An exclusive male-female sexual relationship is a dyadic structure opposed to communitas. The trickster shares this property of communitas for he is known for sexual disruption and violation of taboos. Both the trickster and communitas destabilize dyadic relationships. I suspect that this is partly the basis for the rule of celibacy for Catholic priests, monks, and nuns. My observations suggest that strong contact with the paranormal can strain marital relationships. P.M.H. Atwater, a researcher on near-death experiences (NDEs) and an experiencer herself, noted that divorce is often a consequence of NDEs.[22] Likewise, people sometimes become involved with the paranormal after the death of a spouse. This general idea is further supported by a multinational survey reported in the *Journal of the American Society for Psychical Research* in 1991.[23] Separated, divorced and widowed people had higher rates of paranormal experiences than the married. In short, supernatural contact leads to disruption of relationships, but such disruption also leads to contact or involvement with the supernatural—the pattern is constellational rather than causal.

The lives of ascetics personify troubling philosophical questions that are not easily resolved. Some mystics commune with Jesus or the Blessed Virgin Mary, have ecstatic visions of heaven, and display grace through miraculous powers of healing and clairvoyance; yet they often endure severe physical suffering, battle demons, and undergo mental breakdowns. As in the story of Job, the life of Lydwine of Schiedam brings into stark relief the question of whether God is merciful and just. Some of the most profound religious questions deal with this topic. Carl Jung's most controversial work, *Answer to Job* (1952), dealt with the matter, and in fact, Stanley Diamond's introduction to the 1972 edition of Paul Radin's *The Trickster* is entitled "Job and the Trickster."

Why did God allow such brutal tortures to be inflicted upon St. Lydwine when she was so holy? Such a case, where direct, personal suffering is endured by someone reputedly close to God, poses a philosophical dilemma that is neither abstract nor obscure. The physical trauma impacts not only the mystic but anyone who sees it. This direct, living contact is exceptionally powerful. It is easier for the ecclesiastical authorities to avoid the issue, to ignore or downplay the role of mysticism, rather than confront and explain it. The more one becomes immersed in trickster phenomena, the more salient the questions can become. After deep involvement with Fortean research, investigator John Keel wrote *The Eighth Tower* (1975) asking not: "Does God exist?" but rather the much more disturbing question: Is God sane? Encounters with the supernatural can be profoundly unsettling and provoke questions that raise grave doubts about the legitimacy of religious and scientific authority.

Eruptions of mysticism and the paranormal destabilize the rational world. The phenomena, and the questions they raise, are deeply disturbing. Supernatural events can legitimize what would otherwise be seen as deviance or even madness. It is no accident that the mystic is often cloistered, thereby restricting divinity's contact with the larger world. The necessity for this was recognized long ago, but our now-rationalized society has lost this understanding.

CHAPTER 6

Shamanism And Its Sham

Shamans are premier exemplars of liminality, and they were perhaps the earliest of our ancestors to wield supernatural power. Shamans were central figures in hunter-gatherer societies; their tribes relied on them to help find game, for healing, and to preside at rituals. They were technicians of the sacred.

An enormous amount has been published on shamans, and in the last 30 years there has been an explosion of interest in them, both in academe and among the wider public. Even popular magazines are now published on shamanism. In view of the literature's extent, any summary can give only a general picture, but there are common patterns to be found. The connections between liminality and shamanism are pervasive, and a useful starting point is Mircea Eliade's classic *Shamanism: Archaic Techniques of Ecstasy* (1951). Though he did not use the term "liminal," a quick glance at the headings in his table of contents reveals the links. Some of the examples include "Shamanism and Mystical Vocation," "Initiatory Sicknesses and Dreams," "Shamanic Initiation," "Celestial Ascents. Descents to the Underworld," "Magical Cures. The Shaman as Psychopomp." These are only some of the major headings, and subheadings demonstrate many further commonalities.

Victor Turner discussed the liminality of shamanism saying: "In extreme cases, such as the acceptance of the shaman's vocation among the Saora of Middle India . . . this may result in the transformation of what is essentially a liminal or extrastructural phase into a permanent condition of sacred 'outsiderhood.' The shaman or prophet assumes a statusless status, external to the secular social structure, which gives him the right to criticize all structure-bound personae in terms of a moral order binding on all."[1]

In their initiations shamans may spend long periods alone in the bush. They seek visions, sometimes facilitated by illness or fasting, which can involve death, dismemberment and rebirth. Shamans' ventures into the bush and mystics' retreats into the desert are examples of journeying into the wilderness. Shamans and mystics put themselves outside society, at least temporarily. Shamans contact ancestors and other spirits in séances; they serve as a bridge between this world and the next. Like other liminal persons, shamans are sometimes associated with birds.[2]

Many liminal persons behave oddly, and shamans are no exception. In fact the literature of anthropology and psychiatry in the first half of the twentieth century frequently labeled shamans as schizophrenic.[3] Later reevaluations disputed this view, but in any event, the observations of the earlier anthropologists and psychiatrists should not be dismissed. Their assessments emphasize the truly exotic nature of shamanism and its inherent incompatibility with Western rationality.

Today many who wish to portray earlier cultures favorably neglect the unsavory, disreputable, and irrational parts of shamanism. This gives a distorted picture and introduces an ethnocentric bias often more pernicious than that of the earlier commentators. The current miscreants typically presume that rationalistic approaches can fully explain and rehabilitate shamanism. They cannot. This blindness has unfortunate consequences, and we will return to this point in the chapter on totemism and the primitive mind.

The Trickster and the Shaman

The trickster-liminality connection has already been discussed at length in earlier chapters, and thus the shaman-trickster link should be apparent to the reader. However, the similarities of the trickster and shaman were recognized independently of theories of liminality. For instance, Carl Jung in his commentary in Radin's *The Trickster* specifically said that "There is something of the trickster in the character of the shaman."[4] Joseph Campbell in *The Masks of God: Primitive Mythology* (1959) declared that the trickster "is a super-shaman,"[5] and Weston La Barre in *The Ghost Dance: Origins of Religion* (1970) commented that the trickster "is plainly a shaman, with a shaman's skills and failures."[6]

Though the existence of the trickster-shaman connection is indisputable, trickster stories are not full and direct representations of the shaman in the way we might expect to find in our own culture. As a result there is some confusion as to the exact relationship between the two. Interpretation is required, and it is much facilitated by recourse to Turner's explication of liminality. However those who have not fully grasped that are often perplexed.

One of the most extensive discussions of "The Shaman and the Trickster" appeared as a chapter in *Mythical Trickster Figures* (1993). That article, by Mac Linscott Ricketts, listed many similarities between the two figures. But in the end he concluded that the trickster and shaman are opposites and that the trickster is only a parody of the shaman. There is much to support this interpretation, and he listed many instances of trickster stories satirizing the shaman and even blaspheming. Nevertheless Ricketts seemed unable to grasp that the trickster is multi-vocal: that is, he has a variety of meanings.[7]

He was astute enough to recognize his befuddlement, and candidly admitted that: "Even though (as I believe) the trickster and the shaman represent opposing worldviews, the two are found side by side in nearly every tribe. Evidently, what I see as an inconsistency was not felt to be such by the majority of Indians."[8] Ricketts did not comprehend the trickster as fundamentally paradoxical. He did not understand liminality, or that blasphemy and satire are signals of it.

Ricketts compared the shaman with the Rudolf Otto's conception of the numinous, and counterposed both of those to the trickster. He said "I believe that the trickster ... embodies another experience of Reality: one in which humans feel themselves to be self-sufficient beings for whom the supernatural spirits are powers not to be worshiped, but ignored, to be overcome, or in the last analysis mocked."[9] He goes on to say that "as I see him, the trickster is a symbolic embodiment of the attitude today represented by the humanist."[10] Ricketts gives no hint that supernatural forces may be real, quite the contrary; he declares that the trickster "stands in opposition to ... supernaturalism."[11] In fact Ricketts essentially equates the numinous with only fear of the unknown.[12] His trickster is Promethean, and while there is merit in this view, it is woefully incomplete.[13]

Though Ricketts' work contains valuable insights, it also exemplifies the confusion so many academics encounter with the trickster. The reasons for the confusion are partly found by examining his social position. Ricketts completed his doctoral dissertation on the trickster at the University of Chicago in 1964, and he has since published several articles on it. He is an example of the older, high status (he was chairman of a department of religion and philosophy), white male academic who has assiduously studied the trickster. His social role leads him to a completely rationalistic interpretation. I don't believe that this is due to ignorance or lack of intellectual acuity, but rather it reflects his societal position, which shapes his understanding of the world. Ricketts is a structural rather than an anti-structural person. Scholars who share more in common with the trickster, who are more marginal (e.g., women, minorities, graduate students), show greater insight.

Ricketts' approach and humanist interpretation, especially the deficiencies, wonderfully parallel the modern-day skeptical movement and its publishing house, Prometheus Books, whose founder also edited *The Humanist*. These matters will be covered in the chapter on CSICOP.

The Sham of Shamanism

Some years ago I began compiling accounts of shamanic trickery from the anthropological literature, but the task quickly became overwhelming. Instead I settled for collecting references that cited multiple cases of trickery, and Table 2 provides part of that list. Shamans simulate paranormal events throughout the world, and the sham of shamanism appears to be one of its most pervasive characteristics. However many writers seem to prefer to pass over it, and Eliade's *Shamanism: Archaic Techniques of Ecstasy*, while over 600 pages, simply comments: "the problem of the 'genuineness' of all these shamanic phenomena lies beyond the scope of the present book."[14] This scholarly aversion is common, and Morton Smith of Columbia University commented on the "total and deliberate neglect of the importance of sham. This is characteristic of a great many works of contemporary anthropology and ethnology. It is a reaction against the unsympathetic, either dogmatic or rationalist, approach to primitive beliefs and practices which vitiated the work of many early observers."[15]

Generally, two explanations are offered for the sham of shamanism. Briefly they are: shamans use deception to enhance healing via placebo effects, and shamans use tricks to demonstrate power and compel obedience. These explanations are not incorrect, but they are incomplete.

Placebo healing is one of the benign uses of trickery. Many shamans used sleight of hand to seemingly remove blood, hair or leaves from a patient or extract rocks or twigs that were supposedly implanted via witchcraft. Sometimes they secretly put worms or bloody tissues in their mouths, sucked on the patient, and then spit out the

Author	Reference
Christopher, Milbourne	*The Illustrated History of Magic* (1973, pp. 69–81)
Flaherty, Gloria	*Shamanism and the Eighteenth Century* (1992, pp. 33, 40, 47, 48, 55, 58, 148)
Kirby, E. T.	"The Shamanistic Origins of Popular Entertainments", 1974, pp. 5–15.
	Ur-Drama: The Origins of Theatre (1975)
Lantis, Margaret	*Alaskan Eskimo Ceremonialism* (1947/1971, pp. 88–90)
McClenon, James	*Wondrous Events: Foundations of Religious Belief* (1994, pp. 160–162)
Reichbart, Richard	"Magic and Psi: Some Speculations on Their Relationship" (1978)
Rose, Ronald	"Psi and Australian Aborigines" (1952)
Turner, Edith; with Blodgett, W.; Kahona, S.; & Benwa, F.	*Experiencing Ritual* (1992, pp. 200–203)
Walsh, Roger N.	*The Spirit of Shamanism* (1990, pp. 101–109)
Warner, Richard	"Deception and Self-Deception in Shamanism and Psychiatry" (1980)
Webster, Hutton	*Magic: A Sociological Study* (1948/1973, pp. 474–496)
Weyer, Edward Moffat	*The Eskimos: Their Environment and Folkways* (1932/1969, pp. 437–442)

Table 2 Articles and Books Giving Multiple Citations to Reports of Sham in Shamanism

hidden item. Such practices are not limited to primitive cultures. In the 1970s and 1980s, thousands of Americans traveled to the Philippines to be treated by psychic surgeons, who used similar tricks; a few of the psychic surgeons even came to the U.S. and western Europe to ply their trade. They seemed to extract tissues without leaving a scar, and efforts were made to validate their abilities. All the attempts I am aware of came to negative conclusions. The "extracted" materials were found to be from pigs, cows, and decomposed human tissue but not from the patients.[16]

It is often difficult to know if a shaman is intentionally dishonest. He may believe that his simulations actually cure patients via sympathetic magic. The secretly hidden object, later revealed, is a symbol of that process, and some clients might even share that view. In other cases, shamans undoubtedly intend to deceive. These issues are beginning to interest anthropologists and others, and there is a slowly growing recognition of the sham in shamanism. For instance Roger Walsh, in his semi-popular book *The Spirit of Shamanism* (1990), includes an entire chapter entitled "Shamanic Trickery."

Richard Warner provided one of the best discussions of the matter in his article "Deception and Self-Deception in Shamanism and Psychiatry" (1980). Warner was the medical director of a mental health center and raised some difficult questions about his profession. He pointed out commonalities between shamans and today's psychotherapists, including questions about deceit that apply to both. Warner admitted that many forms of modern psychotherapy have little innate healing capacity, and the benefits have more to do with the therapist than the mode of treatment.[17] This has been demonstrated by a large number of scientific studies, to the chagrin of advocates of various types of psychotherapy. In fact some research indicates that greater training may make one a worse therapist.[18] Similar concerns were also expressed by Robyn Dawes a psychologist and professor at Carnegie-Mellon University, who won the 1990 American Psychological Association's William James Award. His book *House of Cards* (1994) was subtitled *Psychology and Psychotherapy Built on Myth* and was a stinging indictment of his profession.

Despite the serious failings, therapists are needed in society because people have problems. Troubled people are unlikely to be helped by telling them that the planned treatment is objectively ineffective, nor is that information likely to help the therapist. Research indicates that a doctor's confident attitude assists in the healing process. Thus for a therapist to be maximally effective, he must believe in his method, but if a technique is objectively worthless, the therapist must fool himself before he can help his patient. Deception and self-deception are at the heart of the psychotherapeutic process. These facts are not lost on student therapists, and Warner pointed out that some quit in despair when they realize the dilemma.

Needless to say, these issues provoke bitter disputes. Clinicians and experimental psychologists have battled for decades over them.

Some clinicians go as far as denying any validity to scientific attempts to assess effectiveness of therapy. One side questions the validity of science. The other attacks not only therapy but also, implicitly, the entire institutional structure surrounding it (a major industry). Much is at stake. If deception is really necessary in therapy, how much science, and promulgation of scientific knowledge, serves the public interest? If the objective inadequacy of the techniques becomes known, would patients be worse off? I certainly am not going to try solve the dilemma, but I raise it in order to place the issue of deception in a new light. It can be helpful to think about the topic more sympathetically when its benefits are considered. Those who would scorn the shamanic trickery of other cultures should spend some time examining similar instances in our own.

The questions raised by deception in shamanic healing are important, but they should not overshadow larger issues. The shaman illustrates the more general connection between liminality and deception, and this crucial nexus has received little recognition. Van Gennep's and Turner's discussions of liminality did not include trickery, fraud, or deception, and none of those terms are listed in the indexes of *The Rites of Passage* or *The Ritual Process*. Even Barbara Babcock's superb exposition of the trickster did not substantially address deceit. Yet unquestionably, the shaman and the trickster are deceptive and are quintessentially liminal beings. The trickster-shaman-liminality complex signals deep connections that will be a continuing focus.

In the coming chapters we will explore liminality in conjunction with fiction, drama, and myth, with the keeping of secrets, and the emergence of ego consciousness. In all of these, deception plays a role. Furthermore, the innate ambiguities of language and interpretation of texts can all lead to the matter of deception. These are trickster issues, and as I will show, they are directly relevant to the paranormal.

Skepticism of Shamanism

The role and function of skepticism vis-à-vis shamanism has received too little attention. Some writers seem to suggest that primitive peoples were in thrall of the shaman, that they were completely superstitious and saw all shamanic tricks as being supernatural. This is unlikely. It is probable that some people in all cultures realized that shamans engaged in trickery at times. The primitives were not stupid, and skepticism was almost certainly needed. An ineffective shaman could be a real liability to a tribe, and some methods must have been available to limit his power. Skepticism could serve as a check.

Paul Radin, in *Primitive Man as Philosopher* (1927), devoted a full chapter to skepticism among the primitives, though he did not discuss trickery. He pointed out that a number of primitives expressed doubts about the power of the gods, and probably have done so for millennia. Likewise, Ricketts' thesis that the trickster mocks the shaman, and shamanic powers, supports the idea that the primitives were more skeptical than generally supposed. They did not see themselves entirely at the mercy of the gods or fully under the spell of the shaman. They satirized them both.

Howard Higgins, an anthropologist with the Canadian Museum who studied the Tahltan Indians of northwest British Columbia, prepared a good discussion of shamanic trickery and skepticism. In 1985 Higgins wrote a short series of articles for the *Linking Ring*, the monthly magazine of the International Brotherhood of Magicians.[19] He was a magician himself, and he witnessed another who pretended to have paranormal powers. Higgins surmised the methods used in the tricks, though others in the audience seemed to believe that the man commanded supernatural forces. Higgins also performed tricks, and he had to reassure even close friends that he was not a witch.

He explained that this was not an indication of gullibility because the Tahltans readily accepted his admission of trickery. He pointed out that the Tahltans could easily believe that a shaman or witch might use both trickery and supernatural powers. These were not mutually exclusive, and exposure of a trick did not necessarily discredit a shaman. Higgins reported a striking case of telepathy among the Tahltan, and he seemed convinced of its genuineness. Earlier peoples did not make the sharp distinction between trickery and paranormal events that we do. They understood that they could exist side by side, and in this their understanding was perhaps more sophisticated than our own.

Other Trickster-Shaman Links

Aside from deception, there are other links between shamanism and the trickster that should be briefly mentioned. A number of commentators have mentioned that some shamans are bisexual or homosexual, but the extent is unclear. Waldemar Bogoras' work *The Chukchee* (1904–09) is often cited in this regard, and a few others have mentioned the connection.[20] Walter L. Williams' 1986 book *The Spirit and the Flesh: Sexual Diversity in American Indian Culture* reports that berdaches (men who wore women's dress and adopted at least some of their roles) were typically viewed as sacred and as having supernatural power. Many, but not all, became shamans. Anthropologist Holgar Kalweit cited a number of reports of shamans' sexual encounters with spirits.[21] Thus sexual abnormality is reported in the lives of many shamans, in accord with the trickster constellation.

Liminality is also a source of creativity, and a few words might be said about shamans as creative innovators. Several authorities have suggested that shamans were among the first artists,[22] and some of their cave drawings were probably used in rituals. Drama too may have shamanic origins. Theatre professor E. T. Kirby suggested that shamans' performances were the predecessors of theatre, a thesis he defended in his book *Ur-Drama: Origins of Theatre* (1975).[23] (Dionysus is the god of theatre, and as such, the shaman's role in its establishment is an instance of Hermes serving as midwife to the birth of Dionysus.) Given all this, shamans almost certainly played a significant role in the development of the arts.

In summary, the relative outsiderhood, the liminality, the "crazy" behavior, the unusual sexual lives, the direct attempts to engage supernatural powers, and the deception, define the trickster constellation as well as the life of many shamans.

As mentioned in earlier chapters, social status is an important issue in theories of the trickster. This is true with shamanism, but the matter is not straightforward. It complicated by the fact that a shaman's status depends upon the complexity of his or her society. Fortunately Michael Winkelman has explicated the topic in his work on magico-religious practitioners, and that will be covered in the next chapter. Winkelman's work helps explain problematic aspects of shamanism, especially in regard to status.

Part 3

Overview

The paranormal's implications for society are emphasized in this Part. The focus is the group, rather than the individual. The perspective here is sociological rather than psychological.

Social processes influence us as individuals at an unconscious level. We need to become aware of them if we are to understand where our own thoughts come from. This is especially true in regard to magic, religion, and the paranormal.

Anthropologist Michael Winkelman produced a monograph entitled *Shamans, Priests and Witches* in 1992. He described his extensive cross-cultural study of the status of magico-religious practitioners, i.e., people who use supernatural power. He showed that as cultures become more complex, those who most immediately engage the supernatural lose status. Their positions are marginalized. Issues of status and marginality are central to understanding the paranormal, and they are also directly relevant to the trickster and anti-structure.

Max Weber was one of the giants of sociology. His concept of rationalization describes the rise of modern civilization. Part of rationalization entails disenchantment, i.e., the suppression of magic, miracles, and supernatural phenomena. Weber was eminently clear on this, but very little attention has been given to his ideas in regard to the paranormal. This is altogether astounding because his theory of rationalization has proven to be one of the grandest and most comprehensive visions in sociology. It describes cultural trends over thousands of years. It is widely known not only within sociology, but also in other academic disciplines. It crucial for understanding the structure of society.

Weber's concept of charisma was an integral part of this. In its pure form, charisma involves supernatural power, a fact that Weber clearly stated. Again amazingly, scholars almost universally ignore that. If they do acknowledge it, they seem puzzled. For Weber, charisma was central to understanding authority, power, and domination. Authority is required in all societies, and he identified three types: bureaucratic (found in our society today), traditional (found in tribal and feudal cultures), and charismatic authority. Charisma is the primordial base; traditional and bureaucratic authority involve attenuated forms of charisma, and sociologists are more comfortable discussing them.

We will return to Weber's ideas many times in this book because they have extraordinary applicability. They will be especially pertinent in Part 5 with discussions of totemism, French structuralism, and literary theory.

The third chapter in this Part is devoted to cultural transformation, and it draws upon the work of anthropologist Anthony F. C. Wallace, who was a leading theorist on cultural revitalization movements. Wallace's description of cultural transformation has remarkable parallels with van Gennep's ideas in *The Rites of Passage*. The supernatural played a role in many cultural transformations, and those are illuminated by theories of the trickster, liminality, and anti-structure.

Winkelman, Weber, and Wallace drew from history and anthropology. They enlightened us about a range of cultures, from simple hunter-gatherer societies to today's post-industrial world. Their theories have great generality.

The work presented in this Part is sociological; it is formulated primarily at the level of groups. As such, it is a bit more abstract than some of the other sections of this book. Part 4 presents a number of concrete examples from modern society, and those will help clarify the ideas.

The problems of parapsychology cannot be understood without considering wide historical and cultural contexts. The works of Winkelman, Weber, and Wallace provide them. The implications of their work are profound.

CHAPTER 7

Michael Winkelman on Magico-Religious Practitioners

The supernatural and its place in society are central topics of this book. Thus the people who directly engage supernatural forces are of particular interest, and their roles and social positions tell us much. Michael Winkelman wrote an enlightening monograph on the topic entitled *Shamans, Priests and Witches: A Cross-Cultural Study of Magico-Religious Practitioners* (1992). Winkelman is an anthropologist at Arizona State University. In 1982, while still a graduate student, he published a paper integrating findings of parapsychology with anthropological theories of magic. The paper appeared in *Current Anthropology*, a journal devoted to debate and dialogue, and a number of eminent anthropologists responded. Winkelman also carried out ESP experiments during his anthropological fieldwork, and he published them in the *Journal of Parapsychology*.[1] He later served as president of the Society for the Anthropology of Consciousness (SAC), an affiliate of the American Anthropological Association. The SAC has an interest in mediumistic and mystical traditions, possession trance, indigenous healing practices, shamanism, and related topics.

In his monograph, Winkelman differentiated the roles of shaman, shaman/healer, healer, medium, and priest, all of whom are involved with the manipulation of supernatural powers (he also covered witches and sorcerers, but those will not be discussed here). For his analysis, he selected a stratified, representative sample of 47 cultures from the Standard Cross-Cultural Sample, a database used in anthropological research. He examined 98 variables in computer statistical analyses. Some of his analyses were suggested by previous works, but earlier anthropologists had utilized smaller samples that were convenient but perhaps biased. Winkelman's sample was large and representative, and thus we can place confidence in his findings.

A primary focus of his investigation was the practitioners' statuses in relation to the complexity of their societies. The interrelationships between the individual and society are often theoretically ambiguous and confusing, and Winkelman's work helps clarify that territory. He explains that "The least complex societies are typified by the hunting and gathering economies without hierarchical political integration; the more complex societies are typified by agriculture, social stratification and hierarchical political integration."[2] Hunting and gathering societies are typically much smaller than those based on agriculture, and the lives of the hunter-gatherers are marked by greater contingency. They need to be mobile, to move to find game and avoid famine. Unlike agricultural societies, hunter-gatherers are unable to stockpile large caches of food to tide them over lean years. They are more dependent upon the vagaries of nature. Agriculture requires long-term planning and care of crops over a period of months, unlike hunting parties that might be a few hours or days long. Thus hunter-gatherer societies are typified by greater instability, fluidity, uncertainty, and more contact with the wilderness; they are perhaps more part of nature than separate from it, and they participate in it more than trying to control it. Agricultural societies are less mobile; they exert more control over nature and are less subject to its vagaries.

The specific roles designated in Winkelman's analysis are very helpful for understanding. However, the reader should be warned that most literature on shamanism does not make these particular distinctions, and often all these roles are lumped under the term "shaman." A graphical summary of his findings is presented in Figure 2, and I will describe them.

Shamans

Under Winkelman's classification regime, shamans are typified by use of altered states of consciousness (ASCs) in which they command spirits to do their bidding, and they display a variety of paranormal powers. Divination, healing, and finding game animals through magical means are primary activities of the shaman. They come to their vocations after involuntary visions, serious illnesses, or vision quests. These individuals are typically part-time practitioners who also assist with their tribes' subsistence efforts. They generally hold high status in their societies and are regarded as healthy, charismatic leaders.

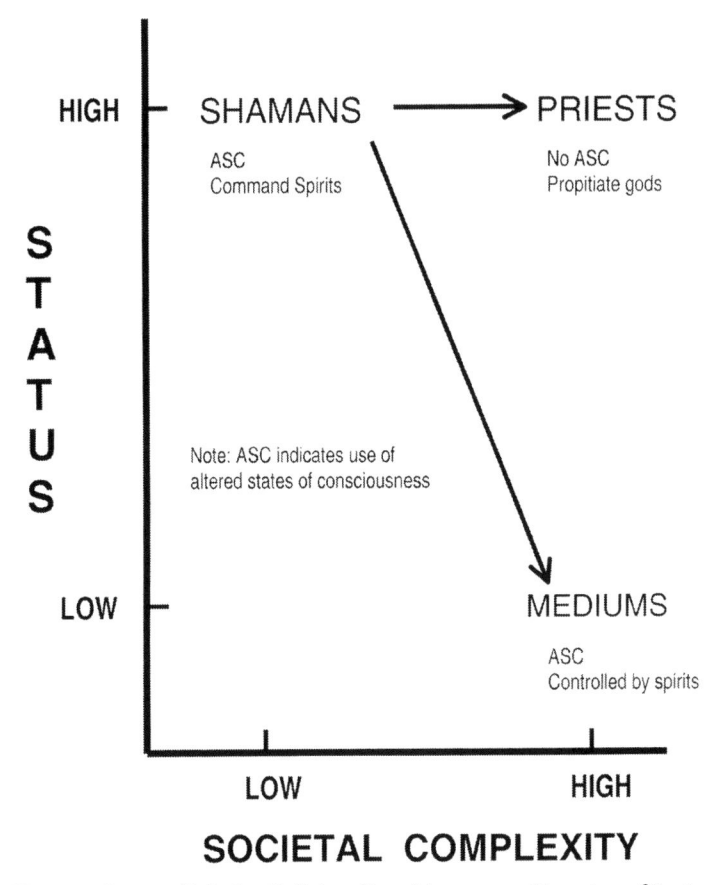

```
                    HIGH ─┤  SHAMANS ──────▶ PRIESTS
                              ASC                No ASC
                              Command Spirits    Propitiate gods
    S
    T
    A
    T
    U              Note: ASC indicates use of
    S              altered states of consciousness


                    LOW ─┤                         MEDIUMS
                                                   ASC
                                                   Controlled by spirits
                          └──────┼─────────────────┼───
                                 LOW              HIGH
                              SOCIETAL COMPLEXITY
```

Figure 2 Status of Magico-Religious Practitioners as a Function of Societal Complexity (Based on Wikelman, 1992)

Shamans are found in hunting and gathering societies with no social classes and little or no political hierarchy beyond the local level.

Shaman/Healers

Shaman/Healers use altered states of consciousness and obtain the help of spirit allies thereby, and they may also utilize impersonal supernatural power (mana). Their primary activities are healing and divination. Like the shamans, they come to this vocation after vision quests or serious illness. They hold only moderate status in agricultural societies with priests present, but high status if there are no priests.

Healers

Healers also are primarily involved with divination and healing but make limited or no use of altered states of consciousness in the course of their work. The gods are superior to them, and they may make offerings to propitiate the gods. Healers may have impersonal kinds of power such as mana and utilize rituals, spells, and formulas. Typically a healer's recruitment is by voluntary selection and involves payment for training. They generally hold high socioeconomic status and power and are integrated within the institutional structures of society. They are found in agricultural societies that have a political hierarchy beyond the local level.

Priests

Priests make little or no use of altered states of consciousness for their endeavors. Much of their work involves ritual, worship, and propitiation of the gods. They have no control over spirits. Priests are selected through social inheritance or political appointment and are generally full-time professionals who enjoy very high social and economic status. Their profession typically has hierarchically ranked positions. Priests are found in agricultural societies with political integration beyond the local level.

Mediums

Mediums use ASCs, specifically possession trance during which spirits communicate. The spirits control the mediums, and thus mediums are not held personally responsible for their actions during trance. Mediums' primary functions are healing, divination, and worship and propitiation of spirits. They are found in complex societies that also have healers and priests. As a result, mediums have very low status and are the only category here consisting primarily of women who are often described as crazy, neurotic, or hysterical. They frequently receive no remuneration for their efforts.

Implications

Winkelman notes that "systematic differences in magico-religious practices can be organized around the principle that beliefs and practices in more complex societies indicate a displacement of responsibility, repression of awareness, and reduction of direct ego control over information revealed or actions taken; practices and beliefs in simpler societies indicate a more direct ego contact with supernatural power and experiences."[3] Of the practitioners considered here, shamans and mediums make the most use of ASCs; more than any of the others, they directly and intentionally engage supernatural powers. Based upon the findings of parapsychology, we can expect shamans and mediums to make the most use of psi. They also have the greatest number of trickster characteristics and are particularly associated with deception.

Winkelman's analysis clearly identifies important relationships between societal structure and the status of psi practitioners. The findings are crucial to understanding where cultivation of psychic functioning will be welcomed and where shunned, and the trends can be seen even in Western culture. The high status and visibility of priests and medical doctors is an example, as is the social invisibility of mediums. Supernatural powers have been recognized for thousands of years. Yet when societies become complex, the practitioners who attempt to directly engage them are shunted to the margins; they are denigrated as "crazy," "epileptic" or "deviant." This labeling, sanctified by establishment science and medicine, helps preserve the existing hierarchy.

Direct contact with psi and the supernatural is anti-structural, and in our society it is found with the marginal. The institutions of science and medicine are among the elite, and they are hierarchical in structure.

Those who expect parapsychology to be soon accepted by scientific establishments should not overlook the profound implications of Winkelman's findings. Hostility to psi is usually attributed to ideologies such as materialistic rationalism, but that is entirely insufficient to explain it. The matter is not primarily an ideological dispute. The source of antagonism toward parapsychology is much more fundamental; it is a consequence of the structure of society. Of this, almost everyone is unconscious.

CHAPTER 8

Max Weber, Charisma, and the Disenchantment of the World

Max Weber (1864–1920) is one of the giants of sociology, and his work forms a substantial part of the core of that discipline. He had extraordinary vision and a vast knowledge of history and cultures. He is considered a founder of the sociology of religion, and his best known work *The Protestant Ethic and the Spirit of Capitalism* (1904–05) retains its influence and is still debated today. Weber was one of those exceptional figures who underwent a creative illness.[1] While in his thirties, he had a breakdown that left him incapacitated for several years and intermittently thereafter. Nevertheless his output was immense, and in his lifetime he produced thousands of pages. Much remained unfinished at the time of his death, and later a number of scholars collaborated to compile, edit, publish, and translate his work.

Weber strived to address fundamental sociological issues, including the crucial topics of authority and domination. Authority is required for any civilization or society to exist; authority serves as a foundation. Authority establishes laws, rules, determines what is true, specifies what will be done, by whom, and when. It is a broad concept that any comprehensive sociological theory must address. In his massive two-volume work *Economy and Society* (1913),[2] Weber differentiated three types of authority: bureaucratic, as seen in today's society; traditional, as in feudal and primitive cultures; and something he called charismatic authority.

The term charisma refers to an extraordinary power, and Weber defined it thus: "The term 'charisma' will be applied to a certain quality of an individual personality by virtue of which he is considered extraordinary and treated as endowed with supernatural, superhuman, or at least specifically exceptional powers or qualities. These are such as are not accessible to the ordinary person, but are regarded as of divine origin or as exemplary."[3] Charisma can produce great good or great evil—both Hitler and Ghandi were charismatic leaders. Such persons have had an exceptional impact on history, but surprisingly many introductory sociology texts quickly skip over charisma. Even entire books have been devoted to it, but as I will show, sociologists subtly avoid confronting its full implications.

Weber's concept of pure charisma is of primary interest here. Though sociologists may discuss other types, it is pure charisma that they typically ignore. This is an example of why it is so important to consult original sources and not rely upon summaries of others. Reading Weber and Victor Turner directly, one discovers that the properties of pure charisma are virtually identical with those of liminality, anti-structure and communitas. Weber drew predominantly from sociology and history, whereas Turner's sources were primarily from anthropology; thus the concepts were derived largely independently. The remarkable parallels between the two formulations indicate their considerable explanatory power, and I will review some of the commonalities. As with Turner, I will directly quote Weber rather extensively. I do this to not only demonstrate the clear overlap, but also to emphasize that Weber's explicit points on the supernatural have been willfully ignored.

In many passages, Weber's writings on pure charisma describe anti-structure. For instance he states that "in a revolutionary and sovereign manner, charismatic domination transforms all values and breaks all traditional and rational norms."[4] He also says: "Since it is 'extra-ordinary,' charismatic authority is sharply opposed to rational, and particularly bureaucratic authority, and to traditional authority... It recognizes no appropriation of positions of power by virtue of the possession of property, either on the part of a chief or of socially privileged groups."[5] This is further elaborated, as Weber tells us that: "In radical contrast to bureaucratic organization, charisma knows no formal and regulated appointment or dismissal, no career, advancement or salary, no supervisory or appeals body, no local or purely technical jurisdiction, and no permanent institutions in the manner of bureaucratic agencies."[6]

Weber says specifically that charisma "cannot remain stable, but becomes either traditionalized or rationalized, or a combination of both."[7] Because of their instability, both pure charisma and anti-structure (liminality) are opposed not only to structure but, almost paradoxically, ultimately to themselves.

Charisma is also intimately linked with communitas and with mysticism. We are told that: "Pure charisma is specifically foreign to economic considerations. Wherever it appears, it constitutes a 'call' in the most emphatic sense of the word, a 'mission' or a 'spiritual duty.' In the pure type, it disdains and repudiates economic exploitation of the gifts of grace as a source of income, though, to be sure, this often remains more an ideal than a fact."[8] He later explains that "In order to live up to their mission the master as well as his disciples and immediate following must be free of the ordinary worldly attachments and duties of occupational and family life. Those who have a share . . . in charisma must inevitably turn away from the world."[9] He tells us that "charisma rejects as undignified all methodical rational acquisition, in fact, all rational economic conduct,"[10] and like Turner, Weber cited Saint Francis as an exemplar!

Pure charisma, like liminality, is directly linked with the supernatural. It is "guaranteed by what is held to be a proof, originally always a miracle."[11] The leader "gains and retains it solely by proving his powers in practice. He must work miracles, if he wants to be a prophet."[12] The role of altered states of consciousness was also recognized as critical, and Weber mentions "the ecstatic states which are viewed, in accordance with primitive experience, as the pre-conditions for producing certain effects in meteorology, healing, divination, and telepathy . . . We shall henceforth employ the term 'charisma' for such extraordinary powers."[13]

Weber also discussed more attenuated kinds of charisma, that allowed its accommodation by more stable, bureaucratic cultures. For instance some of the more moderated, rationalized versions are referred to as pseudocharisma, lineage-charisma, charisma of office, and manufactured charisma. The transition from pure charismatic authority, involving miracles and supernatural power, to one of the more stable forms is a source of ambiguity and causes confusion among scholars. Turner faced similar difficulties as he tried to distinguish the liminal from the liminoid.[14]

Disenchantment Of The World

The concept of rationalization was one of Weber's seminal contributions to sociology, and it is directly related to charisma. In his usage, rationalization has several related meanings that are a bit difficult to summarize because it affects so many aspects of culture. Briefly, it involves instrumental use of objects and requires planning. Talcott Parsons explains that "Rationalization comprises first the intellectual clarification, specification and systematization of ideas."[15] This of course requires abstraction and drawing of clear distinctions, both of which are antithetical to the trickster. In law, rationalization leads to a growing body of rules and regulations, and the duties to enforce and interpret them lay in the offices (established legal positions) rather than individual personalities. For production of goods and services, it begets standardization and interchangeability, both of machines and of people. A regimentation emerges. There is increasing specialization in education and occupations. Social structure takes on greater and greater complexity, leading to ever growing hierarchy and differentiation. Bureaucracies act to maintain and advance themselves; they take on a life of their own, and people become alienated.

These aspects of rationalization are well understood in sociology, and there is an enormous amount written on them. But there is another feature—"the elimination of magic from the world."[16] Weber recognized that a direct product of rationalization was *die Entzauberung der Welt* or the disenchantment of the world.[17] Another scholar of Weber, S. N. Eisenstadt, explains that this is "a concept which denotes the demystification and secularization of the world, the *attenuation of charisma*" (emphasis added).[18] Rationalization-disenchantment is a long-term process, extending over thousands of years through which there have been stagnations and even reversals of the trend. Details of Weber's rationalization theory have been criticized, and critics have pointed to counter-examples, but the broad sweep remains valid when a sufficiently long time span is considered. The overall trend is unmistakable.

Weber noted that in ancient times as priests became differentiated from magicians, injunctions were placed against the use of magic. He specifically commented on the "rational" training required for priests in contrast to the "irrational" initiations of magicians. This is consistent with the findings of Winkelman presented in the last chapter.

The rise of Protestantism was one step in the global rationalization process, and its contrasts with Catholicism are instructive. Catholicism has the stronger mystical component, whereas Protestantism largely disavows mysticism and monastic orders. Protestantism has no priests who serve as mediators between God and humanity. In the Catholic Mass with transubstantiation, bread and wine become the body and blood of Christ, but in Protestantism, they are only symbols. Protestantism is more "text-based," with God being mediated more through the written word of the Bible. Protestantism fostered the Higher Criticism, which disputed the reality of miracles. Many now look upon these differences as only arcane theological disputes, but in reality they have profound implications for our world.

A set of factors merits contemplation here: Weber has immense stature in sociology; his ideas are universally known therein; he remains influential in other disciplines. Charisma has had enormous impact in the history of the world, and miracles played central roles (e.g., the miracles of Moses, Jesus, and Mohammed gave them legitimacy). Given all this, it is altogether astounding that social scientists ignore the question of the reality of supernatural phenomena. In fact, the vast majority of scholars writing on Weber's notion of charisma give no hint that it involves such phenomena; if they do, it is typically in extremely vague, abstract terms.[19] Even sociologists who write on the paranormal avoid mentioning it, even though Weber explicitly cited telepathy as a property of pure charisma. Only by reading Weber directly does one discover the importance of magic, the miraculous, and supernatural phenomena. This near-universal avoidance by academe is an important clue to the nature of the paranormal.

Winston Davis, a professor known for his writings on religion and East Asian Studies, summed up the current situation: "if there is any attitude that is universally regarded as irrational and anti-modern, it is the outlook of the magician."[20] Weber noted that "the magician is permanently endowed with charisma."[21] Davis elaborates: "The conflict between the magician and the secularist is every bit as intense as the struggle Sir James George Frazer depicted between the magician and the priest of old. Not only theologians, but sociologists and intellectual historians seem convinced that this *must* be a battle to the finish."[22] He also comments: "We are told that in the modern world, magic must be sequestered or else it will cause the maladjustment of individuals or the dysfunction of the entire social organism."[23] Even casual reading of the academic literature will confirm Davis' observations.

Academe today is both a product of and an agent for the disenchantment of the world. It has steadily become more bureaucratic and hierarchical. Davis noted that "Weber believed that the very progress of civilization inevitably led to the permanent anesthetizing of the human spirit."[24] Anti-structure, pure charisma, and supernatural phenomena are needed for the vitality of culture. In academe they are marginalized, occasionally denounced but generally ignored.

All these ideas illuminate the trickster. Weber states that "Bureaucratic authority is specifically rational in the sense of being bound to intellectually analyzable rules; while charismatic authority is specifically irrational in the sense of being foreign to all rules."[25] The trickster is explicitly a crosser of boundaries, a violator of rules, a denizen of the irrational. These ideas also raise matters pertinent to psi. In discussing Weber's notion of disenchantment, Davis noted that one factor "less obvious from the annals of intellectual history, may be even more important: the disenchanting effect of the routines of everyday life in industrial society."[26] Davis is perceptive. "Routine" is antithetical to spontaneity and synchronicity. As will be described later in the book, William Braud's research has shown that spontaneity facilitates the occurrence of psychic phenomena. Rigid structures of thought, behavior, and belief all conspire to reduce magic, suppress the trickster, and marginalize the paranormal.

At this point something needs to be said about a small misunderstanding by Weber on the topic of magic. Magic is never actually eliminated from the world; it is only marginalized. It is removed from the conscious attention of cultural elites. The bureaucratic institutions of government, industry, and academe now ignore it, but it is still found in popular and low culture. As will be explained in coming chapters, cultural elites relegate magic to fiction, and large industries now flourish by portraying magic and the paranormal in and as fiction.

Despite the small (but significant) error, Weber provided us with grand vistas on history and sociology, and from them we can see patterns of the paranormal. Miracles (paranormal phenomena) are found in conjunction with pure charisma. Pure charisma is a source of primordial power, but it's unstable; like liminality it's dangerous; it can overturn established orders. It needs to be attenuated and rationalized. In all this, Weber's ideas are compatible with those of Victor Turner.

However, Weber's general formulations on rationality and disenchantment have additional implications—far beyond what he, and most others, have recognized. We will encounter those ramifications in a variety of contexts, and it may be helpful to give some idea of the coming discussions. Here I can outline them in only broad, general terms; much more detail will be given later. The concepts and terms may be difficult for those who have little prior familiarity, but some forewarning may be helpful even so. These are central to foundational issues being debated in academe today.

One reason that the full force of Weber's ideas has not been recognized is that they ultimately implicate the limits of rationality—the very foundations of Western thought. Science ignores those limits, and it is at those limits that the supernatural erupts. But it is not only the supernatural that is of interest, the problem of meaning, the idea of objective reality, and the validity of logic are all directly related to rationalization and to each other. These matters are entirely ignored within science, but they are at center stage in the humanities—particularly in postmodernism and deconstructionism. When these ideas are raised in regard to science, scientists become anxious, panic, viciously lash out, and display an unconsciousness of the fundamental issues.[27]

In post-structuralist literary theory, meaning is a central concern. By meaning, I am not referring to some grand purpose for an individual or for humanity, but rather the simpler and more prosaic concept discussed by linguist Ferdinand de Saussure. The connection between a signifier and its signified, between a word and its referent, is the issue. Science today considers meaning to be entirely unproblematic. It assumes that a word can be unambiguously attached to an item or event. Ambiguity is repressed from consciousness. Deconstructionists recognize that meaning is problematical. They point out that a reader and writer can have very different interpretations. They emphasize the ambiguity inherent in language. Scientists steadfastly refuse to acknowledge the problem. Deconstructionists see the fundamental difficulty, and a few even vaguely suggest that a theory of literature requires a theory of telepathy. With this, magic and meaning are joined.

In order to explore and explicate this, future chapters will examine the precursors to deconstructionism. It is well recognized that structuralism immediately preceded deconstructionism, but the precursors to structuralism have rarely been fully understood. The linguistic root receives attention, to the neglect of the anthropological influence. Most assume that deconstructionism's consequences are limited merely to text. They're not, and the implications for the real world are uncovered by considering the anthropological root.

Furious debates about postmodernism, deconstructionism, and post-structuralism revolve on the issue of power. Deconstructionists assert that there is no objective reality, and that all attempts to define and control the world can be reduced to plays for power. Scientists maintain that there is an objective reality that, in principle, everyone can know, and that it does not depend upon power to force agreement. Weber's contribution is of exceeding importance here because his work extensively addressed issues of authority, power, and domination. The concepts of bureaucratic, traditional, and charismatic authority are central to the debates—especially charismatic authority, because it is the primordial source. It is the wellspring of supernatural power.

Another issue we will meet in future chapters is the reluctance to examine foundations too closely. Existence of society requires collectively held fundamental premises, beliefs, and assumptions. When they are questionned or challenged, disruption ensues. Western science adheres to the myth of objective reality, but it does not comprehend the foundations of that myth. Rationalization (and our society generally) presupposes the validity of Aristotelian logic, but that has severe limits. One way to demonstrate them is through paradoxes generated by reflexivity. Reflexivity is found in diverse areas, but there is a subtle and pervasive avoidance of the topic. These should be central issues for science and knowledge, and as I will show, the paranormal is fundamental to them.

In summary, Weber's concepts of charisma, rationalization, and disenchantment are crucial to understanding the structure and stability of societies. They also explain why the paranormal is marginalized. The implications are even deeper; they address the very foundations of Western thought.

CHAPTER 9

Cultural Change and the Paranormal

In times of great cultural change, trickster and anti-structural manifestations are particularly apparent, and the supernatural is an important part of them. In 1956 University of Pennsylvania anthropologist Anthony F. C. Wallace published his classic paper "Revitalization Movements." It is one of the most illuminating works on cultural transformation, and it has been widely cited. Wallace compiled a database of several hundred such movements from five continents and analyzed their patterns of development. For his analysis, "revitalization movement" meant "a deliberate, organized, conscious effort by members of a society to construct a more satisfying culture,"[1] and he provided a number of examples to explain his meaning. Both Christianity and Islam originated in revitalization movements, and there have been thousands of others throughout history.

Wallace delineated the process saying: "The structure of the revitalization process, in cases where the full course is run, consists of five somewhat overlapping stages: 1. Steady State; 2. Period of Individual Stress; 3. Period of Cultural Distortion; 4. Period of Revitalization (in which occur the functions of mazeway reformulation, communication, organization, adaptation, cultural transformation, and routinization), and finally, 5. New Steady State."[2] This formulation is strikingly parallel to van Gennep's three phase model of separation, transition (or limen), and incorporation, as presented in *The Rites of Passage* (1909). Wallace's period of revitalization is essentially equivalent to the liminal phase of van Gennep.

Wallace defined his concept of the "mazeway" as a person's "mental image of the society and its culture, as well as of his own body . . . it includes perceptions of both the maze of physical objects of the environment (internal and external, human and nonhuman) and also of the ways in which this maze can be manipulated . . . The mazeway is nature, society, culture, personality, and body image, as seen by one person."[3] In essence, it is a person's picture of the structure of his or her existence. The metaphor of the *mazeway* is particularly apt for our consideration because a maze is simply a combination of *passageways* delimited by *boundaries*—rites of passage and boundaries being primary themes of this book.

Wallace chose an organismic analogy for human society, which he viewed as composed of, not only individuals and groups but also the very cells and organs of people's bodies. He described his framework as "holistic" saying it assumed a "network" of intercommunication (years later the New Age movement used the same terms). He went on to explain that a stress on one level would stress all levels.

When society or some part of it is subjected to high stress, there will be an effort to ameliorate it. During the stress, not everyone attempts to change; reactionary forces try to maintain the status quo. In what could have been written by psychiatrist Ernest Hartmann 35 years later, Wallace comments: "Rigid persons apparently prefer to tolerate high levels of chronic stress rather than make systematic adaptive changes in the mazeway. More flexible persons try out various limited mazeway changes in their personal lives."[4]

Some of the characteristics of cultural distortion parallel those described for shaman initiates undergoing their individual transformations. Wallace notes that during these periods "Some persons turn to psychodynamically regressive innovations ... [including] disregard of kinship and sexual mores ... states of depression and self-reproach, and probably a variety of psychosomatic and neurotic disorders."[5] Such deterioration can potentially lead to the death of a society.

If the stress is not relieved by modifying discrete parts of the culture, a more radical change is needed. Such alterations can be abrupt. During the process, cultural mazeways are demolished and rebuilt.

The supernatural plays a crucial role, and Wallace states: "With a few exceptions, every religious revitalization movement with which I am acquainted has been originally conceived in one or several hallucinatory visions by a single individual. A supernatural being appears to the prophet-to-be."[6] Wallace acknowledges that many people believe that such visions are pathological hallucinations, but he says that "the religious vision experience per se is not psychopathological but rather the reverse, being a synthesizing and often therapeutic process performed under extreme stress by individuals already sick."[7] Wallace even acknowledges the similarity of revitalization to shamans' transformations in rites of passage. (There are also many parallels to Henri Ellenberger's concept of creative illness.[8]) Wallace explains that the prophet generally "shows evidence of a radical inner change in personality soon after the vision experience: a remission of old and chronic physical complaints, a more active and purposeful way of life, greater confidence in interpersonal relations."[9] Such a person often develops charisma.

Wallace recognized the crucial role of paranormal phenomena, saying: "Followers defer to the charismatic leader not because of his status in an existing authority structure but because of a fascinating personal 'power,' often ascribed to supernatural sources and validated in successful performance, akin to the 'mana' or 'orenda' of ethnological literature."[10] Thus the leader derives power from outside the structure (i.e., via anti-structure) and gains legitimacy by paranormal manifestations. Wallace discussed supernatural encounters, focusing primarily on the leader's, but he also mentioned that some of the other participants have "hysterical seizures" and ecstatic visions. He noted that "Like the prophet, many of the converts undergo a revitalizing personality transformation."[11]

Revitalization attempts are not always successful; in fact they can lead to destruction, sometimes hastened by the supernatural. Oracles, diviners, and spirits are not altogether reliable, and their advice occasionally has had particularly nasty consequences. Anthropologist Weston La Barre surveyed some of them in his book *The Ghost Dance* (1970). In the late 1800s the Dakota Sioux were being pushed to extinction, and they undertook a ghost dance to revive their culture. After a shaman instructed them to wear magic shirts to protect them from soldiers' bullets, they went into battle. They fought valiantly, and with renewed confidence, but the shirts afforded no such protection, and the Sioux were massacred. The Xosa of South Africa provide another example. In 1856 spirits promised them that if they made sacrifices, the spirits would help them drive out the English. The Xosa then destroyed their animal herds and all their grain, and consequently nearly all of them starved to death. Their reliance on the spirits proved disastrous. These are just a couple of the many examples summarized by La Barre.

Revitalization occurs in periods of cultural liminality. The trickster constellation manifests during such times, as is clear from Wallace's descriptions. The disregard of sexual mores, general disruption, and a highly visible role of the supernatural, including the sometimes unconscionably bad advice of the spirits, are all trickster characteristics.

The "increasing incidences of such things as alcoholism"[12] indicates destructuring of consciousness.

Recent Examples In The World Today

Revitalization movements are not limited to ancient societies or primitive peoples. The Nation of Islam in the U.S. is an example today. It is not only a religious movement but also a political and social one. Its leaders unashamedly report paranormal experiences. A spiritual being appeared to Malcolm X while he was in jail; Louis Farrakhan reported being taken aboard a flying saucer.[13] (This connection between political activism and the paranormal is seen more generally. A 1992 survey conducted by the Roper Organization discovered that people active in political and social causes are more likely than average to report paranormal experiences.[14])

Dramatic transformations are not limited to small, marginal groups. The collapse of communism and the dissolution of the former U.S.S.R. in the early 1990s were accompanied by an explosion of interest in the paranormal. There were numerous accounts of macro-PK, spiritual healing, diviners, and new religions, all to the alarm of some high status scientists. In fact Sergei Kapitza, president of the Physical Society of the U.S.S.R., lamented the conditions in an article for *Scientific American* entitled "Antiscience Trends in the U.S.S.R." (1991). This burst of popularity of the paranormal was seen throughout Eastern Europe, and the whole region underwent exceptional change. This is a dramatic recent example of the association of anti-structure with the supernatural.

A similar revival of occult interests occurred in the People's Republic of China after the repressive "Cultural Revolution" and pogroms of Mao. In the mid and late 1970s, there was a revitalization of many aspects of culture; curiosity in psi burgeoned, and many people reported amazing paranormal events.[15]

The same pattern, though less abrupt, was seen in the U.S. in the 1960s and 1970s. That era was marked by the civil rights movement, the anti-war movement, the sexual revolution, manned space exploration (boundary crossing), the drug culture (emphasizing altered states of consciousness [ASCs]), and the growth of Eastern religions and meditation (more ASCs). This period of anti-structure also saw surging interest in the paranormal. Some of the same people who were involved with the anti-war movement later became active in paranormal and spiritual pursuits.[16] Victor Turner recognized the liminal aspects of this period and specifically discussed the hippies.[17] Ernest Hartmann noticed that: "the late 1960s was a period when certain thin-boundary characteristics were valued more highly than they usually are."[18]

In the last 20 years, one of the most publicized supernatural manifestations in the world was the apparitions of the Blessed Virgin Mary at Medjugorje. Although Marian sightings are by no means uncommon, Medjugorje received extended international attention over a period of years. It was undoubtedly one of the most publicized sightings ever. It is no exaggeration to say that it reached public consciousness on a worldwide scale. I suggest that it is no coincidence that it occurred in then Yugoslavia, foreshadowing some of the most vicious, fractionating (dramatically destructuring) fighting seen in the world at that time.

UFOs and Cultural Stress

Several theorists have commented on UFOs in relation to cultural stress and transformation. Carl Jung discussed "transformations of the collective psyche" on the very first page of the "Introductory" section of *Flying Saucers: A Modern Myth of Things Seen in the Skies* (1958). Carl Raschke, a religious scholar at the University of Denver wrote an essay: "UFOs: Ultraterrestrial Agents of Cultural Deconstruction" (1981), which succinctly stated his thesis with the title. He specifically cited the trickster in relation to UFOs, and noted that tricksters "perform the service of cognitive deconstruction."[19]

Martin Kottmeyer is arguably the premier UFO theorist in the U.S. (Though he is exceptionally knowledgeable and has published many articles, he is little known outside a small circle of specialists). In his article "UFO Flaps" (1995–96), he reviewed the political and social conditions during periods that had relatively high levels of reported UFO sightings. He concluded that the reports increased when there is a loss of national pride. For instance, a dramatic increase occurred after Sputnik was launched in 1957, and after anti-U.S. demonstrations in Vietnam in 1966 there was also an upsurge. Kottmeyer also discussed several other instances.

When I read his paper, I was struck by the congruences with my own ideas. Kottmeyer's concept of "loss of pride" is very close to "loss of status," a key issue in this book.[20] But there is another important facet of his theoretical analysis—paranoia. UFOs are indisputably associated with paranoia, and I will discuss that in the chapter on paranoia.[21]

The data make it easy to dismiss UFO reports as only psychological aberrations of individuals or groups under stress. But such explanations are too simplistic because psychological problems do not account for the well-documented physical aspects. Even skeptics of ufology seem to agree that with the Watergate scandal, 1973 was a time of national shame, and they admit that year also had an elevated level of UFO reports. October of 1973 saw the Coyne helicopter case in Ohio[22] and the Eddie Doyle Webb case in Missouri,[23] both are impressive, evidential cases with physical effects. Another loss of international status occurred with the Iran hostage crisis. Near its end, in December 1980, the Cash-Landrum case occurred in Texas.[24] Three victims received severe radiation burns, and mysterious helicopters were seen by a number of witnesses. There is no reason to think that the mental states of the victims and witnesses can explain the phenomena. These cases cannot be dismissed as fictional myths, and the skeptics largely ignore them.

Summary

Transitions occur in all societies, from those of thousands of years ago to our own. Whether dramatic and full blown, or relatively mild and limited, cultural change and revitalization are complex processes, but they have commonalities. Aspects of liminality and anti-structure are seen in them. There is often a loss of faith in the established order. Those on the margins are likely to be the first to suffer from the problems of incipient change. Their protests can induce the establishment to try to further marginalize and discredit them. As a crisis progresses, corruption and deceit in the establishment leads to further distrust. Individuals abandon their old ways of doing things and look for new ones. Those under stress may drastically alter their lifestyles and accept a change in status. In the terminology of Anthony Wallace, mazeways are demolished and reconstructed. Of particular interest for this book is the fact that the paranormal and supernatural become prominent during times of transition. Charismatic leaders may arise who demonstrate paranormal powers, attracting followers, and challenging the legitimacy of the establishment.

Whether within individuals, small tribes, or large cultures, the same pattern is found. Wallace's work on cultural revitalization substantially parallels van Gennep's work on rites of passage and Turner's explication of liminality. Disruption, loss of status, transition, deception, disregard of moral boundaries, and a prominent role for the supernatural are typical aspects of cultural change, and they are also all part of the trickster constellation.

Any comprehensive theory of the paranormal must explain its role in cultural transitions.

Part 4

Overview

This Part presents concrete, modern examples of the more abstract, theoretical ideas presented in earlier sections. The cases include: phony psychics, UFOs, magic tricks, hypnosis, fiction of the supernatural, modern-day witchcraft, government disinformation, the organization of parapsychology, and more. At first glance these subjects don't seem related; they are in wildly different categories. But they all involve the paranormal, and they are illuminated by the trickster, liminality, and anti-structure.

Deception is pervasively associated with all branches of the paranormal, including UFOs, Bigfoot, and laboratory parapsychology. Thus the trickster assumes particular importance here.

Deception is highlighted in the first two chapters, and in the very last two. The first chapter reviews prominent psychics who have been caught in trickery. The second chapter discusses magic tricks, magicians, and their subculture. Magicians' connection with the paranormal is far more complex than most people assume, and additionally, magicians have many liminal aspects. The next to the last chapter discusses government disinformation, and the final one covers hoaxes. Both are significant problems in the UFO field. They play a major part in shaping ufology, and the public's perception of it.

One chapter is devoted to CSICOP and the debunkers. They are a force within academe and are aggressive agents for the rationalization and disenchantment of the world (in Weber's senses). Their activities, beliefs, and institutions have striking contrasts with those of paranormal practitioners found in Spiritualism, modern-day witchcraft, and the New Age movement.

This Part is particularly concerned with institutions and how the paranormal is or is not accommodated by them, particularly those of government, industry, and academe. The term anti-structure is an important clue vis-à-vis the paranormal, and it is especially relevant to the paranormal's relationship to institutions.

Briefly, strong manifestations of the paranormal are found in small groups; rarely are large organizations involved. Groups that achieve strong psychic functioning are marked by instability, and they resist institutionalizing. This pattern is seen in Spiritualism, modern-day witchcraft, and psychical research.

Large institutions do not neglect the supernatural. In fact there are sizeable industries devoted to it, but they portray it as fiction in books, movies, and television. Fictionalizing subtly discourages serious consideration of the paranormal.

CHAPTER 10

Prominent "Psychics"

In the last 150 years, *the* most widely known "psychics" have been as ambiguous as they were prominent, and some are still the subject of debate, despite being dead for over a century. As it happens, allegations of trickery follow nearly all of them, and a summary is presented in Table 3. The general public associates psychic phenomena with all these people, even those who were professional magicians (e.g., Davenport brothers, Kreskin, Dunninger). It is difficult to assess whether most of these characters had genuine abilities, but that is not a primary concern here. Rather, it is their substantial influence on the public's perception of the paranormal that is of interest. They accentuate the ambiguity surrounding the paranormal. Questions arise not only about their psychic powers but also regarding their sexual orientations, sources of money, and marital statuses.

These are fascinating and colorful individuals, and book-length biographies have been written about them all. Many have undeniable charisma. They inspired devoted, unquestionning followers, and equally fanatic antagonists. Ironically, their enemies have sometimes been their most effective publicists, and the debunkers have often done the most to keep the psychics' names alive.

Parapsychologists have an ambivalent relationship with these characters, and in most cases they generally shun them because of their bizarre beliefs, odd behaviors, and sometimes cult-like followings. Yet these individuals have had an impact on scientific research. Because of the massive publicity they received, along with the allegations of fraud, serious psychical research was tainted by association. Similar figures will continue to emerge; they will continue to play salient roles in shaping belief and skepticism regarding the paranormal. As such, we need to understand them; they merit study regardless whether or not they ever produced convincing evidence of psi.

Performer	Reference with Report of Trickery
Fox Sisters *	Self-admitted, Earl Wesley Fornell (1964)
Davenport Brothers #*	John Nevil Maskelyne (1910)
Daniel Dunglas Home *	F. Merrifield (1903) Count Perovsky-Petrovo-Solovovo (1912, 1930)
Helena Petrovna Blavatsky *	Report of the Committee (1885) Vsevolod Sergyeevich Solovyoff (1892)
Eusapia Palladino *	Self-admitted, Hereward Carrington (1909)
Margery #*	William McDougall (1925 & 1926/1967)
Arthur Ford	William V. Rauscher with Allen Spraggett (1975) Allen Spraggett with William V. Rauscher (1973)
Joseph Dunninger #*	David Price (1985)
Kreskin *	David Marks & Richard Kammann (1980)
don Juan Matus	Richard de Mille (1976, 1980)
Uri Geller #*	Self-admitted, Uri Geller (1975)
Sathya Sai Baba	Venu K. Kodimela (1992)

Table 3 Prominent "Psychics" and Allegations of Their Trickery

Listed in The Encyclopedia of Magic and Magicians by T. A. Waters (1988).
* Listed in *Who's Who in Magic* by Bart Whaley (1990).

The Fox sisters became prominent in 1848, when odd sounds were heard in the home of Mr. and Mrs. John Fox in Hydesville, New York. Their daughters, Kate and Margaret, then 12 and 13 years old, discovered rapping sounds that gave messages from what purported to be a deceased person.[2] Visitors soon flocked to the farmhouse, and newspapers put the sisters on the front page; even Horace Greeley became involved. In short order, the spiritualist movement spread through the U.S. to Europe and beyond. The new religion gathered millions of followers, from all strata of society, and the Fox sisters became the most celebrated of mediums. However, near the end of their careers, during a period of alcoholism, Margaret claimed that as a young girl she had produced the raps by cracking her toe knuckles. She later retracted the confession, but whatever the truth of her statements, the sisters are forever tainted by charges of fraud.

Spiritualism has several trickster elements, its frequent association with deception being only one. Mediums, per their name, mediate between this world and the next, and it is no accident that trickster gods also often serve in that capacity. Spiritualism has other trickster and anti-structural properties, and later chapters will address them in more detail.

In 1855 Ira Erastus Davenport (1839–1877) and William Henry Harrison Davenport (1841–1911), two brothers from Buffalo, New York, began performing spiritualistic effects professionally on stage. They would enter a cabinet similar to a wardrobe, and their hands and feet were bound. After the lights were put out, instruments played within the cabinet, ghostly hands appeared outside of it, and sometimes the Davenports seemed to float over the heads of their audiences. Their personal lives were turbulent. William married a number of times (once secretly to Adah Isaacs Menken, a love-goddess of that era), and he had a severe problem with alcohol.[3]

There is little doubt that the brothers engaged in trickery, but their true beliefs about spiritualism are still puzzling. Joe Nickell, a CSICOP investigator, examined a scrapbook of the brothers, and from his analysis it is plausible to think that Ira Davenport actually believed in spiritualism.[4] The brothers generated enormous publicity, entertained royalty, and biographies were written proclaiming their miraculous powers. Many others followed their lead, and conjurors quickly stirred up controversy and capitalized on it.

John Henry Anderson and Henri Robin, two prominent magicians, exposed the Davenports' act in their own performances. John Nevil Maskelyne and Samri Baldwin began their careers doing exposés, later becoming eminent magicians themselves. Maskelyne went on to father a magical dynasty, and Samri Baldwin did handcuff escapes decades before Houdini. Early in his career, Harry Kellar traveled with the Davenports and went on to become the most famous magician of his era in the U.S. Thus the Davenports, who presented themselves as spiritualists, had an extraordinary, if unintended, effect on conjuring. Despite the magician detractors, or perhaps partly because of them, the Davenports were the most successful performing stage mediums of their day.[5] They publicized spiritualism but also contributed to its ambiguity; people were left wondering: were the manifestations real or fake?

Daniel Dunglas Home (1833–1886) is called the medium who was never caught in fraud. The reports of his phenomena are amazing, and Eric Dingwall succinctly summarized Home's life as "the problem of miracles in its most acute form."[6] Home elongated his body, levitated both himself and large tables, and materialized spirit hands. He could hold red-hot coals in his bare hands without any ill effect and even passed them to others, conferring his immunity on them. Sir William Crookes, the eminent British physicist who invented the Crookes tube and discovered the element thallium, investigated and endorsed him. Home attracted the attention of royalty throughout Europe and gave séances for Czar Alexander II, Napolean III, and Queen Sophia of Holland. He did not charge money for his séances, but he did accept gifts, some of which were lavish. Elizabeth Barrett Browning was much taken with him, but her husband Robert believed Home to be a fraud and wrote a poem about him: "Mr. Sludge, 'The Medium'." There were many ambiguities in his personal life, and Dingwall suggests that Home likely had some homosexual tendencies, but rarely, if ever, expressed them. It is true that absolute proof of trickery was never obtained against Home; however, there were several serious detailed allegations (see Table 3). Even today debunkers persist in trying to discredit him.[7]

Helena Petrovna Blavatsky (1831–1891), co-founder of the Theosophical Society, still retains her notoriety for her paranormal manifestations. Born a granddaughter of a Russian princess, Blavatsky began traveling the world at age 17, later claiming to have spent time in Tibet, though that has been questioned. Her life was frequently in turmoil. She deserted two husbands; several of her devoted disciples became bitter enemies, and at times she lived near poverty. Her sex life still provokes wild speculation. She claimed to be a virgin,[8] though many say that she had given birth to a son.[9] There were rumors that she was wildly promiscuous, a lesbian, a transvestite, and a hermaphrodite.[10] The sexual scandals around her and her close followers are very amusing, and Marion Meade recounted some of them in her *Madame Blavatsky: The Woman Behind the Myth* (1980). Whatever the truth, there is no question that this part of her life was marked by ambiguity. Blavatsky's psychic phenomena were exotic. Materializations and levitations were frequently reported. Her followers received apported letters, purportedly from "ascended masters," though many suspect that HPB wrote them herself. The Society for Psychical Research sent Richard Hodgson to India to investigate, and he found so much trickery that he concluded that she should be considered one of the world's greatest practical jokers.[11] His report continues to be debated, even a century after it was written.

Though it is easy to dismiss HPB as a charlatan, she was far too fascinating for that. Her life story is amazing, and religion professor Robert Ellwood writes that she can be regarded as "a fraud and confidence artist, or a sage of sages, or a compulsive liar, or a rare psychic and intimate of supernormal entities, or a gluttonous and overbearing old tartar with a fishwife's tongue."[12] HPB continues to be the subject of biographies, and at least two more appeared in the early 1990s.

HPB should not be considered a mere opportunist, capitalizing on the gullibility of those surrounding her. She sometimes privately admitted that she used tricks.[13] Vselovod S. Solovyoff published a letter of hers (with her permission!) in which she admitted that she would lie about her mahatmas, though the interpretation is ambiguous, as she succeeded in muddying the issue.[14] Her anti-structural characteristics can be seen in other ways. Political intrigue followed Blavatsky, and in India she was suspected of being a Russian agent, fomenting unrest. Whether this was true or not, among her successors in the Theosophical Society were Annie Besant, a central figure in the Indian independence movement, and C. W. Leadbeater, a sex pervert. HPB and her immediate followers were disruptive of the social order, and paranormal phenomena were an impetus in establishing the Theosophical Society.[15]

Robert S. Ellwood, Jr. provided an extended analysis of HPB in his book *Alternative Altars: Unconventional and Eastern Spirituality in America* (1979). He was an Episcopal clergyman, a member of the Theosophical Society of America, and professor in the department of religion at the University of Southern California (his wife, Gracia Fay Ellwood, has written on the paranormal). Drawing on the work of Victor Turner, Ellwood pointed out that Blavatsky was a liminal character and that her life identified with archetypal forms, particularly the trickster and shaman. His analysis is particularly valuable because it explicitly discussed liminality in conjunction with deception and the paranormal. Both HPB and her colleague Henry Steel Olcott assumed a voluntary loss of social status and became wanderers; in fact her entire life was marked by travel. Though she was the catalyst for founding the Theosophical Society in 1875, HPB and her teachings were not its sole focus. She lacked administrative ability and never held the top position in the society.

Eusapia Palladino (1854–1918), an Italian peasant woman, was one of the most celebrated physical mediums in the history of psychical research.[16] She levitated tables, produced paranormal breezes and rapping sounds, and materialized spirit hands, among many other phenomena, and she submitted to extensive testing over a period of years. Palladino was impulsive and had little self-control, especially when in trance, and she warned researchers that she would cheat if given a chance. Despite her warnings, some investigators intentionally loosened controls, allowed her to cheat, and then dismissed her, proclaiming her a fraud. The British Victorian researchers considered her a coarse character and were often shocked by her overt eroticism and sexual remarks. She attracted wide attention, and the *New York Times* published a number of articles about Palladino during her visit to the U.S. for testing. Magicians were involved in that endeavor, and Howard Thurston, the most eminent conjuror of his day, endorsed her phenomena as genuine.[17] Nevertheless, because of the allegations of fraud and attendant publicity, the case of Eusapia Palladino helped discredit psychical research in the eyes of many. Yet the controversy over Palladino continues still, and in the early 1990s the *Journal of the Society for Psychical Research* carried an extended debate on her.[18]

Mina Crandon (1889–1941), also known as "Margery," was the most famous physical medium of the 1920s. The wife of Boston surgeon Le Roi Crandon, 16 years her senior, she held séances that captured enormous public attention. *Scientific American* magazine had offered prizes totaling $5000 for demonstrations of certain psychic phenomena. Margery applied to be tested, and a prominent committee was appointed to assess her claims. She produced innumerable dramatic materializations, levitations, and movements of objects for the committee. Ectoplasm appeared to emerge from her bodily orifices, including her vagina, but subsequent examination of the photographs indicated that some of it was actually tissue cut from animal lung, and there was other evidence of fraud as well. Rumors circulated that some investigators were sexually involved with her, thus providing a motive for complicity in deception.[19]

One of the members of the *Scientific American* committee was Harry Houdini, another trickster figure of archetypal proportions, and one who was obsessed with spiritualism.[20] His assistant, James Collins, later admitted that under Houdini's orders, he hid a folding ruler inside a testing cabinet, leading others to suspect that Margery had smuggled it in. Collins' actions allowed Houdini to "honestly" deny planting it himself.[21] The trickster is seen on both sides of the Margery affair.

The Margery case was the most divisive in the history of U.S. psychical research. Leaders of the American Society for Psychical Research (ASPR) became her partisans, but the most capable ASPR investigators, including Walter Franklin Prince and Harvard professor William McDougall, left and founded a rival society in Boston.[22] As a young man J. B. Rhine attended one of Margery's séances and was so disgusted by what he witnessed that he published an exposé describing the deceptions he saw.[23] This was a turning point in his career, and the Margery affair led Rhine to chart a new course for parapsychology by restricting his work to the laboratory, using statistics and testing ordinary people.[24] Thus Margery had a major, albeit indirect, impact on the course of psychical research for over half a century.

Arthur Ford (1897–1971) was a renowned medium, who in 1929 gained notoriety for cracking a secret code that Houdini had left with his wife Bess. According to Houdini's plan, if a medium was able to ascertain the code's meaning, it would indicate that Houdini was speaking from beyond the grave. In a dramatic séance, Ford communicated the meaning, and the case received enormous publicity. But there were cries of fraud, and magicians and spiritualists long debated whether Ford was truly successful.[25] Almost 40 years later, he came to international attention again, when he conducted a televised séance with the prominent maverick Episcopal bishop, James Pike. He provided Pike with ostensible communication from his son who had committed suicide. After Ford's death, William Rauscher, Ford's literary legatee, and writer Allen Spraggett reviewed his private papers and found many old obituaries clipped from newspapers. These contained numerous small details that Ford had given in séances. After he made that discovery public, Rauscher received a letter from a Jay Abbott, who had been closely acquainted with both Ford and Bess Houdini. Abbott provided evidence of a romantic link between the two and indicated that the cracking of the Houdini code was deceitful. Rauscher is an Episcopal priest and a magician with a wide knowledge of fraudulent mediumship, and he was the driving force behind M. Lamar Keene's exposé *The Psychic Mafia* (1977). Yet Rauscher remains convinced that Ford demonstrated genuine psychic ability in some instances.

In addition to deception, there were other trickster and antistructural aspects to Ford's character. He had a long personal battle with alcoholism. His sex life raised speculation, and his biographers noted that "people were always falling in love with him, men as well as women."[26] Ford was the motivating factor for establishing Spiritual Frontiers Fellowship (SFF) in 1956, which grew to be a large organization of clergy and lay people that worked to bring respectability to psychic areas. Despite his influence, Ford always remained in the background, and the SFF never was focused on him.

Mentalists Joseph Dunninger (1892–1975) and Kreskin (b. 1935) are conjurors, yet many people believe them to be genuinely psychic, a belief they both encouraged. Among magicians, the two are known for their publicity skills. Dunninger was the foremost mentalist of his day, and he had a real knack for associating with people who enhanced his credibility. For instance, along with Houdini he published exposés of spiritualism, and later he was appointed Chairman of the *Scientific American* Committee for the Investigation of Psychic Phenomena.[27] Berthold E. Schwarz, a kindly but gullible psychiatrist and writer of books on the paranormal, frequently lauded Dunninger's psychic abilities. His association with Houdini, *Scientific American*, and the praise from a psychiatrist undoubtedly convinced many that Dunninger's act was based on psychic ability rather than trickery. His personal life was filled with ambiguity. He lived with Chrystal Spencer for many years, but during that time he promised to marry a Betty Devery. In 1944 Chrystal won a lawsuit and was declared his common-law wife. But she admitted that there were weeks when she did not know where he was or what he was doing, and she had to compete with his mother for his affection. Many other oddities of Dunninger's life were revealed in Maurice Zolotow's entertaining *It Takes All Kinds* (1952).

After Dunninger's heyday, Kreskin (George Kresge, Jr.) became an internationally known mentalist, and his winning and persuasive manner is now widely acknowledged. He was so charming that even Prometheus Books, the publishing house of the debunking movement, published one of his books (though many skeptics were outraged by it).[28] Kreskin is a somewhat solitary man. He has never married, keeps his distance from other conjurors, and is not seen at magicians' conventions; however, he is rumored to furtively visit magic shops late at night, by special appointment. Both Dunninger and Kreskin fostered the belief that they are actually psychic. Their press material and the writings of Walter Gibson, who ghosted books for them, promoted their reputations as psychics.[29] I've spoken to magicians who knew

Dunninger and Kreskin, and the general, though not universal, impression is that they both believed themselves to actually be psychic.

Don Juan Matus, a Yaqui sorcerer with supernatural powers, was introduced to the reading public by Carlos Castaneda in his *The Teachings of Don Juan: A Yaqui Way of Knowledge*. The University of California Press published that work in 1968 with a foreword by Walter Goldschmidt, chairman of the anthropology department of the University of California at Los Angeles (UCLA), who had also served as president of the American Anthropological Association. In 1973, Castaneda was granted a Ph.D. from that department, with a dissertation essentially identical to his popular book *Journey to Ixtlan: The Lessons of Don Juan* (1972). This was the beginning of a lucrative literary career, and Castaneda continued to produce a steady stream of books well into the 1990s. Some were bestsellers, and *Publishers Weekly* reported that by 1977 nearly four million copies of his books had been sold.[30]

Don Juan Matus, Castaneda's "teacher," had telepathic and PK powers, and Castaneda described them along with amazing feats of other sorcerers.[31] With the seal of approval of the UCLA anthropology department, many assumed the books to be factual accounts. But Castaneda largely invented them! Primarily through the efforts of psychologist Richard de Mille, overwhelming evidence was marshalled that Castaneda did much of his "fieldwork" in the UCLA library, and there is no good evidence don Juan ever existed.[32] As such, he is the only fictional character listed in Table 3. Nevertheless, he may well be the most influential, and many people were introduced to paranormal ideas through Castaneda's writings.

De Mille's books, *Castaneda's Journey* (1976) and *The Don Juan Papers* (1980), are nicely crafted and enormously entertaining, and they show a true sympathy for both the trickster and the paranormal.[33] In fact the first chapter of his *Castaneda's Journey* is titled "The Day of the Coyote," and it opens with an epigraph from a poltergeist report from the *Journal of the American Society for Psychical Research*. Even though Castaneda tried to erase his personal history, de Mille was able to reconstruct some of it, and his biographical analysis is useful and witty. Both of de Mille's books have extended discussions of Castaneda as trickster, with intriguing insights into his personality. Castaneda never responded, and his mystique continues to this day.

This landmark hoax severely embarrassed the UCLA anthropology department, and it made it difficult for anthropology students everywhere to investigate paranormal topics because their professors feared being similarly tainted. This helped shield the paranormal from scientific investigation, and de Mille even commented that "I can't help wondering how many prospective readers of serious psi literature may have been shunted off in another direction" by Castaneda.[34]

Uri Geller (b. 1946) burst upon the psychic scene in the 1970s with his seeming power to bend keys and spoons with PK and also for his ESP. He was born in Israel, and when he was about 10 his parents divorced; after that he lived in a kibbutz and later went to Cyprus with his mother and stepfather. He returned to Israel and began performing on stage displaying his paranormal abilities, which even he admits were augmented by tricks. He came to the attention of paranormal researcher Andrija Puharich, who helped arrange for tests of his psychic abilities at Stanford Research Institute by Harold Puthoff and Russell Targ. Those results were reported in *Nature* and the *Proceedings of the IEEE*, major scientific journals of international standing (IEEE stands for the Institute of Electrical and Electronic Engineers).[35] Those papers sparked enormous controversy, and the fallout persists. Books have been written attacking and defending Geller, and there have been direct allegations of cheating.[36] He has acquired enormous wealth, reputedly through mineral prospecting, and he now lives in a mansion that has a helicopter landing pad. A fictionalized movie has been made of his life.

Geller drew the attention and spite of magician James Randi, who in the last quarter of the twentieth century was the most prominent spokesman for the debunking movement. Both Geller and Randi have appeared on numerous TV shows, and Randi even wrote a book denouncing Geller. The conflict has continued for over 25 years, becoming so intense that the two battled in lawsuits around the world. Randi was forced out of the Committee for the Scientific Investigation of Claims of the Paranormal (which he helped found), because of the legal suits provoked by his statements.[37]

Sathya Sai Baba (b. 1926), a Hindu holy man with millions of followers around the world, is one of today's best known miracle workers.[38] He reputedly materializes precious metals and gems, is clairvoyant, has turned water into gasoline, and even raised the dead. But he has not allowed controlled tests of his abilities, and there is much evidence indicating trickery.[39] Many of his materializations of small objects have been recorded on video, and magicians confirm that they certainly *look* like magic tricks, though the resolution and video quality were insufficient for definitive proof. A number of devotees have lived in close proximity with Sai Baba and later became disillusioned, some bitterly so. One was Meenakshi Srikanth who posted an article on the Internet in 1993 entitled "Sri Sathya Sai Baba: The Good, the Bad and the Ugly." He reported that Sai Baba had sodomized a number of his students and that some were familiar with the magic tricks he used. Tal Brooke, another former devotee, also recounted Sai Baba's homosexual advances on himself and others.[40] Elements of the trickster constellation appear in the person of Sai Baba.

Summary

I know of no psychics more prominent than those listed in Table 3, and serious allegations of deception follow them all. There are few of comparable public visibility without such taint (e.g., Edgar Cayce, Jeane Dixon, Eileen Garrett, Ingo Swann). Even if one wishes to disregard the relatively weaker testimony, the overwhelming majority of the most widely known psychic performers have a reputation for trickery. This is simply a cultural fact.

These characters exemplify the patterns of liminality, antistructure, and the trickster. Deception and psi are not the only trickster qualities to manifest in these personalities. None were long-term employees in large bureaucratic institutions; they didn't fit into the normal work-a-day world. They had odd life-styles; marital situations were nonstandard; they did not hold regular jobs; unusual sexuality was common, and several had problems with alcohol. Many were charismatic. These are liminal, anti-structural people.

These people have been exceptionally effective in drawing attention to themselves and stimulating discussion about their phenomena. At the same time, their antics and deceptions serve as an excuse for status-conscious scientists to ignore them and to marginalize their phenomena. This presents a paradox—for the paranormal, publicity fends off detailed examination.

CHAPTER 11

Conjurors and the Paranormal

> Everything that deceives may be said to enchant.
> Plato[1]

The terms *magic* and *conjuring* are defined as the influencing of the physical world via supernatural means, but they are also synonymous with legerdemain, trickery, and sleight-of-hand.[2] The two definitions seem to have little in common, but there are actually deep connections between them. The links are obscure, but that obscurity is a clue to their nature. Primitive peoples often did not make a distinction between the two kinds of magic, and it behooves us to understand why. To clarify this it is helpful to examine magicians who perform tricks, especially those who have been involved with the paranormal.[3]

Magicians' embroilment in paranormal controversies didn't start with the modern-day skeptical movement or even with Houdini's attack on spiritualism. Over 400 years ago the first English-language book describing practical conjurors' methods, Reginald Scot's *The Discoverie of Witchcraft*, also attacked beliefs in divination, alchemy, astrology, the Catholic Church, exorcism and precognitive dreams. But by no means were all magicians debunkers. John Wilkins' *Mercury: Or the Secret and Swift Messenger*, one of the first books discussing mentalist methods, spoke favorably of communications from spirits and angels. *Hocus Pocus Junior* and the first magic magazine ever published also gave favorable comment to the paranormal. This dichotomy of opinion is not limited to hundreds of years ago; many conjurors have since endorsed the reality of paranormal phenomena while others have been some of the most vocal critics.[4] This peculiar association of conjuring and the supernatural spans centuries, even millennia. The fact that the controversy over the existence of psi continues even within the magic community indicates an especially problematic situation.

At present, many people believe that magicians are almost all skeptical about paranormal phenomena. This impression has been fostered by an effective propaganda campaign by debunkers. The impression is untrue, the campaign intentionally misleading. Many of the greatest names in the history of conjuring endorsed the reality of psychic phenomena, and a list of them is provided in Table 5. In addition I identified many more in a two-part article in *The Linking Ring*, the monthly magazine of the International Brotherhood of Magicians.

Author or Editor	Year	Title	Description
Scot, Reginald	1584	*The Discoverie of Witchcraft*	First practical English-language work on conjuring.
Anonymous	1634	*Hocus Pocus Junior*	First original work devoted solely to conjuring.
Wilkins, John	1641	*Mercury: Or The Secret and Swift Messenger*	One of the first works describing mentalist methods.
Ady, Thomas	1655	*A Candle in the Dark*	Written against the witchcraft persecutions
Decremps, Henri	1784	*La Magie Blanche Dévoilée*	Regarded as the most important work on magic since Scot's of 1584.
Locke, W.	1791	*The Conjuror's Magazine*	The first magic magazine.
Pinchbeck, W. F.	1805	*The Expositor; or Many Mysteries Unravelled*	First original work on magic published in the U.S.

Table 4 Major Historical Works on Conjuring That Also Addressed the Paranormal

Magician	Reference
Abbott, David P.	Abbott (1908)
	Hyslop et al (1913)
Baldwin, Samri S.	Baldwin (1895, p. 104)
Bellachini, Samuel	Zöllner (1881, pp. 213–214)
Dickson, Abb	Zorka (1976)
Evans, Henry Ridgely	Evans (1897, pp. 12, 32)
Gibson, Walter B.	Gibson & Gibson (1969)
Goldston, Will	Goldston (1933)
Jansen, Harry (Dante)	Rauscher (2000, pp. 61–62)
Kellar, Harry	Rinn (1950, p. 387)
Lewis, Angelo (Professor Hoffmann)	Lewis (1886)
Maskelyne, John Nevil	A Spiritualistic Expose–II (1885)
	Maskelyne (1885, 1910)
McGill, Ormond	McGill (1977)
Miller, Katlyn (Katlyn)	Katlyn (1982, 1989)
Oursler, Fulton	Oursler (1964, pp. 184, 482–484)
Parsons, E. A. (Henry Hardin)	Hyslop et al (1913)
Price, Harry	Price (1925)
Robert-Houdin, Jean Eugene	Lee (1866, pp. 162–163)
	Goldston (1906, p. 22)
Thurston, Howard	Thurston (1910)

Table 5 Magicians Who Endorsed the Reality of Psychic Phenomena

All of the above persons were of sufficient prominence to be included in *The Encyclopedia of Magic and Magicians* by T. A. Waters (1988). Names in parentheses are stage or pen names. All references give first-person accounts.

Anti-structural Aspects of Conjuring

Conjuring, by its nature is liminal and anti-structural. The magician's role is one of the margin and outsiderhood, yet I do not recall ever seeing any academic theorist of liminality discuss magicians. This seems to have been completely overlooked. Historically, conjurors have been associated with mountebanks, itinerant entertainers and other unsavory figures—persons not part of the establishment.[5] The art is seen more in the interstices than as part of the structure, and today conjuring remains apart from most institutional affiliations. Whereas music, painting, and drama are taught in virtually all colleges and universities, magic never became an element of the established curriculum. Magic courses are rarely found even in adult education programs and are virtually never offered for college credit. Few libraries have substantial holdings on the topic; even major universities seldom have much more than do small-town public libraries. Despite this, the literature on conjuring is vast, and the *Master Index to Magic in Print* (published 1967–1975) compiled by Jack Potter and Micky Hades gives one an appreciation of the literature's extent. This *Index* contains nearly 6000 pages. No trick methods are described; it is only an index. Almost all major magic libraries are in private hands. Many of the important works are not listed in *Books in Print*; they can be obtained only from sources known to magicians.

Conjuring has low status compared with the other arts, despite it being one of the oldest forms of entertainment. There are night clubs, symphony halls and recording studios devoted to music, and theatres to drama, but there is almost nothing comparable for the art of magic. Many magicians are forced to travel to earn a living, and even the biggest names may stay in any one venue for only a week; long engagements are rare.[6] Conjurors are also marginal to show business. Rock stars, movie actors, and TV personalities receive more attention. (There is one exception to this, namely Houdini—the greatest showman ever. Today all schoolchildren know his name. He was a trickster figure of extraordinary proportions.) Although a number of prominent people have made magic their hobby (e.g., George Bush, Norman Schwarzkopf), the *role* of conjurer is marginal.

Magicians' organizations are distinctive, and they are not comparable to unions or other professional groups that have objective criteria for qualifications and competence. In many magic societies, rank amateurs and seasoned professionals are all involved, and the groups are usually headed by those with amateur status. Because of the secretive nature of magic, much information cannot be given to outsiders; revealing secrets destroys the effects. However at meetings and conventions, performers can find people with whom they can share ideas and discuss methods. Conjuring is a hobby that cuts across class lines, and magic conventions often promote great camaraderie. There is temporary leveling or even inversion of outside statuses; within magic, carnies may be held in higher regard than medical doctors. Thus magic fraternities provide a measure of communitas.

Trickster Characteristics of Conjurors

The relationship between the trickster character-type and magicians seems obvious, but surprisingly, there is almost no literature addressing it. As far as I can tell, virtually all those pursuing psychological theories of the trickster have missed this exemplar.[7] Within magic, there has been only fleeting mention of the association.[8] Though the logo of the International Brotherhood of Magicians includes the image of the Roman god Mercury, few members seem to be aware of it or what it signifies.

Mythological trickster characters are typically male, and this is reflected in conjuring. In fact women constitute only 5% of the membership of the International Brotherhood of Magicians, the largest magic organization in the U.S.[9] Trickster figures are also frequently solitary creatures, and sociologist Michael Carroll has shown that many trickster animals have habits of isolation.[10] Likewise, magicians are somewhat solitary. Long hours of practice alone typify the early years of many conjurors, and they generally perform solo or, at most, with a small supporting cast; rarely are large groups involved.[11]

The trickster issue of sexuality can be raised. Though I know of no formal survey of magicians' sexual preferences, in my experience, conjurors are relatively open about acknowledging the homosexuality and unusual sexual behavior of some of their fellow entertainers. On the basis of statistical percentages, their sexual preferences almost certainly differ from the general population. A fair number of magic performers incorporate ribaldry in their acts, and magic magazines not infrequently carry discussion of "blue" material and its appropriateness, or otherwise, for various venues. Magicians' affinity for the crude was illustrated by an incident in a promotional effort for Oreo cookies. In 1991, the International Brotherhood of Magicians (IBM) and the Society of American Magicians (SAM) helped arrange auditions for magicians to work in grocery stores to promote Oreos. In the one-page flyer sent out, auditioners were warned, with emphasis in capital letters, not to use profanity or vulgarity. The magic organizations deemed it necessary to bring this point to the conscious awareness of their members who were auditioning. I wonder whether any other group of performers would require such a warning, since it was clear that the Oreo promotions were to be in grocery stores.

Supernatural And Liminal Features of Conjuring

Magic performances are a bit like modern religious ritual; for some they seem silly, childish, or puzzling, but for others they can evoke uneasy feelings of the supernatural. Interpretation poses problems for audiences. Although virtually all academics understand that stage magicians use tricks, not all of the general public does. I have been cautioned by religiously conservative people that legerdemain is demonic, and I know quite a few magicians who have received similar warnings, including some who primarily perform at children's parties. Yet even sophisticated audiences do not completely escape the ambiguity.

More than any other form of entertainment, magic evokes ideas of supernatural power. Trickery played an important role in the supernatural manifestations of shamans. Some of the earliest written accounts of conjuring describe methods used to promote religious belief, such as the temple tricks of the Greeks described by Hero of Alexandria.[12] The association between trickery and the supernatural is longstanding, yet full comprehension of magic's appeal remains something of a puzzle and is perhaps paradoxical. Demonstrations of power can be threatening, but also amusing.

Conjuring illusions have parallels with mystical experiences. Many classic stage illusions feature themes of death, dismemberment, and supernatural beings. Cremation, decapitation, impaling, and levitation are all part of the stage performer's repertoire. Similar imagery is found in shamanic visions, LSD trips, visionary experiences, certain psychotic episodes, and even some UFO accounts. Rogan Taylor's book *The Death and Resurrection Show* (1985) discusses the parallels at length. Mystical experiences are more common than most people realize, and they can have great impact. Like mysticism, conjuring provides immediate and direct experience. Whereas books, TV and film can provide similar imagery, conjuring loses its power with the distance and abstraction inherent in those media.

Bizarre Magic

Bizarre magic is a small, modern-day subspecialty of conjuring in which dark supernatural themes are explicit. Performers sometimes don hooded robes, at altars with chalices of (stage) blood, and other performances involve phony séances where evil entities manifest. Bizarre magic emerged from pseudo-spiritism and mentalism around 1967,[13] and though there may be only a few hundred aficionados, there have been several periodicals and quite a number of books devoted to the topic. The spectators are primarily insiders such as mentalists and other bizarrists. In much of this genre the supernatural element is too strong for lay audiences and is thus not commercially viable.

This branch of magic raises clear, pertinent questions; the problem of explaining magic's appeal and even its existence is most acute here. The attraction cannot be accounted for as a wish to "evoke a sense of wonder or the mysterious" rather the performances provoke a sense of danger and dread—a more immediate version of horror than encountered in movies or in books. The psychology behind it can illuminate important issues.

Much bizarre magic is not performed to entertain, influence or educate the public. It seems to be more for the gratification of the performers and a very small cultic audience. The supernatural has an undeniable impact on them; many display a preoccupation and fascination with occult and supernatural themes, and some of the most active participants in this genre are noted for their anti-religious feelings. Issue number 666 of *Genii*, a general-interest magic magazine, carried tricks by bizarrists including one using a St. Christopher's medal,[14] and others involved the theme of the beast of the Biblical Book of Revelations.

The writers in that issue of *Genii* (April 1992) ridiculed religion and parodied rituals. The question is: why? Perhaps they were trying to reassure themselves that such powers are not "real." After all they spend countless hours writing about paranormal phenomena, simulating them, and attending conventions with like-minded persons. They cultivate a mystique, groom their public personas, and encourage nonmagicians to see them as controlling occult forces. The paranormal is often destabilizing (anti-structural), and their "rituals of protection" (i.e., of parody and ridicule) may help them maintain their equilibrium. They may wish to avoid a too sustained involvement with the occult. If the supernatural did not hold such power, a few words of rational explanation should banish any problem.

On the other hand, perhaps some of the aficionados become desensitized and wanted a stronger "kick," a more immediate contact with supernatural themes. Perhaps they needed to deal with emotionally charged issues that are only partly conscious.

These proffered explanations are not complete, but they point directions that explanations can be sought. Later chapters will discuss the wide appeal of supernatural horror fiction, and that is pertinent to understanding bizarre magic.

Mentalism

Mentalism is the branch of conjuring devoted to simulating psychic phenomena. Mentalists perform mind-reading feats, predict newspaper headlines, and demonstrate telepathy. These performers are some of the most trickster-like within the magic fraternity. As with other trickster characters, they typically perform alone, and I can think of no instance in which a mentalist used a large cast for public performances. During their acts, much of the audience believes they are witnessing genuine psi because mentalists intentionally blur the distinctions between the genuine and the fake. Much of their literature encourages performers to foster belief in the paranormal and even to claim that they possess genuine psychic abilities themselves. Mentalists have had a long association with mediums and psychics, and some do readings at psychic fairs and séances at spiritualist camps.

There are far fewer mentalists than regular magicians, and there have been some antagonisms between the two groups. Episcopal priest William Rauscher[15] and atheist James Randi, both magicians and both upholders of orthodoxy, have suggested that mentalists do a disservice and mislead the public, leaving them vulnerable to charlatans, and giving them a false view of the world. Magic historian David Price[16] as well as J. B. Rhine[17] expressed opinions similar to Rauscher and Randi. Needless to say, mentalists have not always accorded these views a warm reception, and Marcello Truzzi, a sociologist and mentalist, has provided a useful analysis of some of the conflicts.[18] Truzzi pointed out that what is and is not "psychic" is a very difficult distinction to make, especially outside of the laboratory. He noted that a certain amount of illusion in life is healthy, and that even those mentalists who do psychic counseling may be providing as much or more of a service than psychiatrists and other so-called mental health professionals. The ethical issues are fuzzy.

Because of the antagonisms, mentalists formed a group of their own, the Psychic Entertainers Association. It has several hundred members and holds an annual convention. The original name of their bulletin, *Psychic Entertainers News & Information Service*, was selected for its acronym, which is appropriately tricksterish.

In playing the role of "psychic," many mentalists come to wonder whether they might, in fact, possess genuine abilities. Even vocal debunker Ray Hyman has admitted that he once believed himself to be gifted in reading palms, though he eventually rejected the notion.[19] Yet Hyman has come to devote much of his professional career to attacking the paranormal, which, in its way, attests to its influence over him.[20] A number of con artists have commented in their autobiographies that it is helpful for them to believe their own story line; such beliefs allow them to be more sincere and thus more effective. Similar beliefs may assist mentalists.

Understandably, many magicians are cynical of performers who claim real psychic abilities; they are dismissed as frauds or, more charitably, as those who unfortunately came to believe their own publicity material. Mentalists' statements to the general public can rarely be trusted; however, a number have written works circulated only among insiders in which they state their belief in the efficacy of psychic practices, though they do not rely on them for performing.[21] The demarcation between trickery and genuine psychic sensitivity is not always clear, even to mentalists. An example is contact mind reading, a technique in which the performer holds on to a person who knows the location of a hidden object. By noting the person's unintentional bodily cues, the mentalist is able to locate the object. In these performances, the distinction between psi and sensory acuity is blurred, and such an exercise has been recommended as training for genuine telepathy by both George Newmann,[22] an eminent mentalist, and psychical researcher Hereward Carrington.[23]

In a 1978 article in the *Journal of the American Society for Psychical Research*, Richard Reichbart suggested that the act of simulating psi may stimulate the real. If he is correct, psi is extremely subversive. The distinctions between true and false, reality and fantasy, are undermined. Understandably this suggestion provokes furious reactions, or contempt, especially from those who despise ambiguity and wish their world to be well structured. Strong protective beliefs are needed. The mentalist-magician antagonism is a symptom of one of the subversive manifestations of the trickster—the blurring of imagination and reality.

Hypnosis

Hypnosis is a liminal and trickster phenomenon in a host of ways. It deserves a section for itself, but it makes sense to include it in this chapter; after all, magicians and mentalists have undoubtedly publicized the phenomenon far more than have psychologists. In fact, the

Amazing Kreskin is probably one of the most famous hypnotists, and some psychologists even consider him an eminent authority.[24]

Hypnosis highlights the confusing interrelationships among conjuring, liminality, and the paranormal. Hypnotism has been known for thousands of years under a variety of names (e.g., animal magnetism, mesmerism, suggestion), but it is ambiguous, and even its definition is problematical. Psychologists continue to debate whether hypnosis involves a special state or if it is essentially indistinguishable from ordinary consciousness. Some attribute hypnotic effects to mere "suggestion," doubting that a hypnotic trance exists. The disputes have been intense, and in one form or another, they have continued for over 200 years, but they are not resolved.[25] All this has resulted in a somewhat marginal position for hypnosis within psychology. Its public image also suffers from some ambiguous and even unsavory affiliations.

Authorities today credit Franz Anton Mesmer as beginning the first sustained investigation of the phenomenon. In his time hypnotism was associated with traveling clairvoyance. That association continued, and from the earliest days of the Society for Psychical Research in the 1880s to the laboratory-based parapsychology of the 1960s and 1970s, hypnosis was used to facilitate ESP in experiments.

The relationship between hypnotism and psychical research is far too extensive to cover here. But to give just a glimpse of the links, I call attention to the book *Hypnosis* (1972) by Erika Fromm and Ronald Shor, a book that gives no coverage to the paranormal. Yet on the first page of Chapter One, 23 historically important persons are listed who made significant contributions to hypnosis. Among those were Vladimir Bechterev, Pierre Janet, Henri Bergson, Sigmund Freud, Frederic Myers, Charles Richet, William James, and William McDougall. All of these people (more than a third of those listed) also contributed to psychical research. Additionally, psychical researchers have published important chronicles of the history, and here again we encounter the scholarship of Eric Dingwall, who edited a four-volume series titled *Abnormal Hypnotic Phenomena* (1967–1968). Alan Gauld, a president of the Society for Psychical Research, wrote the 738-page *A History of Hypnotism* (1992).

In the popular mind also, hypnosis is connected with the paranormal. During the 1950s there was an explosion of interest with the Bridey Murphy reincarnation case. Businessman Morey Bernstein hypnotized Virginia Tighe, a Colorado housewife who recalled details of a life in Ireland during the first part of the nineteenth century. Bernstein's book *The Search for Bridey Murphy* (1956) raised a storm of controversy.[26] A few decades later, hypnosis was used to retrieve "memories" of UFO abductions, suggesting the dubious reliability of the practice.

Hypnosis blurs a variety of psychological boundaries. It calls into question who is in control—hypnotist or subject?—thereby blurring the distinction between self and other. Hypnosis challenges the division between mind and body with its startling cures of warts and skin diseases. It is sometimes used as analgesia for surgery, eliminating the need for drugs. The line between the conscious and unconscious is blurred when subjects are hypnotized to regain repressed memories, but hypnotists can implant false ones, thereby blurring the distinction between fantasy and reality. The "memories" of abductions by extraterrestrial aliens is but one instance. These few examples are only a smattering, and there is a vast literature on all these matters. The concept of liminality can be fruitfully applied to them.

Hypnosis and illicit sex have long been associated. Men's magazines sometimes carry advertisements for books teaching how to hypnotize and seduce women. This unsavory association is nothing new. During Mesmer's heyday in Paris, the King of France appointed a commission to investigate the so-called animal magnetism. The committee included Benjamin Franklin, Antoine Lavoisier, Joseph Ignace Guillotin and others, and in 1784 they issued a report that was made public. They disparaged Mesmer's idea of a magnetic fluid, and they asserted that imitation and imagination could explain the phenomenon. The commission also produced a secret report, meant only for the eyes of the king. It warned that mesmerism could lead to sexual immorality.[27]

Another trickster quality of hypnosis is seen in stage demonstrations, which, like spirit mediumship, sometimes involved deception. Subjects occasionally performed amazing feats, but other times the effects were more mundane. The phenomenon is not reliable, and performers could not count on producing some of the more spectacular demonstrations, and they resorted to using confederates who faked being hypnotized.[28] The deceptions enhanced audience appeal, but they also helped marginalize hypnotism in the eyes of establishment psychologists. In fact Wesley Wells in an article in *The Journal of Abnormal and Social Psychology* (1946) opened with the statement: "Public exhibitions of hypnosis on the stage and over the radio are an affront to science." Hypnotism's affiliation with the paranormal in the popular press additionally contributed to its scientific marginality, and

Wells also decried "the association of hypnosis with magic, witchcraft, and telepathy."[29]

Magicians have plenty of connections with hypnosis, and I will mention a few for illustrative purposes. Will Goldston, a prolific magic writer, published a magazine titled *The Magician*. For its first five volumes (1904–1909), it was subtitled *A Monthly Journal Devoted To Magic, Spiritualism, Hypnotism & Human Progress*. Another striking example of the same nexus is seen in the person of Ormond McGill. He authored *The Encyclopedia of Stage Hypnotism* (1947) a manual used by numerous stage performers. He was also involved in debates on psychic phenomena. Beginning in January 1937, he wrote a monthly series entitled "The Psychic Circle" for *The Tops*, the magazine of Abbott's Magic Novelty Company. McGill not only held a positive view on the reality of psi, but he even gave advice on how to develop psychic abilities. He also wrote books on how to fake them. In the 1940s he toured as Doctor Zomb. His performances often commenced with a hypnosis demonstration; after that was over, lights were turned out, and a ghost show began. Glowing monsters appeared on stage and spirit forms flew over the audience.[30] In the 1970s he published several popular books describing his travels and encounters with supernatural phenomena.[31] McGill exemplifies the combination of the genuine and fake, in both hypnosis and the paranormal. He is but one of many similar individuals in the magic field. These people cross boundaries and deal in both the authentic and the spurious; they do not fit into the usual categories. Parapsychologists don't trust them; debunkers can't label them as gullible without looking foolish themselves. Consequently academics, parapsychologists, and debunkers largely ignore them.

In short, the trickster constellation is strikingly obvious in the phenomenon of hypnosis. It is associated with deception, lowered sexual inhibitions, psychological boundary blurring, paranormal manifestations, and marginality—all trickster attributes.

Exemplar Magician-Tricksters

Magicians heavily involved in paranormal controversies often manifest strong trickster qualities, and their biographies can be particularly illuminating. A number of such persons could be examined, but three exemplars are James Randi, Tony 'Doc' Shiels, and Eric J. Dingwall—the debunker, the hoaxer, and the investigator, respectively. All are extreme types, and all have had an intense, almost life-long involvement with the paranormal. The three are exceedingly bright, creative, and controversial, and each has published a number of books. Each displays a trickster constellation in almost archetypal form. The all-too-brief sketches that follow emphasize trickster qualities to the exclusion of others.

James Randi

James (The Amazing) Randi (born Randall James Hamilton Zwinge, 1928) is the individual most widely associated with the modern-day skeptical movement, and he has made countless public appearances, the world over, as a debunker. Randi has many fans among high status scientists. In 1986 the MacArthur Foundation bestowed upon him a "genius" award along with $286,000, and in 1989 he was given an award by the American Physical Society for "Promoting Public Understanding of the Relation of Physics to Society." Randi has been involved with the paranormal almost his entire life, and his entry in *Current Biography Yearbook 1987* tells how he publicly confronted phoney spiritualists when he was still a teenager. In his early days he produced a newspaper astrology column and pretended to be a psychic. He abandoned that and eventually achieved fame with his attacks on Uri Geller.[32] In 1976 the Committee for the Scientific Investigation of Claims of the Paranormal (CSICOP) was formed, and Randi quickly became one of its most visible members.

In the early 1980s Randi began his Project Alpha. He recruited two teenage magicians, Steve Shaw and Michael Edwards, who posed as psychics and visited a number of researchers, demonstrating their purported abilities of psychically bending spoons, producing psychic photographs, and moving small objects. They were able to convince a few nonprofessional investigators of their talents, but many professionals remained unconvinced by the boys, some vocally so. Nevertheless, in January 1983 Randi called a well-attended press conference and claimed that he had fooled the parapsychologists. This garnered wide coverage by television, newspapers, and magazines, and the Project helped to ridicule and marginalize parapsychology.[33]

Like many tricksters, some of Randi's antics have caused problems for himself. He was forced to resign from CSICOP because his accusations provoked lawsuits against the Committee.[34] One of the most publicized involved physicist Eldon Byrd, a friend of Uri Geller. On May 10, 1988 Randi made a presentation for the New York Area Skeptics in Manhattan. After his lecture, during the question and answer period, a member of the audience confronted him with a tape recording, which allegedly had Randi speaking in explicit sexual terms with young men (the recording was not played during the public meeting). I was present and watched as pandemonium almost broke out. Randi did not completely regain his composure. He accused Byrd of distributing the tape and went on to claim that Byrd was a child molester and that he was in prison. He made the same assertion in an interview with *Twilight Zone Magazine*.[35] This was untrue, and in a jury trial he was found guilty of defaming Byrd.[36]

Randi has never been married, but his sex life has received published comment regarding rumors of pederasty, including from a longtime friend James Moseley.[37] Randi threatened lawsuits over them, but he never carried through.

Randi has written a number of books on the paranormal, and they are not known for their accuracy. I documented some of his errors in my overview article on CSICOP.[38] He was infuriated by that and wrote me an unpleasant letter demanding a correction. I asked him to explain any mistakes I made, but he was unable to do so, and I didn't hear from him again.

He has allied himself with atheistic causes, and much of his life has been devoted to battles against supernatural ideas, at considerable personal sacrifice. The fights left their mark, and Carl Sagan's (sympathetic) introduction to Randi's book *The Faith Healers* (1987) described Randi as an angry man and labeled his book a "tirade." All in all, Randi is more a Promethean figure than a Hermetic one.

Tony "Doc" Shiels

Tony "Doc" Shiels (b. 1938), is an artist and musician and also a mentalist and magician who has authored a column for British magazine *Fortean Times*. He presents himself as "investigator" but is actually a marvelous hoaxer, and Issue No. 8 of *Strange Magazine* (Fall 1991) exposed some of his hoaxes of aquatic monsters. Because of his expertise at hoaxing, it is perhaps fortunate that he is less known than my other two exemplars.

Shiels was one of the originators of bizarre magic,[39] and his performances and writings are noted for the unusual. Shiels describes himself as a surrealist and has written: "Performing, writing, and thinking about trickery, illusion, legerdemain, hocus-pocus, and all such stuff, actually seems to make the genuine thing happen ... To perform a 'trick' is, in effect, to act out a piece of sympathetic magic."[40] While this may indeed be true, in view of his archetypal tricksterhood, it is difficult to know whether Shiels actually believes this or uses it only as a magician's patter line. I suspect that he believes it. I've had some correspondence with him, and he demonstrated an exceptional understanding of the trickster. He incorporated it into his surrealist worldview.

In the Introduction to Shiels' book *Monstrum!* (1990), Colin Wilson noted that some of Shiels' "writing seems suffused with a touch of alcoholic euphoria," and Shiels acknowledges that "A mixture of Scottish and Irish blood, plus regular lashings of Guinness and whiskey, pursues its eccentric course through my constantly hardening arteries."[41] We may assume that altered states of consciousness play a part in his life. Sexuality is also a prominent feature; Shiels' artwork contains erotic imagery, as do his books on magic, which carry pictures of voluptuous nude women. He has taken photographs of his nude daughters, and that sparked rumors with veiled hints of incest.[42]

Colin Wilson comments on Shiels' charm and accords him "an immense natural goodness and amiability."[43] Shiels' writings are indeed charming and friendly; they display none of the anger and bitterness found in those of Randi. Shiels shows more of a Hermes personality rather than the Promethean demeanor of Randi.

Eric J. Dingwall

Anthropologist Eric Dingwall (1890–1986) was one of the brightest and most knowledgeable characters in the history of psychical research, and also one having a decided taste for the bizarre. He wrote a book on chastity belts (1931), one titled *Male Infibulation* (1925), and edited another (illustrated) on female sexuality;[44] his book *The American Woman* (1956) primarily focused on the sexual life of middle and upper class American women. He cataloged erotica at the British Library, and he also investigated black magic, sexuality, and transvestism in Haiti.[45] His explicit interest in the relationship between psi and sexuality was so discomfiting to his colleagues that criminologist and Society for Psychical Research (SPR) president D. J. West felt compelled to comment on it in the obituary he wrote of Dingwall.[46]

Dingwall held both Ph.D. and D.Sc. degrees, but he considered himself to be an unsophisticated person. He described his ability to communicate with the primitive and the insane, a talent he found lacking in most highly educated people.[47] This is a subtle trickster attribute. The trickster has the ability to communicate effectively across markedly different cultures. Dingwall's comment indicates an awareness of the issue, though he did not relate it to the trickster.

Dingwall was a conjuror of long standing, and Milbourne Christopher, an eminent magic historian, dedicated his *Mediums, Mystics & the Occult* (1975) to Ding. At the time of his death Dingwall was the oldest member of the Magic Circle, the prestigious London magic society. He investigated and wrote extensively on psychical research and especially on physical mediumship, where trickery is an especially severe problem. Although he was often highly critical, he made positive statements regarding the existence of psi.

Dingwall had an uneasy relationship with organized psychical research. For a short time he was research officer of the SPR, but that did not last. In his reminiscences on Dingwall, SPR president Alan Gauld described his mischievous and disruptive nature,[48] and that is evidenced by the reports of the Annual General Meetings of the SPR, which frequently noted his complaints about how the society was run. In later years, D. J. West tried to convince others to elect Dingwall to the Council, but he was unsuccessful.

Dingwall was also a member of CSICOP and the Rationalist Press Association,[49] and his numerous trickster elements seem to have been balanced by his almost rabid rationalistic beliefs. For instance in one of his essays he blamed parapsychologists for the rise of interest in occultism, and he also commented that "Christianity, unbelievable as it may be to the rational mind, has been supported by the occult superstitions of darker ages."[50] His strong beliefs may have provided him some structure when grappling with the paranormal.

Dingwall was seen as an "individual" rather than as one who found identity by holding a position in some institution. Although he was employed by several organizations, his private means allowed him to independently pursue personal interests. His anti-structural qualities can be seen in a variety of contexts.

I have referred to a number of Dingwall's works in preparing this book, and in them I have found exceedingly rich detail, illuminating case studies, but lacking strong, explicit theoretical orientation. His emphasis was on the concrete rather than the abstract.[51]

Lessons of the Exemplars

None of these three personalities can be described as "normal"; they really are unusual characters. None have held long-term, prominent positions in structured institutions; they are known for individual achievements rather than for directing the work of organizations. All three could be described as disruptive and were known for rocking the boat. Unusual sexuality is prominent in their lives, and all have been intensely involved with magic and the paranormal. Shiels used trickery to fake paranormal events; both Randi and Dingwall spent much of their time exposing similar attempts. Randi and Dingwall display strong rationalistic beliefs which may afford some structure and protection; Shiels' surrealist worldview perhaps does not furnish the same benefits.

The writings of Randi and Dingwall give much specific detail and rather little on theory, and this perhaps signals another similarity between magicians and mystics. Both are characterized by relatively low levels of abstraction. Magic books and magazines are filled with specific methods for tricks, but very little space is devoted to theoretical ideas. The major magic histories—*The Illustrated History of Magic* (1973) by Milbourne Christopher, *The Great Illusionists* (1979) by Edwin Dawes, and *Magic: A Pictorial History of Conjurers in the Theater* (1985) by David Price—give exceptional, sometimes excruciating, detail, but they offer scant theoretical perspective. At least in the open literature, there is relatively little theoretical work on deception per se (though there is much on the psychology of it). This is puzzling given the vast literature on conjuring and the practical applications (such as defense intelligence). The subject of deception appears somewhat resistant to useful abstraction and theorizing.[52]

Summary

Conjurors fake paranormal phenomena; illusions of the supernatural are their stock-in-trade. Major stage productions incorporate themes of death, dismemberment, and rebirth. Mentalists counterfeit ESP. None of this is new. Shamans in earlier cultures did the same thing. The paranormal has been affiliated with trickery for thousands of years, and this is an important clue to its nature.

Debates still rage whether famous "psychics" were really only magicians, and conversely, conjurors are often suspected of having psychic powers. They intentionally blur the lines between genuine-spurious and fact-fiction. Some encourage the public to believe in psi, even when they don't themselves.

Many famous magicians in history believed in paranormal phenomena; others were among the most vociferous debunkers. For over a century conjurors have played major roles in the public debates on the paranormal. Their visibility often eclipsed the scientists. The controversy over the reality of psi rages even within the magic community, and that indicates an especially problematic condition.

Conjuring has trickster qualities in addition to deception and the paranormal. There are other liminal features. Magic is a marginal art. Unlike music or drama, there are no university departments devoted to it, and outside Las Vegas, there are almost no performance halls dedicated primarily to magic. Magicians often work solo; rarely do they use a large cast. Conjurors' employment is generally temporary, and most are forced to travel from engagement to engagement. Marginality, solitariness, and travel are all associated with the trickster. Further, magicians have been among the most effective promoters of hypnosis—a liminal phenomenon par excellence.

Conjuring and deception are pertinent to theoretical issues addressed in later chapters, and it may help the reader to give some idea of the topics to come. Briefly, deception takes advantage of people's assumptions. Assumptions are simply abstractions and representations of the world, and they are necessarily incomplete. The issues of abstraction and representation will be discussed later, in conjunction with literary theory and related topics. Deception is somewhat resistant to abstraction; so is mystical experience.

CHAPTER 12

CSICOP and the Debunkers

> I am an enemy to all the gods.
> Prometheus[1]

The Committee for the Scientific Investigation of Claims of the Paranormal (CSICOP, pronounced "sigh cop") is the most aggressive antagonist of the paranormal today. As such, analysis of the group provides a wealth of insight. CSICOP's personnel, its organizational structure, its operations, and its demographics tell us much about the paranormal and its status in our culture.

The Committee was founded at the 1976 convention of the American Humanist Association. It quickly grew, and its magazine *The Skeptical Inquirer* has a circulation of over 50,000.[2] A survey of its readership found that 54% have an advanced degree and 27% hold a doctorate.[3] CSICOP's Fellows have included Francis Crick, Murray Gell-Mann, Leon Lederman, Glenn Seaborg, and Steven Weinberg, all Nobel laureates, as well as paleontologist Stephen Jay Gould, psychologist B. F. Skinner, astronomer Carl Sagan, writer Isaac Asimov, zoologist Richard Dawkins, and philosopher Sidney Hook, among others. CSICOP is headquartered just off the Amherst Campus of the State University of New York at Buffalo in a new 25,000 square foot office building costing $4,000,000, a figure they surpassed in their fundraising for the project.[4] The Committee has spawned more than 65 local and international groups with similar aims. All this is an impressive accomplishment, and CSICOP is highly visible within academe and elite culture. Its success is in marked contrast to scientific parapsychology. The circulation of the *Journal of Parapsychology* is 757.[5] Understandably, many see the Committee as a legitimate scientific authority on the paranormal.

While it purports to be impartial, CSICOP's early rhetoric revealed its actual agenda. In an interview for *Science* magazine, Lee Nisbet, Executive Director of the Committee, articulated its position: "It's [belief in the paranormal] a very dangerous phenomenon, dangerous to science, dangerous to the basic fabric of our society . . . We feel it is the duty of the scientific community to show that these beliefs are utterly screwball."[6] Since the early days, CSICOP has slightly tempered its rhetoric but not its stance. It still aggressively denounces the paranormal and labels it as irrational. CSICOP serves as a force for marginalizing the supernatural, and that is its primary function.

Parapsychologists, not surprisingly, sometimes see CSICOP as the enemy. However, such an attitude keeps them from recognizing the larger picture. The Committee only exemplifies pervasive patterns and personifies social forces at work today. CSICOP benefits parapsychology because its antagonism is explicit rather than hidden, and detached examination can clarify issues. The Committee should become an object of study and contemplation.

CSICOP can be profitably compared and contrasted with those who intentionally attempt to elicit paranormal phenomena. A number of such groups will be covered in later chapters, including parapsychologists, spiritualists, the New Age movement, and modern-day witchcraft. Please remember CSICOP when reading about them, because they provide stark contrasts with the Committee and its constituency. CSICOP upholds the status quo. It is structural rather than anti-structural; it values hierarchy over communitas; it desires stability rather than liminality. Nevertheless, because it directly confronts the paranormal, it cannot escape a certain influence from it, and as I will show, the trickster manifests with both the supernatural and its opponents.

In 1992 I published a 45-page overview of CSICOP. I identified four distinguishing features of the Committee: association with high status scientists, heavy dominance by males, pervasive anti-religious sentiment, and an active role by magicians. That paper was largely descriptive; it had extensive documentation but little interpretation. The presentation here is more interpretive. Those wishing greater detail about specifics of CSICOP might seek out my earlier paper.

CSICOP and Science

CSICOP purports to be scientific, but for many years it had an official policy against conducting research itself. The genesis of that policy is amusing. In 1975, before CSICOP was founded, philosopher Paul Kurtz produced a manifesto denouncing astrology, and 186 scientists signed it. That generated intense media coverage and served as a springboard to establish the Committee. Kurtz went on to urge newspapers to label their astrology columns as follows: "*Warning: If taken seriously, this column may be dangerous to your health!*" (Kurtz's emphasis).[7] At that time, Kurtz was editor of *The Humanist*, and he had allowed some scientifically erroneous attacks on astrology to be published in the magazine.

Under pressure to defend his position, Kurtz was challenged to undertake a scientific study to confirm or dispute some astrological findings of Michel Gauquelin. He and a few colleagues accepted the challenge. Very early on, Dennis Rawlins, an astronomer and member of CSICOP's Executive Council, warned them of serious problems with their approach, and he later volunteered to assist with the calculations for the project. Data were collected and analyzed, and the results supported Gauquelin's findings that the position of Mars at a person's birth was related to sports ability. Rawlins understood that Kurtz's method was flawed and was unconvinced by the data, but he also said that the outcome, favorable to Gauquelin, should be frankly acknowledged. Kurtz was enraged by that advice, and he refused to heed it. Rawlins charged Kurtz with covering up the mistakes, and he repeatedly tried to bring the problems to the attention of other CSICOP members. Rawlins was rebuffed and eventually forced out of the Committee, and a number of other CSICOP members resigned because of the cover-up. Rawlins published a 32-page exposé in the October 1981 issue of *Fate* magazine, and that same month CSICOP adopted a formal policy of not conducting research.[8]

After the scandal became public, sociologists Trevor Pinch and Harry Collins published a study of CSICOP. They explicitly warned the Committee that if they actually conducted research, they would no longer be able to hold the views of science that they did. Scientific processes are not nearly as objective as commonly thought, and social factors play a significant role in interpreting results. This is entirely counter to CSICOP's ideology. If one does research, one runs the risk of obtaining uncongenial results, a danger Kurtz by then undoubtedly understood. In any event, the Committee's policy accorded with the advice of Pinch and Collins to not undertake research.[9]

Instead of scientific investigation, CSICOP's primary efforts are directed to influencing public opinion. Its magazine carries innumerable articles decrying the media's treatment of the paranormal and describing CSICOP's attempts to combat the favorable coverage. The priorities are particularly striking in its *Manual for Local, Regional and*

National Groups (1987). Seventeen pages are devoted to "Handling the Media" and "Public Relations"; in contrast only three pages are given to "Scientific Investigation." No scientific references are cited in that section, and the reader is referred to Paul Kurtz's book *The Transcendental Temptation* for an explanation of the scientific method. That volume is by no means a scientific handbook, and among other things, it suggests that Jesus and Lazarus had a homosexual relationship.[10] This is an example of promoting an essentially religious work as a scientific text, a tactic CSICOP frequently accuses their opposition of using.

CSICOP's actual function can be seen by contrasting it with scientific organizations such as the American Physical Society, the American Anthropological Association, and the American Chemical Society. These and hundreds of others share some common characteristics. Their goals, organizational structure, operations, and demographics indicate how scientific societies advance their fields. Table 6 lists some contrasts between them and CSICOP.

Table 6, by itself, should alert any reader that scientific research is not a high priority of the Committee. This is not surprising, given that of the four members of its board of directors, only one, James Alcock, is a scientist.

Though it has a building worth several million dollars, a paid staff, and a good size library, CSICOP has no research program. In fact for the first 15 years of its existence, none of the scientist-members of its Executive Council ever published a report of a parapsychology experiment in a refereed journal. CSICOP has not established a laboratory in which researchers might attempt to elicit paranormal phenomena; it makes no effort at research similar to that of a scientific organization. However, occasionally a member conducts an ad hoc test of a psychic during an afternoon and writes up a brief report for a popular periodical.

The Committee should not be criticized too harshly for all this, because scientists firmly ensconced in the academic establishment rarely if ever explicitly address paranormal claims, but CSICOP does. Their willingness to confront the paranormal acknowledges its importance, at least indirectly, and this has consequences. To some extent, CSICOP holds a betwixt and between status. It is headquartered just off a university campus, and that is symbolic of a larger pattern. CSICOP serves as a buffer between the academic establishment and claims of the paranormal. The claims are not brought inside academe but handled at its border. The most eminent scientist-members have

Scientific Societies	CSICOP
Scientific societies publish technical, peer-reviewed journals that are primarily geared for specialists in the discipline.	CSICOP publishes no journal. It produces a popular magazine carrying cartoons and caricatures and recommends that technical papers be submitted to scientific periodicals.
Scientific journals are edited by specialists who have training in the discipline and who have made technical contributions to that field.	The *Skeptical Inquirer* is edited by a journalist.
Scientific societies are headed by eminent scientists who have made major contributions to their fields.	CSICOP is headed by a philosopher-businessman who has never published any empirical research on the paranormal in a refereed scientific journal.
Heads of scientific societies typically serve for a year or two.	The chairman of CSICOP has held his position for over two decades.
Scientific societies' governing boards are typically elected, and their members serve for a few years.	Many members of CSICOP's board of directors and executive council have maintained their positions for decades.
Scientific societies' governing boards are typically elected, and their members serve for a few years.	Many members of CSICOP's board of directors and executive council have maintained their positions for decades.
Scientific organizations arrange conferences for specialists. Calls for papers are printed in journals, and submitted papers are refereed.	CSICOP puts on conferences for the general public with particular emphasis on the media. Calls for papers are not issued. Presentations are geared for the general public rather than technical specialists.
Scientific organizations promote professional development among students in academic departments.	CSICOP promotes lay organizations.
Status in scientific organizations depends upon publication of papers in professional journals of an appropriate specialty.	Status in CSICOP is dependent upon status in science or the media, but it is unrelated to investigation of the paranormal.

Table 6 Characteristics of Scientific Societies Contrasted With Those of CSICOP.[11]

virtually nothing to do with the running of CSICOP; they serve as mere figureheads. They lend their names to campaigns but rarely comment publicly on the paranormal. When they occasionally do, they reveal a vast ignorance. Consequently, the scientists are not the main debunkers; that task is relegated primarily to journalists, magicians, and philosophers. The most active are Kendrick Frazier, journalist and editor of *The Skeptical Inquirer*; Joe Nickell, writer; Martin Gardner, writer-magician; James Randi, magician; Philip J. Klass, journalist; Paul Kurtz, philosopher and chairman of CSICOP. The four psychologists who are active debunkers, namely Ray Hyman, James Alcock, Susan Blackmore, and Richard Wiseman, certainly do not rank among the more eminent of the scientists.

Although markedly different from scientific societies, the Committee still has some parallels with science. For instance, CSICOP is particularly attuned to status issues. The Committee honors high-status scientists, invites them to conventions, gives them awards, and writes favorable articles about them. CSICOP's members[12] are typically recruited because of their prestige rather than for their research on the paranormal. Their status allows the Committee to speak with a voice of authority, and those who disagree are portrayed as marginal or without scientific standing, and thus can be disregarded.

Structure, status, and hierarchy are now central to science, and to bureaucracies generally. In the classic, *The Sociological Imagination* (1959), C. Wright Mills devoted an entire chapter to science's "bureaucratic ethos." Many years of training are required before one becomes a practicing scientist, and there are many levels of status after becoming a practitioner (ranks of professorships, grades of schools, and varying levels of professional honors). The hierarchy is international in scope. Those who have been most amply rewarded by this system give it their allegiance. They have spent their lives building and climbing the edifice that will perpetuate their legacy. The personalities most suited to operating in the hierarchical institutional structures have great vested interests. They obtain positions of influence, award grants and honors, and permit publication of papers. Max Weber pointed out that bureaucracies are part of the rationalization process. They help disenchant the world and are inimical to pure charisma, which involves manifestations of supernatural power. Considering all this, it should be no surprise that sociologist James McClenon found that the so-called elite (i.e., high status) scientists were some of the most hostile to parapsychology.[13]

Anti-religion and Rationalism

In my 1992 overview of CSICOP I provided an extended discussion of religious factors affecting the Committee. Later, some of its members and supporters complained to me privately that I devoted too much space to that. It was obviously a sensitive issue for them, and they were clearly uncomfortable with the implications.

CSICOP is pervaded with anti-religious sentiment, and I easily compiled a list of 29 members who had publicly identified themselves as holding nontheistic or atheistic views. This constituted more than 25% of the official membership of the organization. That percentage was not unexpected given the group is composed primarily of academics, but it was the aggressive *public* profession of religious unbelief that was so striking. Those people vigorously promote their religious opinions, and a number of them contributed to periodicals such as Madalyn Murray O'Hair's *American Atheist*.

As an organization, CSICOP is formally allied with atheistic groups. It shares a building, personnel, office equipment, and fund raising with the Council for Democratic and Secular Humanism (CODESH). The two organizations overlap extensively, and both are headed by Paul Kurtz. When I visited their offices in 1991, I sat in the reading area that happened to be next to a copy machine. Several times I overheard employees inquiring whether copies should be charged to CSICOP or CODESH, further illustrating the lack of demarcation between the organizations. Some might be puzzled why such a long cumbersome name was selected for the Council and also why the acronym CODESH was used, rather than CODASH, with "A" for "and." When one knows that "kodesh" is Hebrew for holy, it makes sense. The acronym was obviously chosen as a slap at the Jewish religion.[14] Someone probably complained because the name was changed to the Council for Secular Humanism as of June 1996.

The Council publishes *Free Inquiry*, a magazine that belittles religion; it also published the *Secular Humanist Bulletin*, which was edited by Tim Madigan, a cofounder of Catholics Anonymous. Kurtz founded the Academy of Humanism to honor eminent people who have held secular humanist beliefs; roughly a third of the Academy members were affiliated with CSICOP. Another organizational connection is the Rationalist Press Association (RPA) in Great Britain, with several of its Honorary Associates being CSICOP Fellows. In addition, the *American Rationalist* was edited by CSICOP member and employee Gordon Stein.

The explicit affiliation of rationalists with debunker organizations is in keeping with historical precedent. Rationalism is inherently antagonistic to the paranormal and supernatural, and this was seen in the early days of the societies for psychical research. A century ago, the RPA served in a capacity similar to Prometheus Books today. Under their imprint, Watts & Co., the RPA published a number of volumes attacking spiritualism and psychical research. This long antagonism is inherent, because fundamentally, the debunkers are a force for the rationalization and disenchantment of the world (in Max Weber's terms).

CSICOP is an exceedingly rich example of rationalization and its consequences. As discussed in the chapter on Weber, rationalization is a long-term, ongoing process. It is particularly marked in academe, but it is also found in religion. The marginalization of mysticism and miracles in mainline Protestant denominations is an example. In fact virtually all religions acknowledge supernatural power but put strictures around it. They keep it somewhat distant. Early peoples understood that the supernatural was dangerous. It needed to be hedged off from the mundane world. There were rules, prohibitions, and taboos surrounding it. The process continues today, but at an unconscious level. Establishment religion and CSICOP, each with their own means, discourage engagement of the phenomena. Both impose taboos. Religions decree occult dabbling a sin; CSICOP marginalizes it by ridicule. Both enforce the taboo, but in slightly different ways.

The skeptical movement exemplifies trends in scientific and academic thinking. It makes them explicit. Many social scientists and psychologists have been predicting the demise of religion for decades and have largely avoided studying it. The eminent sociologist Peter Berger stated "in recent years sociologists, with very few exceptions, have shown very little interest [in religion], probably because they have sworn allegiance to a scientific 'progressivism' that regards religion as a vanishing leftover from the dark ages of superstition and do not care to invest their energies in the study of a moribund phenomenon."[15] Many psychologists are even puzzled by people who believe, yet a 1994 survey by *U.S. News & World Report* found that 93% of adult Americans believed in God or a universal spirit.[16] Obviously many social scientists cannot comprehend a vast realm of human experience. They are isolated from ordinary people, and their alienated, ivory-tower existence destroys their understanding.

Even scholars sympathetic to religion are heavily influenced by the trends. For instance, Peter Berger, who is actively religious himself, in his book *A Rumor of Angels* (1990) refers to the supernatural saying: "It is impossible to know for sure whether any such rediscovery [of the supernatural] will remain the property of more or less *isolated cognitive minorities*" (emphasis added).[17] Yet a 1993 survey by *Time* magazine showed that 69% of adult Americans believed in angels.[18] Clearly, it is the academicians who are the "isolated cognitive minorities." Berger specializes in the sociology of religion. His ignorance of basic data of human experience is comparable to a physicist who doesn't know the density of water, and publicly flaunts it. Yet Berger is typical! This is difficult for ordinary people to understand, but much academic work is marked by extreme abstraction, and that is inimical to comprehension of the supernatural.

In some ways, the skeptics are more astute than the average academic, and philosopher-businessman-debunker Paul Kurtz probably has a greater intuitive feeling for the problems posed by the supernatural than do the vast majority of religious scholars. Most of them no longer comprehend the numinous and the supernatural and the deep problems they present. Many consider the supernatural to be only a crude superstition, and the issues have been banished from the awareness of academe, even though they were extensively discussed at the beginning of the twentieth century. In *The Idea of the Holy* (1917), the eminent German religious scholar Rudolf Otto recognized that "In truth the enemy has often a keener vision in this matter than either the champion of religion or the neutral and professedly impartial theorist. For the adversaries on their side know very well that the entire 'pother about mysticism' has nothing to do with 'reason' and 'rationality'."[19]

The personality dynamics of some skeptics may make them unconsciously sensitive to crucial issues. Perhaps they feel the subversive, destructive, chaotic potential of the trickster, anti-structure, and the paranormal.[20] Sociologist Nachman Ben-Yehuda in his book *Deviance and Moral Boundaries* (1985) noted: "The sense of awe and bewilderment experienced repeatedly in science fiction and occultism necessarily brings one very close to what O'Dea (1966) called existential 'breaking points,' or to a liminal situation, that is, a state of existential transit . . . It becomes impossible to encounter either science fiction or occultism and remain indifferent to them, *unless one is well shielded by some other strong belief*" (emphasis added).[21] He went on to state that "occult-related phenomena [ghosts, possession, reincarnation, trances, séances, automatic writing] can have a deeper, more pervasive experiential impact on an observer than science fiction."[22] As will be discussed in the chapter on totemism and the primitive mind, these passages hint at the power of the numinous.

Whereas religions place strictures against dabbling in the supernatural, atheists and rationalists prefer to banish (i.e., repress) the ideas entirely. Yet the supernatural is found in all cultures, and it cannot be effectively eliminated with rationalistic incantations such as: "extraordinary claims require extraordinary evidence." The paranormal is part of the human condition, and its repression has consequences. John Wren-Lewis, a mathematical physicist and religion professor, writing in the *Journal of Humanistic Psychology* discussed the antagonism to parapsychology and noted that "*the plain fact is that the clearest evidence of strong emotion nowadays comes from those who have antireligious feelings*" (Wren-Lewis' emphasis).[23] He wrote this in 1974, even before CSICOP was formed. Others have recognized these strong feelings. John F. Schumaker, a clinical psychologist as well as a debunker, reported that based on data from his own studies "people with traditional religious beliefs had significantly fewer symptoms of mental illness than the atheists."[24] He concluded that there was a need for paranormal belief, and that those lacking it had higher levels of stress and anxiety.

Some authors have noted the irrational behavior of skeptics when they confront paranormal claims. Walter Franklin Prince's book *The Enchanted Boundary* (1930) was devoted entirely to the matter. Prince was an Episcopal clergyman and one of the most careful and respected psychical researchers in the first decades of the twentieth century. His extensive and detailed analyses demonstrated over and over that when many critics cross into the realm of psychical research and attempt to examine the evidence, they lose the common sense and good judgement that they display in other activities. CSICOP's inability to mount a systematic scientific research program and their choice to denounce, rather than investigate, the paranormal indicate the power of the enchanted boundary. In essence, Prince's enchanted boundary is the limen of van Gennep and Turner.

The Trickster Figure

The sheer volume and intensity of the debunkers' activities suggests something other than dispassionate inquiry; rather, one suspects the operation of some energetic, unconscious, archetypal process. The trickster figure Prometheus illuminates this, and he has much in common with the skeptics. Prometheus was not a god, but a titan, who stole fire from the gods for the benefit of humanity. He shares some, though not all, of the qualities of Hermes. In his book *Hermes and His Children*, Rafael Lopez-Pedraza explains: "Prometheus in no way shows the undignified, weakened side of Hermes; on the contrary, he wants to rule the world, but because of the undifferentiated energy of his Titanic nature, it becomes only a power-ridden ambition. He shows only a suspicious and boastful rebellion against the archetypal forms of life, forms he is keen in finding ways to blackmail or destroy. He shows a lack of tolerance, which we feel in the many ways of missionarizing so predominant in today's life, so different from the variety in a Hermes attitude.

"Hermes thieves and then sacrifices to the gods all that he has thieved, whereas Prometheus sacrifices to the gods and within that sacrifice he cheats and thieves. If the Hermes sacrifice seems to be the religious sacrifice *par excellence*, then the Prometheus sacrifice is just the opposite—it is openly anti-religious. From this we can assume that the anti-religious function in man is Promethean."[25]

Lopez-Pedraza's comments were made in regard to a psychological understanding of Prometheus and were totally unrelated to the psi controversy. In light of that, they are all the more striking when one knows that Prometheus Books is the most active publisher of debunking works and a major purveyor of atheistic and anti-religious tracts; it was founded by Paul Kurtz, chairman of CSICOP.[26] (In keeping with the trickster constellation, Prometheus Books also publishes a number of titles that challenge conventional sexual morality.)

Although the above aspects of Prometheus are not flattering to the skeptics, he does have many positive attributes. For his theft of fire, Prometheus was chained to a rock by order of Zeus, and an eagle ate his liver. It grew back daily, but to Prometheus' agony, it was eaten again and again. Prometheus suffered for helping humans and upholding their dignity; he defied the gods who could be vain, unreliable, vengeful, and even malicious. Their powers needed to be curtailed.

The trickster's influence on CSICOP is also seen in the disproportionate number of magicians in the organization. In my 1992 study, I found that at least 13 magicians had been official members of CSICOP (approximately 10% of the official membership). This goes back to the beginning, and in fact, the immediate predecessor to CSICOP was RSEP (Resources for the Scientific Evaluation of the Paranormal), a group of magicians including Martin Gardner, Ray Hyman, James Randi, and Marcello Truzzi. Truzzi and Hyman are also professors, and Gardner is a writer, but all three have made substantial contributions to conjuring and are well recognized therein. Randi and Gardner have been some of the most effective promoters of CSICOP, and they have been leading figures in the popular-level debates on parapsychology.

CSICOP's Contributions to Scientific Parapsychology

I have focused on CSICOP's social role and given little attention to its contribution on technical matters in parapsychology. That is a minor aspect of its activities. Nevertheless, two of its members deserve special mention. Psychologist Ray Hyman has provided detailed comment on various parapsychological experiments, and he must be considered the preeminent outside critic on technical matters. Though I must add that some of his critiques are seriously marred by flaws, a number of which have been documented.[27] Martin Gardner has incisively criticized shortcomings in controls against deception in parapsychological studies. He is an exceedingly important figure in the skeptical movement, and his work will be addressed later in this book.

The Committee has made a valuable contribution in emphasizing the paranormal's frequent association with deception. They were a strong influence for my interest in that topic. I have published a number of critical papers myself, and CSICOP members Philip J. Klass and Martin Gardner provided valuable help on some of them. Many of my colleagues in parapsychology ignore the problem of deception, and most have been unwilling to seek training in conjuring to help exclude trickery in their studies. Indeed, in my 1990 survey of 23 former presidents of the Parapsychological Association, only 4 had ever taken a course in magic and only one owned more than eight books on the topic.[28] Their training of students perpetuated what I have labeled the "legacy of magical ignorance."[29] The 988-page *Handbook of Parapsychology* edited by Benjamin Wolman (1977) is revealing. Its 30-page index contains no entries under "conjuring," "deceit," "deception," "fraud," "legerdemain," "sleight of hand," or "trickery." All entries under "magic" and "magicians" refer to the anthropological or occult types. It is perhaps not too strong to say that such neglect has been pathologically naive.

Summary

CSCIOP was founded during a period of surging popular interest in the paranormal, and its expressed purpose was to combat that tide. The Committee has since become the most visible institutional body addressing the issues; it speaks with the voice of establishment science. The Committee is a fascinating organization and deserves far more analysis than it has heretofore received.

CSICOP is a valuable specimen for anyone studying the role of the paranormal in our culture because its hostility to the paranormal is overt, not hidden. CSICOP's social position, its demographics, its operations, and its constituency tell us much about the supernatural in the world today. The Committee's primary function is to marginalize the paranormal. Yet almost paradoxically, its activities serve to emphasize the paranormal's importance because it has expended such great energy in its endeavor.

Analysis of CSICOP illuminates many issues, but here I'll select only three for brief summary comment: the trickster figure, the Committee's concern with status, and rationalization (in Max Weber's sense). These are central to this book.

Trickster characteristics manifest overtly with CSICOP. Magicians have been involved in paranormal controversies for hundreds of years, and many conjurors are now associated with the Committee. In fact James Randi and Martin Gardner have been the most effective publicists for the skeptical movement. The mythical Prometheus is a trickster associated with humanism and with anti-religious feeling. Thus it is entirely appropriate that CSICOP's Chairman, Paul Kurtz, used his name for his publishing company, Prometheus Books.

Status consciousness is one of the Committee's salient characteristics. CSICOP goes to considerable lengths to assure its status and respectability in the eyes of scientific, academic, and media elites. It has gathered an impressive roster of members, including five Nobel laureates (though none of them have ever published research on the paranormal). The readership of its magazine, *The Skeptical Inquirer*, is very highly educated, with 54% holding an advanced degree. The Committee is an influential voice, and it reflects and reinforces beliefs of scientific elites.

Because CSICOP is so status conscious, scientific investigation is inappropriate for it. If a serious, sustained effort were undertaken to investigate the paranormal, that by itself would confer status upon the topic. It would signal the paranormal to be worthy of study. Instead, the Committee belittles such efforts, and its magazine carries cartoons and caricatures that ridicule researchers.

Perhaps the Committee's most striking feature is its intimate affiliation with rationalist and anti-religious organizations. Such groups have long opposed paranormal claims and psychical research. The explicit connection with rationalist belief manifests a fundamental pattern, for CSICOP is an aggressive agent for the rationalization and disenchantment of the world. As Max Weber explained, those require the attenuation of charisma, and the elimination (or marginalization) of the magical and miraculous. The Committee furthers those ends, and it provides a living example of Weber's theories.

Rationality and rationalization have limits, but those are rarely recognized. In its (unconscious) avoidance of scientific research, CSICOP subtly signals the limits of science and rationality. Science is part of the foundational myth of much of academe. But rational methods cannot fully establish their own foundations, and probing them provokes anxiety. As will be explained in later chapters, wariness toward the supernatural is nothing new for humankind; it goes back millennia. There have always been taboos, prohibitions, and restrictions surrounding the supernatural. There are undoubtedly good reasons for this. Religious orthodoxy decrees dabbling in the paranormal to be a sin; CSICOP ridicules such dabbling. The effect is the same. Both religious orthodoxy and atheists enforce a taboo; both shun paranormal phenomena, and this commonality is key to understanding them.

CHAPTER 13

Small Groups and the Paranormal

James McClenon is a sociologist who has extensively studied the paranormal and is one of very few who have published scholarly books and articles on the subject. His book *Wondrous Events: Foundations of Religious Belief* (1994) noted that many dramatic paranormal manifestations involve small groups of people. Some of these phenomena are spontaneous, often occurring to the dismay of those present, but other groups seek to induce paranormal occurrences. In either situation, typically small numbers of people are involved; rarely are large organizations engaged. The implications of this simple observation have not been fully appreciated.

Groups that intentionally try to elicit paranormal phenomena have some common characteristics, and they deserve closer inspection than they have heretofore received. Examples include sitter groups conducting séances, psychotronics hobbyists trying to use electronic devices to amplify psychic abilities, UFO aficionados that attempt telepathic contact with flying saucers in order to induce them to appear, and treasure hunters who use channeling and map dowsing. There are numerous others, but rarely are many people involved in any given undertaking.

A number of groups are quite open, and studying them presents few problems (although some are secretive). Some publish newsletters, and in others insiders have written books about their experiences, and participants are publicly identified with the paranormal. There is considerable information readily available for analysis. Even if most material is from an insider's "biased" perspective, it can still be valuable.

Parapsychologists have neglected these groups in the past and even actively avoided them for fear of being tainted in the eyes of establishment science. However, much useful information is lost by such policies. Nevertheless the avoidance is understandable; trickster and anti-structural features are abundant in these groups. All of the above mentioned endeavors have con artists, tricksters, and hoaxers, and they play particularly visible roles. Irrational beliefs abound; psychic battles sometimes develop; paranoid ideas, rumors of death hexes and magical attack are common. Further, groups that strive to elicit strong psi frequently become unstable. Often interpersonal tensions develop, and the groups dissolve.

At this point I am not concerned whether these groups actually induce real paranormal events. Attempts to engage the phenomena have consequences.[1] The dynamics of the process need to be understood because similar problems will frequently arise when others elicit, or believe that they have elicited, strong, real phenomena, some of which can be quite disconcerting. Anyone who tries to produce large psi effects faces the same difficulties.

Groups tend to reinforce their members' beliefs and expectations, and when this involves the paranormal, the effects can be insidious. If paranormal manifestations persist and grow, the usual rules of what is possible, reliable, etc. no longer apply. The trickster constellation strengthens. One consequence is the blurring of distinctions between subjective and objective, between imagination and reality. The problems are not limited to groups of "marginals." I have watched as medical doctors, high ranking military officers, university professors, and other normal, respectable people were overtaken by preposterous occult beliefs. The full force of this perhaps cannot be appreciated unless one experiences it firsthand. Trickster-induced irrationality is not trivial, and the skeptics' charges, if anything, are often understated. A full analysis of the patterns of such irrationality could be very fruitful.

There are numerous historical examples of occult groups available for detailed study. Here I will discuss a few recent cases in order to emphasize that direct encounters with the supernatural are not limited to distant times and places.

Legend-trips

"Legend-trip" is a term folklorists use to designate a short journey taken by a small group of teenagers to visit a spooky place. It typically begins when someone recounts a story about an allegedly haunted site; the group decides to visit it, usually traveling some distance by car. Hundreds of these accounts have been collected from college students, and the reports have been archived. Pennsylvania State University folklorist Bill Ellis has had a special interest in them, and he reviewed a number of cases in his paper "Legend-Tripping in Ohio."[2] The trips are typically made by those between the ages of 16 and 18, a period of often turbulent transition as teenagers take their first jobs or prepare to leave home for college. Legend-trips are very short, typically less than one-night duration, and they are explicitly taken for the purpose of exploring the supernatural.

Though Ellis did not mention it, legend-trips display parallels with rites of passage described by Turner and van Gennep. In addition to geographic boundary crossing (highlighted by the name legend-*trip*), the adventures sometimes involve vandalism, such as toppling of gravestones. Drinking, drug use (altered states of consciousness), and sexual experimentation are reported, as well as attempted contact with supernatural forces. The parallels with the liminal periods of initiations in primitive cultures are striking. Though legend-trips are much attenuated compared with initiations of the primitives, they share the key properties of liminality and anti-structure. Disruption (vandalism), lowered sexual inhibitions, and contact with the supernatural are all part of the trickster constellation; additionally, personal transition, travel, and altered states of consciousness appear.

Elisabeth Kübler-Ross And Shanti Nilaya

Psychiatrist Elisabeth Kübler-Ross is internationally acclaimed for her pioneering work on death and dying, and she is probably the most well-known person associated with the topic. Born in 1926 as one of triplets, as a young woman she studied medicine and eventually specialized in psychiatry. She emigrated to the U.S. and worked with the terminally ill. In 1969 her book *On Death and Dying* appeared and became a best-seller. This led to innumerable invitations to speak, and she spent much time traveling in order to lecture. By her own account, she had many interpersonal conflicts and many battles with establishment medicine (and established institutions generally). Her personal life was tumultuous, and her husband divorced her. Her memoir *The Wheel of Life* (1997) seems generally candid and quite illuminating.

The paranormal was central in her life's mission. After she began working with the dying, spirits spontaneously appeared to her and gave her advice and encouragement. She continued to seek their counsel, both during séances and when she was alone. In 1976 she met spiritualist medium, Jay Barham, and shortly thereafter they founded Shanti Nilaya, a healing and growth center near San Diego, California. The center drew a clientele that included many psychotherapists. Séances were a common attraction, and in some of them "spirit entities" engaged in sexual "therapy." During one séance, a light was turned on abruptly, and Barham was discovered to be naked. Kübler-Ross dismissed the incident saying that a spirit had cloned his body. Despite the exposure, a number of followers continued to participate, and the therapies started to become violent. Some participants were held down, beaten, and even partly suffocated.[3] Eventually Kübler-Ross recognized Barham's deceptions, and before she confronted him, she discussed the situation with her most trusted co-workers. Three of them then admitted that they had been party to the fraud, claiming to have fallen under the medium's control after he had entranced them.

The case shares anti-structural and trickster features found in many others. Sex in the séance room is encountered in countless cases.[4] In my own experience with occult groups, I've noted that a disproportionate share of the people involved had experienced a recent major transition (e.g., divorce, completion of an education program, a geographical move). They were looking for change and reintegration and hence were especially open and vulnerable to promises of hope. The prevalence of psychotherapists visiting Kübler-Ross's center suggests that many of the participants were concerned with human change, not only in themselves, but also as a primary career interest.

Shanti Nilaya lasted only a few years. During that time her house burned down, and arson was suspected. She later moved to rural Virginia and tried to set up a center for babies infected with AIDS, but local opponents vandalized her property. She was not able to establish a long-term existence for that center either. Though she helped inspire the hospice movement and bereavement groups, she did not establish and direct any long-lasting institution, despite her sizeable following around the world. This is in keeping with the anti-structural nature of her work.

Kübler-Ross's life was devoted to exploring, and even denying, the life-death binary opposition. She often proclaimed that there is no death. Kübler-Ross was suffused with liminality, but she did not understand that nor its implications. From the earliest times, there have been specialists who facilitated the transition between life and death. Today we have morticians, funeral directors, priests, ministers, and rabbis. Kübler-Ross was different from those professionals. She had no ritualized religious approach and did not use rational, detached, scientific methods in studying the matter. She immersed herself in the realm and tried to chart the life-death transition anew, essentially outside of conventional religious, medical, and scientific frameworks. She entered this liminal area "unprotected," didn't grasp the consequences, and frequently fell victim to the trickster.

SORRAT

The Society for Research on Rapport and Telekinesis (SORRAT) was founded by John Neihardt, a professor of English at the University of Missouri and author of *Black Elk Speaks*, a widely known work on the Sioux Indian medicine man.[5] In the early 1960s, Neihardt gathered a group of friends, family members, and students and began holding Victorian-style séances. This was in the Bible Belt, and not surprisingly, some of the members encountered severe opposition from their families and university authorities. Despite the persecution the group persisted, and many large-scale PK phenomena were reported over a period of years, some quite dramatic. There were levitations of tables and people, psychic photography, and apports; items mysteriously entered sealed containers, and innumerable rappings from floors and tables communicated and intelligently responded to questions.[6]

SORRAT members wrote to J. B. Rhine telling him about their activities, and in the late 1970s W. E. Cox, one of Rhine's long-time associates, moved from North Carolina to Rolla, Missouri in order to study the group. At that time, many phenomena centered around Dr. John Thomas Richards, a former student of Neihardt and a medium, and now a writer and English teacher. Cox's research focused on Richards and his wife Elaine, and through his efforts many phenomena were caught on film. Pens wrote by themselves; small objects materialized and dematerialized; balloons inflated without any apparent source of air pressure, and numerous other events were filmed. These occurred in or near a "mini-lab," an inverted fish tank kept in the basement of the Richards' home. Sensors in the mini-lab detected when events occurred and triggered a spring-wound camera to record them. However, the phenomena happened when no one was around, or so it was claimed. This gave rise to suspicions that some human was actually responsible, and the quality of the films didn't add to their credibility. Some of them looked as though they were produced using frame by frame photography. Virtually all had a silly, surreal quality, like a small theatre of the absurd.

Cox's reports attracted additional investigators to Rolla, but they usually stayed only for a day or two. I spoke to several who were impressed with what they had witnessed, and none put forward any substantial evidence for fraud. In 1981 I spent five nights at the home of the Richards, who were exceptionally gracious hosts. During my visits I heard hundreds of intelligently communicating raps, for which I have no explanation, though these were under uncontrolled conditions. I was also shown a mini-lab film in which Zener cards emerged from their box, sorted themselves into suits, and then jumped back into the box, penetrating the cardboard! However bizarre, this seemed to be an ideal phenomenon to test because good controls could be easily implemented. All that was needed was to glue a box closed and record a number of security features that would indicate if someone had tried to enter it via normal means.

When I returned to North Carolina, Richard Broughton and I prepared three boxes of cards. We glued them shut and embedded hairs in the glue. We microscopically examined features of the boxes and made photographic records of precautions. After preparation, we randomly selected one of the three boxes and sent it to Missouri along with a request for the SORRAT entities to sort the cards. The remaining two boxes were to serve as controls, and if the cards were sorted successfully, the control boxes would be offered to skeptics to see if they could duplicate the feat without disturbing the security markers. After several misadventures, the box was returned to us, and we found clear evidence of attempted deceit. At that point I abandoned research with the SORRAT.[7]

Since my study, others investigated, and additional accounts of deception were revealed. Other tricksterish and anti-structural features of the group have been reported. Loren Parks spent some time with the SORRAT and commented on the sexual undercurrents he observed during one of their séances.[8] John Thomas Richards has since published a fictionalized account of the early years of the group (*The Year of the Sorrats*, 1992), and one can glean from it that many participants joined during periods of tumultuous change in their lives, and there were strong interpersonal tensions.[9]

Despite the problems, the SORRAT is of continuing interest because of its longevity (well over 30 years) and because it still reports strong phenomena (though many outsiders question its genuineness). Dr. and Mrs. Richards remain pivotal figures, but the SORRAT maintains only informal and fluid membership. It has no formalized hierarchy with designated officers, written constitution or bylaws, and the group is not affiliated with any larger organization. The phenomena continue to play a central role, and the SORRAT remains nondogmatic. Given its long existence, this group could be profitable for study because it exemplifies the marginality and other anti-structural qualities associated with the paranormal.

As a final note on the SORRAT, I should mention that my research with them was some of the very first that I undertook as a professional parapsychologist. In retrospect, I have to attribute much of my interest in the psi-deception problem to that experience. I had observed psychic tricks and fraudulent mediumship previously, and I knew that I could be fooled. But I must admit that I was shocked and bewildered to discover the deceit with the SORRAT. The people did not seem like the kind who would try to dupe me. SORRAT members were warm and friendly, invited me into their home, and were quite unlike charlatans I had met elsewhere. The experience made me realize how others could be lulled into complacency, and it reinforced my view that extremely strict controls are required in psi research. Looking back, my SORRAT investigation was exceptionally valuable, though dismaying at the time. I still do not understand the motives for the deception, and I remain puzzled, and intrigued, by the SORRAT.

Psi Tech

Psi Tech is a for-profit corporation started in 1989 by government-trained remote viewers to provide services to science and industry (particularly Fortune 500 companies). The Chairman was Major General Albert N. Stubblebine III, former head of the U.S. Army Intelligence and Security Command, and while in the army he had been a strong supporter of its psychic programs. Major Edward A. Dames served as president, and David A. Morehouse was vice-president.

Some historical background may be helpful in understanding the company. In 1972 physicists Harold Puthoff and Russell Targ began to investigate psychic abilities at Stanford Research Institute (later renamed SRI International) in Palo Alto, California. During the early stages of their work, they met Ingo Swann, an artist and psychic from New York City who was participating in experiments at the American Society for Psychical Research. He was also tested by Dr. Gertrude Schmeidler of the City College of New York and found to be able to psychically influence thermistors (electronic devices that can measure temperature). Puthoff carried out some preliminary and successful experiments with Swann, but he did not find them altogether appealing. Swann asked to try to perceive distant geographical sites. He showed some remarkable success, and the process was dubbed *remote viewing*.[10][11]

The program quickly caught the attention of the CIA, which began funding them, and the results prompted the agency to request an operational program to utilize remote viewing for espionage. At some point, Swann developed a training program, and a number of military and intelligence personnel were taught how to do remote viewing. In the late 1980s some of those people retired and formed Psi Tech.

It was an auspicious start, and the company seemed to have great promise. These were not marginal individuals, unsuccessful in life, who did not fit into the everyday world. These were career officers, accustomed to discipline. They were used to taking orders and working in a bureaucratic environment. They had been taught a skill and used it operationally for some years. They understood the need to work as a team.

At the beginning, Psi Tech kept a low profile, but in late 1991 they made it known that they had donated their services to the UN for searching for Iraqi weapon sites. Ed Dames began appearing on television and radio programs.[12] A few months later, in April 1992 in Atlanta, Georgia, Psi Tech made one of its most detailed public presentations at TREAT IV (Treatment and Research of Experienced Anomalous Trauma), a conference devoted primarily to UFO abductions. In his talks there, Ed Dames made a number of amazing statements. He claimed that remote-viewing data indicated that there were cities on Mars, that various kinds of extraterrestrial aliens were visiting underground caverns on earth, and that Psi Tech would locate Mozart's grave. Dames spoke of angelic and extraterrestrial beings that were not unlike those described by eighteenth-century mystic Emanuel Swedenborg.[13] Dames later publicly predicted that a nest of pregnant extraterrestrial alien hybrid women would emerge from a cavern in New Mexico in late summer of 1993. Privately he made claims that were even more bizarre. Present at the TREAT conference were General Stubblebine and Colonel John Alexander, who was reputedly head of a non-lethal weapons program at Los Alamos National Laboratory. Their continuing public association with Dames enhanced the seriousness of his claims. Many observers took the statements at face value, while others suspected Dames' revelations were some kind of government disinformation program. Others thought that the Psi Tech people had lost all capacity for rational analysis. In any event, this was a period of growing public interest in UFOs, and word of Dames' talk spread rapidly among UFO groups. His claims accelerated the rumors about conspiracies and government cover-ups of UFOs and ET aliens.

I suggest that it was no coincidence that within a year of its appearance in the news, all figures publicly associated with Psi Tech had marital difficulties and were either divorced or separated (Stubblebine,[14] Dames, Morehouse, John B. Alexander, member of the Board,[15] and Ryan Wood, sales executive.[16]) Further, David Morehouse, one of the Psi Tech viewers, experienced what might be termed a "Dionysian" period and was hospitalized in a psychiatric ward of the Walter Reed Army Medical Center. He faced charges of sodomy in a court martial, but to avoid prosecution he was allowed to resign his commission under other than honorable conditions. The instability in the personal lives of those involved, and the loss of their rational faculties, should be cause for concern.[17]

Psi Tech did not live up to its early promise, and it now has a much lower profile. Even with the impressive rank of its first Chairman (Major General), its initial reputation crumbled quickly with its failed predictions. There were feelings of disaffection and even threats of lawsuits between associates. The emotions persist, and as I write this, Dames' web site still denounces some of his former colleagues. The entire situation demonstrates a breakdown of the normal, rational, critical abilities expected from highly trained military officers. Considering the lives of the members, and that of the organization, Psi Tech shows unmistakable anti-structural characteristics.

Summary

The groups discussed above consciously attempted to engage paranormal powers and supernatural beings, and dramatic phenomena were reported by SORRAT, Psi Tech, and Kübler-Ross's group. All share clear anti-structural and trickster characteristics. Psi, disorder, lowered sexual inhibitions, and deception were all present. The groups display a pattern of descent through the archetypes—from Apollo, characterized by order and structure; through Hermes, the trickster; to Dionysus, dangerous license and sensuality (these are living examples of Hermes serving as midwife to the birth of Dionysus). In addition, the phenomena led the groups to make bizarre claims that provoked ridicule and brought discredit upon them. Thus the trickster appeared, and marginality was induced again and again.

CHAPTER 14

Alternative Religions and Psi

> For rebellion is as the sin of witchcraft.
> I Samuel 15:23[1]

In our culture, psychic phenomena are hospitably received in Spiritualism, the New Age movement, and modern-day witchcraft. The three movements share common elements, and in a variety of fashions, they are at odds with the establishment. None of them have institutionalized in the manner of government, industry, academe, or mainline religion. Few of the groups within these movements have buildings or permanent paid staffs, and if they do manage to institutionalize, it is usually only briefly. None of the movements acknowledge any central authority; control is local. The movements are marginal and antistructural in many ways, but it is within them that one can find discussion of, training in, and use of psychic abilities.

Spiritualism

The religion of Spiritualism is dated as beginning in 1848 in Hydesville, New York with the mysterious rappings discovered by the Fox sisters, Kate and Margaret.[2] The rappings communicated intelligently and purported to be from the spirit of an itinerant pedlar who had been murdered in the Foxes' house. Word spread rapidly and crowds as large as 500 persons soon flocked to their home to listen to the rappings. In short order the family came to nationwide attention. Many others began contacting the spirits, and a new religion was born. Spiritualism's central tenet was that humans could communicate with the deceased through mediums. The religion presented itself as scientific and empirical. No faith was required—one only needed to consult a medium and witness the phenomena.

Mediums didn't just give general, vague messages and spout platitudes; they provided verifiable information for their sitters that was seemingly unknown to the medium, except by spirit contact. Mediums also levitated tables and produced messages on slates without any anyone touching them. These apparently miraculous occurrences led to their philosophies and exhortations becoming markedly influential. Most mediums were not prominent in other areas of life, and their views would have otherwise gone unheeded. Their paranormal phenomena convinced many of the legitimacy of Spiritualism. In Max Weber's terms, these were manifestations of pure charisma.

The followers of Spiritualism numbered in the millions, and the movement was broadly based, reaching from plebians to the highest levels of society.[3] Horace Greeley, Cornelius Vanderbilt, and Sir Arthur Conan Doyle were among the supporters; Lincoln attended séances in the White House. D. D. Home gave séances for Czar Alexander II, Napolean III, and Queen Sophia of Holland. It is curious that despite its extraordinary following and wealthy supporters, Spiritualism did not develop a hierarchical structure nor even a strong central organization. Cornell University history professor R. Laurence Moore in his *In Search of White Crows: Spiritualism, Parapsychology, and American Culture* (1977) noted that in America, Spiritualists built only one church structure of any size, and the vast majority met in homes or in rented halls. In addition, a recent analysis of the architecture of Spiritualist summer camps showed that they were far more liminal than those of orthodox Christian groups.[4] Considering the available resources and the prominent social status of many participants, the anti-structural characteristics are remarkable.

Mediums frequently went into trance and allowed spirits to speak through them, a phenomenon shared with shamanism. Altered states of consciousness played an important role in both Spiritualism and shamanism.

Spiritualism inherently blurs the life-death binary opposition and calls into question the boundary between the two. Mediums served as mediators between those oppositions—a function that some trickster gods also fulfill. Further, it was the Fox *sisters* who are given credit for founding the movement, and women were prominent from its beginning, thereby inverting the usual male-female hierarchy. Important male mediums were involved, but women played a much larger role in Spiritualism than in the established religions.[5]

Other trickster qualities can be seen in Spiritualism. Its subversive tendencies are highlighted in the titles of Ann Braude's *Radical Spirits*

(1989) and Howard Kerr's *Mediums, and Spirit-Rappers, and Roaring Radicals* (1972). Spiritualism was associated with abolitionism, women's rights, and free love. A number of its followers were advocates of what now would be termed holistic health, thus challenging the medical establishment. The darkened séances provided opportunities for sexual liaisons; divorces of various mediums attracted public attention and disrepute, and segments of the Spiritualist movement advocated birth control rights. Mediumistic trickery hardly needs mention.[6] The trickster characteristics of disruption, deception, lowering of sexual inhibitions, and display of paranormal powers are all prominent in Spiritualism.

Spiritualism still exists today but with a much smaller following than in the nineteenth century. Robert Ellwood, a professor of religion at the University of Southern California, studied Spiritualism and provided an insightful discussion of it in his book *Alternative Altars: Unconventional and Eastern Spirituality in America* (1979). Ellwood has a real appreciation of Victor Turner's concept of liminality. He noted that Spiritualist congregations are fluid, and many who attend services are not members. The churches now draw from lower, marginal classes, and they attract few large families to services. Even the church buildings change hands frequently, further evidencing Spiritualism's ineffectiveness at institutionalizing. Spiritualism has an inherently marginal, anti-structural nature.

The New Age Movement

The New Age movement is a loose network of people and organizations involved with such causes as holistic health, channeling, spiritual seeking, Eastern religions, personal transformation, and ecological awareness, among others. It is amorphous, unstructured, and impossible to define crisply. The New Age is more ambiguous than the other two movements discussed in this chapter, and many aspects of it are not religious, but some are.

According to *The New Age Almanac* (1991),[7] the New Age movement emerged as a recognizable entity circa 1971, though many of its ideas had long been part of American culture. Those ideas, however, were somewhat submerged and did not receive much attention from science and academe. James Webb points out in *The Occult Establishment* (1976) that the ideas were kept alive among the beats, hippies, etc., that is, on the margins of society.[8]

Mediumship and channeling (a newer name for mediumship) played a major role in establishing, defining and maintaining the New Age.[9] The works by and about Edgar Cayce, the "sleeping prophet," brought many their first exposure to New Age ideas. The books of Ruth Montgomery, who reported contacts with discarnate entities, attracted others, as did the Seth books by channeler Jane Roberts. Helen Schucman's *A Course in Miracles* (1975), another channeled work, drew still more to the New Age. Thousands of others, who gained no national attention, became channelers, and groups formed around many of them. The burgeoning popular interest in shamanism is yet another instance of New Age influence. In all of these examples, altered states of consciousness play a central role.

Marilyn Ferguson, one of the most articulate persons expressing the ideas of the New Age, noted that there is no central authority defining the movement. In her book *The Aquarian Conspiracy* (1980), she emphasized its informal, fluid networks, decentralization of power, and lack of structured hierarchies. New Age concerns typically include feminism, the environment, and alternative healing, and women play major roles.[10] In addition, it is open to astrology and other forms of divination. All of this is a bit subversive to the establishment. Overall, its properties define it as anti-structural.

Modern-Day Witchcraft And Neo-Paganism

Modern-day witchcraft and neo-paganism saw an explosion of growth in the 1960s and 1970s, similar to the New Age movement. Some might consider witchcraft as part of the New Age, but with its strong emphasis on ritual and magic it has a sufficiently distinct identity to warrant separate comment. A central feature of witchcraft and neo-paganism is the use of ritual magic for practical ends, and as such, direct contact with the supernatural is salient. There is a great diversity of beliefs, and an individual practitioner or group may borrow from a variety of traditions. For instance, Egyptian, Eastern and extraterrestrial concepts may be merged into one system. Neo-paganism is highly syncretic. The movement has an intellectual component, and some of the practitioners have produced sophisticated scholarly works describing the religion. Notable are Margot Adler's *Drawing Down the Moon* (1979) and Aidan Kelly's *Crafting the Art of Magic* (1991).

Women play major roles in the groups, and primary worship of the goddess, as opposed to a masculine god, is a common feature. Witchcraft is organized around the coven, which typically has from 3-

20 members, and if one becomes too large, others "hive off."[11] Some groups are involved with umbrella organizations that facilitate networking, but those hold no theological or institutional power over the individual coven. There is no central authority. Because of this anti-structural nature, many covens do not have a long-term existence, though some continue for years.

There are other anti-structural aspects to witchcraft. Drugs and explicit sexuality are part of some neo-pagan religious rituals, though not as much as some of the popular media portray.[12] A number of practitioners have an interest in parapsychology, and I know several who were influenced by the writings of J. B. Rhine. Modern witches are frequently aligned with feminism and ecology. In all of these areas, their beliefs challenge the status quo and dogma of established science and religion, and Aidan Kelly states: "Neopagans tend to be extremely anti-authoritarian."[13]

Anthropologist Tanya Luhrmann provided a detailed commentary on magical practices in her *Persuasions of the Witch's Craft* (1989). That book was based on a study of witchcraft practitioners in England. During her investigation, she took courses on ritual magic, practiced assigned exercises, participated in rituals, and came to have anomalous experiences. The exercises evoked modes of thought similar to those of the mystics mentioned by Victor Turner. She tells us that a: "feature of esoteric knowledge is that magicians often say that the truths of the Mysteries are conveyed through images. The classic training manual in the Western Mysteries grandly asserts that the mind cannot comprehend the truths of the Mysteries rationally, but that the human can understand them when they are couched in imagery. Witchcraft is said to engage a different mode of thought than analytic rationality. In that mode, 'verbal understanding is limited; [the mind] communicates through images, emotions, sensations, dreams, visions and physical symptoms'. [Luhrmann quoting Starhawk (1979, p. 21)] There is knowledge that has content, but is understood in terms of images and communicated neither verbally nor in rational terms."[14]

"In magic, non-ordinary states have a practical, this-worldly purpose. Magical rituals are meant to concentrate forces and direct power. According to the theory, this happens only when magicians sink into altered states of consciousness in appropriate ritual conditions and visualize images with great intensity. In order to manipulate the subtle currents and interconnections of their world, magicians are said to need to step outside the normal ways people think and communicate, to step over the barrier which Western conceptions of subjectivity and objectivity place between self and world. They are trained in techniques intended to make this possible."[15]

"Theirs is a conceptual world of images, myths, symbols and their associations, in which poetic evocation is more highly valued than analytic evaluation, and the force of a poetic analogy is strong."[16]

Clearly, such uses of altered states of consciousness tend to be subversive to Western rationalistic conceptions of reality. Indeed Luhrmann even noted that practitioners' understanding of ritual magic is in non-rational terms. The very practice of it leads to anti-structural thought. Magic denies the primacy of verbal, rational knowledge. Luhrmann's own reaction to all this is particularly instructive, and she was very frank about her preconceptions and motives. She explicitly rejected psi, saying: "The only reason I continued to think of myself as an anthropologist, rather than as a witch, was that I had a strong disincentive against asserting that rituals had an effect upon the material world . . . The very purpose of my involvement . . . would have been undermined by my assent to the truth of magical ideas."[17] Even so, few anthropological works have as much insight as hers, and Luhrmann's candid admission reveals academia's fundamental hostility to psi and her need to align herself with academe.

Summary

All three of these movements have loose boundaries. It is often difficult to tell if someone is part of them or not. Many who attend Spiritualist services are also members of established religions; New Age followers are drawn from all faiths. Witchcraft and neo-pagan groups are perhaps more distinct, but ambiguity reigns there as well with vast differences among them. Within covens, beliefs and rituals can change with the whim of the high priestess or priest. There is no higher ecclesiastical authority or common text that solidifies dogma or mandates what, how, or when rituals must be performed.

These three movements have striking similarities. In all altered (i.e., destructured) states of consciousness play a major role. Women are prominent, as are the issues of feminism, the environment and healing. None recognize a central authority for their movement, and they engage in virtually no institution building. All of the movements are considered subversive by the establishment; they court direct involvement with paranormal and supernatural phenomena, and all display elements of the trickster constellation.

The most vocal opposition to these movements comes from two sources: establishment scientists (exemplified by CSICOP) and conservative and fundamentalist religious groups. Both of these antagonists are typified by large, male-dominated, status conscious, hierarchical institutions—the antithesis of the targets of their scorn. Both have produced massive amounts of literature denouncing the New Age proponents and modern pagans, and similar attacks were directed at the Spiritualists of the nineteenth century. While some of the political and social goals advocated by the "deviants" have been partially incorporated into science and mainstream churches (e.g., feminism, ecology, alternative healing), the establishments' most vehement attacks remain directed at paranormal and supernatural practices.

CHAPTER 15

Institutions and the Paranormal

Sociologist Nachman Ben-Yehuda published an excellent book in 1985 entitled *Deviance and Moral Boundaries: Witchcraft, the Occult, Science Fiction, Deviant Sciences and Scientists*. It remains underappreciated, perhaps because his analysis mixed science, science fiction, and the occult, topics that many academics wish to keep separate. Comparing materials from such diverse areas is not always welcome, but it can provide unexpected insights.

Ben-Yehuda commented that occult groups typically engage in little or no successful institution building. This is an exceedingly important observation, but almost no one has recognized its implications. Few groups that directly engage paranormal phenomena have been able to institutionalize, and that is an anti-structural property of the phenomena. In this chapter I will examine a variety of examples involving institutions and the paranormal and show how they conform to anti-structural patterns.

The word institution has several meanings. Here I will use it to refer to an organization that has paid staff, buildings, grounds, etc. Institutions have some stability and legal identity apart from the people who form them. Institutions may be large or small. Those of government, industry, and academe are a pervasive part of our lives, and we are rarely aware of their full influence over us. We take them for granted as a natural part of the order of things. They are largely responsible for the statuses we hold (e.g., schools attended, places of employment), with whom we associate, where we live, etc. Their power is subtle.

The paranormal's relationship to institutions can be studied via several avenues. One approach is to examine groups that began with a direct focus on paranormal phenomena, review how they became firmly established, and note changes in paranormal activities. Another method is to study the positions of paranormal practitioners (e.g., psychics, healers, mediums) in relation to modern institutions. Briefly, the practitioners are likely to be found more outside of institutions rather than being part of them. A third approach is to observe how business and academe treat paranormal themes. They are not neglected, but the situation is curious. The entertainment industry gives the paranormal extended coverage, but in fiction. Within academe, the supernatural is discussed in departments of literature, folklore, and religion. These institutions serve important functions in relation to the paranormal—by what they present, and by what they ignore.

Paranormal Groups, Individual Practitioners, and Institutions

A number of groups formed for the purpose of producing paranormal phenomena and later institutionalized with paid staff, buildings, and offices. The examples can be divided into two classes: those that maintain a focus on directly engaging the phenomena and those that shift away from that.

Of the first type, Spiritualist camps are some of most institutionalized. Several own buildings and grounds and have a number of mediums associated with them for months or years. These camps maintain a commitment to their visitors to produce phenomena such as spirit messages, apports, and materializations. Unfortunately, the groups also have a reputation for being rife with fraud. There have been damaging exposés, and one of the most graphic was *The Psychic Mafia* (1976) by M. Lamar Keene, who had been a highly successful medium. The association of Spiritualism with fraudulent mediumship is so widely known that the camps are assured of maintaining their marginal status, even within the larger paranormal subculture.

The second type of group also began with a focus on paranormal phenomena, grew, and eventually succeeded in institutionalizing. As they evolved, emphasis shifted away from training or display of psychic abilities and toward "spiritual development" and "personal growth." Two prominent examples are the Theosophical Society (TS), founded by Helena P. Blavatsky in 1875 and the Association for Research and Enlightenment (ARE), founded by Edgar Cayce in 1931. Blavatsky gained wide notoriety for fraudulently producing messages from "ascended masters." She was discussed in the earlier chapter on prominent psychics. Cayce did distant healings and clairvoyant diagnoses, but he escaped any serious charge of deception. Both organizations are now devoted to spiritual development and have buildings, professional staff, publishing facilities, and produce magazines and books. Psychic manifestations are downplayed. Even though the ARE has thousands of members, there is no permanent role of "psychic" within its institutional structure. The ARE and TS are largely monuments to an earlier era and are frequently staffed by gray-haired, elderly people. Within the paranormal subculture, they have a higher status than the Spiritualist camps.

Many large organizations with paranormal interests do not, qua institutions, directly engage the phenomena themselves. National societies for dowsers, astrologers, and psychotronics specialists are typically loose confederations of groups and individuals. Such national organizations might recommend certain practitioners, but as a corporate body they rarely provide paranormal services to clients. The same is true of local societies.

Spiritualist churches were discussed in an earlier chapter. Compared with ordinary churches, they are rarely successful at institutionalizing. Further, they are often independent entities and do not answer to any larger ecclesiastical body. The more respectable of them tend to emphasize mental phenomena rather than the more dramatic and dubious physical manifestations. The churches may have a number of psychics and mediums loosely affiliated with them who typically donate their services; rarely are they employees.

The individual psychic practitioner's relationship to modern institutions is also worth noting. The large majority of professional psychics that I know work out of their homes, though a few have small offices. They operate as individual consultants rather than through corporations. Psychic fairs may employ many psychics, but these often last only a day or two, again displaying transient, anti-structural qualities. Numerous police departments use psychic detectives—even some that deny doing so. The psychics generally volunteer their time, and I know of no police force that has employees with the job description of "psychic detective." Of course psychics have lives apart from their paranormal roles, and some are employed full-time by large corporations, but in ordinary capacities. Their paranormal activities are conducted off the job.

There is one major business that now hires psychics—the telephone psychic hot lines. These have become popular in the last ten years due to heavy television advertising. The industry grosses at least hundreds of millions of dollars annually.

One of the most prominent and successful companies was the Psychic Friends Network, which was endorsed by singer Dionne Warwick. Its infomercial was the second most lucrative of all infomercials aired in 1995.[1] The owner, Baltimore-based Inphomation Communications Inc., was reported to annually gross $125 million at its peak, and they had more than 1000 psychics working for them. In 1998 Inphomation was forced to declare bankruptcy, and court filings and newspaper coverage gave inside details about the company. The founder, Michael Lasky, was accused of shady business practices and numerous lawsuits were filed against him.[2]

There are still a number of other hot lines with celebrity endorsers, and they continue to attract callers. But the industry in general has an unsavory reputation, and public utility regulators have received many complaints about the companies for deceptive advertising.[3]

Freelance writer Sherry Amatenstein published a short account (really a small exposé) of her experience as a phone psychic with one hot line (unnamed). She had no problem getting the job, even though she didn't believe herself to be psychic. There was no test to pass. The company charged callers $3.99 a minute to talk with her, and she received $.25 of that. This translates to $15.00 an hour for her, a mere six percent of the $239.40 an hour paid by the clients. When Amatenstein was not on the phone, the company's representatives called frequently, urging her to try to keep people on the line in order to maximize billings. The primary concern was profit, not service.

Amatenstein had real sympathy for her callers, and soon had second thoughts about what she was doing. She discovered that the clients "had one thing in common: vulnerability." She said that: "They needed to talk, some so badly that they called over and over. What had initially seemed like a harmless way to earn spare cash turned out to be serious business. I felt guilty and ashamed of myself." For a few minutes of consolation, clients were spending hundreds of dollars, dollars which most could ill afford. Amatenstein lasted only about three days on the job.[4]

I have personally known others who worked on the hot lines and who believed themselves to have genuine abilities. They did not stay with it for very long and returned to doing private readings on their own. I suspect that the industry has an extremely high turnover of personnel.

The telephone hot line psychics are, in effect, high-priced, untrained counselors. There is little or no emphasis on producing or verifying real ESP, and there is little reason to think that much really occurs.

The hot lines have a deservedly sleazy reputation for preying on vulnerable people. The psychics, too, are poorly treated, and underpaid; they are pushed to increase profits with little regard for the welfare of their clients. In short, the hot lines' high visibility, combined with their disreputability, help assure the marginality of the paranormal.

The Paranormal In Entertainment Media

Throughout history, art, literature, and drama have portrayed supernatural themes. In the secular culture today, the paranormal makes its most prominent appearance in fictional TV programs, books, and movies. The industries devoted to such fiction are massive. In terms of capital, manpower and resources, they dwarf the organized groups devoted to direct contact with paranormal phenomena. Millions of dollars are available for projects with stories of ghost busters, witches, exorcists and the like. The contrast between the fiction industries and the reality from which they borrow is comparable to no other area. For instance, police officers and medical doctors often appear in exciting television shows and movies, but their industries are far larger than those that portray them in fiction. Contemplation of this state of affairs gives clues to the nature of psi.

The entertainment industry's treatment of psychic themes is instructive.

Anthropologist David Hess analyzed Hollywood films in his book *Science in the New Age: The Paranormal, Its Defenders and Debunkers, and American Culture* (1993). He noted that paranormal heroes tend to be marginal or exotic, and he was not the only one to detect this trend. Psychologist Keith Harary also reviewed Hollywood's portrayal of psychics and found them often presented as odd or unusual; frequently there was a negative taint.[5] Harary's paper was presented at a parapsychology conference, and in the published discussion that followed, D. Scott Rogo noted that psychics are similarly viewed in many cultures. The comments after Rogo's suggested that his observations were not particularly welcome, and the other conference-goers seemed to want to ignore the implications. Yet Rogo was clearly correct, and though characters in film are often exaggerated, they do reflect a reality that some would prefer to deny. Hollywood recognizes that the paranormal is associated with marginality, which suggests that the producers are more perceptive than the scientists.

Supernatural horror fiction is exceedingly popular. Bookstores devote much shelf space to it, and the novels of Stephen King and the movies based on them gross untold millions. Many other writers specialize in this genre and make a good living doing so. Paranormal motifs are particularly common in horror films,[6] and this needs an explanation. Folklorist William Clements analyzes interstitiality in relation to horror in his paper "The Interstitial Ogre" (1987). He notes that many horror figures are "symbols of disorder"[7] and that "their essence is their interstitiality. They articulate ultimate defiance to humanity by challenging... the founding constructs upon which all of culture rests."[8] He is not alone in this recognition; in *Power and Paranoia* (1986), film critic Dana Polan talks of "what Julia Kristeva calls 'the powers of horror': the fear in the presence of that which 'disturbs identity, system, order. What does not respect borders, positions, rules. The in-between, the ambiguous, the composite'."[9] He elaborates that "For Kristeva, in other words, the power of horror is the horror of all those experiences that might suggest to the human subject the ultimate nothingness or foundationlessness of all his/her being."[10] The above quotations refer to classification and foundations, and it is through them that the implications of liminality, interstitiality, and anti-structure can be extended. The next Part of this book will do that.

Horror fiction contains graphic, concrete imagery of monsters, ghosts, and ET aliens, and that reinforces the culture's perception of the paranormal. Clements notes that "the very fact that these beings are presented in literature or films labeled as 'fantasy' reminds that the threat... is unreal."[11] Polan likewise concludes that "by treating all this as mere fiction... holds the threat at a distance, writes it within the limits of a reason."[12] In fact that may be its most important function. To suggest that such things are actually real, no matter in how veiled a manner, is to provoke an extraordinary level of unconscious anxiety in many. Indeed, some of the most terrifying films are those that are not overly exaggerated.

Even fictional portrayals can be uncomfortable for some. CSICOP has capitalized on the uneasy feelings evoked by the paranormal, and in their fund-raising letters, they have denounced fictional TV shows with paranormal themes. They imply that even fiction gives the topics credibility, and that rationality is thereby subverted. An example is the television program *The X-Files* which has dark plots of government cover-ups, UFO abductions, conspiracies, psychic characters, and the like. It attracted a devoted following, and *X-Files* conventions were held in large cities around the country. Chris Carter, the producer of the show, was invited to a CSICOP conference, and he received sharp criticism there. Neil deGrasse Tyson, a Princeton University astrophysicist, accused him of misleading the public and hindering attempts to improve scientific literacy.[13] The attack came despite the fact that the show is explicitly fictional and that Carter made it clear that he was only a storyteller. Even so, some people are unsettled by stories like the *X-Files*. For others though, fictional accounts are reassuring; they help reinforce the idea that paranormal events are just that: fiction.

Tabloid newspapers constitute another branch of the entertainment media, and they highlight many issues. Tabloids are liminal entities; they blur the distinction between news and entertainment, between fact and fiction. Culturally, they are of low status, both in terms of news content, as well as in entertainment, and of all the major media, they give the greatest coverage to paranormal topics. Indeed, many of them feature it on their front pages.

Though the tabloids have long been fixtures in popular culture, and few take them seriously, they rouse the anger and indignation of CSICOP and other debunkers. No matter how blatantly silly the tabloids may be, the skeptics' periodicals carry articles denouncing the tabloids' coverage of the paranormal. CSICOP's attacks are not light-hearted spoofs; they take the tabloid stories as a real menace, and have done so for more than 20 years. This is curious because even magazines and newsletters of the paranormal subculture give little attention or credence to the tabloids. The readers of *The Skeptical Inquirer* are even less at risk of uncritically accepting the stories; of its readership, 83% have some type of college degree and 54% have an advanced degree.[14] Why then does CSICOP raise such a furor over the tabloids?

It makes no sense to maintain that the debunkers' attacks are provided to educate their readership or a wider public. The function of the denunciations lies elsewhere. The skeptics' tirades effectively reinforce the marginality of the paranormal by emphasizing its association with the tabloids and their excesses. Thus boundaries are strengthened, the paranormal kept at bay.

There is one popular-style periodical in the U.S. that deserves special mention because it has been devoted exclusively to the paranormal for more than 50 years—*Fate* magazine. That longevity makes it highly pertinent to issues here. *Fate* was founded in 1948. For nearly all of its life, until the early 1990s, it was a digest-size magazine published on pulp paper. The cover art was often crude and lurid, especially in its early days. It carried tawdry advertisements for voodoo practitioners, lucky charms, removal of curses, and the like. Its format and production quality assured its marginality.

The magazine's content was mixed. There were credulous reports, along with some by professional parapsychologists, but what many people don't know is that many skeptics published full articles in *Fate*. These included CSICOP members Susan Blackmore, L. Sprague de Camp, Kendrick Frazier, Martin Gardner, Philip J. Klass, Larry Kusche, Lawrence Jerome, David Marks, Joe Nickell, James Oberg, Dennis Rawlins, Robert Sheaffer, Gordon Stein, and Marcello Truzzi. There were many critical and debunking articles by others as well. *Fate* is certainly more effective than *Skeptical Inquirer* in warning people about psychic scams because *Fate* is read by far more people likely to be prone to them.

Ray Palmer and Curtis Fuller founded the magazine, and in 1955 Fuller bought Palmer's share and became the sole owner. In 1989 ownership went to Carl Llewellyn Weschcke, who also owns Llewellyn Publications, one of the largest publishers of occult books.[15] For its entire existence, the magazine was owned by individuals not a conglomerate.

Though *Fate* meets the definition for being an institution, it still might be described as anti-structural. Its marginality and its ownership are factors in that. The surprising and ambiguous mix of credible, highly skeptical, and credulous articles were packaged in way that assured that *Fate* was outside the mainstream media. That formula has allowed the magazine to continue for more than half a century. In appearance, style, and content, it conforms to anti-structural characteristics. *Fate*, in its own way, marks the paranormal's marginality.

The Supernatural In Academe

Academe does not totally neglect the paranormal. Sociologists, anthropologists, psychologists and folklorists are allowed to study *beliefs* about paranormal events, but there is a taboo against attempting to verify their reality. In academe today, serious consideration of the supernatural is almost exclusively limited to the arts and humanities. Yet even there we find ambivalence; the accounts studied are of "long ago" or "far away" and usually explicitly fictional (or metaphorical). The fact that no academic departments study the reality of the claims subtly implies to the students that the phenomena are not real.

Everyone knows that universities have departments devoted to the sciences, but those outside academe often are unaware that many state-supported schools have long-established departments of religion. Despite the much-acclaimed warfare between science and religion, both have been incorporated into the academy. Science and religion are clearly demarcated. Science studies the empirical world, religion the spiritual. The paranormal, though, incorporates both; it is the middle ground. Spiritual beings that convey information about the empirical world subvert the boundary between science and religion.

Laboratory-based parapsychology tries to test aspects of the supernatural, thereby suggesting that it is, at least in part, based in reality. Of course, such research is not long welcome in the academy. There are no extant university departments of parapsychology. In a few universities, occasionally a professor will teach a class on parapsychology, but this is done typically out of personal interest. The class rarely if ever becomes part of the established curriculum, and when the professor retires or loses interest, the course is dropped from the offerings. There are universities with classes, even a few for credit, teaching the development of psychic abilities. These are exceptions and are almost always in low-status schools or in temporary or experimental programs. None are firmly embedded as part of the formal academic establishment.

Later chapters will give more detail about parapsychology in academe, but an illustration can be helpful. Discussion of paranormal phenomena sometimes provokes extreme reactions, and parapsychologists have frequently endured prejudice and unfair rejection of their work. An amusing example is seen in a review of the book *Wondrous Events: Foundations of Religious Belief* (1994) authored by James McClenon. The reviewer, William Sims Bainbridge, is a well known sociologist of religion, a former Harvard professor, and director of the sociology program of the National Science Foundation.

Bainbridge's review, less than a page long, appeared in the December 1995 issue of the highly respected *Journal for the Scientific Study of Religion* (*JSSR*). It is a remarkable document, revealing a wonderfully primitive, visceral reaction. So much so, that after first reading his review, I almost wondered whether that style might be common in the pages of the *JSSR*, but it's not. I checked. The 1995 volume reviewed 81 books, and only three others received strongly negative assessments. However, their reviewers clearly explained the deficiencies, and they completely avoided sarcasm and ridicule.

More than just not liking *Wondrous Events*, Bainbridge denounced the "shriekingly bizarre events" it analyzed. So enraged, he was unable to articulate *any* substantive failing, though he implied that McClenon's prose was a bit stilted (even though that is frequently taken as a badge of merit in academic circles). His most extended barrage was aimed at McClenon's photographs of such things as fire walking and psychic surgery, claiming they were only appropriate for "a lurid exploitation paperback of the kind sold to subnormals at the supermarket checkout." Bainbridge's annoyance with the illustrations of psychic surgeons is remarkable considering that similar practitioners in innumerable cultures have been active for thousands of years and held prominent religious positions.

Bainbridge was astute enough to realize that simply giving scientific attention to the paranormal automatically enhances its respectability. Thus he spoke of "the supermarket checkout" (home of the tabloids) and "subnormals"—rhetorical tactics guaranteed to reinforce the paranormal's outsider status vis-à-vis the academy. Like the scatological stories of the trickster, McClenon's graphic illustrations of the paranormal are unwelcome in polite company.

Bainbridge's review was aimed at more than just *Wondrous Events*, for near the end of it he asked: "How can the University of Pennsylvania Press publish the half of this book that is utter trash and still pretend to be an academic press?" Thus he targeted not only the author but any university press that might consider publishing similar works. At the end his text, Bainbridge's name was followed not only by his affiliation with the National Science Foundation (NSF), but an additional, prominently positioned note called attention to that affiliation. No other review in the 1995 *JSSR* carried anything similar. The implications will not be lost on the readers as the NSF is a major funding source for academic research.

In contrast to Bainbridge's high status, McClenon has spent much of his professional career examining the paranormal. He is one of very few academics who have published original research on the subject in scholarly books and articles, and more than any other researcher I know, he has maintained extended, personal contact with paranormal practitioners and experiencers. McClenon teaches at Elizabeth City State University, a small school in the South whose student body is largely composed of low-income African Americans.

Parapsychologists can point to other instances of prejudice, and in 1992 anthropologist David Hess published a number of accounts from them. He specifically discussed the notions of academic boundaries and their maintenance, and he compared parapsychologists with Marxists and feminists who also sometimes face opposition in the academy. There are parallels, but those groups have been far more successful in gaining tenured positions in universities than have parapsychologists. Further, Marxists and feminists are overtly hostile to establishment political views, and they represent a tiny fraction of the general population. On the other hand, parapsychology has no political agenda, and the public has enormous interest in it. The relative success of the Marxists and feminists compared with parapsychologists is striking.

The ambivalence toward the paranormal is found even among academics who are sympathetic to it. This is nicely illustrated in an article titled "The Reality of Spirits: A Tabooed or Permitted Field of Study?" (1993) by Edith Turner, a University of Virginia anthropologist and the widow of Victor Turner. In 1985 she attended a healing ritual in Zambia and saw a spirit form emerge from the body of a sick woman. Later she had some ESP experiences herself. She was quite open about all these, but few anthropologists seem willing to acknowledge similar occurrences. Turner commented that she "began to see how anthropologists have perpetrated an endless series of put-downs as regards the many spirit events in which they participated— 'participated' in a kindly pretense."[16] She was frank enough to admit that "There seems to be a kind of force field between the anthropologist and her or his subject matter making it impossible for her or him to come close to it, a kind of religious frigidity."[17]

Turner called for anthropologists to more fully participate in the cultures they study, but she also explained that if an anthropologist "went native" he or she was academically doomed. She seemed to want to portray this as a thing of the past, but clearly it is not. Going native, especially regarding the paranormal, has severe consequences for a professional career. Anthropologists continue to distance themselves from the phenomena, in order to maintain their status within academe. They explain away the paranormal in stilted, abstract, academic frameworks.

The really telling aspect of Edith Turner's article was that despite her plea for greater openness, she made only the scantest reference to similar paranormal experiences in our own culture. And of course she made absolutely no mention of parapsychology. This failure, whether inadvertent or deliberate, is a powerful example of what parapsychology faces.

Summary

This chapter can be summarized succinctly: paranormal phenomena and established institutions do not find each other congenial. This statement is best understood in conjunction with the material from which it was derived, so I will briefly review some of it here.

The Association for Research and Enlightenment and the Theosophical Society were founded upon the works of Edgar Cayce and Helena Blavatsky, both of whom were famous psychics. The organizations now do not emphasize production of paranormal phenomena. The few institutions that directly provide psychic services, e.g., Spiritualist camps and telephone psychic hot lines, have very low status and are widely viewed as disreputable.

Although kings, presidents, and CEOs have consulted psychics, the prophet, clairvoyant, healer, and psychic counselor hold no position within the modern, large, bureaucratic institutions of government, industry, and academe. Psychics, rather, are typically self-employed.

Major institutions do more than ignore the paranormal, some work to marginalize it. Two of the most active are the entertainment industry and academe. Entertainment media frequently portray the paranormal in and as fiction. That consigns it to the realm of the imagination and subtly reinforces the idea that it need not be taken seriously. Academe addresses the paranormal and supernatural in literature courses. All universities have such classes, but none of them have departments that study the reality of the phenomena, and that sends an unstated message to the students. Academe is a product of, and an agent for, the rationalization and disenchantment of the world, and that entails marginalizing the paranormal. The efforts are sometimes overt, as with the Bainbridge review, but more often the pressures are exceedingly subtle, signalled by what is neglected, ignored, and left unmentioned (e.g., parapsychology in Edith Turner's article).

These examples confirm the anti-structural nature of the paranormal described in earlier chapters. It will be seen again in the next chapter on the organization of psychical research. Given the enormous interest and widespread acceptance of the existence of psi (according to any number of polls), the structural position of its practitioners within the culture is curious.

These patterns of the paranormal are anti-structural, and they are easily overlooked precisely because of that. This condition has existed for millennia, and it continues today. Parapsychologists need to recognize that words of rational explanation are unlikely to have a substantial effect on the place of the paranormal in our culture. Further, it is altogether unrealistic to expect the scientific establishment to study the phenomena. Those who believe that parapsychology's academic acceptance can be gained by presentation of evidence and rational discussion are simply naive. The problem is far deeper than ideology or belief. The evidence is ubiquitous that the phenomena inherently become marginalized. As a consequence, direct investigation of them can only be effectively conducted in the margins.

CHAPTER 16

Anti-Structure and the History of Psychical Research

The histories of psychical research societies and parapsychology laboratories are stories of promising beginnings, rapid initial growth, encounters with tricksters, internal conflict, stagnation and decline. No such institution today can be said to be thriving, and virtually all extant are less impressive than in their early years. This anti-structural pattern is pervasive and is quite curious in light of the tremendous popular interest in the field. To put this in context, one only need remember that the movies *Ghostbusters* (1984) and *Ghost* (1990) each grossed well over $200,000,000.[1] Interest from the media continues, and very few ordinary scientists or scientific laboratories ever receive the publicity given to psychical researchers. In my experience, a parapsychologist in an established laboratory may turn down more media appearances in a year or two than an average scientist may receive in a lifetime. This popular fascination with psychic phenomena is not a recent development; indeed paranormal and supernatural themes are found in some of the most influential art and literature ever produced. It is puzzling that all this attention does not translate into long-term institutional support for scientific parapsychological research.

This state of affairs cannot be attributed to a supposed lack of practical applications for psi because many non-utilitarian endeavors obtain continuing support from established institutions. Drama, music, art, and literature all have strong sponsorship, and all universities have departments devoted to them. Much scientific research has little direct application and captures no public interest whatever, yet it garners steady funding, often from large bureaucracies. But there *are* applications for psychic abilities. Psychic detective work and psychic spying are widely known. The use of psi for healing is frequently reported.

Even if one is a complete disbeliever and attributes all reports of psi to fraud and delusion, one still needs to explain the lack of establishment support in light of the massive public interest. After all, many forms of psychotherapy have flourished despite scant evidence for their efficacy.[2] Commercial and academic empires have been built on them, and they have become institutions even while antagonizing others in the scientific establishment.[3] There is even evidence that advanced training in therapy makes one a worse therapist,[4] but such findings have little impact on the legitimacy granted psychotherapy by the establishment, including insurance companies, courts of law, academia, and government agencies.[5] Similarly, billions of dollars have been expended on medical procedures that were later found to be of dubious value. In summary, even if all psychic phenomena were spurious, we would normally expect psi practitioners to be integrated into the bureaucracies of government, academe, and industry.

The psychical research societies also subtly reflect this state of affairs. Even those organizations now provide little or no money for actual research, and what funding they do provide typically constitutes a tiny fraction of their budgets. Those who have published little research often hold political power within the societies.

The major parapsychology groups illustrate the anti-structural pattern. Histories of the organizations are illuminating. (Let me be clear here. By parapsychology I mean the study of psychic phenomena with scientific methods, followed by written reports that are submitted for review and publication in refereed journals.)

SPR

In 1882 the Society for Psychical Research was founded and soon attracted some of the most prominent people in England.[6] Members included: J. J. Thompson, discoverer of the electron; William Crookes, discoverer of thallium; Andrew Lang, the eminent folklorist; Arthur Balfour, a later prime minister; Camille Flammarion, noted French astronomer; classicist Gilbert Murray, physicist Sir Oliver Lodge, psychologists William James and William McDougall, and Nobel laureates: Henri Bergson, Lord Rayleigh, and Charles Richet; and these were only some of the presidents! Other members included: Charles Lutwidge Dodgson (Lewis Carroll), Sigmund Freud, Marie Curie, J. Venn, Heinrich Hertz, William Ruskin, F. C. S. Schiller, William

Gladstone, Alfred Tennyson, Robert Louis Stevenson, and Alfred Russel Wallace. Although most of the research was conducted by a small group of dedicated members, many prominent figures participated directly. They were not mere figureheads. Despite the activity of this stellar list, psychical research was not integrated into academia.

In the early days, some of the most intense controversies swirled around the trickery of physical mediums. Many Spiritualist members of the society were offended by the exposés conducted by the scientists of the organization, and they left a few years after the founding.[7] Although the SPR is still in existence, it continues to slowly decline, and its journal ranks as the poorest quality of the four major journals in the field.[8] Yet to its credit, it has managed to publish its journal continuously since 1882.

Duke And The FRNM

The career of J. B. Rhine at Duke University and his Foundation for Research on the Nature of Man (FRNM)[9] illuminates the paranormal in regard to institutionalization and anti-structure. Duke was established in 1924, building upon the small, denominational Trinity College, which was already in existence. Duke's president, William Preston Few, hired William McDougall to establish the new department of psychology. McDougall brought in J. B. Rhine who began his work there in 1927. Science historians, Seymour Mauskopf and Michael McVaugh, covered this early period in their book *The Elusive Science* (1980). They were alert to the factors that allowed Rhine to obtain his post and stated: "There was surely no other university in the United States where he could have been given a position in the psychology department and been allowed to devote himself to psychical research."[10] They went on to specifically comment: "The *institutional fluidity* inevitable in the establishment of a new school may have helped to make this possible" (emphasis added).[11]

Duke received enormous publicity following publication of Rhine's book *Extra-Sensory Perception* in 1934. Waldemar Kaempffert, the recognized dean of newspaper science writers, gave it extensive, favorable comment in *The New York Times*. His writings and those of others generated a huge popular interest in Rhine's work.[12] Considerable funds were raised, and in the early years Rhine had almost four times as much money for research as all rest of the psychology professors put together.[13] Not surprisingly the Duke psychologists developed some hostility toward him.

Rhine encountered the problem of trickery early on (this is rarely noted by parapsychologists). The very first issue of the *Journal of Parapsychology* reported positive results from a woman who had been caught cheating, a fact not mentioned in the published paper.[14] There were some rumors about others cheating, and Rhine addressed them.[15]

After the flurry of publicity in the mid-1930s, the fortunes of the laboratory fluctuated; there were times of modest growth, but in other periods the laboratory nearly closed. For its first years, Rhine's laboratory was nominally part of the psychology department, but in 1947 the connection was officially severed. The Parapsychology Laboratory was made an independent center and placed outside the traditional academic structure. Though the laboratory was still on the Duke campus and Rhine maintained his faculty rank, the last graduate degree for work in parapsychology at Duke was awarded in 1948.[16]

In 1965 Rhine retired, and shortly thereafter the laboratory moved across the street from the Duke campus to the Foundation for Research on the Nature of Man (FRNM), which Rhine had established earlier.[17] The break with the university occurred at a time of growing popular interest in the paranormal, and a large number of young researchers were then entering the field. Some were later to be among the fields' most prominent scientists of the 1970s and 1980s. During the mid-1960s, Rhine's laboratories at Duke and the FRNM produced a number of successful experiments. It was a time of excitement and growth, but in September 1967, tensions came to a head, and many of the young researchers walked out, thus manifesting the anti-structural pattern.

Popular interest in the paranormal continued, and the early 1970s saw a further intensification. There were new books, TV shows, and magazines devoted to occult matters. Another wave of young researchers entered parapsychology. The issue of trickery became salient, and magic performers Kreskin and Uri Geller attracted much attention, blurring the distinctions between real and simulated psi in the public mind. The problem irrupted in the laboratory as well. The FRNM "confirmed" the psychic abilities of Bill Delmore, who later admitted to being adept at card manipulation.[18] More serious, the director of research, Walter J. Levy, M.D., was caught faking results in 1974. Shortly thereafter, the laboratory began to decline, and when I arrived in 1980, the building was in disrepair. Many carpets were worn literally all the way to the flooring, and large holes had been knocked in walls with the gypsum from the sheetrock crumbling about. The building was infested by rats (not escaped experimental animals), and occasionally they would scurry about the offices. The director laughed about the rats, and he seemed at home with them and with the building's condition generally.

Maimonides Medical Center And PRL

Another active laboratory of the 1970s was the Division of Parapsychology and Psychophysics at Maimonides Medical Center in Brooklyn, New York. It was run under the aegis of psychiatrist Montague Ullman, with the research directed by Stanley Krippner. It was one of the more successful centers in eliciting psi, and it produced numerous publications, yet it was forced to close in 1979.[19] A full history of the laboratory has not been written, but a glimpse behind the scenes of that earlier time can be found in the October 1993 issue of the *Journal of the American Society for Psychical Research* (*JASPR*), which was devoted to reminiscences on Charles Honorton. Honorton had left Rhine's lab, where he had been an instigator of the discord in 1967, and at age 21 he began working at Maimonides, becoming the most active researcher in the lab. Most of the Maimonides parapsychology researchers were young, and many volunteered their time without pay. Even Stanley Krippner was forced to work at three other part-time jobs to make ends meet.[20] Internal tensions were acute, and there was an unusually high turnover of personnel. Even a decade and a half after the lab closed, the intensity of emotion remained for some of the workers. The October 1993 *JASPR* included embittered attacks on the deceased Honorton by Keith Harary and Michael Smith, which must be among the most virulent ever published in a professional journal.

When the Maimonides laboratory closed in 1979, some of the staff moved to New Jersey and established Psychophysical Research Laboratories (PRL) which had no affiliation with any institution. It was led by Charles Honorton and supported by the James S. McDonnell Foundation, and it also achieved a reputation for successfully eliciting psi. There were internal conflicts in this laboratory also. Ephraim Schechter gave an extensive and dispassionate overview in the March 1993 *Journal of Parapsychology*,[21] but his short piece in the October 1993 *JASPR* issue seethed with veiled hostility. Honorton did not have a Ph.D.; in fact he held no degree at all. Schechter, who was his subordinate, obviously chafed at that.

I was employed at PRL from 1984 until it closed in 1989 and was able to observe the anti-structural aspects of the lab. During its existence, a total of 14 full-time employees worked there for periods longer than six months. Only one of the 14 was married when he came to the laboratory and remained so during his entire employment. In a brief comment, which was not elaborated upon, Honorton hinted that he did not believe that happily married people were the most suitable employees for psi research. In many ways, Honorton lived an anti-structural existence himself. Often he did not produce the written reports requested by funders, and when they were completed, they were invariably late. He told me that it was his experience that when a laboratory's future became uncertain, stronger experimental results were seen. It was only a few months before the closing of PRL that a ganzfeld study with Juilliard students was conducted, which was one of the most successful of the PRL ganzfeld sequences.[22] Honorton lived for his work; everything else was secondary for him. There were a number of amusing anti-structural aspects to his life, which I may someday relate.

ASPR

The historical tribulations of the American Society for Psychical Research have been well documented by others.[23] But it is worth summarizing them because they exemplify the problems faced by psychic research organizations. The society was started in 1885 under the impetus of British physicist William F. Barrett. It published a few issues of its *Proceedings* in the 1880s, but because of insufficient financial support, in December 1889 it requested to become part of the Society for Psychical Research in England. James H. Hyslop, who had taught philosophy at Columbia University, revived the ASPR as a separate organization in 1907. Hyslop was supremely dedicated and wrote thousands of pages for books and journals, but he lacked diplomacy. The organization only hobbled along, and by 1914 it had only about 600 members.[24] Many blamed Hyslop for the lack of growth because his irascibility alienated many supporters. Yet he succeeded in establishing the ASPR as a scientific organization, something his more "diplomatic" (and ineffectual) colleagues were unable to accomplish.[25]

Hyslop died in 1920, and within a few years the ASPR was taken over by partisans of the notorious medium Margery. The capable scientists including William McDougall and Walter Franklin Prince left the ASPR and established the Boston Society for Psychic Research.

Meanwhile, the ASPR shifted to a more popular orientation, and it maintained little intellectual integrity. In 1941 there was a "palace revolution" lead by the eminent psychologist Gardner Murphy and George H. Hyslop, son of James. Murphy revived interest in serious research in the 1940s and 1950s, but the budget was limited. In fact by 1950 the total annual expenditures were only $14,000; by 1960 they were $25,000, and that included publication of the *Journal*.[26] It was indeed a small operation.

During the 1960s and 1970s, the ASPR had an active research program under the direction of Karlis Osis. He and his assistants published a number of scientific papers. Subsequently, there was a decline in the research output. In his reminiscences, Osis noted that it seemed to parallel the failing health and ultimate demise of Gardner Murphy, who died in 1979.[27] Murphy had protected and promoted research, but other members of the board of directors of the ASPR seemed hostile to it. During the mid-1980s there were still persons on the staff who conducted and published original research, notably Michaeleen Maher and James Matlock, though both were employed as librarians. Political infighting was particularly intense at the Society during that time, and Matlock and Maher were deemed unnecessary. Eventually, Patrice Keane, who had never published a scientific paper in a refereed journal, was promoted to position of Executive Director with a salary several times that which had been paid to the active researchers, and today the ASPR has no scientific research program.

The ASPR published the *Journal of the American Society for Psychical Research* continuously from 1907 to 1997. For year 1989 the total paid circulation was 1747.[28]

Funding

The funding sources for psychical research reflect the antistructural nature of psi. The greatest support for open (i.e., nonclassified) research has come from wealthy *individuals* such as James S. McDonnell, Thomas Welton Stanford, Charles Ozanne, Frances Bolton, Thomas Baker Slick, Jr., John E. Fetzer, George W. Church, Jr., W. Clement Stone, Arthur C. Twitchell, Jr., Marie Higbee, William Perry Bentley, James Kidd, Arthur Koestler, Chester F. Carlson, and Robert Bigelow. Overall, large philanthropic institutions have made comparatively modest contributions. Some of the people listed above established foundations to support parapsychology, but after their deaths, professional philanthropists took control, changed the focus of the foundations, and eliminated support for parapsychology. Unlike other areas of science, it is not institutions (e.g., corporations, government agencies, philanthropic foundations), but rather individuals, who have provided the primary financial backing for psychical research. This is simply another manifestation of anti-structure and the anti-institutional nature of psi.[29 30]

There is one important exception to the trend described above, and that is the government-sponsored work related to psychic spying. Between 1972 and 1995 a parapsychological research program was conducted at SRI International and then at Science Applications International Corporation (SAIC). The work was carried out within prestigious institutions, was government-supported for more than two decades, and produced successful psi experiments. News reports indicate that $20 million was spent during that period, and that made it by far the most heavily-financed research group in the history of parapsychology.[31 32]

Despite first-glance impressions, closer inspection shows that this program encountered the anti-structural tendencies found with other psi research organizations. First of all, the funding may sound substantial, and for parapsychology it was. The director of the program from 1985 until its close was physicist Edwin C. May. He told me that the SRI funding from 1972 to 1989 averaged $750,000 per year, but there were huge variations.[33] For extended periods they had no support at all, and the program often faced an uncertain future. The $750,000 figure should be put in perspective. In the 1980s my brother-in-law worked as a research chemist at a major chemical company. His personal budget for himself and one technician was on the order of $300,000 per year. Assuming rough equivalence, the SRI budget would support 2.5 scientists and 2.5 technicians a year.

The funding came from the U.S. government, primarily the CIA, DIA, and other intelligence agencies. Those are unquestionably heavily bureaucratized (i.e., structured). This seems to contradict my claim that funding for parapsychology is primarily from individuals; however, those agencies have important differences from other parts of government. They overtly deal in secrets, and they are the only part in which deception is formally institutionalized. Their support for parapsychological research far exceeded that of other agencies. This is yet another confirmation of the affinity of psi and deception, and it is altogether compatible with trickster theory.

The ultimate demise of the program is also instructive, and Ed May described it in a 1996 article in the *Journal of Parapsychology*.

Though the program successfully demonstrated psi, had well-satisfied clients, and had a number of supporters in the U.S. Congress, during its final years it could not find a sponsorship home within the intelligence community. Rather, the funding came from a Defense Appropriations bill passed by Congress. No intelligence agency wanted the program as part of its budget.

Eventually Congress asked the CIA to take over the program. But the CIA didn't want it, so they commissioned a study. They selected the American Institutes for Research (AIR) to prepare a report. It was released to the public in late 1995 and concluded that remote viewing was not useful for intelligence operations. It turned out that the president of AIR was one David Goslin, who had previously been the administrator in charge of an earlier study of parapsychology for the National Research Council (NRC). Serious charges of bias and unethical activity were raised against that report, and the charges were never answered.[34] The NRC administrators had requested an independent evaluation of parapsychology by the eminent Harvard psychologist Robert Rosenthal. When he returned with a positive assessment, they tried to get him to drop it. Rosenthal and his colleagues at Harvard were shocked, and he refused to go along with the cover-up. That didn't faze the NRC because when they issued their final report, they not only ignored Rosenthal's findings but didn't even mention them. This was a blatant suppression of data.[35] Goslin was thus an ideal choice for the CIA because he was well acquainted with the administrative tactics for keeping unwanted information out of reports, and assuring the conclusions desired by his sponsors.

It is clear that the CIA preordained the conclusion. But Ed May pointed out that they seemed to have very good reasons for not wanting the program, reasons that had nothing to do with the effectiveness of remote viewing. The SAIC program was linked with an operational remote-viewing team at Fort Meade, and that had been micromanaged by a staffer from the Senate Appropriations Committee. That resulted in very low morale, and everyone admitted the weaknesses in the operational program in its last years. May also noted that the CIA likely did not want to be saddled with a program that might cause it future embarrassment, because it had endured some recent public relations debacles with the exposure of Aldrich Ames, a CIA employee who sold U.S. secrets to foreign agents.

All this ultimately contributed to the demise of the program, and despite the good intentions of individuals in Congress and elsewhere, the bureaucracy finally ejected remote-viewing research.

Parapsychology Since 1970

The above overview of parapsychology covered more than a century, but a more focused inquiry is also illuminating. A review of the last 30 years shows many of the same anti-structural patterns. One of the reasons I wrote this book was to explain what happened to parapsychology, a field that seemed to have so much promise in the 1970s and 1980s.

To explain what transpired, I need to describe the social and cultural trends that affected the field. In order to make the task manageable, I will limit coverage to the United States, and my approach here will be rather impressionistic. I was employed professionally in parapsychology from 1981 to 1989, and I have some first-hand knowledge of activities behind the scenes. That is helpful for interpreting the field, but my biases undoubtedly creep in.

I am here specifically concerned with direct attempts to elicit the phenomena in the laboratory or observe them firsthand in the field such as in poltergeist and haunting investigations. There are other approaches to parapsychology; for instance, some conduct surveys of paranormal belief. Others investigate events after the fact, such as by interviewing people who have had near-death experiences or who claim to remember previous lives. The field also attracts quite a number of commentators, theorists, and philosophers. While those all make contributions, they keep the phenomena at a distance; interviewer-researchers and commentators do not directly engage them.

Unless one closely follows the research by reading the journals and attending professional conventions, one is unlikely to have any idea of the size and scope of the field of parapsychology. This is even true for most scientists and critics. John Wheeler, a Nobel laureate in physics, provided an amusing example. In 1979 he attacked the field in an emotional speech and urged the American Association for the Advancement of Science (AAAS) to withdraw the membership of the Parapsychological Association (PA). He estimated that there were as many as 200 workers in parapsychology, each being supported at $100,000 annually, for a total expenditure of perhaps as high as $20,000,000 per year.[36] Wheeler's attack revealed his complete ignorance of the field, including its size and level of funding. At a conference the year before, Charles Tart, a former president of the PA, had presented a survey of parapsychology research centers and found *total* research funding to be $552,000 annually.[37] The actual support was less than 3% of what Wheeler had guessed.

Wheeler's error is somewhat understandable given the media's massive attention to the paranormal. His ignorance is typical, and his vehement assault is important. The irrational antipathy coming from the very highest echelon of the scientific establishment deserves notice.

Parapsychology is tiny. To put it in context, it can be compared with the field of psychology, and Sybo Schouten, a Dutch researcher, presented some useful figures on the two. Drawing upon a survey done in 1983 and 1984, he reported that approximately 34,000 psychologists were employed in research activities in the U.S. (several times that many are involved in teaching, counseling, etc.). In contrast, for most of the past 100 years in parapsychology, there have been no more than 5 to 10 persons employed in full-time research at any one point.[38] The Parapsychological Association is the professional organization of the field, and in 1991 it had 251 members. In contrast, the 1991 membership of the American Psychological Association (APA) was 72,202. But these comparisons don't tell the entire story, because the vast majority of APA members are, or have worked as, full-time professionals in the field. They have extensive training in it and spent years of their lives pursuing advanced degrees from accredited institutions. This is not true for parapsychology, which has no degree-granting programs. Virtually all of its researchers are professionally trained in other disciplines. The level of institutionalization and bureaucratization of parapsychology is miniscule compared with other sciences, but the hostility it provokes is extraordinary.

The 1970s

The progress of parapsychology needs to be understood in the context of larger cultural forces. The 1960s and early 1970s are instructive. Those years were marked by social tumult. Civil rights and anti-war protests were frequent; the environmental movement was beginning, manned space flight was underway, and the sexual revolution was in full swing. The baby-boomers were coming of age. It was a time of idealism, particularly for those from the college-educated middle class in their late teens and early 20s. A counter-culture was thriving; that was a liminal phenomenon, and not surprisingly, it included a paranormal component. Those same years were ones of growth and innovation for parapsychology, but also ones of instability.

The 1970s had a wide general interest in the paranormal, even outside the counter-culture. Movies, TV programs, books, and adult education courses all reflected the popularity. The movie *The Exorcist*

(1973) did surprisingly well at the box office, and books such as *The Secret Life of Plants* (1973) and *Psychic Discoveries Behind the Iron Curtain* (1970) were bestsellers. Adult education programs had courses on witchcraft and psychic development. Interest in direct, overt use of psi was widespread; the CIA began funding research to develop psychic spies. *Psychic* magazine had begun in 1969, and it flourished in the 1970s. It was a popular bimonthly on slick paper, something of an upscale version of *Fate* magazine. It regularly carried interviews with parapsychologists and reported on their work. There were also several similar, more short-lived, newsstand periodicals. Uri Geller received enormous media attention for bending spoons and keys, and in 1976 CSICOP was founded.

In 1978 Tart identified 14 parapsychological research centers (13 of which responded to his questionnaire); this might seem promising until ones learns that half of them had budgets less than $17,000 per year. Some centers had only one researcher funded for full-time work, and many were staffed with volunteers or with workers paid exceptionally poorly (I knew people who made less than $300 per month for nearly full-time work). Some volunteered for months for free, and not surprisingly there was a high turnover of personnel.

In the 1970s, professors, their associates, and students were major contributors to the research effort. Some of the more notable included: John Bisaha at Mundelein College in Chicago, Charles Tart at the University of California at Davis, Robert Morris at the University of California at Irvine and, earlier in the decade, at Santa Barbara, Gertrude Schmeidler at the City College of New York, Douglas Dean at Newark College of Engineering, Ian Stevenson and J. G. Pratt at the University of Virginia in Charlottesville, Carroll Nash at St. Joseph's University in Philadelphia, Lendell Braud at Texas Southern University, Rex Stanford at St. John's University in New York, John Palmer at John F. Kennedy University in Orinda, California, Irvin Child at Yale. These professors and their students made substantial contributions to the literature. Some of the students, particularly those of Bisaha, Morris, Palmer, and Schmeidler continued to be active in the field and became leaders in it.

There were also several laboratories not affiliated with academic institutions. Some that employed full-time researchers were: the Foundation for Research on the Nature of Man (FRNM) and the Psychical Research Foundation (PRF) both of Durham, North Carolina, the American Society for Psychical Research (ASPR) in New York City, the Division of Parapsychology and Psychophysics at Maimonides

Medical Center in Brooklyn, New York, Stanford Research Institute in Menlo Park, California, and Mind Science Foundation in San Antonio, Texas.

A sizeable number of individuals and small informal groups also carried out research in a grass-roots effort. The quality varied enormously; much of it lacked controls or appropriate statistical analyses, but some of these independent efforts produced creditable studies.

New scholarly journals became available. In 1974 *Psychoenergetic Systems* was begun under the editorship of Stanley Krippner and was produced by Gordon and Breach, a major scientific publisher. In 1978, after breaking from CSICOP, Marcello Truzzi founded *Zetetic Scholar* to provide a forum for debate for both proponents and skeptics of the paranormal. *Parapsychology Review* started in 1970 as a means for parapsychologists to communicate with their colleagues as well as with an audience of interested laypersons who might not read the technical journals. This growth and diversity seemed propitious.

The 1970s were a time of innovation; many new experimental procedures and theoretical models were developed. Remote viewing, the ganzfeld technique, and electronic random number generators became widely used. The major theoretical work included: retroactive PK, task-complexity independence, observer effects, quantum mechanical theories, conformance behavior, and lability and inertia. These theoretical efforts remain crucial to understanding psi but are virtually unknown outside the field. They will be discussed in a later chapter.

Before 1970, when Rhine dominated the field, much research was directed at the psychic abilities of ordinary people. In the 1970s more effort was devoted to talented individuals. These included: Uri Geller, now the most famous, Lalsingh Harribance, Bill Delmore, Ingo Swann, Pat Price, Felicia Parise, Hella Hammid, Malcolm Bessent, Blue Harary, Alexander Tanous, Olga Worrall. With very few exceptions, researchers were extremely naive regarding trickery. Both Geller and Delmore later admitted to being adept at magic tricks, and research done with them had serious flaws.

The 1980s

The cultural tenor of the 1980s was decidedly different than that of the 1970s, and parapsychology felt it. In society, business success became more highly valued among the middle class baby-boomers. Less idealism was evident, and corporate and individual greed were frequent topics of pundits. The baby-boomers were sometimes referred to as the "Me Generation." The number of volunteer workers at parapsychology laboratories dwindled rapidly.

The 1980s saw a move away from popular interest in the paranormal in the larger society, and that was accompanied by a decided change within the New Age and psychic subcultures. Those who had previously been interested in psychic matters shifted their attention to more "spiritual" concerns that might be characterized as "a search for meaning." This was subtly foreshadowed when California-based *Psychic* magazine changed its name to *New Realities* in 1977. Channeling came in to vogue, but unlike spiritualism, there was little emphasis on verifiable information or physical phenomena. Channelers spouted "philosophy," made dire predictions of earth changes, and gave general advice, but that was about all. The number of books published on paranormal topics dropped precipitously between 1980 and 1982.[39] With the general shift away from psychism and toward the search for meaning, the books of Joseph Campbell became popular. There were new magazines, printed on high quality paper, catering to that general trend.

The beginning of the 1980s appeared extremely promising for parapsychology. The 1970s had produced a number of innovative lines of research. The field had attracted new researchers, greater attention, and more financial resources than ever before.

Academe seemed receptive. During the first years of the 1980s there were four laboratories affiliated with universities and staffed with full-time researchers. These included the Experiential Learning Laboratory in the Electrical Engineering department at Duke University, headed by psychologist Edward F. Kelly; the Communication Studies Laboratory in the School of Computer and Information Science at Syracuse University with psychologist Robert L. Morris; the McDonnell Laboratory for Psychical Research at Washington University, St. Louis, led by physicist Peter Phillips; and the Princeton Engineering Anomalies Research (PEAR) laboratory headed by Robert G. Jahn.

By 1986 only one remained. The Duke laboratory was unceremoniously closed. Robert Morris moved to Edinburgh, Scotland. The MacLab, which had focused primarily on macro-PK, met the most ignominious fate. It was a victim of James Randi's highly publicized Project Alpha and closed shortly thereafter.[40] Only the Princeton University lab stayed the decade. Robert Jahn was the dean of the School of Engineering and Applied Science at Princeton, and undoubtedly it was his personal clout and connections that kept the laboratory alive.

There was opposition to his work at Princeton, and Philip Anderson, a Nobel laureate in physics, was a particularly vocal detractor.

Professors at other schools continued to contribute, but the level of their efforts began to decline. Gertrude Schmeidler, Irvin Child, and Carroll Nash retired. Charles Tart, Rex Stanford, and Lendell Braud were not as active as they had been in the 1970s. John Palmer left John F. Kennedy University in Orinda, California, and it was generally agreed that after his departure the University did not attract the quality of students that it had in the 1970s, some of whom are still active in the field today. James Crandall at the University of Idaho conducted studies. Stanley Krippner at Saybrook Institute in San Francisco had a few graduate students with an interest in the field. Norman S. Don, Charles Warren, and Bruce McDonough at the University of Illinois at Chicago began carrying out research, but they had no students as collaborators. Student research dropped dramatically. Overall, professors had less prominence in the field than they did in the 1970s, and no one was taking the place of those who retired.

The laboratories dominated the decade. There were six labs active through the decade that employed two or more full-time researchers. Four of the laboratories were independent, and only two were affiliated with larger institutions, a subtle, continuing indication of the anti-structural nature of the field. Conferences and journals were heavily influenced, even dominated, by personnel from these laboratories. Experimental research was at center stage, and field studies and theoretical development played a minor role.

The following briefly describes the six major laboratories of the 1980s.

Mind Science Foundation (MSF), in San Antonio, Texas, was founded in 1957 by Thomas Baker Slick, Jr., a businessman with inherited wealth from oil.[41] During the 1980s William Braud, Helmut Schmidt, and Marilyn Schlitz were the most well known psi researchers affiliated with that foundation. Schmidt was the father of random number generator (RNG) research in parapsychology. Braud did extensive work on psi and biological organisms. Both were exceptionally innovative, and their work will be discussed in a later chapter. The parapsychology budget for MSF was on the order of $300,000 per year in the 1980s.[42] Despite the substantial contributions of the MSF researchers, in the early 1990s the Foundation shifted support away from parapsychology. Schmidt retired, and Braud and Schlitz moved to California.

Science Unlimited Research Foundation (SURF) was also in San Antonio, Texas. It was funded by George W. Church, Jr. of Church's Fried Chicken, a fast-food chain located in the southern part of the U.S. Gary Heseltine and Rick Berger were the best known researchers affiliated with SURF in the 1980s. Much of their work used electronic random number generators. The budget was approximately $100,000 per year.[43] This was the smallest of the six labs discussed here, and SURF was not exclusively devoted to parapsychology. Some of Heseltine's time was spent developing computer technology for people with disabilities.

Psychophysical Research Laboratories (PRL) was in Princeton, New Jersey, and I mentioned it briefly earlier. It was funded primarily by the James S. McDonnell Foundation. At its peak, the laboratory had seven full-time employees and annual expenditures of approximately $300,000. The main researchers included: Rick Berger, Pat Barker, Charles Honorton, Marta Quant, Ephraim Schechter, Mario Varvoglis, and myself. PRL was the leader in ESP ganzfeld research, and it also developed a standardized random number generator and testing package for Apple II computers.[44]

Princeton Engineering Anomalies Research (PEAR) laboratory is at Princeton University. Its best known researchers have been Angela Thompson, Brenda J. Dunne, York H. Dobyns, Roger D. Nelson, and Robert G. Jahn, who was dean of Princeton's School of Engineering and Applied Science. The laboratory is housed in a few small offices in the basement of the engineering building. A *New York Times Magazine* article reported that its 1989 budget was $250,000.[45] PEAR primarily focuses on PK effects on delicate physical systems. Its prestigious Princeton affiliation gives PEAR high public visibility, but within the field the poor quality of its remote-viewing research is notorious.[46]

The Foundation for Research on the Nature of Man (FRNM) in Durham, North Carolina was founded by J. B. Rhine, and in 1995, 15 years after his death, it changed its name to the Rhine Research Center. In the 1980s K. Ramakrishna Rao served as director. The major researchers during that period included John A. Palmer, H. Kanthamani, Richard S. Broughton, Debra H. Weiner, Shanti Krishna, James R. Perlstrom, and Nancy L. Zingrone. I was there in the early 1980s as a research fellow, as were Leonard George and Marilyn J. Schlitz. The primary research included testing of children in classroom situations, ganzfeld, and RNG studies. During the 1980s the FRNM's approximate annual expenditures ranged from $250,000 to $300,000.[47] The

Center also publishes the *Journal of Parapsychology*, which is included in its budget.

SRI International (formerly Stanford Research Institute) in Menlo Park, California had a parapsychology program that was headed by Hal Puthoff until 1985, at which point Edwin C. May took over. Russell Targ was there early in the decade. Other researchers included Nevin D. Lantz, Beverly S. Humphrey, G. Scott Hubbard, Wanda L. W. Luke, James P. Spottiswoode, Christine L. James, Larissa Vilenskaya, Dean Radin and Keith Harary. Much of the work was classified, but based on that which had been released, the focus was on remote viewing and RNG research. Its history, funding, and demise were discussed earlier.

At the peak, in the mid 1980s, these six laboratories probably employed no more than 25 to 30 full-time researchers. Four of the laboratories (PRL, MSF, SRI, PEAR) had facilities comparable to research centers for other sciences. The FRNM remained in an old house across from the Duke campus. SURF was in a converted warehouse in a commercial/industrial park.[48]

The 1980s provided the opportunity to build a more professional community. The quality of the research substantially improved in terms of methodology, peer review, sophistication of analysis, and controls against deception. Studies became more technically advanced. For instance, meta-analysis, a technique for evaluating groups of statistical studies, was introduced and widely used. The development and testing of electronic random number generators were taken to new levels. Theoretical issues received less attention than in the 1970s as more focus was placed on methodological improvements.

During the 1980s the field became more attuned to issues of deception, and researchers generally shifted away from high-profile special subjects who might bring taint of fraud. Researchers tested ordinary people with efforts aimed at improving replication rates of experiments. The period was marked by steadily improving methods and more stable infrastructure to support the research.

There were, however, drawbacks to the advances. The growing sophistication meant fewer people could follow the research and understand it. Reports and discussions grew increasingly technical, and they seemed distant from real-world concerns. This is not a problem in normal science where funding comes from institutions that call upon other scientists for evaluation and recommendations, but much of parapsychology's support came from wealthy individuals who were not scientists.

Around 1989 two of the laboratories (PRL, SURF) closed, and the SRI work was curtailed and then revived and moved to SAIC in 1991. Mind Science Foundation's parapsychology researchers left in 1992. Ed May resigned from SAIC in 1995 just before massive news coverage was given to the government's psychic spying program. Despite the publicity, funding was nowhere in sight to support his research.

The same general decline was also seen in the publications of the field. Truzzi's *Zetetic Scholar* stopped in 1987. *Psychoenergetic Systems* changed its name to *Psychoenergetics* in 1981 (Volume 4), and the last issue (Volume 6, No. 1) appeared in 1988 with yet another name, *Theoretical Parapsychology. Parapsychology Review* ceased in 1990. Even the circulation of the long-established *Journal of Parapsychology* declined from 1311 in 1979 to 904 in 1990.

Through the 1990s, only the Rhine Research Center and PEAR remained viable. Today in parapsychology there are probably fewer than 10 full-time researchers employed in the U.S. The decline is seen with other measures as well. In 1985, 51 papers were printed in the convention proceedings of the Parapsychological Association's annual convention, with 46 of them of U.S. origin. In 1996, there were 24 papers printed, but only 15 were from the U.S. The trend continues, and the PA membership steadily becomes older, grayer, and attracts few new researchers or observers.

Summary

The pattern of initial growth, internal discord, stagnation, and decay for any one organization, or even several, would not be unusual, but the pattern is universal in psi research. Many other groups and laboratories outside the U.S. could be given as illustrations. I know of *no* counter example. Those groups that attempt to scientifically study paranormal phenomena by directly engaging and interacting with them, tend toward disruption, encounters with fraud and trickery, and loss of institutional affiliation and support. The research activities have *never* produced the growth that a normal business or scientific discipline might expect. Further, none of the groups ever became fully ensconced within a larger organization; at best, affiliations were temporary and tenuous. Those that remained viable in research for a few decades were led by individuals with prestige and personal power, such as Gardner Murphy, J. B. Rhine, and Robert Jahn. After they depart, decline is inevitable.

This history is very curious given the intense public interest in psi and the high percentage of people who report paranormal experiences. The pattern suggests that large structured institutions are inimical to direct attempts to engage psi. The consequences for parapsychology are profound.

CHAPTER 17

Unbounded Conditions

Bigfoot sightings, cattle mutilations, and UFO flaps are some of the largest paranormal manifestations. With them, no clearly defined group of people is involved but rather participation is "unbounded." Any number of people can be witnesses; the phenomena occur over indefinite areas and for indeterminate periods of time. These are often exotic and confusing, and the conditions surrounding them are ill defined and unstructured. Examples of more structured occurrences include: séances held in predesignated rooms with known participants, ritual magic ceremonies that cast magic circles of protection with specified procedures, various cultures' rituals to propitiate spirits of the dead, and parapsychology's laboratory methods to constrain and designate the phenomena to be observed. In these examples the participants are known to each other, the locations and times of activities are clearly demarcated, and the beliefs, expectations, and paradigms are understood.

In unbounded cases, roles and identities of players may be ambiguous. For example, during major UFO flaps, reports of "men in black," visitations by government agents, and sightings of phantom helicopters are common, but their relationships to the original UFO sightings typically remain obscure. Strange characters emerge who may or may not be part of some orchestrated disinformation campaign, and hoaxers sometimes infiltrate research groups in order to make their plots more effective.

These unbounded situations are overlooked or avoided by most researchers, especially by those in laboratories, or with tenured academic positions, or with established reputations in respectable areas. Unbounded phenomena are messy; gathering reliable information is difficult, and trickster manifestations are acute. These factors conspire to discourage scientific investigation, despite the intriguing reports.

Another drawback to studying such phenomena is that they intrude into the personal lives of investigators. The full impact of this perhaps cannot be appreciated unless one has had direct experience. A couple examples may help illustrate the possibilities.

Ralph Steiner—A Case Study

In June 1992, Ralph Steiner, a journalist in the San Francisco Bay Area, began investigating "Sandy," a woman who claimed to have been abducted by ET aliens.[1] He was called into the case because he had been researching government-UFO connections, and there were reports of government harassment in this one. A few days after his initial interview with her, Sandy disappeared from home and later turned up in Las Vegas, Nevada. She claimed to have been kidnapped and drugged by government agents and was warned to keep quiet. She returned to California, and Steiner discovered that Sandy had been previously diagnosed with multiple personality disorder. Steiner readily admits that this was only one of several warning signs that he consciously chose to ignore. But the case was only beginning.

Events continued, and her husband and a friend of theirs corroborated Sandy's reports. Unmarked helicopters were seen. The three claimed long contact with the CIA and other government agencies; they all reported being harassed by government personnel, possibly a rogue group outside the law. Sandy believed that she was part ET and that the agents knew of her condition. Steiner came to suspect that her psychological problems were caused by a government project. At the time, quite a few other investigators across the country held similar suspicions about other cases.

As Steiner puts it, he was sucked into the "belief system vortex," and he now recognizes that he was in the grip of a paranoiac idea. Sandy established a strong emotional bond with him, and they would spend many hours on the phone. During those conversations, she displayed extraordinary telepathic abilities and was able to tell him exactly what he was doing, though she was more than 40 miles away. He began having odd sensations in his solar plexus. He encountered apparent PK when electronic equipment, which had previously worked well for years, began to malfunction inexplicably. There were problems with his phone, leading him to suspect that it was tapped. One of Steiner's colleagues had brief contact with Sandy and afterwards was visited at her place of work by a sinister figure who warned her away from the case. During the warning a helicopter ominously hovered low overhead. This confirmation, from another investigator, was compelling and unsettling.

About two months after Steiner began his investigation, Sandy called him frantically, saying that she had been taken aboard a space ship and that the aliens had removed the outer covering of her eyes. This was physical evidence, and Steiner immediately summoned a cab to bring her to his home. When she arrived, she was wearing sunglasses, and when she took them off, Steiner saw that her eyes were almost completely black. For the next few days, Sandy stayed at the homes of Steiner's friends and associates, and she sat for a number of sessions where her eyes were photographed close up. Analysis showed that Sandy was wearing very large black contact lenses.

Steiner's friends locked him in a room and confronted him with the facts, and he slowly began to examine them realistically. His capacity to rationally assess the case had slipped his grasp, and he did not regain it overnight. With the help of his friends he did, and he now realizes that in less than two months he came very close to losing his job, his journalistic reputation, his marriage and family, and his entire career. It is remarkable that Steiner had the ability to look back and write about the events with such clarity. He made an exceptional contribution in doing so.

If Sandy was the sole hoaxer, the case would not have been particularly noteworthy, but at least two other people were involved. There are still unexplained aspects to the hoax, and the motive remains opaque. Steiner now believes that this elaborate charade was orchestrated to discredit researchers, sow dissention, and kill the credibility of genuine cases. The perpetrators remain a mystery.

Salient aspects of the case include: elaborate deception, a nearly catastrophic loss of status, strong psi functioning, and great difficulty discerning illusion from reality. These formed a powerful trickster constellation and reinforced conspiratorial ideas. In passing I should mention that the helicopter-trickster connection was previously recognized by Dennis Stillings in a 1988 article entitled "Helicopters, UFOs, and the Psyche."

John Keel and the Mothman

The Steiner case seems surreal, but it is not unique. A quarter century earlier John Keel encountered similar events. Keel (born Alva John Kiehle, 1930-) is an unusual character who has some affinity with the trickster. Though primarily a writer, he is also a magician and is listed in *Who's Who in Magic*.[2] As a teenager he edited a periodical called *The Jester*.[3] While in his twenties he traveled around the world investigating the odd and unusual, including magicians, monks, the Indian rope trick, and reports of levitations, all of which were recounted in his book *Jadoo* (1957); more recently he has written a column for *Fate* magazine. His taste for the bizarre never left, and as a journalist and author he chronicled innumerable odd paranormal events that the vast majority of other investigators chose to ignore because they did not fit into the accepted categories.

Keel has lived much of his adult life in New York City. He knows magicians, media people, and a wide swath of various paranormal subcultures in and around that area. He was a frequent guest on the Long John Nebel radio show, and he took part in research conducted by Karlis Osis at the Parapsychology Foundation in the 1950s.[4] Keel was primarily a free-lance writer. Despite the massive popular interest in the paranormal topics he covered, there was not enough work in that to keep him employed over the years; so he also wrote for photography and electronics magazines, among others. He was never a long-time employee of a large corporation.

In the late 1980s and early 1990s, Keel ran the New York Fortean Society (NYFS). The group was named after Charles Hoy Fort (1874-1932), who compiled books of odd facts (e.g., fish falling from the air) and provided preposterous, tongue-in-cheek explanations for them, thereby annoying some scientists. Fortean "organizations" are some of the most anti-structural of any in the paranormal subculture, and the NYFS fit this pattern. It was very loosely run, and the bulk of the work fell on Keel's shoulders. It published only a few issues of a newsletter and sponsored irregularly scheduled lectures. These were held in a room rented in a run-down building in Manhattan and attracted a small but diverse audience. After adjournment the participants would move to a deli down the street, where some of the NYFS members bought something to eat and others brought their own food to consume on the premises. One of my friends described the NYFS as the cheapest bunch of guys she ever met. I attended regularly.

In 1966 and 1967 Keel kept busy investigating UFO activity in West Virginia and on New York's Long Island. His book *The Mothman Prophecies* (1975) tells of that time in his life, and it effectively conveys the surreal nature of unbounded paranormal phenomena. Point Pleasant, West Virginia was then a center of activity with sightings of UFOs and also of a bizarre, winged monster with red eyes, dubbed the mothman. Keel began interviewing people in the area and staking out locations where there had been sightings. Soon unknown individuals began impersonating him; his phone was bugged and had other problems, and during his day-to-day activities an extremely odd, emaciated person appeared in his vicinity. It seemed like he was being monitored. It was difficult for him to tell fantasy from reality, and he readily admits that he was concerned about his mental stability during his investigation. *The Mothman Prophecies* is disturbing, and two researchers in the paranormal, one eminent in parapsychology, the other a nuts-and-bolts ufologist, independently described it to me as the scariest book they ever read.

Keel spoke frequently with UFO contactees who reported receiving mental messages from flying saucers. Much of the time they made no sense, but sometimes the messages seemed telepathic. Keel would think of a question, and immediately one of his stable of contactees would call him on the phone with the answer; at other times they seemed precognitive and predicted what would happen to him. The contactees began prophesying a large power blackout for December 15. A number of their other predictions failed to occur, but this was persistent. The blackout didn't happen, but on that date a bridge at Point Pleasant collapsed at rush hour and killed more than 30 people. Keel had known some of the victims, and the entire string of events shook him. He saw much of it as evil. It wasn't until years later that he wrote the book, and only with the prodding of an editor.[5]

Keel is one of few who recognized that UFO sightings should not be studied as discrete events in isolation and that their effects are not limited to a circumscribed time and place. The consequences could extend for weeks or months and be profoundly destabilizing to the personal lives of those who become enmeshed in the phenomena. Some who had impressive sightings later experienced other paranormal activity such as poltergeist occurrences. When the paranormal events continued, neighbors, friends, and the media learned of it. Stresses built and the victims and their family became "tainted," looked upon as odd, different, even somewhat dangerous. Keel noticed that marital break-ups were frequent in the situations. Some experiencers displayed a decided tendency to paranoia, and Keel even entitled one of his chapters "Paranoiacs Are Made, Not Born." He was perceptive enough to recognize the same tendencies within himself.

Keel concluded that the battle cry of the phenomena must be: "Make him look like a nut!"[6] He saw the phenomena marginalize experiencers, who became irrational, made wild claims, and whose lives were left in shambles. These were trickster manifestations. Keel suggested that others should be discouraged from pursuing the phenomena because of the irrationality they induce. He went so far to say that "the CIA/air force plan to debunk, downgrade, and ridicule flying saucers was, in retrospect, the most responsible course the government could take."[7] In essence, he urged further rationalization and disenchantment of the world (in Max Weber's senses of the terms).

The experiences of Steiner and Keel are instructive. Both investigated events under unbounded conditions and became entangled in the phenomena of their study. They recognized the difficulty of remaining objective. Both reported strong telepathic occurrences. Both had problems with their phones. Both became paranoid and concerned about their own mental health. Neither was employed by a research organization geared to study such events. They operated with little institutional support.

Frameworks

Strong supernatural manifestations are frequently disorienting. There is a natural tendency to put the phenomena into some kind of framework, to reduce ambiguity, to understand them, and establish their limits. One of two classes of interpretations is often adopted. The phenomena are either believed to be of a religious or otherwordly nature (e.g., caused by spirits, demons, gods, or ETs), or they are attributed to a human conspiracy.

The first class of interpretations explains communications of trance mediums as from spirits of the dead, credits UFO experiences to ET aliens in "nuts and bolts" spacecraft, or ascribes poltergeist effects to unconscious minds. ETs, spirits, demons, and the unconscious have common properties, and such attributions create frameworks that socially construct reality and make it easier to speak about anomalous events. For instance, I have been in a number of UFO groups discussing ETs, and if one simply replaced the word "extraterrestrial" with "spirit" one could carry on virtually identical conversations with spiritualists.

The second class of explanations, conspiracy theories, is closely related. There are real similarities between religious and conspiratorial beliefs, and in fact, philosopher Sir Karl Popper commented that conspiracy theorizing "comes from abandoning God and then asking: 'Who is in his place?'"[8] He noted that rationalists are particularly prone to it.

Both religious and conspiracy theories put the phenomena in frameworks, and some structure and limitation are thereby imposed. Action can be taken. Gods can be propitiated, dangerous humans avoided. Outsiders may see such beliefs as paranoid or as a crackpot religion, but it is not unreasonable to adopt such perspectives when confronted with strong manifestations of autonomous intelligent power.

It can be difficult to differentiate synchronicities and other psychic phenomena from those due to a conspiracy. A minor experience of my own may illustrate the idea. In the Fall of 1989 I was asked to comment on an early version of "The Controllers," a manuscript by Martin Cannon on government mind control that went on to become something of an underground classic in some ufology circles. Within a few days of beginning my written commentary, I was called by a hospital in New York City and asked if I would take part in an experiment. They wanted to inject me with sodium pentothal and monitor my brain waves. This was startling because I had not before, or since, been asked to take part in anything remotely similar. I did not really suspect that was part of some conspiracy to monitor my activity, but I was taken aback.

Psi phenomena, including synchronicities, are somewhat "ideoplastic," that is, they respond to, and are shaped by, the ideas, beliefs, and anxieties of the observers—a fact demonstrated in both laboratory and field studies. The phenomena also display a measure of independent intelligence. This is unlike most natural sciences, which deal primarily with nonconscious entities. When an investigator studies something that can be intentionally deceitful, and has intelligence-gathering capabilities of its own, the usual paradigms of science are inadequate. New frameworks and perspectives are needed. Indeed, in some circumstances, science may not be useful; rather, approaches taken from the field of intelligence may be more appropriate. UFO researcher Jacques Vallee made this point in his book *Messengers of Deception* (1979).

Paranoia is an occupational hazard of paranormal investigation, and there is an affinity between conspiracy theories and the occult.[9] This occurs in many contexts. I have known witchcraft groups that engaged in magical battles and cast spells against others, fearing themselves to be under magical attack. I have heard rumors of psychotronics practitioners directing death rays against rivals (psychotronics mixes electronics and occultism). The level of paranoid conspiracy theorizing is even greater in the unbounded paranormal areas such as crop circles,[10] cattle mutilations,[11] and ufology.[12] Some of the rumors in the UFO field during the 1980s and early 1990s described sinister government treaties with ET aliens that allowed biological experimentation on citizens; others told of underground alien bases. Government personnel spread a number of these stories, as will be described in the next chapter. There was serious speculation that President John F. Kennedy was killed because he was about to reveal the truth of the ETs.[13] The dynamics of these beliefs are similar to those of witchcraft and sorcery accusations extensively documented by anthropologists in other cultures.[14]

Paranoia and conspiracy theories subvert established structures, and they thrive when there is disorder and uncertainty about the established system's viability. Paranoia is directly related to anti-structure and liminality, and a future chapter will be devoted to that nexus. Paranoia and conspiracy theorizing cannot be reduced to just psychological explanations; they fundamentally involve more than that.

Summary

Paranormal phenomena associated with unbounded conditions inherently lack clear limits, constraints, and boundaries, and hence they are particularly hospitable to the trickster. They display an extraordinary richness of surreal qualities. They blend fantasy and reality. They are almost universally ignored by those in the establishment. The task of studying unbounded paranormal phenomena falls to a small number of independent researchers—another symptom of the phenomena's anti-structural nature.

These phenomena intrude into the lives of investigators. The researchers participate in them and cannot remain on the side as observers. The subject-object distinction is subverted, and the consequences are often unpleasant.

Status is an important concept here. The phenomena induce marginality in those that become enmeshed in them. Researchers who seriously study the phenomena are tainted and suffer a loss of prestige. Further, trying to describe the phenomena with the most obvious frameworks, i.e., religious beliefs and conspiracy theories, tend to make one appear odd.

The phenomena are almost incomprehensible to the modern rationalistic mind, but people in earlier cultures understood them. The primitives grasped the ideas of "participation" and the contagion of taboo violation. These concepts illuminate unbounded paranormal phenomena far better than scientific theories accepted today.

CHAPTER 18

Government Disinformation

> If I put you over at Justice, I want you to find the answers to two questions for me. One, Who killed JFK? And two, Are there UFOs?
> President Bill Clinton to Webb Hubbell[1]

The epigraph above exemplifies the UFO problem today. What does the government know? Who can be trusted to reveal it? Even the president seems puzzled. But is the epigraph from a real conversation? Hubbell was a friend of the president and later pleaded guilty to bilking clients and served time in prison. Can he be believed here? Or was he just telling a story to help sell his book? These are exactly the kinds of questions found throughout the UFO field. Ambiguity, disreputable claimants, paranoia, and distrust of authority permeate ufology. Even the association with the Kennedy assassination is not uncommon.

One reason I prepared this chapter is that mainstream journalists and academics ignore the role that government disinformation has played in fostering belief in UFOs, aliens visiting earth, and official cover-ups. Those beliefs are held by rational, thinking people who have spent much time investigating them. I am not the only one to recognize the importance of disinformation for that. So has James Oberg, a founding member of CSICOP and a consulting editor for *Skeptical Inquirer*, and he is one of the trio of CSICOP's primary UFO debunkers (the others being Philip J. Klass and Robert Sheaffer). Oberg is also a NASA scientist and a leading expert on Soviet space affairs, and as such he undoubtedly has wide contacts in the intelligence world. In an open letter regarding government disinformation activities, Oberg wrote: "from my own experience, they seem to have played a tremendous role in inciting and enflaming public interest in UFOs."[2] It is truly remarkable how widely this factor is ignored.

On the other hand, the widespread belief cannot be accounted for only by deceptive practices of the government. The situation is much too complicated to be explained by that alone. Yet there *is* considerable government activity. Intelligence agents really are involved with the paranormal. Secrecy and paranoia surround them. Many of the same shadowy figures are connected with parapsychology, ufology, and even cattle mutilations, but the statuses of those individuals are often unclear. Are they who they claim? Do they really work for some intelligence agency? If so, are they acting in an official capacity? There are disturbing, even ominous, signs of illicit activities.

I want to make it clear that I am not proposing the existence of a massive orchestrated government conspiracy. The government is not monolithic; many parts operate independently and even at cross-purposes. But groups and individuals associated with various agencies have been deceitful on the paranormal. It is often unclear whether they were acting in an official capacity.

There is always a middle ground between official policy and individuals' activity. No organization operates with only explicit policies, stated rules, and distinct chains of command. Established codes and regulations cannot cover all situations. Individuals may take advantage of that for their own purposes. Additionally, some official goals must be kept hidden. At times, direct orders may not be forthcoming, but hints are given as to what needs to be done.

All this promotes ambiguity and uncertainty and is congenial to the trickster. The field of intelligence is particularly hospitable because it is one of institutionalized deception. When its operatives dabble in the paranormal, they ipso facto strengthen the trickster constellation.

Of all paranormal areas, disinformation is most prevalent in ufology, and UFO phenomena have an incredible number of liminal and trickster properties. Several will be introduced in this chapter, and the next one will address more. Ufology is a marginal field. Deception, ambiguity, paranoia, and conspiracy theorizing are its salient features. Boundary blurring is pervasive. Fact and fiction are mixed. Liars are prominent. Statuses of operatives are often unclear.

There is an added complexity: government UFO activities are mixed with remote viewing and cattle mutilations.[3] Several paranormal phenomena are blended, and that makes the situation of special interest for this book.[4] But the mix is repulsive for those in the establishment. The marginality and disreputability are amplified, making the situations unpleasant to investigate for mainstream scientists and journalists.

Anti-structure assures that no stable, recognized institutions study all these topics and identify reliable information. Researchers must spend much time evaluating the reliability of sources because qualified authorities are difficult to identify. Investigators are often fooled by glib claimants and hucksters who only seem to be credible.

Countless trickster manifestations are found in government disinformation activities. They provide concrete examples of some central issues of this book. However those wishing a clear, unambiguous view will be disappointed. Emphasis in this chapter is on obscurity, rather than lucidity; on messes, rather than order; on confusion, rather than clarity. Uncertainties are seen in motives, roles, purposes, statuses, identities, etc. UFO research requires a high tolerance for ambiguity if one is not to succumb to premature conclusions, or paranoia.

The limits of science and knowledge quickly become apparent when one investigates intelligence agencies. Full answers are impossible to obtain, and when they are offered, the agencies have such a long history of lying that they cannot be trusted. The full story of many cases cannot be known, and any comprehensive picture must include this inherent ambiguity.

Many examples of government UFO involvement are available, but I will focus on relatively recent ones that have substantial documentation. As I will show, government agencies have promoted mythological beliefs, but the consequences are rarely recognized. They are not always healthy for the larger society.

Historical Comment

Intelligence agencies' interest in UFOs is not a recent development, and this is superbly documented in the book *Clear Intent: The Government Coverup of the UFO Experience* (1984) by Lawrence Fawcett and Barry J. Greenwood. The authors were leading members of Citizens Against UFO Secrecy (CAUS), a group that waged a long legal battle for release of documents on UFOs using the Freedom of Information Act (FOIA). Greenwood edited their newsletter *Just Cause*. Fawcett and Greenwood are among the most reliable researchers in ufology, but they have not attracted much media attention, and they are not even especially well known to casual followers of UFO research.

Clear Intent describes the CIA involvement with the National Investigations Committee on Aerial Phenomena (NICAP), a civilian organization begun in the 1950s that went on to become the largest UFO group of its time. Roscoe Hillenkoetter, the first director of the

CIA, served on the Board of Governors of the organization, and he was by no means the only CIA employee in it. There were many others. Fawcett and Greenwood report that "CAUS uncovered a number of disturbing bits of evidence relating to NICAP that should cause other UFO groups considerable concern."[5] They then proceed through a litany of CIA personnel involved in NICAP from its inception until its demise. They explain how those people controlled the organization in the 1960s and 1970s, and when Donald Keyhoe started pressing the government for public disclosure, he was ousted as Director in a cabal led by Joseph Bryan, former Chief of the CIA's Psychological Warfare Staff. After that NICAP became less active and more inept scientifically; it slowly disintegrated and finally went out of business.[6] The evidence for deliberate malfeasance is only circumstantial, and it is possible that the culmination of the leadership's ineptness just happened to follow Keyhoe's political activism. Fawcett and Greenwood admit that the connection is speculative, but there is plenty reason for suspicion.

Undoubtedly the CIA had a legitimate interest in NICAP, if only because of Hillenkoetter's involvement. His membership must have attracted the KGB's attention. That in turn would make NICAP, and the UFO subculture generally, of interest to U.S. intelligence agencies and to the FBI. In fact, Fawcett and Greenwood even report that "NICAP received several overtures from the Soviet KGB."[7]

In 1997 Gerald K. Haines, a historian at the National Reconnaissance Office, published an article entitled "A Die-Hard Issue: The CIA's Role in the Study of UFOs, 1947-90." It appeared in *Studies In Intelligence*, a journal produced by the CIA for the U.S. intelligence community, and the article was posted on the Internet.

Haines admitted that the CIA had an interest in UFOs for many years and also had a policy of denying that interest. In 1952 the CIA sponsored a panel headed by H. P. Robertson, a physicist from California Institute of Technology. The panel expressed concern that a surge of UFO reports could clog channels of communication and that it might also lead to hysterical behavior. It "recommended that the National Security Council debunk UFO reports and institute a policy of public education to reassure the public of the lack of evidence behind UFOs . . . the panel also recommended that such private UFO groups as the Civilian Flying Saucer Investigators in Los Angeles and the Aerial Phenomena Research Organization in Wisconsin be monitored for subversive activities."[8] This is revealing, for it shows that ufologists' paranoia about the government had a basis in reality.

Haines readily acknowledged that the CIA withheld information and misled people about that, but he had little to say about any active disinformation programs. He admitted that in the 1950s and 1960s the Air Force made "misleading and deceptive statements to the public in order to allay public fears and protect an extraordinarily sensitive national security project [the U-2]."[9] When he discussed more recent activities, Haines was not as forthcoming. He carefully avoided mentioning Fawcett, Greenwood, *Clear Intent*, or CAUS. On the other hand, he gave four citations to William L. Moore, who will be discussed shortly. Moore is a self-admitted liar who claimed to be an informant for the government. Haines gave no hint of Moore's unreliability. Although in ufology it is common to cite Moore's work without caveats, in any other field such practices would themselves be considered dishonest. One may surmise that Haines was not completely candid, and some may suspect him of deliberately spreading misinformation.

Haines alluded to some intriguing projects. For instance, he stated that "The CIA reportedly is also a member of an Incident Response Team to investigate UFO landings."[10] Here Haines seems to admit that he didn't have full access to the CIA activities regarding UFOs. Why else would he use the word "reportedly?" He went on to comment that "The lack of solid CIA documentation on Agency UFO-related activities in the 1980s leaves the entire issue somewhat murky for this period."[11] This is a direct acknowledgement that he did not have access to all relevant information.

Haines made another startling admission. He wrote that "During the late 1970s and 1980s . . . some in the Agency and in the Intelligence Community shifted their interest to studying parapsychology and psychic phenomena associated with UFO sightings."[12] He also reported that "There is a DIA Psychic Center and the NSA studies parapsychology."[13] These statements confirm the government interest in the link between UFOs and parapsychology, but Haines said nothing more about it.

Rumors Of ET Aliens

Rumors allege that ET aliens have landed on earth and are held captive by, or are in league with, the government. There are innumerable variants of the story, some exceedingly bizarre. For many years, the rumors were considered completely fringe, but in the 1990s they gained mainstream attention. The establishment media did not completely sneer at them, and for a while they were given some respectable coverage on major network TV shows. The motifs also appeared in popular culture, with captured aliens featured in science fiction movies and elsewhere (e.g., the 1996 movie *Independence Day* grossed over $300 million).[14] A centerpiece of the stories was the now-infamous Roswell incident, and the popular fascination with UFOs in the 1990s cannot be understood without some familiarity with it.

On July 8, 1947, the Army Air Forces base near Roswell, New Mexico released a statement saying that it had captured a crashed flying disk. The story appeared in a number of newspapers, but it was quickly retracted, and instead it was claimed that the object actually was a misidentified weather balloon. Today, proponents, skeptics, and even the Air Force agree that this second explanation was a fabrication and that something else crashed near Roswell. There is no consensus on what it was, but from the currently available evidence, the most likely candidate is a downed balloon from the then-classified Project Mogul. Robert G. Todd, probably the most capable researcher on the case, was the first to suggest this, and he uncovered a variety of information to support that idea.[15] The Mogul hypothesis received additional support from a 1995 report issued by the Air Force.

After the fabricated cover story was released, the incident seemed to be forgotten. But in 1950 Frank Scully, a writer for the entertainment industry's *Variety* magazine, published *Behind the Flying Saucers*. He claimed that the government had discovered a crashed saucer with dead aliens in New Mexico. It was later revealed that two of Scully's primary informants, Silas Newton and Leo GeBauer, were veteran confidence artists, and after that exposure, the stories of crashed saucers largely disappeared from public view, though they circulated among a fringe of UFO buffs. Then in 1980, Charles Berlitz and William L. Moore revived the story with their book *The Roswell Incident*. These two writers had previously collaborated on an ostensibly nonfiction, but non-credible, book about the U.S. Navy making a ship disappear and inadvertently sending sailors into some other dimension.

In December 1984, Moore's close collaborator, Jaime Shandera, received a roll of undeveloped film. Processing showed photos of the now-notorious "MJ-12" documents, which discussed a purported crashed saucer in possession of the government. The "12" of MJ-12 referred to 12 highly placed, now-deceased individuals charged with managing the cover-up. There is overwhelming evidence that the MJ-12 documents were hoaxed, and in 1989 Moore publicly admitted to lying about some of his UFO activities.[16] He is widely suspected of forging the documents, and his admission of deceit didn't enhance his credibility. On the other hand, it didn't diminish interest in Roswell; if anything, it stimulated it.

The debate over MJ-12 consumed a massive amount of the time of UFO researchers.[17] It was a major component of the conspiracy theories surrounding the Roswell case. If a crashed saucer had been retrieved, and the public was not informed, there must have been an intense scientific effort to study it and keep the findings secret. A high-level group of scientists, engineers, and military personnel would have been formed to manage the project. MJ-12, or similar group by any other name, became a centerpiece of theorizing by ufologists. It established a governing paradigm for many researchers. They gathered snippets of evidence and tried fitting them into this framework, and indeed, a cover-up of a crashed saucer seemed to explain many events as well as the obvious disinformation spread by government agents.

In the late 1980s the J. Allen Hynek Center for UFO Studies (CUFOS) began supporting the work of Kevin D. Randle and Donald R. Schmitt on Roswell. The two produced books and numerous articles, but in 1995 a reporter for a Milwaukee magazine discovered that Schmitt, the CUFOS Director of Special Investigations, had extensively lied about his background. Some months later, after checking, Randle publicly repudiated all Schmitt's work.[18]

The above mentioned individuals (GeBauer, Newton, Moore, Schmitt) are not minor players in the Roswell drama, but rather *the* most prominent promoters of the case. However, they are by no means the only ones with dubious credibility, and there are a number of entertaining stories of "witnesses" who came forward but were later shown to be liars. The affair exposed the extraordinary gullibility of many UFO investigators.

The Roswell saga began with a lie by the government, and over a period of half a century it was boosted by con artists and dishonest researchers to become the most celebrated of all UFO cases. In the 1990s it generated countless articles, several books, TV programs, and even full-length movies. Three museums opened in the Roswell area to capitalize on the publicity. A General Accounting Office inquiry was carried out at the request of New Mexico Congressman Steven Schiff. All this activity culminated in a massive celebration on the July 4th weekend of 1997, the fiftieth anniversary of the supposed crash. In short, the Roswell incident received more sustained media attention than any other UFO case in history.

The above review might suggest that the Roswell affair and attendant publicity can be chalked up to a phony cover story, dishonest writers, con artists, and general gullibility. However, the matter is not nearly so simple. The stories from government personnel did not stop in 1947; they continue, and the ambiguity only grows.

The U.S. Air Force Office of Special Investigations (AFOSI) is a major source for reports of government involvement with aliens. Their Special Agent, Richard C. Doty, was, and is, particularly active. The AFOSI has the task of conducting criminal investigations and counterintelligence operations. It is remarkably successful in avoiding public examination of its own activities.

Rick Doty's saga is long and convoluted. Through the 1980s he was briefly mentioned in the UFO literature, but by 1989 the focus had intensified. That year several researchers made revelations. Particularly important were Linda Moulton Howe's book *An Alien Harvest*, Robert Hastings' exposé of William L. Moore, Moore's subsequent confession, and a one-page report by Philip J. Klass.

Richard C. Doty and William L. Moore (coauthor of *The Roswell Incident*) are intimately tied to Roswell and the MJ-12 papers. Doty's activities must be considered in conjunction with those of Moore. In June 1989, researcher Robert Hastings published an exposé of William L. Moore in the *MUFON UFO Journal*. It contained some devastating findings. Hastings reported that Moore had posed as a government agent during his interactions with Lee Graham, a researcher who has had a long-time interest in UFOs and in experimental aircraft. Graham is known for his openness and integrity, and he has voluntarily provided colleagues of mine with massive amounts of documents to support his statements. Graham has filed many FOIA requests and has had extensive dealings with government personnel about them. Moore visited Graham, became friendly with him, and showed him an identification card that appeared identical to those of the Defense Investigative Service (DIS), an agency quite familiar to Graham. Graham even wrote a letter to the DIS inquiring about Moore, and Hastings reproduced it in his report.

Hastings also discussed a questionable MJ-12 document that had been circulating in the UFO community. The AFOSI had declared it a forgery, and Hastings found confirmation of that conclusion. He reproduced a letter from Richard Hall who had asked Moore directly about the document, and Moore admitted that he had retyped it and done a cut-and-paste job on it. Of course there was no legitimate need for him to have done that, and it further eroded his credibility.

In short, Moore had impersonated a federal agent, and he had forged at least one government document. Yet he was one of the most prominent people in the UFO field.

Shortly following Hastings' exposé, the annual MUFON symposium was held, and Moore made a presentation that must rate as one of the most fantastic in the history of those conventions. Moore claimed to be an informant for the government and admitted to intentionally misleading UFO researchers. His story is amazing. He alleged that in September 1980 someone in the intelligence community approached him claiming to speak for a small group dissatisfied with the government's cover-up policy on UFOs. They wanted to help Moore. In the bargain Moore was to provide information on the Aerial Phenomena Research Organization (APRO) and other UFO researchers. Moore agreed to this, expecting to learn more about the government program. Richard Doty was to serve as liaison with Moore.

Paul Bennewitz was one of the UFO researchers Moore was asked to spy on. Bennewitz was a physicist and president of Thunder Scientific Corporation, a manufacturer of humidity measuring devices in Albuquerque, New Mexico. He was an enthusiastic UFO buff and prone to leap to conclusions on that topic, and he may have been a bit psychologically unstable. He had taken pictures and movie footage of UFOs over Manzano Weapons Storage Area where nuclear weapons were kept. Using his computer and electronics skills, Bennewitz also detected some unusual electromagnetic signals seemingly from that area, and he concluded that all these were due to alien technology. He was not shy in telling people about it; in fact he contacted Kirtland AFB and informed them.

Bennewitz was interviewed by Richard Doty and Jerald D. Miller, an investigator for the Air Force's former Project Blue Book (that project was devoted to UFOs; it closed in 1969). He was subsequently invited to Kirtland AFB to make a presentation of his findings to several high-ranking officers. Further, security patrols had sighted UFOs in the general area, around the time Bennewitz took his photos, according to a document obtained by Fawcett and Greenwood through the FOIA. The document indicated that the information about the sightings came from Major Ernest Edwards, but it was signed by Richard Doty.[19]

Bennewitz's activities may have alarmed someone, because Moore alleged that an intense disinformation campaign was waged against him. Moore became friendly with Bennewitz to observe the operation. He asserted that Bennewitz was fed with bogus information and was put under surveillance, including wiretaps. As he grew paranoid and more unstable, Moore reported back on the progress of Bennewitz's psychological deterioration. Bennewitz told people that aliens were coming through walls and injecting him with chemicals, and eventually he was hospitalized for psychiatric care.

Moore's confession caused an uproar. At the end of his talk, he did not take questions from the audience but rather answered queries he had prepared himself. One asked if he had ever been on the payroll of the U.S. Government, and he denied it.[20] Another asked if he had shown Lee Graham a fake ID, and he did *not* deny that.

Moore's confession didn't diminish belief in a cover-up, but rather stimulated it. His claims were further evidence of a grand government scheme that was starting to crack open. The controversies over MJ-12 and Roswell heated up.

Don Ecker of *UFO* magazine continued the investigation into Moore's mysterious connections. In a 1992 article he reported that Moore admitted that he was still a "controlled informant." Ecker's investigation led to even more interesting links, and he identified one key player in the drama as C. B. Scott Jones, whose activities will be described below.[21] Shortly after Ecker's article appeared, a white paper was released by Robert J. Durant which detailed many of Jones' connections and showed that Moore had developed contacts among government intelligence operatives dealing with UFOs, as well as in the parapsychology area.[22]

Moore's clearest, undisputed tie to the intelligence world is Richard C. Doty. Moore's credibility is poor, but we need not depend on him for information on Doty. Linda Moulton Howe's *An Alien Harvest* (1989) has a detailed description of her interaction with Doty.

In the 1970s Howe was a reporter on environmental issues in Colorado, and in 1979 she began researching animal mutilations for a documentary film. In the course of her investigation, UFO stories began trickling to her, and after her program was aired in May 1980, that turned into a flood. She has since become a prominent figure in ufology and has shown incredible energy, tenacity, and dedication in spreading her findings. Her public presentations, and her networking behind the scenes, have been major factors in publicizing the allegations of government cover-ups of the ET aliens. Her integrity is above reproach, but even her friends sometimes become exasperated at her for uncritically accepting information from government personnel.

In 1983 Howe began work on a UFO documentary for television company HBO. She heard that Doty had some information on a 1977 case at Ellsworth Air Force Base in South Dakota, and she flew to Albuquerque to talk with him on April 9, 1983. Due to some apparent miscommunication, he did not meet her as promised; so she contacted Jerald D. Miller, Doty's colleague who had been with Project Blue Book. Finally Howe connected with Doty who took her to an office on Kirtland AFB for their meeting. It began by Doty telling her: "You know you upset some people in Washington with your film *A Strange Harvest* [on cattle mutilations]. It came too close to something we don't want the public to know about."[23]

After some discussion of the Ellsworth case, Doty pulled out an envelope, opened it, and handed Howe several sheets. He told her that she could read them but not take notes. The top page was titled "Briefing Paper for the President of the United States of America." The documents catalogued a number of crashed disks found in the southwest part of the U.S. Bodies had been retrieved, and in one crash an alien had survived and lived in captivity until 1952. The documents went on to describe attempts to fly one of the alien craft. It was also stated that the aliens were able to manipulate human DNA.

Doty led Howe to believe that their meeting was part of a government program to slowly release information to the public and that she was to play a role in it. He promised her film footage for her documentary. Howe informed the executives at HBO, and they were excited by the prospect. But when the promised footage didn't arrive, the entire project was cancelled, which may have been the AFOSI goal all along. The purpose of this is unclear, but this incident is not unique. In his book *Revelations* (1991), Jacques Vallee reported other instances where Air Force personnel dangled film and then jerked it away.[24]

Linda Howe was not the only one to receive this kind of information from Doty. Peter Gersten heard similar stories from him. Gersten was a New York attorney, the legal adviser for CAUS, and he had brought lawsuits against various federal agencies to force them to comply with the FOIA. He had met with Doty in January 1983, a few months before Linda Howe's visit, and heard his disturbing reports. Among other things, Doty told Gersten that the National Security Agency was in communication with the aliens. The Gersten-Doty meeting was summarized by Linda Howe, who reports: "Doty claimed the government and ETs have made an agreement. The aliens could conduct animal mutilations and human abductions in exchange for teaching U.S. experts about alien advanced technologies."[25]

Doty's 1983 activity with Howe and Gersten was not a one-time project by a lone practical joker. Indeed, his UFO involvement went back some years, even before he met William Moore. He told Gersten that his interest started at Ellsworth AFB in 1977. Various allegations about what Doty did and said about that case have been published, but it is universally agreed that he played some role, and probably a central one. In any event, the case appears to be a hoax, at least in part, and it wasted the time of a number of investigators. In 1984 Robert Pratt published an exposé of the case.[26]

Linda Howe's April 1983 meeting with Doty was not the last time she was shown documents by Air Force personnel. She reported that in the Fall of 1986 she met with Captain Robert Collins, who was also stationed at Kirtland AFB, and he also showed her documents about an ET alien held captive by the government. At that time Collins admitted that he had worked with Moore for years behind the scenes.[27] Thus Doty was not working alone; others in the Air Force were involved. Additionally, persons who were aware of his UFO investigations had to include Major Ernest E. Edwards, Captain Robert Collins, Jerald D. Miller, and the high ranking officers who met with Bennewitz: Brigadier General William Brooksher, Colonel Jack W. Sheppard, Colonel Thomas Simmons, Colonel Frank M. Huey, Lt. Colonel Joe R. Lamport, and Major Thomas A. Cseh. Civilians at the meeting included Dr. Lehman and Ed Breen.[28]

Doty's efforts had a substantial effect on the popular fascination with UFOs. Linda Howe was tireless in bringing his message to a wider public. She is one of the most energetic people I've ever known, and through her talks, writings, and behind the scenes efforts, many ufologists were persuaded that a breach in the cover-up had occurred. Material was leaking out. The staggering implications could not be over-estimated. Many abductees also learned of her work and became convinced that the government was in league with the aliens in the abductions. Linda Howe was a bona fide journalist with many awards for her work. She appeared on innumerable television shows with literally millions of viewers. Still the Air Force did nothing to counteract Doty's claims, and that confirmed the worst fears of many.

All this intensified the focus on the Roswell incident, and the publicity reached a crescendo in the 1990s. New Mexico Congressman Steven Schiff asked the Defense Department about it. He was given the brush-off and was not pleased with that. He then turned to the General Accounting Office (GAO) and requested them to investigate. The Defense Department could not ignore the GAO.

In 1995 the Air Force issued a 975-page report on the Roswell incident in response to the GAO inquiry. The focus of that report was the search for documents regarding Roswell. Considerable effort was expended, and the Air Force's final report contained long lists of boxes that were examined in various archives. To facilitate the hunt, the Air Force investigators reviewed the published literature on Roswell for clues. In fact, the section in their report entitled "Search Strategy and Methodology" discussed various popular accounts and specifically mentioned two of William Moore's works.

There was one glaring omission: Richard C. Doty. Doty was one publicly-identified, living government employee who claimed to have knowledge of, and documents pertinent to, the alleged Roswell crash. He had shown Linda Howe pages discussing Roswell, and Howe had published a sworn statement attesting to that. The whole furor over Roswell, and its emergence into the wider popular culture, had its genesis in the efforts of Moore and Doty. Moore could be discounted. But Doty said he was acting in an official capacity. In the final analysis, his activities played a major role in the instigation of the GAO inquiry.

The Air Force response to the GAO was overseen by one Colonel Richard L. Weaver, who signed the report. It seems highly unlikely that he and his colleagues would have been unaware of Doty's activities and their repercussions for the Roswell affair. Weaver had known Doty while they were stationed in Germany. Doty was even identified as a key player in the myth of ET aliens in Curtis Peebles' book *Watch the Skies!* (1994), published by the Smithsonian Institution Press.

How was it that Doty was so neglected? Was his credibility so low that he could be disregarded? Could he be ignored without fear of raising embarrassing questions from the establishment media? Apparently so. Doty's integrity is seriously challenged by the testimony of Linda Howe and Peter Gersten, and there are other reasons to distrust him. Philip J. Klass reported that while Doty was stationed at Lindsey Air Station in West Germany he "was charged with falsifying official documents and telling falsehoods to his commanding officer. A formal investigation confirmed these charges and Doty was 'decertified' as a Special Agent of the Air Force Office of Special Investigations."[29] Klass did not give his source for this information, but he is a respected journalist who has many contacts in the military and defense industry. I was able to locate a well-placed source who confirmed the information.

Given Doty's outlandish claims to Linda Howe and his general unreliability, it is tempting to dismiss his hoaxings as products of a lone individual. But that is too easy. There are many reasons to be suspicious. As NASA scientist and CSICOP skeptic James Oberg noted, various agencies have undoubtedly used stories of UFOs to conceal projects and activities. It is reasonable to suspect that the AFOSI was one of those agencies, and I will review some of the reasons to think that to be the case.

Doty was apparently involved with the dubious Ellsworth UFO case before he entered AFOSI. Why then was he made a Special Agent? Given the sensitive nature of that agency's work, an extensive background check must have been done, and his caper at Ellsworth must have come to light. It is plausible that Doty was recruited by AFOSI precisely because of that. His personal interest in UFOs may have been useful to AFOSI, and his unreliability could have been an asset because he could be easily discredited if he was caught in something that might embarrass the agency.

The plausibility of this scenario is strengthened by the case of Simone Mendez. Her story appeared in *Just Cause* in 1991, after documentation supporting her report became available via the FOIA.[30] It leaves many questions unanswered, but it implicates the AFOSI.

At age 21, Airman Mendez was a telecommunications specialist stationed at Nellis AFB. She held a Top Secret security clearance and worked in a message center that handled sensitive, classified materials. She sometimes spoke to her co-workers about her interest in UFOs, and one morning in October 1981, one of them brought a copy of a Top Secret message about UFOs to her home. Mendez kept the copy for several months—an obvious and serious violation of regulations. She eventually concluded that it was a likely hoax and was not too concerned about it. When she returned it to the message center, the AFOSI and FBI began an intense, long-term investigation.

That was traumatic for her, and she was briefly hospitalized because of the stress. Mendez lost her security clearance and was given clerical jobs. But in 1987 she was approached by the AFOSI who wanted her to work for them. They told her that they knew about the earlier investigation of her. She accepted the offer but had mixed feelings about working for them. In the summer of that year she attended the MUFON annual symposium, but before she went, the head of counterintelligence for the base told her that she should prepare a briefing on it after her return. She did so and presented a report.

The Mendez case further demonstrates the AFOSI interest in UFO matters, and it raises questions. Despite her poor judgement in the past, the AFOSI actively sought her out. Why was she recruited? I have no answer. However, it parallels the Doty case. In both the AFOSI recruited UFO buffs with questionable activities in their past.

There are other reasons to be suspicious of AFOSI. As mentioned above, Doty offered film footage to Linda Howe, but it was never delivered. This was not unique. In 1973, film producers Alan Sandler and Robert Emenegger discussed potential television documentaries with the Air Force. While at Norton Air Force Base in a meeting with the head of AFOSI, they were told about footage of a UFO landing at Holloman Air Force Base. The details were murky, and it was unclear whether it was of a simulation or of an actual event. They fully expected to see the footage, but the offer was abruptly withdrawn. Emenegger went to Wright-Patterson AFB to speak with Colonel George Weinbrenner about it. Weinbrenner's response was bizarre. He started talking in a loud voice about a Soviet MIG, and then walked over to a bookshelf, took down a book on UFOs, and handed it to Emenegger, but he continued to talk about the MIG. Linda Howe quotes Emenegger describing the experience as "like a scene from a Kafka play."[31] Weinbrenner never did answer the question about the status of the film.

This doesn't prove a connection between the cases, but it raises reasonable suspicions, suspicions that the Air Force has not allayed. The pattern of dangling film, and then jerking it away, suggests a standardized method to sow confusion and damage the credibility of UFO investigators.

In any event, there is circumstantial evidence that Doty's UFO activities were officially sanctioned. Further, identifiable Air Force personnel were aware of some of Doty's UFO activities, including Jerald Miller and Robert Collins; undoubtedly there were others. The allegations of Air Force activity against civilians (e.g., Bennewitz) provided sufficient grounds for a formal investigation. However, the Air Force may not have wanted Doty's work to be investigated. Projects could have been jeopardized, especially if they deliberately harmed civilians. There are more reasons to think that the Air Force tried to cover up Doty's work.

In the late 1980s, CIA personnel had a meeting with Richard Weaver and Barry Hennessey, whom Doty indicated was once his superior officer. The CIA asked about Doty. The Air Force seemed embarrassed by this, because when I called Colonel Hennessey and inquired whether he had attended such a meeting, after a long, long, long pause, he responded with something like: "There wasn't any reason to have such a meeting."[32] I did not press him and let the matter drop. I can only conclude that Hennessey was being intentionally misleading. Colonel Weaver later admitted to me that he had attended the meeting and was asked about Doty.[33]

Thus years before Weaver authored the 1995 Air Force report on Roswell, the CIA pointedly made him aware of Doty's UFO activities.

Here I want to review key points. It was the Air Force that spread the rumors about Roswell, not just in 1947 but also by Doty's work in the 1980s. It was Air Force personnel who spread the rumors that a live ET alien had been captured; it was Air Force personnel who said that the aliens could manipulate human DNA, and it was Air Force personnel who claimed that the government had an agreement with the aliens. It was Air Force personnel who focused the public interest on the MJ-12 papers. Given all this, if Doty had done the hoaxing entirely on his own, the Air Force could have, and should have, made that clear. He used his military position and government property for those ends. Doty was a government agent; he claimed to be acting under orders of his superiors. Ipso facto, his activities were official (albeit possibly illegitimate). The failure to explain the situation makes the Air Force culpable.

If Doty was operating under the orders of his superiors, and that fact became known, it could have had severe political repercussions for the Air Force. The Roswell affair sowed wide distrust of the government, distrust that went as high as the President of the United States. It is understandable that the AFOSI would want to obscure any role it played in that.

Concerns over Doty should have been addressed in the 1995 Air Force report, but he was not mentioned. The question naturally arises: Did the head of the Air Force Roswell investigation, Colonel Richard L. Weaver, carefully steer the inquiry away from any embarrassing areas? The vast bulk of his report focussed on Project Mogul, the project that, years before, Robert Todd had identified as the likely source of debris that figured prominently in the case. Weaver published hundreds of pages regarding Project Mogul, but nothing on Doty.

Suspicion must fall on Weaver, and a few words should be said about him. He and I exchanged a number of letters about the Roswell report, his role in it, and about Doty. He always responded promptly to my queries, and I have no reason to distrust any information he gave me. Weaver spent most of his military career with the AFOSI and acknowledged that he had known Doty in the mid-1980s when they both were stationed in Germany. He admitted that Doty was not interviewed for the Roswell investigation. He also stated that he was unaware of any role Doty may have played in Roswell. I think that he is probably telling the truth here. There were many rumors about Doty, but most Roswell promoters seemed to be embarrassed by his connections. Other than Linda Howe's writings, there was little published linking him *directly* to Roswell, though the indirect links were numerous. Even if Weaver had known of Doty's activities, I must admit that he could conceivably have dismissed them as not worth investigating.

Weaver may have interpreted his task as limited to finding credible evidence of an actual saucer crash at Roswell. If so, it would be convenient, and reasonable, to completely ignore any Air Force projects involving phony stories of UFOs. That would meet the bureaucratic requirements, but such would not provide an intellectually honest account of the Air Force involvement with the Roswell story. The tax-paying public deserved better. After all, it was Air Force personnel who spread rumors about aliens and about Roswell, and government facilities were used for that purpose. The repercussions were enormous.

Doty really couldn't have been overlooked. After all, Linda Howe had published accounts that raised serious questions, not just about the Air Force, but particularly the AFOSI. Further, Jacques Vallee in his book *Revelations* specifically called for an explanation of Doty's activities,[34] and Vallee too raised questions about the AFOSI. In addition, Curtis Peebles had mentioned Doty as a key player in promoting the myth of aliens.

I asked Weaver if he knew anything about phony UFO stories the Air Force might have used, and whether he could talk about them if he knew. He denied that the Air Force had any UFO projects, and without my suggesting it, he volunteered to take a polygraph test.

It is possibly true that the Air Force never used phony UFO stories, but that is difficult to believe. Perhaps Weaver knew that he should not broach the subject during his investigation. It is quite plausible that he could have willfully ignored, and perhaps actively blocked, any investigation of such activities. He could thereby claim ignorance.

Weaver deserves sharp criticism for his neglect of the Doty matters. But he was a member of the Air Force, near retirement, and undoubtedly sensitive enough to avoid probing areas that might cause his employer problems. The Air Force investigated itself. The outcome was no surprise.

Other Sources

It is far too simple to explain the resurgence of the Roswell story as only a creation of Doty and his colleagues. That story and many related ones are too pervasive to be explained by a single source. Doty and Collins are not the only identifiable government people who have spread rumors about ET aliens. Dr. Bruce Maccabee, an optical physicist with the U.S. Navy, has passed on similar ones.

Maccabee appears credible; he has a doctorate in physics, long held an official position with the government, authored numerous professional papers, and appeared on many TV shows. In 1991 Maccabee published an article stating that "a credible intermediary" told him that a person who works with the Joint Chiefs of Staff reported that there are hundreds of people with high security clearances working on a project regarding extraterrestrial aliens. The aliens have bases in the U.S. and are now apparently "out of control." Project personnel were alarmed by the many reports of people being abducted by UFOs.[35]

The genesis of the story, true or not, could shed considerable light on these rumors, which have been circulating for years. One would think that extraordinary measures would be taken to have the informants come forward and tell what they know. If the story was not true, that also would be important. It might point to the source of rumors that have consumed the time of innumerable researchers. Maccabee is a prominent and influential figure within ufology, and his affiliation with the Navy gives him considerable prestige. He served as president of the Fund for UFO Research (FUFOR), a group particularly active in trying to inform and influence politicians regarding UFOs. Why wasn't every effort made to obtain congressional immunity from prosecution for the informants? Nothing like this happened. Instead, FUFOR promoted the half-century-old Roswell case with its many dubious claimants and secondary witnesses with failing memories. This diverted attention from current projects that could be investigated directly.

Maccabee's other activities also raise suspicions. He endorsed the authenticity of the UFO photos from Gulf Breeze, Florida taken by Ed Walters. Walters was a convicted felon, and he also was discovered to have been proficient at making phony ghost photographs before his UFO photos, and he had a reputation as a practical joker.[36] Walters appeared on the *Oprah* television talk show on September 7, 1990. There Philip J. Klass confronted him and pointed out that he had claimed to have been abducted by a flying saucer. Walters denied it. However Walters had published that claim earlier.[37] Klass was correct. So either Walters was lying on national TV or he "forgot" about his abduction, but in either case his credibility was destroyed. Nevertheless, Maccabee was impressed by Walters, and he contributed a foreword and a 45-page "Investigation and Photo Analysis" section for Walters' book *The Gulf Breeze Sightings* (1990).[38] Did Maccabee really believe that Walters' photos were genuine? Or was Maccabee intentionally touting material he knew to be false in order to discredit ufology generally, throw investigators off the path, and keep them busy with bogus cases? Given the evidence, these are plausible suspicions.[39] In 1993 a widely circulated report by the Associated Investigators Group (AIG) titled "The Fund for CIA Research" (a take-off on the Fund for UFO Research) raised many of these same issues. Further, it documented Maccabee's heavy involvement with the CIA on UFO matters and pointed out that he had hindered civilian access to documents on UFOs.[40] Maccabee's tight association with the CIA was again confirmed when it was revealed that the CIA had commissioned him to prepare a report for U.S. presidential science advisor John Gibbons.[41]

The motivations of Maccabee will probably never be known for certain. My own guess is that he really believed in the cases he promoted. He seems easily influenced by persuasive personalities.[42] When in their thrall, he shows little capacity for independent analysis. In any other field, his endorsements would have utterly destroyed his reputation and career. Not so in ufology. He is still regarded as a leading expert within the field.

Doty, Collins, and Maccabee are not the only government employees to promote the stories of ET aliens. Some amazing claims were made at the 1992 conference on Treatment and Research of Experienced Anomalous Trauma (TREAT) held in Atlanta, Georgia in April. That conference was devoted to UFO abduction phenomena, and one of the presenters was government-trained remote viewer Major Edward A. Dames (U.S. Army, retired). He claimed to have located an underground cavern of ET aliens in New Mexico. This startling announcement received wide attention among UFO researchers and was congruent with similar rumors circulating in the late 1980s and early 1990s that can be traced to Richard Doty and Paul Bennewitz. If Dames was just an isolated individual, his reports might be easily ignored. However he was president of Psi Tech, and John B. Alexander, then head of a non-lethal weaponry program at Los Alamos National Laboratory, sat on the Board of Directors of Dames' organization. Major General Albert N. Stubblebine, III (U.S. Army, retired), former head of the U.S. Army Intelligence and Security Command, was the Chairman of Psi Tech. Both Alexander and Stubblebine attended the TREAT conference, and their prominent association with Dames gave the claims considerable credibility.

Alexander is exceptionally well connected in paranormal areas. He has written articles on parapsychology and was a president of the International Association for Near-Death Studies. He was the Army liaison for a review of remote-viewing research by the National Research Council, the research branch of the National Academy of Sciences. He also served with the office of the U.S. Army Inspector General on an investigation of the Cash-Landrum UFO case. But there are even more convoluted associations involving ufology, near-death studies, parapsychology, rumors of aliens, and John Alexander. There are even some bizarre connections with the Kennedy assassination, through the person of one Gordon Novel. This character has many curious associations with the CIA and was somehow able to evade the extradition attempts of prosecutor Jim Garrison during his investigation of the Kennedy assassination.[43] Garrison concluded that Novel's intelligence associates were protecting him.[44] Whatever the truth of the matter, other peculiarities in his background are disturbing. Novel was convicted of illegally transporting electronic surveillance equipment in Nevada. Later in Georgia, he pleaded guilty to illegal possession of firearms. After being charged with fire bombing in Louisiana he jumped bail, but after recapture, his trial ended in a hung jury.[45] Novel achieved even more notoriety for making a dubious claim of having seen a CIA photograph of J. Edgar Hoover engaging in homosexual activity.[46] Recently Novel has been reported in the company of John B. Alexander and Harold Puthoff, and in fact Alexander has flaunted the association, perhaps in an attempt to intimidate others.[47]

Martin Cannon, an investigator who has written on government mind control projects, received a call from Alexander's wife on May 30, 1993. She left a message on his answering machine saying: "Martin, as an ex-friend I have to warn you. John and Hal [Puthoff] are really pissed off at you. And they've given the matter over to Gordon [Novel] to handle. Watch out." Cannon had no idea what had provoked the threat, but in his book *The Controllers* he had suggested that perhaps some UFO abduction accounts were actually due to screen memories imposed on the victims of a government mind control program in order to conceal other atrocities. Cannon was well aware of Alexander's interest in UFO abductions and of Novel's background. He was quite alarmed, and the day he received the message, he called and played me the tape. I suggested that he alert a number of people in the media, and he also notified the FBI.

But Cannon was not the only one targeted by Alexander. Armen Victorian of England is one of the most effective researchers to use the U.S. Freedom of Information Act (FOIA) to uncover government involvement in paranormal areas.[48] Victorian requested some information about research at Los Alamos National Laboratory, but it was denied him. Undeterred, he placed a second request, seeking copies of all paperwork relating to the denial. Victorian thereby obtained a memorandum written by John Alexander to Gilbert Ortiz, dated 28 September 1993. In that memo, Alexander discussed Victorian and specifically complained about his role in the exposé of Bruce Maccabee, the Navy physicist who spread rumors of ET alien bases on earth that are known to the U.S. government (the mentioned exposé was that by the Associated Investigators Group, 1993).[49]

Alexander's memo revealed that the CIA had requested "British Intelligence and the police to assist in resolving problems with" Victorian. Alexander did not discuss court action, legal remedies, or regulations that might be used to deny information. Rather it implied retaliation by government agents without due process, a serious abuse of power. Victorian subsequently reported that his home and car were broken into, computer disks and other records stolen, and that someone tampered with his mail.[50] After an account of all this appeared in the January 1, 1995 edition of British newspaper *The Observer*[51] his problems seemed to stop.

There are other players in this extended drama of remote viewing, UFOs, and threats against civilian researchers. One is Cecil B. Scott Jones, whose multitudinous connections were documented in a 24-page paper by Robert J. Durant in 1992. That exposé, "Will the *Real* Scott Jones Please Stand Up?", was widely circulated in the UFO and parapsychology research communities.[52]

Jones was exceptionally connected in government circles, and Durant pointed out that he was on a first-name basis with the U.S. Secretary of Defense. Jones spent much of his career in Naval Intelligence and later went to work for Senator Claiborne Pell, head of the Senate Foreign Relations Committee. He served as Pell's Special Assistant from 1985 to 1991, concentrating on New Age, parapsychological, and UFO topics. His contacts in the New Age and paranormal subcultures are as impressive as his government connections. He served as president of the American Society for Psychical Research (ASPR) and on boards of many organizations. During his employment as Special Assistant, part of his work included escorting Prince Hans-Adam of Liechtenstein to UFO conferences and parapsychology laboratories. The prince is extraordinarily wealthy, and the *Wall Street Journal* estimated his personal fortune at over two billion dollars. He also holds the majority voting interest in the Bank of Liechtenstein, which controls additional billions.[53] He has been an important funder of UFO research.

After he left Pell's employ, Jones could be found at the Washington beltway office of his Human Potential Foundation, which was funded by Laurance Rockefeller and Pell. Jones had ample support for his own activities, but as Durant noted, information and money seemed to flow to Jones, but not from him. Some doubted whether he acted for the benefit of civilian paranormal research.

Jones installed Patrice Keane as the Executive Director of the ASPR, and John Alexander aided him in political efforts there. None of these three ever published a scientific paper in a refereed parapsychology journal, and under Keane's direction the ASPR established no research program, and its financial plight became increasingly grim. Some saw parallels between Jones' activity at the ASPR and the CIA's involvement with NICAP when it went defunct.

Jones made one of his most curious presentations at the International Symposium on UFO Research in May 1992 in Denver, Colorado. The title of his talk was "Controlling Government Response: Self Interest in a Nation State System," and it was published in the symposium's proceedings.[54] The paper began vaguely but moved to focus on the devastating 1908 explosion in the Tunguska region of Russian Siberia, which was probably caused by a large meteorite.

Jones spoke in general terms about government interests and then segued to UFOs and how the government might handle them. About midway though the paper he cautioned UFO researchers that "if there is an intent to embarrass governments for acts of commission and omission on this subject, we can expect a domestic response equivalent to the international one when a massive loss of face potentially is involved, i.e., war—a readiness to destroy property and take lives."[55] This was an electrifying statement, but Jones proceeded calmly to describe how Psi Tech had remote viewed the Tunguska event. They reported a crash of an egg-shaped object with consciousness that was monitored by humanoid controllers a long distance away, presumably off the earth. Jones' paper was a bizarre combination of topics. A clear threat aimed at civilian UFO researchers was coupled with a discussion of government-developed remote-viewing technology.

Word spread fast, and I heard about his talk only a few hours after he made it. Jones' statements stoked the fires of paranoia in the UFO subculture. In March 1992, about two months previous, a relatively new, aggressive group, Operation Right to Know, had protested the government cover-up in front of the White House, and they were making plans for more demonstrations.[56] Further, there were already wild rumors circulating of concentration camps being prepared for dissidents who might object to the government's handling of the UFO problem or perhaps for those who had contact with the aliens. Also stories flew that the government used Psi Tech to hunt down people so they could be killed. Jones had extensive contacts in the paranormal subculture, and it is unlikely that he was unaware of these rumors.

Jones was not a marginal individual. He had access to the highest levels in government. He associated with some of the wealthiest and most powerful people in the world. In fact some of them financed his activities. When he spoke, people listened. His clear, but unstated, message was that they should not probe too deeply. With his credentials, and calculated ambiguity, he fed the paranoia and reinforced the belief that the government possessed a crashed saucer.

It is difficult to know what to make of Jones' activities and statements. He could be seen as a courageous former government employee coming forward with the backing of several wealthy and powerful people who believed that the UFO cover-up should end. That was the most obvious interpretation, and it was consistent with much other data.

Cattle Mutilations

The cattle mutilation phenomenon overlaps with UFO government disinformation programs. As mentioned previously, Richard Doty took Linda Moulton Howe to Kirtland Air Force Base and informed her that some people in Washington were upset with her work on cattle mutilations. But there are other connections with the government, cattle mutilations, and UFOs, particularly in the person of one Karl Pflock.

Pflock worked for the CIA from 1966 to 1972, and he later served as a Deputy Assistant Secretary of Defense. In the late 1970s and early 1980s he investigated cattle mutilations, and during part of that period he presented himself as "Kurt Peters." The purpose for his deception is not clear, but he was unmasked by Ian Summers and Dan Kagan in their book *Mute Evidence* (1984).[57]

Between 1989 and 1992 Pflock worked for BDM International, a defense contractor. For what it's worth, a file obtained from the FBI showed BDM had had an earlier interest in cattle mutilations.[58] During Pflock's time at BDM, Major General Albert N. Stubblebine, III (Chairman of Psi Tech) also worked for the company. With the BDM interest in mutilations along with their employing both Stubblebine and Pflock, coupled with Richard Doty's ominous warnings to Linda Howe, the paranoia went wild.

In the 1990s Pflock investigated the Roswell case and received support from the Fund for UFO Research. The Fund's close ties to the CIA via Bruce Maccabee raised more suspicions. Further, Pflock was married to Mary E. Martinek, who was on the staff of New Mexico Congressman Steven Schiff, who had prodded the General Accounting Office to investigate the Roswell case. Some suspected that she was placed in that position so she could intercept evidence sent to Schiff from civilians and direct his attention away from sensitive areas.

With all these coincidences, suspicions of Pflock were reasonable; after all, why would someone with such high-level experience and contacts in the defense industry be so active in the marginal areas of cattle mutilations and ufology? Why did Pflock present himself as someone else? Many suspected that he gathered information from civilian researchers so that his superiors could assess the effectiveness of their cover-up strategy and modify it as needed. Pflock had been employed by the CIA, an agency known for lying, and he had used a false name. All this didn't enhance his credibility, and suspicions about him were based on real, if not conclusive, evidence.

Of all the personalities discussed here, I suspect that Pflock is what he says he is. He is now generally open about his background, and he has published summaries of his career.[59] He is a writer and editor with unusually diverse interests: he has contributed to *Fate* magazine, served as an editor for *Libertarian Review*, was a contributing editor to *Reason*, and science columnist for *Eternity Science Fiction*. His circuitous career path produced a pile of coincidences and connections, which, while suspicious, are probably innocent. He perhaps adopted a false name to avoid tipping competitors that he was planning to write on cattle mutilations.

What Is the Meaning of All This?

This confusing excursion into personalities and activities describes but a tiny fraction of government-paranormal connections. The above examples were selected because there is substantial documentation on them. All of these cases raise far more questions than answers, but unlike in other sciences, the questions will probably never be resolved. Why do government personnel continue to report ET alien contacts? Why do Dames, Maccabee, Doty, Moore, Alexander, and Pflock have direct links with intelligence agencies? Why are the same people involved in both parapsychological and UFO matters? Why have Maccabee, Moore, Doty and Dames spread rumors that there are ET aliens on earth? If these were not connected, then why did Alexander, in the course of his official duties, complain about the report on Maccabee by the Associated Investigators Group? If the above-mentioned individuals were acting as private citizens rather than as government employees, then why was Linda Moulton Howe brought to Kirtland AFB and shown documents in the offices of AFOSI? Why has Maccabee had such a long association with the CIA? Why did Jones issue such an ominous threat to UFO researchers? Were all these people intentionally deceptive? Or were they pawns in a larger game? A more elaborate scenario suggests that someone recognized them to be ambitious but credulous and incompetent. They may have been assisted in achieving positions of prominence so that their natural blundering would discredit the field.

The implications are disturbing. Some suspect that intelligence agencies purposely create confusion among paranormal researchers, to taint the field and make it unpalatable for mainstream scientists and journalists to investigate. Perhaps the agencies want to protect a breakthrough and harness it for their own purposes. Or have they come into possession of ET alien technology that they are trying to duplicate? Some worry that the aliens have taken control. Possibly government personnel are manipulating public belief in order to establish a new mythology or cult. In any event, the government has spent at least moderate amounts on paranormal research in classified programs. Little was allotted for open research. Why? Do they want to keep some discovery from the public? These are largely speculations, and they can be spun endlessly. More prosaically, perhaps the rumors of crashed saucers were spread in order to confuse the U.S.S.R. and other hostile countries. Maybe some were cover stories used to protect experimental aircraft. Others may have been covers for retrievals of crashed Soviet satellites. However, it is implausible that these mundane suggestions could account for many of the incidents mentioned above. Why was Martin Cannon threatened? Why did Maccabee spread rumors of the government cooperating with the aliens? Why did Jones issue such an ominous warning? Why did Dames claim to have located an alien base? All these happened after the end of the cold war. I know highly capable people of independent means who have spent years investigating these areas on a full-time basis and have not reached solid conclusions. We will probably never know the full truth.

My own guess is that much of the nefarious activity is due to the nature of the paranormal. When the intelligence agencies toyed with the paranormal and with mythologies, they had little idea what they were dabbling with. Engaging supernatural powers can lead to problems in distinguishing fantasy from reality and right from wrong. Dames' judgement may have been impaired by his heavy involvement in remote viewing. Likewise, Maccabee and Alexander perhaps lost whatever critical faculties they demonstrate in other areas of their lives. Jones may have been in the grip of some paranoid idea accompanied by the grandiose delusion that he could divine the secret government agenda about UFOs.

Historically, many groups that attempted to engage paranormal phenomena became unstable. There is little reason to think that secret government projects would escape that fate. They too are probably prone to paranoia and conspiracy theorizing. Because of the secrecy surrounding their work, and the importance of it, they could be susceptible to delusions of grandeur, a common accompaniment of incipient paranoia. The projects were classified and probably received little critical peer review. The resulting isolation would exacerbate the problems. With the general irrationality and loss of judgement, it is plausible that criminal activity was tolerated (e.g., against Paul Bennewitz). The bureaucratic embarrassment about dabbling in the paranormal would help assure that those cases would not be investigated. The establishment media could be subtly dissuaded from investigating by marginalizing the field and promoting unreliable operatives such as Doty and Moore.

Summary

Government disinformation mixed with the paranormal creates situations of incredible ambiguity. I have tried to sketch a few of the intricacies, and it is clear that no simple theory will explain them all. In such circumstances the trickster provides the best way to think about the conditions. A quick review of his characteristics may help explain the relevance of all this to the larger perspectives discussed in this book. We have here, with the intelligence agencies, institutionalized deception, which they mix with supernatural and mythological themes. Blurring of boundaries and categories is seen in a variety of contexts. Statuses of government operatives are unclear, and sometimes they deliberately misrepresent themselves. Fact and fiction are commingled.

Most people think that UFOs, remote viewing, and cattle mutilations are entirely separate domains, and when these marginal topics are blended, establishment academics and journalists are repulsed. But the mixture is an ideal exemplar for this book. It displays boundary blurring, marginality, and deception, which are trickster characteristics.

UFO and cattle mutilation research efforts are extremely marginal, and intelligence agencies can easily penetrate and disrupt them with little hindrance or consequence. The few investigators who venture into these areas are particularly vulnerable to manipulation. They cannot pursue their studies in a manner typical of normal science; intelligence agencies muddy their work.

Any legitimate analysis that tries to explain beliefs about UFOs must recognize that the UFO subculture is awash in disinformation spread by government personnel, and that has played an enormous role in shaping the subculture. That influence is far more extensive than I have described above. Virtually all UFO investigators who make regular public presentations are from time to time approached by people who claim to have seen materials or documents while in military service that confirmed that the government has UFO projects. It is impossible to estimate the number of such people, but it must be considerable. Even CSICOP skeptic James Oberg reported that "I have my own list of people who have privately talked to me over the years and who were involved in government activities leading to a number of well-known 'UFO cases'."[60] These low-profile informants are a major source of UFO beliefs held by millions of people. Their information circulates quietly throughout the culture and contributes to the distrust of the establishment.

Government disinformation on the paranormal provides superb case material for study, and it is a gold mine for theoretical exploration. For instance, the topic illustrates the limits to knowledge and the limitations to science. Full connections, motivations, etc. cannot be known. Powerful establishments have vested interests in keeping it that way. It is impossible to obtain a full and coherent picture. This is simply a statement of fact, and this fact must be incorporated into any theoretical understanding of the cultural manifestation of the supernatural.

Government groups interact with the civilian organizations; each feeds the other information, much of it on both sides of dubious reliability. The dynamic appears very similar to Umberto Eco's bestselling novel *Foucault's Pendulum* (1988), which describes the paranoia and intrigue surrounding, what turns out to be, a remnant of an ancient laundry list. I only half-jokingly refer to that book as perhaps the best ethnography of U.S. ufology.

Despite their marginality, UFO phenomena draw enormous popular interest. Government and academic establishments have little understanding of this because they view UFOs as beneath serious consideration. Establishment minions don't recognize that the disinformation sown by personnel from the Air Force and other agencies undermines trust in the government.[61]

Scientific perspectives are not altogether useful in understanding this situation where secrecy and deception are so pervasive. Literature provides a more useful picture than science here, and the next Part of this book will examine that topic.

I will briefly preview some ideas to help orient the reader and explain how ufology can be relevant to other areas. Postmodernist theories suggest that the world can be understood as though one was reading a book or text. This metaphor (i.e., the world is text), allows one to ask new questions that would not be generated by traditional scientific paradigms. Reading requires interpretation, and postmodernist and post-structuralist theories emphasize the variety of interpretations that can be placed on any text. The uncertainties inherent in the UFO phenomena, and exacerbated by government disinformation, provide superb examples for theories that emphasize ambiguity and multiple interpretations. By the way, the study of interpretation is known as hermeneutics, a term derived from Hermes, the trickster of the Greeks.

CHAPTER 19

Hoaxes and the Paranormal

Hoaxes plague the paranormal, but few think deeply about them. They are regarded as nuisances, not fit for scientific consideration in themselves. At best they are viewed as minor contaminants to serious investigation, and most researchers want to ignore them and study "more important" things. This view is pervasive, but naïve, because hoaxes hold a key to the paranormal and supernatural.

In hoaxes, trickster motifs appear: e.g., deception, comedy, and a loss of status by victims. There is often a general air of disreputability and unsavoriness surrounding them. Those fooled are seen as gullible, the perpetrators as untrustworthy. Even skeptics who investigate come to bear a bit of the taint, as their colleagues tend to see their efforts spent on rather inconsequential matters.

Hoaxes considered in the abstract give only limited insight, because, as I have noted before, deception is resistant to abstraction. The topic needs to be explored with concrete examples. Furthermore, like many magic tricks, once a hoax is exposed it appears so simple that one wonders how anyone could have been fooled.

I will present a UFO hoax that I helped investigate, but before I do, I want to be clear that I am not suggesting that all UFO reports can be dismissed as intentional fraud or honest mistakes. On the contrary, the evidence is clear that some UFO phenomena have a physical event-level reality. Well-documented cases have not been satisfactorily explained in conventional scientific terms, despite considerable efforts by debunkers. Nevertheless, hoaxes pervade ufology, and they illuminate the nature of UFOs and other paranormal occurrences.

The reader may need some background in ufology, and I will make a few introductory comments.[1] Hundreds of thousands of sightings have been reported, the vast majority by honest people. However, these are not the cases that capture the attention of the mass media and engage UFO researchers for extended periods. On the contrary, it is typically the dubious cases with outlandish aspects that garner the greatest interest. The most famous is the Roswell incident, which started with a lie by the U.S. Army, as discussed in the last chapter.

The evidence indicates that UFOs are not "nuts and bolts" craft driven by "flesh and blood" humanoid aliens. They are something quite different. The direct sightings are not the only, or even the most important, aspect; social and cultural circumstances surrounding UFO events must be considered as part of the phenomena. One should examine effects of UFOs and observe the conditions around their manifestations. This is an indirect approach, but it provides more insight than studying the sightings themselves.

UFO phenomena are fundamentally liminal, interstitial, betwixt and between, and anti-structural. UFOs inhabit the realm between heaven and earth (a binary opposition), much like spirits and angels, and they share common properties with them. In this domain we also find the blurring of imagination and reality, another binary opposition.

Ufology's position in relation to other sciences and to the larger culture is important. UFOs generate enormous popular interest, and some of the top grossing movies of all time feature flying saucers. The movie *E.T.* (1982) grossed $400,000,000 and *Independence Day* (1996) grossed $316,000,000.[2] In the mid and late 1990s, images of aliens and flying saucers were common in magazine and television advertisements. Yet there is no generally recognized institution that speaks as the scientific authority on UFOs, and amazingly little support is available for research. Scientific ufology is impecunious, even compared with parapsychology. The largest UFO organization in the U.S. is the Mutual UFO Network (MUFON), and its 1992 tax return listed total expenditures of $172,048 which included the costs of publishing its magazine and conference proceedings. Very few academics have published quality studies, and the best research comes from independent workers. These are all anti-structural characteristics. *Nota bene*, anti-structure and marginality typify the UFO culture, including its (extremely limited) scientific culture. Hoaxes are a feature of anti-structure (a.k.a., liminality) and are both products of and contributors to it.

Among those few individuals who scientifically study UFOs, there is some reluctance to dwell upon the fraud issue for fear of it tainting the rest of the field and dissuading others from taking it seriously. As a result, the proponents' histories give a distorted picture. On the other hand, those of debunkers are often so casually done as to be misleading and unreliable.

The paranormal, by its nature, is enmeshed in frauds and hoaxes, especially in cases with high public visibility. Nowhere is this better seen than in ufology. The field is a gold mine for researchers who understand this, and a cesspool for those who do not.

Its entire history is permeated with fraud and con artists, and it makes the physical mediumship of nineteenth-century Spiritualism pale by comparison. Furthermore, I have never encountered an area in which it is so difficult to obtain reliable information. It is nearly impossible to convey the extent of these problems to someone who has not been involved. It takes several years of relatively intense reading and research to appreciate the field's complexity.

The following example is one that I investigated. The hoaxers have not yet admitted to their handiwork, but sufficient evidence has been presented on both sides for a reasonable person to draw conclusions. However, exposés of hoaxes are often not satisfactorily convincing for everyone. Even a full confession by perpetrators can be inadequate to convince die-hards that they had been hoodwinked, and I expect the following case to continue that pattern.

The Linda Napolitano (Cortile) Hoax—A Case Study

The purported UFO abduction of Linda Napolitano[3] is truly exotic, even for a UFO abduction. Government agents were involved; the UN Secretary General was a key witness; Linda was kidnapped in the interest of national security; the CIA tried to discredit the case, and the ETs helped end the cold war. Or so the story goes. The most complete version of the tale is reported in Budd Hopkins' book *Witnessed: The True Story of the Brooklyn Bridge UFO Abductions* (1996),[4] and three years prior, two colleagues and I released a 25-page critical report. It was widely printed in UFO periodicals and posted on the Internet.[5]

The chief investigator of the case, Budd Hopkins, is the most active spokesperson advocating the physical reality of UFO abductions. Prior to the Napolitano affair he had published two books on the topic and made innumerable appearances on radio, television, and at conferences. He is so famous that characters in books and television shows have been based on his life. Hopkins is an artist by profession but devotes a considerable portion of his time to ufology, and though he is not a trained scientist, he works closely with academics. He has collaborated extensively with David Jacobs, professor of history at Temple University, and his most illustrious supporter and colleague is John E. Mack, M.D., former head of the psychiatry department at Harvard Medical School and a Pulitzer Prize winner.

From the time he first went public with the Napolitano case, Hopkins made it clear that he considered it to be the most important evidence for the physical reality of UFO abductions, and in his book, he compares it to a flying saucer landing on the White House lawn. The case's significance is strengthened by the support it received from leaders of the two largest UFO organizations in the U.S., the Mutual UFO Network (MUFON) and the J. Allen Hynek Center for UFO Studies. Not only the magnitude of the claims, but also their endorsement by the field's leadership, have profound implications for understanding the nature of ufology and the UFO phenomena.

Several independent parties investigated the affair, and the available written material now provides a variety of perspectives. In addition to our own work, journalist Patrick Huyghe wrote an extensive article on the case for the April 1994 issue of *Omni* magazine, and Jim Schnabel's book *Dark White* (1994) covered the affair; both of these are critical.[6] Entertainment writer Greg Sandow supported Hopkins in a two-part article for the Spring and Summer 1997 issues of *International UFO Reporter*.

Linda Napolitano is a vivacious New York City housewife with a husband and two sons, and at the time of her celebrated abduction she was in her early 40s. In mid-1989 Linda joined Hopkins' support group for UFO abductees. She was just another member, but that soon changed. On November 30, 1989 at approximately 3:16 a.m., a large, brightly lit spaceship was witnessed hovering over her apartment building in lower Manhattan, and Linda and three small beings were seen floating up into it. At that very time, the UN Secretary General, Javier Perez de Cuellar, and his two bodyguards, "Richard" and "Dan," were passing by in a motorcade a few blocks away en route to a heliport, and as the spaceship appeared, their car stalled. The three watched as Linda ascended into the ship; afterward, the craft flew over the Brooklyn Bridge and plunged into the East River. Then, Richard, Dan, and the Secretary General were also abducted by the aliens and taken to a beach where they met Linda. After about an hour, all were returned to Manhattan, and later in the day Linda called Hopkins. He put her under hypnosis, but apparently she remembered little of the event.

The story became more exciting when in February 1991, over a year later, Richard and Dan sent Hopkins a letter describing their experience. They were severely traumatized but were still concerned about the fate of the woman they had seen taken into the craft. A few days after Hopkins received that letter, the two visited Linda in person, but they declined to meet directly with Hopkins. In April of that year, Richard and Dan kidnapped Linda. They forced her into a Mercedes, and Linda noticed that it was accompanied by a Rolls Royce; later under hypnosis she was able to recall part of its license plate number, and it was eventually traced to a diplomatic mission at the UN. During the kidnapping, they drove around New York for several hours; Linda was questioned and then released. In October Dan kidnapped her again, took her to a beach house on Long Island, and tried to kill her. But at the last moment Richard miraculously saved her. Dan was put in a mental institution, but he escaped, and Richard again rescued Linda from his clutches. Other sinister figures followed Linda, and the situation became so ominous that Hopkins raised money to hire a bodyguard for her.

Despite the wild activities, Hopkins had no direct evidence for any of this. He relied on Linda's reports and letters from Richard and Dan, but the only way he could contact the two was via a mail drop, or through Linda who met with them and spoke to them on the phone. Richard and Dan sent Hopkins letters and audiotapes, and they even sent him presents. But they steadfastly refused to meet with him, and they never have. Hopkins also received letters purportedly from Perez de Cuellar, but Hopkins never verified their authenticity, though he was convinced that they were genuine.

The story grew even more intriguing when Linda's niece, Lisa, a doctor of podiatric medicine, took an x-ray of Linda's head, because it was suspected that the aliens had implanted a device. The x-ray showed a small object with a curly, wire-like protuberance in Linda's nose, but the circumstances were odd. Lisa used a machine designed to x-ray feet, and in his book Hopkins quotes her as saying that she had never x-rayed anyone's head before and was not sure "how much to raise the amperage and kilowatts."[7] It is unclear whether Hopkins ever met Lisa or only spoke with her on the phone or whether he verified that she had a medical license. Unfortunately, before he saw the x-ray, the aliens apparently abducted Linda and removed the object because a later examination found no trace of it.

In November 1991 Hopkins received a letter from Janet Kimball (a pseudonym), a retired telephone operator. She was driving home from a retirement party for her boss on the morning of November 30, 1989. As she crossed the Brooklyn Bridge, her car stalled, and her lights went out. She saw an extremely bright object above Linda's apartment building, and even though she was over a quarter mile away, it was so brilliant that she had to shield her eyes. Janet saw a woman and three beings float up into the object, which then flew away. Other cars had also stopped on the bridge, and some of the people got out and ran around screaming. Janet, though, had the presence of mind to rummage through her purse to find her cigarette lighter in order to illuminate her watch and check the time.

Janet had also written to Hopkins in July, almost five months earlier, but received no reply (Hopkins typically had a large volume of unopened mail from readers of his books). The second time she wrote she marked the outside of the envelope "Confidential Re: Brooklyn Bridge." This odd marking attracted Hopkins' attention, but apparently not his suspicions. He interviewed Janet only once in person, and in a restaurant, away from her family members who may have given inconvenient information. She agreed to talk with another investigator, but backed out. As far as can be ascertained, Hopkins didn't even verify that the retirement party occurred on the date and time she claimed.

Linda's saga had romance. Richard's heroic efforts to rescue Linda led him to fall in love with her, and the two came to realize that they had been abducted together many times since their early childhood. As they grew up, the aliens arranged sexual liaisons, and Richard believed that he had fathered Johnny, one of Linda's children.

Hopkins began touting the case in 1992, and it got mentioned in the *New York Times*, the *Wall Street Journal*, *Omni* magazine, and *Paris Match*. He also published short articles on it in UFO magazines. In the middle of that year I became involved when Richard Butler and Joseph Stefula, whom I had known through a local UFO group, asked me for assistance. Butler had had abduction experiences, and he attended Hopkins' support group for abductees. There he had met Linda, who told him her story and asked his advice about threats from Richard and Dan. Butler called on Joe Stefula because the two agents apparently worked for some government office. Stefula was a Chief Warrant Officer in the U.S. Army (retired) and former operations officer for criminal investigations at Fort Dix, New Jersey. He had numerous contacts in law enforcement agencies, and he also had a long interest in UFOs.

A number of elements raised suspicions. The story was outlandish on the face of it. No credible, multipli-witnessed abduction had ever been documented. The purported involvement of the UN Secretary General made the claims even more unlikely. Anyone familiar with ufology knew the field to be rife with fraud and hoaxes, and the implausible aspects alone should have been cause for grave concern. An added twist came when our colleague Vincent Creevy told us about the science fiction novel *Nighteyes* by Garfield Reeves-Stevens.[8] This was first published in April 1989, and it contained many striking parallels with Linda's story (including alien-arranged sexual liaisons between a government agent and the female protagonist), suggesting that the hoaxers had based some of their ideas on it. In fact, Hopkins admitted in his book that, before the Linda case, he had never heard of such alien match-making,[9] and the fact that it had been portrayed previously in *Nighteyes* further suggests that the hoaxers borrowed ideas from that book.

Small details of the case also provoked questions. Why had Richard and Dan written to Hopkins before they contacted Linda? They knew the location of her apartment but would have had no reason to think Hopkins was involved. A most amusing detail was that Linda had not reported the kidnappings or the attempted murder to law enforcement authorities, even though she had made the allegations publicly in front of media representatives and hundreds of other people at the 1992 MUFON convention. Hopkins had amassed a great deal of material from Richard and Dan that could help police identify them. In fact, Hopkins even had a picture of Dan. If the two existed, they could almost certainly be found. However, if Linda was lying and filed her claims with the police, she could be criminally prosecuted. Her failure to make the allegations official made the case extremely dubious.

We contacted Hopkins during our investigation, and he agreed to a meeting with us, and he invited others to attend including Walter Andrus, the head of MUFON, and Jerry Clark, vice president of the Hynek Center. A few weeks before that meeting, we toured Linda's neighborhood in order to become more familiar with the location of the events. Her apartment complex had a guardhouse that was manned 24 hours a day, and video cameras were positioned at various locations around the complex. We discovered that the New York Post had a loading dock two blocks away that was open until 5:00 a.m. We talked with the guards and people at the loading dock and others in the vicinity, but no one knew anything about the UFO event. According to Hopkins' witnesses, the ship was extremely large and bright. So it seemed odd to find no one who had heard of it.

The meeting revealed much about Hopkins' methods and the mentality of ufology's leaders. We asked Hopkins if he had checked with the apartment complex guards or with the New York Post loading dock personnel to see if they remembered seeing a UFO. He hadn't. We learned that Hopkins didn't even know the weather conditions the night of the abduction. He had done nothing to verify the most rudimentary facts. During questioning, Linda admitted that she had lied about several aspects of the case, and Penelope Franklin, one of Hopkins' closest collaborators, staunchly supported her in doing so.

Stefula brought along a colleague who had years of experience in dignitary protective services. He made an independent, detailed presentation on motorcades carrying important political figures. He explained that in such operations checkpoints are established, and if they are not passed on time, several authorities are notified. If even one car stalls, a whole network of people is informed. At the end of his presentation he suggested that Hopkins ask Richard and Dan the meaning of several specialist terms. If they were whom they claimed, they would know the definitions. Hopkins apparently never asked them the meaning of the words.

At the meeting we played our trump card. We suggested that Linda report the kidnapping and attempted murder to the police, and we stated that if she didn't, we were prepared to file a request for a federal investigation. We explained that Linda had publicly alleged that federal officials had committed crimes, and that anyone could now make such a request. At that, Hopkins, Jacobs, Andrus, and Clark all appeared to panic. They said that a worldwide government conspiracy may be attempting to suppress knowledge of earth's visitation by ETs. If the crimes were reported, we might never learn the truth about the Napolitano affair. In fact Clark committed his position to writing and said that the case "involves a political figure of international stature . . . banging on the wrong doors could alert the relevant agency that two of its agents were leaking a huge secret."[10] This reasoning was silly, but revealing. Even if there was such an effective, orchestrated conspiracy, Hopkins had already widely publicized the case, including the alleged crimes, and any report from us would amount to nothing. If Linda's claims had merit, there was a chance for a conspiracy to be exposed. Government agencies commonly investigate each other, and there are often bitter rivalries among them. There was nothing to lose. The attitude of the leading ufologists struck me as exceedingly odd, but because they had been given inside information by Hopkins, a few days later I called Andrus, Clark, Jacobs, and Mack to be sure that they believed Linda's story about the kidnappings and attempted murder. All assured me that they accepted her report.

Stefula, Butler, and I wanted a simple test of Linda's honesty. Would she stand by her claims when there were real penalties for lying? To force the issue, and up the stakes, I wrote to the office of the Inspector General of the U.S. Treasury and Stefula called the Secret Service requesting an investigation of Linda's allegations. Eventually the Secret Service interviewed Hopkins and Linda. I don't know exactly what transpired during that interview, or what Hopkins and Linda told them, but as far as we could tell, the Secret Service took no further action. I can only surmise that Hopkins' and Linda's claims did not warrant an investigation and that they tried to avoid one. In any event, Hopkins was furious, and I received a letter from the Hynek Center rebuking me and bitterly complaining that I had provided law enforcement the name, address and phone number of one of their vice presidents who had been given secret information about the alleged crimes. I didn't understand their anger, but I gather that their private mythology had just collided with real-world considerations, and that was none too pleasant for them.

In January 1993 we released a report on our findings, and Hopkins and his supporters wasted little time in replying. The March/April 1993 issue of the Hynek Center's magazine *International UFO Reporter* was almost entirely devoted to personal attacks on us.[11] Hopkins made a number of false statements about us, and though we informed him and the magazine of them, no apology or correction ever appeared. Nevertheless, I found his vehement denunciation, including profanity, quite hilarious. And one of my favorite passages read: "And then there's the third and strangest member of the New Jersey trio, George Hansen. In my brief meetings with him, certain personal characteristics were immediately obvious. First of all, George is the epitome of the fanatic college debater who will use any tactic to win, no matter what the human cost. His ego is always on the line, and apparently he would rather destroy an innocent person than lose what he perceives to be the abstract argument. He has learned to wear the protective paraphernalia of written academic discourse as a coat of chain mail to conceal the inner man. All this, because the soul of George Hansen is, essentially, the soul of a hater."[12] I bought copies of the magazine and gave them to friends.

After our exposé, Hopkins seemed even more firmly committed to the case. Through his contacts in the media, he arranged for a brief personal meeting with Perez de Cuellar in November 1993 at Chicago's O'Hare airport, while the former Secretary General had a temporary stop-over between flights. Hopkins describes the meeting in his book, and though Perez de Cuellar said little about the case, the statements he made were denials. Of course Hopkins interpreted them as support for his belief.

After our critique appeared, Hopkins discovered a few other "witnesses." One was a "Cathy Turner" who was brought to his attention by "Frank Turner," Cathy's nephew, in 1993, nearly four years after the event. Ms. Turner didn't clearly recall the year of her sighting, and she even said that it may have occurred near one of the bridges going to Queens (miles north of the Brooklyn Bridge). After spending much time interviewing her, Hopkins convinced himself that her testimony strongly supported the Linda case. He went on to make conference presentations and wrote an extended article about this "witness."[13]

For several years, the Linda case captured the imagination of ufologists and garnered endorsements from many of them. By the time Hopkins' book appeared in 1996, their interest and support had faded. The reviews in the UFO magazines were generally positive, but considering the magnitude of the claims, most were not ringing endorsements. Some reviewers even appeared slightly embarrassed, and a number of ufologists seemed to want to forget the affair. Frank Turner, Cathy's nephew, became friendly with Linda, but after a period he was greatly disillusioned and vocally skeptical. His comments appeared on the Internet, and there were hints that others close to Linda also had doubts.

Analysis

Hopkins' book probably is about as accurate as he could make it, though not as complete, and there is no reason to think that there was any duplicity on his part. In fact, the story is so unlikely that no refutation is really needed, and I believe that any reasonably judicious reader would find the claims ludicrous. Nevertheless, it may be helpful to keep in mind some of the salient points against the case. First, Hopkins did not attempt to find witnesses in Linda's neighborhood, and he didn't even check with the guards at her apartment complex, though in New York City, even at 3:16 a.m., such a bright object should have been seen by hundreds, perhaps thousands, of people. All major witnesses sought out Hopkins rather than the other way around. Second, Perez de Cuellar denied knowing Linda. Third, Linda failed to file police reports of her kidnappings and attempted murder. Fourth, the case has innumerable unique features with no parallel in the history of ufology, though there are many similarities to the novel *Nighteyes*.

Hopkins and his defenders argued that if this was a hoax, it was an incredibly complicated one. There is a grain of truth in that, but it is wildly overstated. The Napolitano case was more lengthy and elaborate than the average UFO hoax, but there have been others that required greater effort. The Napolitano case was not a technically difficult or expensive operation, nor would it have required a lot of time or coordination. It was carried out over a period of years and could have been undertaken like a hobby, perhaps plotted when Linda's husband and sons were out of the apartment for a few hours or when she was visiting friends. Linda was not the only one involved with the deception, but she was the linchpin. Male friends could have helped prepare the "Richard" and "Dan" audiotapes that were sent to Hopkins. Maybe Linda typed "their" letters as she had worked as a temporary secretary and would have had access to a variety of typewriters.

The riskiest part of the hoax was probably Janet Kimball, the supposed witness whose car stalled on the Brooklyn Bridge. She refused to be interviewed by anyone but Hopkins. He presented no evidence to corroborate her story as to why she was on the Brooklyn Bridge at 3:16 a.m.

Some have objected that the hoax explanation is not plausible because there is no reasonable motive for such an extended effort. This is a common refrain, and in my investigations of other paranormal deceptions, I've often heard the questions "Why would anyone perpetrate a hoax? What motive could there be?" After a few experiences investigating them, I discovered that motives are often difficult to discern and comprehend.

I admit that the motives in the Napolitano case are a mystery, but some speculation might ease concerns about them. Perhaps Linda began with a relatively innocent tall tale that got out of hand. At the beginning, she may have only wanted a bit of attention and some excitement in her life. But as the case became known, Linda was mentioned in magazines, invited to conferences, appeared on TV, was provided a bodyguard, and even dined with royalty (the Prince of Liechtenstein was friendly with Hopkins). The initial impetus for the hoax remains unknown, but as it progressed, benefits appeared.

Rumors suggested that the hoax was done for revenge. Several people privately told me about dissatisfaction among Hopkins' group of abductees (e.g., women scorned). Linda may have started the tale on her own and then been encouraged by others who had been slighted by Hopkins and who realized what she was doing. A few parts of the hoax may have operated independently of Linda; Hopkins had a number of colleagues with inside information about the case, and it is possible that one or more of them joined in for their own purposes. Such scenarios are speculative, but they are not implausible.

Implications of the Hoax

The Napolitano affair is an important example because the field's leaders vetted the case and committed their views to writing. Hopkins shared his evidence with them, and subsequently Walter Andrus, Jerry Clark, David Jacobs, and John Mack all supported the integrity of Linda and her story.[14] These leaders have many decades of experience among them.[15] They play substantial roles in publicizing cases, endorsing their credibility, and setting the agenda of the field. Andrus, as International Director of MUFON, and Clark as an editor with the Hynek Center, also control the content of membership magazines. These persons have a long history of supporting what were later shown to be hoaxes. Their actions, in light of their vast experience, prominence, and influence, tell us something about the nature of ufology.

The victims played important roles in the hoax, and they cannot be separated from it when analyzing the affair. In fact Hopkins' role was more important than those of the perpetrators. He was the target, and his responses determined the hoax's progress. The hoaxers preyed upon his beliefs and expectations, and subtly manipulated him into ignoring glaring inconsistencies. His colleagues fared little better. With the manifest loss of critical judgement, some outsiders thought that the victims were willing participants. This became so extreme that several people told me that they suspected Hopkins of being in on the scam. Wealthy persons were supporting him, and some observers thought that he needed to maintain excitement in order to assure their continued backing. I very much doubt that Hopkins consciously took part in any deceit, and in other paranormal deceptions I have investigated, skeptical outsiders voiced virtually identical suspicions to me privately. Victims are often perceived as being dishonest, but in the vast majority of cases, they are oblivious to their contribution. Nevertheless, in many minds, the distinction between the hoaxers and the hoaxed is blurred, this being a subtle effect of the trickster.

The question remains, just why did the victims get hoodwinked? What made them susceptible? They had a long familiarity with ufology and its many frauds. How are we to understand those people? It is not wrong to accuse them of gullibility, but that is too simplistic, and it provides little insight. Further, it will not do to claim that the victims were psychologically abnormal, ineffectual, or despirited human beings grasping for the merest bit of meaning in their lives. Most are highly successful in other areas. The ufologists who endorsed the case are not generally cultish in any usual sense of that word; they have no common rituals, central charismatic leader, dogma, etc. Furthermore, they are not charlatans who are out for a fast buck and then disappear. Hopkins' supporters had no direct financial interest in the case; in fact they stood to lose prestige if they were wrong. The traditional explanations of debunkers do not suffice. Nevertheless the victims were caught up in the story and were unable to summon their critical, analytic capabilities. This is disturbing, and it deserves the careful consideration of everyone interested in ufology.

Belief and Social Roles

The victims held beliefs compatible with major features of the hoax, and that made them vulnerable. Yet to attribute their gullibility to belief is insufficient. Everyone has beliefs, and everyone has areas of gullibility. Beliefs are complex; they are not all or none things; they can be ambiguous and unstable. Sometimes they are vigorously espoused and then quickly abandoned.

The UFO subculture illustrates the complexities of belief. That subculture is typified by exotic ideas that are held, discussed, and then discarded. I have known many who believed in benevolent space brothers, evil government conspiracies, interdimensional time travel, and black helicopters and clouds that change into flying saucers. A few months later they adopted a completely different outlook, and then someone else picked up the rejected ideas. This is common, in fact, more the rule than the exception. Fluidity of belief is not so characteristic of the establishment ufologists (e.g., those who hold offices in organizations). It is so prevalent among members of the subculture generally that it must be considered a fundamental characteristic of the subculture. Dhwani Shah, an undergraduate at Rutgers University, called attention to it in his 1996 thesis *UFOs and the Experience of the Sacred: Discovering Living Myths in Post-Modernity*. Lability, ambiguity, and ambivalence characterize beliefs in the UFO subculture and are some of its anti-structural (liminal) aspects. In ufology, belief has some of the same properties as the institutions; both are weak and tenuous.

Hopkins and his supporters were convinced that extraterrestrial beings are visiting earth. They also believed (perhaps less strongly) that there is an extensive government conspiracy to suppress the truth of alien visitations. Linda's story about Perez de Cuellar confirmed and reinforced both beliefs. The notion that ETs have landed on earth has some respectability, but it is easy for many outsiders to dismiss the conspiracy idea as delusional. But the belief is not completely unjustified. Government officials have suppressed data on UFOs and have spread disinformation; some have made threats against civilians. Documents released under the Freedom of Information Act demonstrate international cooperation in nefarious actions against investigators (e.g., against Armen Victorian. See the last chapter.) The established system does operate something like a conspiracy. Furthermore, conspiracy theory provides a framework in which to make sense of a large amount of data, not only in this case but also in many others.

That being said, the idea of a massive, highly orchestrated, international conspiracy functions as a myth, and among the U.S. ufological hierarchy it is socially unacceptable to examine the myth's foundations too closely. This taboo explains the lack of basic reality testing, such as MUFON's and the Hynek Center's opposition to a federal investigation of Linda's kidnappings. An investigation could disconfirm their myth.

Grandiosity frequently accompanies conspiratorial thinking and paranoiac belief. That occurred in the Linda case, and the hoaxers capitalized splendidly on it. One of *Hopkins'* abductees was chosen by the aliens for their demonstration of power to earth's political leaders. Hopkins was thereby cast in a central role in the drama, and his colleagues would share in the glory of proving to the world the reality of the ETs. This would be the ultimate accomplishment for any ufologist. Even if there was only a slim chance of the case being proven, the payoff was extraordinary, and it would make their lives' work worth all the effort.

There is another reason that Hopkins and his supporters failed to critically examine the evidence. At some unconscious level, they must have recognized their hopes and beliefs to be unrealistic. To the extent that they vaguely understood this, it was to their credit. Had they pushed for a federal investigation, and Linda was proven to be lying, they would have looked silly. If they firmly believed in a vast government conspiracy, they might have joined a survivalist anti-government group. It was to their benefit that they did not act in accord with their expressed beliefs.

Despite the indications of their unconscious doubts about the case, they made ludicrous statements supporting it, and that remains puzzling. The victims' actions suggest that they were almost playing along with the hoax. They seemed to unconsciously subscribe to the agenda and carry out their roles, sometimes with great vigor. Part of the explanation can perhaps be found in considering social roles and group behavior. Roles (social positions) induce behavior that is not consciously, rationally planned but rather just accepted as "normal." A person's role in society exerts an overwhelming influence on one's actions and beliefs. When one is immersed in one's own culture, the influence, though pervasive, is difficult to perceive. It is more easily observed other cultures.

Hopkins' partisans have dedicated their lives to UFO research; they identify with the field, and others identify the field with them. These people are inseparable from those roles. Hopkins attained a prominent position in ufology through many years of effort. He had received awards for his work, made numerous presentations to the media, and his presence at conferences was sure to draw many who might not otherwise attend. Ufology is a tiny field with a tenuous existence, and an attack on Hopkins has greater repercussions than one on a comparable person in a larger field. The field's welfare is partly linked to that of Hopkins'. His comrades too are closely identified with ufology and with the extraterrestrial hypothesis; an attack on either is, in some sense, an attack on them personally.

The leaders firmly believed in the value of ufology, despite its shabby treatment by establishment science. They understood the need for supporting what little institutionalization there was in the field, in order to build a base for further research and progress. If there was continuous infighting about all pieces of evidence, no foundation could be built for scientific advancement. Some compromises have to be made, some agreement reached.

Hopkins' associates tried to uphold ufology's reputation and defend its institutions. In contrast, Stefula and I, and to a lesser extent Butler, were seen as outsiders and troublemakers trying to besmirch its status. That perception was not altogether wrong. Butler and Stefula were sympathetic to the extraterrestrial hypothesis (ETH), but I was not. (The ETH is essentially misnamed, and the "hypothesis" in actuality is more of a foundational premise. U.S. ufologists rarely test the ETH; rather they assume it and derive ideas accordingly.) I thought it worthwhile to lower the status of the ETH. My role was that of an outsider, and I had no commitment to the field as it was formally organized in the U.S. Our side had no institutional affiliation to defend. Our opponents understandably viewed us as people who could not be trusted.

I am not saying they consciously weighed and evaluated their social roles when they supported Hopkins. The victims were unable to step outside their roles as defenders of ufology and examine matters in a more detached manner. This was probably exacerbated by the field's marginality. Marginal groups usually need members to strongly identify with them in order that the groups remain viable. Less identification is required for a more established discipline. With marginality, paranoia can emerge, which may serve to draw the group together and unite it, but it can also undercut rational reality testing. For Hopkins' supporters, short-term preservation of harmony took precedence over critical analysis.

The idea of social roles applies to all normal areas, and there are countless examples of them leading to irrational actions. Also, paranoia and grandiosity afflict the normal world. Nevertheless, in ufology the problems of hoaxes and paranoia are extreme, and some additional explanation is needed.

Ufology differs from normal science in the subject matter. It lies in the realm of the liminal, the paranormal, and the supernatural. It is an enchanted area where the rules of the rational world do not apply. Those with only a casual acquaintance with UFO phenomena may not realize that descriptions of extraterrestrial aliens are virtually identical to those of fairies, demons, and other mythical figures. Jacques Vallee amply documented this in his book *Passport to Magonia* (1969). However, many leading U.S. ufologists still abhor such ideas. They see them as discrediting their field. Instead they have conceptualized the phenomena as ET "flesh and blood" humanoids traveling in "nuts and bolts" flying saucers, thereby rationalizing them, keeping them in the normal world and apart from the supernatural. Those ufologists are correct in seeing that associations with the supernatural taint their field and make it unattractive to establishment scientists. However, by suppressing the paranormal aspects, and removing them from ufology's purview, they misunderstand the nature of the phenomena and become vulnerable to them. Ufologists' perennial victimization by hoaxers is but one example.

Roles and Fantasy

Two factors, identified above, help explicate the connection between UFOs and hoaxes. The first is the matter of social roles; the second is the mythical and magical character of UFO phenomena. The same factors are seen in childhood pretending and in fantasy role-playing games.

Children often pretend to be someone else: a mother or father, policeman, fireman, shopkeeper, etc., and this is a natural part of human development. We learn who we are and how to behave by mimicking roles of others; we search for role models. Even as adults we take roles, e.g., parent, employee, sports enthusiast, homeowner, etc. These roles produce different thoughts and behaviors by us, and they significantly shape our lives.

Children experiment with more exotic roles; they play make-believe monsters and sometimes become truly frightened. As adults we don't completely outgrow our fascination with that. We attend horror movies, watch tales of the supernatural on television, and read horror fiction.

Fantasy role-playing games (FRPGs) are an adult version of childhood play, and they can be profitably compared with ufology and its hoaxes. This is not meant to demean ufology, but to illuminate it. The similarities are sufficient to command attention, but the differences between them are also important. Both FRPGs and UFO hoaxes have liminal aspects.

Large-scale, organized, adult fantasy role playing emerged in 1974 with the commercial publication of *Dungeons & Dragons* (D & D), the best known of the genre. It was invented by E. Gary Gygax and David L. Arneson, quickly became popular, and spawned hundreds of variants. The book *Heroic Worlds: A History and Guide to Role-Playing Games* (1991) by Lawrence Schick describes an amazing number of them.[16] Gary Alan Fine prepared an excellent, readable sociological study of FRPGs in his book *Shared Fantasy: Role-Playing Games as Social Worlds* (1983).

In a FRPG, players assume roles of characters, such as monsters, wizards, and other mythical creatures. Players use magical powers and instruments. Generally 4 to 12 people take part, one being the game master who establishes situations and terrain, interprets rules, and settles disputes. Dice determine a character's talents and abilities and outcomes of battles, spells, etc. A game can be temporarily halted, picked up again, and may extend over a period of days or even weeks. It becomes a shared fantasy, wherein the players voluntarily suspend normal, rational considerations. In most cases there are no winners or losers, in contrast with more traditional games like Monopoly.

A sizeable industry now supports the FRPG subculture. There are glossy magazines, gaming shops in many cities, and conventions that draw thousands of people. Even in its early days it did well, and Fine reports that: "By August 1978, only four years after the publication of *Dungeons and Dragons*, TSR Hobbies had a full-time staff of eighteen employees, and by September 1979 was grossing over two million dollars annually."[17] This can be contrasted to MUFON, the largest UFO organization in the U.S., which has approximately 3500 members. In the last few years, its annual convention has attracted 300-1000 people. Although it has been in existence for 30 years, MUFON is still headquartered in the home of Walt Andrus, its founder and International Director. Its total expenditures for 1992 were $172,048. Thus the FRPG industry is far more structured, organized, and financially viable than that devoted to investigating UFO phenomena.

FRPGs have some liminal aspects, despite the organized commercial structure supporting them, and in the context of the topics covered in this book, they are worth considering. Two liminal components of FRPGs are the blurring of fantasy and reality and the invocation of magical beings. These are also seen in science fiction and fantasy, but role playing takes them a step further. The games give more direct contact with supernatural ideas than does literature alone. Live people are involved; they participate in a drama; props may be used, and some physical action is required. Unlike reading, FRPGs engage more than just the mind and imagination; there is interaction with the physical world, albeit limited. As such, FRP gaming is a more blurred, interstitial area than fantasy literature or science fiction film.

FRPGs have other liminal and anti-structural features. The players are frequently high school or college age (i.e., those who are often in periods of transition) and usually unmarried. Within the subculture there is a rapid evolution of rules, and many groups invent their own versions. There is no central authority that everyone acknowledges as legitimate. The rules are not nearly as rigid as say chess or bridge. In fact FRPG rules do not cover all contingencies, and game masters have wide discretionary power. They can void the published rules to keep things running smoothly. Rules can be even further transgressed, and

Fine tells us that "cheating in fantasy role-playing games is extremely common—almost everyone cheats and this dishonesty is implicitly condoned in most situation[s]."[18] Cheating is frequent despite there being no winners or losers in the game. The winner-loser binary opposition is eliminated, and that reduces the structure compared with other games. The goal is more diffuse than a typical contest. Players' statuses are thus more equal, and Victor Turner's concept of communitas applies to FRPGs.[19] Players' outside roles and positions are discarded, and a new "world" established. Fine tells us that "As a new gamer I was struck by how little I learned about the private lives of others—even others to whom I felt close. One didn't talk about occupations, marital status, residence, or ethnic heritage."[20]

Another liminal feature of FRPGs is the use of the creative imagination. Some New Age guided-imagery exercises instruct students to meet magical beings and ask them for help with real-world problems; in FRPGs entities are also invoked. *The Aquarian Guide to the New Age* (1990) by Eileen Campbell and J. H. Brennan commented on FRPGs' striking similarity to New Age techniques in this regard.[21] It is probably no accident that FRPGs became popular during the same period that saw the growth of the New Age movement.

In the early years of FRPGs, some of the media trumpeted the dangers, and a few commentators suggested that players may not always be able to tell the difference between fantasy and reality. Fantasy role playing taps archetypal images that hold considerable psychological power. Those images and ideas can become immensely attractive, even somewhat addictive, to people playing the game. Even so, the problems seem to have been overblown, but in 1994, twenty years after first publication of *D & D*, Kurt Lancaster authored a paper in the *Journal of Popular Culture* entitled "Do Role-Playing Games Promote Crime, Satanism and Suicide among Players as Critics Claim?" He concluded that the games did not, but the question still gets asked. There is a perception that the games pose risk. In any event, players do become engrossed, and Fine discussed the problem of overinvolvement. Players can identify with their game characters, and sometimes they prefer not to separate themselves from those roles. A gamer may become depressed for several days after the death of a fantasy character, but this might not be much different than a sports fan whose team loses an important game.

D & D participants play with otherworld ideas and supernatural entities, but within a structured setting. There are boundaries: the time and place are set, the players are known, and the Dungeon Master settles disputes. The liminality is contained.

Ufology is more unstructured; there are fewer rules about what is and is not possible, and the powers of the otherworld figures are almost unbounded. UFO phenomena can happen without warning, at any time or any place. The ETs can be anywhere, and some ufologists believe that ETs tag certain people and track them for their entire lives. There is no escape. Paranoia is rampant, with a fear of the ETs or the government, or of ETs and government working together. Abduction accounts involving both ETs and government personnel are not uncommon.

Both ufology and *D & D* allow direct, immediate involvement with powerful otherworld beings and mythological motifs. Both endeavors have been known to engross the participants. Most "players" are able to successfully detach themselves from involvement, but occasionally the "game" becomes obsessive and interferes with real-world pursuits. The problems are far more severe with UFO phenomena than with FRPGs.

Lessons From the Linda Napolitano Case

Ufology does not have the same protective mechanisms as FRPGs; it is not clearly separated from the real world. The Napolitano case is essentially an unbounded version of *Dungeons & Dragons*. The victims interpreted the hoaxers' handiwork as due to beings with virtually unlimited magical powers. They believed that ETs could pass through walls, make themselves invisible, and even control world events. The magical beings included not only the ET aliens, but also the pantheon of agents of an unreachable, evil government conspiracy determined to prevent humankind's knowledge of the ETs. Thus the interactions of Hopkins, et al., with the hoaxers conform with those between humans and gods. Humans question and provoke the gods only at the greatest peril. The proper approach is to appease, mollify and supplicate them. It should be no surprise that the simplest reality tests of the Napolitano story were not made. Hopkins' failure to search for witnesses actually makes sense in this context.

Intermediaries were crucial in the hoax, and readers should recall that mythological tricksters often serve as intermediaries. Dan and Richard were the primary intermediaries between the evil government conspirators and the rest of the world. Like trickster deities, their reality status was ambiguous. Linda was the main link between Hopkins and the two agents. She was the medium through whom they communicated.

In fantasy role playing, the players accept the rules, and when there is a question, the game master settles it. In the Linda case the terrain was not so set; nevertheless, Hopkins and his supporters felt that neither the basic evidence nor the foundational assumptions were to be questioned. Our challenges disrupted the situation, and Hopkins, along with the leaders of MUFON and the Hynek Center, pleaded and even ordered (Hopkins' term) us to cease investigation, despite the massive publicity given the case. It was preposterous for them to think that they possessed any authority to give such orders. Their mindset was worrisome, and it signalled some detachment from everyday reality. They seemed to perceive themselves to be in the position of a Dungeon Master who decrees the rules and regulations in a closed, artificial society, cut off from the outside world.

Observers might now see Hopkins and his supporters as deserving only scorn and derision. That would not be completely fair. Hopkins should be given credit for daring to study matters shunned by orthodox science. His efforts, writings, and life provide abundant material for analysis. Further, Hopkins has a true interest in aiding UFO abductees, and he has spent enormous time and effort in that. Unlike professional therapists who profit from the afflictions of others, Hopkins assists abductees without charge. He is exceptionally dedicated, and his good intentions probably made him more vulnerable than he otherwise would have been.

Almost all leaders of U.S. ufology remain oblivious to the phenomena's nature. But this has nothing to do with their IQ, education, or professional achievements in other areas. Actually, high accomplishment in established fields may make them more vulnerable, as they may assume that the rational methods effective in those areas will yield results on the UFO problem. When they pursue the UFO topic, they enter an unbounded, liminal domain, unaware of its dangers. The problem is compounded by the wish to see ufology gain respectability (i.e., rise in status). In order to further that cause, most investigators embrace a rationalized interpretation of the phenomena (nuts and bolts craft with flesh and blood aliens). As a result, the blindness is exacerbated, and those people become especially susceptible to hoaxes.

Benefits of Fraud and Hoaxing

Much of this chapter has been devoted to one case, but a few remarks on more general issues are in order. Because hoaxes, trickery, and deception play such major roles in the paranormal, they must have positive aspects. We must develop a sympathy for frauds if we are to understand them. It behooves us to recognize their benefits, to view them in a more positive light. Prejudice can blind us to their contributions, and hoaxers should not necessarily be denounced, reviled, and made pariahs.

Deceits can serve a variety of purposes, some quite unsuspected, even by those who expose them. The beneficiaries are not always obvious, and it is not always the skeptics who are the most cunning. The potential benefits are multiple, and I will outline a few of them.

Outrageously blatant fraud can serve as a warning that not everything is as it seems. For example, unconscious deception by a spiritualist medium can attract the attention of family and friends. It can be symptomatic, a plea for help to reintegrate dissociated aspects of the personality.[22] When a hoax becomes obvious, it alerts some people (typically outsiders rather than victims) that the reported phenomena are not altogether real. Astute observers can refrain from investing time, effort, money, and emotional commitment in gullible investigators pursuing chimeras. Investigators can lose their grip on consensual reality, be embarrassed, and suffer damage to their reputations, but others are duly warned.

Hoaxes give an opportunity to assess competence of investigators and the progress of a paranormal discipline. Frauds will continue to be perpetrated in all branches of the paranormal; individuals will continue to be duped. What is important though, is how such cases are handled. If experts in a field generally treat the reports skeptically, they demonstrate that their discipline has achieved some level of maturity. When leaders uncritically embrace claims, and open criticism is suppressed, the field does not deserve to be called scientific. Thus beneficiaries of a hoax may be the outside observers far removed from it, and hoaxers can inadvertently provide a public service.

Hoaxes can be perpetrated with the intention of being exposed. For instance, a successful psychic may be inundated with unwanted media attention which results in people calling and demanding readings, contact with deceased relatives, help locating a missing family member, or for healing. The attention can be distressing and even overwhelming. To reduce public interest, a psychic may discredit himself by committing some trick sure to be caught. Likewise, families enduring poltergeist activity can face similar problems. These families can be overrun by media intruding into their lives. A publicized instance of fraud can dissolve the interest, allowing them more private time to work out interpersonal problems, which are often important components of poltergeist outbreaks.

Paranormal abilities can bring other unwanted complications; for instance, some people see psychic power as a threat. Additionally, a psychic may develop a bit of paranoia and worry that others may fear his abilities. Paranoia can afflict both a psychic and possible enemies, and a publicized exposure of fraud may relieve the worries of both. It can be safer to be perceived as a practical joker or a fraud, than as a witch.

Similar ambiguity can benefit groups. A coven using magic may be seen as dangerous, but if it cultivates a reputation for being fraudulent, or insignificant, it can proceed with less interruption from outsiders. Psychic treasure hunters and mineral prospectors might wish to be seen as inconsequential or even nutty so as not to attract the interest of possible competitors. An intelligence agency with a psychic spying program might encourage publicity of frauds in order to discredit the very idea of psychic spies and convince people that nothing of substance is worth investigating. Such operations need not be aimed at enemies; they could be directed at congressional committees and news media that might take it too seriously and give the program unwanted attention.

Fraud can be used for exactly the opposite purpose too, that is, to seek the publicity that comes with an exposure. The apropos maxim is: any publicity is good publicity, as long as they spell your name right. Denouncing a psychic as fraudulent can attract new clients, contrary to debunkers' expectations. But this benefits both the debunker and the psychic; the skeptic can feel superior, and the psychic can gain business. Both win. In fact, I have a mentalist acquaintance who asked James Randi to expose him, in order to generate publicity. Some people have speculated that James Randi was Uri Geller's publicity manager (this was before Geller's lawsuits against Randi). Randi's efforts undoubtedly helped keep Geller's name before the public.

As seen above, the purposes and consequences of hoaxes are innumerable and multifaceted. From an outsider's viewpoint, the motives may be indeterminate. Even denunciation and exposure may be the desired outcome. Anyone who thinks that hoaxers' motives can be rationally inferred is simply naive.

Summary

The purpose of this chapter was two-fold: first, to present a case study showing the complexities of hoaxing, and second, to give further insight into UFO phenomena. The next Part of this book develops theoretical issues. In order to help prepare the reader, my concluding remarks here will address some of them, including marginality, rationalization, participation, and ambiguity. With the examples from this chapter, the abstract formulations to come should be more easily comprehended.

UFOs are liminal and anti-structural; they are found betwixt and between the heavens and the earth (a binary opposition). They have properties in common with angels, spirits, fairies, and demons. These are all interstitial, and when one enters this realm, one must tread cautiously because other binary oppositions can become blurred. The imagination-reality opposition is especially vulnerable.

Hoaxes are liminal productions. They lower the statuses of the victims, and loss of status is one of the defining characteristics of liminal conditions. Marginality is another trickster quality, and hoaxes help marginalize not only the victims but the whole field of ufology.

Hoaxes assist the rationalization and disenchantment of the world. They help consign the paranormal to the realm of fraud and gullibility, so that the phenomena receive little serious study. With the taint they induce, hoaxes protect the paranormal from close examination.

Anti-structure is a trickster quality, and it manifests in ufology's inability to effectively institutionalize its research. The failure is not a shortcoming of the leaders in the field, but rather it is a direct consequence of the phenomena studied.

In hoaxes, victims and investigators are often active participants. Hoaxers may shape their plots to fulfill the expectations of the dupes, and the dupes' responses thereby help determine a hoax's progress and direction. Thus an investigator's beliefs and expectations can influence the events generated by the hoaxer. This in effect constitutes a blurring of observer and observed, and it causes problems for objective inquiry because the investigator unwittingly participates in the phenomena. The topic of participation will be discussed in the next Part. It involves a blurring of subject and object, of self and other.

Ambiguity is a salient aspect of hoaxes. The actions and products of hoaxers can be interpreted in several ways. They can mean different things to different people. They show the difficulty in establishing an objective perspective from which to understand the events. Motives and purposes may be impossible to determine, and ambiguous, uncertain situations may never be resolved. Ambiguity is a trickster characteristic, and it is a central issue in post-structuralist literary theory, as will be discussed in the next Part.

In Western culture today, ambiguity, hoaxing, liminality, anti-structure, and the paranormal are all to be avoided, overcome, or shunned. They destabilize the rational world. They have not been given the theoretical attention they deserve. There are subtle taboos surrounding them, and that is a clue to their nature.

Part 5

Overview

We have seen that the trickster is associated with a confusing and exotic array of data, concepts, and implications. His purview includes ritual clowns who eat excrement, the collapse of cultures, side effects of strongly functioning psychic ability, magic tricks, and many others. Several readers of early drafts of this book found it difficult to perceive an overall theme; the ideas seemed scattered, even incoherent. This is indeed how the trickster appears in our current rationalistic paradigms.

It is the task of scholarship to interpret and reconcile the trickster with a logical, scientific worldview. The ideas must be at least partially distilled and translated in order for the implications to be grasped and the meaning comprehended. Any attempt will necessarily be incomplete, but that does not mean that we should abandon the effort.

An effective philosophical perspective should provide some frame of reference. We need to have some structure in which to think, perceive, analyze, some known or accepted base from which to start, a foundation. This is a bit problematic, because the trickster laughs at the idea that such is even possible in an absolute sense.

We will make some extended explorations into what appear to be four unrelated topics: first, reflexivity and its logical paradoxes; second, the limits of ESP and PK as considered from the findings of laboratory-based parapsychology; third, primitive thought, primarily explicated in regard to totemism; fourth, literary theory, particularly the deconstructionist and post-structuralist varieties. The central issues are abstract.

The basic issue is the rational versus the irrational. The rational typically refers to the use of reason, but I will use a slightly more restricted definition, specifically reasoning with rigorous adherence to Aristotelian logic.

Reflexivity is important because it poses paradoxes for logic. It reveals limits of rationality. It is a topic that is subtly avoided.

Several approaches to logic exist, but that of mathematician George Spencer-Brown is fruitful. His book *Laws of Form* (1969) opens by drawing a boundary, dividing an area into two pieces, and then exploring the consequences of crossing that boundary. His is an extremely simple procedure that is basically mathematical, and logic can be derived directly from it. Boundary drawing is so rudimentary that it is usually overlooked, but it has deep consequences. Spencer-Brown noted that the simple act of drawing distinctions is fundamental to structures "underlying linguistic, mathematical, physical and biological science."[1] He didn't elaborate upon this statement, but he recognized the power of his formulation.[2]

Making a distinction, differentiating one thing from another, carves out an item or event from a larger, more amorphous background. That process gives an identity. In making a distinction, some representation is required, whether simply mental, or more concretely as with gesture, speech, artistic portrayal, or writing. For instance, naming both makes a distinction and creates a representation. Naming, classification, and abstraction are processes of boundary drawing; they are required for thought. They lie at the root of information, communication, and even notions of self and objective reality.

Classification and making distinctions are social processes. Early humans used totemism as an important classification scheme. It structured innumerable societies, and it was linked to magic. It didn't appear logical to many twentieth-century scholars, and they considered it irrational. Yet it survived for thousands of years. Magic is still frequently disparaged, but parapsychology's data indicate that it actually works.

The muddled academic discussions about totemism and magic were important precursors to structuralism and deconstructionism. Structuralism helped explicate the order and communications of societies. It provided a link between anthropology, on the one hand, and literary theory, on the other. Deconstructionism was structuralism's successor. It has been applied mostly to texts; it emphasized ambiguity and challenged fundamental assumptions. Like totemism and magic, it was denounced as irrational.

Binary opposition was important in primitive classification, and it has been introduced already. It was a key concept in structuralism.

Oppositions are distinctions. In liminal conditions, oppositions and statuses are blurred or inverted.

Magic, the paranormal, and the supernatural are intimately tied to issues of boundaries, distinctions, and foundations. The phenomena violate boundaries, blur distinctions, and overturn foundations. Conversely, when boundaries are violated, or distinctions are blurred, or

foundations overturned, the supernatural erupts into the world. This is why the phenomena are so difficult to deal with within a rationalistic worldview.

CHAPTER 20

Reflexivity and the Trickster

> The result *and the sense* of the fraud is . . .
> not that it *simulates*, but that it *masks*, the genuine phenomena.
> Kurt Gödel, referring to the paranormal[1]

Reflexivity is one of the most abstract concepts presented in this book, and it is a frequent source of paradox and confusion. The concept is not difficult, but it often seems so, and because of that, few have recognized its generality. Common patterns can be seen in diverse areas when one understands properties of reflexive operations. Mathematical logic, literary theory, ethnomethodology, meditation, Lacanian psychoanalysis, and postmodernism carry examples of reflexivity, and they show some surprising commonalities.

The ideas of reflexivity, mirroring, reflection, self-reference, and projection are interrelated. Though some of these terms are often used interchangeably, it can be helpful to make distinctions. Self-reference is the source of a number of paradoxes. One of the best known is: "This statement is false" (Epimenides' paradox); the sentence refers to itself, and, if it is false, then it's true. On the surface, this seems trivial or even silly, but the consequences are profound. This paradox confuses subject and object; it explodes that distinction. Reflection is a slightly different idea; when one is reflective, one is aware of oneself. Being reflexive is a further step—one is aware of one's awareness. Reflexivity is the turning of some function or process back upon itself, as in using awareness to learn about awareness or using logic to study logic.

At first glance, reflexivity appears innocuous, but as it is pondered, scholars often become vaguely apprehensive. When restricted to mathematical logic or literary theory, the feelings are typically muted, but when consideration moves to concrete matters, researchers often encounter manifestations that are more ominous and then turn away.

Sociologists have offered some of the most intriguing comments. Bruno Latour warns that "Given the pressure of a scientific career, reflexivity is equivalent to suicide."[2] Hugh Mehan and Houston Wood note that: "The reflexivity of reflexivity lies behind Garfinkel's... statement that... Ethnomethodology is only 'for whoever has the nervous system to withstand it... for whoever can take it'."[3] Sociologists have recognized reflexivity to be dangerous, a way to make trouble, something to be avoided, and Malcolm Ashmore's book *The Reflexive Thesis* (1989) contains a substantial listing of quotes supporting this point. He also listed some of the names for the problem of reflexivity: "the abyss, the spectre, the infinite regress; paradox, aporia, antinomy."[4] These evoke the numinous.

Barbara Babcock, the preeminent theorist of the trickster, has written a number of papers dealing with reflexivity; in fact it was the topic of her doctoral dissertation. She noted that it is not a new idea, and numerous variants have been presented in many contexts. She points out that: "Reflexivity is a problematic concept, a paradoxical concept, and as Wittgenstein says, 'a concept with blurred edges'."[5] It necessarily leads to some ambiguity. Babcock is one of the very few who has understood its connection to liminality. The "blurred edges" she cites is only one brief allusion, and she has significantly developed other facets of the issue.

Manifestations of reflexivity frequently have some paranormal or mystical aspect in the milieu. It may emerge as something of a side issue or seem totally unrelated, but this frequent association indicates a fundamental connection. The lives of the people involved sometimes show this. As such, there will be an extended discussion of one person in whom reflexivity, paradox and the paranormal converge, namely Martin Gardner.

Although reflexivity has at times been topical in intellectual culture, almost nothing has been written on it in regard to parapsychology. The current ways of thinking in that field do not easily lend themselves to considering reflexivity or seeing its importance. Yet telepathy blurs the distinction between self and other (subject and object) and raises the question: "Who's thoughts am I thinking?" (a paranoiac query). Our society promotes rationality and leads us to view ourselves as discrete, independent entities. Psi challenges that idea by subverting the distinction between subject and object. Psi is intrinsically paradoxical, and paradox models are needed in conceptualizing psi phenomena; reflexive models provide them.

Sociology

Reflexivity is difficult to study directly. A more fruitful approach is to investigate its consequences by examining the social and intellectual environments where it is confronted. A few sociologists advised this tack, and Malcolm Ashmore quotes Steven Yearley saying "What I think is interesting about reflexivity is the way people evade the implications of the paradox, and I think it's other people's evasion that is interesting and instructive rather than that we should create an experience out of facing the anxiety itself. So why I seem to run down reflexivity is because with these paradoxes my feeling is that the best thing to do is *not* to confront them."[6] Ashmore also quotes Trevor Pinch warning him that reflexivity "presents peculiar 'political' problems since the audience for your work will be the people you study. Be warned—you are bound to make an enemy of everyone!"[7] This counsel is useful; however, I do not intend to fully follow Yearley and Pinch. I expect to antagonize people. I will accept Yearley's advice to notice where reflexivity erupts, and observe how it is handled, alluded to, and avoided.

The sociology of scientific knowledge (SSK) and ethnomethodology are two branches of sociology that have considered reflexivity at some length. The germane writings from those fields are especially valuable because they deal with reflexivity in real-world situations and not just in terms of abstract logic or in literary texts. This has enormous repercussions, including how ethnomethodology is conducted today.

Ethnomethodology

Ethnomethodology was founded by Harold Garfinkel, a professor of sociology at the University of California at Los Angeles. In its early years in the 1960s, ethnomethodology was quite radical, and many sociologists disavowed it. Since then, it has been tamed; its fundamental challenges have been largely repressed by sociology's collective memory, and ethnomethodology is now incorporated into the establishment, with introductory college texts devoting at least some space to it. Its roots can be traced to the phenomenology of Edmund Husserl. Though ethnomethodology shows little overlap with semiotics or structuralism in its intellectual predecessors or in its personnel, there are remarkable similarities in the salient issues.

Garfinkel's *Studies in Ethnomethodology* (1967) is one of the classic works of the field. It is egregiously written. In fact, anthropologist Anthony F. C. Wallace commented that "In some passages, normal English grammar is almost completely abandoned" and "Where one expects clear technical exposition, one finds instead the creative ambiguity of a prophet exhorting his followers and confounding the heathen." He suggests that it should be "read not as technical prose but inspirational literature."[8] Fortunately, *The Reality of Ethnomethodology* (1975) by Hugh Mehan and Houston Wood is much more accessible, and it provides a sophisticated discussion with many concrete examples. Their book addresses a multitude of issues including reflexivity and paranoia.

Ethnomethodologists took as their subject matter the interactions of everyday social life and how people make sense of them. That sounds innocuous enough, but ethnomethodologists probed foundations. They recognized that for orderly common activity, people must share a large body of assumptions, meanings, and expectations, though these are not consciously recognized. In order to make them explicit (i.e., bring them to conscious awareness), breaching experiments were invented, and those involved violating, in some way, typical patterns of behavior. For instance students might be given an assignment to return home and act as though they were boarders (e.g., being very polite, using formal address, and not showing undue familiarity), and later record their reactions and those of their family. These exercises often caused parents and siblings to become angry and upset.

Garfinkel was explicit about his aims. He said "Procedurally it is my preference to start with familiar scenes and ask what can be done to make trouble."[9] He stated that it was his intention to provoke "bewilderment, consternation, and confusion; to produce the socially structured affects of anxiety, shame, guilt, and indignation; and to produce disorganized interaction should tell us something about how the structures of everyday activities are ordinarily and routinely produced and maintained."[10] These breaching experiments have commonalities with anti-structure and the trickster; they all violate the *boundaries* that *frame* experience.

Another ethnomethodology exercise was to have students record a brief, everyday conversation (maybe only 5 or ten sentences long) and prepare a transcription of it on the left-hand half of a sheet of paper. On the right half of the sheet, they would proceed to explain it, and in doing so they often came to realize that the conversation was nearly unintelligible to outsiders. Their explanations were typically much longer than the original conversation. The next step was to have them explain the explanation. The students would soon recognize that this could become an infinite process, demonstrating the impossibility of specifying all aspects required for complete understanding. This could be applied to any communication, and as Mehan and Wood put it: "*all* symbolic forms (rules, linguistic utterances, gestures, actions) carry a fringe of incompleteness."[11]

These kinds of experiments and demonstrations led ethnomethodologists to explore issues of abstraction, reflexivity, and participation (i.e., becoming part of the phenomenon). I will describe some of them, but the reader should be aware that today summaries of ethnomethodology often give them little or no notice. The topics proved too subversive. In fact several recent reviews note that analysis of conversations is now the major part of ethnomethodology. That keeps it safe by restricting it to text so that it cannot wreak havoc in the outer world.

Ethnomethodology applied to sociology (i.e., reflexively) was not always flattering or welcome, especially when the incompleteness of sociology's assumptions was pointed out. These challenges irritated other sociologists. Mehan and Wood report: "Ethnomethodology investigates everyday life. Social science colleagues sometimes ask me to tell them about ethnomethodology. I have developed presentations using videotapes of everyday scenes. I find that sociologists have had little experience at such observations. This incompetence is remarkable . . . They have no interest in the scenes themselves. It is only when they are discussing abstracted concepts that they feel secure. I am often made to feel as if I have breached some deep taboo by even suggesting that the problem of social order is related to everyday interactions."[12]

Mehan and Wood note that "because alone among the sciences it treats meaning itself as a phenomenon, ethnomethodology exhibits several novel characteristics."[13] Meaning is a concern shared by literary theory, and as I will explain later, it is one that scientists avoid.

Ethnomethodologists pointed out that one is part of that which one observes, i.e., one participates in processes of observation. The issue of participation has some intriguing connections. At least since Levy-Bruhl's *How Natives Think* (1910) it has been associated with the nonrational. Mehan and Wood mentioned an article by Edmund Leach reviewing an anthology containing several papers critical of contemporary practices in anthropology. In that review, Leach spent some space discussing the issue of participation, one that ethnographers necessarily face. He commented: "But God forbid that we should propose the search for mystical experience as a proper substitute for the pretensions of objectivity. I have no wish to muddle up my scholarly concerns with the ethics of a Franciscan friar."[14] As he typically does, Leach strikes at the heart of the matter with sparkling, unexpected comparisons. The references to mystical experience and a Franciscan friar are altogether appropriate. Mysticism subverts subjective and objective, and friars are permanently liminal persons. Reflexivity entails participation and raises the issue of the irrational.

Mehan and Wood say that their theoretical perspective "within ethnomethodology commits me to the study of concrete scenes and to the recognition that I am always a part of those scenes. Social science is committed to avoiding both of those involvements."[15] They are correct, but few social scientists wish to acknowledge the consequences. The abstraction and distancing found in all science endow a certain status and privilege from which to judge and comment on others. In order to maintain that position, scientists must not get too "dirty," too closely associated with their objects of study. Ethnomethodologists understand that they necessarily participate in the phenomena they observe. Mehan and Wood comment that "Ethnomethodology can be seen as an activity of destratification."[16] This destratification is a leveling of status, and that is also associated with liminal conditions (a.k.a., anti-structure). Thus social leveling via participation and reflexivity has been recognized by theorists from entirely separate disciplines, demonstrating its validity. As I will show shortly, this same issue of status leveling irrupts in the sociology of scientific knowledge.

As befits those who deal with reflexivity, ethnomethodologists have had some amusing encounters with tricksters. Garfinkel was one of the faculty members who approved Carlos Castaneda's Ph.D. dissertation.[17] But this was not the only instance of his being duped in the course of his professional work.

The longest chapter in *Studies in Ethnomethodology* was devoted to "Agnes" who was born a boy. At puberty he developed no facial hair, and his breasts began to enlarge. Garfinkel became interested for theoretical reasons. He hypothesized that a person strives to develop a clearly defined sex role because that is what others expect, and by conforming to those expectations, social life becomes easier. Garfinkel spent time interviewing Agnes in order to illuminate that process. Agnes then underwent surgery to remove her penis and become a woman.

The medical doctors and Garfinkel believed that the condition was congenital, but unbeknownst to them, the boy had regularly stolen Stilbestrol from his mother, and taken it for years. His gender ambiguity was intentionally induced. Agnes had chosen to be sexually ambiguous for years. All this was discovered after Garfinkel wrote his book, and it falsified his hypothesis in a very embarrassing way.

Mehan and Wood's *The Reality of Ethnomethodology* is not completely free from gullibility either. It favorably cites Castaneda and another hoax-like work, *Keep the River on Your Right* by Tobias Schneebaum. Schneebaum told a story of Akarama tribesmen in South American engaging in homosexual activity and cannibalism, which anthropologists knew were not part of their tradition. In any event, Schneebaum dropped strong hints that the book should not be taken as fully factual, and Mehan and Wood should have recognized them, but they didn't. Richard de Mille revealed the embarrassing mistake in his highly entertaining and instructive anthology *The Don Juan Papers* (1980). He showed Schneebaum's account was largely fantasy, and he also included a statement by Schneebaum, essentially admitting as much.[18] Despite such slips by Mehan and Wood, I highly recommend their volume, though I suggest reading in it conjunction with de Mille's.

These three embarrassments for ethnomethodology—"Agnes," Schneebaum, and Castaneda—have clear trickster and liminal elements. The Anges and Schneebaum cases involved deception and sexual ambiguity. The Castaneda affair, by far the most famous, highlighted deception and the paranormal. It seems no accident that they were found with ethnomethodology, a reflexive discipline.

Several important themes coincide in early ethnomethodology: tricksters, leveling of status, participation, and challenges to foundational assumptions.

Sociology of Scientific Knowledge (SSK)

The sociology of scientific knowledge (SSK) also confronts reflexivity. It is a relatively new branch of science, emerging in the last 30 years, and many of the prominent SSK practitioners reside in Britain. It contrasts with older versions of sociology of science, which studied scientists, their institutions, and their social relations. SSK goes further and explores the nature, content, and truth of scientific knowledge. *Social Studies of Science* is the leading journal of the field; it has covered reflexivity and occasionally discussed parapsychology.

Researchers in SSK often take an ethnographic approach; they are more likely to conduct case studies rather than using survey questionnaires, which are more detached and distancing vis-à-vis the subjects. The practitioners sometimes become participant observers involved with the day-to-day activities of scientific laboratories. With this firsthand knowledge, they don't have to rely on scientists' interpretations and explanations of how they establish facts. Instead, the sociologists develop their own understanding of the process. Steve Woolgar, a leading figure in SSK, says that SSK researchers: "adopted the stance of an anthropologist joining a strange tribe, engaging in prolonged participant observation . . . This afforded the possibility of being deliberately sceptical about just those knowledge claims which seemed most evident and obvious to members of the tribe."[19]

Of course sociologists who discuss the "truth" of scientific knowledge appropriate the customary roles of laboratory scientists and philosophers. SSK practitioners assert that scientific facts are socially constructed, and some even challenge the philosophical idea of "fact." This is consistent with strains of postmodernism, and SSK is associated with relativist perspectives; it opposes positivist, realist, and objectivist positions in the philosophy of science. Needless to say, SSK has sparked considerable debate and antagonism.

SSK innately involves reflexivity, and a number of its practitioners have addressed the topic. Ashmore's already-mentioned book *The Reflexive Thesis* falls within the field, but he was not the only one to cover the issue. Steve Woolgar edited a volume entitled *Knowledge and Reflexivity: New Frontiers in the Sociology of Knowledge* (1988) with a number of useful contributions. The reader should be warned that the SSK discussions of reflexivity are formidable; they invoke such concepts as similarity, distance, and representation. They tread into arid philosophical areas where it is difficult to grasp any substance. Yet the articles are worth the effort, because the patterns and insights they identify can be overlooked when contemplating matters that are more concrete.

Two essays in *Knowledge and Reflexivity* are of particular interest: one by Woolgar and another by Bruno Latour. Neither is easy to summarize.

Representation and status are inherently part of the scientific process. Woolgar explained that a physicist tries to objectively describe (represent) electrons; he is "distant" from them. Similarly, an ethnographer portrays an exotic primitive people; the more exotic they appear, the more distant they are. The ethnographer and the primitive (like the physicist and electron) share little in common. Both the physicist and ethnographer seem "objective," and their accounts are privileged and taken as true by readers. This is illustrated when an ethnographer's explanation of primitives' "superstitious" behavior is accepted as correct, but the primitives' own understanding is ignored.

The physicist and ethnographer enjoy a higher status than the objects of their inquiry.

Participation is of theoretical interest in SSK. In much of sociology, participant-observation is carried out among marginal or low-status groups such as religious cults, the poor, or ethnic minorities. Sociologists dare not undertake comparable research with bankers, CEOs, or college presidents. Likewise, anthropologists may study primitive peoples, i.e., socially distant and "inferior." However with SSK, there is not so much social distance between the observers and the observed. In fact the status of the objects of study may equal or exceed that of the researcher, at least initially. Scientists traditionally are assumed to be the final arbiters of scientific knowledge. But when they become objects of study and are described (represented) by sociologists, their legitimacy and reliability are called into question. Sociologists demonstrate that scientists are not as objective and rational as many people thought and that they are influenced by subjective and social factors in evaluating data. This naturally calls into question the authority, objectivity, and rationality of science, and it has the potential of reducing the status of scientists. As in liminality, there is a leveling or even inversion of status. Again we see the connection between reflexivity, status reduction, and participation—a connection also found in ethnomethodology. It is no accident that participation arose in Levy-Bruhl's discussions of primitive mentality. Participation raises issues not only of status but also of the basis of rationality. These are discomforting matters, and Woolgar admitted that "Most social scientists tend to steer well clear of any sustained examination of the significance of reflexivity, despite frequently acknowledging its relevance in general terms."[20]

Bruno Latour's essay in *Knowledge and Reflexivity*, "The Politics of Explanation: An Alternative," holds a number of insights about information, abstraction, and explanation. Latour is from France, and the influence of French philosophy is apparent in his writing. Among other things, he explains why Garfinkel and the deconstructionists are so hard to understand, a charge that more than one commentator has made against Latour himself. Impenetrability is a frequent consequence of reflexivity, so here I will not try to summarize his presentation, but only his conclusions.

Latour concludes that when reflexivity is applied on a limited basis in the academic enterprise, it is often sterile and leads to little productivity. However he suggests that greater application of it should produce interdisciplinary pollination. Hybridization and increased understanding across academic boundaries should result. I was very pleased to see this conclusion, because my own readings convinced me that an interdisciplinary approach was required to make progress with the topic of reflexivity (and of psychic phenomena). His explicit mention of "boundaries" (and their disruption) confirms the importance of them for understanding the repercussions of reflexivity. In short, Latour's essay marks him as a major theorist of the topic.[21]

Replication of scientific experiments is one of the thorny problems tackled by SSK. It is a foundational issue of science. Most scientists accept the simple idea that valid experiments must be repeatable by others. But when the matter is closely examined, all sorts of complexities arise. What is replication? Who determines whether it is accomplished? How is it described? In controversial areas, simply doing more experiments doesn't resolve issues about putative effects; there are continuing arguments about what is required for a satisfactory experiment. Slight changes in conditions may have important consequences, and those can be debated endlessly. Conducting more experiments can lead to what has been termed the "experimenter's regress." Do objective observations establish fact, or is it only social agreement? Further, written reports are not always sufficient to explain an experiment's procedure. Sometimes direct personal training is required to teach the skill and convey the necessary information for successful replication. Abstract text is inadequate. SSK raises all these issues, and in a subtle but profound way it strikes a blow against the foundational myth that science is a fully objective process.

Harry Collins and Trevor Pinch are two of the leading sociologists who have investigated replication, and their work features prominently in both Ashmore's and Woolgar's books on reflexivity. Collins and Pinch are of added interest, because they have also studied the paranormal. In fact four of their books on sociology discuss parapsychology: *Sociology of Scientific Knowledge: A Source Book* (1982), *Frames of Meaning* (1982), *Changing Order* (1985), and *The Golem* (1993). Additionally, they have written on CSICOP, and relatively early in his career Collins even carried out an investigation of psychic metal bending by children. He took part in a 1986 symposium sponsored by the Parapsychology Foundation, contributing a paper entitled "Scientific Knowledge and Scientific Criticism." Parapsychology provided Collins and Pinch a natural choice for case material because replication has been a central issue in the field for decades.[22]

With SSK, and especially with its attentiveness to reflexivity, we see a constellation of ideas: loss of status, participation, questioning of foundations, representation, and, as an apparent side issue, the paranormal. However abstractly formulated in SSK, these same matters lie at the heart of liminality and the trickster.

Experimenter Effects in Psychology

While Robert Rosenthal was analyzing an experiment for his Ph.D. dissertation in the mid-1950s, he was dismayed to discover that his data indicated that he had unintentionally biased his subjects (he had inadvertently "participated" in the experiment). This initially unwelcome discovery shaped his career, and he went on to study experimenter expectancy effects. After completing his doctorate, he conducted experiments with several lower echelon researchers. Each carried out the same procedure, but they were told to expect different results. Rosenthal demonstrated that significant biases could be thereby induced.[23]

Experimenting on experimenters is innately reflexive, and it raises the question of whether experimenters can objectively investigate the world. How extreme are their biases? The philosophical point disconcerted many psychologists, and Rosenthal received some sharp criticisms. In addition, some researchers claimed that they were unable to repeat his results (the replication problem). In the end, Rosenthal largely prevailed, and experimenter expectancy effects are now accepted as real. Nevertheless, his work raises questions about the ultimate validity of experimentation, but as with ethnomethodology, the especially troubling ones, the true foundational issues, are largely ignored.

Rosenthal went on to investigate how teachers' expectancies influence their pupils. In a number of studies, grade school students were given an intelligence test, and afterwards teachers were told that some of them should intellectually bloom in the coming months. Unknown to the teachers, the "bloomers" were not selected by the test, but instead were designated randomly. Months later, another test was administered, and the randomly selected bloomers had increased their objective test scores more than the other students. Somehow the teachers had unconsciously transmitted their expectations to the students, who fulfilled them. This has sometimes been referred to as the Rosenthal-Pygmalion effect.[24] It attracted enormous attention (I remember my parents discussing it at the dinner table); it showed the relevance of psychological research in a way that everyone could understand.

Rosenthal later became one of the pioneers in the development of meta-analysis, a procedure to quantitatively evaluate large numbers of statistically-based studies. Much early work with meta-analysis was done in psychology, and it is now frequently used in medicine and other fields.

As in other instances of reflexivity, there is often a connection with the paranormal. This is true with Robert Rosenthal. In fact, the very first psychology experiment he conducted, while still in high school, was an ESP test, and he had even written to J. B. Rhine about it.[25] This was not to be his only contact with the field. In the mid 1980s he was commissioned by the National Research Council (the research arm of the National Academy of Sciences) to provide a report on several areas of interest to the U.S. Army. When he came to positive conclusions about parapsychology, the NRC pressured him to remove that section. He refused, and they tried to suppress his findings.[26]

Meditation

"Meditation" encompasses a wide range of practices; in some forms, a person may simply sit quietly with eyes closed and just observe what happens. Images, ideas, and feelings will emerge from the unconscious and display themselves to conscious awareness. Consciousness is used to observe consciousness, and thus the process is reflexive. Meditation blurs the area between the conscious and the unconscious.

Daniel Goleman gives a very useful overview of meditation in his book *The Meditative Mind* (1988). Goleman taught at Harvard, wrote for the *New York Times* for twelve years covering behavioral and brain sciences, and he was author of the best-selling book *Emotional Intelligence* (1995). He also spent two years in the Far East studying meditation. Goleman distinguishes between concentration, "in which mind focuses on a fixed mental object" and mindfulness "in which mind observes itself."[27] Mindfulness fits the definition for being reflexive. Concentration though is not far removed from it. Mind observes a "mental object," i.e., a product of mind; thus even in concentration, mind is inwardly attentive of itself.

A number of meditative schools speak of encountering the void or the abyss. Malcolm Ashmore noted that those are other names for the problem of reflexivity. Adept meditators sometimes speak of the ineffable. Douglas Hofstadter's *Gödel, Escher, Bach* (1979) briefly discusses

Zen, a meditative discipline, saying "Zen is the fight against reliance on words."[28] (The same issue is raised in other contexts in which reflexivity is engaged. The obscurity of the writings of Garfinkel and of the deconstructionists also challenges the hegemony of words.)

Goleman reports that many traditions have warnings about the dangers of meditation and the need for purification before one engages in it. This signals a liminal, anti-structural domain, and this makes sense. In meditation, the outer physical world is disregarded. Its structure, order, and routine no longer hold the conscious mind to the regularities of existence.

Paranormal powers sometimes accompany meditative practice, and Goleman notes that they are explicitly addressed in the literature of the classical schools. Typically there are warnings against pursuing them; thus they are taboo within an already liminal domain. Meditation has had a long association with mysticism, and it is an integral part of mystical practice. Numerous mystics have displayed paranormal abilities. But the evidence regarding meditation and psi is not merely anecdotal. A number of laboratory studies have shown that meditation enhances ESP scoring in experimental tests.[29]

Like other liminal activities, meditation became prominent in the U.S. in the late 1960s and 1970s. That period saw the burgeoning interest in the paranormal (and the emergence of ethnomethodology, SSK, and deconstructionism). The Transcendental Meditation movement attracted the Beatles and a number of movie stars. Academe began to take notice, and in 1969 Charles Tart published the anthology *Altered States of Consciousness*. It became a widely used text, and it had a section devoted to meditation. Tart, by the way, has authored several books and many papers on parapsychology.

In summary, meditation has a number of liminal features. It blurs the boundary between conscious and unconscious; its traditional schools warn of dangers; it is associated with mysticism and paranormal abilities. Many forms are inherently reflexive.

Mathematical Logic

Mathematical logic might seem to have little in common with sociology, meditation, or literary criticism, but reflexivity is found there as well. Kurt Gödel, the foremost mathematical logician of the twentieth century, demonstrated the importance of reflexivity for mathematics. Born in Moravia in 1906, he attended the University of Vienna and took part in meetings of the Vienna Circle, a group of influential philosophers of science, though he later made it known that he did not accept the doctrines associated with the Circle. In 1931 Gödel published his Incompleteness Theorem, which rigorously showed that any consistent logical system of sufficient complexity is necessarily incomplete. There exist true statements about the system that must lie outside of it; they cannot be proven from within. The proof made use of self-reference; it used logic to study limits of logic and thus was reflexive. With this proof, Gödel brought the issues of self-reference and reflexivity to the foundations of mathematics. For several decades prior, mathematicians had attempted to provide a fully logical basis for mathematics, and Gödel demonstrated that was impossible. His proof was revolutionary.[30]

By any measure Gödel was a brilliant though odd character. He suffered a nervous breakdown in 1934 and several times again during that decade. This period might be seen as a time of creative illness, to use Henri Ellenberger's term.[31] Gödel emigrated to the U.S. and took a position at the Institute for Advanced Study in Princeton, where he remained from 1940 until his death in 1978. His social circle was quite limited, and he had no teaching responsibilities at the Institute, which further assured his rather isolated existence. His precisely logical mind sometimes led to problems in the normal social world where ambiguity plays a role. Near the end of his life, he was paranoid of doctors and medicine.

Gödel had a more than passing interest in parapsychology. Several members of the Vienna Circle, including Gödel apparently, took part in séances. His biographer, John Dawson, found a memorandum of his that appeared to be a record of a séance. Gödel also believed his wife to have the ability to predict numbers generated by chance.[32] His private papers demonstrate that he maintained an interest in such topics, including demonology, over a period of decades.[33] Gödel considered himself a Platonist, and his biographer Hao Wang noted that "he had spoken of rocks having experience and the spirits hiding out today," though Wang was not sure how serious he was.[34] At any rate, in Kurt Gödel we find yet another example of the conjunction of reflexivity and the paranormal.

Initially, few recognized the importance of Gödel's incompleteness discovery (though John von Neumann did immediately). It took some time for many to grasp its implications, and it is only in the last two decades that they have come to significant public awareness. Scholars in other fields are taking notice; for instance, semiotics professor Floyd

Merrell has referred to Gödel as "perhaps the greatest 'deconstructor' the Western World has seen."[35] The attention given Gödel has been largely due to efforts of several popular authors. These have included Douglas Hofstadter with his classic *Gödel, Escher, Bach* (1979), William Poundstone with *The Recursive Universe* (1985) and *Labyrinths of Reason* (1988), Rudy Rucker's *Infinity and the Mind* (1982) and *The Fourth Dimension* (1984), Jeremy Campbell's *Grammatical Man* (1982), Raymond Smullyan's *Satan, Cantor, and Infinity* (1992), and John Casti with *Searching for Certainty* (1990).

Though these writers discuss reflexivity primarily in the context of mathematical logic, some of them have ventured further. Rudy Rucker in particular has pushed the boundaries, and he has discussed some intriguing connections with the paranormal. His *The Fourth Dimension* addresses spiritualism, synchronicity and telepathy, though he was unfortunately unaware of the scientific research on the matters he raised. In his *Infinity and the Mind* he acknowledges that "Infinity commonly inspires feelings of awe, futility, and fear,"[36] a clear hint at the numinous.

Rucker is an interesting character; he is a descendant of Georg Wilhelm F. Hegel, the German philosopher; he holds a doctorate in mathematics, has written science fiction, and was a co-author of *Mondo 2000: A User's Guide to The New Edge* (1992) which included "cyberpunk, virtual reality, wetware, designer aphrodisiacs, artificial life, techno-erotic paganism," and more. Such montage and mixing of diverse categories is typical of liminal and postmodern productions. This creativity extends to his mathematical writings, and it is an example of the hybridization and interdisciplinary pollination mentioned by Latour in reference to reflexivity.

There is one more person who has been instrumental in popularizing the topics of reflexivity and self-reference—Martin Gardner. He contributed blurbs to books by Hofstadter, Poundstone, Smullyan,[37] Campbell, and Rucker, and he wrote a foreword to *The Fourth Dimension*.[38]

Martin Gardner

The person of Martin Gardner illuminates reflexivity. His work covers mathematics, magic, literary criticism, the paranormal, religion, and paradox, and he exemplifies the cross-pollination and hybridization that can accompany reflexivity. Gardner is a lively, fascinating, and paradoxical character, and as such this section may provide a respite from the abstract philosophical matters that dominate this Part.

Gardner has also been the single most powerful antagonist of the paranormal in the second half of the twentieth century, and any cultural analysis of the paranormal must grapple with him. His innumerable books, articles, and life provide a wealth of material for examination.[39] These illuminate the paranormal in a way rarely seen; for the antagonist not only instinctively identifies the weaknesses of the other, but also possesses some of the qualities he despises. Much is to be gained by studying him.

Gardner is an extraordinarily prolific and influential writer; his work has appeared in many magazines, and major publishing houses have produced his books. His recent anthology, *The Night Is Large* (1996), included a list of 56 of his books, and that was incomplete. For much of his career he lived in the New York City area and developed important contacts in the publishing industry. His influence is evidenced by the fact that he was allowed to review one of his own works in the pages of the *New York Review of Books*.[40]

His greatest fame came from the Mathematical Games column he wrote for *Scientific American* for a quarter century, and upon his retirement from it, several magazines carried articles about his career.[41] After he retired, Douglas Hofstadter carried on for a while in the same vein preparing a similar series entitled "Metamagical Themas." Gardner's writings educated generations of mathematicians, computer and physical scientists, and engineers, and many who read him as children are now in positions of power. He has been celebrated by mathematicians, with Volume 22 (1990) of the *Journal of Recreational Mathematics* dedicated to him. Also, a book of essays, *The Mathematical Gardner* (1981), was prepared in his honor.[42] But mathematics is not the only area in which he has achieved fame.

Gardner established his reputation in the paranormal in 1952 with his book *In the Name of Science*, which proved to be a landmark in debunking polemics. That work took a popular rather than scholarly approach; it contained no footnotes or list of references, and it established an aggressive, belittling style now common among debunkers of the paranormal. In 1957 the book was revised and released under the title *Fads and Fallacies in the Name of Science*, and it remains in print.

His numerous contacts in New York publishing helped him to promote the skeptical movement publicly and assist it behind the scenes. He aided C. E. M. Hansel in getting his academic, highly skeptical *ESP: A Scientific Evaluation* published in 1966; that book was probably the most detailed critique of the scientific parapsychology literature to that time. Undoubtedly Gardner has helped others. He was a founding member of CSICOP, and his circle of friends, including Marcello Truzzi, James Randi, and Ray Hyman had formed a loose group called RSEP (Resources for the Scientific Evaluation of the Paranormal) that was CSICOP's immediate predecessor. Gardner also served as something of a father figure to magician James Randi, who went on to become the most visible spokesman for CSICOP. With these efforts and others, Gardner is justifiably referred to as the godfather of the skeptical movement.

Gardner was born in 1914 in Oklahoma. His father was a geologist and oilman and pantheist; his mother was a devout Methodist. As a teenager, Gardner embraced a strain of Protestant fundamentalism. He attended the University of Chicago intending to study physics, but he got sidetracked and majored in philosophy instead. He studied under Rudolf Carnap, who had been a leading figure in the Vienna Circle, and Gardner later edited a book of his. While at the university, Gardner underwent a religious crisis and rejected his high-school fundamentalism. The transition was painful, and in order to deal with it, he wrote a semi-autobiographical novel *The Flight of Peter Fromm*. That work remained unpublished until 1973, years later.

That book is narrated by Homer Wilson, a secular humanist professor, who tells the story of a young divinity student at the University of Chicago, Peter Fromm. Peter slowly rejects a literalist interpretation of the Bible and embraces a basically rationalistic one. The book is largely devoted to a discussion of Protestant theology, and Gardner shows great familiarity with the writings of Tillich, Barth, Niebuhr, Bultmann, Kierkegaard, and others. He obviously spent an enormous amount of time reading and pondering them. *The Flight of Peter Fromm* was engagingly written, and it was of sufficient merit to receive a review in the *Journal for the Scientific Study of Religion*.[43]

Thousands of others have undergone such transformations, but Gardner's writing is valuable because it so clearly explains the issues, a characteristic of his prose generally. Both the book and his later commentaries on it express an antagonism toward ambiguity in religious matters. Much of his crisis of faith revolved around the literal truth of the resurrection of Christ, the Virgin Birth, and other miracles, and he was unable to accept the evidence for them. His striving for clarity led him to confront issues that many try to avoid.

The book was reprinted in 1994, by Paul Kurtz's Prometheus Books, with an afterword in which Gardner discussed his early fundamentalism and reported that when he reread the book in order to prepare the afterword, that "it was agonizing to recall the doctrinal zigzags of my youth."[44] There is no question that religious issues have had a profound impact on his life, and he has a continuing preoccupation with them.

During his Chicago years, scholarship consumed Gardner. John Booth, a leading chronicler of magic and magicians, knew him as a young man and commented on his then "monk's existence . . . [living] in a single plain room furnished only with a cot, desk and chair. In a few shoe boxes were filed stacks of cards on which he had laboriously summarized the total of all the knowledge that he felt he possessed."[45]

The philosophical bent never left Gardner, and he seems to prefer books, ideas, and abstractions to direct personal contact. Several have commented upon his shyness; though an active correspondent, Gardner almost never attends conferences. He has never made a presentation at a CSICOP convention, and when the Mathematical Association of America honored him at its annual meeting, he did not attend.[46] As a writer, Gardner is a more solitary figure than those in academe who regularly interact with students and colleagues on a daily, face-to-face basis.

One cannot understand Gardner and his involvement in the paranormal without considering the entire corpus of his writings including those on conjuring, mathematics, logic, paradox, and religion. He freely intermixes these and does not treat them as separate, clearly demarcated fields of inquiry. This boundary blurring befits a trickster character. His views on the paranormal are intricately linked not only with religion, conjuring, and philosophy, but can even be seen in his writings on mathematics. Both in his person and in his work, he brings together topics that others keep separate.[47]

Critic

In the last half-century, Gardner has been *the* most prolific and influential critic of the paranormal, and many of his essays on it have been compiled into anthologies including *Science: Good, Bad and Bogus* (1981), *The New Age: Notes of a Fringe Watcher* (1988), and *On the Wild Side* (1992). A number of his other collections carry pieces on the paranormal as well. His commentary on psychical research runs the gamut from obscure figures in its history such as Johann Zöllner,

Douglas Blackburn, and Leonora Piper to more modern, laboratory psi research conducted at Duke University, Stanford Research Institute and elsewhere.

Gardner's role as paranormal critic cannot be appreciated without knowing his background in conjuring. Magic has been his life-long hobby, and he began writing on it while still a teenager. Though he does not perform publicly, he has made innumerable contributions to that field.[48] Among other periodicals, Gardner contributed to *The Jinx*, a newsletter edited by Ted Annemann, perhaps the most creative mentalist of the twentieth century. A Gardner piece appeared in the 1938 Summer Extra issue, and the cover story of the immediately following number, August 1938, was devoted to a critique of Rhine's work by Annemann. This kind of article is not uncommon in the magic literature, but parapsychologists are almost completely unaware of it. Gardner though has had a long exposure to that venue of criticism, and that helped shape his life.

Gardner's interest in magic was not limited to mentalism, and he produced the 574-page *Encyclopedia of Impromptu Magic* (1978), which was compiled from his numerous magic magazine columns. Much of that material is pertinent for close-up situations, where a magician performs within a few feet, or even inches, of spectators. Knowledge of close-up magic is required for evaluating demonstrations of claimed PK such as bending keys or spoons or levitating small objects. Stage magic, on the other hand, is largely irrelevant for such assessments. Thus Gardner is particularly well qualified to comment on deception and the paranormal.

Much of his criticism of psychical research focuses on possibilities of cheating. He has an ability to quickly spot methods magicians might use in overcoming controls. His attacks are usually on the mark, but they are not always recognized as such by those whom he criticizes, investigators who typically have no knowledge of conjuring. Nearly all of Gardner's criticisms have been leveled at reports of individuals gifted with psychic powers. He avoids commenting on experiments that test groups of ordinary people who claim no special abilities, though such studies constitute the bulk of formal parapsychological research. The problem of deception is much less severe in research with groups than with investigations of a talented individual.[49]

Though little of his criticism is directed at work published in the refereed parapsychology journals, a notable exception is his book *How Not to Test a Psychic: Ten Years of Remarkable Experiments with Renowned Clairvoyant Pavel Stepanek* (1989). Stepanek, a clerk and resident of Prague, was extensively tested in the 1960s, but he is little known outside parapsychology. He obtained outstanding results in a set of tedious card experiments in which he was asked to guess which face of a card was uppermost inside a container (typically the cards had a green and a white side). This was a binary decision with a 50% chance of being correct on a trial. Many papers were published on Stepanek in the parapsychology journals as well as one in *Nature*, and for some years the research was considered landmark work in the field.

Gardner attacked it from the perspective of a magician. He suggested ways that subtle sensory cues coupled with cheating could explain the results. He also addressed potential randomization flaws on which Stepanek might have capitalized. Overall, he convincingly demonstrated that the investigators did not use sufficiently strict controls and did not understand methods a magician might use to cheat. The parapsychologists' responses were surprisingly weak. Only Jurgen Keil attempted a defense, and that was brief.[50] Given the voluminous research with Stepanek, the limited response to Gardner is surprising. This is partly explained by the cogency of Gardner's assault, but also because the Stepanek work has relatively little relationship to other major research in the field either theoretically or procedurally. As the original studies were published in professional parapsychology journals, Gardner's attack constitutes one of the strongest indictments of the field on its inability to institute adequate safeguards against trickery.[51]

How Not to Test a Psychic is an extremely detailed, technical work, and because the potential readership is small, I was surprised that the book was published. I would be more surprised to learn that even 10–15 people read it with any thoroughness. It is to his and his publisher's credit that the critique saw print. Considering the breadth and depth of his effort, the only comparable attack from a CSICOP member focussing on a particular line of research is Ray Hyman's 1985 critique of the ganzfeld, which was substantially refuted.[52] Gardner demonstrated a capability to address a sophisticated research effort. He proved himself a formidable critic on certain technical matters, far more so than a number of professional psychologists who have published skeptical books on psychical research.

All this is not to say that Gardner's critiques are without flaws, and there have been some ethical questions raised about his methods. Gardner wrote to Stepanek and suggested that he give an interview describing how he cheated. Gardner offered to help publicize it and arrange for a documentary film that would bring him money and fame. Stepanek refused, a fact that tends to support his honesty. Some may see Gardner's attempt as one of bribery to suborn testimony. He seems to have been embarrassed by the matter, and when his letter to Stepanek became known, he threatened to sue if it was published.[53]

Another facet that detracts from Gardner's full credibility is that he has been unwilling to submit to the discipline required for scientific publication. He has chosen to publish his work in unrefereed, popular forums where he is not subject to peer review and full and open rebuttal. Unfortunately this led him into errors that he might not have otherwise made.

A most surprising series of mistakes is found in his comments on the statistics of the Stepanek work. His remarks reveal an ignorance and carelessness entirely unexpected from someone who has written so clearly on probability and someone so honored by mathematicians. For instance, on page 67 of *How Not to Test a Psychic* he cites a study where Stepanek achieved 2636 hits out of 5000 trials giving a deviation from chance of 136, but Gardner claims that this is very close to chance level. In fact, as the original report states, that score gives a $z = 3.85$ with a $p = .00012$ (2-tailed). This is a very significant result, and anyone familiar with these kinds of calculations, even seeing just the raw score, should immediately recognize the outcome to be significant. It is hard to understand how Gardner made this mistake.

This is not the only such error; on page 98 he cites a series with 225 hits in 400 trials, 25 hits above chance, and he again claims this to be at chance level, which clearly it is not ($p = .007$, one-tailed). Ironically, in the paragraph immediately preceding this claim, Gardner cites an earlier Stepanek series with 400 hits out of 800 trials. He goes on to say that this "tends to cast suspicion on the reliability of the data" because the result was exactly at chance. He correctly gives the probability of obtaining exactly that score ($p = .028$). This is of marginal significance at best, and the value is much larger than those p-values he incorrectly claimed were at chance.

This is not an isolated example, and throughout his book, Gardner voices suspicion of any score close to the expected mean and suggests that there may be some problem with the data. Of those instances I noticed, all those of which he was suspicious had associated probability values of .028 or greater and some as high as .09. There were hundreds of runs with Stepanek, the large majority not particularly close to the exact mean chance value. Gardner gives the reader no reason whatever to suspect that the number of scores very close to the expected mean was any greater than chance would allow. He could have made a calculation to address the matter, but he failed to do so. His complaints are simply examples of selective reporting, a well known statistical fallacy.

Several places in the book Gardner admits that he had friends do calculations for him. Surprisingly, those were very simple computations that are typically taught the first few weeks of any introductory class in statistics. Ironically, back in 1979, Gardner was interviewed and asked about mathematics in parapsychology. He stated "I'm going to do a column that will discuss this whole aspect of contemporary parapsychology, and the need for a more sophisticated understanding of some of the statistics involved."[54,55]

Statistics is not the only area where Gardner is less capable than might be expected. His comments on more general scientific matters also reveal deficits. For instance, he asserted that "There is no way a skeptic can comment meaningfully on the Honorton and Schmidt experiments, because there is no way, now that the tests are completed, to know exactly what controls were in force."[56] In fact, since that statement was made, a number of skeptical psychologists have published assessments of both Honorton's and Schmidt's work. Similar evaluations are made in all other areas of science and have been for decades. Journal articles contain a great deal of information that allows assessment, and that is why the details are published. Reviewers frequently contact authors when additional information is required. This happens in all sciences. Gardner was amazingly uninformed about how scientific research is actually conducted, reported, and evaluated.[57]

One should remember that Gardner has a strong background in philosophy, but he has not had the advantage of carrying out day-to-day scientific research. He has only a philosopher's idealized conception of science, and his remarks must be interpreted in that light. In the last 25 years, sociologists have demonstrated that the process of science is rather different than philosophers thought, and that is particularly germane for skeptics of the paranormal. Trevor Pinch and Harry Collins, two prominent researchers in the sociology of scientific knowledge (SSK), have shown that participating in scientific research changes one's understanding of it. To illustrate their point, they investigated CSICOP and concluded that if the Committee wished to maintain its philosophical view of science it should not engage in research, and in fact, CSICOP established a policy against conducting research itself.[58] Gardner is not oblivious to SSK and its ramifications, and he has been a critic of Collins and Pinch, particularly on the topic of relativism, but he has not addressed their findings on CSICOP.[59]

Gardner is also sometimes beyond his ken when he discusses technical and theoretical issues of parapsychology. He has complained that PK effects in experiments typically rely upon statistical deviations for detection rather than direct movements of mechanical objects. That objection is laden with assumptions about how psi works. Vast amounts of research demonstrate that psi does not act like a mechanical force, and several plausible theoretical explanations have been presented to explain that. Gardner seems totally unaware of them. Yet when parapsychologists respond to his uninformed remarks he replies offering gratuitous comments such as "I find it puzzling that Rao and Palmer cannot understand such simple reasoning."[60]

Even in magic, his knowledge is spotty in some areas. For instance, he has asserted that "Conjurors are indeed the enemy [of psychic researchers]."[61] Through his popular writings, Gardner has been largely responsible for the canard that magicians are generally skeptical of the existence of psychic phenomena. Perhaps his relative isolation keeps him away from a broad cross-section of magicians. In fact studies have shown that the majority of conjurors believe in the paranormal, and a number of eminent ones have participated in psychical research.[62]

The general style of his criticisms is unlike that found in scientific journals. His are often biting, derisive, personal, and peppered with words such as "laughable," "ridiculous," with allusions to "youthful indiscretions," and references to parapsychologists as "Geller-gawkers." He makes liberal use of innuendo. The prestige endowed by his long association with *Scientific American*, coupled with the low status of his targets, allow him tactics that otherwise would be considered reprehensible. He is aware of it, and he frankly acknowledged that he and his colleagues "felt that when pseudoscience is far enough out on the fringes of irrationalism, it is fair game for humor, and at times even ridicule."[63] Gardner popularized H. L. Mencken's aphorism "one horse-laugh is worth ten thousand syllogisms," using it as an epigraph for his *Science: Good, Bad and Bogus*, making it something of a motto for debunkers.

His extensive sarcasm and ridicule should alert readers that something other than detached, dispassionate analysis is involved in his critiques. Even though he is skeptical, Gardner undeniably has a deep fascination with the paranormal. He has expended enormous intellectual effort, professional time, and personal energy on it. Paranormal claims enrage him and occasionally provoke his naive and emotional outbursts. This says something important about the phenomena. Even skeptics do not remain untouched by them. Gardner is a particularly important example because he directly confronts claims and deals with them in an extended fashion. As such, he has more immediate contact with the paranormal than those academics who simply dismiss it or comment on more abstracted issues such as belief in psychic abilities. Over seventy years ago, Walter Franklin Prince described the "enchanted boundary" and explained that when skeptics cross it they generally display a loosening of intellectual judgement and emotional restraint.[64] Gardner is an example.

Gardner is at least somewhat aware of the psychological factors affecting his views of parapsychology. In his essay "Science: Why I Am Not a Paranormalist" he explained that the idea of telepathy makes him uneasy: "I also value the privacy of my thoughts. I would not care to live in a world in which others had the telepathic power to know what I was secretly thinking, or the clairvoyant power to see what I was doing." He also wrote that "PK opens up even more terrifying possibilities. I am not enthusiastic over the possibility that someone who dislikes me might have the power from a distance to cause me harm."[65] These statements raise a fundamental issue—paranoia. Though I am not suggesting that Gardner is paranoid, his concerns are paranoiac, and it is to his credit that he recognizes potentials of psi that most parapsychologists wish to ignore. Paranoia is an important issue, and it is intricately linked to mirrors and reflexivity. A later chapter is devoted to it.

Gardner and Religion

Many people are surprised to learn that Gardner is not an atheist. He believes in God and in prayer as can be seen in his *The Whys of a Philosophical Scrivener*. But because so many have been amazed when I told them this, I suspect that some of them thought that I misinterpreted Gardner or somehow took him out of context. So I wrote to him, and he confirmed his belief in "a personal god, prayer, and life after death" (letter to author, 16 Nov 96). The religious crisis of his youth led him to reject his Protestant fundamentalism, but he did not reject God.

Gardner's virulent attacks on the paranormal are not based solely on its frequent association with deceit. Nor is his antagonism founded only on the unpleasant ramifications of psi. Gardner's antipathy has deeper roots. His essay "Prayer: Why I Do Not Think It Foolish" is revealing; for in it he says: "It is possible that paranormal forces not yet established may allow prayers to influence the material world, and I certainly am not saying this possibility should be ruled out a priori . . . As for empirical tests of the power of God to answer prayer, I am among those theists who, in the spirit of Jesus' remark that only the faithless look for signs, consider such tests both futile and blasphemous . . . Let us not tempt God."[66]

Nor is the above quote an isolated example. He also objects to interpreting miracles in terms of parapsychological concepts. He goes on to say that "If I were an orthodox Jew or Christian, I would find such attempts to explain biblical miracles to be both preposterous and an insult to God."[67] Obviously he feels that attempts to explain the workings of God in scientific parapsychological terms diminish the concept of divinity. God is to be exalted, not tested.

These statements cannot be ignored if one wishes to understand his views of parapsychology. The importance of them should not be underestimated, because he has stated that "Of my books, the one that I am most pleased to have written is my confessional, *The Whys of a Philosophical Scrivener*, with my novel about Peter Fromm running second."[68] Obviously Gardner's opposition is of a different order than most CSICOP followers, and I suspect that few of them appreciate this basis of his opinions. A rationalist debunker encountering the above passages might unconsciously skip over them, or perhaps think them to be in jest, because in the vast bulk of his writings on the paranormal Gardner gives no inkling of his underlying religious feelings. Despite his influence among debunkers, his *Whys* was not reviewed in the pages of the *Skeptical Inquirer* or the parapsychology journals. Perhaps they didn't know quite what to make of it.

Gardner's position is profoundly contrary to those of rationalists and secular humanists, with whom he frequently allies himself. Most of them would assert that every topic is open for scientific scrutiny; full investigation and inquiry should be encouraged. Religious restrictions on science are regressive, irrational, and squelch the search for truth. A rationalist is likely to believe that the only inherent harm in researching God or the paranormal is wasted time and effort. Badly conducted psi research resulting in positive, though invalid, findings simply furthers delusion. That should be combatted, but research is not a threat simply because of the content. Gardner, however, opposes investigation of a topic on religious grounds purely because of the subject matter. This deserves exploration.

Gardner's position can be traced back to his teenage Protestant fundamentalism. Protestantism draws a sharp demarcation between God and man; Gardner wants to uphold that and does not want man to appropriate the role of God. The binary opposition is not to be blurred.

Max Weber's concept of rationalization helps illuminate this. Weber recognized the crucial differences between an immanent and a transcendent God. An immanent God can be found within the material world. The transcendent God is above and beyond it; He may intervene, but there is a clear distinction between the material and the divine. Weber pointed out that the immanent-transcendent dichotomy is reflected in the Catholic-Protestant split. The divine is closer to the human in Catholicism than in Protestantism. Catholicism is more mystical; it has monastic orders and a priesthood. With transubstantiation in Catholicism, the bread and wine become the body and blood of Christ. Protestants see bread and wine as only symbols. In Protestantism, faith alone is required for salvation. That keeps it strictly mental; the divine is separated from the physical.

Protestantism has an intellectual tradition that critiqued miracles and dismissed them, and Gardner can be considered to fall loosely within that tradition. Attacking miracles is a step in the disenchantment process. Gardner and the Protestants are not full rationalists; they don't seek full disenchantment of the world. They leave room for mystery, and Gardner does not want to intrude upon it.

Gardner's attitude toward mysticism is ambivalent, but he does describe himself as "a mystic in the Platonic sense."[69] To his credit, he does not ignore the issue of paradox; he acknowledges it in at least some religious contexts. He recognizes the numinous, and in his *The Whys of a Philosophical Scrivener* he discusses Kurt Gödel and a few paragraphs later covers Rudolf Otto and the *mysterium tremendum*, directly mixing mathematics and religion. Of the numinous he says "It is the secret of the book of Job,"[70] indicating an understanding that few have today. Yet he doesn't fully explore the numinous either in his novel or essays, though in Otto's formulation, the numinous is the source of supernatural phenomena. Gardner is clearly ambivalent toward miracles and mysticism; he does not completely disparage them. His fascination is evinced by the last chapter of *The Flight of Peter Fromm*, which has a generally favorable discussion of Francis of Assisi.[71]

Reflexivity is pertinent to understanding Gardner's religious beliefs. Gardner is known for his clear writing, and that is one of the keys to his professional success. He is able to take complex topics and explain them simply. His religious thought shows this same striving for clarity, but he perhaps does not fully appreciate its consequences. Clarity and precision have costs, and reflexivity is central to understanding that. Reflexivity subverts clarity, and it is no accident that the writings of the deconstructionists and ethnomethodologist Harold Garfinkel are so obscure. Gardner serves as a counterpoint to them.

One of the most capable expositors on reflexivity and ambiguity is Bruno Latour, a prominent figure in the sociology of scientific knowledge, and his essay "The Politics of Explanation" discusses the issues at length. As will be explained in the chapter on literary theory, deconstructionism calls into question the correspondence between an object and its representation, between a text and its referent. Deconstructionists assert that there is no unambiguous connection between them, either in principle or in practice. Latour explains several aspects of reflexivity, and one "is based on the idea that the most deleterious effect of a text is to be naively believed by the reader as in some way relating to a referent out there. Reflexivity is supposed to counteract this effect by rendering the text unfit for normal consumption (which often means unreadable)."[72]

Latour specifically addressed the story of the empty tomb in the Gospel of St. Mark. He goes on to say that "The good reader of such a text is not the one who asks the silly question 'What *really* happened there? Would I find traces of the empty tomb if I were to go to that place in Jerusalem and dig the ground?'"[73] This is *exactly* the problem Gardner wrestled with in *The Flight of Peter Fromm*. Peter wondered what *really* happened with the resurrection, and whether Christ's bones could be found. Gardner never fully shook the effects of his teenage Biblical literalism and as a result rejected Christianity. Yet he is too sophisticated to be a rationalist, and he is more philosophically astute than most deconstructionists.

Paradox is one of the ramifications of reflexivity, and we encounter it here. Gardner chooses to embrace paradox rather than succumb to ambiguity. He believes in the power of prayer and life after death, yet he aggressively opposes scientific investigation of them. He allies himself with Paul Kurtz, a secular humanist and prominent publisher of atheist material. Gardner has even served as a co-chairman of a joint fundraising drive of CSICOP and CODESH (Council for Democratic and Secular Humanism). The religious man and atheist banded together to ward off the supernatural.

Gardner seems to recognize that there are limits to what can be known and expressed about the world via rational means. He accepts some things on faith alone. But he has rejected the path of direct experience, which both mysticism and science can provide. Gardner is a mystic only in the intellectual sense, and he has never been a practicing scientist. He works in an abstracted world where text is primary. He vehemently opposes using science to empirically address religious issues. That would blur a major binary opposition. He is comfortable with CSICOP because it doesn't really do science. Instead it ridicules attempts to study the paranormal scientifically.

Gardner's religious beliefs seem to have colored his relations with parapsychologists, and he has had a particularly strong antipathy toward J. B. Rhine. (Like Gardner, Rhine had an early formative interest in religion, and Rhine had planned to enter the ministry before switching to science. He later went to the University of Chicago.) In a conversation with me, Gardner referred to Mauskopf and McVaugh's book *The Elusive Science* as a "hagiography." This characterization is absolutely absurd, and I was puzzled by it. When I saw his remarks about tempting God, I recalled that Rhine had written of a potential role for psi in prayer and that he had even carried out a PK experiment pitting ministerial students against others who had a reputation for being good at shooting craps. This was dubbed the "Preachers versus Gamblers" study and was instigated by William Gatling, a Duke divinity student.[74] Gardner may have construed that research as "testing God" and therefore blasphemous.[75]

Gardner's religious concerns were overt in his attacks on parapsychological research at Stanford Research Institute. He was exceedingly incensed that some of those involved had a background in Scientology, and he wrote scathing denunciations, complaining about their religious affiliations, suggesting that they should not be trusted.[76] His religious biases are apparent in other contexts as well. He argued that science writer Forrest Mims should not become a columnist for *Scientific American* because he was a creationist, even though his views would have no impact on his work for the magazine.[77] Gardner perhaps recognized the bias resulting from his own religious convictions but projected it onto his opponents.[78]

Gardner's views on the paranormal are intricately linked to his ideas about miracles, prayer and God. When he says that we should not test God, he in effect invokes the primitive taboos against illicit contact with the supernatural. In our rationalized world, most people do not consciously recognize the taboos, but if they do, they are dismissed from serious intellectual consideration. Yet the taboos still exist, and in his own way, Gardner is an agent for maintaining them.

Gardner serves as a border guard to keep the paranormal out of science and academe. He belittles parapsychological researchers in order to ensure their marginal status. By emotional attacks and biting sarcasm he warns others to stay clear of the realm. He portrays the paranormal as unsavory, "unclean," and unsuited to be part of elite culture. His writings, actions, and life constitute an important case study of how taboo continues to be enforced.

As such, Gardner's social position merits analysis. He serves as a buffer, protecting the rationalized world, but in directly grappling with paranormal claims, he is tainted by them. This is reflected by his position in society. For most of his life he remained largely outside the usual bureaucratic structures of employment found in government, industry, and academe. Though for many years he wrote a column for *Scientific American*, he was primarily a free-lance writer. Though widely read and cited by scholars, he never held an academic appointment; he doesn't even have an advanced degree. His reputation was made through his individual efforts, rather than by establishing a group or leading an organization. Thus Gardner can be considered an interstitial or anti-structural character. This is fitting for someone who directly engages the paranormal. That activity is unsuitable for a person firmly emplaced within an established bureaucratic organization. Gardner's social position is thus compatible with his function.

I grew up reading his *Scientific American* column and learned much from him. Despite his biases, he has a great many insights about religion and the paranormal, and when he writes about them, few equal his clarity or incisiveness. He has an ability to creatively combine ideas from unexpectedly diverse areas, and the paranormal is frequently part of the mix. His efforts give psychic phenomena a certain visibility and prominence they might otherwise lack. He has untiringly pointed out the frequent association of deception and psi, which many parapsychologists choose to ignore. His writings brought repeated examples to my attention, and he was an important influence in my thinking about parapsychology (especially after learning the subject sufficiently to recognize what had been left out of his accounts!). He has thought about dangers of the paranormal, which many are reluctant to confront. It is his intelligence, breadth of knowledge, sophistication, and intensity of feeling that make him such a fascinating and important character.

Above all, he is paradoxical, and the issue of paradox involves more than just his mathematical interests. It and other trickster manifestations are seen in both his philosophy and his life. A believer in prayer and a personal god, he allies himself with atheists. Though an aggressive debunker of the paranormal, Gardner promoted mentalist Stanley Jaks as having genuine psychic abilities.[79] A superb writer on issues of probability, his criticisms of statistics in parapsychology might be charitably described as undistinguished. Describing himself as a Platonic mystic, much of his writing is grounded in Aristotelian logic. These paradoxical aspects involve the core of his being.

Reflexivity Summary

By now the reader may have lost the threads of my exposition. With the long biographical sketch and the diversity of topics from meditation to mathematical logic, this chapter may seem a hodgepodge collection. I will try to summarize the guiding ideas and again bring the issues of liminality and the trickster into view.

Reflexivity reveals the limits to logic, objectivity, knowledge, communication, representation, and a host of others. The problem of limits also applies to reflexivity itself. There are limits as to what can be said about it in any straightforward manner. The reader may have noticed that I talked more "around" reflexivity than addressing it directly. That was necessary because to learn about it one must observe the vicinity in which it is applied.

Anti-structure (a.k.a. liminality) involves a leveling or inversion of social status. This is also found in applications of ethnomethodology and the sociology of scientific knowledge. Scientists are extremely leery of these, for if science is applied reflexively (using science to study science), scientists face a lowering of their status, power, and prestige.

In science, reflexivity is found in the *margins* (where the trickster resides). Ethnomethodology and SSK provoke strong hostile reactions from the establishment. Ethnomethodology was eviscerated after its real challenges were recognized, and that is now conveniently forgotten. Currently many scientists loath SSK, ridicule it, and pray for its demise. The antagonism toward Bruno Latour is but one example. In psychology, reflexivity revealed experimenter effects. Researchers played with them for a few years, and then largely abandoned that effort; there was no substantial follow-up. The general pattern is unmistakable; after the initial intense interest and furious disputes, virtually all scientists pull away from reflexive disciplines, and the fundamental questions are left on the margins.

Reflexivity leads scientists to recognize that they are part of experiments; they "participate" in them. This poses problems, particularly in replication. When personal qualities of an experimenter influence a result, the outcome is not fully objective. The results are marked by instability. Accusations of nonreplicability have been lodged against studies involving reflexivity. The same charge is made against parapsychology.

Academics have avoided reflexivity, and some of the most astute have issued warnings. Trevor Pinch said "in terms of actually doing concrete research it's debilitating to actually think about problems of reflexivity,"[80] and Malcolm Ashmore indicated that "to advocate a self-reflexive stance is . . . merely a way of making trouble *for oneself*."[81] Reflexivity courts disruption, a trickster quality.

When reflexivity is applied, some aspect of the paranormal is often found in the vicinity. Gödel had his interest in demons, and Garfinkel was had by Castaneda. Harry Collins, Trevor Pinch, and Robert Rosenthal got involved with parapsychology, and Martin Gardner has battled it for half a century. These may all seem incidental, but that's unlikely. Reflexive blurring of subject and object allows connections undreamt of by Western rationality. So does psi.

Martin Gardner is found on the margins of science. He is not part of it, but only a commentator. He freely mixes mathematics, religion, and the paranormal—ignoring the traditional academic boundaries. He also exemplifies paradox. He extolls the scientific method, except when it comes to religion and the paranormal. With all these qualities, and with his exceptional contributions to conjuring, he must be considered a trickster.

Reflexivity also brings religious issues to the fore. Those feature prominently in Gardner's writing. To a much lesser extent Kurt Gödel, Bruno Latour, and Rudy Rucker have alluded to them. Meditation, typically a reflexive practice, is a universal part of esoteric religions.

The topics associated with reflexivity are varied, and even this summary may seem scattered, and not quite coherent. The commonalities of the topics are found at an abstract level, and they are not always easy to recognize. Reflexivity courts the ineffable; it exposes foundational assumptions that are usually banished from conscious awareness.

The victims of ethnomethodological breaching experiments were often unable to explain their discomfiture.

At the risk of being repetitious, I want to briefly list again some of the links between the trickster (and liminality) and reflexivity. The trickster blurs the distinction between subject and object, and so does reflexivity; both thereby subvert objectivity. The trickster is a paradoxical creature, and reflexivity generates paradox. The paranormal has trickster qualities, and it is found in the vicinity of applications of reflexivity. The trickster has deep religious implications, and reflexivity evokes religious issues; both are pertinent to the numinous. Manifestations of reflexivity generate ambiguity, paradox, and uncertainty; they provoke feelings of unease, worry, and even paranoia. The trickster does too. The issue of limits is fundamental to the trickster, and reflexivity reveals limits.

All these issues can be grasped with further attention to order, structure, boundaries, classification, foundations, and limits. The following chapters continue this exploration.

In closing, I can only quote Hugh Mehan and Houston Wood who concluded: "Reflexivity will exhaust us long before we exhaust it."[82]

CHAPTER 21

Laboratory Research on Psi

Experimental parapsychology is included in a section covering reflexivity, the primitive mind, and literary theory, and readers may think that odd. A brief explanation is in order. Reflexivity begets paradox; it blurs the distinction between subject and object. Psychic phenomena do also. Primitive notions of magic and divination are compatible with parapsychology, and some psi experiments have been modeled on those practices. Psi can be seen as communication, and literary theory deals with information and communication in a more fundamental way than do the sciences. In particular, semiotics and structuralism can provide new views on psi as communication. These few sentences are, of course, much too brief, and given the topics, it is almost impossible for them not to seem disjointed, if not incoherent.

Throughout this book I have returned to the themes of structure, stasis, boundaries, and stability and counterposed them to antistructure, transition, boundary blurring, and instability. It is helpful to keep all these in mind while reading this chapter. The primary issue here is the limits of psi. ESP (extrasensory perception) and PK (psychokinesis) transcend the usual barriers of distance and time. They overcome boundaries. Clairvoyance can operate over thousands of miles, and accurate premonitions have occurred days and weeks before events. Even so, psi doesn't happen all the time; in fact it seems rather rare. Some experiments work; others don't. Psychics are neither omniscient nor omnipotent, and many factors restrain their abilities. Psi obviously has limits, but they cannot yet be specified.

The issues are difficult to explain to those who have little background in parapsychology. In order to overcome this potential problem, I will describe some laboratory studies and discuss their rationales in the context of limits. These concrete examples should help illustrate the conceptual ambiguities. I realize that it is probably foolhardy to try to introduce experimental parapsychology in the context of its most advanced theoretical issues, and I don't know of anyone who has made such an attempt. Yet I am going to try, and ultimately I hope to stimulate the reader to pursue some of the field's technical material.

Many people are surprised at the extent and variety of parapsychological research. This is odd, because with television programs and movies, there is a wide awareness of psychic phenomena, yet the vast bulk of the scientific work remains unknown to the general public. Many have an interest in psychic phenomena but few have read anything substantial about them. Several factors contribute to this state of affairs. Much of the research is buried in professional journals that are not easily available, and only a small amount of it has been reported in popular books. Of the popular accounts, a fair number are unreliable, and most of the so-called skeptical literature is particularly naive, and frequently misrepresents the research. Prominent skeptical scientists, with no familiarity with the paranormal, have felt compelled to publicly comment on parapsychology, further confusing the lay public.

The few scientists who actually carry out psi experiments generally give a higher priority to scientific publication than to popularizing. Most have little inclination to spend time explaining their work to a larger public. This is particularly true with advanced, theory-based research, which is especially difficult to communicate because the results don't fit within current frameworks of understanding.

Many popular books leave the reader with the impression that ESP is something like mental radio. The term "telepathy" helps foster this idea, and while this is a useful way to initially present and comprehend the data, it is misleading. ESP and PK can be conceptualized in terms of information, but it is a mistake to think of them as energy being transmitted. I will try to clarify why that is.

In the 1970s several models were developed that grappled with psi in a new way. Notable were Evan Harris Walker's quantum mechanical theory, Rex Stanford's conformance behavior model, and William Braud's concepts of lability and inertia. These helped clarify some crucial aspects of psi. They were informational models, and as will be described in the following chapters, they have some commonality with structuralist thought. As with structuralism, I will accent information—instead of energy, force, or power. I will focus on correspondences, correlations, and patterns—instead of causes. This way of thinking is unusual, and readers should not become alarmed if they do not immediately grasp it.

Psi and Boundaries

The limits of psi are problematic. ESP and PK transcend the usual barriers of time and distance; thus they conflict with conventional views of how the world works. This is nothing new. A half century ago, C. D. Broad, an eminent Cambridge philosopher and former president of the Society for Psychical Research, acknowledged that psi violates what he called basic limiting principles. He explained that: "There are certain limiting principles which we unhesitatingly take for granted as the framework within which all our practical activities and our scientific theories are confined. Some of these seem self-evident. Others are so overwhelmingly supported by all the empirical facts which fall within the range of ordinary experience and the scientific elaborations of it . . . that it hardly enters our heads to question them."[1]

Briefly and crudely summarized, these include: an event cannot precede its cause; a person's mind cannot *directly* affect the material world except the nervous system; mental life depends upon the brain; we obtain knowledge of the world only through the senses. These give the general idea of Broad's points though he described them more elaborately and included a few qualifications. In any event, parapsychologists and their critics agree that psychic phenomena violate commonsense expectations about what is possible. It is this that makes psi so controversial; however, as I will explain, the problem of limits is even more subtle and pervasive than this suggests.

The Definition Problem

The very definition of psi reflects the problem of limits, and one of the occasionally voiced, though invalid, objections to parapsychology is that psi is negatively defined. True, psi is defined in terms of what it is not. The Parapsychological Association's position paper "Terms and Methods in Parapsychological Research" states: "When an event is classified as a psi phenomenon, it is claimed that all known channels for the apparent interaction have been eliminated."[2]

This definition requires psi to circumvent known boundaries. It specifies that all normal alternative causes be ruled out before psi can be deemed to have occurred. Thus psi is defined by what is excluded. Difficulty is built into the definition, but it suffices until the phenomena are better understood. The definition's advantage is that it emphasizes the matter of limits. Psi is placed in opposition to other causes known to science. Despite its drawbacks, the definition reflects the current state of knowledge, and it guides researchers. Before psi is inferred to have occurred in an experiment, normal modes of influence and communication must be excluded. Much of the effort in formal research is devoted to that task. Anyone making a scientific claim for a psi occurrence shoulders a similar burden.

The Role of the Laboratory

Lay persons who are sympathetic to parapsychology, in principle, often do not appreciate research. It seems too distant from real-life events to have much meaning for them. There is some truth in this complaint. The laboratory is artificial, but necessarily so. Special training is required to understand the research, and much of it must be translated for the wider public. Indeed, in the last 30 years parapsychology has become more technical and probably lost a base of support from members of the general public because of it. In addition, the advanced theoretical development has been unappealing to available funding sources. Psychic spying, research on healing and life after death attract more support. Yet the theoretical research will likely prove much more important for fundamental understanding. There has been considerable progress, but it is almost completely unappreciated.

Regarding the laboratory, there is a crucial point for our concern here. The essence of any laboratory, be it for physics, chemistry, biology, or parapsychology, is to limit and constrain phenomena. It is under controlled conditions that limits are investigated most effectively.

John Pierce, a researcher at Bell Laboratories, spoke to this in his book *Symbols, Signals and Noise* (1961). He pointed out that much scientific progress has come from studying phenomena in artificial, man-made environments. Humans learned more about fire by observing it in furnaces than they did by watching forest fires. Physics progressed much more rapidly by studying electricity in wires, capacitors and resistors than by observing lightning. Hydraulics advanced more from studying water flowing in pipes than by watching ocean waves. Small effects under controlled artificial conditions often reveal more than large phenomena in natural settings. This is also true in parapsychology. Field studies and case collections emphasize the dramatic manifestations of psi. Seemingly trivial and mundane examples tend to be discounted, but those hide profound clues. Indeed, the laboratory has revealed important but subtle psi effects that would have been otherwise overlooked.

The laboratory has additional advantages. It gives more reliable evidence than do field studies and collections of anecdotal reports. In laboratory work, phenomena are recorded in progress; whereas anecdotal reports are often obtained days, weeks, or even months after the events. In the lab, standardized forms and machines help register results and minimize unconscious human error. Lab experimenters can implement safeguards against fraud, which is often difficult or impossible in field situations. Laboratory precautions can exclude subtle sensory cues that cannot be eliminated in field settings. Experimenters use mathematical statistics to determine if chance coincidence might account for results; whereas that typically cannot be assessed in field studies. In addition, statistical probabilities can be directly transformed into measures of information, thereby allowing a standard basis to compare various types of phenomena.

I will discuss some specific examples to illustrate these general points.

J. B. Rhine and His Legacy

Serious scientific investigation of psychic phenomena has been ongoing since 1882 with the founding of the Society for Psychical Research in England. But it wasn't until the work of J. B. Rhine at Duke University in the early 1930s that a systematic, laboratory approach was effectively institutionalized. The history of parapsychology cannot be understood apart from Rhine, and from the 1930s through at least the 1960s, he was the undisputed leader of the field. Rhine was a dyed-in-the-wool experimentalist who placed a high value on collecting quality data, but he had little interest in theories. He believed that experiments, guided by simple hypotheses, would eventually point the way to a theory.

Rhine's work and that of his followers was squarely in the laboratory. The *Journal of Parapsychology*, which he founded, published little on spontaneous cases, mediumship, or life after death (also termed "survival" research), and that policy continues to this day. Rhine did not disparage such work, but he believed that with limited resources it was best to investigate the psychic capacity of the living. The limits of human abilities needed delineation before survival-related concepts were explored. This was a pragmatic decision on Rhine's part. With regard to spiritualist ideas, Rhine adopted a psychological perspective. If accurate messages were received from a medium purportedly communicating with deceased persons, ESP of the medium might account for the messages, and the communicating spirits could be construed as unconscious aspects of the medium's personality. Even if spirits somehow ultimately are found to be the cause of some phenomena, ESP and PK, by definition, subsume them. Many commentators have failed to understand this point. ESP is simply the obtaining of information without the use of the known senses. If spirits provide information, the process is still without the use of the senses, and hence classified as ESP.

Rhine became internationally known for his ESP card tests with the still-famous symbols: circle, cross, wavy lines, square, and star. Those symbols were designed by Karl Zener, a psychologist at Duke. They were printed on cards and were arranged into decks of 25, with five of each of the five symbols.

Rhine's subjects typically did runs of 25 trials. For telepathy experiments, a sender would shuffle a deck of Zener cards, look at them and try to mentally transmit them to a receiver. He or she would then record the order of the cards on a sheet of paper. The receiver, who would be in another room or another building, would mark guesses on a similar sheet. After the experiment, the two sheets would be compared to determine how many guesses were correct. With clairvoyance tests, the procedure was similar, except the person in the role of the sender shuffled the cards but did not look at the faces until after the receiver finished guessing. In precognition experiments, the cards were not shuffled or recorded until the receiver had made the guesses. In a run of 25 trials, five correct guesses (hits) were expected by chance. If a subject was able to consistently score more than five hits per run, it was evidence of ESP, and the overall odds against chance were computed using mathematical statistics.

Rhine and his colleagues carried out hundreds of thousands of trials, and typically the scores were only slightly above chance. In some series, the average was 5.4 hits (a typical result; though in extremely rare cases people guessed nearly all 25 cards correctly). By chance, 5.0 were expected, but because there were so many trials, the outcome was very significant and the odds were millions to one against chance. The best summary of that early work is found in the book *Extra-sensory Perception After Sixty Years* (1940) by J. G. Pratt, et al. This classic remains one of the most detailed, technical treatments of the subject in book form. The volume is of added interest because critics' comments were invited and included in it.

Rhine also investigated PK after meeting a young gambler who told him that tumbling dice could be influenced mentally. Rhine tried some preliminary experiments, throwing dice by hand, and obtained encouraging results. Eventually machines were built for the research. Sometimes subjects tried for high numbers and sometimes for low ones, or they might try successively for ones through sixes (the target face was varied in order to counter possible bias of the dice). Typically several dice were tumbled simultaneously in order to enhance interest of the subjects.

Rhine and his colleagues conducted tests with a wide variety of conditions. Several ESP experiments were done over intercontinental distances. Precognition tests were carried out with guesses made days or weeks before targets were selected. Some of these studies were strikingly successful, and the supposed barriers of space and time did not reduce the scores. The findings led many researchers to conclude that psi is space-time independent. The evidence is not completely overwhelming on this, but most parapsychologists consider distance and time not to impose limits on ESP.[3] In my opinion, this is at least a good, first-order approximation. Other factors affect ESP far more than distance or time.

A central feature in Rhine's work was the use of random sequences (e.g., shuffled cards and falls of dice), and virtually all parapsychological laboratory work has since relied on some source of randomness. The studies use mathematical statistics for evaluation, and the methods are identical to those found in psychology, biology, and medical research.

What surprises many people is that psychic research was one of the very first fields to make use of randomization and statistics, and Rhine was by no means the earliest. In fact, Ian Hacking, a philosopher of science and a sneering disbeliever, admitted that in psychical research "we find the first faltering use, by many investigators, of a technique that is now standard in many sciences and mandatory in much sociology and biology."[4] He pointed out that Charles Richet, a Nobel laureate and SPR president, was an early pioneer in using probability to evaluate experiments as far back as 1884, a half century before Rhine.[5]

As in other scientific fields, randomization allows a great variety of procedures, and parapsychology is not restricted to cards and dice. Some experiments have tested psychic healing, psychic influence on mechanical and electrical devices, and on animal behavior. Though Rhine didn't explore all of these himself, his methodology set a foundation for others; his procedures had a lasting influence, which can still be seen today.

Like other scientists, parapsychologists are interested in the generality of their findings. As such, most experiments test a number of people rather than a single person. In fact the large bulk of the research published in professional journals involves numbers of subjects, typically ordinary people who claim no special abilities and who volunteer their time. A smaller percentage of studies has focussed on the talents of an individual, often a reputed "star." Stars have advantages—they are more likely to be successful than ordinary people, and experiments can be designed to maximize their talents. But they are risky because some are tricksters, and these often attract considerable media attention and taint the field.

For the last several decades, few psi experiments have used cards or dice; many alternatives have been introduced.

One innovator was Douglas Dean, a British chemist who emigrated to the U.S. He was assistant director of research at the Parapsychology Foundation in New York City between 1959 and 1962. Dean later served as president of the Parapsychological Association (PA), and it was largely through his efforts that that the PA became affiliated with the American Association for the Advancement of Science in 1969.

Dean's telepathy tests were different than Rhine's. He used a plethysmograph to measure blood volume in the finger of a telepathic receiver. In another room, a sender had cards with peoples' names on them; some of the people were known to the receiver and some were not. At randomized intervals, the sender looked at a randomly selected card. When the receiver knew the person named on the card, the blood volume changed significantly, but no change was found when the sender looked at names unknown to the receiver. Dean's work demonstrated that ESP could function at a physiological level, probably below conscious awareness.

Experiments like those of Rhine and Dean substantially increased our knowledge of psi, but like all scientific approaches, they had limitations. Several researchers recognized that the methods didn't capture the essence of all psychic phenomena. Other parapsychologists had collected and analyzed thousands of reports of spontaneous experiences. Precognitive dreams were among the most frequently reported, and some were dramatic. In many cases, dream content matched future events so strikingly that the dreamer had no doubt that a psychic event had occurred.

Many of those experiencers were not intentionally trying to use ESP, had no knowledge of the kind of information about to come to them, and were in an altered state of consciousness when it did. In contrast, in the card experiments participants were awake, concentrating, and knew the possible targets. Card experiments are "forced-choice" procedures because the receiver knows the range of possible targets (e.g., the five Zener symbols). A few investigators were dissatisfied with the differences between the laboratory and real-life settings. "Free-response" methods are an alternative; with them the receiver does not know the possible targets.

The dream studies conducted at Maimonides Medical Center in Brooklyn, New York are some of the best known examples of free-response experiments. They were carried out in the 1960s and 1970s and were directed by Stanley Krippner. He has held many leadership positions in the field including the presidency of the Parapsychological Association. Krippner has written and edited important books on parapsychology, probably more than anyone else alive today. Currently he is at the Saybrook Institute in San Francisco.[6]

The Maimonides dream experiments were designed to reproduce conditions of real life that facilitate ESP (e.g., the dream state, receiver ignorant of target material). I will briefly describe the method.

A variety of photographs and art prints were collected and given identification numbers. This established a "target pool" before any tests were run. The receiver came to the laboratory in the evening and was introduced to the other participants. He or she was put to bed and fitted with electrodes to monitor rapid eye movement (REM), which indicates a dream is probably underway. One experimenter used a random process to select a picture from the target pool and then delivered it to the sender, who was in a distant room. During the night, the other experimenter monitored the REM activity, and when a period began, signaled the sender with a buzzer, to alert him that sending should commence. After observing some REM, the experimenter woke the receiver via an intercom, and asked about the dream; this was recorded on tape and later transcribed. The receiver was not aware of the possible targets (unlike the forced-choice experiments), and the primary experimenter, who monitored the receiver, did not know the target being sent. (This is a conceptually simple, idealized description, and there were a number variations in method, e.g., some were precognitive.)

At the end of several sessions, the dream reports and the targets were given to an outside "judge" who had no previous contact with the experiment. The judge tried to match each report with its target. The judge gave numeric ratings and rankings to the pictures, which permitted statistical evaluation.

In these experiments, one trial took a full night and required at least four people (two experimenters, a sender, and a receiver). It was time-consuming and expensive. Some experiments had as few as seven trials (though a full week's work). In contrast, in experiments with forced-choice card guessing, subjects might complete 100 trials in less than an hour, and sometimes in only a few minutes. The scoring rate (percentage of hits) for the dream studies was typically much higher than for the card experiments, but the dream experiments required much more effort per trial.

The book *Dream Telepathy* (1973) by Montague Ullman, Stanley Krippner and Alan Vaughan describes these experiments. In addition, Irvin Child, former head of the Yale University psychology department, summarized the studies in an article in the November 1985 issue of *American Psychologist*, the flagship journal of American Psychological Association. Child pointed out that a number of skeptical psychologists had severely misrepresented that research when they purported to give a scientific assessment of parapsychology.

The Maimonides studies attracted attention and brought free-response methods to the fore in parapsychology (though they had been used previously), and such methods are now some of the most common in the field. There are variations; for instance in remote viewing, geographical sites are targets, and subjects gain impressions while awake. At Stanford Research Institute, Ingo Swann, Russell Targ, and Harold Puthoff developed remote viewing with funds from the CIA and other government agencies. It became the heart of the U.S. government's psychic spying program.

Helmut Schmidt and RNGs

In the 1960s Helmut Schmidt, a German physicist then at Boeing Scientific Research Laboratories in Seattle, began experimenting with electronic random number generators (RNGs).[7] These are essentially electronic coin flippers, and he demonstrated that humans could influence their output by PK. Schmidt eventually left Boeing and moved to Durham, North Carolina to work at Rhine's Institute for Parapsychology. After a several years in North Carolina, he moved to San Antonio, Texas and joined the Mind Science Foundation; he has since retired.

In 1974 Schmidt published a paper comparing two different RNGs, one simple and one complex. The simple generator was based on a Geiger counter and a sample of radioactive strontium-90. The complex generator used an electronic noise generator for randomness. The simple generator produced one binary digit (1 or 0) per trial, but the complex generator produced 100 of them, tallying them and using a majority vote to determine the final 1 or 0.[8] The generators were connected to circuits that controlled two light bulbs, and each time a button was pressed, one of the two bulbs was lit, depending upon the output of one of the RNGs. A 0 designated one light, and 1 designated the other. Both generators were used in the experiment, but on any trial only one generator operated when the subject pressed the button and wished for one bulb to light. The active generator for each trial was randomly chosen, and during the experiment neither the subject nor the experimenter knew which generator functioned for a trial. Schmidt found no significant difference between the two generators; PK seemed to work equally well on both of them.

This was just one of many RNG experiments conducted by Schmidt, and because of his work, electronic RNGs have become a basic tool of parapsychologists. Electronic devices allow automatic recording and easy checking and tallying of results. Since they can be automated, human error can be largely excluded. The application of RNGs has led to not only technical advances but also to greater theoretical understanding, as I will describe later.

RNGs stimulated a variety of tests, and in the 1980s several were built for personal computers. Simple programming languages permitted random numbers to be easily incorporated into experiments. For instance, RNGs were used in video games to control whether "laser cannons" fire. The subjects playing the games were asked to use PK to increase the firing rate. Many other psi tests also used RNGs.

Now that some experiments have been described, conceptual topics can be discussed. Later a few more studies will be presented in order to illustrate additional concepts.

Classification Issues

The terms (categories) "telepathy," "clairvoyance," "precognition," and "PK" probably do not designate separate underlying processes. They are convenient labels for events, but examination of the supposed distinctions reveals their shortcomings. For instance, in telepathy experiments, does a receiver obtain information from the mind of the sender? Or instead, does he or she use clairvoyance to get information directly from the cards or other targets? Perhaps a telepathic receiver really uses precognition. In ESP experiments, receivers often learn of the target material (e.g., order of the cards, picture, geographical location) after the experiment is over. Maybe this information is carried back in time to the receiver, even in an experiment labelled telepathic. The situation grows even more confused, and disconcerting, when PK is considered. Telepathy might act via an "active agent," in which the sender somehow "implants" thoughts by PK. Douglas Dean's plethysmograph experiment suggests that a receiver can be influenced unawares.

Early parapsychologists recognized the ambiguities, but theory building was a low priority for them. They gave conceptual problems only secondary attention, and hence most researchers thought about psi in a way that was not completely explicit. Many assumed it to be a form of communication, with some channel and a signal transmitted along that channel. Parapsychologists usually presumed that psi operated like other physical and biological processes, and this was later labelled the psycho-biological perspective. This seemed a natural way to conceive of the phenomena, and the traditional terminology (e.g., senders, receivers) subtly conspired to maintain those modes of thinking. (I plead guilty to perpetuating those dubious terms. I use them because they help describe experimental procedures.) Nevertheless, a body of experiments indicated that neither did ESP act like some form of "mental radio" nor did PK behave as an energy projected from the body. They acted more like a unitary process, quite different from other physical operations. Active researchers knew that psi did not fit with models from other disciplines. They wrote about it, but even so, most persisted in thinking along traditional lines.

The implicit assumptions didn't stop theoretical development, but the emphasis was on experiments. Parapsychology was a small field (for most of its history, probably fewer than 10 full-time researchers in the U.S.), and with Rhine's commanding presence, theoretical work was not a high priority. Rhine kept the field focussed on experiments, and without his leadership it may well have disintegrated. Yet the focus had a price.

New Approaches

The late 1960s and the 1970s were years of growth for parapsychology, and spurred by several factors, that period proved to be a watershed for theoretical development. With Rhine's retirement as director of the Institute for Parapsychology, his dominance in the field lessened, and new laboratories were established by those who found Rhine's approach too restrictive. The influx of new researchers broadened the field, and established scientists from other areas brought perspectives from their disciplines. Physicists introduced quantum mechanics to parapsychological problems; biologists undertook more studies of psi in animals, and computer technology allowed new and more sophisticated experiments. During that fruitful but turbulent period, older experiments were reevaluated, and alternative theoretical models were developed.

Helmut Schmidt and Evan Harris Walker, a physicist with the U.S. Army at Aberdeen Proving Grounds in Maryland, produced some of the most important theories. They were based on quantum mechanics and attracted the attention of a number of scientists. Other theories were introduced as well. Rex Stanford proposed his psi-mediated instrumental response (PMIR) and conformance behavior models. J. E. Kennedy published conceptual articles on task complexity, redundancy, and experimenter effects. William Braud introduced the ideas of lability and inertia in relation to psi processes. All were developed in the 1970s.

These theoretical efforts occurred in tandem with experiments that explicitly probed the limits of psi and raised questions as how to best conceive it. The driving topics included psi-mediated experimenter effects, retroactive PK, the goal-oriented nature of psi, divergence, task-complexity independence, conformance behavior, and the source of psi problem. Probably only a few dozen people in the world have a working knowledge of these terms. They will be explained below. They are interrelated, and one cannot draw clear distinctions between them, but all speak to the problem of boundaries, constraints, and limitations. Their meaning and implications are difficult to grasp without extensive familiarity with the literature of experimental parapsychology. As a result, most receive little or no coverage in introductory texts, and since the early 1980s, they have attracted relatively little notice, even within the field.

To illustrate the points, several additional experiments need to be presented. Some were quite clever and produced striking results, and the reader can profit even if he or she chooses to concentrate on the experimental procedures and ignore the conceptual ambiguities. Nevertheless, theoretical issues are central here, and as with all scientific experiments, varying interpretations are possible. Yet when all parapsychological research is viewed together, a picture emerges that is decidedly odd.

Experimenter Effects

Parapsychologists had long known that some of their colleagues were more successful than others in obtaining positive results. They suspected that this was due to differences in interpersonal skills, abilities to make people feel comfortable yet highly motivated in experiments. The experimenter effect was so well recognized that Rhine urged new people coming into the field to try some preliminary tests in order to determine whether or not they could elicit psi in a lab. If a potential parapsychologist was unable to do so, Rhine counseled that the person might be more effective in something other than experimental psi research.[9] Other parapsychologists experimentally tested experimenter effects, and it turned out that they involved more than just social skills. In some studies, experimenters unconsciously exerted a psychic influence on scoring patterns.

In the early 1950s Donald J. West and George W. Fisk had an interest in the issue. Fisk was a British physicist who spent many years in China and later served as editor of the *Journal of the Society for Psychical Research*. West is a psychiatrist, criminologist, and former president of the Society. Each had conducted a number of studies. Fisk frequently obtained positive results, but West did not. They decided to collaborate and explore the differences in results. They set up an experiment that resulted in one of the most frequently cited papers on psi experimenter effects; it was published in 1953.

Twenty subjects were each sent 32 sealed packs of 12 clock cards (clock cards have the face of a clock printed on them and a hand pointing to one of the hours). West and Fisk each prepared half of the targets for each subject, and the subjects were unaware of who had prepared any of the packs or even that two different experimenters were involved. Fisk sent out all the packs, and in random order. It turned out that the cards prepared by Fisk were much more successfully guessed than those prepared by West. The tabulated results showed that no single subject was responsible for the overall outcome.[10]

The experiment was generally well conducted, but unfortunately the report gave essentially no details about precautions against cheating. However, there were no especially extreme scores that might provoke such suspicions. Furthermore even if one of the subjects did cheat, it would be expected that all packs were vulnerable (the authors report that even if the subjects had known the packs to have been prepared by two experimenters "they would not have been able to tell which were which."[11] Thus while the experiment was not perfectly controlled, cheating seems unlikely.

The question arises—were the subjects the ones responsible for the results? Some probably were, for one of them did very well on targets sealed by both Fisk and West. Had Fisk or West left some kind of residue that either stimulated or inhibited psychic ability? This might be a possibility, but later work by other experimenters found similar patterns in precognition experiments where the targets were not selected until after the guesses were made. Significant differences were found between experimenters who checked the results, and it appeared that it was the experimenters' psychic influences that were at work. These kinds of findings provoked discussion.[12]

In 1976 two major reviews appeared on experimenter effects in psi research. One was by Rhea White in the *Journal of the American Society for Psychical Research* and the other by J. E. Kennedy and Judith Taddonio was published in the *Journal of Parapsychology*. These were independently written, but covered much of the same material, indicating that the matter had come to the fore.[13] White, a librarian, had worked at Rhine's laboratory in the 1950s. She later served as editor of the *Journal of the American Society for Psychical Research* and now edits her own periodicals and databases. Over the years she has produced a number of important reference books for the field as well as significant conceptual articles. Kennedy was a young researcher at Rhine's lab who published several major theoretical papers in the 1970s. He was one of a trio who caught laboratory director, Walter J. Levy, M.D., faking results in 1974.

Part of the stimulus for their papers on experimenter effects came from parallel concerns in ordinary psychological research. In the preceding 10 years, Robert Rosenthal's study of experimenter bias (previously mentioned in the chapter on reflexivity) attracted considerable media interest, and it sparked lively debates. Experimenter effects alarmed psychologists. They often compared groups in experiments, and an investigator might unconsciously treat one group differently than another. If a procedure allowed an experimenter's bias to be unintentionally communicated to the subjects, results could be contaminated. Similar problems arise in medical research with the well-known placebo effect. The problems in parapsychology are even more severe than in psychology or medicine. The West and Fisk study indicated that experimenter effects can be due to psi.

Experimenting about experiments is a reflexive activity, and experimenter effects are one of the problematic manifestations of reflexivity. They challenge the validity of experimental methods in all fields. They raise problems that people want to avoid. As discussed in the last chapter, experimenter effects in ordinary psychology were difficult to replicate, and the replication problem in parapsychology is even more severe. One cannot be sure that only the putative subjects use psi; experimenters and others may contribute psi influences. This, of course, exacerbates problems of replication. Experimenter effects also raise the issue of participation. Psi permits (and maybe requires) experimenters to psychically participate in experiments, even unwillingly. They cannot fully separate themselves from their task.

Participation is a crucial issue for parapsychology. It is also found in ethnomethodology and in the sociology of scientific knowledge. It will again be addressed in the next chapter on primitive mentality, particularly with the work of Levy-Bruhl.

Non-Intentional Psi

Some people seem lucky and have a knack for being at the right place at the right time. Parapsychologists noticed this and suspected that those people used their psychic abilities unconsciously. The idea initially appeared straightforward, and a number of experiments tested it.

In 1975 Rex Stanford and his colleagues published a paper on non-intentional PK. Stanford is a professor of psychology at St. John's University in New York, and he has been an active experimentalist and theoretician in parapsychology for many years. Earlier in his career he worked at Rhine's laboratory and then with psychiatrist Ian Stevenson at the Division of Parapsychology at the University of Virginia Medical School. Rex has an identical twin brother, Ray, an artist and psychic who has written a number of books on paranormal topics. Ray has also made substantial contributions to paleontology by discovering previously unknown fossilized species.

In Stanford's experiment 40 male college students were each given the long, boring task of tracking a slow-moving pursuit rotor, for up to 45 minutes. Unknown to each student, a random number generator was running during the time he was being tested. If at any point during the 45-minute session the RNG produced a sufficiently extreme result, the student was released from the tracking task, and given an interesting one—rating erotic pictures. It turned out that a significant number of students escaped the boring tracking task and had the opportunity to view the erotica. They were not aware that they were in a parapsychology experiment at the time. Apparently they used PK unconsciously to influence the RNG; that seemed to be the most reasonable interpretation, at least initially.[14]

Martin Johnson at Lund University in Sweden conducted another study on non-intentional psi in 1971 and 1972 (ESP in this one).[15] Johnson was in charge of a psychology course, and he prepared an examination for his students. Each copy of the exam was pasted to an envelope. Unbeknownst to the students, inside each envelope was a sheet with some randomly selected answers. Each student had a different set answers, and the sheets were covered with aluminum foil to assure the answers couldn't be seen. The students were not told the contents of the envelopes or even that they were participating in an ESP test. They did significantly better on the questions that were answered in their own envelopes.

That outcome raises a question. If, as much evidence indicates, ESP is not limited by distance, why didn't the students use ESP to learn the answers to all the questions equally well (e.g., by telepathy from the teacher, or from answers in other students' envelopes)? Why did they score higher on questions that had answers in their own envelopes? Of course one could suggest reasons that were somehow compatible with the findings. But this and other research suggest that it wasn't necessarily the subjects' psychic abilities that accounted for the results. The experimenter's desire for a successful outcome, coupled with his own unconscious psychic ability, may explain the result. Johnson randomly selected answers for each envelope and in distributing the envelopes for the test, perhaps they were matched with students who knew those particular answers. This entire procedure can be construed as a complex random process, and his psi may have influenced it. A number of conceptually comparable studies also suggest that experimenter psi can operate in such circumstances.

Task-Complexity Independence

Early laboratory researchers suspected that ESP and PK were aspects of a unitary process. One way to investigate that idea combined ESP and PK tests into one experiment by using hidden targets. Karlis Osis published one of the earliest of those experiments in 1953 while he was working at Rhine's laboratory at Duke.[16] Osis was a major figure in parapsychology, and he deserves some introduction. He was born in Latvia and obtained his Ph.D. in psychology in Germany. He immigrated to the U.S. after WWII and first did manual labor because of his poor English, but during that time he tried some ESP tests with animals. Rhine had an interest in that and invited Osis to work at Duke. After his stint there, Osis served as director of research for the Parapsychology Foundation in New York City and later in a similar capacity at the American Society for Psychical Research. He is one of very few who made a nearly life-long career in parapsychology, and he was an innovator. He pioneered research on ESP in dreams;[17] he studied near-death experiences long before Raymond Moody and Elisabeth Kübler-Ross popularized the topic,[18] and he investigated the effects of distance on ESP performance. Osis was one of few who devoted himself almost exclusively to research and had little to do with administration, teaching, or management.[19]

Osis' testing procedure used dice, and it was simple and straightforward. Lists of target faces (numbers 1 through 6) were prepared by utilizing tables of random numbers. On each list, 16 targets were indicated. Each list was placed in an envelope, and a similar but blank sheet was clipped to the outside. Subjects threw a die for each trial, trying to make the uppermost face of the die match the associated target in the envelope. The throws' outcomes were recorded on the outer sheet.

If ESP and PK act like perceptual and motor processes, then in Osis' study, one presumes that a person first uses ESP to learn the target face and then uses PK to affect the fall of the die. If this is so, PK scores with hidden targets should be much lower than those with targets known to the subject. For instance, if ESP and PK were independent and each worked accurately 10% of the time, then they would work together only 1% of the time (.10 x .10 = .01). The scores would be much reduced.[20]

Osis found that scores on hidden targets were about the same as for known targets, indicating that PK may not be comparable to other forces in nature. This preliminary experiment was certainly not sufficient to prove the conclusion, and further, it was not as well controlled as formal studies in parapsychology, a fact Osis made very clear in his report. (Better controls would include machine tumbling of the die, sealed envelopes with target lists covered with aluminum foil to assure opacity, and greater monitoring by the experimenter. It should be noted, however, that Osis and his wife contributed the bulk of the trials, which partly mitigates the shortcomings.) The conclusions were strengthened when a variety of later studies pointed in the same direction.

Hidden-target PK experiments are now seen as testing the effects of what is called task complexity. Complexity in this sense refers to the amount of apparent information required to duplicate a psi task by normal human sensorimotor activities (e.g., in the Osis experiment, one first needed to learn the identity of the target and then influence the fall of the dice; two steps were required). Making a task more complex did not lower the scores, and this was confirmed with other studies with high complexity that still achieved success.

These experiments stimulated theoretical work, and in 1974 Helmut Schmidt suggested that psi was "goal oriented." He stated: "This suggests that PK may not be properly understood in terms of some mechanism by which the mind interferes with the machine in some cleverly calculated way but that it may be more appropriate to see PK as a goal-oriented principle, one that aims successfully at a final event, no matter how intricate the intermediate steps."[21] This idea spurred others.

In June 1978 J. E. Kennedy published another important conceptual paper entitled: "The Role of Task Complexity in PK: A Review" in the *Journal of Parapsychology*. Kennedy asked whether there was any substantial difference between a subject throwing a die and wishing for a six in a PK experiment and an experimenter conducting a study and desiring a significant result. Both attempt to influence random processes.

Kennedy pointed out that any experiment involves a hierarchy of goals: a subject aims for success on each individual trial; each subject wants to do well on the sum of his or her trials; the experimenter desires a statistically significant experiment, and each experiment is typically part of a larger line of research that the investigator hopes to be successful. The goals are not contradictory, but they do cause problems for interpretation. If an experimenter is the primary source of psi, and the subjects do little more than generate random data, statistical significance might be detected only when a study is analyzed overall. For instance, it is possible that no individual subject achieves a significant result yet the entire experiment could be statistically significant. The pattern of the data generated randomly, via random number tables and subjects' guesses, may conform to the experimenter's expectations. Kennedy suggested that in order to maximize psi in an experiment (statistically speaking), all parties involved should give particular focus and effort to each individual trial rather than on the overall experiment. He elaborated upon this idea in a paper on redundancy published the next year.[22]

Retroactive PK

Precognition is one of the greatest impediments to incorporating psi into conventional scientific theories. Violating the time barrier subverts the usual notion of cause and effect (i.e., causes precede effects). That poses real problems. Identical questions are raised by some PK experiments on pre-recorded targets conducted by Helmut Schmidt. He found that PK could work backward in time, and this was dubbed retroactive PK.[23]

Schmidt used an electronic random number generator (RNG) to control the rate of clicking sounds produced by an electronic device. These were played through headphones. In preliminary experiments Schmidt showed that humans could increase the rate of clicks by using PK to influence the RNG. He carried this further, and instead of playing the clicks directly for subjects, he recorded them onto audiotape. In addition, a second record was made on paper punch tape. For the experiment, half of the tape-recorded sequences of clicks were played to subjects, and the remaining half served as controls. The experimental and control sequences were selected by using a deterministic random process (finding the square roots of a succession of primes, taking the twelfth digits, and then using their parity [even or odd] to designate target or control). The subjects listened to the tapes through headphones and tried to increase the rate of the clicks. Schmidt set the sound level very low so that they needed to stay alert while listening. The test runs had significantly more clicks than the controls. The PK effect on pre-recorded trials was about the same magnitude as the real-time PK efforts.

Schmidt's experiment directly challenges the notion of cause and effect. Even though the experiment was conducted a quarter century ago, few people are aware of it, and when I tell people about it, they often think that they misunderstood what I said. The outcome assaults common sense.

Retroactive PK experiments allow very strong controls against cheating. Schmidt analyzed his results by using the paper tape. Since that tape was not available to the subjects, even if they somehow managed to alter the magnetic tape, it would have made no difference.

The method can be extended to protect against fraud by a single experimenter. One experimenter can record the sequences to be influenced (e.g., zeroes and ones on a tape or disk or other media), make a duplicate copy of them, and then give the copy to a second experimenter. A third experimenter, who does not have a copy of the tape, could randomly select segments to serve as target and control runs. The third experimenter can give a copy of his selections to the first or second experimenter. Then the tapes may be given directly to subjects to take home. Even if a subject had electronic and computer skills and changed a tape, it would make no difference. Results are evaluated with the copies held by experimenters. Further, experimenter fraud requires collusion by two experimenters.

In the March 1986 issue of the *Journal of Parapsychology* Schmidt published an ingenious experiment along with Robert Morris and Luther Rudolph. Schmidt was at Mind Science Foundation in San Antonio, Texas and the other two were at Syracuse University in New York.[24] Their procedure was similar to that described above though rather more involved, and the reader is urged to examine the original report, which was one of the most tightly controlled parapsychology experiments ever conducted. It was a success, and later experiments continued this line.[25]

Elmar Gruber, a young German researcher, carried out an intriguing extension of this kind of experiment.[26] Instead of using an RNG to produce target sequences, he used a photoelectric device to monitor people walking into a supermarket. When they passed the device, it recorded a click on a magnetic tape. The taped sequence of clicks was divided into experimental and control periods (by using shuffled black and white cards), and the experimental portions were later played to subjects, who did not know that the clicks had been pre-recorded. As in Schmidt's experiments, subjects listened to the clicks through headphones and tried to increase the click rate. Gruber did a second series of experiments, but instead of recording passers-by in a supermarket, his device monitored cars driving through a tunnel. In both series of experiments, Gruber found the rate of clicks in the experimental periods significantly exceeded that of the control periods. It appeared as though his subjects could affect the past. At least there was a correlation between the subjects' intentions and the movement of shoppers and automobile traffic.

Theoretical Issues

The situation is perplexing. With experimenter effects, nonintentional psi, and retroactive PK, one worries just how far a person's psychic influence can go. Indeed, some may wonder whether any scientific progress can be made at all! How can anyone know who caused a psi effect in an experiment? It seems that subjects, experimenters, checkers, and outside observers might all influence the outcome. Could skeptics inhibit positive results by using their abilities unconsciously? Doesn't all this invalidate parapsychology?

The problems are real but not too severe. After all, a similar situation is found in psychology. When psychologists try to explain human behavior, they consider a multitude of factors including: personality traits, upbringing, birth order, physiology, brain structure, beliefs, cultural background, and literally hundreds of other variables. These all interact and interfere with each other. No one factor or specifiable group of them absolutely predicts human action. Yet psychologists continue to carry out studies, and they make some progress.

Likewise, progress is made in parapsychology. In many real-world cases there is little hesitation in attributing an effect to a specific individual. In mediumship and poltergeist cases, paranormal events typically occur only when a certain person is present. If a psychic has consistent results in healing, again there is little dispute in saying that the healer is the primary cause. Or if a person describes a distant, unknown location in considerable, accurate detail, there would be no problem in saying that that individual had a psychic experience. In such cases, it makes sense to attribute the psychic effects to the obvious source.

By studying such seemingly gifted individuals, or even ordinary people, common patterns can be found. Of course, one must be cautious in interpreting results from only one experimenter (who may have certain expectations that may cause bias), but when a variety of investigators find a similar pattern, the potential for experimenter influence recedes. In such cases, results can be reasonably attributed to subjects.

In fact, a number of psychological factors have been found to influence ESP performance. I have already mentioned that altered states of consciousness facilitate it. Extroverts tend to do better than introverts, and those who believe in ESP tend to get higher scores than those who don't. Being spontaneous in guessing helps also. There is an enormous amount of research on these topics, and it is far too vast to summarize here. John Palmer published a 185-page overview article on ESP research findings in Volume 2 of the series *Advances in Parapsychological Research* edited by Stanley Krippner. That is a good starting point for anyone wishing to become more familiar with the scientific research on psychological variables that influence ESP.

As mentioned earlier, experimental work consumed most of the resources of the field, and much of the empirical research has been dominated by a psychological approach typical of that found in psychology departments at American universities. It proved effective in identifying variables that affected psi performance, but it was limited. It was reductionistic; it focussed on individuals, and it did not lend itself to useful integration. There was a need for a broader understanding.

Three Models

Between 1970 and 1980 three important theoretical developments were introduced in parapsychology. These were the quantum mechanical theory of Evan Harris Walker, the conformance behavior model proposed by Rex Stanford, and the concepts of lability and inertia advanced by William Braud. There were other, related formulations presented during the same period, but these three were among the most influential. These models are particularly valuable because their inventors were involved with ongoing laboratory research. Both Stanford and Braud were active experimentalists, and Walker maintained close contact with researchers in laboratories, and their models guided a variety of experimental research. The field was long afflicted with philosophers and others who offered opinions, ideas and speculations, but had little contact with data. The work of Walker, Stanford, and Braud was a refreshing change.

Evan Harris Walker's Quantum Mechanical Theory

Evan Harris Walker is a physicist who worked for the U.S. Army at Aberdeen Proving Grounds in Maryland. He is now retired. His relevant papers began appearing in 1970, and since then he has published a number of them describing models of quantum mechanics (QM), consciousness, and psi. His work prompted others to propose alternatives, but his theory was by far the most developed, and it stimulated much discussion and experimentation. Within parapsychology, his work falls under the rubric of "observational theories," which typically have some direct or tangential relation to QM. The label "observational theory" is loosely used and one not preferred by Walker.

Since its beginning, QM has had unresolved conceptual difficulties that fostered many rival interpretations. It violates common sense;

it poses paradoxes; it overturns notions of cause and effect. An initial glance suggests that it may be relevant to understanding precognition and retroactive PK. Furthermore, in some interpretations of QM, consciousness plays a role, allowing a possible influence by a human observer.

For decades, speculations on QM and psi have appeared in scientific, philosophical, and popular literature. In 1956 Indian philosopher C. T. K. Chari published an article titled "Quantum Physics and Parapsychology" in the *Journal of Parapsychology*.[27] In 1960 the eminent physicist Pascual Jordan commented on the possible relationship in the *International Journal of Parapsychology*,[28] and in the 1970s the connection was more widely popularized by such books as *The Roots of Coincidence* (1972) by Arthur Koestler.

The significant scientific development began in the 1970s with the theoretical work of Walker and Helmut Schmidt. As described earlier, Schmidt pioneered the use of electronic random number generators (RNGs) in psi testing; he also proposed theoretical models, but the bulk of his contributions were in experimental research. Walker concentrated on theoretical problems, and he produced the more encompassing body of theory, with connections to a variety of areas.

Within QM there is a controversy about what causes "state vector collapse," in other words, what constitutes a "measurement" or an "observation." Though the concept of measurement is a central issue, the problem is not satisfactorily resolved among physicists. There are competing interpretations. For instance, some suggest that a measurement is complete when a meter records the outcome of a QM process, but not everyone agrees that is sufficient. Some argue that something else, perhaps human consciousness, is required. The matter has been debated for decades, and Walker addressed the problem in a long paper, "The Nature of Consciousness," in the journal *Mathematical Biosciences* in 1970, and the following year he participated in a debate in the pages of *Physics Today* with his paper "Consciousness as a Hidden Variable."

Walker noted that quantum processes could occur in the brain. Synapses, the junctions of neurons where nervous impulses are transmitted, include a tiny gap between cells called the synaptic cleft. Walker calculated that the synaptic cleft was small enough to allow electrons to cross it via quantum tunneling, a process subject to random quantum uncertainty.[29] Walker extended his ideas, and estimating the number of synapses in the brain, their firing rates, and electron tunneling rates; he computed information rates for the unconscious, consciousness, and also the will, which he suggested was responsible for collapse of the state vector. He thereby incorporated brain processes, QM, and consciousness in an attractive formulation.

Walker went on to apply his ideas to psi, and at the 1972 meeting of the Parapsychological Association he gave a paper entitled "Application of the Quantum Theory of Consciousness to the Problem of Psi Phenomena." He argued that psi is caused by the will, thereby tying it to his theory of consciousness and the collapse of the state vector. His model focussed on measures of information, and he conceived both ESP and PK not as energetic processes, where energy is transmitted, but rather as informational ones.

In 1974 he presented one of his most important articles, "Foundations of Paraphysical and Parapsychological Phenomena," at a Parapsychology Foundation symposium on quantum mechanics. In that paper Walker reanalyzed data of Haakon Forwald. Forwald was a Norwegian-born engineer who became a naturalized citizen of Sweden and who obtained over 500 patents. He had conducted PK experiments with cubes of different sizes and materials in order to study physical parameters. He began in 1949, and through the 1950s and 1960s Forwald's work appeared in refereed professional journals, and he collaborated with a number of researchers during that time. His data were especially valuable because they quantitatively measured the operation of psi in relation to physical variables.

Forwald's equipment dropped cubes mechanically; they tumbled down a ramp and came to rest on a flat surface marked with a grid. A subject wished for the to cubes fall to one side or the other of the grid's centerline, depending upon the designated target side for a trial. These were referred to as placement studies. After the cubes came to rest, their distances from the centerline were measured and tallied. Forwald discovered that the material of the cubes affected the net deviation from the centerline (taking into account both the hitting and missing cubes, i.e., whether a cube fell on the specified target side for a trial). He surmised that the psi influence on the cubes was related to the materials' nuclear properties, and he developed some equations of mechanical forces to describe the results.

Walker took a different perspective; instead of analyzing classical forces, he used quantum mechanics. The Heisenberg uncertainty principle states that as the position of a particle becomes more precisely known its momentum becomes more uncertain, and Walker calculated the quantum uncertainty for cubes. One of the implications of those calculations is that for a sufficient number of bounces, the final position, i.e., the upward face, is in principle indeterminate. That is, even knowing the initial position and all forces acting on a die, the upward face of the final resting position cannot be calculated. It is, in principle, random. Extending such computations and incorporating his model of consciousness, he analyzed Forwald's placement studies. Walker calculated the amount of deviation expected by his theory and found startlingly good agreement with the Forwald data.

Walker's work attracted considerable attention, including that of critics. In the December 1984 issue of the *Journal of Parapsychology* he published a long response and further explained his theory. One of the critics was Martin Gardner, godfather of the skeptical movement, who was discussed extensively in the last chapter. In a 1981 article, Gardner had objected to Walker's use of the Forwald data because Forwald often served as both experimenter and subject.[30] Walker answered, noting that there had been some replication of Forwald's findings, and more importantly, the data had been collected and published years before Walker developed his theory. As such, it is unlikely that the close fit of theory and data would be due to any bias of Forwald.

Gardner's critique had its problems, and he may not have fully understood the debates among physicists, a point Walker illustrated in his reply. For instance, Gardner stated that "In QM it is not the human observer who collapses wave packets but the observing instruments,"[31] a view disputed by a number of Nobel laureates. In a footnote he acknowledged Eugene Wigner's position contradicted his own, and Gardner may not have been aware that Wigner allowed the possibility that consciousness could influence the physical world, an idea Gardner vehemently disputed in his attack on Walker.[32] Wigner had made the statement in a 1962 article "Remarks on the Mind-Body Question," and the following year he won the Nobel Prize. More recently Gardner has given QM additional attention, and he has further criticized Wigner, saying "I never liked his approach to quantum mechanics ... From Wigner's point of view there is a sense in which even the entire Universe is not 'out there' unless there are humans to observe it."[33]

In any event, Gardner was forced to admit that if Walker's assumptions were correct "a scaffolding exists on which to hang a theory of ESP and PK."[34] In addition Gardner begrudgingly admitted that "Walker's theory also accounts for the embarrassing fact that parapsychologists have been unable to detect a PK effect on a delicately balanced needle ... assuming the subject is not a superpsychic."[35]

Coming from such a committed debunker, these remarks can only be seen as high praise.

Despite Gardner's typical patronizing tone and disparaging remarks, he brought into focus crucial underlying philosophical assumptions. Though Walker largely refuted Gardner, Gardner's critique was useful for its exposition, and several people told me that they were more impressed with Walker's theory after reading Gardner's presentation of it.

As an aside, Gardner's point about a delicately balanced needle raises the issue of macro-PK, a topic I have so far neglected in this chapter. Nearly all formal parapsychological research concentrates on statistically based experiments (i.e., those incorporating a source of randomness, as in card-guessing ESP tests and PK studies with dice). The reader may wonder how these esoteric experiments and theories apply to poltergeist phenomena or other macro-PK effects, such as levitation of tables. Richard Mattuck, a physicist at the University of Copenhagen, extended Walker's theory in this regard. In 1976 he presented a paper "Random Fluctuation Theory of Psychokinesis: Thermal Noise Model," and later he and Walker collaborated on further refinements. They suggested that the mind may reorganize energy already available in the environment, for example, random movement of molecules due to heat. In their model, human consciousness imposes coherence (order or information) on random noise. Useful energy is the product of that. The Walker-Mattuck model allowed the levitation of an object of only about 10 grams, but they did point a way that larger forces might be accommodated with further revisions of the theory.[36]

There is another incompatibility between macro-PK and other types of psi. Unlike ESP and PK detected with statistics, macro-PK appears to be severely limited by distance. In almost all cases, the person putatively responsible for an event is within a few meters of it.

Macro-PK phenomena have received little attention from laboratory researchers, who view them with suspicion because of their frequent association with fraud. There is very little quantitative data on macro-PK, and few theories address it; most consider only statistical effects. An exception is the work of Kenneth Batcheldor, a British psychologist who spent decades studying macro-PK in séance-like situations. He gathered groups to hold sessions to elicit macro-PK. They interpreted their séance phenomena not as caused by spirits of the dead, but rather by the unconscious minds of the participants. Batcheldor died in 1988, and in 1994 Patric V. Giesler compiled and edited his notes discussing his theoretical ideas. Some of the salient issues included ambiguity, indeterminacy, and elusiveness. These are congruent with, and even reinforce, the theoretical perspectives discussed in this book.[37]

Psi appears to be essentially independent of space and time, but if people in the future can influence the past (e.g., precognition, retroactive PK), how can we know whether an experiment is ever finished? If a study is conducted and published, could someone later read it and alter the outcome? This, in a nutshell, is the divergence problem. Fundamentally it is a problem of boundaries and limits, and one not encountered in the usual frameworks of science. The term, in this usage, was introduced by Helmut Schmidt in his 1975 article "Toward a Mathematical Theory of Psi."[38] Schmidt borrowed the term from an analogous divergence problem in quantum electrodynamics.[39]

Several researchers have offered ideas to limit divergence. Some suggest that only the first observer causes a psi effect (e.g., the subject watching a set of lights controlled by an RNG in a PK test), but others propose that diminishing contributions come from later observers. Walker argues that those suggestions are simply ad hoc and fail to deal with the space-time independence. He addressed the matter in the *Journal of Research in Psi Phenomena* (1977), noting that not only subjects but also experimenters and later observers play potential roles. He pointed out that any result obtained in an experiment incorporates the effects of future observers, though the experimenter has little or no control over them. Walker used his theory to calculate the potential influence of future observers, by making some plausible assumptions about the strength of their effects. He concluded that while there is a problem, it is not too severe.[40]

The issue of divergence highlights two problematic areas: the definition of observation, and the social aspect of psi. Because the definition of "observation" is not included in the formalism of QM, defining consciousness is problematical. Within parapsychology a number of experiments explored the notion of observation by varying the amount of information available to an observer, using multiple observers, and by comparing animals and humans as observers. These were tentative steps, and the issue is still open for theoretical speculation.

In Walker's theory, observing an event (i.e., becoming consciously aware of it) collapses the wave function, and it is there that PK can operate. For his formulation, consciousness is essentially equivalent to awareness, though he admits that that is not yet completely defined, and that the concept needs more development. One objection to Walker's model is that psi often appears to act unconsciously. Nevertheless consciousness seems somehow involved, and it may play an important role, perhaps somehow limiting or restraining psi. Becoming fully aware of an object or event in some sense stabilizes it in the mind. If the event is spoken of, artistically portrayed, or written about, it becomes "firmer." Such representations give the object or event attention; awareness of it is enhanced. It is through representation that other people can learn of the item or event.

If awareness is required in the operation of psi, some interesting theoretical connections arise. To be aware of something is to distinguish it from its background, to make a distinction. Becoming aware entails the construction of a mental representation; part of the brain's information processing capacity is allotted to that task. Thus the issue of "representation" can be tied to Walker's theory. In nearly all sciences, representation is assumed to be unproblematic; the fundamental questions about it are ignored. The issue is central to semiotics and literary theory, and in the argot of semiotics, Walker's theory establishes a connection between the signifier and signified.

The second matter highlighted by divergence is that psi has a social aspect: multiple people may affect a paranormal event. In Walker's formulation, the act of observing collapses the wave function, and it is there that PK operates. When more than one person observes an event (whether in the present or future), there is a collective effect because of psi's space-time independence. Reporting an event to others makes those persons observers and links them to it.

I am not aware of anyone discussing divergence explicitly in terms of social factors, but it suggests connections between parapsychology and other disciplines. When groups are involved, representations are made collectively, bringing to mind Durkheim's notion of "collective representations." For social activity some level of consensus and coherence is required, and consciousness might be seen as a collective function, a social process. Walker did not elaborate on the implications of divergence as much as he might have, but he did make some provocative statements about the consensus required for "fundamental laws of nature."[41]

The topic of divergence stimulates speculation about psi. For instance, strong psi effects may operate so that relatively few people learn of them. If they do become known, they may be of such a nature as to be easily dismissed. They may be surrounded by fraud, or reported only by those who have a reputation for gullibility. Similarly this may explain why secrecy and ambiguity surround many groups engaging in occult practices. Such speculations could be multiplied endlessly, and that is why it would help to have some clear limits on psi.

Walker's theory was truly innovative; it was a radical departure from previous theories. There had been nothing comparable in parapsychology before its arrival. Like all important new works, revisions have been and will be made, elaborations are required. The theory remains controversial among psi researchers, and maybe it will be ultimately rejected. Nevertheless Walker made several exceptional contributions. Perhaps most importantly, he formally introduced randomness and uncertainty into theories of psi. He tied his theory to physical processes (e.g., tumbling dice and brain activity) in a way that had not been accomplished before, and he went to considerable effort to link his theories to quantitative data.

Further, Walker directly addressed some of the most problematical aspects of psi including its independence of space, time, and task complexity. Any successful theory must accommodate these.

Rex Stanford's Conformance Behavior

Walker's theory was from physics, and it was not immediately well understood by many in other disciplines. Some of the general ideas were discussed within parapsychology, and a few researchers began formulating them in terms congenial to other fields. One of those was psychologist Rex Stanford, who was introduced earlier.

In the 1970s Stanford began rethinking the vexing conceptual difficulties of psi. He questionned the traditional models that many parapsychologists adopted implicitly, wherein ESP was conceived as something transmitted, and PK was thought to be a capacity to act upon the environment. Psi was usually assumed to be similar to other psychological and biological processes (e.g., perception) which involve some transmission (e.g., light, sound). The traditional conceptions have been referred to as transmission models, communication models, and psycho-biological models. Sometimes these were explicit in the theorizing about psi, but often they were not.[42]

Stanford proposed a model that he called "conformance behavior." He strived to simplify and clarify the crucial components of the psi process and look at them anew, by discarding the usual assumptions. His model was abstractly formulated; it had two parts: a disposed system and a random event generator (REG). By "disposed system" Stanford meant an organism that had a need or disposition (presumably his use of the term "disposition" was more comprehensive than "need" and included negative human moods, feelings, and expectations). By "random event generator" Stanford referred to systems like those discussed by Walker. Stanford's random processes were those that could affect the disposed system, perhaps even very indirectly. The conformance behavior model obviates the idea of sending and receiving information. It simply postulates that the random process affects an event in accord with the disposed system. The model does not specify how that happens, but only that it does; that is how the universe is built.

Stanford's model requires no conscious intent to use psi, and it subsumes synchronicity, i.e., meaningful coincidence. He gave an example of a person forgetting to change subway trains on the way to visit friends. Because of that forgetfulness, the person encountered the very people he was planning to visit. Had he been alert and changed trains, he would have completely missed his friends. Here the subway rider had the goal of (i.e., disposition toward) meeting friends. Various contingencies provided a result that conformed to that goal.

Stanford's conformance behavior model was not nearly as developed as Walker's, and it was criticized, somewhat justifiably, for lacking much predictive value. But what it lacked there, it compensated with clarity and simplicity. It was couched in terms more congenial to psychologists and was more easily adapted to testing by them. It stimulated experiments that otherwise might not have been conducted, such as those of Gruber, described earlier. Stanford's model helped emphasize the then-new ideas of the goal-oriented nature of psi and the fundamental role of randomness.

William Braud's Lability and Inertia

William G. Braud is a psychologist who was a leading experimenter in the field in the 1970s and 1980s. For much of that period he worked at the Mind Science Foundation in San Antonio, Texas, along with Helmut Schmidt. Braud published many innovative and successful experiments. He was the first to report an ESP ganzfeld study, but he is rarely given credit for that.[43] Braud was known for methodological rigor. I had the good fortune of serving as a reviewer of several of his papers, and it was difficult to find much to criticize in them. He undertook his theoretical work with a very strong grounding in empirical data and experience (somewhat like Victor Turner in anthropology). He did not start with some grand philosophical scheme.

Because Braud is known as an exemplary experimentalist, his conceptual insights have been largely overlooked. His most important theoretical contributions addressed the matters of "lability and inertia." Lability is the ready capacity for change, "the ease with which a system can change from one state to another, the amount of 'free variability' in the system."[44] Inertia is the opposite: the tendency to resist change. Braud's model proposed that the magnitude of a PK effect should be directly related to the amount of lability in the target system, and the likelihood of an ESP event should be proportional to the amount of lability in the brain or mind of the percipient.

Braud drew upon the theorizing of Walker and Stanford, and he gave them explicit credit. In fact his first paper on the topic was titled "Lability and Inertia in Conformance Behavior," thus incorporating Stanford's phrase.[45]

Braud understood that lability is directly related to randomness, which was central to the models of both Walker and Stanford. He explained how many systems and processes can be described in terms of lability and inertia, and he reviewed a number of lines of research that indicate that psi has more influence on labile systems than on inert ones. The concept has great applicability, including to areas not immediately obvious. ESP in altered states of consciousness is an example. Meditation, progressive relaxation, hypnosis and other altered states have been found to enhance ESP in the laboratory. They are typified by an inward focus, with the outer physical and social environments given diminished attention. The physical and social worlds have a stability and a capacity to structure and organize a person's attention. In contrast, in dreaming and meditation, the mind can quickly flit from one idea to another. There is less patterning of cognitive processes in those states, and less structure to them. The imagery is labile; it changes rapidly.

Braud's concept also subsumes research on "response bias avoidance behavior." In ESP card-guessing tests, subjects tend to call some symbols more frequently than others. Those preferred symbols are the response bias; the calls (responses) are biased (the symbols are not called equally often). When a subject made a guess that he or she made relatively infrequently (i.e., avoided the response bias), the guess was more likely to be correct than those guesses of symbols called more often. Thus when a subject broke from the usual pattern (i.e., the usual structure), ESP was more likely to manifest.

Novelty also facilitates ESP. Novelty, by definition, is a change from an old pattern. In many ESP card experiments and PK dice studies, the first part of a run was likely to have especially strong scoring. Again, the beginning of a run is a break from whatever was happening before. As an experiment continues, it becomes less novel and more routinized, and scores typically decline. Thus transition periods produce better psi scores than more routine conditions.

Braud carried out additional experiments to test the model. He set up a PK study with two different targets: a candle flame, and an electric lamp with a DC power supply. A small fan was placed near the candle flame, causing it to flicker. The electric lamp gave more stable illumination. These were monitored by a photocell attached to an amplifier, and in another room a chart recorder and a digital readout device displayed the output. The subjects and experimenter were in the second room with the recording devices and were able to watch them. During randomly selected periods the subjects were asked to increase the activity of the flame or electric light and in other periods to reduce the activity. With the "high aim" and "low aim" conditions, a subject's performance could be evaluated statistically. The analysis showed that the subjects influenced the candle flame (the labile target) but not the electric lamp (the inert target).

Braud frequently used biological organisms in his PK experiments (e.g., cells, small animals, humans). He argued that they should be especially suitable because of their natural variability and unpredictability. Inanimate systems generally have less lability. His experiments with organisms as PK targets were quite successful.[46]

Braud's concept provides an encompassing vision. It integrated and extended the work of Walker and Stanford. Braud showed the great generality of their ideas and explained where they apply. He discussed physical and biological systems but did not carry the idea to higher levels such as small groups of people, societies, and large cultures. Those too show a similar pattern.

Braud's model guided much of my thinking since I became professionally active in parapsychology. His two papers allowed me to see the theoretical possibilities inherent in Victor Turner's concept of anti-structure. Both "anti-structure" and "lability" referred to instability and transition, and that suggested linkages to psi. Further, Braud's work depended upon Walker's, which focussed on information rather than energy, force, or power. Likewise, Edmund Leach's conception of structural anthropology was also formulated in terms of information. The common language expressing the ideas clarified the shared patterns across seemingly unrelated fields.

Conclusion

This has been an all-too-short presentation of parapsychology. The scientific journals contain over a century of material, and much more of it bears on the topics in this book. It's too vast to present it all here.

Both parapsychologists and their critics acknowledge that psi experiments are not fully repeatable. Psi is detected only intermittently, and the effects are usually weak. Some researchers succeed; others don't. If the results were strong and robust and anyone could easily replicate them, there would be no controversy, and this book would not have been written.

The replication problems signal psi's profound properties, but introductory texts give the implications scant treatment, and few researchers consider them at length. I presented some of the perplexities in this chapter because I don't believe that they should be minimized in order to make the field appealing to other scientists or to a popular audience. If progress is to be made, the troubles must be confronted. I will summarize some of the key issues.

In any given psi experiment, it is difficult, if not impossible, to fully determine who causes any result. Experimenters, subjects, checkers, and others may all contribute some influence even without conscious intent. ESP is not blocked by distance or time. Retroactive PK suggests that persons in the future can influence the past. It is probably impossible, in principle, for a researcher to control all factors that affect an experiment. "Participation" may be far greater than an investigator envisions.

The future may show that these problems can be overcome, that clear limits can be demonstrated, and that high levels of replicability can be achieved. Indeed, progress has been made. Research demonstrates that a variety of factors affect psi including: belief in ESP, personality traits, spontaneity, and altered states of consciousness, among others. So far, psychic phenomena can be influenced, if not fully controlled. Some believe that continuing experiments along traditional lines will solve the control problem, and I think progress will be made by such efforts. Nevertheless, everyone agrees that psi violates commonsense assumptions. Any theory must accommodate those violations.

One consequence of the research findings is that psi experiments must be understood as social processes. Many people potentially influence a result, even inadvertently and even in the future. Social forces must be taken seriously. They have an autonomy that cannot be comprehended reductionistically. So far, most parapsychology studies have focused on psychological variables (i.e., characteristics of individuals). This is not sufficient; a final result cannot be determined by summing the contributions of known individuals. There is a complex interplay, and a more sophisticated understanding of social processes is needed. This will be broached in the next chapter.

Boundaries and limits are two recurring themes in this book, and they help provide a broader perspective needed in considering psi. The trickster is central to this effort, for like psi, he is not easily constrained; he crosses and blurs boundaries. He is paradoxical, ambiguous, and causes problems for rational understanding.

Psi requires a broad perspective for understanding. Any comprehensive theory must accommodate RNG results as well as cultural trends in the paranormal. The commonalities must be discerned. The work of William Braud provides a beginning. Labile systems, i.e., those that readily change, are more amenable to psi influence than are stable systems. This is a general property. It appears at the micro-level with electronic random number generators and tumbling dice. The same pattern is seen at higher levels. Persons who break out of routine, and who act spontaneously, find psi more likely to manifest. Small groups and larger cultures undergoing significant transition have elevated levels of paranormal activity. Liminality and anti-structure have properties of lability and randomness (by the way, Hermes is the god of luck, and of dice).

Though ESP and PK involve information, there is no reason to think that anything is transmitted. ESP is not like mental radio. Instead, more abstract ideas of information and communication are required for modelling it. Structuralism, semiotics, and literary theory provide some alternatives, and they will be discussed in the next two chapters. Briefly expressed, the ideas are: individually and collectively, we detect and impose pattern and order on our existence in myriad ways. Through classification, social structure, rational thought, and many other mechanisms, we bring order and intelligibility to our world.

Liminality and anti-structure break down established classifications and categories; they subvert structure; they allow new forms to emerge. It is under those conditions that information is created and destroyed. Those conditions are also the home of the trickster and of psi.

CHAPTER 22

Totemism and the Primitive Mind

Note: In years past, anthropologists used "primitive" and "savage" to designate what is now referred to as preliterate. The words were sometimes, but by no means always, used in a derogatory sense. The two terms were so frequently used in the writings on totemism that it seems best to continue with them because they are consistent with the large bulk of the relevant literature. Little new material on totemism has appeared since those terms were in fashion.

During the last decades of the nineteenth century and the first two of the twentieth, totemism engaged some of the era's most formidable minds including Emile Durkheim, Andrew Lang, Wilhelm Wundt, Arnold van Gennep, Herbert Spencer, Marcel Mauss, and Sigmund Freud. Totemism was the base for the religious and social organization of many societies, but it was also one of the most vexing aspects of primitive cultures. It commanded extended discussion and debate in books and professional journals. Today the matter is almost entirely forgotten. Most introductory anthropology texts allot totemism only a few sentences, and when I checked the subject in the 1997 *Books in Print*, I found only ten items listed. Two were first published over 30 years ago, and the remainder over 70 years ago. This astounding neglect gives an important clue to the nature of the topic.

This situation makes it difficult to explain totemism, because without a set of common examples, the overall picture cannot be conveyed, yet if examples are presented with no sense of direction, they seem incoherent. For the first few pages of this chapter I will give an introductory overview. It may seem dry and abstract, but the remainder of the chapter should be a bit easier.

Totemism was central to the worlds of many primitive peoples, but because it was so fundamental, encompassing and varied, it cannot be neatly defined. It is perhaps best explained by example. A tribe might be divided into a bear clan, an eagle clan, and others. Each clan has different rights, responsibilities, taboos, marriage restrictions, etc. In some cultures all objects in the world are categorized in relationship to totem animals. For instance, certain kinds of rocks and trees belong to one clan, others to other clans. One clan might own the rain, another streams. Clans may be restricted from eating certain foods, but at ritual occasions they may be required to eat them. A clan may revere its totem animal or consider it a relative or a guardian spirit. A person may see himself as part of the totem, and the totem as part of him. Death of a member of a totem species could be viewed as death of a family member.

Such arrangements are vastly different than our own, and from our perspective, they confuse rational categories; boundaries are blurred (e.g., between people and animals). The primitives recognized a wide range of magical interconnections, but magic was particularly problematic for the early scholars who grappled with the primitive mentality. Many who thoroughly studied totemism and magic readily acknowledged that they found them incomprehensible. Even in 1994, after an extensive review, anthropologist Andrew Duff-Cooper concluded that totemism "remains essentially problematical today."[1] All this subtly signals the limits to Western rationality, and this is a key to the nature of totemism.

Primitive classification schemes, and their incomprehensibility to the modern academic mind, are central to understanding the rationalization and disenchantment of the world (in Max Weber's usage of the terms). The non-resolution of the debates on totemism indicates the presence of foundational issues. Those are relevant to anthropology, sociology, linguistics, literary theory, and, I propose, to psychical research.

The basic issues, though transmogrified, are now seen in deconstructionism, post-structuralism, and cultural studies. Those areas also raise questions about rationality. The intellectual antecedents of those fields can be traced (in part) to the early discussions of totemism (though few recognize it). That lineage must be understood to fully appreciate the implications. Totemism provides a direct challenge to the Western worldview, but so does deconstructionism. As I will explain in the next chapter, the fundamental ideas involve magic and the irrational.

In order to keep the discussion to a manageable length, I will emphasize the topic of classification. Totemism classifies items, structures society, and organizes the world. This general interpretation has wide support among eminent figures in social science, and it will be the focus here. When classification, statuses, and structures are dissolved we have conditions of liminality, anti-structure, and communitas. That is how totemism relates to other topics in this book.

British structural anthropologist Rodney Needham recognized the intrinsic relation between classification and liminality. He translated Emile Durkheim and Marcel Mauss's *Primitive Classification* (first published in French in 1903), and in his introduction to that work Needham explicitly referred to festivals such as saturnalia where rules and taboos are violated. He stated that "The theme of reversal is itself one of the most pervasive and fundamental problems in social anthropology, and it is so only in the context of the classifications within which its instances are discerned."[2] Needham did not use the term *liminal* (the word was then not as commonly used by anthropologists as it is today), but he recognized that festivals typified the breakdown of a variety of boundaries. A few years later the ideas received more attention from Victor Turner and Barbara Babcock.

"Boundary" is a recurrent theme in this book. Classification and categorization establish boundaries. Something as simple as applying a name to a tribe of people, a group of trees, a species of animal, or a mountain range constitutes a process of classifying. Naming sets a person, idea, or group apart from others. It gives an identity. It makes a distinction. For social life, distinctions must be agreed upon, and the anthropological terms "cultural category" and "collective representation" emphasize the shared nature of distinctions. Such notions initially appear trivial, but they form the basis of thought and language. Communication is a shared process, and by its nature calls attention to distinctions. Even modern information theory is based on the difference between 0 and 1 (i.e., bits, short for binary digits, are used to measure and convey information).

Anthropologists recognized that our perceptions and categories are often organized around binary oppositions. Differentiation (i.e., making distinctions) is central to this. French anthropologist Claude Levi-Strauss developed the ideas, noting that oppositions form structures out of a more undifferentiated whole. He noted that there are parallels between structures. This was a simple observation with deep consequences, and using his structural approach, anthropologists and others demonstrated the existence of common patterns across an amazing array of areas including kinship, myth, and linguistics.

Levi-Strauss revived interest in totemism in the 1960s in an attempt to understand the seemingly irrational beliefs of the primitives. Though he continues to be widely cited, his writings are perhaps not too well understood; they are couched in abstract terms. Levi-Strauss did not fully comprehend the issues himself, because he did not realize the efficacy of magic per se (i.e., involving psi).

Although Levi-Strauss is the best-known anthropologist associated with structuralism, equally important are the contributions of Rodney Needham of Oxford and Edmund Leach of Cambridge. Needham translated many important works, including Robert Hertz's essay "The Pre-eminence of the Right Hand" (originally published in 1909) which is one of the most important papers on binary classification schemes. Needham also edited a significant collection of essays on binary oppositions: *Right & Left* (1973). In 1979 he published *Symbolic Classification*, an accessible introduction to the topic.[3] Needham also translated Levi-Strauss' *Totemism*. Edmund Leach was the foremost interpreter of Levi-Strauss. His works are always a delight to read, with many pungent comments and sparkling insights.

Many who have used structuralist ideas focussed on how society is strengthened and made stable. Less attention has been given to the dissolution of structure, but that also shows commonalities. In this book we are more interested in the breakdown of structures and in their nascent formation, rather than in their stable forms. Structural breakdown, i.e., dissolving into more undifferentiated conditions, and structure emerging from those conditions, are anti-structural (a.k.a., liminal, interstitial) by definition. They are characterized by the blurring of binary oppositions.[4] The primitives looked upon liminal conditions as dangerous situations that needed to be hedged off from the mundane world. There were rituals to separate the elements of oppositions and thereby reinforce the order of the world.

Above are some of the main ideas that connect magic, totemism, structuralist thought, and liminality. These concepts are difficult to absorb on the first encounter. To help, I will present something about the history of the ideas and the personalities who articulated them.

The understanding of totemism and the development of structuralist thought did not occur quickly. It took decades, with rapid advances within a span of a few years and then long periods of quiescence during which little of importance was written.

Totemism Debates, 1869–1918: The Rationality Battles

In 1869 John Ferguson McLennan called attention to the relationship between totemism and marriageability classes. The primitive was not allowed to marry or have sexual relations within his or her totemic group (i.e., the rule of exogamy). This imposed limitations on sexual behavior. It also served to specify important relationships and obligations between groups. Neither totemism nor exogamy was found in all primitive cultures nor did they necessarily occur together, but their conjunction was frequent enough to demand attention, and the debates sparked by McLennan continued for over 50 years.

Sir James George Frazer was an important figure in those debates. He was best known for his work *The Golden Bough*, which was first published in 1890 in two volumes. Frazer had a gift for writing, and his books and articles stimulated broad interest in anthropology in the literate public.[5] *The Golden Bough* was later expanded, ultimately being presented in a series of 13 volumes; a one-volume abridgement was also published and remains in print.

Frazer's work on totemism is lesser known. As early as 1885 he had written an article on it for *Encyclopaedia Britannica*, and a few years later that served as the basis for a book. In 1910 he published a four-volume set entitled *Totemism and Exogamy* with over 2200 pages, and an additional fifth volume, *Totemica*, appeared in 1937. Frazer's work called attention to the obscure connection between rules of marriageability and totemism. Violation of exogamy (i.e., incest) was looked upon as extremely dangerous, and breaking of this taboo warranted extreme punishment, often death. In many primitive cultures, the entire cosmology was intricately tied to the social structure. Breaking rules concerning social relations was seen as having effects in the larger cosmos; there were magical interconnections, and violation of taboos had cosmic consequences.

Frazer was an armchair theorist who compiled and summarized the work of others. In fact, he had no direct encounter with the people of his theories, and when William James asked him about the primitives he knew, Frazer replied "But Heaven forbid!"[6] Frazer viewed earlier cultures as lower forms on an evolutionary chain (Western European being the highest). Even in his own day, Frazer's work was not well regarded by all anthropologists, and his influence among them was limited; he had a greater impact in the humanities.[7] Despite, or perhaps because of, the limitations of his perspective, his work called attention to how different we are from the primitives; they appear irrational. Frazer recognized it to be extremely difficult to comprehend their viewpoint, and he seems to have understood this better than those who have had more sympathy for them.

Frazer wrote during a time when the long war between science and religion was particularly intense in intellectual circles. This was partly due to the rise of Darwinism, but also the growing field of anthropology was demonstrating some embarrassing parallels between the primitive gods and the Judeo-Christian one. These were not detached scholarly discussions, rather the debates struck at the core of the participants' lives. Many rationalists studied magic and religion with the goal of defeating superstitious beliefs, including Christianity, which they saw as regressive. Frazer understood his role in this, and a number of his colleagues used his writings to attack religion.[8]

To the rationalists, magic was particularly vexing; it appeared entirely superstitious. However, it was not extinct in their own society, and the then-rising popularity of Theosophy, occultism, and spiritualism alarmed them. They viewed those movements as a dangerous throwback to the primitive past. The scientific evidence compiled by the Society for Psychical Research (SPR) lent credibility to magical ideas, and the formation of the SPR was prompted by some who were sympathetic to religious concerns.[9] Needless to say, this was not welcome to many rationalists, and Frazer's friend, rationalist Edward Clodd, denounced the SPR in his presidential address to the Folk Lore Society.[10] The Rationalist Press Association (RPA) and its imprint Watts & Co. were active in the battles; not only did they attack religion, but they were some of the strongest adversaries of psychical research.[11] By the way, Frazer is one of the anthropologists frequently invoked by modern-day debunkers of the paranormal.[12]

The science-religion war was central to the development of the social sciences and intellectual culture of the twentieth century. It established social patterns, determined who would achieve status and influence in academe, and who would indoctrinate students. The battles determined the kinds of thought and behavior that were to be acceptable and rewarded. Whether or not they admitted it, like that of the primitive, their own intellectualism was intimately tied to social structure.

Andrew Lang was one of Frazer's sharpest critics.[13] Lang was a folklorist, journalist, anthropologist, and one of the leading men of letters of his day. He was also a psychical researcher and served as president of the Society for Psychical Research and also of the Folk Lore Society.[14] His position in anthropology was forgotten for many years, but there has been some belated recognition. Oxford anthropologist Rodney Needham dedicated his book *Remarks and Inventions* (1974) to him. In 1994, Lang's nearly-lost manuscript *Totemism* was first published along with an extensive commentary by Andrew Duff-

Cooper.[15] An additional example of Lang's influence is that Arnold van Gennep credited his own interest in ethnography to him.[16]

Lang offered a completely different perspective on totemism than Frazer, and in his books *Social Origins* (1903) and *The Secret of the Totem* (1905) he argued that totems were used to differentiate groups. Lang noted that this was not a new idea, and in fact, it had been suggested by Garcilaso de la Vega (1539–1616), author of *History of the Incas*.

The notion that totems differentiate groups seems trifling, but it's not. It emphasizes that totemism is ultimately about classification. Totems connected social classes to the larger world. Such sociological paradigms radically contrast with psychological perspectives. For instance James Frazer took a psychological approach; he saw the person as a separate entity and considered magic and religion to be products (errors) of individual human minds. His perspective has been labeled individualistic rationalism. Sociological approaches recognize the massive impact and primacy of social relationships on human thought. These provide very different insights than psychological paradigms, but they have had limited influence outside a small section of the social sciences. Individualistic rationalism continues its dominance today and so pervades our thinking that most do not grasp other ways of thought.

Lang was by no means the only, nor the most important, figure to adopt a sociological approach. Emile Durkheim, one of the greatest sociologists of all time, also advocated that perspective. He and his colleague and nephew, Marcel Mauss, illuminated totemism in their book *Primitive Classification* (1903). One of their major points was that *we classify things because we live in groups* and not the other way around, which argues that we live in groups because we classify things. Living in groups (i.e., the social) is primary. Durkheim expanded the ideas in his classic *The Elementary Forms of the Religious Life* (1912), devoting well over a hundred pages to totemism, and saying that "the fundamental notions of the intellect, the essential categories of thought, may be the product of social factors ... this is the case with the very notion of category itself."[17] Making categories is fundamentally, and above all, a social process. Categories, distinctions, and classification schemes are not just mental models stored in our brains. They have far deeper foundations; they are encoded in our social structure, in our statuses and relationships. Although some now consider Durkheim's original premise as overstated, it remains a very good first approximation.

Durkheim's ideas are not fully grasped by most sociologists. This was true historically, and it remains so today. Roscoe Hinkle noted the "exasperated incomprehension" that early American sociologists found when reading Durkheim.[18] The problem persists, and even French sociologist Raymond Aron frankly admitted that he had "a great deal of difficulty entering into Durkheim's way of thinking."[19] Most people implicitly assume a psychological viewpoint and try to analyze society as a collection of individuals, each having a brain, and a mind arising from that brain. In such formulations social forces are mere secondary, theoretical abstractions.

In contrast, sociological paradigms assert that mind arises from social interaction. They argue that the very development of self emerges from society. Thus self is an emergent property of the group rather than the other way around. George Herbert Mead, in his *Mind, Self & Society* (1934), came to similar conclusions, and his work formed the basis of the symbolic interactionist perspective in sociology.

Jungian psychiatrist M. Esther Harding took this general approach in her *The 'I' and the 'Not-I'* (1965). Harding was particularly interested in the emergence of individual thought from that of the collective, and she drew upon the writings on the primitive mind by Lucien Levy-Bruhl (discussed shortly). She pointed out that development of ego and separation from collective thought takes not just a few months or years, but is a lifelong process.

Those who adopt such perspectives recognize that we humans are so pervasively influenced by social interactions, relationships, and statuses that we are unaware of it. We actually make very few fully conscious, reasoned decisions. The vast majority are foreordained by our roles and positions in the social order. This has led several theorists to assert that "the unconscious is the social."[20] This is compatible with notions of group minds, a concept now anathema in virtually all of academe.[21] The individualistic rationalism of Frazer's time continues to hold sway.

Sigmund Freud was also drawn to the problem of totemism, and in 1913 he published *Totem and Taboo*. In many circles this is undoubtedly the best known book on totemism, and it's one of the most severely flawed. Freud could hardly ignore totemism and its connection to exogamy because the Oedipus complex was central to his theories. By definition, violation of rules of exogamy is incest, and it is associated with taboo. The first chapter of his book was entitled "The Savage's Dread of Incest." Freud understood that the strong emotion of dread is a consequence of taboo. It was associated with things sacred and consecrated but also with the "uncanny, dangerous, forbidden, and unclean."[22]

Freud knew that totemic beliefs posited magical connections between things, and he frankly admitted that they were beyond his comprehension. Totemic classification schemes seemed confused, to be irrational, and Freud compared them to neurotic and infantile thought. In fact the subtitle of his book was *Resemblances Between the Psychic Lives of Savages and Neurotics*. All this gave him entree to address religion and the sacred. In order to explain all these entangled issues, Freud invented an ingenious story about the primal horde. He claimed that our primate ancestors lived in small groups dominated by a strong father, who did not allow other males to have sexual congress with females in the group. One day, the other males banded together, killed the father, and ate him. Then out of guilt they renounced sexual contact with group's females, thereby establishing exogamy. Although bizarre, this is a remarkably clever formulation. It ties together motifs of religion, sacrifice, sexuality, and exogamy. Unfortunately, there is no evidence to support it, and anthropologists quickly recognized it to be a myth of origins, another just so story.[23]

Despite the shortcomings, Freud's ideas are still useful. He understood that boundaries, limitations, and restrictions are required for social life, and that they must be enforced. Taboo accomplished that. The male-female binary opposition established categories fundamental for society. Different rights and responsibilities were assigned to males and females. Freud correctly saw that sexual relations and restrictions had parallels with other domains of primitive life. Other boundaries had to be maintained. There was a similarity between sexual prohibitions and others, but taboo involved issues far removed from the sexual sphere, and Freud's formulation was insufficient. It didn't work to reduce all thought and behavior to sexuality. Edmund Leach's essay "Magical Hair" (1958) pointed out that Freud's perspective often provided insights compatible with ethnographic findings, but it also led to ludicrous mistakes.[24]

The question remains: just why was Freud compelled to invent the bizarre story of the primal horde? The primitives knew that taboo violations could unleash supernatural forces, and Freud probably feared that there might be something to that. He revealed his anxiety to Carl Jung. Jung tells how Freud said to him "'My dear Jung, promise me never to abandon the sexual theory. That is the most essential thing of all. You see, we must make a dogma of it, an unshakable bulwark.' He said that to me with great emotion, in the tone of a father saying, 'And promise me this one thing, my dear son: that you will go to church every Sunday.' In some astonishment I asked him, 'A bulwark—against what?' To which he replied, 'Against the black tide mud'—and here he hesitated for a moment, then added—'of occultism.'"[25] Jung pointed out that the choice of words "bulwark" and "dogma" showed Freud to be suppressing doubts on a highly emotional issue. There is no question that Freud was markedly ambivalent on the paranormal. One can find statements demonstrating his belief and about an equal number denying it. In his 3-volume biography, Ernest Jones included a 33-page chapter "Occultism" describing Freud's extreme vacillation on the topic.

The occult provokes uneasiness. That it did so in someone as insightful and influential as Freud emphasizes the importance of the problem, even if it was unresolved. His attempted resolution led to errors and excesses. Freud and his followers readily embraced a shoddy myth of origins rather than fully address the sacred. In his own way, Freud signalled the danger of the sacred; he established a taboo. The potential ridicule and derision of being labelled neurotic or infantile is still sufficient to keep rational, academic, status-conscious scholars from approaching the supernatural too seriously. Even Ernest Jones expressed a condescending attitude toward Freud's interest in the occult.

Lucien Levy-Bruhl, a French philosopher who made substantial contributions to anthropology and sociology, was another who grappled with totemism and primitive classification. As a philosopher, his interest was more in primitives' thought than in their institutions. His first book on the topic, *How Natives Think*, was published in 1910 but not translated until 1926; it was followed by *Primitive Mentality* in 1922 and several others.

Levy-Bruhl's work was poorly regarded for some decades. His choices of terms, particularly "prelogical" and "mystical" seem to have confused some readers, and others took offense at them. Many mentions of Levy-Bruhl are so short that they are misleading. In reality, he was an exceptionally deep thinker, and fortunately there has been some rehabilitation of his reputation. Rodney Needham dedicated his book *Belief, Language, and Experience* (1972) to his memory. In 1985 Princeton University Press reprinted *How Natives Think* with a superb introduction by C. Scott Littleton, explaining the importance of Levy-Bruhl's ideas to relativist perspectives in anthropology.

Levy-Bruhl posited that primitive thought was governed by what he called the law of participation. For the primitive, all things in the universe had mystical interconnections. In our view, this confuses categories, and there are many examples. For instance, the primitive conception of death is drastically different than that of the modern academician. Levy-Bruhl pointed out that "To us, a human being is either alive or dead: there is no middle course, whereas to the prelogical mind he is alive in a certain way, even though he be dead,"[26] and also "To them, there is no insuperable barrier separating the dead from the living."[27] The primitive not only communicates with the deceased, but the dead can harm the living and vice versa. To us, the life-death binary opposition is sharply drawn, but not so for the primitive. In addition, Levy-Bruhl pointed out that divination practices displayed similar confusion of categories.

He also said important things about abstraction in relation to the law of participation. He understood that "classification . . . takes place at the same time as abstraction and generalization."[28] In discussing our Western mode of thinking, he noted that "Our wealth of social thought is transmitted, in condensed form, through a hierarchy of concepts which co-ordinate with, or are subordinate to, each other."[29] In contrast, primitive thought is not so condensed, and "in prelogical mentality memory plays a much more important part than it does in our mental life."[30] Levy-Bruhl underscored the importance of exceptional memory found among primitives, and he cited a number of examples. Abstraction was less important for them, because they had comparatively little need of it. He noted that many early cultures did not count beyond two or three, yet they had methods to designate and remember much larger quantities. For instance they sometimes counted by using points on the body, each point being associated with a positive integer. This form of abstraction was linked to the concrete. Both concepts and numbers were designated by concrete symbols.

Levy-Bruhl did not analyze the thought of religious mystics, and he avoided discussing Christianity and Judaism, perhaps to not give offense. In fact he went so far as saying "I shall make use of this term [mystic]—not referring thereby to the religious mysticism of our communities, which is something entirely different."[31] On this point, Levy-Bruhl was wrong. There is an essential similarity between the primitive and mystic; both display a relatively low level of abstraction, as pointed out by Victor Turner.

The law of participation is difficult to communicate in abstract terms, and Levy-Bruhl admitted it. He realized that "It is useless to try and explain the institutions and customs and beliefs of undeveloped peoples by starting from the psychological and intellectual analysis of 'the human mind' as *we* know it. No interpretation will be satisfactory unless it has for its starting-point the prelogical and mystic mentality underlying the various forms of activity in primitives."[32] The primitive mentality is essentially incommensurate with rationalistic academic discourse.

Levy-Bruhl drew attention to the differences between the primitives and us, and some saw that as disparaging earlier cultures. He clearly did not mean it that way, and the charges of ethnocentrism hurled at Levy-Bruhl were misdirected. In fact his critics were far more guilty of it. Littleton pointed out that their rationalist assumptions made it impossible for them to really grasp the primitives' perspectives. Those same assumptions also made magical practices incomprehensible. Littleton astutely recognized that mystical participation is still found today, and he cited Margot Adler's *Drawing Down the Moon*, which covers modern-day witchcraft and Robert Ellwood's *Alternative Altars* which discusses Theosophy, Spiritualism, and the like. Few academics have any comprehension of those magical practices, despite the fact that a number of their neighbors and students engage in them.[33] The academy denounces magical thought as infantile; yet magic still flourishes. Since the time of Levy-Bruhl, the incomprehension among academics has only grown, and now they don't even recognize their own failure (which, at least, Freud, Frazer, and Levy-Bruhl acknowledged). In a somewhat attenuated form, the same pattern is seen in academe's treatment of religion. A consideration of religious scholarship can throw light on the issues of magic and the supernatural, and we will now turn to it.

The writers mentioned above concerned themselves with primitive cultures, but the fundamental issues are not limited to those; the irrational appears in the major religions of today. This matter is widely avoided, but one who directly addressed it, and its innate paradoxes, was German religious scholar Rudolf Otto.

Otto's classic work, *The Idea of the Holy*, first appeared in 1917. That book primarily drew upon religious scholarship of the Judeo-Christian tradition, but also some from Eastern thought. Otto cited almost no ethnographic data. Yet the issues he dealt with were surprisingly similar to those of Durkheim, Freud, Weber, Frazer, Lang, etc. The core issues were in the air during the first two decades of the twentieth century. His work, derived from modern religions, can be compared with that on the primitives, and the striking overlap demonstrates an important part of the human condition.

The "numinous" was one of Otto's key concepts. He used it to designate, in the words of his translator, "that aspect of deity which ... eludes comprehension in rational ... terms."[34] The numinous evokes an awe or dread that is unique to religion, and there are two parts to it: the supreme goodness and majesty of God on the one hand, and God's wrath on the other. This wrath is irrational, and for illustration, Otto cited the Book of Job saying that "it is concerned with the non-rational in the sense of the irrational, with sheer paradox baffling comprehension."[35] Here paradox is underscored, and that calls forth the trickster. He is a paradoxical, irrational character, who played a central role in the religions of many primitive societies. It is no accident that Stanley Diamond's introduction to Radin's *The Trickster* was primarily concerned with the Book of Job.

Otto had much to say about the numinous, and among other points, he stated: "Its antecedent stage is 'daemonic dread' (cf. the horror of Pan) with its queer perversion, a sort of abortive offshoot, the 'dread of ghosts'. It first begins to stir in the feeling of 'something uncanny', 'eerie', or 'weird'. It is this feeling which, emerging in the mind of primeval man, forms the starting-point for the entire religious development in history. 'Daemons' and 'gods' alike spring from this root, and all the products of 'mythological apperception' or 'fantasy' are nothing but different modes in which it has been objectified."[36] These, of course, refer to real experiences that many people now call "paranormal."

Freud raised some of the same issues in *Totem and Taboo*. He didn't use the term numinous, but he did refer to holy dread. He understood the dual aspect of the divine and commented that "taboo branches off into two opposite directions. On the one hand it means to us, sacred, consecrated: but on the other hand it means, uncanny, dangerous, forbidden, and unclean."[37] Freud also recognized the feeling accompanying it and stated "Our combination of 'holy dred' would often express the meaning of taboo."[38] Freud's followers essentially explained these as infantile thought, though Freud included qualifications. At any rate, as explained earlier, this interpretation itself establishes a taboo.

Emile Durkheim also addressed the numinous and holy dread, though he did not use those terms. He noted that primitives divided the world into the sacred and profane, and that rituals were needed to keep them separate. The sacred had a contagious quality that could infect the profane world and cause destruction. For instance, animals were not allowed to be killed with weapons made from wood of their totem group (e.g., certain woods were sacred vis-à-vis certain animals). If they were, a taboo was violated, supernatural powers unleashed, and ritual purification was necessary. The forces needed to be contained "Since, in virtue of this extraordinary power of expansion, the slightest contact, the least proximity, either material or simply moral, suffices to draw religious forces out of their domain."[39]

The primitives' awareness of this extreme danger is discussed at length by Durkheim, and he commented that "Owing to the contagiousness inherent in all that is sacred, a profane being cannot violate an interdict without having the religious force, to which he has unduly approached, extend itself over him and establish its empire over him. But as there is an antagonism between them, he becomes dependent upon a hostile power, whose hostility cannot fail to manifest itself in the form of violent reactions which tend to destroy him."[40] This describes the irrational power of the sacred.

Durkheim recognized that those undergoing initiation were particularly endowed with this supernatural quality and said: "The initiate lives in an atmosphere charged with religiousness, and it is as though he were impregnated with it himself."[41] He also noted that the dead were similarly imbued with the power. Both initiates and spirits of the dead are liminal beings; they are found at the boundary between the rational and irrational. They are surrounded with rituals and strictures, and "What makes these precautions necessary is the extraordinary contagiousness of a sacred character."[42]

Durkheim, Freud, and Otto were all speaking of the same fundamental phenomenon. Otto's formulation was a bit more restricted because he primarily addressed Western religions. He perhaps did not fully appreciate the extent to which taboo, the numinous, and holy dread operated throughout primitive societies. Their world had a much wider realm considered sacred than is so in ours. The numinous was more pervasive.

Freud, Durkheim and Otto all recognized the importance of the numinous; they understood that religion established the foundation for many cultures. Holy dread, taboo, and the numinous were *the* religious phenomena that served to uphold and stabilize societies. These were the fundamental source of religious power. Incredibly, the matters are given almost no discussion today. Otto was particularly perceptive and noted: "with a resolution and cunning which one can hardly help admiring, men shut their eyes to that which is quite unique in the religious experience, even in its most primitive manifestations. But it is rather a matter for astonishment than for admiration!"[43] These words are even more true now than when they were written eighty years ago.

This state of affairs should command extended analysis. The problem is severe in academe, and science is particularly antipathetic to the mystical and irrational. But this is found not only among academics. Today the liberal denominations of Protestant Christianity substantially downplay the supernatural and the wrath of God. Responding to secular trends in society, those denominations have become more rationalized, and their conceptions of deity largely lack the mystical and irrational aspects.

All this is part of the rationalization and disenchantment of the world, and as Max Weber recognized, this has been progressing for millennia. Protestant Christianity eliminated priests and largely did away with monastic orders. Unlike priests, Protestant ministers do not serve as mediators between their human congregations and the divine realm. Otto also noted the decline of the miraculous in religion. He commented: "on the more enlightened levels, 'miracle' begins to fade away; how Christ is at one with Mohammed and Buddha in declining the role of mere wonder-worker; how Luther dismisses the 'outward miracles' disparagingly as 'jugglery' or 'apples and nuts for children'; and finally how the 'supernaturalism' of miracle is purged from religion as something that is only an imperfect analogue and no genuine 'schema' of the numinous."[44] Here Otto himself contributes to the rationalizing trend whether he recognizes it or not, equating the decline of the miraculous with progress toward enlightenment. This is not fully compatible with his other statements.

Rationalization strengthens the boundary between the human and the divine. God is pushed ever further into heaven. Supernatural contact between humans and gods is minimized and repressed. The irrational is shunted from consciousness. Otto referred to ghosts and miracles as aspects of the numinous, though as degenerate forms of it. Both are now embarrassments in academe; they seem superstitious. Nevertheless, ghosts and miracles continue to be reported. They have not been cleansed from the world. Max Weber was perceptive regarding rationalization, but his formulation needed a slight elaboration. Rationalization did not really entail the elimination of magic from the world, but rather the elimination of the conscious awareness of it among cultural elites. Even with liberal Protestant churchmen, there is often an embarrassed silence regarding the efficacy of petitionary prayer, which is a magical practice by any reasonable definition (such embarrassment is not seen among conservatives). Although magic has not been expunged from the Western world, it has been forced to the margins, repressed, and although individuals are well aware of it, it has no place in our major bureaucratic institutions of government, industry, and academe.

The writers covered above produced a foundation for understanding the role of the supernatural in society. Amazingly, this work emerged in a mere decade and a half; Table 7 lists the crucial works. (The profusion of the 1903–1917 period is often obscured by writers who do not list dates of original publication in references they cite. Many give only the date of the copy they have most readily available. Such laxity is a disservice to readers and misleads them. Readers then fail to appreciate the historical context and the full implications of the writings.)

Several salient themes emerge from this early work. The scholars recognized that it was difficult to comprehend totemism and magic. Even though they were labeled as irrational, there was a grudging admission that the primitives' beliefs and practices allowed their societies to function. Nevertheless, many scholars displayed a revulsion toward magic. They decried similar beliefs in their own culture, and people holding such views were compared to neurotics and infants. The taboos surrounding magic and the sacred were still operating, and the scholars who enforced them were unaware of doing so. Not surprisingly, discussion of the fundamental issues faded from academe.

Levi-Strauss and the Second Era of Totemism Debates

The debates on magic and religion continued within anthropology of course, but since that early period, relatively little of consequence was published. In 1962 Oxford anthropologist E. E. Evans-Pritchard prepared a review and critique. He presented it in a series of lectures that were later published as *Theories of Primitive Religion* (1965). He spent considerable time discussing Durkheim, Frazer, and Levy-Bruhl, and the fact that their works were then half-a-century old is a subtle indication of the fertility of the earlier period.

Evans-Pritchard meant his lectures for a general audience, and thus they are relatively accessible. Evans-Pritchard was not an advocate of a particular theoretical school but rather made a wide range of contributions; accordingly, he was well positioned to offer diverse insights. His writings are generally lucid, and his books *Social Anthropology and Other Essays* (1962) and *A History of Anthropological Thought*

Year	Author	Title
1903	Emile Durkheim & Marcel Mauss	*Primitive Classification*
1905	Max Weber	*The Protestant Ethic and the Spirit of Capitalism*
1909	Arnold van Gennep	*The Rites of Passage*
1909	Robert Hertz	"The Pre-eminence of the Right Hand"
1910	James George Frazer	*Totemism and Exogamy*
1910	Lucien Levy-Bruhl	*How Natives Think*
1912	Emile Durkheim	*The Elementary Forms of the Religious Life*
1913	Sigmund Freud	*Totem and Taboo*
1913	Max Weber	*Economy and Society*
1916	Ferdinand de Saussure	*Course in General Linguistics*
1917	Rudolf Otto	*The Idea of the Holy*

Table 7 Important Works for Understanding the Role of the Supernatural In Society[45]

(1981) provide excellent overviews of anthropology, especially of theory.

Evans-Pritchard pointed out that the first anthropological theorists faced considerable obstacles. The cultural evolutionist paradigm, modeled on Darwinism, was prominent at the beginning of the twentieth century, and it had severe flaws. Further, during anthropology's early decades, ethnography was not a developed discipline, and anthropologists did little or no fieldwork themselves. They relied upon reports of explorers, missionaries, travelers, writers, and the like. The descriptions of totemic beliefs appeared extremely foreign, and yet as more and better ethnographic data became available, the situation grew more confused. There was much controversy, and writers were diffident about their interpretations. In their antagonism toward religion, many theorists avoided consulting relevant religious scholarship. Totemism began looking untractable, and the topic languished for decades.

Evans-Pritchard was very critical of Frazer but more sympathetic to Levy-Bruhl. Evans-Pritchard argued successfully that we are not substantially different from the primitives and that there are many irrational aspects in our culture today. One of his primary criticisms was that Levy-Bruhl made too sharp a distinction between the civilized and primitive mind. Evans-Pritchard was right in this, yet, for all the force of his argument, he did not effectively deal with the differences between the primitives and us in regard to magic. Though magic is alive today, Max Weber was correct—rationalization and disenchantment continue. We really are different from the primitive, and Frazer and Levy-Bruhl were right in bringing this point to the fore.

Evans-Pritchard delivered his lectures in 1962, and that year the eminent French anthropologist Claude Levi-Strauss published two important works: *Totemism* and *The Savage Mind*. In them he tackled the problem of classification. Years earlier he had achieved some fame for his study of kinship structures, and Levi-Strauss was about to attract even more attention with a series of books on myth, but in the interim, he addressed classification. He understood his studies of kinship, totemism, and mythology as attempts to find underlying patterns of human thought, and the issue of classification was central to that effort.

Levi-Strauss needs a bit more introduction than most others. He was exceptionally influential, but it is difficult to give a comprehensive background to his ideas because he drew from so many sources. He acknowledged his youthful interest in geology, but also in Freud, Marx, Marcel Mauss, linguists Ferdinand de Saussure and Roman Jakobson, philosopher Henri Bergson, among others. He cannot be easily situated.

Ambiguity is an innate part of his thought. In fact Levi-Strauss admitted that he didn't understand some of the anthropological theorizing that his work stimulated, and conversely some of those who borrowed his ideas admitted that they didn't fully understand him either![46] Edmund Leach's *Claude Levi-Strauss* (1970) is perhaps the best introduction to his work, though Levi-Strauss might not agree.

Levi-Strauss was the leading figure in the French intellectual movement known as structuralism, which flourished in the 1960s. It encompassed anthropology, philosophy, literary criticism, religious studies, psychoanalysis, and others. Because it was so diverse, it is difficult to summarize. In 1966 a symposium on structuralism was held at Johns Hopkins University, and papers from it were compiled into the volume *The Structuralist Controversy* (1970).[47] That collection includes a diversity of approaches. Michael Lane's *Introduction to Structuralism* (1970) presents articles on some of the wider ideas.

As an intellectual movement, structuralism was short lived, and I suspect that the vast majority of my readers never heard of it. Its descendants are deconstructionism and post-structuralism, and those now have currency. They are commonly discussed in academe, and the terms sometimes appear in the popular media, but very few, even in academe, understand from whence they came. The intellectual lineage is important for understanding the controversies, their implications, and the severe deficiencies of most presentations.

Levi-Strauss' work serves as a bridge from totemism and primitive mentality, on the one hand, to literary theory and post-structuralism on the other. At a fundamental level these all concern communication, representation, and the limits of logic.

Levi-Strauss recognized that the problem of classification arises because the mind grasps the world in chunks. It perceives contrasts, differences, and opposites. He was familiar with the anthropological works on binary oppositions, and he recognized the similarities with the ideas of Swiss linguist Ferdinand de Saussure. Saussure pointed out that in language, sounds must be distinguished from each other; they are in opposition. They thereby designate differences in their referents in the world. Patterns of differences are seen. Binary oppositions such as life-death, man-woman, like sounds of language, form structures. The similarities are at an abstract level.

Binary contrasts are perceived, but the parallels and relations among them are not observed directly. Those are encoded in totems. For instance, it is not that members of the eagle clan are like eagles and members of the bear clan are like bears, rather the relation between the eagle clan and bear clan is like the relation of the eagle and the bear. The eagle is associated with heights and the sky, the bear with the ground and caves. Thus totemism can serve as a method of abstraction and can express properties that are not directly observable. The parallels between structures allow a kind of generalization about relationships. Harvard psychologist Howard Gardner, writing on Levi-Strauss, points out that "Consciously, of course, people are aware of concrete manifestations rather than of relations *per se*; but the tendency to perceive relations is fundamental."[48]

Levi-Strauss found inspiration in the writings of Henri Bergson, a Nobel laureate and also a president of the Society for Psychical Research. Bergson had written on the interplay between the discrete and the continuous (wholistic), and Levi-Strauss cited passages showing

Bergson to have had a more wholistic understanding than typically found among academics.[49] Bergson saw the continuous and discrete as complementary and refused to choose between them. In such refusals, tensions are generated between separatenesses and unities; intermediaries are needed to resolve them.[50]

Admittedly, these ideas are a bit vague, and the relationships between Levi-Strauss' schemas and the real world are sometimes difficult to grasp. Howard Gardner commented that his "major argument about the nature of thought and society centers on the role of contradiction, opposition, and paradox in the experience of man."[51] The problems of explication are a direct consequence. Others who are sympathetic to the ideas also acknowledge the difficulties. Kathleen Ashley, a scholar of medieval studies who has also written insightfully on tricksters, noted that "Structuralist theory . . . founds itself upon ambivalence and ambiguity,"[52] and Edmund Leach, readily admitted the obscurity of Levi-Strauss but said that he "often manages to give me ideas even when I don't really know what he is saying."[53]

Levi-Strauss compared both myth, and the primitive mind, with a bricoleur. This is a French term that refers to something like a handyman, though there is no exact English-language equivalent. (Trickster scholars and some post-structuralists are introducing the word to English-language readers.) A bricoleur collects a hodgepodge of materials and then incorporates them into a work, or he makes do with things immediately at hand. No outside theoretical or conceptual structure guides the fabrication of a bricolage (the product of a bricoleur). Like a bricoleur, myth works with materials directly available, concrete images rather than abstract concepts. Many mythologists consider the trickster to be a bricoleur. This is appropriate as Levi-Strauss notes that there is something a bit devious about the bricoleur.[54] Some think that Levi-Strauss was a bit devious himself, and a number of writers have commented on his sometimes-seeming intellectual sleight of hand. His foremost British interpreter, Edmund Leach, commented on his structural approach saying "some English-speaking readers might begin to suspect that the whole argument was an elaborate academic joke . . . we must try to take the matter seriously. This is rather difficult."[55] [56]

There are limits to clarity in discussing these issues. Categorizing lies at the very root of our thought and communication. Beyond some point, we are forced to the inarticulate; the ineffable of mysticism is not far away. Levi-Strauss has been accused of being Jungian, and indeed the deep structures of which he speaks are not so very different from the archetypes of Jung. Both had important things to say about the trickster and about binary oppositions. Both dealt with fundamentally difficult issues, and both are known for their obscurity. They drew upon very different sources: Jung researched alchemy, and Levi-Strauss studied natives of the Americas. The parallels reflect real underlying patterns, but by their nature we may be unable to fully grasp them by rational means.[57]

It is probably no accident that Levi-Strauss's ideas came to the fore in the 1960s, a time of rapid cultural change, a period of antistructure. During the same decade Mary Douglas, Victor Turner, and Edmund Leach also made lasting contributions to understanding magic and the primitive mind.[58] That period was intellectually hospitable to addressing those issues in academe, and a similar interest was seen in the wider culture.

The reader might be puzzled as to why I gave all this attention to Levi-Strauss when his writings are so ambiguous. In grappling with totemism, primitive classification, and the deep structures of the human mind, Levi-Strauss was forced into areas of ambiguity. This should not be seen as a failure so much as an illumination of the problem.

Structuralism's successor, deconstructionism, probed foundations even more explicitly and raised disconcerting problems. As will be described in the next chapter, it asserted that all communication is ambiguous. All statements are open to interpretation. The idea of objective reality is only a myth. Deconstructionism is justifiably labelled as irrational, but so are primitives' beliefs in magic.

Rationalization and the Disenchantment of the World

The intellectual history of totemism includes: charges of irrationality and erroneous thinking hurled at the primitive, the acknowledged incomprehensibility of totemism to academicians, unresolved debates, and ambiguous scholarly theories. The muddle-headedness occurred because the scholars failed to comprehend the inherent limitations of Western rationality. All this needs to be seen in light of rationalization (in Max Weber's sense), which has been a dominant process in the development of Western civilization. Totemism must be understood in opposition to rationalization. Totemism incorporates magical interconnections. Rationalization entails the elimination of magic and severs magical interconnections (in reality, only the conscious awareness of them).

Just because totemism is "irrational" does not mean that it was maladaptive. On the contrary, it survived for thousands of years. Most cultures did not rely upon our science and logic. Their success should make us examine our prejudices regarding the rational. Western logic requires entities to be discrete, separate, distinct, differentiated. We assume a clear distinction between subject and object. The primitives did not; they understood themselves as mystically connected to the cosmos. They participated in it. (The issue of participation also arises in conjunction with reflexivity, a source of paradox for Western logic.)

For social life, there must be shared assumptions, symbols, and meanings. Rationalists assume an objective reality exists and that it provides the required foundation. It is assumed that the objective world is independent of our representations of it—that representations (e.g., thoughts) do not affect it directly. The scientific enterprise accepts and upholds these ideas. Admittedly they usually produce a good, first-order approximation of reality. But they don't always apply. The practice of magic and the data of parapsychology demonstrate that fact.

The agenda of rationalization faces an almost insurmountable problem—the serious study of magic has a magical influence. Thus the disenchantment process must eliminate not only magic, but also serious consideration of it. A number of techniques have been developed to assure that it remains marginalized and outside the awareness of academe. Freud linked magic to the infantile and the neurotic, and his followers aggressively promoted that view. In our society, "magical thinking" is disparaged, and it is now used as an epithet by debunkers to discredit those who show an interest in the paranormal. Such belittling discourages use of magic by status-conscious persons.

Anthropologists writing about early cultures face a problematic situation. Without a doubt, totemism can justifiably be called irrational. But to make that explicit leaves one open to charges of ethnocentrism or even racism. Today the designation "irrational" is considered derogatory, and those who wish to instill a neutral or positive attitude toward primitive societies find it is easier to ignore the problems posed by totemism and magic. Those are seen as remnants from a superstitious past, embarrassments, and best forgotten in the effort to increase the respect for earlier peoples. However, scholars who ignore the issue come to believe that they hold an unbiased view of the primitives, but they are blinded by their own beliefs. At least the ethnocentrism of Frazer was overt.

A vast number of academics who write on magic today are not only unable to grasp it, but unlike the earlier commentators, they do not realize their failure. They almost universally ignore or deny the intrinsic efficacy of magic (i.e., psi). It is problematic, and merely thinking about it raises their anxieties. Making this explicit is, of course, not welcomed by those who have devoted their careers to fostering rationality. As such, it is unreasonable to expect academe to explore totemism much further. Nevertheless, some progress can be made with structuralist methods.

I do not wish to make academic science a scapegoat for the sins of rationalization, and it would be wrong to attribute the problems solely to that quarter. As I explained earlier, similar trends are seen in much of religion. Mainline liberal Protestant Christians may profess a belief in miracles, but ones that happened long ago and far away. The miraculous is placed at a distance. Even Rudolf Otto's writings show some leeriness toward supernatural phenomena. Both establishment science and orthodox exoteric religion display the same trend. One can only conclude that the roots of rationalization, the downplaying of miracles and mysticism, must be far deeper than just ideology and belief. They are inherent in the structure of our society. The primitives' taboos against contact with supernatural forces are with us still, though in veiled form.

Totemism Summary

This chapter covered a cluster of topics of preeminent importance for the social sciences: religion, magic, social restrictions on sexual behavior, taboo, and classification. These are all relevant to the trickster. It is no accident that early sociologists and anthropologists devoted so much effort to magic and totemism. It is also not happenstance that the trickster played a major role in the mythologies of many primitive peoples.

Durkheim, Frazer, and Freud wrote about the numinous, the sacred, the supernatural. They did not shy away from the irrational aspects. Today anthropologists know that totemism formed the basis for social organization of many cultures, but they almost completely ignore it. The early academic debates are forgotten, quaint relics of a bygone era, and many presume the issues to have been resolved. They weren't.

Even more amazing is the neglect of taboo, holy dread, and the numinous. Order and stability of society were maintained through these. Academics now dismiss them as vague emotional responses, even though they are central to the religious experience of all humankind.

Totemism *is* a difficult topic. Not only is it extremely varied, but the issues blend and blur together, and they are nearly impossible to arrange coherently. Totemism deals with classification and shared meaning.

Magic and religion need to be understood in relation to issues of foundations, classification, and boundaries. The primitives recognized that when foundations are upturned, classification schemes violated, or boundaries blurred, then supernatural powers erupt. A liminal, antistructural condition is created.

The primitives also understood that taboos could be violated in order to release magical power. Society would be partly deconstructed in the process. This might be done inadvertently, or intentionally with ritual protection. In either case, danger and chaos were invited. Foundations were suspended. This was magical, numinous.

Like totemism, the trickster has been difficult for scholars to comprehend; he resists being placed in our rational categories. He disrupts; he crosses boundaries; he thrives in paradox and ambiguity. He is associated with the supernatural. Theories of the trickster and those of totemism illuminate each other.

Today academic debates regarding the paranormal are not much different than those on magic a century ago. They are laced overtly and covertly with religious issues, so much so that detached, dispassionate examination is the exception. The discussions, of totemism and magic, previously, and the paranormal today, need to be understood in this light.

CHAPTER 23

Literary Criticism, Meaning, and the Trickster

> In the beginning was the Word, and the Word was with God, and the Word was God.
>
> John 1:1[1]

The trickster is a literary figure. He is central to the problem of meaning. In fact, the term hermeneutics (the study of interpretation) is derived from the name Hermes, the trickster of the Greeks.

Meaning is the explicit concern of literary criticism, an innately reflexive discipline—it uses language to study language. Literary critics have long pondered the limitations of language and developed some understanding of them, and it is no accident that they have generated the most important insights on the trickster.

The trickster is also intimately involved with magic (psi). Though magic and meaning are not quite identical, they are closely related, and at times they blur into each other. The similarity is profound; one can work through the other. Hermes is the messenger god and is central to information, language, and meaning, but also to limits, and to reflexivity. These issues cannot be neatly disentangled, which is in keeping with the trickster.

Literary criticism is a vast area, and I cannot attempt to survey it. Instead I will focus on that small part which involves structuralism and its intellectual descendants—deconstructionism and post-structuralism. They fomented controversy, but they are still not too well understood despite the resulting publicity.

I introduced the French structuralist movement in the discussions of Claude Levi-Strauss, but structuralism encompassed far more than anthropology. It also included literary criticism, religious studies, psychoanalysis, philosophy, and linguistics, and there were many variants of it.[2] It was not a closed, self-consistent school, nor is it particularly easy to define. Readers who have only a passing familiarity with structuralism should not feel intellectually inadequate if they failed to grasp its central issues. Even Levi-Strauss admitted that he didn't understand some of the uses to which his ideas were put. Ambiguity is an important issue in the structuralist lineage; it's not to be neglected or lamented. Ambiguity highlights the limits of language, and the failure of meaning.

As a movement, structuralism is dead. Its ideas cannot now be effectively understood without considering deconstructionism and poststructuralism. I will provide a brief overview of these and some of the people involved with them.

Concepts from the structuralist lineage are now almost exclusively applied to literary endeavors. That restrains the ideas, restricts them to text, and that makes them safe for academe.[3] This chapter will escape those shackles and cover anthropological ideas that receive little attention by literary theorists. One commonality between literary and anthropological concepts is the theme of binary opposition—a theme also found with the trickster and in primitive classification.

Structuralism, semiotics, deconstructionism, and poststructuralism all display the influence of French philosophy, which has a strongly rationalistic bent. It is marked by abstraction and little empirical content, and many decry it for that reason. However, the extremes make both the strengths and weaknesses of rationalism apparent. The excesses are instructive. As I will show, deconstructionism is the logical culmination of rationalism. This will surprise some and be abhorrent to others, because deconstructionism lays bare the pretensions of rationality.

Structuralist Theory

Structuralism emphasizes patterns of differences. Communication systems use patterns of matter or energy as signals. For example, computers utilize strings of 1s and 0s (bits); they may be printed on paper (matter) or put in the form of electronic impulses (energy). It is the arrangement that is important. But the "meaning" of the information lies outside the formal system. Meaning requires interpretation, because the same "information" can mean quite different things to different people. It is here that ambiguity and the trickster enter.

Two key aspects of communication and information can be identified: distinction and representation. Communication requires differences; one entity (e.g., event, person, idea) must be differentiated from others. Something *is* only in relation to something else. This wholistic concept is a fundamental tenet of structuralism. The second aspect, representation, is an inherent part of this process. In representation (e.g., gesture, drawing, speech, writing), one thing is taken to indicate another. It is not the thing, but only an indicator of it. Language is a form of representation; a name is used to represent something, and we have few effective ways to communicate without using names for things.

Structuralists saw culture and all its products as a form of communication. For example, social statuses differentiate people; they serve to form a structure because individuals have separate roles. A person's position in the structure communicates who he is, both to himself and to others. Edmund Leach's book *Culture & Communication* (1976) provides an introduction to the ideas and explains the premise from an anthropological perspective.

Many things can be seen in terms of communication, and structuralists' search for commonalities in such diverse areas as kinship, language, and myth might seem unlikely to be fruitful. Yet analogous explorations in physics and engineering produced spectacular results. For instance, buildings in earthquakes; electrical circuits with resistors, inductors, and capacitors; and certain hydraulic systems are all governed by the same mathematical equations. What is learned in one area applies to others. Edmund Leach was the foremost English structuralist, and as an undergraduate he studied engineering. He mentioned that his familiarity with binary arithmetic helped him appreciate structuralist ideas about binary oppositions.[4] Structuralist theory cannot claim the magnitude of success attained by the physical sciences, but if its ideas are rejuvenated, further developed, and more widely disseminated, it should produce some surprising insights.

Structuralism has some compatibility with parapsychology. Both express themes of interrelatedness not found in other sciences. Sociologist Michael Lane described structuralism saying that "its fundamental tenet, lies in its attempt to study not the elements of a whole, but the complex network of relationships that link and unite those elements."[5] He went on to say that "structuralism is effectively anticausal. The language of structuralist analysis in its pure form makes no use of the notions of cause and effect: rather, it rejects this conceptualization of the world in favour of 'laws of transformation'."[6] Psi does not conform to causal patterns, and transition and transformation are liminal processes and ones hospitable to psi. If structuralist ideas and parapsychology are to inform each other, development will be required, but the fundamental outlook is so similar that it demands investigation.

Ferdinand de Saussure

Ferdinand de Saussure, a Swiss linguist, was a most influential figure for structuralism. His best known work is *Course in General Linguistics*. He died in 1913 before he could write the book, but two of his colleagues gathered his students' notes and formed them into a volume that was published in 1916. This constituted a major reconceptualization, and today it is recognized to have been an important advance in linguistics.

Saussure pointed out that language is a system of differences. Various sounds are in opposition to one another; they are differentiated amongst themselves. He emphasized language as a *system*. Saussure explained that: "to consider a term as simply the union of a certain sound with a certain concept is grossly misleading. To define it in this way would isolate the term from its system; it would mean assuming that one can start from the terms and construct the system by adding them together when, on the contrary, it is from the interdependent whole that one must start and through analysis obtain its elements."[7] British linguist Geoffrey Sampson in his *Schools of Linguistics* (1980) noted that Durkheim's influence can be seen in the writings of Saussure. Durkheim showed that social facts have an independent existence and that social phenomena cannot be reduced to that of a collection of individuals. Saussure saw language as a social fact with an existence independent from any individual. As a system, language is shared; as a system of collective representations, it has a life of its own. This collectivist, anti-reductionist approach typifies both Durkheim and Saussure.

Saussure raised issues that are often glossed over in texts on linguistics. He grappled with the problem of how sounds (speech) are connected to concepts and ideas. He pointed out that "Psychologically our thought—apart from its expression in words—is only a shapeless and indistinct mass . . . without the help of signs we would be unable to make a clear-cut, consistent distinction between two ideas. Without language, thought is a vague, uncharted nebula."[8]

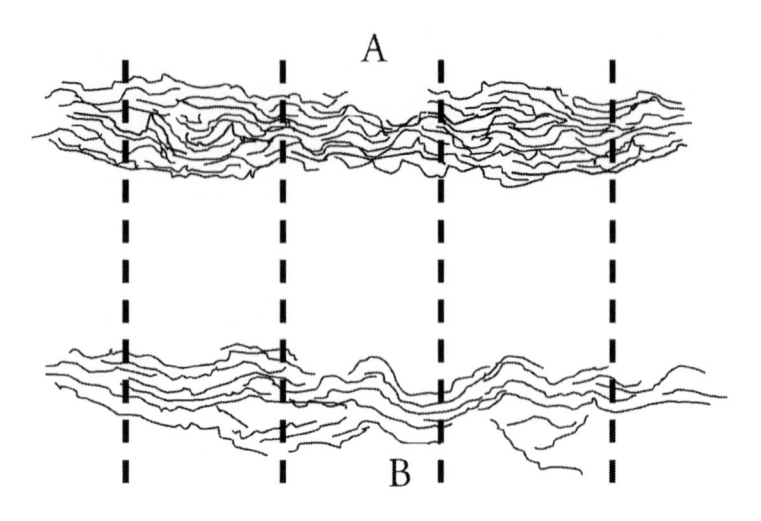

Figure 3 Ideas (A) and Sounds (B)
(Following Saussure, 1916/1959, p. 112)

He illustrated the model with a diagram, and Figure 3 is patterned after his. The top irregular area designates thought, and the bottom designates sounds; between the two is a nether region. The vertical lines divide all three areas, showing the associations of thoughts and sounds. Saussure explained that "language works out its units while taking shape between two shapeless masses,"[9] and he further commented that "Linguistics then works in the borderland where the elements of sound and thought combine; *their combination produces a form, not a substance*" (Saussure's emphasis).[10] Thus language has a betwixt and between quality.

Edmund Leach

Edmund Leach explained the importance of distinctions vis-à-vis language in a famous essay entitled: "Anthropological Aspects of Language: Animal Categories and Verbal Abuse" (1964). That paper is of special merit because it displays the real power of structuralism to illuminate connections of seemingly disparate topics. Leach ranged over taboo, profanity, and the valuation of animals, among other matters. In discussing the development of language, Leach "postulate[d] that the physical and social environment is perceived as a continuum. It does not contain any intrinsically separate things."[11] He went on to say that "Language gives us the names to distinguish the things; taboo inhibits the recognition of those parts of the continuum which separate things."[12] He illustrated his ideas with several very simple diagrams.

Figure 4 The Continuum (Following Leach, 1964, p. 35)

Figure 5 Things, that is, items that are named (Following Leach, 1964, p. 35)

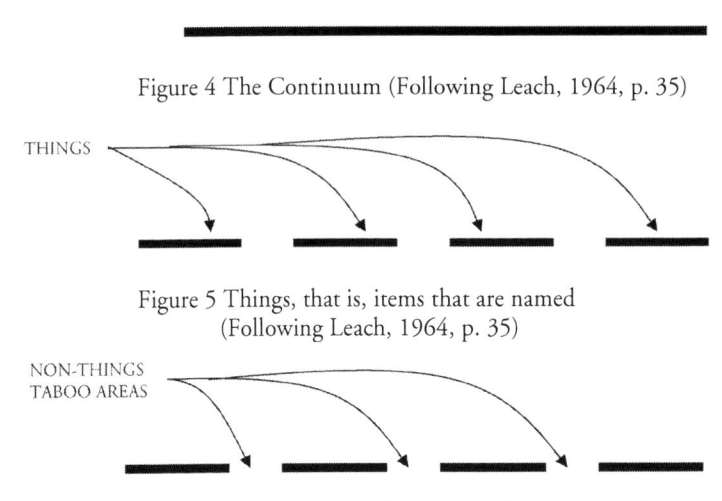

Figure 6 Taboo Areas (Following Leach, 1964, p. 35)

Leach's formulation shows the interplay between the continuous and the discrete, a theme pondered earlier by Levi-Strauss and Henri Bergson. We also see that language plays an important role in making distinctions, as names make designations. But Leach went further and said that "by suppressing our recognition of the nonthings which fill the interstices, then of course *what is suppressed becomes especially interesting*" (emphasis added).[13] In our modern, rationalized world, the suppression has triumphed over the interest, and many have missed the deep implications of Leach's paper. Leach was an anthropologist rather than a linguist, and as such he emphasized the world as much as he did language. Most other theorists focus on language or text. The consequences of the usual one-sidedness are typically neglected, but we will explore them a bit later.

Semiotics and Umberto Eco

Semiotics is the study of signs and symbols, and it has much in common with structuralism; the two shared ideas and leading exponents. Semiotics' groundwork was developed independently by Ferdinand de Saussure and American philosopher Charles Sanders Peirce. Neither Peirce nor Saussure lived to see the fruits of their labors in semiotics; Peirce died in 1914, the year after Saussure.[14]

Like structuralism, semiotics is not too well known, and I have encountered a number of Ph.D.s in the sciences who did not know what the word meant, even though there are professional academic journals devoted to it. Semioticians also see culture and its products as a system of communication, and they study patterns in order to discover hidden messages, even in such things as food, dress, toys, and buildings. For instance, our choice of foods depends upon the time of day, our social class, religious observances, and other factors. The selections usually have nothing to do with nutrition. Food choices mark differences, and as such they can be seen as a form of communication about other aspects of our lives. The book *Structuralism & Semiotics* (1977) by Terence Hawkes provides an accessible introduction and explains the overlap of the fields.

French literary critic Roland Barthes, a leading figure in both semiotics and structuralism, promulgated Saussure's ideas. Barthes considered the problem of meaning. In his book *Mythologies* (1957) he followed Saussure saying that a signifier and its signified together constitute a "sign"[15] and thus produce meaning. Meaning is not simply information, but more than that; it is a wholistic concept involving a representation and its object.

Here again, a distinction is drawn, this time between the signifier and the signified, another binary opposition, but the terms are united via meaning. It is commonly assumed that there is a simple, objective correspondence between the signifier and signified even though they are separate entities. It is assumed that language is only a set of names for things, events, and concepts. These assumptions are incorrect, but few recognize the extent of the implications. This lies at the heart of deconstructionism, and magic.

Saussure identified a realm betwixt and between the signifier and signified, and that suggests the trickster is lurking. In fact semiotics can be considered the trickster's domain. Umberto Eco, a professor at the University of Bologna, in his book *A Theory of Semiotics* commented that "*semiotics is in principle the discipline studying everything which can be used in order to lie*" (Eco's emphasis).[16] Ergo the signifier is the tool of the trickster. His book *The Limits of Interpretation* (1990) devotes an entire chapter to a theoretical consideration of fakes and forgeries.[17] Eco recognized the importance of deception, but I don't think that he made much progress with it. For instance his discussion of fakes and forgeries is primarily about classifying them, but it goes little further than that.

Despite his limited success in addressing deception theoretically, Eco's fiction demonstrates profound understanding. I heartily recommend his best-selling novel *Foucault's Pendulum* (1988) for anyone with an interest in the topics covered in this book. It tells the story of intrigue, conspiracy, and paranoia surrounding what ultimately turns out to be a remnant of an ancient laundry list. I only half-jokingly refer to it as the best available ethnography of modern-day American ufology. Eco really does understand much about the occult, secrets, and deception. His success with *Foucault's Pendulum* suggests that these topics are expressed more effectively via fiction. Malcolm Ashmore recognized a similar pattern vis-à-vis reflexivity; he noted that much involving that topic is presented in fictional terms. Some topics may inherently limit what can be meaningfully said about them in any straightforward manner.

Deconstructionism

Deconstructionism is a major component of postmodern thought, and it has been one of the most controversial areas in the humanities in the last 30 years. It can be explicated from several angles, but I will speak to it primarily within the theoretical perspectives of structuralism and semiotics, its two immediate predecessors.

Saussure noted that signifiers are completely arbitrary; they have no necessary connection to the signified. He assumed a relation exists but didn't really specify how it was accomplished. Deconstructionism seized on this idea. Its proponents assert that the signifier is completely separate from the signified, and that no text has any clear referent; all are ambiguous. Furthermore, meaning is neither to be found objectively in a text, nor in some exterior reality, nor is it given by the writer; rather, meaning is imparted by the reader, with each one producing a different interpretation. This comes down to an attack on objectivity. Deconstructionism, like reflexivity, leads to paradox. For if it is asserted that no objective meaning can be found in any text, then that applies to deconstructionism as well. Opponents therefore suggest that deconstructionists' own writings have no real meaning and thus need not be considered seriously.

Virtually all philosophical positions lead to absurdity when taken to their limits. Deconstructionism is no exception, but it is valuable because it explicitly challenges limits. However, as its advocates came to realize the full force of it, they pulled back from the extreme view. They sensed that its innate subversiveness could undermine their own positions. One of the symptoms is the poor writing and impenetrable jargon that fills much of deconstructionism's literature. Also, the adoption of term "post-structuralism" hints at some leeriness of fully embracing deconstructionism.

French philosopher Jacques Derrida is regarded as the founder of the movement, and he first emerged as a force in the mid 1960s during the debates on structuralism. In the 1970s deconstructionism took hold in the U.S. largely due to the efforts of Paul de Man, who served chairmanships in Yale University's French and comparative literature departments. Derrida held temporary appointments at Yale, and with their collaboration, de Man soon became the leading literary proponent of the movement.

It is altogether appropriate that deconstructionism found its most hospitable reception among literary critics, because literary criticism is an innately reflexive discipline. Reflexivity forces literary theorists to confront limits, and deconstructionism is aggressive in exposing them. The central issue can be conceptualized as the problem of representation, i.e., the relationship between the signifier and signified. This is similar to reflexivity, where distinguishing the subject and object is made problematic.

The consequences of this idea are not limited to a few arcane works of literary scholars. In discussing anthropological interpretation, de Man writes in *Blindness and Insight*: "a fundamental discrepancy always prevents the observer from coinciding fully with the consciousness he is observing. The same discrepancy exists in everyday language, in the impossibility of making the actual expression coincide with what has to be expressed, of making the actual sign coincide with what it signifies."[18] Deconstructionism calls attention to ambiguity and uncertainty, and at its core, it is about the problem of representation in all forms.

The issues are also relevant to the sciences, but few are aware of it. In his essay "Science versus Literature" (1967) Roland Barthes explains: "As far as science is concerned language is simply an instrument, which it profits it to make as transparent and neutral as possible:

it is subordinate to the matter of science (workings, hypotheses, results) which, so it is said, exists outside language and precedes it. On the one hand and *first* there is the content of the scientific message, which is everything; on the other hand and *next*, the verbal form responsible for expressing that content, which is nothing. It is no coincidence that, from the sixteenth century onwards, the corporate blossoming of empiricism, rationalism and an evidential religion (with the Reformation), that is, of the scientific spirit in the widest sense of the term, should have been accompanied by a regression in the autonomy of language."[19]

Barthes is describing rationalization (in Weber's sense), though he does not use the term. Like magic, the problem of meaning is banished from the consciousness of science. Deconstructionism raises the issue overtly. It points out that meaning is neither neutral nor transparent. It asserts that language precedes science and thus has primacy over it. This is subversive, a reversal of privilege; it lowers the status of science.

Rationalization separates things; it makes clear-cut distinctions; it makes things "objective." In deconstruction, the process is taken to its ultimate conclusion. The signifier and signified are separated, and any objective connection between them is denied. Meaning is voided.

Formal logic is similar. In it symbols are independent of any particular meaning. There is a continual interplay of symbols, which refer only to each other; this gives logic considerable power, but at the cost of direct meaning. In essence, deconstructionism completes the rationalization of the world, in its literary manifestation.

Deconstructionists and post-structuralists understand that there must be shared symbols, assumptions, and meanings for social life to occur. They typically assert that those are established by power. Power dictates and enforces meaning, which is used to dominate others. Power, and its abuse, are frequent themes for those who draw on post-structuralist ideas. They frequently lament hierarchies, citing the usual binary oppositions: men over women, white over black, straight over gay. Virtually every minority group has protesters who now use this obscure academic idiom. Because of its intentional obscurity, it is only mildly subversive to the establishment.

The issue of power again leads back to Max Weber. Weber's discussion of authority was about power and domination. He identified three types of authority: charismatic, traditional, and bureaucratic. Pure charisma, the most fundamental, involves supernatural power. The other types are rationalized forms of it. One need only recall Weber's insight that the process of rationalization calls for the elimination of magic from the world (in actuality, elimination of the *conscious awareness* of magic by cultural elites). With the process of disenchantment virtually complete in the academy, deconstructionists (and everyone else) display an almost complete amnesia as to the primitive foundations of their school of thought. Nearly all have forgotten the taboo areas, the liminal regions, those betwixt and between categories, the anomalous, the supernatural. This has consequences, because it is there that the trickster manifests. The obscurity of the deconstructionists' writings, coupled with the violent controversy surrounding them, are subtle indicators of his effects. The suppression from consciousness of archetypal forces allows supernatural power to operate unimpeded.

The deconstructionists have also detached themselves from the world (more precisely, extinguished the *conscious awareness* of their attachment). They cannot fathom the consequences of their ideas, because, after all, all is text. When they look into the abyss they see nothing. University of California historian Page Smith described this in his book *Killing the Spirit: Higher Education in America* (1990): "For decades professors have been destroying their students' illusions, their 'false consciousness,' their naive adherence to certain obsolete values (religion being one of the most obvious). Now the shoe appears to be on the other foot. Derrida is destroying *their* illusions, especially *their* illusion that they are engaged in objective, scientific investigation of the world. What they are really doing is imposing their own, ultimately baseless, views on their students and their colleagues, and there is no independent, 'objective' evidence that their illusions are any better than those of their students; they may well be worse. The students' illusions had at least enabled the students to live a reasonably ordered existence. Undoubtedly there is a vertiginous thrill in looking into the abyss. Derrida may well be the professors' equivalent of a teenager's horror movie, the difference being that the teenager can walk out of the movie house into a moderately real world, whereas it is not yet clear that professors can assemble a post-Derridarian world out of the lumber of the deconstructed one. All we can say is that the human psyche, like the rest of nature, abhors a vacuum and *something* will fill it."[20] That "something" will almost certainly be supernatural, and academe hasn't a clue.

An archetype suppressed is not an archetype subdued; it erupts elsewhere. In fact the trickster manifested in the lives of leading deconstructionists, and the results were not pretty. Roland Barthes did what he called "linguistic studies" while having sex with young boys in Morocco. Michel Foucault infected some of his followers with AIDS.[21]

Yet even now he is the object of something of a secular canonization effort, with references to him as "Saint" Foucault, and even a "hagiography" (the author's term) has been written. The archetypal influence persists.

Paul de Man is an even better exemplar. After his death it was discovered that he had collaborated with the Nazis in Belgium, and that he was a bigamist who abandoned his children. David Lehman's revealing study *Signs of the Times: Deconstruction and the Fall of Paul de Man* reports that "When the twenty-eight-year-old de Man embarked for the United States in 1948, he left behind a crowd of angry creditors and the prospect of a lawsuit. He had ruined his father and had earned himself a local reputation for dishonesty. Ortwin de Graef noted that Editions Hermes [de Man's publishing house] was 'appropriately' named—Hermes being the patron of thieves in Greek mythology. The Belgian sociologist Georges Goriely recalled de Man, the friend of his youth, for conferencegoers at the University of Antwerp in June 1988. 'A charming, humorous, modest, highly cultured man,' said Goriely. But a scoundrel. 'Swindling, forging, lying were, at least at the time, second nature to him.'"[22] The trickster archetype is striking, and the life of de Man confirms the aphorism that philosophy is largely autobiography.

Deep down, most deconstructionists and post-structuralists are rationalists. They deny the mystical and supernatural. For them everything is detached; there are no magical interconnections. They will undoubtedly dismiss the above manifestations as mere coincidence, having nothing to do with deconstructionism and its ideas. They never understood the intellectual roots of their beliefs.

The case of Jacques Derrida is also instructive. To his credit, he at least briefly addressed the paranormal; he did not completely repress it. His paper "Telepathy" was first published in 1981, and it is extremely odd.[23] Basically, it is a confused hodgepodge of fragments of writings from Freud (letters, notes, etc.). It is even more obscure than Derrida's usual writings. Fortunately, Nicholas Royle, the translator of the article, provided some commentary. He admitted that "Derrida cannot see very clearly in 'Telepathy',"[24] adding "It is frightening. Reading Derrida is frightening. As he says in 'Telepathy', he scares other people and he scares himself."[25] Telepathy seems to disconcert him, though he does not know why. Some of his other writings shed some light on this. In his *Specters of Marx* (1993), Derrida asserted that "There has never been a scholar who really, and as scholar, deals with ghosts . . . There has never been a scholar who, as such, does not believe in the sharp distinction between the real and the unreal, the actual and the inactual, the living and the non-living."[26] This is a direct confession of his rationalism and reveals his inability to comprehend alternatives. Yet he has a vague sense that rationalism is insufficient.

Derrida is an elderly academic white male, comfortably ensconced in the exceedingly ethnocentric rationalistic French intellectual culture. It is not surprising that he is so grossly ignorant of the paranormal and its implications. When he ventured into that foreign territory, being oblivious to any useful scholarship, he lunged for the only thing he knew relevant: the antiquated writings of Freud. (As discussed in the chapter on totemism, Freud was very ambivalent about the paranormal. It upset him.) Obviously unsettled by what he encountered, he was unable to articulate it.

Nevertheless, Derrida's article attests to the importance of telepathy. But the topic renders him almost incoherent; he doesn't know what to do with it. Royle commented that "Derrida implies that a theory of telepathy, especially insofar as his 'own' text promotes the possibility of such a theory, is inextricably linked to the question of writing."[27] Royle proposed "'Telepathy' as a name for literature as discursive formation."[28] Derrida and Royle seemed to recognize telepathy as important for communication, but they were at a loss as to how to think about it.

Although the blind rationalism of Derrida is typical, awareness of the liminal regions has not been completely suppressed in the academy, and a few have drawn on deconstructionist theory in conjunction with the trickster. The taboo has been partly overcome, fittingly, in theories of criticism of two minority (i.e., marginal) literatures, that of the American Indian and the African American.

When American Indian literature and deconstructionism are mentioned, the name of Gerald Vizenor invariably arises. Vizenor is a mixed-blood (his preferred term) intellectual and Berkeley professor, and the trickster is central to his personal and professional lives. When only 20 months old, his father was murdered, and he was raised sometimes by relatives and at times by his impoverished mother. As an adolescent he was caught in petty theft.

The absent father, impoverished mother, and thievery are part of the Hermes archetype. Vizenor has a betwixt and between status because he is of mixed blood. He is also a communicator and mediator between the American Indian and White cultures. His eminence is attested by the Winter 1985 issue of *American Indian Quarterly*, which was devoted to his work. It contains a number of articles related to trickster issues. Trickster themes pervade his writings, and his essay "Trickster Discourse: Comic Holotropes and Language Games" (1989) relates trickster ideas to those of deconstructionism. Vizenor's writings are difficult going without a substantial background; even Barbara Babcock refers to his "enigmatic, incomprehensible, ambiguous, ambivalent language."[29]

Fortunately, Kimberly Blaeser has provided a superb presentation of his ideas in her book *Gerald Vizenor: Writing in the Oral Tradition* (1996). Blaeser is particularly well suited for the task; like Vizenor she is a mixedblood, lived on the White Earth Indian Reservation in Minnesota as a child, and is a poet. She applies deconstructionist and poststructuralist ideas in an accessible manner. Hers is one of the best descriptions I have found of the contrasts between the rationalistic Western European outlook and that of Native Americans.

She points out that ambiguity is key to Vizenor's writings, and that Vizenor blurs a variety of concepts and boundaries and makes them problematical. She tells us "Truth, Vizenor repeatedly illustrates, may lie outside the realm of simplistic distinction between fact and fiction."[30] He calls into question the distinction between history and myth, and his writings mix them in a confusing fashion. This is undoubtedly tied to his life experiences, and Blaeser reports that "In Vizenor's writing the trickster figure becomes nearly synonymous with and a metaphor for the tribal mixedblood, whose symbolic role it is to subvert the artificial distinctions of society."[31]

The trickster is central to Blaeser's exposition, and she quotes Vizenor describing the trickster: "It's Life, It's Juice, It's Energy!"[32] An entire chapter, "Trickster Signatures," draws heavily on the work of Barbara Babcock, and Blaeser states that "Many of Babcock's claims about the trickster dynamic seem very much like those of Vizenor."[33] Blaeser's is one of the best applications of Babcock's ideas that I have seen. By itself that is a high recommendation, but I would also recommend it to anyone still hypnotized by the Western rationalistic worldview. Those who do not comprehend the alternatives could benefit by reading Blaeser.

Although the trickster is a focus of her book, Blaeser has little explicitly dealing with magic or the supernatural. She did, though, briefly discuss the magical power of words.

Karl Kroeber, a professor of English at Columbia University, raised related matters in his article entitled "Deconstructionist Criticism and American Indian Literature" (1979). He discussed deconstructionism, focusing on ambiguity and transformation. He stated: "it has been argued that transformative processes are crucial to the language of all literature. This is the central tenet of deconstructionist critics, who perceive no fixed meaning to words constituting a text."[34]

In our rationalized world, the signifier and signified are clearly separate, but in primitive worldviews, this distinction is not so strong. They recognize a connection between the two, particularly in the magical power of words. Kroeber notes that American "Indians' respect for this efficacy was profound, appearing, for example, in the belief that one's personal name is so potent that it must be scrupulously concealed. If someone knows my name, he has power over my life."[35]

The trickster lives in the liminal area betwixt and between the signifier and the signified, and Kroeber pointed out that it was difficult for natives to explain him to ethnologists. Kroeber noted that American "Indians saw European 'philosophy' as defective because [it was] unable to recognize meaning in the world."[36]

Henry Louis Gates, Jr., the chairman of the Afro-American Studies Department at Harvard University, produced an extended treatment of the trickster, deconstructionist ideas, and literary criticism. Gates did his undergraduate work in the early 1970s at Yale, then the center of deconstructionist thought in the U.S. His book *The Signifying Monkey* (1988) is subtitled "A Theory of Afro-American Literary Criticism," and at the heart of his theory lie the Yoruba trickster god Eshu-Elegba and the Ifa divination system.[37] Here we have a most instructive confluence: a theoretician from a minority (marginal) culture, a trickster god, a magical divination system, the topics of ambiguity and chance, and a deconstructionist influence.[38]

Gates focuses on Eshu-Elegba's intricate ties with language, but in no sense does he reduce him to that. Fully recognizing his multiplicity, Gates explains: "Esu is the sole messenger of the gods . . . he who interprets the will of the gods to man; he who carries the desires of man to the gods. Esu is the guardian of the crossroads, master of style and of stylus, the phallic god of generation and fecundity, master of that elusive, mystical barrier that separates the divine world from the profane. Frequently characterized as an inveterate copulator possessed by his enormous penis, linguistically Esu is the ultimate copula, connecting truth with understanding, the sacred with the profane, text with interpretation . . . He connects the grammar of divination with its rhetorical structures."[39]

In the Ifa divination system, a diviner manipulates 16 palm nuts, and their resulting configuration designates verses to be chanted. There are thousands of these enigmatic, riddle-like lyrical poems, and because they are ambiguous, they need interpretation. Gates points out: "Ifa is the god of determinate meaning, but his meaning must be rendered by analogy. Esu, god of indeterminacy, rules this interpretive process; he is the god of interpretation because he embodies the ambiguity of figurative language,"[40] and "Legba, like Esu, is the divine reader, whose interpretation of the Book of Fate determines precisely what this book says."[41] This divination system is explicitly recognized as ambiguous, but Gates sees that all communication systems have the same property. Like the Ifa divination, all texts are open to interpretation.

As have many others, both Kroeber and Gates remarked on the pervasiveness and centrality of trickster tales in earlier cultures. That tells us something very profound about the societies from which they come. Likewise, the little attention the tales receive in our own deserves notice. The primitives understood things that we do not. Minority scholars recognize the trickster's importance, but establishment minions have no glimmer of it.

Magic and Meaning

A moderate size literature deals with the trickster and magic, and some addresses the trickster and meaning, but relatively little explains the conjunction. Nicholas Royle's and Jacques Derrida's writings on telepathy make some vague allusions. Henry Louis Gates' exposition makes the connection explicit for Eshu-Elegba, though he gives meaning far more attention than magic.

Both magic and meaning can be understood in terms of binary oppositions. Magical and supernatural phenomena occur with the blurring and mediation of binary oppositions, as described in earlier chapters. Meaning can also be cast in oppositional terms. Saussure postulated that meaning was found in the union of the signifier and signified.

Both magic and meaning have a betwixt and between aspect, and both engage ambiguity. In science, meaning is assumed to be entirely unproblematic, and magic is simply denied. Both magic and meaning fall outside formal logical systems. Both pose profound challenges to rationality, and deep consideration of them exposes the limits of our way of thought.

Both magic and meaning are unstable. Psi occurs more in conditions of uncertainty, instability, and transition than in stasis. Meaning must be continually reinforced if ambiguity is to be kept at bay.

Levi-Strauss addressed some of these ideas in his *Introduction to the Work of Marcel Mauss* (1950). He discussed the concept of *mana*, which roughly means magical power. Speaking of it he said "always and everywhere, those types of notions, somewhat like algebraic symbols, occur to represent an indeterminate value of signification, in itself devoid of meaning and thus susceptible of receiving any meaning at all; *their sole function is to fill a gap between the signifier and the signified*" (emphasis added).[42] He expanded on the idea, though in quite abstract fashion, but he recognized that magic works in the gap between the signifier and signified.

The connection between magic and meaning is also illustrated by parapsychology experiments.

In psychometry experiments a psychic makes statements about owners of concealed objects. The owners then are given a list of all the statements and asked to pick which ones pertain to themselves (i.e., select the ones that have *meaning* for them). If the psychic was successful the owners select the statements made when the psychic was focussed on their own objects. The "magical process" (the psychic's reading) is interpreted by the objects' owners, who impart meaning to them. This parallels the Ifa divination described by Henry Louis Gates, Jr.

Synchronicity is a type of psi. It is defined as *meaningful* coincidence. Two unrelated events occur that an observer sees as meaningful. The occurrence of psi is inferred because of the meaning.

In abstract form, psi experiments (with the exception of macro-PK studies) can be represented as two strings of numbers (e.g., binary numbers, strings of binary oppositions). One of the strings is randomly determined (e.g., shuffled cards, tumbled dice, electronically generated random numbers). The other string may be selected in a variety of ways (e.g., guesses made in an ESP test). When an above-chance correlation is found between the two strings, psi is inferred (i.e., magic happened). There is a *meaningful* relationship between them.

In psi experiments, divination practices, and synchronistic events, humans ascribe meaning to the relationship between a random process in the outer world and a mental image, impression, or intent inside a person. The person perceives the relationship, but there is no known physical cause for it. Magic (psi) is inferred when meaning is found.

Jacques Lacan

Before finishing with structuralism and literary theory, French psychoanalyst Jacques Lacan (1901–1981) should be introduced. He was an anti-structural, trickster character who was prominent among structuralists and among the literati. He came to greater public attention during the 1968 student and worker uprisings in France. His work can serve as something of a transition from this section on literary and anthropological issues, to the more psychologically oriented work covered in the next Part.

Lacan's writings are some of the most difficult I've encountered. To his credit, Lacan recognized that many of his statements were obscure. He meant them to be that way! Sociology professor Edith Kurzweil explains in *The Age of Structuralism* (1980) that "Lacan makes much of the fact that he cannot be systematized, that he cannot be 'understood,' that to understand him is to reify and misconstrue him, because 'misunderstanding' is an inherent part of 'understanding.'"[43] One of the tenets of deconstructionism is that there is no single meaning to a text, and Lacan's style amplifies that principle.

Because of this situation, it is imperative to find informed interpreters who are familiar with Lacan's intellectual culture, and who can at least partly translate his message. MIT sociologist Sherry Turkle provides a useful interpretation in her *Psychoanalytic Politics* (1978),[44] and I have found Stuart Schneiderman's *Jacques Lacan: The Death of an Intellectual Hero* (1983) especially helpful. Schneiderman was an American professor of English who became a psychoanalyst, and during his training he was analyzed by Lacan. Schneiderman's broad background in the humanities allowed him to effectively convey the wider implications of Lacanian thought, more so than commentators grounded in the sciences or medicine. This is valuable because like Freud, Lacan's ideas attract cultural theorists, who apply them to many contexts beyond the clinic. Schneiderman did so himself with his *An Angel Passes: How the Sexes Became Undivided* (1988). The Introduction to that book has a number of intriguing insights on literary issues, the problem of meaning, and angels.

Lacan personified trickster and an anti-structural qualities in his private and professional lives. Turkle and Schneiderman both compared him to a bricoleur, with Schneiderman saying that Lacan's work had "the quality of being fragmented and somewhat disjointed, even fictional at times."[45] Lacan did not restrict himself to psychiatry or the sciences, and early in his career he wrote for surrealist publications. His sex life was unconventional, and it is rumored that "his mistresses were almost as legion as his followers."[46] Lacan considered himself a hysteric, and the boundary between his conscious and unconscious was perhaps rather thin, as reflected in his unrestrained behavior. He shocked people with his antics. For instance he once arrived unexpectedly at a dinner party and ate the food remaining on the guests' plates.[47] More respectable analysts accused him of being narcissistic and having unresolved oedipal conflicts. He precipitated schisms in the psychoanalytic community, and in the 1960s the International Psychoanalytic Association expelled him and his followers. He went on to establish the Freudian School in Paris, but during his final illness he tried to dissolve that institution.[48] That action too provoked bitter feuding, which generated enormous publicity and some notoriety for psychoanalysis. Lacan's anti-structural nature was apparent to his end.

Trickster figures usually have some connection with the paranormal, but I am not aware of any with Lacan. However, his biographer Elizabeth Roudinesco, in the first paragraph of her Preface, said that Lacan's is the story of "a doctrine that, following on from Freud's, tried to rescue humanity from the universe of religion, dreams, and the occult, even if this meant revealing the inability of reason, knowledge, and truth to bring about such a deliverance."[49] I have found no indication that Lacan had anything like Freud's understanding of the occult; he seems to have been oblivious to it. There were some early religious influences, and Roudinesco referred to the "stifling religiosity" of his childhood.[50] His younger brother entered a monastery and became a theologian.[51] Lacan's doctrines may have been, in part, a reaction to all that. In any event, if the paranormal had been mixed into his volatile personality, it might have been too much for him. French intellectualism is strongly rationalistic and that may serve a protective, limiting function.

Psychoanalysis perhaps has more affinity with the trickster than do other types of psychotherapy. Through free association, unconscious material is brought to consciousness; this boundary crossing operation is somewhat reflexive with the mind examining the products of the mind. Lacan's practice and philosophy had additional reflexive and anti-structural features. To the chagrin of many other analysts, he advocated that an analyzand should analyze the psychoanalyst, thus turning the tables. The inversion of roles puts the two on an equal footing, leveling their status. Lacan had other controversial ideas; for instance, Schneiderman reports that he "did not think that psychoanalysis was a respectable profession; he judged it to be a subversive and revolutionary occupation"[52] and that "Lacan as an analyst was not trying to establish any sort of communication with his patients; nor did he think it a good idea that they understand each other."[53] More orthodox analysts desired respectability; they wanted to understand their patients so they could help them to adjust to society. Lacan rejected that.

Lacan was antagonistic to institutions, including one he founded. He viewed institutionalization, codification, and hierarchy as inimical to psychoanalysis. Turkle notes that according to Lacan "No institution . . . but only the analyst can authorize him- or herself in the analytic vocation."[54] This caused rifts. Many analysts had spent years in training; they had an allegiance to their institutions and a vested interest in maintaining the status quo. If anyone could become an analyst, professionalism, and accompanying financial rewards, would be threatened.

Scientific psychologists generally view psychoanalysis as a marginal endeavor. Lacan probably understood this better than other analysts who coveted the imprimatur of the scientific establishment. He wanted no rapprochement, but rather "tended to dismiss scientific psychology as alien to his enterprise, as a product of what he saw as the worst tendencies of American life."[55]

Psychoanalysis served as a mythology to some extent; it invented a jargon that brought issues to consciousness but also obscured them. Freudianism focused primarily on sexuality and symbolized many of its ideas in those terms (the sexual tension of the male-female binary opposition being central). For instance, a variety of conflicts could be interpreted in terms of unresolved oedipal complexes, whether or not there was anything like a father figure involved.

Binary opposition is a common theme in the structuralist lineage, and it is used to explore a variety of concepts. Schneiderman mentioned that psychoanalysts need not restrict themselves to the male-female opposition and that the life-death opposition can serve as an axis for another system of symbolization. He and Lacan didn't really understand the implications of that, but that makes their comments all the more interesting. The literary and psychoanalytic practitioners did not grasp binary oppositions as clearly as say Edmund Leach or Rodney Needham, who understood the primitive roots.

The life-death binary opposition is a major one for all cultures. The demarcation between the two is always surrounded by rituals, taboos, and is associated with the supernatural. Lacan and his followers, like Freud and his, believe that the supernatural is nothing more than symbolic. They are wrong of course, and it is amusing to see how they avoid the issue with their naive rationalism. Nevertheless, some of their concepts are useful, and just because the psychoanalysts fail to comprehend the full implications of their own ideas doesn't mean that they should be neglected by theorists of the paranormal. However, the relevant writings of Lacan and Schneiderman are obscure, but it can be stimulating to briefly dip into them as a source for ideas. They are only direction markers, and it would be a mistake to anchor anything to them.

Schneiderman concludes that "analysis has as its major task the repairing of the relationships people have, not with other people, but with the dead."[56] This provocative statement opens many possibilities, and he has more to say. He comments that "Unfortunately our passion for science and rationality has prevented us from appreciating the role the dead play for the living... We usually think of the dead as phantoms and ghosts, to which no mature adult would give credence. They become relegated to the world of children, infidels, and savages, these ghosts. But as the affair of children, they come to inhabit the unconscious, and Freud identified the unconscious with the infantile."[57] As discussed in the chapter on totemism, this passage is itself an instance of taboo enforcement. Challenging the life-death demarcation is greeted with hostility and derision in science. Even in parapsychology, research on survival of bodily death is a relatively marginal area. Spiritualism and mediumship directly defy the idea of a clear boundary between life and death, and they are even more anathema to respectable academics. Schneiderman unwittingly displays the force of the taboo, for despite his insight, when he writes of ghosts he must add the protective incantation: "to which no mature adult would give credence."

Lacan's ideas about therapy and death raise other intriguing connections. Schneiderman notes that "Relations between the living and the dead never take place in an atmosphere of communication leading to interpersonal and mutual understanding. In place of this humanistic model for therapy, Lacan proposed one based on the elements of theft and sacrifice. Prometheus is the most striking example of this."[58] I am unable to follow him here, but Schneiderman recognizes the potential of a trickster figure (Prometheus). Schneiderman later discussed Norman O. Brown's *Hermes the Thief*.[59] Although the ideas are not fully developed, the point is that trickster figures are relevant to psychoanalysis, therapy, and exploring the unconscious. This signals a nexus of religious issues, life and death, sacrifice, and supernatural beings. To express their ideas these psychoanalysts chose not the language of modern science but rather that of ancient mythology.

The life-death opposition also offers possibilities for reconsidering hysteria. Freud understood it in terms of sexuality, but again, that explanatory framework is not the only one available. Schneiderman points out that "the dead have far more appeal to the hysteric than anything about the living has and that hysteria is a failed attempt to stay in touch with the dead."[60] Hysteria is an interesting example, especially in light of the history of French psychiatry and the work of Jean-Martin Charcot. Charcot revived the use of hypnosis with his treatments of hysterics, who were associated with somnambulism and also clairvoyance. Here again we see a confluence of liminal elements (hypnosis, hysteria, clairvoyance), and Schneiderman links them to the life-death binary opposition. This is fitting because spiritualist mediums were often accused of being hysterics.

The life-death opposition is not the only one relevant to the paranormal. Others include: internal-external, self-other, and imagination-reality. Lacan's ideas are pertinent to those too. He wrote about mirrors, the imaginary, the real, and the symbolic. A later chapter will discuss the imaginal realm, a combination of imagination and reality developed by Henry Corbin. Some of Lacan's ideas are at least vaguely related. Edith Kurzweil refers to "his central concept of the *imaginary* (this highly idiosyncratic concept has its roots in the *mirror-stage*, where it is said to form a 'Borromean knot' with the *real* and the *symbolic* . . . he has never quite explained how this *imaginary* functions."[61]

Lacan also wrote on paranoia, in fact it was the topic of his doctoral dissertation. I will briefly draw upon Lacan's notions on it in a later chapter.

The above ideas are not fully formed; indeed, they are only allusions to possibilities that might be developed. Yet they flag issues that need new ways of understanding. Lacan's obscurity is not necessarily a drawback. It can stimulate exploration and perhaps point a new way, without being unduly constrictive. His ideas might pollinate those in related areas. Ambiguity has its benefits.

The difficulty in understanding Lacan hints that the issues are inherently problematic and ones that rationalists wish to avoid. Lacan raises many matters related to the supernatural, and then seems to intentionally obscure them. It is to our advantage that he tries to address them, for it shows the difficulties one may encounter.

Summary

To date, literary theory has had no impact on parapsychology, not surprisingly because literary concerns seem far removed from those of the sciences. Nevertheless literary theory has much to say. It deals with information and communication in ways that science does not.

Literary theory intrudes into anthropology, particularly in the structuralist lineage. Semiotics and structuralism help show the relationships between literary ideas, on the one hand, and social structure on the other. These perspectives are primarily concerned with stable systems; they give less attention to ambiguity, uncertainty, liminality, and dissolution of structure.

Literary criticism emphasizes interpretation, i.e., the determination of "meaning." When we interpret, we reduce ambiguity and uncertainty, we perceive order and structure in the world. When we cannot effectively interpret, our world becomes chaotic and disorganized. In most of our day-to-day activities, interpretation is straightforward, and meaning poses little problem. We generally give it little thought. Closer examination reveals difficulties.

Deconstructionists emphasized ambiguity. Some of them intentionally made their writings difficult to understand, perhaps to illustrate the problem of meaning. The issue is subtle, and we are usually unconscious of it. A person's background influences how a message is understood. Choice of words, what is given prominence, who is speaking, what is left unsaid, all have implications. There are many layers of meaning, and they are not the same for everyone. Science assumes that meaning is unproblematic—that it can be objectively, impersonally, and rationally determined. Deconstructionists argued otherwise.

Deconstructionism provoked violent controversies. It probed foundations, challenged the status quo, and attacked the myth of objectivity. The attackers eventually realized that deconstructionism could be turned back upon themselves. They blunted their weapon, and that was signalled by the adoption of the term post-structuralism.

One root of the structuralist lineage traces back to the totemism debates at the beginning of the twentieth century. Those addressed rationality and the supernatural. This root is almost entirely forgotten, but the implications are profound.

Probing foundations and questionning basic assumptions are the beginnings of liminal conditions. Those are governed by the trickster; they have a power of their own. The primitives understood that; most academics do not. Deconstructionists and post-structuralists are really rationalists who are oblivious to the liminal realms and taboo areas. It is no accident that the lives of Barthes, Foucault, de Man, and Lacan were marked by unsavory trickster qualities.

Today, most who draw upon concepts from the structuralist lineage have little understanding of anthropology. Edmund Leach explained that non-things, that is, things that are not named, are taboo. They lie betwixt and between "things." Those interstitial areas are rarely examined. Psi is one of those "non-things"; psi is defined by what it is not.

The paranormal shares a central concern with literary criticism—interpretation. Many divination systems require interpretation. Likewise many psychic readings are ambiguous and also need to be interpreted. The situation is especially clear with formal psi experiments. In virtually all such tests, at the heart is some random process, and the outcome of that process is "interpreted" as being "significant" (i.e., meaningful) or not. If an experiment achieves statistically significant results, psi occurred, by definition. Magic (psi) and meaning are essentially equivalent in psi experiments.

Obviously interpretation does not involve psi (magic) in the vast majority of instances. For most of everyday life interpretation is relatively straightforward. Yet at limits, in ambiguous situations, the parallels become apparent, and meaning can be seen as equivalent to magic (or psi). Perhaps clarity and precision help keep psi at bay.

Part 6

Overview

The two chapters in this Part cover the imagination and paranoia. Analysis of binary oppositions is again employed. A key opposition is imagination-reality, and it has deep parallels with others such as representation-object and internal-external. The boundaries between the elements are not as clear as one might expect.

The "imagination" is not as simple an idea as commonly thought. A number of disciplines have addressed it including psychology, sociology, literature, anthropology, and religion, among others. I will draw upon all of them and mix concepts that seem wildly disparate. Undoubtedly this will disconcert those who prefer to stay within firmly established categories, but the trickster demands the commingling.

Clairvoyance and PK also blur the distinction between mental representation (imagination) and object (reality). Pretending blurs the same distinction, as well as that between falsehood and truth. So does deception. Pretending and deception have important functions in the mental development of primates and young human children. They are crucial for growth of self-awareness and formation of ego.

Paranoia often signals the fear of loss of the boundary between internal and external. Telepathy, clairvoyance, and PK blur the same boundary. Paranoia is frequently associated with the paranormal. Witchcraft accusations, fear of being psychically spied upon, and rumors of government cover-ups of UFOs are examples. The paranoia-paranormal affiliation is common, but parapsychologists have given it remarkably little attention.

CHAPTER 24

The Imagination

Imagination, fiction, and the like are commonly thought to be clearly separated from reality and fact. This is usually a good assumption. Yet upon closer examination, the situation is more problematic. There are many situations where they are blended. Myth is often defined as truth expressed fictionally. ESP and PK call into question the sharp demarcation of mind (imagination) and matter (reality). In deception, fact and fiction are often mixed. There are a number of other circumstances with similar blurring, and it makes sense to explore them for commonalities. This is a speculative chapter, and the ideas are not fully developed. I hope to point directions for future elaboration.

Earlier Parts of this book examined a variety of phenomena in terms of binary oppositions. I will continue using that structuralist approach because it gives useful ways to think about things. It encourages comparisons that might be otherwise overlooked.

The binary oppositions in Figure 7 are found in many contexts, and they show a similar pattern. Typically, one element in a pair has a privileged position, and the elements in the top row generally have the higher status. When that status is challenged, or the elements are blurred, there is a threat to stability and clarity. As individuals and as societies, we have methods to assure that these oppositions are clearly demarcated. When they are not, a liminal, anti-structural condition is developed. Instability is courted, and the trickster reigns.

With the paranormal, the privileged position is often reversed. For instance, billions of dollars are devoted to paranormal fiction in movies, TV shows, and books. Gross national expenditures for scientific research on the paranormal are tiny (the inverse of normal occupations). In UFO research, hoax cases generate far more attention than genuine ones.

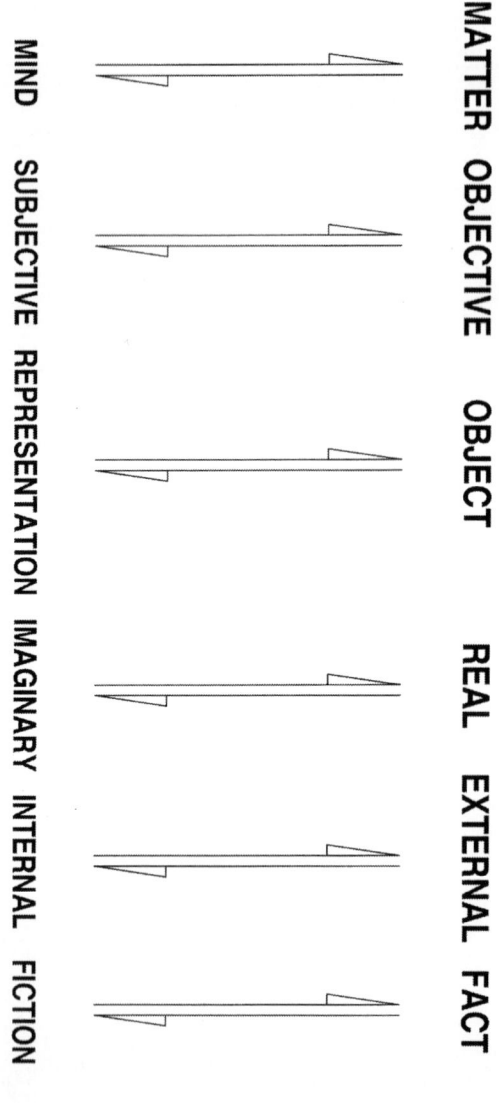

Figure 7 Binary Oppositions

Note: The elements in the top row generally have a higher status than those in the bottom row. The arrows indicate that the statuses reverse in liminal conditions.

This chapter continues to explore how binary oppositions are demarcated and how they become blurred or inverted. The broad concept of representation will again be invoked. Representation is addressed in several seemingly disparate areas, including semiotics, research on animal deception, studies of the imagination, and theories of fiction.

The idea that imagination and reality can, in principle, be blurred raises a severe challenge to the Western worldview and provokes anxieties. It disputes the notion of a fully objective reality. This problem should not be minimized or slyly avoided. It must be confronted directly because it is a fundamental issue of psi.

Imagination

The usual idea of the imagination is simplistic—it's all in the head. To say something is "just imagination" is to deprecate it. Even when it is not meant that way, a message is conveyed that the matter is not serious or important. In other words, "the imagination" has low status.

The imagination has received extensive discussion through the centuries, but new conceptions keep being proposed. Some are not too well developed and display a bit of confusion, and some have nothing to do with imagery. We must cross disciplinary boundaries if we are to understand the imagination. We need to ponder ideas from anthropology, religious scholarship, sociology, analytical psychology, and others. Indeed, many readers will probably consider my conglomeration of theories and examples as illegitimately mixing concepts that have nothing to do with each other (but this is fitting for the trickster). The perspectives on the imagination are diverse and not yet cohesive; most seem to have been developed independently, with little overlap or cross fertilization from outside a theorist's field.

The imagination is valued in fantasy and fiction. Thus we might expect some useful insights from theories of fiction. This may alarm some readers who may think that I am disparaging the reality of the paranormal. If people read this chapter separately from the rest of the book, they might conclude that I was debunking the paranormal. The ideas are easily misunderstood. My intention is not to belittle paranormal phenomena but to emphasize their ambiguity and explore the consequences of that.

Status has been an issue throughout this book, and it is key in understanding the imagination. Francis Galton, a cousin of Charles Darwin and a prominent 19th-century scientist in his own right, made an intriguing study of mental imagery. He asked people to visualize their breakfast table and describe the image that appeared to them in their mind's eye. He reported "To my astonishment, I found that the great majority of the men of science to whom I first applied protested that mental imagery was unknown to them, and they looked on me as fanciful and fantastic in supposing that the words 'mental imagery' really expressed what I believed everybody supposed them to mean ... They had a mental deficiency of which they were unaware, and naturally enough supposed that those who affirmed they possessed it, were romancing."[1] Galton found that imagery was frequently reported by women and children.

Galton was not the only one to find a relationship between social position and imagery. Yale psychologist Jerome Singer found parallel results with fantasy daydreaming. He conducted a study in the 1950s and discovered that Jewish and African Americans had higher daydreaming frequency than those of Anglo-Saxon descent.[2] This finding supports the association of imagery with marginal, low-status groups.

C. Wright Mills' book *The Sociological Imagination* (1959) is a classic in its field. Mills was not a psychologist, and not surprisingly, he did not discuss mental imagery. His concept was a bit different. He defined the sociological imagination as a quality of mind that "enables its possessor to understand the larger historical scene in terms of its meaning for the inner life and the external career of a variety of individuals."[3] It allows one to accurately perceive large social forces that shape individuals and societies, but most people typically do not understand the idea. Mills noted that the acquisition of the sociological imagination "by individuals and by the cultural community at large is slow and often fumbling; many social scientists are themselves quite unaware of it."[4] Though Mills' use of the word imagination did not involve imagery as such, it emphasized a broad, wholistic perspective.

John Macionis pointed out in his introductory text *Sociology* (1989) that persons in socially marginal positions have an above-average ability to take a sociological perspective and understand patterns in society that are not immediately observable. He also noted that certain periods foster the sociological imagination and stated specifically that "the 1930s stand out as a decade of heightened sociological awareness" and that "People very quickly develop a sociological perspective when the established patterns of society began [sic] to shake and crumble."[5] He mentioned the 1960s as a similar era. Both marginality and periods of transition foster the sociological imagination; both are anti-structural. The sociological imagination itself may be a bit subversive. For society to function smoothly, there must be shared, though arbitrary, values and customs, and these must be accepted without much conscious questioning. The sociological imagination brings these patterns and values to consciousness, and, as such, serves a function of liminality.

In summary, several lines of research indicate that one's imagination is linked to one's social position, to one's status. A key finding is that the imagination is more developed in anti-structural conditions and persons.

The Religious Imagination and Personification

Gods and supernatural beings are part of all cultures. They are typically personified i.e., endowed with human characteristics. But gods are more than mere persons. In monotheistic religions, God is considered as "totality," though it is difficult or impossible to speak of that concept directly. The religious imagination grapples with the problem, and it deserves special comment. It cannot be fully distinguished from social and psychological concepts because they blend into each other. It is a mistake to try to completely disentangle them.

Emile Durkheim, one of the founders of the sociology of religion, suggested that gods and religious institutions are collective representations of society (here again we encounter the broad but seminal concept of "representation"). In his *The Elementary Forms of the Religious Life* (1912), he went so far as to say that "At bottom, the concept of totality, that of society and that of divinity are very probably only different aspects of the same notion."[6] The gods reflect the values and structure of society, but most people usually do not consciously recognize the implications. It is beneficial for society for them not to. In fact Macionis comments that "the ability of the sacred to legitimate and stabilize society rests on one major condition: *the socially constructed character of the sacred must go unrecognized*" (emphasis by Macionis).[7] In other words, religion must partly obscure its own nature.

The gods are perceived as having a force and will of their own. These collectively shared representations (images) are personified, and we need to contemplate the topic of personification. It is an essential aspect of myth (the trickster, for instance, is a personified being). Imagination and personification go together; they need to be understood jointly. Both are poorly regarded by scientists. Both have low status. Hence most scholars ignore them.

James Hillman is one of the most insightful writers on personification. He is a primary exponent of analytic psychology (analytic psychology follows a Jungian tradition and differentiates itself from Freudian psychoanalysis), and he has written a bit on parapsychology.[8] Hillman has been a controversial figure among Jungians, and he has some parallels with French psychoanalyst Jacques Lacan, who was introduced in the earlier chapter on literary criticism. The two recognized the importance of many of the same fundamental issues. Hillman, like Lacan, has written on paranoia.[9] Hillman also discussed the imagination, and "the imaginary" was part of Lacan's theorizing. Both were critical of most therapeutic practices and of scientific conceptualizations of therapy. Both challenged the establishment, and both were accused of irrationalism. Lacan's and Hillman's writings are relevant far outside the clinic, and cultural theorists have drawn upon them.[10] Fortunately Hillman is much easier to understand than Lacan.[11]

Hillman's book *Re-Visioning Psychology* (1975) is probably his most important work. Its first chapter is entitled: "Personifying or Imaging Things." There he demonstrated his grasp of the broad psychological trends in history, and he addressed the devaluation of personified and anthropomorphic thinking. He explained that this is not something recent. The trend extends over centuries, and it is especially pervasive in academe. He noted that "psychologists in general denigrate personifying, labelling it a defensive mode of perception, a projection, a 'pathetic fallacy,' a regression to delusional, hallucinatory or illusory modes of adaptation."[12] Psychologists are active agents for marginalizing personification. Their activity indicates a deep antagonism, and that signals the importance of the topic.

Hillman did not cite Max Weber, but the trend he identified is clearly part of the rationalization and disenchantment of the world. Personification does not fit with the Western worldview. It is not just marginalized but pathologized.

The general attitude is seen in literary areas as well, even though personification is common in literature. Academic discussions of metaphor and allegory emphasize that they are only analogs. Hillman comments that "*allegory is a defensive reaction of the rational mind against the full power of the soul's irrational personifying propensity.* Gods and demons become mere poetic allusions" (Hillman's emphasis).[13]

Hillman would suggest that the imagination perceives in a wholistic, autonomous, personified manner. He says: "Where imagination reigns, personifying happens... Just as we do not create our dreams, but they *happen* to us, so we do not invent the persons of myth and religion; they, too, happen to us. The persons present themselves as existing prior to any effort of ours to personify."[14] The realm appears to have an independence, and it is not fully subject to conscious rational control. This is essentially confirmed by anthropologist Michele Stephen, who studied religion in New Guinea and advanced some ideas about religious imagination. She proposed the idea of the "autonomous imagination," which functions outside of conscious awareness and is "experienced as an external, independent reality, but it displays a much greater freedom and richness of imaginative inventiveness, and a different access to memory."[15] She recognized that the forces perceived seem to have a life of their own. Her formulation is consistent with, but developed seemingly independently of, Hillman.

Hillman explains that "anthropomorphism, animism, personification—contain one basic idea: there exists a 'mode of thought' which takes an inside event and puts it outside, at the same time making this content alive, personal, and even divine."[16] This is a blurring of the internal-external binary opposition. All this typifies the primitive mentality, but imagery-based perception has not been eliminated from Western culture, and Hillman recognized the importance of images for "Gnosticism, Neoplatonism, alchemy, Rosicrucianism, and Swedenborg."[17] These are not from primitive cultures but from our own. They are still alive and practiced today, but they have virtually no presence in the academy. They are viewed as marginal by science and by establishment religion.

The above formulations of the imagination are still rudimentary. They were developed by people in diverse disciplines, and apparently in relative isolation. They are a hodgepodge collection, but commonalities are found. A number of facts cohere: the devaluation of personification in Western elite culture, the prevalence of fantasy in marginal groups, a deficiency in imagery ability among high status professional males, and the rise of the sociological imagination in periods of cultural stress. In view of these factors, we can conclude that the imagination is anti-structural. The widespread, subtly negative attitude toward fantasy, imagery, and the imagination indirectly acknowledges its power and the need to keep it constrained. (The trickster demonstrates the power of personified thinking. He is a personified concept, and it is through him that common patterns in so many diverse areas can be recognized.)

The Imagination, Psi, and the Imaginal Realm

The imagination, imagery, and the paranormal go hand in hand. They are found together in mystical traditions stretching back millennia, in long occult traditions, and in scientific parapsychology. Ghosts, demons, angels, spirits, visionary experience, and altered states of consciousness all involve imagery. Mediums go into trance to see and talk with spirits of the dead. Mystics cultivate altered states of consciousness, and occultists induce them in order to cast magical spells. Hypnosis can produce hallucinations and has also been used to facilitate ESP. Parapsychologists have demonstrated that dreams, ganzfeld, and other methods that alter consciousness and stimulate imagery also enhance ESP receptiveness. In short, imagination and imagery are important in many psi events.[18]

Questions about many paranormal experiences have typically focussed on whether they were "real" or occurred "only in the imagination." People on both sides of the psi controversy have expended tremendous energy in defining and maintaining this boundary. In fact, that is the purpose of laboratory-based parapsychology. In laboratories, much effort is taken to assure that psi really happens and that results are not due to fraud, error, or delusion.

The existence of psi suggests that imagination and reality are not clearly separable. This is a disconcerting idea, but it must be explored if one wishes to understand the paranormal. The binary oppositions of internal-external, subjective-objective, fantasy-reality are fundamental to the Western worldview, and anything that proposes a blurring of them is dismissed as irrational. Yet psi engages both the mental and physical worlds, both the imagination and reality; there is an interface, an interaction.

There is one formulation that begins to recognize that the paranormal has a quality of being "betwixt and between" reality and imagination. This is referred to as the imaginal realm. It is based upon the work of Henry Corbin, a French Islamic scholar who wrote on mysticism. In 1972 he published a paper, entitled "Mundus Imaginalis" (Latin for imaginal world). Those who have adopted his idea typically now refer to it as the imaginal realm, rather than using the Latin term.

Corbin's "world" is not precisely defined (despite his claim) and perhaps cannot be. Its description is couched in mystical and mythological terms, in language almost impenetrable to a rationalistic mind. It is accessed through the imagination and mystical visionary states.

Corbin drew primarily from the Islamic mystical tradition, but his concept is quite compatible with others, and he cited Emanuel Swedenborg as an example of someone who accessed the imaginal realm.

A few researchers have utilized Corbin's ideas. Kenneth Ring, a University of Connecticut psychologist and one of the foremost investigators of near-death experiences (NDEs), explored the imaginal realm in relation to UFO experiences and NDEs.[19] Folklorist Peter Rojcewicz, a professor at the Juilliard School, incorporated it into his thinking and discussed what he calls "crack" phenomena, i.e., those that fall into the crack at the borders of reality.[20] Rojcewicz briefly cited Victor Turner's notions of betwixt and between and the liminal in support of his thesis. He also discussed Jung's idea of the psychoid, which somehow combines the mental and physical. Like the imaginal realm, the psychoid is ambiguously defined. Dennis Stillings also explored the concept and helped promote it by editing an anthology entitled *Cyberbiological Studies of the Imaginal Component of the UFO Contact Experience* (1989). Fred Alan Wolf, who is both a physicist and a performing magician as well as a writer, provided an extensive discussion of the imaginal in his *The Dreaming Universe* (1994).[21]

The social position of these theorists merits note. None of them have published much in professional parapsychology journals, though they all have some familiarity with psychic research. All acknowledge the existence of psi, but unlike most parapsychologists, they are also familiar with ufology. They are marginal figures in a marginal discipline. They have a broader perspective than most, and they do not neglect some of the more bizarre phenomena that many others wish to ignore. These people established needed groundwork, but yet have only scratched the surface.[22]

Corbin's work, by itself, is of very limited usefulness because his writings are vague, grounded in mysticism, and lack substantial links to scientific theories or empirical evidence. There are additional problems; for instance, he insisted that the imaginal is distinctly separate from fantasy, but he seemed unable to describe just how. He was wrong. Reality, the imaginal, and fantasy blur into one another. Fantasy and reality are perhaps carved out of the imaginal. Another problem is that the term *imaginal* can be easily misinterpreted. For instance, a number of people misunderstood Kenneth Ring as saying that UFO experiences occur only in the imagination, something he clearly did not say or imply. But the terminology, almost intentionally, invites confusion.

Despite the problems, the vagueness of Corbin's concept has benefits; it easily accepts extensions, refinements, and borrowings. It can accommodate a wide range of phenomena that do not fit into most other classification schemes. The idea of the imaginal realm provides flexibility; fluidity is easily included, and ambiguity is explicitly recognized. The grounding is from a base that is sympathetic to paranormal phenomena and does not view them as hallucination or fantasy.

High-Strangeness Cases

The term imaginal has been applied to near-death and UFO experiences, especially those with bizarre elements. Some of those can be described as highly strange; they have odd aspects that don't seem to fit together. In 1990 I presented a short paper at a parapsychology conference entitled "Demons, ETs, Bigfoot, and Elvis."[23] I pointed out that the usually assumed classes of paranormal phenomena are not distinct. NDEs can occur in conjunction with UFO experiences; Bigfoot has been sighted during UFO flaps; there are accounts of Bigfoot making bedroom visitations. Fairies and uniformed military personnel have been encountered in ET abduction experiences. Poltergeist phenomena are found in the lives of crop circle investigators and UFO witnesses. Shamans in primitive societies claimed to have sexual encounters with spirits that produced babies who were brought to them at night when others were not around to observe. Similarly, many UFO abductees report having parented hybrid ET-human children, undoubtedly unaware of similar accounts from other cultures hundreds or thousands of years ago.

The melange of experiences described above will undoubtedly strike most readers as bizarre. Those who have not immersed themselves in investigations of such cases can be tempted to dismiss the events as "not firmly established" or "only imagination." They are often quickly and cheerfully explained as hallucination, caused by stress, and occurring only in the brain of those reporting them. This attitude is psychologically protective for the inquirer, but it leads to serious misunderstanding of the nature of the occurrences.

The experiences have low status, and that is subtly reinforced in several ways. Though there is a fair amount of written material about such events, it is often relegated to obscure magazines and books by writers of dubious integrity, printed on low quality paper by slightly disreputable publishers, or published by the authors themselves.[24]

Crude drawings or blurred photographs sometimes accompany the articles. Few libraries collect such material. All this signals that there is "something wrong," and it is easy to dismiss the reports, yet when one meets experiencers, they tell stories very similar to the "disreputable" accounts.

In academic circles, serious, or even casual, consideration of such things evokes murmurs of disapproval. This is even true within the "orthodox" paranormal fields. Many researchers avoid high-strangeness cases, because they legitimately worry about respectability. Indeed, loss of status typically accompanies direct engagement of, or even serious attention given to, this kind of phenomena. Few academics really get to know such experiencers. Those few who do, typically have one, and only one, narrowly defined area of study (e.g., NDEs, OOBEs, apparitions, or UFO sightings). As a result, experiencers are often reluctant to tell of their more bizarre encounters, especially those falling outside a researcher's category of interest.

Further, the few scientists who do investigate often try to maintain a stance of a detached, impartial observer, and they naively expect to gain people's trust by doing so. Researchers who are more astute realize the need to become part of a subculture, and participate in it, in order to understand the phenomena, but this is frowned upon by academe. One's position as a respectable academic would be undermined by too close an association with the objects of study.

Kenneth Ring is one who dared to investigate mixed categories of the imaginal and paranormal. He carried out extensive psychological tests on near-death experiencers and UFO abductees. He found that the experiences often had profound transformative effects on peoples' lives. He also discussed the strong parallels that both NDEs and UFO abductions had with shamanic initiations. Ring is a psychologist and was apparently unfamiliar with the anthropological work on liminality. Yet it was encouraging to see that he recognized commonalities among NDEs, UFO abductions, and shamanic initiations, all of which are liminal phenomena.

In the last chapter of his book *The Omega Project* (1992), Ring speculated about the meaning of his research and the implications of NDEs and UFO abduction experiences for the wider society. He went so far to say that they may "presage the *shamanizing of modern humanity*" (Ring's emphasis).[25] The shaman is a liminal being, and in effect, Ring suggested that humanity is undergoing some transformative process. It is easy to lapse into apocalyptic rhetoric when discussing this, and some saw his comments as rather florid.[26] Even so, Ring recognized an important pattern. Anthony F. C. Wallace's paper on cultural revitalization mentioned that in times of transition, a number of people are likely to have visionary experiences.

While Ring was conducting his research during the late 1980s and early 1990s, other scholars made some parallel speculations regarding cultural transition. That time period saw publication of a number of books on postmodernism, but most made little impact outside the academy. The works were generally abstract, drawing on deconstructionism and other philosophical ideas, but the thrust was nearly identical to Ring's point. They too discussed social and psychological transformation.

The concept of the imaginal is not far advanced, and it needs to be buttressed with other work, particularly theories of the trickster, liminality, and anti-structure. The concept explicity merges (and blurs) imagination and reality. Thus the imaginal realm is a liminal area, and it is governed by the trickster. The implications need to be recognized because the trickster poses risks, and the imaginal realm is not immune from them. It is easy to lose one's grip on reality; critical judgement can dissolve. Imaginal experiences can cause one to mistake fantasy for reality, and can lure one into becoming a victim of hoaxes or into paranoia. The phenomena seep into the lives of investigators, as discussed in the chapter on unbounded conditions. Researchers in academia face a loss of status if they have substantial contact with imaginal events. These are some of the reasons that this area has been so little explored, and any further theorizing needs to recognize that.

Fiction

Academics can more safely study paranormal and imaginal events through literature, fiction, and folklore. That keeps the phenomena constrained and restricts them to "stories" and "text." As discussed in the chapter on institutions, massive industries are devoted to portraying them in and as fiction. Emphasizing that they are fiction reduces anxiety about them, and reinforces the boundary between imagination and reality.

Fiction helps constrain liminal and imaginal phenomena, but fiction retains a power to influence. It is not as innocuous and inconsequential as it might first appear. Some of it has been politically and religiously suppressed. Scientists' tendency to ignore fiction deserves examination.[27]

Horror fiction is particularly germane to our concerns. Horror supports a sizeable industry, and there has been considerable scholarship devoted to it. Monsters of horror are often interstitial; i.e., they lie between accepted categories. They display properties considered mutually exclusive. Some are sexually ambiguous with both male and female characteristics; others blur the boundary between the living and dead, such as ghosts or walking corpses; Bigfoot exists between ape and man; others combine plant and animal qualities with some plants demonstrating cunning intelligence. All these merge properties in ways not found within our usual classification systems. The same can be said of imaginal creatures. William Clements, a professor of English at Arkansas State University published a valuable essay titled "The Interstitial Ogre" (1987) in which he discussed fictional monsters, and he pointed out that they violate human categories. He explained that "For while they may also represent psychic repressions, sexual tension, the threat of nuclear destruction, or emotional catharsis, their essence is their interstitiality. They articulate ultimate defiance to humanity by challenging, merely through the nature of their being, the founding constructs upon which all of culture rests."[28]

Clements understood that subversion of categories is the fundamental quality of horror monsters, but he was also aware that fiction can reflect cultural anxieties and stresses that can result from changes in structure (e.g., in times of economic recession, some people lose their jobs and status). Stephen King confirms this message in his *Danse Macabre* (1981) where he comments that while "Horror movies and horror novels have always been popular . . . they seem to enjoy a cycle of increased popularity . . . [in times that] almost always seem to coincide with periods of fairly serious economic and/or political strain, and the books and films seem to reflect those free-floating anxieties . . . which accompany such serious but not mortal dislocations."[29] Such strains occur during periods of anti-structure. The popularity of interstitial characters in movies resonates with liminality and anti-structure in the culture.

Likewise, some paranormal experiences include bizarre, category-defying imagery. It becomes very easy for others to dismiss them by saying that experiencers saw them in movies. Fiction often reflects cultural trends, anxieties, and semi-conscious ideas. Fiction is not separate from them. When a culture feels stress and is in a period of transition, so are individuals. Peoples' dream imagery can reflect not only their personal problems but also those of their culture, often in a veiled manner. Commercially successful fiction, and its associated imagery, can become part of the larger culture. They may be adopted as icons, as vehicles for expression of a variety of ideas.

The essence of fiction raises important theoretical issues, supernatural horror especially so. How is it that the untrue can scare us? Noel Carroll, a philosopher at the University of Wisconsin, presents a useful analysis in his book *The Philosophy of Horror* (1990). Carroll began by asking why we become scared when watching a horror movie or reading a horror novel. Why should fiction cause such a reaction when we know perfectly well that it is not real? This seems like a rather inconsequential question, but his exploration is enlightening.

A number of rationales have been offered for this seeming paradox, and Carroll addressed several of them. A commonly invoked explanatory phrase is "the willing suspension of disbelief."[30] Carroll laid out a devastating attack against this notion. He commented that the idea of "will" is specified, but few people, if any, can remember any such act of will when they sit down to watch a movie or read a novel. Suggesting that it is an "unconscious will" at work simply avoids the problem. Further, when we read a horror story, we know that it is fiction; we do not willingly decide to believe it to be real.

Some have argued that we only pretend to be scared, but this too is not the case. As Carroll pointed out, many in an audience don't have to pretend. Speaking of himself regarding *The Exorcist*, Carroll stated "But I, at least, recall being genuinely horrified by the film."[31] The proposed explanation thus fails. (Carroll's choice of *The Exorcist* is not the most compelling, because in the minds of many people, the line between fact and fiction is especially blurred in this case. Being a respectable academic, Carroll did not consider the reality basis of *The Exorcist*.)

Carroll finally suggests that "thought contents, as well as beliefs, can produce emotional states,"[32] and he is right. Images and ideas are not separate from emotion. Even pondering some of them is enough to evoke fear or anxiety. We cannot easily detach our cognitions from our emotions.

The innate ambiguity between emotions and thoughts is a problem of blurred boundaries, and several techniques help separate the fictional from the real and so assure our peace of mind. The context and setting in which a story is told provide a structure to frame it. When we go to a movie theatre or read a work of fiction, we set aside a time and place for the fictional encounter. We are informed by the book cover, word of mouth, or clear implication, that the story is unreal. The labels are explicit. When such markers and context are insufficient, problems can erupt. For instance, Orson Welles' 1938 radio broadcast of the *War of the Worlds* caused a panic even though it was announced several times that it was only a story.

Popular fiction can sometimes promote belief in the paranormal, and this has been of grave concern to CSICOP. In the mid-1990s the TV series the *X-Files* became extremely popular; it included psychics, UFOs, and sinister government conspiracies. CSICOP's magazine, *Skeptical Inquirer*, criticized the program for promoting erroneous beliefs, and the Committee capitalized on the situation by sending out a fundraising letter denouncing the show.[33]

Their concerns seem largely misplaced. The first half of the 1990s saw a rising membership in UFO organizations (which indicated a growing level of relatively committed belief), but the second half saw a marked decline. The immense popularity of the *X-Files* did not translate into more serious, long-term belief in UFO conspiracies. On the other hand, CSICOP's concerns are not entirely off the mark. During periods of liminality in a culture, fiction can work to blur boundaries.

Typically though, horror and supernatural fiction reinforce the separation of imagination and reality. Audiences can witness the events, and then in a somewhat detached manner come to recognize that they have not seen anything quite like what was portrayed. They can discuss matters with others and receive reassurances.

Pretense

Pretending overtly mixes imagination and reality; it blurs that binary opposition. Children's games, theater, deception, and fantasy role playing all involve pretense. Unlike fictional books, pretending involves more than text—the physical world is engaged. It is a more active blurring, and the theoretical work on pretending provides added insight into the imagination-reality binary opposition.

Children pretend. A child may imagine that a stick is a doll, or a doll a baby. Children often simulate activities while imagining they are doing them. But pretending is not limited to humans; it has been reported occasionally among rhesus monkeys and chimpanzees. For instance, one monkey was seen mimicking her mother by carrying a coconut shell as though it were a baby. Such examples are rare among those raised with conspecifics but more common by those raised with humans.[34]

Pretending and deception (like the trickster) are found in all cultures, and we must suspect, if not a direct biological basis, at least some foreshadowing of them in our early evolution. Deception, of course, appears widely; even plants and simple animals use it, e.g., camouflage and mimicry. But conscious deceit is our interest here.

Robert W. Mitchell, a psychologist at Eastern Kentucky University, has explored deception in animals. His writings help us understand its implications for a host of activities. Mitchell noted that "pretense is extremely rare in chimpanzee play but may be rather common in chimpanzee deception" and went on to suggest that "the existence of pretend play in humans may derive evolutionarily from the usefulness of pretense in deception."[35] He discussed the account of a series of deceptions by two chimps, Belle a female, and Rock, a greedy dominant male.[36] After Rock stole Belle's food, she began to hide it. Rock tried to discover her hiding place by watching her, but Belle began to lead him away from her hiding places. The deceits escalated, and Rock learned to watch her surreptitiously. Each tried to deceive the other, in part by being aware of how they appeared to the other and modifying their appearance accordingly. They behaved in ways calculated to mislead. There was intent behind the pretense.

Mitchell analyzed such cases, and he concluded that in many instances, to effectively use pretense for intentional deceit, one must be able to take the other's point of view, to understand what the other sees and experiences. One must imagine what it is like to be another. He explains: "To pretend to be another, one must recognize that one's own actions, usually experienced kinesthetically, are the same as those of another, experienced visually. Both planning and pretending to be another indicate an agility at imaginal representation which can be used to manipulate others."[37] Mitchell commented that: "Once an organism recognizes that the other has a perspective, the organism may come to recognize that that perspective may include the recognition that the organism itself has a perspective. It is at this point that the organism has a self, in the sense that the organism can think about itself from the other's perspective."[38] This suggests the beginning of reflexive self-awareness, which requires an understanding of the self from an outside vantage point. The use of conscious deception was probably an important factor in the evolutionary development of awareness.[39]

Parenthetically, I should add that research on animal deception, intent, and thinking is extremely controversial, and it generates bitter debates. There are pitfalls in inferring mental activities in animals. Individuals of many species can appear to pretend, but it is often difficult to tell if intent is involved. Play fighting has been a source of speculation for decades. When animals fight playfully, do they consciously know that they are pretending or is their behavior genetically programmed? There are arguments on both sides. Perhaps there is a gradation. Even humans do not always realize when they are pretending. Children may play that a monster is chasing them, but they sometimes become truly frightened when doing so. The distinction between imagination and reality is not always clear for them and sometimes not even for adults. Despite the uncertainties and controversies, there is much to learn from the research with animals. Even the disputes and ambiguities might provide clues.

Summary

This chapter has discussed diverse views on the imagination—from primate behavior to religion to fiction. Perhaps some readers will find little cohesion in the mixture. But there has been one central concern—the blurring of imagination and reality, of representation and object, of signifier and signified, and conversely, how each aspect within a pair of opposites is made distinct.

The betwixt and between area is the trickster's realm. This domain is inherently nebulous, ambiguous, and somewhat chaotic. Those who fail to recognize this essential characteristic are doomed to misunderstand the fundamental issues.

Paranormal experiences often involve the imagination; they are also frequently associated with deception. The paranormal and deception are two constituents of the trickster constellation, and this suggests that the imagination shares some of its properties. There is another component of the trickster constellation—sexuality. I have not addressed the sexual imagination, but it is a powerful force. So here we have the trickster elements of deception, sex, and psi, which are all closely associated with the imagination.

There are deep evolutionary connections among mental representation, imagination, awareness, simulation, pretending, and deceit. These cannot be fully explained by the evolution of primate behavior, but that body of work should not be overlooked when contemplating the matters.

Although the imagination has a marginal status, it is too powerful to be ignored. Massive industries are devoted to fiction, and they serve to stimulate, but also to satisfy, the imagination. Horror fiction and other genres incorporating paranormal themes are exceedingly popular. They frighten us, but ultimately we know them to be untrue.

Their explicit fictionality serves to reinforce the boundary between imagination and reality.

All this has implications for understanding psychic phenomena. Psi blurs the distinction between imagination and reality; the same blurring is found with pretense, the playful, and deception. In most situations, society needs clear distinctions. Pretense and the playful have their place, but they must be limited. So too must psi.

CHAPTER 25

Paranoia

> The coyote is the most aware creature there is . . .
> because he is completely paranoid.
> Charles Manson, circa 1969[1]

Paranoia and the paranormal cluster together. Examples include fear of being watched by ESP, witchcraft accusations, ideas that occult societies control the world, and conspiracy theories of government cover-ups of UFOs.

Paranoia has several definitions. Webster's dictionary gives two: "1: a psychosis characterized by systematized delusions of persecution or grandeur usu. without hallucinations 2 : a tendency on the part of an individual or group toward excessive or irrational suspiciousness and distrustfulness of others."[2] I will typically use the term in the second, more general, sense. There are many degrees of paranoia, and conspiracy theories are collective versions of it.

Paranoia's association with pathology gives it a strongly negative connotation, and many people think of it only in that way. Even when the more general definition is used, like the term "delusion," it evokes ideas of mental illness. With all the unfavorable associations, proponents of the paranormal have little incentive to mention the topic. Yet paranoia needs to be studied because it helps explain fear of the paranormal and opposition to psychic research.

Projection and Self-Awareness

The projection hypothesis describes many instances of paranoia. It suggests that one "projects" one's hostilities onto an outside entity. For instance, toddlers' nightmares of monsters can be interpreted as projections of his (or her) hostilities toward the parents.[3] The monsters reflect the toddler's thoughts, and they serve a beneficial function. After the nightmare, the child recognizes (at least partly) that he (or she) needs the parents' protection, and if he killed them, he would be left vulnerable to the actual dangers of the world. The toddler learns his place in the social order, the need for cooperation, etc. This is a natural and necessary development.

Projection has many implications for topics in this book, and it can be formulated more generally in terms of boundaries and binary oppositions. Toddlers' projections indicate a confusion between self and other, between dream and reality, and between internal and external.

The development of self-awareness can provoke fear. Barbara Babcock noted the pattern in her seminal article on the trickster. In reviewing Paul Radin's work she commented that: "Episode 3 also provides the first indication of self-awareness in the statement, 'Trickster got frightened', for, as Radin points out, 'being frightened in Winnebago symbolism is generally indicative of an awakening consciousness and sense of reality, indeed, the beginning of a conscience'."[4]

French psychoanalyst Jacques Lacan made a similar point, though in his typically obscure fashion. Morris Berman succinctly summarized a few of the ideas, noting that: "Lacan has argued that the ego is a paranoid construct, founded on the logic of opposition and identity of self and other. He adds that all such logic, which is peculiar to the West, requires boundaries, whereas the truth is that perception, being analogue in nature, has no intrinsic boundaries."[5] Briefly, Lacan indicates that the emergence of ego (i.e., the development of self as a separate entity) entails some paranoia. Lacan writes: "we call ego that nucleus given to consciousness, but opaque to reflexion," and he goes on to say that "the analytic maieutic adopts a roundabout approach that amounts in fact to inducing in the subject a controlled paranoia."[6] Lacan relates paranoia to reflection, mirroring, and development of self-awareness.

Examples

To explain the issues, I will present a variety of paranoiac conditions and situations. This will be something of a hodgepodge collection, but diverse concrete examples are useful when pondering general principles. I hope that the intentionally jarring juxtapositions of cases and theories will force readers to recognize the abstract commonalities.

Ernest Hartmann explained that some paranoia can be understood in terms of mental boundaries. He reported that his thin-boundary measure correlated with high scores on the paranoia scale of the MMPI, commenting that the scale "is often considered a measure of sensitivity, especially interpersonal sensitivity, when tested in nonclinical populations."[7] Hartmann did not give much more discussion to the matter, perhaps wishing to avoid too closely associating thin boundaries with pathology.

Bigfoot can be partly understood in terms of projection and paranoia. Anthropologist Henry Sharp, in his book *The Transformation of Bigfoot* (1988), tells of a small Chipewyan society in which tensions between two brothers threatened the group's existence. A hunt for Bigfoot brought them together in a common purpose even though neither had a firm belief in the creature. The hostility within the group was projected outward onto a common enemy, and that strengthened the social bonds. Each brother realized that he needed the other as an ally. The fear of Bigfoot was therapeutic and adaptive. This instance, like others, shows that estrangement can beget fear and the recognition of danger.

In many primitive cultures, illness, death, and bad luck are sometimes ascribed to a witch, who may have some unresolved problem with the victim. The cause of misfortune is attributed to an outside source, again illustrating the concept of projection. The witch may not even be aware of being a witch, but can be accused anyway. In our culture, such suspicions are seen as irrational and paranoid because it is believed that one cannot harm another by thoughts alone. (Anthropological definitions of witchcraft vary. A witch typically has an innate ability to cause harm and may do so unintentionally. The term sorcerer generally designates a person who deliberately uses magical practices for negative ends.)

A witchcraft accusation made against a member of one's own society causes severe tensions. If it is not resolved, some people may leave the group to escape the hostility. Thus paranoia serves a destabilizing, anti-structural function. British anthropologist Mary Douglas suggested that witchcraft is "an aggravator of all hostilities and fears" and that it can also be "a brutal midwife delivering new forms to society."[8] Witchcraft and sorcery can fracture groups, thereby stimulating the formation of new ones. With small tribal societies, this promotes diversity, which can have survival value for the species overall. This atavistic function of the paranormal is not accommodated the same way in our society.

The UFO field is characterized by rampant conspiracy theorizing and paranoia, and examples were presented in earlier chapters. Martin Kottmeyer attempted to explain the connection theoretically in his paper "Ufology Considered as an Evolving System of Paranoia" (1989).[9] Carl Jung raised the issue of projection in his book *Flying Saucers: A Modern Myth of Things Seen in the Skies* (1958), suggesting that UFOs could be explained, in part, by that concept.[10]

Some cultural conditions are fertile for paranoia. Historian Curtis Peebles in his *Watch the Skies!* (1994) noted that UFO-related conspiracy theories flourished in times of growing distrust of government. Those are anti-structural periods, and during such times even highly respectable people are freer to voice suspicions of the establishment.

Intelligence agencies are an excellent source of case material for studying paranoia, as they encounter it in extreme form. They are required to be suspicious—that is their job. Those agencies are inherently deceptive, and they are also prime targets of enemies' deceit. They must be continually alert for attempts at infiltration.

James Jesus Angleton was chief of the counterintelligence staff of the CIA. He is mentioned in many books on the agency, and authors either praise him for his penetrating insights or damn him for his destructive paranoia. Author Edward Jay Epstein spent time with him and described some labyrinthine deceits in *Deception: The Invisible War Between the KGB and the CIA* (1989). Epstein explained that Angleton "conceived of deception as the 'mirror image of intelligence.'"[11] Information may be genuine or intentionally misleading, or even both (good information being provided to build confidence in a source). A defector may be real or surreptitiously working for the enemy, or he may genuinely defect but have been fed misleading information by his original employer. Epstein notes that "Angleton found in the CIA that a 'single mind-set' could not deal with this contingent reality."[12] All possibilities must be evaluated, but those who recruit defectors have an interest in believing them to be genuine (personal bonds are established, and promotions are linked to success in recruiting). It is difficult to maintain the necessary critical balance in face of the ambiguity. (Fundamentally, this is a problem in interpretation. As was explained in the chapter on literary theory, interpretation is the realm of the trickster.) In order to address the problem, a formal division was made between intelligence and counterintelligence.

This set up an internal adversarial relationship, but even though it was institutionalized, and therefore somewhat controlled, it created tremendous tensions. The case of Soviet defector Yuri Nosenko was particularly wrenching. People within the CIA could not agree whether he was a true defector, and the controversy continued for years. It nearly paralyzed major sections of the Agency and ruined a number of careers. Former CIA director Richard Helms described the affair as an incubus.[13]

Intelligence agencies' inherent paranoia and deception highlight issues of boundaries and sense of self. If a spy infiltrates an agency and gains a high position (which Angleton long suspected of the CIA, not unreasonably, since it happened to the British), the question arises as to the true loyalty, and thus identity, of the agency. With such an infiltration, the enemy "participates" in the "mind" of the state. However, even if an agency has not been so infiltrated, its suspicion about itself can have severe repercussions. The distinction between self and enemy can be ambiguous to the agency's "self."

Spying, paranoia, and deception cluster together. I will remind the reader that in the U.S., the only government agencies, in fact the only bureaucracies of any size, that substantially supported parapsychological research, were the intelligence services. The trickster constellated here.

Anti-structure and Paranoia

Concepts of anti-structure and the trickster help explain paranoiac conditions that might otherwise seem unrelated.

Marginals, inferiors, and others who live between categories or near boundaries often have an above-average susceptibility to paranoid ideas. By necessity they must be especially sensitive to threats to their well-being. They understand that elites are unlikely to be attentive to their needs and often conceal information from them. Many examples can be cited.

Billionaire Ross Perot ran as a third-party candidate in the 1992 U.S. presidential election. He was outside the long-established Democrat-Republican two-party structure. Perot believed that conspiracies targeted him and included wiretaps and threats against his daughter's wedding. The establishment media ridiculed him, and *Time* magazine even titled one of its articles "Perot-noia."[14] Other anti-structural characteristics clustered around Perot, and perhaps not surprisingly, a disproportionate share of his supporters believed in the paranormal. (This is not unique. New Age beliefs were also linked with anti-establishment political views in the December 1993 elections in Russia.)[15]

Many African Americans are in marginal positions, and some of them suspect that the AIDS virus was developed to target their race. As far as I can tell, this suspicion has little to support it directly, but AIDS has had a devastating effect in Africa. Given the prejudice African Americans have endured, distrust is understandable and often completely justified.

In the 1950s, owners of small businesses (people not part of large bureaucratic organizations) were disproportionately represented among supporters of Joseph McCarthy, who claimed that a communist conspiracy had infiltrated the government.[16]

Most of the people in the above examples are generally not regarded as socially marginal, but they are in positions outside the establishment, and that makes them vigilant to threats.

People who have safe, secure jobs in corporations or tenured positions in academe are prone to discount conspiracy theories as excuses used by marginal or ineffectual groups for their unfortunate plight. Elite news media frequently speak disparagingly of conspiratorial beliefs, and the medical and psychological establishments do their part by denigrating the fears as infantile, narcissistic, delusional, etc. Paranoia and conspiracy theories undermine trust and destabilize social relations; thus establishment authorities have good reason to marginalize those who espouse the ideas.

Establishments too can be vulnerable to paranoia, especially when their security is threatened. They may become fearful of those not clearly part of themselves, especially those who live at the boundaries and whose status is ambiguous. In the European witchcraft persecutions, many poor, elderly women were put to death because they were feared for using magic to do evil. However, those women were actually in much greater danger from the hands of the authorities—a clear instance of projection by people in the establishment. Despite the establishments' overwhelming physical superiority, they still feared magic.

Parapsychology

Little parapsychological literature addresses the connection between psi and paranoia. In fact the word paranoia is not even listed in any of the indexes of the eight-volume series *Advances in Parapsychological Research*. There is, however, discussion about the fear of psi, and that raises at least some of the pertinent issues.

Psychiatrist Jan Ehrenwald was one of the few parapsychologists to comment explicitly on paranoia.[17] More than half a century ago he noted that "the projection hypothesis of paranoic delusions, advanced by the psychoanalysts is nothing else than the reverse of the telepathy hypothesis, its photographic negative, as it were."[18] This suggests an extremely close relationship between the two, and one that is unpleasant to think about.

Ehrenwald went on to speak of personality disintegration in schizophrenia after a paranoiac phase, saying: "At this stage the boundaries of the self are abolished, 'the distinction between the ego and the environment suspended' . . . the patient may himself complain that he is unable 'to tell himself from the outer world' . . . or, from 'things of the outer world' . . . Seen from the angle of the telepathy hypothesis this state marks the end of the patient's struggle to maintain his personality against the impact of hetero-psychic influences of both sadistic-aggressive and trivial kind."[19] This raises the disturbing issue of personality disintegration, and the possibility that telepathy might contribute to it. This is an unsettling thought, and Ehrenwald came in for criticism. Some pointed out that ESP tests with psychotics did not produce substantially higher scores than with normal people. That gives some reassurances, but with the limited research, experimenter effects, and other possible influences in ESP tests, I am not so confident that psi is not a factor in mental illness.

Therapist Helen Palmer discussed paranoia and psi in a 1992 paper that emphasized cases with justifiable fears rather than pathology.[20] She offered herself as an example. Palmer helped organize Vietnam War protests, and she relied upon her psychic impressions to detect informants planted by the government. She had precognitive experiences warning her of harm to colleagues. Her anti-war activism put her at odds with the established power structure, i.e., into an antistructural position.

Other than the writings of Ehrenwald and Palmer, parapsychologists have made little comment on paranoia, but this is understandable. Drawing attention to the association could further marginalize parapsychology. Nevertheless, the problem needs study. I have witnessed a number of instances of apparently strong paranormal phenomena, after which paranoid fears soon emerged in the participants. Many worried about being followed, of phones being tapped, or "accidents" just seeming to happen. The prevalence of paranoiac beliefs in groups intentionally applying psychic abilities warrants contemplation.

Fear of Psi

Several parapsychologists have discussed the fear of psi, and the topic is sufficiently related to paranoia to merit comment. Though the literature is limited, it spans over half a century. The commentators have included Jule Eisenbud, Harvey Irwin, Lawrence LeShan, Charles Tart, and John Wren-Lewis.[21]

Most adopted psychodynamic and psychoanalytic approaches, which are particularly concerned with events and thought processes of early childhood. Psychoanalysts suggest that, at some point, infants believe that their thoughts can influence the world. This has been dubbed magical thinking. During that stage, a child may worry that her (or his) negative thoughts have destructive power, and that can be frightening, especially when anger cannot always be controlled. A child can feel guilty if she suspects that her thoughts hurt others. Eventually children learn that their thoughts do not affect things directly (at least most of the time), and that realization is a healthy progression.

But psi actually exists. The child's fears are not entirely based in fantasy. As such there must be psychological mechanisms to avoid the unpleasant implications. Charles Tart, a psychologist at the University of California at Davis, presented two related theories about unconscious resistance to psi: social masking theory and primal conflict repression theory.

Social masking theory says that for smooth social interaction, we must veil our hostilities and other negative feelings toward others. Likewise, we must block our own recognition of others' negative feelings toward us. If psi operated strongly, and we were continuously aware of others' hostile emotions, the social balance would be upset.

Primal conflict repression theory is closely related. Tart suggests that psychic bonds between mothers and young children are especially strong, but the emotions between them are not always positive. Sometimes mothers become angry, even furious, at their children. But to be good mothers, they try to maintain composure and outward calm. A child may sense the anger telepathically, while his (or her) ordinary senses tell him that his mother is unruffled. Because the child wants and needs to please his mother, it is best for him to ignore the anger he sensed psychically.[22] The child is thereby subtly encouraged to ignore or repress telepathic information.[23]

There are good reasons for repressing psychic awareness. Psi can foment distrust that can destroy social relationships. In fact, some instances of paranoia may be essentially failures of repression. Many social processes work to marginalize the paranormal, and they also reinforce the repression of psychic awareness. This undoubtedly has benefits.

Summary

This chapter has been rather short and terse. Like others, it brings together some seemingly unrelated matters, but they can be linked. Briefly, paranoia is a natural part of the human condition. It is not necessarily, or even primarily, pathological. It arises in processes of separation, and it is seen with both individuals and collectives. In separation processes, fears naturally arise. Separation is required for development of the individual, for differentiated roles in society, and for formation of new groups. Becoming separate, distinguishing ourselves from others, is facilitated with liminal conditions.

Paranoia is a rich area for fundamental concepts. The blurring of binary oppositions of self-other, internal-external, fantasy-reality are all obvious examples. Thus paranoia is the province of the trickster.

Paranoia is frequently associated with occult practices, and it is found with a variety of anti-structural circumstances. Paranoia often emerges with strong psychic functioning, and it can fragment groups successfully producing psi. These facts pose special problems for psychic research. Parapsychologists' theories and practice must take them into account.

CHAPTER 26

Conclusions

Supernatural events have been reported for millennia (e.g., miracles of Moses, Jesus, Mohammed); they have played central roles in history's most important cultural transformations. They are frequently portrayed in the world's greatest art and literature. The majority of the U.S. adult population believes in paranormal phenomena. Yet debates still rage about their very existence. These facts indicate a problematic situation of a very deep order. Parapsychology is engaged in something drastically different than "normal science," and those who pretend otherwise are gravely deluded.

In times past, the supernatural was seen as all-encompassing, providing a ground for existence, but it was also recognized as irrational and dangerous. In academe now, those ideas are viewed as quaint, as artifacts of the emotions, as nonsensical, or due to neurotic or infantile thought. Earlier peoples' understanding of the world was entirely different than that of elite culture today. It makes sense to reevaluate those older, forgotten, marginalized, and discredited ideas. They can expose the limits of "rationality."

This book focused on the paranormal, and by now the reader probably realizes that there is no way to succinctly survey the contents. This summary excludes much. I will simply recap a few key points, review some examples, and try to bring a little coherence to the diversity of topics. Major issues include marginality, binary oppositions, rationality, and rationalization. The trickster is pertinent to them all.

I began this book with the goal of explaining why deception is so frequently encountered with the paranormal, e.g., fraudulent mediumship, UFO hoaxes, the confusion of magic tricks with psychic phenomena. This led me to consider the trickster figure, and as I became familiar with him, I found that he shared a number of other characteristics of the paranormal. As I learned more about his qualities, I began to recall similar ones in the paranormal, properties that others had discounted as happenstance or inconsequential. For instance, paradox, ambiguity, and marginality typify them both. I also discovered that the trickster was an important figure in many "primitive" religions, but curiously, he is now rather neglected.

The Paranormal Today

The paranormal is perplexing. Its place in society, as well as laboratory research, demonstrate the peculiarities. Any comprehensive theory must accommodate, integrate, and explain the oddities. I will review several.

Today few groups make concerted attempts to elicit psi. Some that do include spiritualists trying to contact the dead, practitioners of modern-day witchcraft, and parapsychologists in laboratories. These are usually small efforts; generally, fewer than a dozen persons are involved in any given undertaking.

Spiritualist and witchcraft groups are typically short-lived and are rarely successful at establishing stable institutions with grounds, buildings, and paid staff. There are umbrella associations, but those are loose networks and confederations, which exert no control and have no ecclesiastical power over local groups.

When such organizations do institutionalize, such as spiritualist camps, they develop reputations for fraudulent mediumship and become even more marginal. The telephone psychic hot lines constitute another example. They have very unsavory reputations for preying on poor, vulnerable people in times of need.

Several organizations that began with an emphasis on paranormal phenomena did institutionalize, and were able to maintain relatively untarnished reputations. However, in their evolution they greatly reduced or eliminated attempts to elicit phenomena.

The anti-institutional nature of psi is seen in other ways. Psychics, spiritualist mediums, psychic detectives, and healers virtually never serve in those capacities as employees in industry, government, or academe. Typically they operate as independent agents. Many practitioners do have ordinary jobs in large organizations, but they carry on their psychic activities outside that employment.

Parapsychology shows a similar pattern. It has had only slight success at institutionalizing. It has nary one secure, permanent research laboratory in government, industry, or academe that is assured of continuing after the founder leaves. There are no university departments of parapsychology. A few college professors offer courses and conduct research, but that effort has never become part of the established, ongoing curriculum in the universities. J. B. Rhine's lab at Duke University lasted 30 years, far longer than any other, but it was outside the usual departmental structure. When he retired, the Duke research stopped. Rhine exemplifies the general pattern, and there is no counterexample.

The term anti-structure subsumes these anti-institutional qualities. In some formulations, marginality is a type of anti-structure. It is a salient characteristic of paranormal groups, which in many eyes are seen as strange or even kooky, something avoided by reputable, rational scientists.

Academic psychologists and sociologists do study belief in the paranormal, and they conduct surveys of paranormal experiences. But as a practical matter, they are forbidden (via subtle pressures) to attempt to induce the phenomena and engage them directly (as is done in normal scientific research). It is acceptable to discuss the supernatural in universities, but in courses on literature and religion. The events are presented as long ago and far away, or as explicitly fictional. All this keeps them distant, and it is easy to dismiss them as inconsequential, metaphorical, or delusional.

Low status is vested upon those who conduct parapsychological research. Conversely, organized opposition to investigation (i.e., CSICOP) has attracted the endorsements of many elite scientists, including Nobel laureates—people with little knowledge of the paranormal.

The paranormal does not lack large institutions to promote it. In fact, enormous industries *are* devoted to it—but portraying it as fiction. Those businesses gross hundreds of millions of dollars annually (at least).

In short, marginality and anti-structure (particularly the anti-institutional aspect) are associated with attempts to explicitly engage psi. This has been the case for thousands of years. Michael Winkelman confirmed the pattern in his cross-cultural study of magico-religious practitioners.

Properties of Psi

Laboratory research shows that it is extremely difficult to specify the limits of psi. There are limits, (after all, psi manifests rather rarely) but specifying them is problematical. Both parapsychologists and their critics acknowledge this. ESP scores show little or no decline as distance between agent and percipient is increased, and research demonstrates that telepathy does not act like some kind of mental radio.[1] The definition of psi also poses problems. It is defined by what it is not. Further, one cannot substantively differentiate telepathy, clairvoyance, precognition, and micro-PK. The terms are only labels. They do not designate mechanisms.

Precognition and retroactive PK suggest that an effect can precede its cause. This poses additional problems in specifying limits of psi. Further, psi seems to be unrestricted by the complexity of a task. It is goal-oriented, and the number of intermediate, mechanical-like steps needed to accomplish a job appears irrelevant.

In laboratory studies, it is often difficult to ascertain who caused any psi effect. The experimenters, putative subjects, and even data checkers may contribute some psi influence. Because psi appears to act backward in time, future readers of a journal article might also conceivably contribute (according to some plausible theories). The effects from these future observers are inherently uncontrollable. These are deeply problematical issues, and they are almost sufficient to discredit the field.

Psi accompanies processes of change, transition, flux, and disorder. William Braud's work on lability and inertia showed that physical processes that readily fluctuate are more susceptible to psychic influence than are more stable systems. The pattern extends to individuals and to higher levels of organization including groups and entire cultures. Times of personal change are associated with psychic functioning. Poltergeist phenomena often focus around someone in puberty. Apparitional experiences may occur near the time of a death. Altered (destructured) states of consciousness, labile physical systems, and novelty (as opposed to routine), all facilitate psi. Groups that engage the phenomena are typically unstable and rarely institutionalize successfully. During cultural transitions paranormal phenomena gain greater public prominence. Anthropologists have documented hundreds of instances. The pattern is seen in our own culture. For example, the late 1960s and early 1970s in the U.S. were times of accelerated social change, and they had a surge of popular interest in the paranormal. The dissolution of the U.S.S.R. saw a similar burst.

Above I have outlined two encompassing themes—marginality and transition. The examples range from social, to psychological, to physical processes. Those categories are too scattered for most scientific theories to give much purchase. Structuralist ideas, however, are broad enough to accommodate the diversity. The concept of binary opposition is especially useful.

Binary Oppositions and Boundaries

Binary oppositions and boundaries are two of the key themes of this book, and they are intimately related. Binary oppositions require distinctions, barriers to separate one element from the other. Thus the notion of binary opposition inherently includes the concept of boundary.

Discussions of binary opposition are found in analyses of primitive classification systems, in mystical theology, in Jung's work on medieval alchemy, in structuralist and post-structuralist theories of anthropology and literary criticism, and in the foundations of logic. They are also commonly encountered in analyses of the trickster.

Major binary oppositions found in all cultures include: life-death, heaven-earth, God-human, male-female. Considerable effort is made to demarcate the boundaries between the elements, and that task is a collective endeavor. Funerals mark the division between life and death. Most academics believe the distinction to be clear, but phenomena exist that blur it. Spirit mediumship, reincarnation, near-death experiences, and ghosts all suggest that the boundary is not sharp. Heaven and earth are usually quite separate. Heaven is up, and beyond the reach of ordinary living humans. The expanse between the heavens and the earth is traveled by angels and extraterrestrial aliens—supernatural or paranormal creatures. Trickster deities are also of that realm. The God-human distinction is emphasized in exoteric religious doctrines. Priests mediate between gods and humans, and they are ritually protected when doing so. On the other hand, esoteric religion challenges the dichotomy. Mystics attempt to become one with the divine, and paranormal phenomena frequently accompany mystical practice. The male-female opposition is demarcated by dress and differing roles. Persons who switch, and adopt those of the opposite sex, are often associated with supernatural power (e.g., the berdache of American Indians).

Today scientists and philosophers give little attention to the above oppositions. They assume them to be clear, distinct and unproblematical. Other oppositions now absorb their efforts. These include self-other, mind-matter, subjective-objective. Psi subverts these distinctions. Telepathy and psychic healing suggest that the dividing line between self and other is not sharp. Psychokinesis challenges the mind-matter demarcation. Psi has the properties of the betwixt and between, of transitional spaces, of the liminal and interstitial.

Binary oppositions involve *relationships*. One thing is related to another. In a typical binary opposition, one element has greater power, prestige, or privilege than the other. Status differences are involved. Status is one of the central issues in this book. Social roles and positions designate statuses. They establish the structure of society; they tell us who we are as individuals; they help us differentiate ourselves from others. The human condition decrees that there is always some amount of "distance" between people. When examining any pair of persons, groups, or nations, one member typically has a higher status, and the other, a lower.

Liminality involves an equalizing (or even an inversion) of status, a blurring of distinctions. One of the trickster's duties is to lower or invert status and to induce marginality. Margins refer to positions at or near boundaries.

Boundaries are established in countless ways—in our minds, in marking territory, in establishing personal relationships, in building homes with walls, in denoting time, in festivals celebrating change of seasons, in making rules for morality, in military insignia designating rank, in giving names, in religious prohibitions that demarcate one religion from another, in making laws that specify what is and is not permissible, in dress and adornment that indicate social status. These all involve bringing order and structure to the world. They entail collective effort and collective representations. It is through them that we communicate and organize life.

In broad terms, structuralism addressed the order, stability, and logic of how society is maintained. Classification was a major issue. Liminality concerns the opposite, and it is best expressed with Turner's term anti-structure. Its theories deal with change, transition, instability, transformation, and revitalization.

The Trickster

The trickster is a personification of many of the ideas above. He is a collection of abstract properties that tend to occur together. He has no fixed shape, form, or image. Some of his primary characteristics include disruption, deception, lowered sexual inhibitions, psi phenomena, and marginality. I must admit that I sometimes still find it difficult to think about how all these logically relate to each other. Personification provides a way of organizing this melange that otherwise seems incoherent.

The trickster is found worldwide. Superficially, his tales seem little more than entertaining stories for children, but they encode important truths. The trickster is central to many religious beliefs, and some of the tales are sacred. In fact, a number of cultures permit only a few persons to tell the stories and restrict when they can be told, because they have a power of their own.

The trickster has innumerable internal contradictions, and those are what have made him so difficult for scholars. He seems irrational, and he is. The usual scientific concepts are inadequate to fully explain him. He has many meanings and cannot be reduced to a single interpretation. He resists being placed in any single category. That's why this book covered such a range of topics—from ritual clowns who eat excrement, to experiments with random number generators, to literary criticism. This diversity is the reason so few people have any comprehension of the scope of his relevance, including his pertinence to psi.

Earlier cultures celebrated the trickster, but now he is only a shallow remnant of his previous glory. He is considered merely amusing, entertaining, but of little serious importance. This reflects a deep but subtle change in culture and civilization.

Western Rationality and Rationalization

The dominant cultural myth now is that the world can be entirely grasped by rational means; any exceptions are considered trivial. This goes almost completely unquestioned, particularly within science. The myth generates an aversion to the irrational and supernatural. Those are not only neglected, but society discourages serious consideration of them. Our culture has a variety of mechanisms that lead one to think that the supernatural doesn't really exist and to equate it with the fictional.

How did this come about? After all, the supernatural was recognized for millennia. Were all our ancestors deluded, superstitious, dim-witted, and irrational human beings? A broad view of history, theology, and philosophy is needed to recognize what happened.

Sociologist Max Weber provided a grand vista with his theories of rationalization and disenchantment. They have enormous implications. The terms rationalization and disenchantment hint at the tension between rationalism and mysticism. Weber explicitly stated that rationalization requires the elimination of magic from the world. He understood that the process slowly progressed through time. During some periods, it stagnated and even reversed, but the overall trend is undeniable. (In reality, it is not the elimination of magic that is accomplished, but rather the elimination of cultural elites' conscious awareness of magic.)

Hunter-gatherer societies had shamans who became entranced, commanded spirits, and directly engaged supernatural forces. As societies became more complex, the shaman gave way to the priest. Priests propitiated gods and did not use altered states of consciousness for magical ends. The rise of the priest, in conjunction with the growing societal complexity, was accompanied by a loss of status for those who continued to practice magic, particularly magic that made use of altered states of consciousness. This trend extended over thousands of years. The emergence of Protestant Christianity was a step in rationalization; it moved away from mysticism, monastic orders, and rejected transubstantiation. The trend accelerated in the twentieth century, particularly in Western elite culture, and notably with the growth of the universities.

Weber's theory was intimately tied to issues of authority and power. He identified three types of authority: bureaucratic, traditional, and charismatic. The primordial source of authority accrued from charisma, and pure charisma involved the working of miracles, a point Weber made explicit. It is altogether astounding that academics now completely ignore this. They seem puzzled by charisma, and they avoid talk of miracles. This is a consequent of the rationalization process; for academe is both a product of, and an agent for, the disenchantment of the world.

Aristotelian logic is central to Western rational thought. It requires clear demarcation. This logic posits the law of the excluded middle; something is either A or not-A; no betwixt and between is allowed. This produces a strong type of binary opposition. Discrete objects and sharp boundaries are compulsory.

Rationalization promotes discreteness and separateness in a huge variety of ways—e.g., in selves and persons, as in rugged individualism, in the binary digits (bits) of modern electronics. Time is divided into hours, minutes, and seconds to allow routinization and scheduling. Another manifestation is the growing regimentation and credentialing in modern life.

Rationalization theory helps explain the paranormal's position in our society today. Bureaucracies and large organizations are major forces for ordering our civilization. We rarely notice just how pervasively they influence us. Bureaucratic authority is far removed from, and almost antithetical to, charisma. Large organizations rarely tolerate attempts to consciously and intentionally utilize psi.

The bureaucratic antagonism to psi is not something planned and organized by those in power. It is not a conscious conspiracy. Those who act in concert with the prejudice are not aware of the factors influencing them. This unconscious antipathy is a pervasive social phenomenon found in numerous cultures; thus it is not to be explained by the psychology of individuals. It demonstrates that social forces have an independent existence and that those forces can operate through individuals without them being aware of it.

All this is nothing new. Psychic phenomena have played crucial roles in religion; they emerge in conjunction with esoteric religious practices, but exoteric religions have prohibitions against dabbling with them. Primitive religions had elaborate rituals, restrictions, and taboos surrounding the supernatural. These existed through recorded history and undoubtedly long before. The reasons for the strictures have been forgotten; today scientists denounce them as silly, superstitious, and irrational.

In actuality, the denunciations serve to enforce the ancient taboos. They are only a variant of earlier religious strictures. Both exoteric religion and establishment science try to hedge off or repress contact with the supernatural and limit conscious awareness of it. There are reasons for that, and by now those reasons should be clearer. Psi both accompanies and stimulates change and disorder. Change carries risk, and we should remember that in biology, most mutations are dysfunctional; relatively few are beneficial. Restrictions, prohibitions, boundaries, and structure confer many advantages; they are fundamental not only to culture but to our very beings.

Some may think that I paint an ominous picture of psychic phenomena. Given all the problems, they might suggest that parapsychology be abandoned, forgotten, that it is useless to pursue investigation of this realm.

That is not my position. The supernatural is irrational, but it is also real. It holds enormous power. We ignore it at our peril. It operates not only on the individual psyche, but at a collective level, influencing entire cultures. The witchcraft persecutions and the demagoguery of charismatic leaders are only two of many dangers.

If we fail to recognize the limits of our "rational" way of thinking, we can become victims of it. Parapsychology demonstrates that our thoughts, including our unconscious thoughts, are not limited to our brains. They move of their own accord and influence the physical world.

NOTES

Epigraphs

[1] Derived from a conversation reported in *Helter Skelter: The True Story of the Manson Murders* by Vincent Bugliosi with Curt Gentry, New York: W. W. Norton & Company, Inc., 1974, p. 238.

[2] King James Version

Chapter 1—Introduction

[1] *Catechism of the Catholic Church*, Liguori, MO: Ligouri Publications, 1994. See p. 513, paragraphs 2115–2117.

Chapter 2—Overview of Tricksters

[1] Ricketts (1987, p. 50) states that Daniel Brinton coined the term trickster in his 1868 book *Myths of the New World*. However, Lewis Hyde (1998, p. 355) reports finding no mention of the word in any of the three editions of that book. Gill and Sullivan (1992, p. 308) state that in 1885 Brinton published an article "The Hero-God of the Algonkins as a Cheat and Liar." They assert that "Brinton cited an entry from Father Albert Lacombe's *Dictionaire de la Langue des Cris* (1878)" saying that "This is probably the first time the term was used to suggest a general category." Unfortunately, Gill and Sullivan do not indicate where Brinton published that article. In the May 1885 issue of *The American Antiquarian* Brinton published a 3-page paper titled "The Chief God of the Algonkins, in His Character as a Cheat and Liar" and did use the word "trickster." He also used the word in his *The Lenâpé and Their Legends; With the Complete Text and Symbols of the Walam Olum, A New Translation, and an Inquiry Into Its Authenticity* (p. 130). The original publication date of that book appears to be 1885. Some reprints state that the book was originally published in 1884, but neither the Library of Congress catalog nor the National Union Catalog lists an 1884 edition.

[2] There are many available references on tricksters, and an extensive bibliography appears in *Mythical Trickster Figures* (1993) edited by William J. Hynes and William G. Doty. Some sources that I have found useful include the following— Wakdjunkaga: (Radin, 1956/1972); Eshu-Elegba: (Pelton, 1980; Wescott, 1962);

Ananse: (Pelton, 1980; Vecsey, 1981); Taugi: (Basso, 1987); Kantjil: (McKean, 1971); Monkey King: (Hyde, 1998); Nanabozho: (Messer, 1982, 1983); Ture: (Evans-Pritchard, 1967); Hermes: (Bolen, 1989; Brown, 1947; Lopez-Pedraza, 1977/1989; Stassinopoulos & Beny, 1983); Loki: (Rooth, 1961); and the Spirit Mercurius: (Jung, 1943/1967).

[3] A variety of conflicting and confusing definitions have been given for archetype. It serves no purpose to review them here. The definition I use is frequently accepted.

[4] Radin 1956/1972, p. xxiv.

[5] Bolen, 1989, p. 166.

[6] Bolen, 1989, p. 170.

[7] Bolen, 1989, p. 169.

[8] Bolen, 1989, p. 169.

[9] Stassinopoulos & Beny, 1983, p. 190.

[10] Bolen, 1989, p. 171.

[11] Brown, 1947, p. 8.

[12] Bolen, 1989, p. 181.

[13] Bolen, 1989, p. 168.

[14] Bolen, 1989, p. 186.

[15] Bolen, 1989, p. 173.

[16] Brown, 1947, p. 11.

[17] Wescott, 1962, p. 345.

[18] Wescott, 1962, p. 345.

[19] Wescott, 1962, p. 342.

[20] Pelton, 1980, p. 163.

[21] Wescott, 1962, p. 348.

[22] Wescott, 1962, p. 343. For more on the significance of hair for sexuality and magic, see Edmund Leach's essay Magical Hair (1958/1967).

[23] Wescott, 1962, p. 337.

[24] Wescott, 1962, p. 340.

[25] For a brief discussion, see pages 1 and 2 of Frank Kermode's *The Genesis of Secrecy* (1979).

[26] Jung, 1943/1967, p. 237.

[27] Jung, 1943/1967, p. 217.

[28] Jung, 1943/1967, p. 232.

[29] Jung, 1943/1967, p. 231.

[30] Jung, 1943/1967, p. 231.

[31] Jung, 1943/1967, p. 237.

[32] Jung, 1943/1967, p. 237.

[33] Jung, 1943/1967, p. 237.

[34] Jung, 1943/1967, p. 237.

[35] Jung, 1943/1967, p. 220.

[36] Jung, 1943/1967, p. 237.

[37] Leach, 1964. The UFO is another example. UFOs are often seen as conveying messages from god-like beings. The most famous poem in ufology is Gray Barker's "UFO is a Bucket of Shit."

[38] Roberts, "Does God Lie?" (1988).

[39] Tricksters of the Bible are not limited to the Old Testament. Medieval scholar Kathleen Ashley analyzed both Christ and Satan as tricksters in a 1982 essay. She commented that "in Christ and Satan, I would argue, is a pair of tricksters who have evolved from one idea of the sacred, a God who paradoxically encompasses both good and evil" (p. 127). The issue of opposites is central, and she explored it at length. Ashley utilized concepts of liminality and structuralism, topics explored in the coming chapters.

[40] For discussions of the Harlequin see McClelland, 1964; Taylor, 1985.

[41] Lucille Charles' article "The Clown's Function" (1945), Laura Makarius' "Ritual Clowns and Symbolical Behavior" (1970), and Rogan Taylor's book *The Death and Resurrection Show* (1985) provide useful reviews of clowns from various cultures.

[42] Babcock, 1982.

[43] Wescott, 1962, p. 343.

[44] Carroll, 1984.

[45] Babcock & Cox, 1994, p. 99.

Chapter 3—Ernest Hartmann's Mental Boundaries

[1] There are no credible accounts of witnesses observing someone being physically abducted by extra-terrestrial aliens. The full causes of abduction experiences are unclear, but external factors likely play important roles. Fantasy is an insufficient explanation.

[2] Haraldsson, Houtkooper, & Hoeltje, (1987).

[3] *Parapsychological Research With Children: An Annotated Bibliography* by Drewes & Drucker (1991). See also Palmer, 1977, p. 148.

[4] See Palmer, 1977, p. 133–134.

[5] See Wickramasekera (1991); Pekala, Kumar, & Cummings (1992).

Chapter 4—Victor Turner's Concept of Anti-Structure

[1] A notable, but little known, exception is the work of Peter Rogerson (1986).

[2] The translator's note claims that the book was first published in 1908, but the French *Catalogue General des Livres Imprimes de la Bibliotheque Nationale* and the U.S. *National Union Catalog* both give the original publication date as 1909.

[3] For biographical information on van Gennep see *Arnold Van Gennep: The Creator of French Ethnography* by Belmont (1974/1979). See also Rodney Needham's Introduction to his translation of van Gennep's *The Semi-Scholars*, London: Routledge & Kegan Paul, 1967. See also "Arnold van Gennep: The Hermit of Bourg-la-Reine" by Zumwalt (1982).

[4] For biographical information on Victor Turner, see his posthumously published books *On the Edge of the Bush* (1985) and *Blazing the Trail* (1992) which were edited by his wife.

[5] Turner, 1969, p. 131.

[6] Van Gennep, 1909/1960, p. 114.

[7] Van Gennep, 1909/1960, p. 114.

[8] Turner, 1969, p. 125.

[9] Turner, 1982, p. 26.

[10] Turner, 1969, p. 95.

[11] Turner, 1982, p. 27.

[12] Turner, 1982, p. 27.

[13] Turner, 1982, p. 28.

[14] See Peters, 1982, 1994.

[15] Both Jungian and Freudian analysts have made use of Turner's ideas. The Jungians have adapted them more extensively; for examples see the anthology *Liminality and Transitional Phenomena* edited by Nathan Schwartz-Salant and Murray Stein (1991). Volney Gay, who has more of a Freudian orientation, made use of Turner's ideas in an article "Ritual and Self-Esteem in Victor Turner and Heinz Kohut" (Gay, 1983a). Gay also addressed the trickster in "Winnicott's Contribution to Religious Studies: The Resurrection of the Culture Hero" (Gay, 1983b). Via his interpreters, Donald W. Winnicott's work may provide some useful insights, though his own writing is some of the most impenetrable I've ever encountered. Winnicott introduced the idea of the "transitional object." Gay called attention to its relevance to the trickster, though he did not discuss liminality in that article.

[16] Turner, 1969, p. 116.

[17] Turner, 1974, p. 274.

[18] Turner, 1969, p. 95.

[19] Turner, 1969, p. 111.

[20] Turner, 1969, p. 128.

[21] Turner, 1974, p. 298.

[22] Turner, 1974, p. 273.

[23] As mentioned earlier, a number of women and minority scholars show an appreciation for Babcock's insights on the trickster. A few other writers are beginning to recognize the connection to anti-structure (e.g., Grottanelli, 1983; Koepping, 1985).

[24] Babcock-Abrahams, 1975a, p. 184.

[25] For some reflections on Koestler, see Arthur Koestler and Parapsychology by Brian Inglis, *Journal of the American Society for Psychical Research*, Vol. 78, 1984, pp. 263–272.

[26] Basso, 1987, pp. 7–8.

[27] Ferdinand Demara was the subject of Robert Crichton's *The Great Impostor* (New York: Random House, 1959). Demara performed surgeries, served as an assistant warden of a prison and as a university dean, among other escapades. He had an attraction to monasteries, which provide a containment structure for liminality. Frank Abagnale, another celebrated impostor, tells in his autobiography *Catch Me If You Can* (Frank W. Agabnale, Jr., with Stan Redding, New York: Grosset & Dunlap, 1980) how he was able to pass as an airline pilot, attorney, and college professor. Both Demara and Abagnale had a remarkable ability to adapt to new situations and readily take on new identities, being shape-shifters, at least in a psychological sense. During their childhoods both of their fathers had suffered a severe financial setback and consequent loss of status. Carlos Castaneda shows a similarity. Psychologist Richard de Mille analyzed Castaneda in his *The Don Juan Papers* (1980) and suggested that Castaneda's father did not achieve the status that one might have expected of him. Perhaps that contributed to a trickster constellation and served as one of the subtle influences that led Carlos to perpetrating his hoax.

[28] Brown, 1947, p. 97.

[29] Peacock (1969).

[30] Turner, 1982, p. 26.

[31] See Needham, 1973.

[32] Turner, 1969, pp. 108–109.

[33] Turner, 1969, pp. 109.

[34] Middleton, 1968/1973, p. 380.

[35] Leach, 1962/1969, p. 11.

[36] Otto, 1917/1975, p. 18.

[37] Degh & Vazsonyi, 1973, p. 28.

[38] Douglas, 1966, p. 8.
[39] Douglas, 1966, p. 94.
[40] Makarius, 1973, p. 663.
[41] Makarius, 1973, p. 663.
[42] See Ballinger, 1989; Carroll, 1986.
[43] E.g., Brown & Tuzin, 1983; Girard 1972/1977; Tierney, 1989.
[44] For accounts of Toelken's experiences with, and views on, the trickster, see Toelken, 1987, 1995a, 1995b, 1996; Toelken & Scott, 1981.
[45] Toelken, 1995a, p. 30; also Toelken, 1996, p. 7.
[46] Turner, 1969, pp. 137–138.
[47] Turner, 1969, p. 128.
[48] See Fraser, 1992; Tatro, 1974; for additional references see Boles, Davis & Tatro, 1983.
[49] Bainbridge, 1989.

Chapter 5—Mysticism, Holy Madness, and Fools for God

[1] Bharati, 1976; Otto, 1926/1987.
[2] Turner, 1969, p. 107.
[3] Turner, 1964/1967, pp. 98–99.
[4] Leontius, the bishop of Neapolis on Cyprus, wrote a biography of him in the middle of the seventh century. A translation of this biography can be found in an appendix to *Symeon the Holy Fool: Leontius's* Life *and the Late Antique City* by Derek Krueger, Berkeley, CA: University of California Press, 1996. For shorter accounts of St. Simeon, see Feuerstein, 1991; Saward, 1980.
[5] Wilson, 1989, p. 68.
[6] *Butler's Lives of the Saints*, 1756–9/1981, Vol. IV, pp. 22–32.
[7] Cousins, 1978.
[8] See Babcock-Abrahams, 1975, p. 175; Radin 1956/1972, p. 7.
[9] Willeford, 1969, p. 7.
[10] Turner, 1982, p. 27.
[11] Eliade, 1951/1964, pp. 96–99.
[12] Dodds, 1951/1971, p. 290. Dodds served as president of the Society for Psychical Research.
[13] For a discussion of some amazing capabilities of birds, see *The Human Nature of Birds* by Theodore Xenophon Barber (1993). Besides his interest in birds, Barber is also an authority on hypnosis, another liminal area.

[14] Huysmans, 1901/1979.

[15] The removal of intestines merits note. Wakdjunkaga, the Winnebago trickster, removed his intestines (Radin, 1956/1972, p. 18). Street magicians in India have performed a similar trick (Siegel, 1991, p. 198). E. E. Evans-Pritchard in *Witchcraft, Oracles and Magic Among the Azande* (1937/1950, p. 40) reports that the Azande believe that a witchcraft substance is found in the small intestine. The prevalence of this motif in these diverse situations suggests a deep though obscure connection. Intestines are crucial in transmuting food to excrement (a binary opposition). Divination by entrails might also be recalled.

[16] Feuerstein, 1991, p. 26.

[17] Schiffman, 1989.

[18] Isherwood, 1965, p. 90.

[19] Feuerstein, 1991, p. 14.

[20] Oetgen, 1976, pp. 191–211.

[21] Turner, 1969, pp. 141–142.

[22] Atwater, 1994.

[23] Haraldsson & Houtkooper, 1991.

Chapter 6—Shamanism and Its Sham

[1] Turner, 1969, pp. 116–117.

[2] For an article that addresses shamanism and liminality in relatively technical and abstract terms, see "Crazy Wisdom: The Shaman as Mediator of Realities" by Mary Schmidt (1987).

[3] For a discussion see Lewis, 1971/1989.

[4] Jung 1956/1972, p. 196.

[5] Campbell, 1959/1987, p. 275.

[6] La Barre, 1970/1972, p. 136.

[7] Graduate student Larry Ellis has a useful discussion in his 1993 article Trickster: Shaman of the Liminal.

[8] Ricketts, 1993, p. 93.

[9] Ricketts, 1993, p. 87.

[10] Ricketts, 1993, p. 88.

[11] Ricketts, 1993, p. 88.

[12] Ricketts, 1966, pp. 345–346.

[13] Ricketts was familiar with Barbara Babcock's work and listed it in an earlier article (Ricketts, 1987), but like many male academics of his generation, he failed to grasp its significance.

[14] Eliade, 1951/1964, p. 255.

[15] Smith, 1968, p. 15.

[16] The most controlled investigation of which I am aware is that of anthropologist Philip Singer. He brought Philippine psychic surgeon Philip Malicdan to a laboratory in Michigan. The goal was to determine whether Malicdan could actually enter a human body and remove tissue without leaving a scar, or if he was using sleight of hand. A number of cameras recorded the events; eminent magician Max Maven was on site to observe, and the "extracted" tissues were medically analyzed. The photography expert, magician, and the medical analysis all supported the conclusion that fraud had been attempted. (See Philip Singer, 1990).

Also of interest are his articles: The Ethnography of the Paranormal by Philip Singer and Kate W. Ankenbrandt, 1980; "Hungry for a Miracle:" Psi, Science, and Faith in Psychic Surgery and Parapsychological Anthropology by Philip Singer and Kate Ankenbrandt, 1983.

Observations made in the Philippines in the field were reported by David Hoy, a magician and mentalist very sympathetic to the paranormal, but he also came to negative conclusions. David Hoy, Psychic Surgery: Hoax or Hope?, *Zetetic Scholar*, No. 8, 1981, pp. 37–46.

Several articles in medical journals reported analyses of blood and tissue from psychic surgeries. They were found to be from animals. Patrick J. Lincoln, Disclosing the Bewitched by Serological Methods, *Medicine, Science and the Law*, Vol. 15, No. 3, 1975, pp. 163–166. P. J. Lincoln & N. J. Wood, Psychic Surgery: A Serological Investigation, *The Lancet*, June 2, 1979, Vol. 1, pp. 1197–1198. 'Psychic Surgery' Can Mean Fiscal Excision with Tumor Retention, *Journal of the American Medical Association*, Vol. 228, No. 3, April 15, 1974, pp. 278–280.

All of the above-cited studies investigated the paranormal aspect, i.e. removal of internal tissue without cutting the skin. Health benefits to patients were not assessed. One of the patients in Singer's study was a medical doctor, who was convinced, despite the evidence of fraud, that that Malicdan had removed adhesions from her two caesarean sections.

[17] Some of the same themes are also discussed in *The Mind Game: Witchdoctors and Psychiatrists* by E. Fuller Torrey. New York: Jason Aronson, 1983 (Originally published 1972).

[18] Andrew Christensen and Neil S. Jacobson, 1994.

[19] Higgins, 1985.

[20] *The Chukchee* by Waldemar Bogoras, New York: G. E. Stechert, 1904–1909. See also Jane M. Murphy "Psychotherapeutic Aspects of Shamanism on St. Lawrence Island, Alaska" in *Magic, Faith, and Healing: Studies in Primitive Psychiatry Today* edited by Ari Kiev, New York: Free Press, 1964, pp. 53–83; and Winnebago Berdache by Nancy Oestreich Lurie (1953).

[21] Kalweit, 1984/1988.

[22] E.g., Lommel, 1967.

[23] See also Kirby, 1974.

Chapter 7—Michael Winkelman on Magico-Religious Practitioners

[1] Michael Winkelman, The Effect of Formal Education on Extrasensory Abilities: The Ozolco Study, *Journal of Parapsychology*, Vol. 45, 1981, pp. 321–336.

[2] Winkelman, 1992, p. 7.

[3] Winkelman, 1992, p. 8.

Chapter 8—Max Weber, Charisma, and the Disenchantment of the World

[1] Ellenberger, 1964/1968.

[2] The date 1913 was of the original manuscript, see Ephraim Fischoff's appendix in Weber's *The Sociology of Religion*, Boston: Beacon Press, 1964, p. 277.

[3] Weber, 1978, p. 241.

[4] Weber, 1978, p. 1115.

[5] Weber, 1978, p. 244.

[6] Weber, 1978, p. 1112.

[7] Weber, 1978, p. 246.

[8] Weber, 1978, p. 244.

[9] Weber, 1978, pp. 1113–1114.

[10] Weber, 1978, p. 1113.

[11] Weber, 1978, p. 242.

[12] Weber, 1978, p. 1114.

[13] Weber, 1978, p. 400.

[14] Turner defined the liminoid as an attenuated version of the liminal. The liminoid is found in modern Western societies, the liminal in more aboriginal ones. Turner had some difficulty in making the distinction as can be seen in his essay "Liminal to Liminoid, in Play, Flow, and Ritual" in his *From Ritual to Theatre* (1982).

[15] Parsons, 1963/1964, p. xxxii.

[16] Weber, 1904–05/1958, p. 105.

[17] He adopted the phrase "the disenchantment of the world" from Friedrich Schiller. See H. H. Gerth & C. Wright Mills, "Bureaucracy and Charisma: A Philosophy of History" (in Glassman & Swatos, 1986, pp. 11–15, see p. 11.)

[18] Eisenstadt, 1968, p. liv.

[19] For moderate exceptions see "Charisma and Modernity: The Use and Abuse of a Concept" by Joseph Bensman & Michael Givant in Glassman & Swatos (1986), pp. 27–56; McIntosh, 1970.

[20] Davis, 1980, p. 10.

[21] Weber, 1978, p. 401.

[22] Davis, 1980, p. 10.

[23] Davis, 1980, p. 11.

[24] Davis, 1980, p. 299. Other scholars have echoed this theme; see for instance *Killing the Spirit: Higher Education in America* (1990) by historian Page Smith.

[25] Weber, 1978, p. 244.

[26] Davis, 1980, p. 299.

[27] One example is: *Higher Superstition: The Academic Left and Its Quarrels with Science* by Paul R. Gross & Norman Levitt, Baltimore, MD: The Johns Hopkins University Press, 1994. This book has been highly praised in the pages of *Skeptical Inquirer* and the authors have made presentations at a CSICOP conference. Another examples is: *The Flight From Science and Reason* edited by Paul R. Gross, Norman Levitt, & Martin W. Lewis, New York Academy of Sciences, 1997. A number of CSICOP members contributed to that volume.

Chapter 9—Cultural Change and the Paranormal

[1] Wallace, 1956, p. 265.

[2] Wallace, 1956, p. 268.

[3] Wallace, 1956, p. 266.

[4] Wallace, 1956, p. 269.

[5] Wallace, 1956, p. 269.

[6] Wallace, 1956, p. 270. Wallace, in keeping with his times, referred to the being as a "wish . . . gratified in fantasy (subjectively real, of course)" (p. 274). Despite the bias, his description of the revitalization process is quite insightful.

[7] Wallace, 1956, p. 273.

[8] Ellenberger, 1964/1968.

[9] Wallace, 1956, p. 271.

[10] Wallace, 1956, p. 274.

[11] Wallace, 1956, p. 273.

[12] Wallace, 1956, p. 269.

[13] Even before Farrakhan, leaders of the Nation of Islam believed in the importance of flying saucers. See *An Original Man: The Life and Times of Elijah Muhammad* by Claude Andrew Clegg III (1997).

[14] *Unusual Personal Experiences*, 1992.

[15] Zha & McConnell, 1991.

[16] See Rossman, 1979.

[17] Turner, 1969, p. 112.

[18] Hartmann, 1991, p. 121.

[19] Raschke, 1981/1989, p. 30.

[20] Here I am considering loss of status on a sociological level (i.e., loss of national pride). Parallels are found at the level of the individual person. Donald Warren (1970) of the University of Michigan analyzed some Gallup poll data and found that among adult white males, those with status inconsistency were more likely than average to report seeing a UFO. Status inconsistency refers to a marked difference between a person's actual social rank and that which might be expected. For instance, an individual with relatively low income and high education would be considered status inconsistent, as would a person with high achievement and low education (e.g., Thomas Edison). Warren also noted that the status of women is lower than that of men, and they were twice as likely as men to have seen a UFO.

[21] Paranoia is one of the most prominent characteristics of the UFO phenomenon. In fact, it was Kottmeyer who most effectively brought this to my attention. When I first read his 1989 paper "Ufology Considered as an Evolving System of Paranoia," I vigorously objected, but after becoming more familiar with ufology, I was forced to admit that he had made an important point. I cannot completely agree with his interpretation of the UFO-paranoia connection, but he has unquestionably identified a central issue.

[22] Zeidman, 1979.

[23] Schuessler & O'Herin, 1993.

[24] Schuessler, 1982.

Chapter 10—Prominent "Psychics"

[1] Carlos Alvarado (1993) described how Eusapia Palladino's trickery tainted psychical research, and Harvey Irwin (1987) made the same point regarding Charles Bailey, an Australian apport medium.

[2] Various ages have been given for the sisters in 1848; those here are from Fornell (1964). There is also ambiguity in the spelling of their names. Kate is also given as Catherine and Katherine, and Margaret is also given as Margaretta.

[3] The Davenport Brothers and Adah Isaacs Menken by Ormus Davenport, *Linking Ring*, Vol. 73, No. 12, December, 1993, pp. 64–74.

[4] The Davenport Brothers: Religious Practitioners, Entertainers, or Frauds? by Joe Nickell, *Skeptical Inquirer*, July/August 1999, pp. 14–17.

[5] Christopher, 1962, 1975.

[6] Dingwall, 1947/1962, p. 187. Dingwall's chapter on Home in *Some Human Oddities* focussed on the ambiguities in Home's personal life rather than on evaluating the evidence for his psychic phenomena. Dingwall recognized the importance of explicitly exploring ambiguity.

[7] As recently as 1993, skeptic Gordon Stein published the book *The Sorcerer of Kings: The Case of Daniel Dunglas Home and William Crookes* (Buffalo, NY: Prometheus Books).

[8] Solovyoff, 1892/1976, p. 141.

[9] Meade, 1980, pp. 86–87.

[10] *Madam Blavatsky's Baboon* by Peter Washington (1993/1995), see p. 407.

[11] Report of the Committee, 1885.

[12] Ellwood, 1973, p. 75.

[13] See Solovyoff 1892/1976, pp. 154–155, 286.

[14] Ibid., pp. 176–181.

[15] Bruce Campbell, 1980; Meade, 1980.

[16] Carrington, 1909; Feilding, Baggally & Carrington, 1909; Dingwall, 1950/1962, pp. 178–217.

[17] Thurston, 1910.

[18] E.g., Alvarado, 1993; Wiseman, 1992, 1993; Martinez-Taboas & Francia, 1993.

[19] Tietze, 1973; see also Tabori, 1972, pp. 40–41.

[20] I am not aware of any substantial treatment of Houdini as trickster. The best biography of Houdini is Kenneth Silverman's *Houdini!!! The Career of Ehrich Weiss* (1996). Useful interpretive biographies are Bernard C. Meyer's *Houdini: A Mind in Chains* (1976), New York: E. P. Dutton & Co.; and Ruth Brandon's *The Life and Many Deaths of Harry Houdini* (1993), New York: Random House.

[21] T. A. Waters' *The Encyclopedia of Magic and Magicians* (1988), p. 219, gives some details. A number of Houdini fans have tried to dismiss Collins' statement, but their reasons are unconvincing. Brandon accepts the story as very plausible. Silverman reports the details of the séance but does not render an opinion about who lied.

[22] Tietze, 1973, 1985.

[23] One Evening's Observation on the Margery Mediumship by J. B. Rhine and Louisa E. Rhine (1927).

[24] See Mauskopf & McVaugh, 1980, pp. 75–80.

[25] See Rauscher, 2000.

[26] Spraggett with Rauscher, 1973, p. 198.

[27] How They Do It, *Scientific American*, January 1942, pp. 20–21.

[28] *Secrets of the Amazing Kreskin* by Kreskin, Buffalo, NY: Prometheus Books, 1991 (Second edition). First published 1984.

[29] See J. Randolph Cox's *Man of Magic and Mystery: A Guide to the Work of Walter B. Gibson* (1988), Metuchen, NJ: Scarecrow.

[30] *Publishers Weekly*, Vol. 211, No. 22, May 30, 1977, p. 29.

[31] Richard de Mille (1976/1977, p. 169) compiled a helpful list of "nonordinary events" reported by Castaneda.

[32] De Mille, 1976, 1980.

[33] De Mille was a member of the Committee for the Scientific Investigation of Claims of the Paranormal (CSICOP), but he resigned over the scandal and cover-up of Paul Kurtz's astrology study.

[34] De Mille, 1976, p. 121.

[35] Information Transmission Under Conditions of Sensory Shielding by Russell Targ & Harold Puthoff, *Nature*, Vol. 251, Oct. 18, 1974, pp. 602–607. A Perceptual Channel for Information Transfer Over Kilometer Distances: Historical Perspective and Recent Research, by H. E. Puthoff & R. Targ, *Proceedings of the IEEE*, Vol. 64, 1976, pp. 329–354.

[36] Randi, 1975; Catching Geller in the Act by Eugene C. Emery, Jr. (1987).

[37] The Lawsuits Against James Randi (Parts One and Two), *Saucer Smear*, Vol. 38, No. 8, October 10, 1991, pp. 1–3, No. 9, November 5, 1991, pp. 2–4. Geller vs Randi vs CSICOP: A Tale of Two Press Releases, *PA News*, October/December 1995, pp. 8–9. An End to the Uri Geller vs Randi vs CSICOP Litigation? by Marcello Truzzi, *PA News*, October/December 1995, pp. 9–11.

[38] Haraldsson, 1987.

[39] Beyerstein, 1992; Kodimela, 1992; Haraldsson & Wiseman, 1994.

[40] Brooke, 1976/1990.

Chapter 11—Conjurors and the Paranormal

[1] *The Republic*, Book III–413. Translation by Benjamim Jowett.

[2] Some library classification schemes use the term *magic* to subsume the occult and anthropological uses of the term while reserving *conjuring* to designate that which explicitly involves tricks. General usage does not make this distinction.

Even librarians do not escape the ambiguity though, and I have been amused at the number of times I have found books on magic and conjuring misclassified.

[3] A number of writers on parapsychology often refer to magicians who perform tricks as "stage magicians" to distinguish them from those who practice the occult kind of magic. The use of such terminology reveals a writer as having little knowledge of legerdemain. Stage magic is only a small branch of conjuring. Additional types include close-up magic, parlor magic, mentalism, and bizarre magic, among others.

[4] Birdsell, 1989; Hansen, 1990a, 1990b, 1992c; Truzzi, 1997.

[5] Dawes, 1979; Francesco, 1939.

[6] The very few counterexamples such as the Magic Castle in Hollywood, several long-running shows in Las Vegas, the Le Grand David production in Beverly, Massachusetts, and Paul Daniels' television program, only serve to highlight the general situation. These exceptions are of some interest. Hollywood is a "city of dreams," and Las Vegas is devoted to gambling, Hermes being the god of dice and gambling. Le Grand David is centered around the person of Cesareo Palaez. For a few words on his background see *Commitment and Community: Communes and Utopias in Sociological Perspective* by Rosabeth Moss Kanter, pp. 196–198, Cambridge, MA: Harvard University Press, 1972.

[7] The one exception that I am aware of is the diploma thesis by John Granrose *The Archetype of the Magician*, 1996, C. G. Jung Institute, Zurich.

[8] For discussion within the conjuring literature see Brady, 1966; Burger & Neale, 1995; Rauscher, 1983.

[9] Nardi, 1988.

[10] Carroll, 1984.

[11] Stebbins, 1983/1984.

[12] Hero of Alexandria, 62/1851/1971.

[13] Minch, 1991.

[14] Minch, 1992.

[15] Rauscher, 1984, 1998.

[16] Price, 1983.

[17] Rhine, 1944.

[18] Truzzi, 1997. See also Truzzi's interview with Bluemle, 1994.

[19] Hyman, 1977.

[20] For some comments on Hyman's career see Hansen, 1991.

[21] E.g., see Ruthchild, 1983; McGill, n.d.; Thomas, 1989; Weber, 1953a, 1953b.

[22] Newmann, 1923.

[23] Carrington, 1920.

[24] One of Kreskin's outspoken supporters is University of Kentucky psychologist Robert Baker, who is an active member of CSICOP. For more on the Kreskin-CSICOP connection, see *Skeptical Inquirer*, Vol. 16, No. 1, Fall 1991, pp. 4–6. For Baker's endorsement of Kreskin, calling him a "public educator and benefactor" see Baker's *They Call it Hypnosis*, 1990, p. 142.

[25] For an introduction to the controversies, see the 1986 and 1987 volumes of *Behavioral and Brain Sciences*, Vol. 9, pp. 449–502, and Vol. 10, pp. 519–531. That journal carried a target article on hypnosis by Nicholas Spanos along with a wide range of commentaries.

[26] Bernstein, 1956. For a discussion of the case, see C. J. Ducasse, 1960.

[27] See Secret Report on Mesmerism, or Animal Magnetism by Jean Sylvain Bailly and others (August 11, 1784), which is the first chapter of *The Nature of Hypnosis: Selected Basic Readings* edited by Ronald E. Shor and Martin T. Orne, New York: Holt, Rinehart and Winston, 1965.

[28] For some literature on faking hypnosis see H. J. Burlingame, *Leaves From Conjurer's Scrap Books or, Modern Magicians and Their Works*. Detroit: Singing Tree Press, 1971 (Originally published 1891); Ernest Hart, *Hypnotism Mesmerism & Witchcraft*, Toronto: Coles (Originally published 1893); Karlyn [J. F. Burrows], *Secrets of Stage Hypnotism: Stage Electricity: and Bloodless Surgery*, London: The Magician Ltd, n.d.; William B. Meeker & Theodore X. Barber, 1971; Nelmar [Anthony Nelmar Albino], *Twenty Hypnotic Tricks*, Chicago: Nelmar System, 1933; Wesley R. Wells, 1946.

[29] Wells, 1946, p. 146.

[30] *Ghostmasters* by Mark Walker, 1991.

[31] See Hansen (1992c) for a list of his books.

[32] Randi, 1975, 1982.

[33] For discussions of Project Alpha see Truzzi, 1987; Thalbourne, 1995.

[34] See On Being Sued: The Chilling of Freedom of Expression by Paul Kurtz, *Skeptical Inquirer*, Vol. 16, No. 2, Winter 1992, pp. 114–117.

[35] Truth's Bodyguard, Interview with James Randi by Stanley Wiater, *Rod Serling's The Twilight Zone Magazine*, June 1988, pp. 32–35, 45, see p. 35.

[36] Moseley, 1993.

[37] Moseley, 1991. Moseley has known Randi for many years, and together they were involved in "archeological exploits" in South America in the 1960s. Moseley's zine *Saucer News* (Vol. 12, No. 2, June 1965, p. 21) carried pictures of Randi. See also Beware of False Prophets Peddling False-Memory Hype by Michele Landsberg, *Toronto Star*, February 11, 1996, p. A2, Final Edition. Randi has admitted to tape-recording his explicit homosexual conversations with boys. Copies of tapes were circulated, played in court, and transcripts were posted on the Internet. Randi's explanations of them have been contradictory.

[38] Hansen, 1992a, p. 47.

[39] Minch, 1991.

[40] Shiels, 1989, p. 48.

[41] Shiels, 1990, p. 15.

[42] Letter from Tony Shiels, Fab (*sic*) 2, 1999.

[43] See Shiels, 1990, p. 15.

[44] *Femina Libido Sexualis: Compendium of the Psychology, Anthropology and Anatomy of the Sexual Characteristics of the Woman* by Herman Heinrich Ploss, Max Bartels, & Paul Bartels; edited by Eric John Dingwall, arranged by J. R. Brosslowsky, New York: The Medical Press, 1965.

[45] Dingwall, 1974, p. 284.

[46] West, 1987.

[47] Dingwall, 1974, p. 284.

[48] Gauld, 1987.

[49] Dingwall did eventually resign from CSICOP because of the scandal and cover-up of Paul Kurtz's astrology study.

[50] Responsibility in Parapsychology by E. J. Dingwall, *A Century of Psychical Research: The Continuing Doubts and Affirmations: Proceedings of an International Conference Held at Le Peol, St. Paul De Vence, France September 2, 3, 4, 1970* edited by Allan Angoff and Betty Shapin, New York: Parapsychology Foundation, 1971, pp. 37–52. See p. 37 for quote.

[51] For a biographical sketch, see Eric Dingwall, Devil's Advocate by Guy Lyon Playfair, *Fate*, Vol. 40, No. 4, April 1987, pp. 73–81.

[52] A few parapsychologists have suggested that researchers need to understand the theoretical principles of magic tricks, claiming that would help them avoid being deceived. That proposal is misguided. A more enlightened approach to teaching, by skeptic Ray Hyman, an acknowledged authority on conjuring, uses case studies involving concrete examples (Goldstein, 1994).

Chapter 12—CSICOP and the Debunkers

[1] *Prometheus Bound* by Aeschylus. Translated by Rex Warner. New York: Heritage Press, 1966, p. 41.

[2] Circulation figure from *Skeptical Inquirer*, November/December 1999, p. 21.

[3] Personal communication from Barry Karr, CSICOP Executive Director, August 19, 1991.

[4] The size of the building is unclear. *Skeptical Inquirer*, Spring 1993, p. 249 gave it as 25,000 square feet; the September/October 1995 issue, p. 55, gave 20,000 square feet; the July/August 1995 issue, p. 8, gave 15,000 square feet.

CSICOP announced that it had raised $4,200,000 exceeding its fundraising goal; see *Skeptical Inquirer*, May/June 1995, p. 8.

[5] Circulation figure from March 1997 issue.

[6] Nicholas Wade, A Pyrrhonian Sledgehammer, *Science*, Vol. 197, 1977, pp. 646–647, see p. 646 for quote.

[7] Astrology and Gullibility by Paul Kurtz, *The Humanist*, 1975, November/December, Vol. 35, No. 6, p. 20.

[8] Policy on Sponsoring Research, Testing Individual Claims, and Conducting Investigations of Alleged Paranormal Powers and Phenomena, *Skeptical Inquirer*, Vol. 6, No. 3, Spring 1982, p. 9. The CSICOP Executive Council approved the policy October 22–24, 1981.

[9] Pinch and Collins (1984).

[10] Kurtz, 1986, p. 146.

[11] Kurtz's book *Toward a New Enlightenment: The Philosophy of Paul Kurtz* (1994) contains a list of his publications. Though hundreds of articles are listed, I found no reports of empirical research, of any type, that were published in refereed scientific journals.

[12] I refer here to the Full Members. According to CSICOP's by laws these comprise the Fellows, Scientific and Technical Consultants, Board of Directors, and Executive Council.

[13] McClenon, 1982, 1984.

[14] I wish to thank Jennie Zeidman for bringing this to my attention.

[15] Berger, 1990, p. 4.

[16] Sheler, 1994.

[17] Berger, 1990, p. 182.

[18] Gibbs, 1993.

[19] Otto, 1917/1975, p. 4.

[20] See Stillings, 1984.

[21] Ben-Yehuda, 1985, p. 91.

[22] Ben-Yehuda, 1985, p. 93.

[23] Wren-Lewis, 1974, p. 43.

[24] Schumaker, 1990, p. 82.

[25] Lopez-Pedraza, 1977/1989, p. 61.

[26] For Kurtz's interpretation of Prometheus, see Promethean Love: Unbound, in his *Toward a New Enlightenment: The Philosophy of Paul Kurtz* (1994, pp. 279–291).

[27] Hansen (1991). For other statistical errors by Hyman, see On Hyman's Factor Analysis by David R. Saunders, *Journal of Parapsychology*, Vol. 49, No. 1,

1985, pp. 86–88. See also Rejoinder by Jessica Utts, *Statistical Science*, Vol. 6, No. 4, 1991, pp. 396–403, especially pp. 398, 399.

[28] Hansen, 1990a, p. 56.

[29] Hansen, 1992d.

Chapter 13—Small Groups and the Paranormal

[1] Social repercussions occur even if putative supernatural events are almost entirely due to trickery. A good example is the British crop circle phenomenon. Evidence indicates that hoaxers produce virtually all of the formations. See Schnabel (1993).

[2] Ellis, 1982–83.

[3] For more detail than Kübler-Ross revealed, see the exposé by Coleman (1979).

[4] See Lamar Keene's *The Psychic Mafia* (1976) and Eric Dingwall's account of the lurid "Angel Anna" in his *Some Human Oddities* (1947/1962).

[5] Black Elk was one of the spirits contacted by the SORRAT. In real life, he was a trickster figure; see The Wisdom of the Contrary: A Conversation with Joseph Epes Brown, *Parabola*, Vol. 4, No. 1, February 1979, pp. 54–65, see p. 56.

[6] McClenon, 1994; Richards, 1982; see Duke & Hansen, 1991 for a bibliography of works on SORRAT.

[7] Hansen & Broughton, 1991.

[8] His remarks were quoted by Dennis Stillings in a 1991 issue of *Artifex* devoted to the SORRAT. See Stillings, 1991.

[9] Richards, 1992.

[10] The early SRI work did not escape the problems of trickery. Uri Geller was one of the early subjects, and numerous allegations of fraud followed him. He has been covered in an earlier chapter.

[11] The full story of the secret government psychic programs since the 1970s has not yet been told, but for the past several years, there have been many rumors of books in preparation. The first issue of the 1996 *Journal of Scientific Exploration* (Vol. 10, No.1) carried several reports on some of the recently declassified material and controversies surrounding them. Also of interest are: *Mind-Reach: Scientists Look at Psychic Abilities* by Russell Targ and Harold Puthoff, New York: Delacorte, 1977. *The Mind Race: Understanding and Using Psychic Abilities* by Russell Targ and Keith Harary, New York: Villard Books, 1984. *To Kiss Earth Good-Bye* by Ingo Swann, New York: Hawthorn Books, 1975. *Miracles of Mind: Exploring Nonlocal Consciousness and Spiritual Healing* by Russell Targ and Jane Katra, Novato, CA: New World Library, 1998. *Remote Viewers: The Secret History of America's Psychic Spies* by Jim Schnabel, New York: Dell, 1997. Parapsychology in

Intelligence: A Personal Review and Conclusions by Kenneth A. Kress, *Studies in Intelligence*, Vol. 21, Winter 1977, pp. 7–17, (declassified 1996).

[12] A transcript of a radio interview Dames did with radio station KIRO (Seattle) on November 18, 1991 was published in *Third Eyes Only*, No. 2, April 1992, pp. 88–95.

[13] Dames' talk was tape-recorded, and eventually a transcript was posted on his web site.

[14] Stubblebine became romantically involved with psychiatrist Rima Laibow (a reported UFO abductee), later divorcing his wife. Laibow had organized the TREAT conference. For some information on Laibow, see *Saucer Smear*, Vol. 38, No. 3 (March 1st, 1991), p. 3 and Vol. 40, No. 4 (May 15th, 1993), p. 3.

[15] Alexander was a protégé of Kübler-Ross and did his doctoral dissertation in thanatology under her direction.

[16] Ryan Wood is the son of McDonnell Douglas physicist Dr. Robert M. Wood. Robert Wood is known for his interest in UFOs, and he was the boss of Jack Houck, who in the 1980s popularized metal-bending PK parties. A number of military personnel, including Alexander and Stubblebine, attended those parties, and Alexander later organized parties himself (In 1982 I assisted both Houck and Alexander in organizing parties). Stubblebine was excited by the possibilities of psychic metal bending and became a vocal supporter of it; he subsequently was sometimes referred to as General Spoon-bender. Robert and Ryan Wood later became notorious for touting some ludicrous UFO documents which suggested, among other things, that Albert Einstein, Robert Oppenheimer, and J. Edgar Hoover were killed because of their knowledge and involvement with UFOs.

[17] Jim Schnabel wrote a piece on remote viewing for *Esquire* magazine, but the editors decided not to publish it. He revised the article, focussing on Morehouse, and posted it on the Internet with the title "An American Hero: The Truth About Dave Morehouse and Psychic Warrior" 7 November 1996. Schnabel's report was based in part on his review of 700 pages of legal proceedings against Morehouse. Morehouse claimed that the remote-viewing program caused his problems.

Chapter 14—Alternative Religions and Psi

[1] King James Version

[2] Here I am using Spiritualism (with a capital S) to designate a particular movement. Of course spirits have been consulted for millennia, and there have been thousands of spiritualist (small s) cults.

[3] For the often-neglected role of the lower classes in Spiritualism, see Barrow, 1986.

[4] See William D. Moore (1997).

[5] For more on Spiritualism, see Braude, 1989; Moore, 1977; Nelson, 1969; Oppenheim, 1985; Owen, 1990; Podmore, 1902; Zingrone, 1994.

[6] There is a huge literature on mediumistic trickery, and many of the books by magicians listed in Hansen (1992c) have extensive discussions of it. Keene's *The Psychic Mafia* (1976) has an excellent bibliography.

[7] Melton, Clark and Kelly (1991).

[8] Webb, 1976, pp. 417–487.

[9] For discussions of channeling, see Hastings, 1991; Klimo, 1987.

[10] Hess, 1993.

[11] Guiley, 1989.

[12] Kelly, 1991; Adler, 1979.

[13] Kelly, 1991, p. 5.

[14] Luhrmann, 1989b, p. 255.

[15] Luhrmann, 1989b, p. 181.

[16] Luhrmann, 1989b, p. 171.

[17] Luhrmann, 1989b, p. 171.

Chapter 15—Institutions and the Paranormal

[1] The Top Ten Grossing Infomercials of 1995, *Brandweek*, June 24, 1996, p. 30.

[2] See *Baltimore Business Journal* articles: Lawsuits Forecast Lasky's Troubles by David Harrison and Donna De Marco, February 13, 1998, p. 1; NationsBank sues Lasky by Donna De Marco, March 6, 1998, p. 1; U.S. Trustee Unwinding Lasky Firm by Donna de Marco, March 13, 1998, p. 1.

[3] Psychic Lines Wither as Regulators, Telephone Firms Crack Down on Scams by James McNair, *Knight-Ridder Tribune Business News: The Miami Herald*, January 25, 1999.

[4] My Life as a Phone Psychic by Sherry Amatenstein, *Mademoiselle*, May 1997, p. 56.

[5] Harary, 1992. Harary bitterly complained about the media's portrayal, but that is ironic, because in a letter to *Skeptical Inquirer* (Vol. 15, No. 3, Spring 1991, p. 331) he objected to being called a psychic himself. He did not wish to be tainted by the label, and his own unwillingness to accept the designation subtly reinforced the negative view of psychics. For an autobiographical piece, which perhaps casts some light on his ambivalence, see Researcher Profile 6: Hidden Worlds by Keith Harary, *Exceptional Human Experience*, Vol. 10, No. 1, June 1992, pp. 5–15.

[6] Iaccino, 1994; Carroll, 1990.

[7] Clements, 1987, p. 37.

[8] Clements, 1987, p. 39.

[9] Polan, 1986, p. 161.

[10] Polan, 1986, p. 320.

[11] Clements, 1987, p. 41.

[12] Polan, 1986, p. 161.

[13] The *X-Files* Meets the Skeptics, in *Skeptical Inquirer*, Vol. 21, No. 1, January/February 1997, pp. 24–30. For Tyson's comments see page 28.

[14] Readership statistics from Barry Karr, Executive Director of CSICOP, August 19, 1991.

[15] Melton, 1996.

[16] Edith Turner, 1993, p. 9.

[17] Ibid. p. 11.

Chapter 16—Anti-structure and the History of Psychical Research

[1] *The World Almanac and Book of Facts 1998*, Mahwah, NJ: World Almanac Books, 1997, p. 250. Figures based on box office sales in the U.S. and Canada.

[2] Warner, 1980.

[3] Dawes, 1994.

[4] Christensen & Jacobson, 1994.

[5] It is true that some forms of psychotherapy have come under increasing criticism, and insurance providers refuse support for some. Nevertheless, many of the relatively ineffective forms have been institutionalized and remain so today.

[6] See Gauld, 1968; Oppenheim, 1985.

[7] Gauld, 1968, p. 138.

[8] Psi Experiments with Random Number Generators: Meta-Analysis Part 1, by Dean I. Radin, Edwin C. May & Martha J. Thomson, in *The Parapsychological Association 28th Annual Convention Proceedings of Presented Papers Volume 1*, August 12–16, 1985, The Parapsychological Association, pp. 199–233, see p. 223.

[9] The FRNM changed its name to the Rhine Research Center in 1995.

[10] Mauskopf & McVaugh, 1980, p. 217.

[11] Mauskopf & McVaugh, 1980, p. 217.

[12] For comments on the role of the popular press in publicizing Rhine's work see "Parapsychology's Reliance on a Free Press" by J. B. R.[hine], *Journal of Parapsychology*, Vol. 20, 1956, pp. 266–268.

[13] Mauskopf & McVaugh, 1980, p. 139.

[14] See Hansen, Deception by Subjects in Psi Research, 1990a, pp. 34–35.

[15] The Hypothesis of Deception by J. B. Rhine, *Journal of Parapsychology*, Vol. 2, 1938, pp. 151–152.

[16] Mauskopf & McVaugh, 1980, p. 304–305.

[17] For some reflections on leaving Duke, see "FRNM's First Decade: Lessons in Retrospect" by J. B. Rhine, *Journal of Parapsychology*, Vol. 36, 1972, pp. 317–327.

[18] Gardner, 1989; Hansen, The Research with B.D. and the Legacy of Magical Ignorance, 1992d.

[19] Child, 1985; Ullman, Krippner with Vaughan, 1973.

[20] Krippner, 1975, see p. 253.

[21] Schechter, 1993b.

[22] The ganzfeld method involves partial sensory deprivation. A telepathic receiver is put in a sound proof room and typically has halves of ping pong balls placed over the eyes with red light shown upon them. This creates an unpatterned visual field. White noise (noise without pattern) is played through headphones. A telepathic sender in another rooms tries to transmit an image or idea to the receiver.

[23] E.g., Berger, 1985a, 1985b; Mauskopf & McVaugh, 1980; Osis, 1985.

[24] Members, Publications and Endowment, *Journal of the American Society for Psychical Research*, Vol. 8, No. 11, pp. 527–529.

[25] For biographical information on Hyslop see Anderson, 1985; Arthur S. Berger, 1988.

[26] Osis, 1985, p. 506.

[27] Osis, 1985.

[28] For the following years the *Journal* did not publish its circulation figures, though postal regulations required it. In 1998 I inquired to the Society about the figures, but they did not respond. In fact I was even unable to learn if I was still a member.

[29] This general pattern is confirmed by Karlis Osis' discussion of his years at the ASPR. He quotes Gardner Murphy telling him that "Karlis, money is actually thrown at me now [by foundations], but I cannot get anything for this [psychic research]." Osis went on to describe how they were more successful with individuals. See Osis, 1985, p. 513.

[30] The same pattern was recently demonstrated in Japan. Masaru Ibuka, co-founder of Sony, established a parapsychology laboratory in the company. He died in December 1997, and a few months later the laboratory was closed. See Closing the Dream Factory by Patrick Huyghe, *Fortean Times*, No. 115, October 1998, pp. 44–46.

[31] CIA's Psychic Spies Under Scrutiny by Sally Lehrman, *Nature*, Vol. 378, 7 December 1995, p. 525. The Vision Thing, *Time*, December 11, 1995, p. 48. CIA Psychics and Spooks: How Spoon-Benders Fought the Cold War by Gregory Vistica, *Newsweek*, December 11, 1995, p. 50. In a telephone conversation on 24 August 1998 Ed May indicated that the $20 million figure was slightly understated.

[32] The full story of the secret government psychic programs has not yet been told, but some accounts are available. For a bit more on the history of the SRI research, see the section on Psi Tech in the chapter Small Groups and the Paranormal. The early SRI work did not escape the problems of trickery. Uri Geller was one of the early subjects, and numerous allegations of fraud followed him. He has been covered in an earlier chapter.

[33] Telephone conversation 24 August 1998.

[34] See Palmer, Honorton, & Utts, 1989; May, 1996.

[35] The NRC made Rosenthal's report available, but their published report did not even acknowledge its existence.

[36] See Gardner, *Science: Good, Bad and Bogus*, 1979/1981b, p. 190.

[37] Tart, 1979.

[38] Schouten, 1993. Schouten's data on psychologists came from Census of Psychological Personnel: 1983 by Joy Stapp, Anthony M. Tucker, and Gary R. VandenBos, *American Psychologist*, Vol. 40, No. 12, December 1985, pp. 1317–1351.

[39] See Four Decades of Fringe Literature by Steven Dutch (1986).

[40] See Truzzi, 1987; Thalbourne, 1995. See also MacLab, St Louis, to Shut by Tim Beardsley, *Nature*, Vol. 317, 5 September 1985, p. 6.

[41] For biographical information on Slick, see *Tom Slick and the Search for the Yeti* by Loren Coleman (1989).

[42] The figures for the Mind Science Foundation budget are from two researchers who worked there.

[43] Per Gary Heseltine via telephone conversation and written note, 25 October 1998, 08 December 1998.

[44] The PRL RNG was a modified version of one built by Dutch physicist Dick Bierman.

[45] Questions for the Cosmos by Steve Fishman, *New York Times Magazine*, November 16, 1989, pp. 50–55.

[46] Hansen, Utts, & Markwick, 1992.

[47] Letter from Richard Broughton, 10 December 1998.

[48] Information on SURF from Gary Heseltine via telephone, 25 October 1998; and Rick E. Berger, 15 November 1998.

Chapter 17—Unbounded Conditions

[1] Steiner, 1993.
[2] Whaley, 1990.
[3] Melton, 1996.
[4] Telephone conversation with John Keel, 13 September 1998.
[5] Telephone conversation with Keel, 13 September 1998.
[6] Keel, *The Mothman Prophecies*, 1975b, p. 171.
[7] Keel, *The Mothman Prophecies*, 1975b, p. 168.
[8] Popper, 1963/1984, p. 123.
[9] For some examples of occult and conspiratorial ideas, see *Architects of Fear* by George Johnson, 1983.
[10] The New Millennium by Rosemary Ellen Guiley, *Fate*, Vol. 47, No. 1, January 1994, pp. 30–36.
[11] Ellis, 1991.
[12] Kottmeyer, 1989. Martin Kottmeyer examined ufology as "an evolving system of paranoia."
[13] See Peebles, 1994, p. 277.
[14] For examples see Middleton & Winter, 1963.

Chapter 18—Government Disinformation

[1] *Friends in High Places: Our Journey from Little Rock to Washington, D.C.* by Webb Hubbell, New York: William Morrow and Company, 1997, pp. 282.
[2] *Saucer Smear*, Vol. 44, No. 6, June 20th, 1997, pp. 2–3.
[3] An amusing trickster connection with cattle mutilations can be suggested. On the day Hermes was born, he stole Apollo's cattle and killed some of them.
[4] Under the rubric of "paranormal" I am including psychic and UFO phenomena and cattle mutilations. In cultural terms, these areas are defined as paranormal. In the scientific sense, there is massive evidence that some psychic and UFO phenomena cannot be understood within conventional scientific frameworks. I have seen no reasonable evidence that ET aliens are visiting earth, but some UFOs have produced physical effects that defy explanation. The evidence for

some fundamentally unexplained aspect of cattle mutilations is yet unclear. There has been much less investigation of that phenomenon.

[5] Fawcett & Greenwood, 1984, p. 206.

[6] Fawcett & Greenwood, 1984, p. 207.

[7] Fawcett & Greenwood, 1984, p. 207.

[8] Haines, 1997, p. 72. There are no consistent page numberings on the Internet version of Haines' paper. The quote here appeared just before footnote 33.

[9] Haines, 1997, p. 73. The quote appeared a bit before Haines' footnote 46.

[10] Haines, 1997, p. 83. Quote in Haines' footnote 90.

[11] Ibid.

[12] Haines, 1997, p. 78. This statement appeared in Haines' text after footnote 89.

[13] Haines, 1997, p. 83, footnote 90.

[14] For a brief overview of the pervasive alien motifs in American popular culture in the 1990s, see Dean, 1998. For data on movie grosses, see *The World Almanac and Book of Facts 1998*, Mahwah, NJ: World Almanac Books, 1997, p. 250.

[15] Todd's suspicion that the Roswell crash object was a Mogul balloon was leaked in *Saucer Smear*, Vol. 38, No. 4, May 1st, 1991, p. 4. See also *Skeptics UFO Newsletter*, No. 30, November 1994; Saler, Ziegler, & Moore (1997).

[16] UFOs and the U.S. Government by William L. Moore, *MUFON UFO Journal*, No. 259, November 1989, pp. 8–16, 18, No. 260, December 1989, pp. 8–14.

[17] There is much written about the MJ-12 documents. For a useful reference see *UFOs, MJ-12 and the Government: A Report on Government Involvement in UFO Crash Retrievals* by Grant Cameron and T. Scott Crain, Jr., 1991.

[18] Randle issued an open letter on September 10, 1995. It is reported in *Saucer Smear*, Vol. 42, No. 9, October 10th, 1995, pp. 5–6 and *Skeptics UFO Newsletter*, No. 36, November 1995, pp. 3–4.

[19] Fawcett & Greenwood, 1984, pp. 224–225. Greenwood has since voiced suspicion about these, see *Just Cause*, No. 50, March 1997, p. 5.

[20] Moore did not say that he had never been paid for his services, but only that he was not on the payroll, as pointed out by Jacques Vallee (1991, p. 47).

[21] Source Confesses Role as 'Controlled Informant' by Don Ecker, *UFO*, Vol. 7, No. 1, 1992, pp. 11–12.

[22] See the report "Will the *Real* Scott Jones Please Stand Up?" (Durant [& Hansen], 1992).

[23] Howe, 1989/1993, p. 147. Howe had reported some of this in a letter published in *CAUS Bulletin*, No. 9, December 1987, pp. 2–4. See also *Just Cause*,

No. 16 (New Series), June 1988, pp. 2–7 for material from Howe, Doty, and Barry Greenwood. More material is found in *Just Cause*, No. 13 (New Series), September 1987, pp. 8–9.

[24] Vallee, 1991, pp. 13–42.

[25] Gersten's meetings are reported in Linda Howe's *An Alien Harvest* (pp. 134–136). Gersten confirmed the accuracy of her account in a letter to me postmarked 28 Oct 1998. Briefer accounts appear in *Just Cause*, No. 16 (New Series), June 1988. This includes "Notes on Peter Gersten's Meeting with SA Richard Doty, 1/83 (phone con with Gersten after his trip to New Mexico.)" by Barry Greenwood.

[26] The Anatomy of a Hoax: The Truth About the 'Ellsworth Case' by Bob Pratt, *MUFON UFO Journal*, No. 191, January 1984, pp. 6–9.

[27] Letters and telephone calls with Linda Howe, 15, 29 October 1998 and 5 November 1998.

[28] For more information, see the Epilogue in *Clear Intent* by Fawcett and Greenwood.

[29] Gullibility of Moore, Shandera and Friedman Revealed by New Data on Their Principal MJ-12 Source—Richard C. Doty—"Falcon" by Philip J. Klass, one page, dated 4/14/89.] Klass later reported that "The USAF decided against a court-martial because it would disclose counterintelligence details." *Skeptics UFO Newsletter*, #34, July 1995, p. 6.

[30] Airman Mendez vs the Bureaucracy—A Case of UFO "Espionage", *Just Cause*, No. 28, June 1991, pp. 1–8; Airman Mendez vs the Bureaucracy—Part Two, *Just Cause*, No. 29, September 1991, pp. 1–8.

[31] Howe, 1989/1993, p. 137–143. See p. 142 for quote.

[32] Telephone call to Barry Hennessey, 28 February 1999.

[33] Letter from Richard L. Weaver to George P. Hansen, 18 March 1999.

[34] See Vallee, 1991, p. 229.

[35] Hiding the Hardware by Bruce Maccabee, *International UFO Reporter*, Vol. 16, No. 5, September/October 1991, pp. 4–10, 23; see pp. 10 & 23.

[36] *Gulf Breeze Double Exposed: The "Ghost-Demon" Photo Controversy* by Zan Overall, Chicago, IL: J. Allen Hynek Center for UFO Studies, 1990; *Anatomy of the Gulf Breeze (Walters') UFO Case* by Carol A. Salisberry and Rex C. Salisberry, April 18, 1992.

[37] *Skeptics UFO Newsletter*, No. 5, Sept. 1990, p. 1.

[38] *The Gulf Breeze Sightings: The Most Astounding Multiple Sightings of UFOs in U.S. History* by Ed Walters and Frances Walters, New York: William Morrow and Company, 1990.

[39] James Moseley raised the very same point in *Saucer Smear*, Vol. 47, No. 5, June 15th, 2000, p. 6, saying "Bruce Maccabee is either very gullible indeed, or else he is deliberately spreading disinformation."

[40] The report was printed in *Third Eyes Only*, No. 14, July, 1993, pp. 1–14. The following issue carried a lengthy response by Maccabee.

[41] *Skeptics UFO Newsletter*, No. 24, November 1993, pp. 1–2.

[42] Even Richard Hall, a close colleague of Maccabee at the Fund for UFO Research, admitted that Maccabee was very taken with William Moore and, as he put it: "lacks some perspective." See Hall's letter reproduced in the *MUFON UFO Journal*, No. 254, June 1989, p. 10.

[43] An entire chapter is devoted to Gordon Novel in *The Kennedy Conspiracy: An Uncommissioned Report on the Jim Garrison Investigation* by Paris Flammonde, New York: Meredith Press, 1969, pp. 96–109.

[44] *On the Trail of the Assassins* by Jim Garrison, New York: Warner Books, 1991, see pp. 208–211. (First published 1988)

[45] Bizarre Rome Case Ends with Man Pleading Guilty by Betsy Neal, *Atlanta Constitution*, November 6, 1977, p. 15–B (page depends on edition).

[46] See the review of *The Secret File on J. Edgar Hoover* produced by William Cran and Stephanie Tepper, Frontline, 1993 by Athan Theoharis, *Journal of American History*, Vol. 80, No. 3, December 1993, pp. 1201–1203.

[47] A picture of Alexander with Novel was printed in *Saucer Smear*, Vol. 41, No. 9, December 5th, 1994, p. 6.

[48] Victorian formerly used the name Henry Azadehdel. On June 6, 1989, he was convicted of smuggling orchids into England.

[49] Alexander's memo was reproduced in *Third Eyes Only*, No. 19, March–April, 1994, pp. 33–38.

[50] Britain in the 90s: Up Against the State by Armen Victorian, *Lobster*, No. 28, 1994, pp. 12–13. Victorian sent me copies of police reports he filed. If he had filed false ones, he would have been subject to prosecution.

[51] Secret Service 'Targets' Military Writer by William Goodwin, *The Observer* (London), January 1, 1995, p. 10.

[52] The paper *Will the Real Scott Jones Please Stand Up?* was printed in *Third Eyes Only*, No. 1, Vernal Equinox, 1992, pp. 26–51.

[53] Durant [& Hansen], 1992, p. 7, *Third Eyes Only* printing, p. 34. See also Prince Has a Way To Save Democracy: A Stronger Monarch by Greg Steinmetz, *Wall Street Journal*, July 22, 1997, pp. A1, A6.

[54] "Controlling Government Response: Self Interest in a Nation State System" by C. B. Scott Jones, *Proceedings of the International Symposium of UFO Research* edited by Maurice L. Albertson and Margaret Shaw, May 22–25, 1992, pp. 59–83.

[55] Ibid., p. 68.

[56] Jones' threat seemed to lack substance. A year later another protest was held in front of the White House, and I marched in it.

[57] *Mute Evidence* by Ian Summers and Dan Kagan, New York: Bantam Books, 1984. See pages 346–371.

[58] See letter from Gerald E. Weinstein to Harrison H. Schmitt, 15 January 1979, this from FBI-Albuquerque file, 198-541-B-1, Apr 27, 1979.

[59] His report *Roswell in Perspective* (1994) published by the Fund for UFO Research includes a page and a half summary of his career.

[60] Open letter to Steven Greer, published in *Saucer Smear*, Vol. 44, No. 6, June 20th, 1997, pp. 2–3.

[61] Establishment academics often naively participate in this. An example is the book *UFO Crash as Roswell: The Genesis of a Modern Myth* (1997). Two of its coauthors were Benson Saler and Charles A. Ziegler, who are professors of anthropology at Brandeis University. They analyzed the Roswell case as a myth, but they totally neglected the larger context of disinformation from government sources which permeates the UFO field. They mentioned William L. Moore, but Richard Doty was not listed in the index. A brief biographical mention of Pflock totally omitted his employment with the CIA. Saler and Ziegler were oblivious to the larger cultural context of the myths and the role the establishment played in promoting them.

Chapter 19—Hoaxes and the Paranormal

[1] Those who wish to pursue the literature of ufology might start with John Keel's *The Mothman Prophecies* (1975), Jacques Vallee's *Passport to Magonia* (1969), Martin Kottmeyer's articles, and the British periodical *Magonia*. James Moseley's newsletter *Saucer Smear* is the best social chronicle of the events of U.S. ufology. The writings of Philip J. Klass can provide a much-needed critical perspective, though he often pushes the skeptical view too far.

[2] Figures for the U.S. and Canada; see *The World Almanac and Book of Facts 1998*, Mahwah, NJ: World Almanac Books, 1997, p. 250.

[3] Since the beginning of her notoriety, she has adopted the stage name Linda Cortile, and her proponents use it when referring to her.

[4] The ironic implications of "Brooklyn Bridge" being in the title seem to have escaped Hopkins.

[5] Stefula, Butler & Hansen, 1993.

[6] The Great High-Rise Abduction by Patrick Huyghe, *Omni*, 16(7), April 1994, pp. 60–67, 96, 99.

[7] Ibid., p. 144.

[8] *Nighteyes* by Garfield Reeves-Stevens, New York: Doubleday, 1989.

[9] Ibid., p. 186.

[10] Clark made this statement in a paper he circulated dated October 24, 1992 entitled "The Politics of Torquemada; or, Earth Calling Hansen's Planet." See p. 1.

[11] The cover of that entertaining issue carried a picture of the Brooklyn Bridge, the irony of which was also missed by the Hynek Center. Humorously, the caption mistakenly stated that the Brooklyn Bridge runs to New Jersey.

[12] See p. 11 of House of Cards: The Butler/Hansen/Stefula Critique of the Cortile Case by Budd Hopkins, *International UFO Reporter*, March/April 1993, pp. 8–14, 21.

[13] The Sixth Witness in the Linda Cortile Abduction Case by Budd Hopkins, *MUFON 1996 International UFO Symposium Proceedings Ufology: A Scientific Enigma*, Greensboro, North Carolina, July 5, 6, & 7, 1996, pp. 111–118.

[14] Andrus' major statement is Rejoinder to the Critique of Budd Hopkins by Walter H. Andrus, Jr., *MUFON UFO Journal*, No. 300, April 1993, pp. 8–9; Jacobs, Mack, and Hopkins published comments in the March–April 1993 issue of *International UFO Reporter*. See Stefula, Butler, and Hansen (1993) for discussion of Clark's comments.

[15] John Mack was the only newcomer, with his interest in ufology beginning in 1989. His long career in psychiatry didn't keep him from being duped.

[16] That guide was published by Prometheus Books, the primary purveyor of books debunking the paranormal.

[17] Fine, 1983, p. 28.

[18] Fine, 1983, p. 99.

[19] Turner suggested that full liminality is not seen in modern Western culture, and he proposed the liminoid as an attenuated version of the liminal. Turner's concept of the liminoid was vague and undeveloped compared with the liminal, but it can sometimes be useful to consider his distinction. FRPGs are more liminoid than liminal.

[20] Fine, 1983, p. 55.

[21] *The Aquarian Guide to the New Age* by Eileen Campbell and J. H. Brennan, Northamptonshire: The Aquarian Press, 1990, pp. 124–126.

[22] I wish to thank Dennis Stillings for pointing this out.

Part 5—Overview

[1] Spencer-Brown, 1969/1979, p. xxix. The quote appears in a section entitled "A Note on the Mathematical Approach" which may not be in all editions of the book.

[2] Spencer-Brown participated in psychical research in the 1950s. He raised questions about probability theory and the adequacy of random number tables.

He contributed to the *Proceedings of the First International Conference of Parapsychological Studies, Utrecht, The Netherlands, July 30 to August 5, 1953*, New York: Parapsychology Foundation, 1955, with a paper "Psychical Research as a Test of Probability Theory." Only the abstract was published. The original paper discussed the idea of "retroactive PK" and was one of the first (and maybe the first) to do so. The *Journal of the Society for Psychical Research* for 1953 and 1954 carried discussion of his ideas and comments from him. In 1957 he published *Probability and Scientific Inference* (London: Longmans, Green and Co.) which continued the debate. That book was reviewed by Christopher Scott in the *Journal of the Society for Psychical Research*, Vol. 39, 1958, pp. 217–234. Scott commented on the wild vacillations in his criticisms (perhaps a consequence of Spencer-Brown's crossing the enchanted boundary). Nevertheless, Spencer-Brown raised fundamental issues that deserved discussion.

Chapter 20—Reflexivity and the Trickster

[1] In a letter to his mother, 3 April 1950. Translated and quoted by Dawson, 1997, p. 30. Emphasis is Dawson's.

[2] Quoted in Ashmore (1989, p. 24), citing: "Latour, Bruno, 1978, Observing scientists observing baboons observing . . . New York: Wenner Grenn Foundation for Anthropological Research, July. (Latour 1978:24, n. 14)."

[3] Mehan and Wood, 1975, p. 167.

[4] Ashmore, 1989, p. 234.

[5] Babcock, 1980, p. 2.

[6] Ashmore, 1989, p. 25.

[7] Ashmore, 1989, p. 22.

[8] Wallace, 1968, p. 125.

[9] Garfinkel, 1967, p. 37.

[10] Ibid. p. 38.

[11] Mehan and Wood, 1975, p. 90.

[12] Mehan and Wood, 1975, pp. 208–209. Although their book is jointly authored, Mehan and Wood use the singular voice. In the Preface they say "Whoever enters the form of life this book embodies becomes the 'I' who speaks here" (p. vii). This statement appears to have been derived independently of deconstructionist literary theory.

[13] Mehan and Wood, 1975, p. 6.

[14] Leach, 1974, p. 34.

[15] Mehan and Wood, 1975, p. 209.

[16] Ibid. p. 223.

[17] Edmund Leach was one of the first to call attention to the fictional nature of Castaneda's work. See his review of *The Teachings of Don Juan: A Yaqui Way of Knowledge* (Leach,1969). Leach was not the only British structuralist to comment on Castaneda. Rodney Needham's book *Exemplars* (1985) has a relevant chapter; and it has another chapter on a confidence artist.

[18] De Mille's *The Don Juan Papers* also discusses Garfinkel and the Agnes case.

[19] Woolgar, 1996, p. 828.

[20] Woolgar, 1988, p. 17.

[21] An incident in Latour's career demonstrates the antagonism SSK evokes. Clifford Geertz, the head of the school of social sciences at the Institute for Advanced Study in Princeton, New Jersey, wanted Latour appointed to a position at the Institute. There was such an outcry against him that the nomination was withdrawn, and eventually the school returned $500,000 to the foundation that would have sponsored Latour's position. See Undressing the Emperor by Madhusree Mukerjee, *Scientific American*, March, 1998, pp. 30, 32.

[22] *Sociology of Scientific Knowledge: A Source Book* edited by H. M. Collins, Bath, U.K.: Bath University Press, 1982. Collins and Pinch (1982, 1993). Collins (1985, 1989).

Those interested in the replicability issue in parapsychology may wish to examine *The Repeatability Problem in Parapsychology: Proceedings of an International Conference Held in San Antonio, Texas October 28–29, 1983* edited by Betty Shapin and Lisette Coly, New York: Parapsychology Foundation, 1985.

[23] Robert Rosenthal, 1966, 1994.

[24] *Pygmalion in the Classroom* by Robert Rosenthal and Lenore Jacobson, New York: Holt, Rinehart and Winston, 1968.

[25] Letter and telephone call, 02 & 06 October 1998. See The Silent Languages of Classrooms and Laboratories by Robert Rosenthal, *Proceedings of the Parapsychological Association Number 8, 1971* edited by W. G. Roll, R. L. Morris, and J. D. Morris, 1972, pp. 95–116, Copyright by the Parapsychological Association, Durham, North Carolina.

[26] See the article by Palmer, Honorton and Utts (1989, p. 38) for details.

[27] Goleman, 1988, p. 105.

[28] Hofstadter, 1979, p. 251.

[29] Psi and Internal Attention States by Charles Honorton (1977). A fair amount of this research involved groups of subjects, where the problems of deception were relatively minor.

[30] For a discussion, see *Gödel's Proof* by Ernest Nagel and James R. Newman, New York: New York University Press, 1958.

[31] Ellenberger, 1964/1968.

[32] Dawson, 1997, pp. 29–30.

[33] For his interest in demons, see Kreisal, 1980, p. 218. I examined some of Gödel's private papers now held by Princeton University and found references to demons. Relevant papers on demons in the Princeton University archives are found in the Gödel collection in Box 7A, Folders 03/107 (Theology Notebook 1) and 03/108 (Theology Notebook 3). Unfortunately most, but not all, of his notes were made in an obscure German shorthand.

[34] Wang, 1987, p. 5.

[35] *Deconstruction Reframed* by Floyd Merrell, West Lafayette, IN: Purdue University Press, 1985, p. 64.

[36] Rucker, 1982/1983, p. 2.

[37] Smullyan is a mathematician, philosopher, and also a magician. Poundstone's connection with magic should not go unnoticed. He publicly revealed a number of conjurer's methods in his books *Big Secrets* (New York: William Morrow and Company, 1983) and *Bigger Secrets* (Boston: Houghton Mifflin Company, 1986), to the annoyance of magicians.

[38] Gardner took issue with some of Rucker's ideas on psychic phenomena.

[39] Some biographical material is available. See the September 1979 issue of *The Two-Year College Mathematical Journal*, which carried a long autobiographical piece (Gardner, 1979) and an interview with him (Barcellos, 1979). John Booth's *Dramatic Magic* (1988) has biographical material on Gardner, as well as on James Randi and Walter Gibson. All three have written extensively on the paranormal.

[40] For a reprinting of that review of his *The Whys of a Philosophical Scrivener* and an additional commentary, see Gardner's *The Night Is Large*, 1996, pp. 481–487.

[41] e.g., *Science 81*, July/August, pp. 32–37; *Newsweek*, November 16, 1981, p. 101.

[42] *The Mathematical Gardner* edited by David A. Klarner, Boston, MA: Prindle, Weber & Schmidt, 1981.

[43] Review by Marion Dearman, *Journal for the Scientific Study of Religion*, Vol. 12, No. 4, 1973, pp. 484–485.

[44] Ibid, p. 280.

[45] Booth, 1988, p. 194.

[46] The source of information for his not attending the MAA meeting is John Booth's *Dramatic Magic* (1988), p. 196.

[47] Gardner is not the first to have such diverse interests. Lewis Carroll (Charles Lutwidge Dodgson) wrote on mathematics and logic puzzles, dabbled in conjuring, and was a member of the Society for Psychical Research. Gardner did *The Annotated Alice* (New York: Bramhall House, 1960) which explained the subtleties of Carroll's *Alice's Adventures in Wonderland* and *Through the Looking Glass*. Gardner mentioned that he felt spiritual kinship with Carroll. See *The Universe in*

a Handkerchief: Lewis Carroll's Mathematical Recreations, Games, Puzzles, and Word Plays (New York: Copernicus An Imprint of Springer-Verlag, 1996), p. ix.

[48] See A Bibliography of Martin Gardner in Magic by Dana Richards. In *Martin Gardner Presents* by Martin Gardner (Edited by Matthew Field, Mark Phillips, Harvey Rosenthal, and Max Maven). Published by Richard Kaufman and Alan Greenberg, 1993. Pp. 399–415.

[49] Elsewhere I have discussed the differing safeguards required in research with groups as opposed to that with gifted individuals. See Hansen, 1990a.

[50] Jurgen Keil, How A Skeptic Misrepresents the Research with Stepanek: A Review of Martin Gardner's *How Not To Test A Psychic, Journal of Parapsychology*, Vol. 54, 1990, pp. 151–167. See also Milan Ryzl's letter in the *Journal of Parapsychology*, Vol. 54, 1990, pp. 282–284. Gardner responded to Keil in a letter in the *Journal of Parapsychology*, Vol. 55, 1991, pp. 116, followed by a rebuttal by Keil in the same issue, pp. 116–118. John Beloff reviewed the book in the *Journal of the Society for Psychical Research* (Vol. 56, 1990, pp. 171–175) and seemed to admit the problems with the controls. However, Beloff's ability to evaluate technical merits of experiments, and criticisms, might be charitably described as limited.

[51] My own article "The Research with B.D. and Legacy of Magical Ignorance" (1992) reinforced this message, and Gardner provided helpful information when I prepared that critique.

[52] "The Ganzfeld Psi Experiment: A Critical Appraisal" in the *Journal of Parapsychology*, 1985, Vol. 49, pp. 3–49. That was immediately followed by a rebuttal by Charles Honorton, "Meta-analysis of Psi Ganzfeld Research: A Response to Hyman," pp. 51–91.

[53] Letter from Milan Ryzl, *Journal of Parapsychology*, Vol. 54, 1990, p. 284.

[54] Barcellos, 1979, p. 243.

[55] Parapsychology has suffered a long history of invalid statistical criticisms. Even back in the 1930s Rhine was subjected to attacks from ignorant psychologists. Professional statisticians, who were not as well established as they are today, became alarmed because they recognized that the attacks on Rhine also besmirched their own discipline. Eminent statisticians Thornton Fry, S. S. Wilks, Edward Huntington, and Burton Camp were in touch with Rhine. A statement was prepared and issued by Camp, president of the Institute of Mathematical Statistics, defending Rhine's statistics. For more on this see Mauskopf and McVaugh's *The Elusive Science*, p. 258.

[56] Gardner, 1977/1981b, A Skeptic's View of Parapsychology, *Science: Good, Bad and Bogus*, p. 141.

[57] His statement about the inability to evaluate the Honorton and Schmidt experiments was made 12 years before he published his Stepanek critique. Presumably Gardner would not make such a statement now.

[58] Pinch and Collins, 1984. For CSICOP policy, see Policy on Sponsoring Research, Testing Individual Claims, and Conducting Investigations of Alleged Paranormal Powers and Phenomena, *Skeptical Inquirer*, Vol. 6, No. 3, 1982, p. 9.

[59] Gardner, 1983/1988, Fool's Paradigms, *The New Age: Notes of a Fringe Watcher*, pp. 184–187.

[60] The quote is from *How Not to Test a Psychic*, p. 56. Gardner also raised the point earlier in lengthy a debate on parapsychology in the pages of *Behavioral and Brain Sciences*, Vol. 10, No. 4, 1987, see p. 587.

[61] Gardner, 1988, p. 18.

[62] See the earlier chapter Conjurors and the Paranormal; Truzzi, 1997; Hansen, Magicians Who Endorsed Psychic Phenomena, 1990, Magicians on the Paranormal, 1992.

[63] *Order and Surprise* by Martin Gardner, Buffalo, NY: Prometheus Books, 1983, p. 213.

[64] Prince, 1930.

[65] The two quotes are from pages 57 and 58 of *The Whys of a Philosophical Scrivener*.

[66] Gardner, 1983, p. 239.

[67] Ibid. p. 232.

[68] A Mind at Play: An Interview with Martin Gardner by Kendrick Frazier, *Skeptical Inquirer*, March/April, 1998, pp. 34–39, see p. 38.

[69] Gardner, 1983, p. 330.

[70] Ibid. p. 331.

[71] Though *The Flight of Peter Fromm* was narrated by a secular humanist professor, the author's sympathies were more with his young protagonist who maintained a belief in God. Not everyone understood this, but one who did was Phillip E. Johnson, a law professor at the University of California at Berkeley and a prominent Christian creationist. Johnson bought a dozen of Gardner's remaining copies of the 1973 edition of the novel and gave them to students and friends, resulting in a surprising, almost paradoxical, audience. Paul Kurtz's publishing house, Prometheus Books, reprinted the novel in 1994, and one wonders whether Kurtz understood Gardner's message and whether he was pleased with the readership. Johnson's interactions with Gardner are described in *Reason in the Balance: The Case Against Naturalism in Science, Law & Education* (1995), Downers Grove, Illinois, InterVarsity Press, pp. 236–238.

[72] Latour, 1988, p. 168.

[73] Ibid. p. 167.

[74] Gatling and Rhine, 1946.

[75] Rhine made it clear that experimental parapsychology had implications for religion, and he included a full chapter on it in *The New World of the Mind* (1953).

[76] Gardner, 1988, pp. 57–64.

[77] Gardner, 1992, pp. 111–117.

[78] *Harper's* magazine (March 1991, pp. 28–31) carried a transcript of a telephone conversation between Mims and Jonathan Piel, editor of *Scientific American*, which demonstrated the overt religious discrimination by *Scientific American*.

[79] In an article he wrote under the pseudonym of George Groth for the October 1952 issue of *Fate* magazine. (He Writes with Your Hand, by George Groth, *Fate*, Vol. 5, pp. 39–43.) That issue of *Fate* also carried an article by J. B. Rhine.

[80] Ashmore, 1989, p. 21.

[81] Ashmore, 1989, p. 42.
[82] Mehan and Wood, 1975, p. 159.

Chapter 21—Laboratory Research on Psi

[1] Broad, 1949/1976, p. 10.

[2] Parapsychological Association, 1988, p. 353.

[3] Zoltan Vassy, a Hungarian physicist who has conducted psi experiments, pointed out that several studies show that distance does affect scoring: "Distance, ESP, and Ideology" by Z. Vassy, *Behavioral and Brain Sciences*, Vol. 10, 1987, pp. 616–617. Charles Tart argues that precognition results are weaker than real-time ESP, which would indicate some, though not absolute, limits. See "Information Acquisition Rates in Forced-Choice ESP Experiments: Precognition Does Not Work as Well as Present-Time ESP" by Charles T. Tart, *Journal of the American Society for Psychical Research*, Vol. 77, 1983, 293–310.

[4] Telepathy: Origins of Randomization in Experimental Design by Ian Hacking (1988, see p. 427).

[5] Use of statistics is also seen in the 1885 *Proceedings of the American Society for Psychical Research*, Vol. 1, Report of the Committee on Thought-Transference by H. P. Bowditch, Edward C. Pickering, C. C. Jackson, Wm. Watson, Charles Sedgewick Minot, N. D. C. Hodges, & J. M. Peirce, see pp. 6–49. J. M. Peirce was a Harvard professor and brother of Charles Sanders Peirce.

[6] For an autobiographical account see *The Song of the Siren* by Stanley Krippner (1975).

[7] Most RNGs in parapsychology incorporate a true source of randomness such as radioactive decay or a noise diode. Some work is done with pseudorandom algorithms.

[8] If exactly 50 ones were produced, no decision was made, and another sample was taken.

[9] For example, see *Parapsychology: Frontier Science of the Mind* by Rhine and Pratt (1957, pp. 131–132). See also Rhine's comment "Frustrations over Research Failures" in the *Journal of Parapsychology*, Vol. 37, 1973, pp. 357–360.

[10] A Dual Experiment with Clock Cards by West and Fisk, 1953.

[11] Ibid. p. 185.

[12] After the West and Fisk study, others found that people who checked data could sometimes affect the outcome, and this was dubbed the "checker effect." The overall results are not clear, but there is sufficient evidence to suggest that a checker (even one who has no contact with the subjects) must be considered as a

potential source of an extra-chance scoring effect. The experiments are a bit too involved to present here, but they incorporated a variety of precautions to exclude unconscious, non-psi bias by the checkers. See "The Possible Effect of the Checker in Precognition Tests" by Sara R. Feather and Robert Brier, *Journal of Parapsychology*, Vol. 32, 1968, pp. 166–175. For more on the checker effect, see "The Checker Effect Revisited" by Debra H. Weiner and Nancy L. Zingrone in the *Journal of Parapsychology*, Vol. 50, 1986, pp. 85–121.

[13] A third paper on experimenter effects was published that year by Robert H. Thouless in the *Journal of the Society for Psychical Research*, Vol. 48, pp. 261–266, entitled "The Effect of the Experimenter's Attitude on Experimental Results in Parapsychology." It is of minor importance, but it demonstrates the salience of the issue at that time.

[14] Psychokinesis as Psi-Mediated Instrumental Response by Rex G. Stanford, et al, 1975.

[15] A New Technique of Testing ESP in a Real-Life, High-Motivational Context by Martin Johnson, 1973.

[16] A Test of the Relationship Between ESP and PK by Karlis Osis, 1953.

[17] *Dream Studies and Telepathy: An Experimental Approach*, by Montague Ullman & Stanley Krippner, 1970, see pp. 12, 31.

[18] *Deathbed Observations by Physicians and Nurses*, Parapsychological Monographs No. 3, by Karlis Osis, New York: Parapsychology Foundation, 1961.

[19] For some additional personal information on Osis, see his chapter "The Paranormal: My Window on Something More" in *Men and Women of Parapsychology: Personal Reflections* edited by Rosemarie Pilkington, Jefferson, NC: McFarland & Company, 1987.

[20] A. A. Foster made a similar point in 1940 in regard to blind matching ESP tests in "Is ESP Diametric?" in the *Journal of Parapsychology*, Vol. 4, No. 2, December 1940, pp. 325–328.

[21] "Psychokinesis" by Helmut Schmidt, in *Psychic Exploration: A Challenge for Science* edited by Edgar D. Mitchell and John White, 1974. See p. 190.

[22] Redundancy in Psi Information: Implications for the Goal-Oriented Hypothesis and for the Application of Psi by J. E. Kennedy, 1979.

[23] PK Effect on Pre-Recorded Targets by Helmut Schmidt, 1976. The retroactive PK experiment described here is covered on pages 279–281 of Schmidt's paper, which reported additional experiments.

[24] Channeling Evidence for a PK Effect to Independent Observers by Schmidt, Morris, and Rudolph, 1986.

[25] For more on such experiments, see "PK With Prerecorded Random Events and the Effects of Preobservation" by Helmut Schmidt and Henry Stapp and "Observation of a Psychokinetic Effect Under Highly Controlled Conditions" by Helmut Schmidt, both in the December 1993 *Journal of Parapsychology*.

[26] PK Effects on Pre-Recorded Group Behavior of Living Systems by Elmar R. Gruber, 1980.

[27] Quantum Physics and Parapsychology by C. T. K. Chari, *Journal of Parapsychology*, Vol. 20, 1956, pp. 166–183.

[28] Parapsychological Implications of Research in Atomic Physics by Pascual Jordan, *International Journal of Parapsychology*, 2(4), pp. 5–16.

[29] In a later article Walker revised and extended his discussion of quantum tunneling at synapses. See Quantum Mechanical Tunneling in Synaptic and Ephaptic Transmission by Evan Harris Walker, 1977.

[30] Parapsychology and Quantum Mechanics by Martin Gardner, 1981.

[31] Ibid. p. 62.

[32] Remarks on the Mind-Body Question by Eugene P. Wigner, 1962.

[33] Interview in the Fall 1997 *Mathematical Intelligencer* (p. 39) "A Great Communicator of Mathematics and Other Games: A Conversation with Martin Gardner" by Istvan Hargittai, Vol. 19, pp. 36–40. See also "Quantum Weirdness" by Martin Gardner, *Discover*, October 1982, pp. 69–76.

[34] Gardner, "Parapsychology and Quantum Mechanics," 1981, p. 64.

[35] Ibid. p. 64.

[36] Random Fluctuation Theory of Psychokinesis: Thermal Noise Model by Mattuck, 1977. Thermal Noise Theory of Psychokinesis: Modified Walker Model with Pulsed Information Rate by Mattuck, 1979. The Action of Consciousness on Matter: A Quantum Mechanical Theory of Psychokinesis by Mattuck and Walker, 1979.

[37] In addition to Giesler (1994), see Contributions to the Theory of PK Induction from Sitter-Group Work by Batcheldor, 1984.

[38] Toward a Mathematical Theory of Psi by Schmidt, 1975.

[39] Comparison of a Teleological Model with a Quantum Collapse Model of Psi by Schmidt, 1984. See p. 263.

[40] Comparison of Some Theoretical Predictions of Schmidt's Mathematical Theory and Walker's Quantum Mechanical Theory of Psi by Walker, 1977.

[41] Comparison of Some Theoretical Predictions of Schmidt's Mathematical Theory and Walker's Quantum Mechanical Theory of Psi by Walker, 1977, p. 64.

[42] Are Parapsychologists Paradigmless in Psiland? by Rex G. Stanford, 1977. See also Toward Reinterpreting Psi Events by Rex G. Stanford, 1978.

[43] See The Time Sequence of Psi-Ganzfeld Experimentation (Letter to the editor) by William G. Braud, *Journal of the American Society for Psychical Research*, Vol. 76, 1982, pp. 194–195.

[44] Braud, 1981, p. 1.

[45] Lability and Inertia in Conformance Behavior by William G. Braud, 1980. See also Lability and Inertia in Psychic Functioning by William Braud, 1981.

[46] For a review of some of that see Distant Intentionality and Healing: Assessing the Evidence by Schlitz and Braud, 1997.

Chapter 22—Totemism and the Primitive Mind

[1] Duff-Cooper, 1994, p. xv.

[2] Needham, 1963/1975, p. xxxix.

[3] Although Needham discussed Arnold van Gennep in that volume, he mentioned neither Victor Turner nor Edmund Leach, whose works were directly relevant.

[4] Reversal is another form of anti-structure, for instance, giving greater privilege to women than men, or paupers over kings.

[5] Frazer's output was massive; a hundred-page bibliography of his works was compiled by Theodore Besterman (*A Bibliography of Sir James George Frazer*, 1934). As a matter of historical interest, during the time he prepared that bibliography, Besterman was also serving as the librarian and investigations officer of the Society for Psychical Research. Besterman went on to become an eminent bibliographer. For more on Besterman, see *The Age of The Enlightenment: Studies Presented to Theodore Besterman*, Edited by W. H. Barber, J. H. Brumfitt, R. A. Leigh, R. Shackleton, and S. S. B. Taylor, Edinburgh: Oliver and Boyd, 1967. See especially the final chapter by Sir Frank Francis, director and principal librarian of the British Museum. See also *Theodore Besterman, Bibliographer And Editor: A Selection of Representative Texts* edited by Fransesco Cordasco, The Scarecrow Press, 1992.

[6] Anthropology and the Humanities by Ruth Benedict, *American Anthropologist*, Vol. 50, 1948, p. 587. Frazer's remark needs to be understood in light of his personality. He was quite solitary, and normal social relations were difficult for him. He worked in his library 12 hours a day, seven days a week, did only limited lecturing and played almost no active role in professional societies. His individualistic rationalism seems suited for someone so isolated from usual human contact. Bronislaw Malinowski knew Frazer for over 30 years and described some of his peculiarities in the chapter "The Paradox of Frazer's Personality and Work" in *A Scientific Theory of Culture and Other Essays*, 1944, see especially pp. 181–183.

[7] Edmund Leach's essay, "Golden Bough or Gilded Twig?" (1961), provides an assessment of Frazer's contributions. Leach noted that when the available sources were insufficient for Frazer, he would invent facts to insure a pleasing literary effect.

[8] For a historical perspective on these debates see Robert Fraser's *The Making of the Golden Bough* (1990).

[9] Alan Gauld, *The Founders of Psychical Research*, 1968.

[10] Presidential Address by E. Clodd, *Folk-Lore*, Vol. 6, 1895, pp. 54–81. See pp. 78–81. For follow-up see Protest of a Psycho-Folklorist by Andrew Lang, *Folk-Lore*, Vol. 6, 1895, pp. 236–248, and Clodd's immediate reply on pp. 248–258.

[11] Not all members of the RPA were antagonistic, a few were psychical researchers.

[12] Frazer is invoked in Paul Kurtz's *The Transcendental Temptation* (1986) and Richard Dawkins' *Unweaving the Rainbow: Science, Delusion and the Appetite for Wonder*, Boston: Houghton Mifflin Company, 1998.

[13] Bronislaw Malinowski reported that Lang's criticism of Frazer's *The Golden Bough* "so deeply upset and irritated Frazer that, as he told me, he had to interrupt his work on the subject for several months. After that experience Frazer never read adverse criticisms or reviews of his books" (Malinowski, 1944, p. 183).

[14] Lang was not the only anthropologist and psychical researcher involved in the debates on totemism; another was Northcote W. Thomas. See the bibliography of Andrew Duff-Cooper's *Andrew Lang on Totemism* (1994) for a listing of some of Thomas's works. Psychologist William McDougall also wrote on totemism (e.g., "The Relations Between Men and Animals in Sarawak" by Charles Hose and W. McDougall, *Journal of the Anthropological Institute of Great Britain and Ireland*, Vol. 31, 1901, pp. 173–213. McDougall later served as president of the SPR and mentor to J. B. Rhine.

[15] Needham was instrumental in the publication of Duff-Cooper's work on Lang.

[16] "Andrew Lang: Folklorist and Critic" (in French), *Folklore*, Vol. 23, 1912, pp. 366–369. See also Rodney Needham's 1967 Introduction to van Gennep's *The Semi-Scholars*, p. xiii.

[17] Durkheim, 1912/1965, p. 170.

[18] Durkheim in American Sociology, by Roscoe C. Hinkle, Jr., (1960/1964, p. 269).

[19] *Main Currents in Sociological Thought: Volume II: Durkheim, Pareto, Weber* by Raymond Aron (1967/1970, p. 64).

[20] For some discussion of this idea, see Emile Durkheim and C. G. Jung: Structuring a Transpersonal Sociology of Religion by Susan F. Greenwood, 1990.

[21] William McDougall's *The Group Mind* (1920, New York: Putnam's) was poorly received. For a more recent comment on the idea group minds, see Mary Douglas' *How Institutions Think* (1987). Freud's concept of the superego is by no means identical with these ideas, but it is related. Similarly, it gets little note today. A number of commentators have discussed its decline (e.g., Alexander Mitscherlich's *Society Without the Father: A Contribution to Social Psychology*, Translated by Eric Mosbacher, New York: Schocken Books, 1970 (Originally published in 1963), and Allen Wheelis' *The Quest for Identity*, New York: W. W. Norton & Company, 1958).

[22] Freud, 1913/1961, p. 26.

[23] See Doty, 1986; Evans-Pritchard, 1965/1972. Despite Freud's flawed explanation, he did recognize an important conjunction of features that many others did not wish to acknowledge. More recently Rene Girard has addressed some of these fundamental issues of violence, sexuality, and authority in terms of mimesis. For an attempted revival of some of Freud's ideas, see Robin Fox's *The Red Lamp of Incest* (1980), New York: E. P. Dutton.

[24] The trickster is particularly relevant to psychoanalytic theories because he violates incest prohibitions. Further, the African trickster god Eshu-Elegba is at times associated with long hair, a symbol of magical and sexual power.

[25] *Memories, Dreams, Reflections* by C. G. Jung, 1962/1963, p. 150. For more on this exchange, see *C. G. Jung's Psychology of Religion and Synchronicity* by Robert Aziz, 1990, pp. 93–110.

[26] Levy-Bruhl, 1910/1985, p. 306.

[27] Ibid. p. 302.

[28] Ibid. p. 127.

[29] Ibid. p. 109.

[30] Ibid. p. 109.

[31] Ibid. p. 38.

[32] Ibid. p. 361.

[33] Littleton has an understanding of liminality and the primitive mind, but his openness to them seems to have been accompanied by some dubious judgement. He was friendly with Carlos Castaneda and endorsed his work ("An Emic Account of Sorcery: Carlos Castaneda and the Rise of a New Anthropology" by C. Scott Littleton, 1976). Even in his 1985 introduction to *How Natives Think* Littleton did not seem convinced that Castaneda's work was a hoax and only noted that it "has been called into serious question" (p. xlvii). More recently Littleton suggested that Castaneda may have been abducted by extraterrestrial aliens and that Don Juan Matus was perhaps an ET alien. Littleton cited the work of John Mack, David Jacobs, and Budd Hopkins in support of the idea (Letter, *The Excluded Middle*, No. 7, 1997, p. 6). Littleton's deficient judgement is compelling evidence of the dangers of the liminal that face academics. Contact with liminality can make it difficult for one to distinguish fantasy from reality, making one an easy victim of hoaxes.

[34] Translator's Preface To The Second Edition by John W. Harvey (1949), see Otto, 1917/1975, p. xvi.

[35] Otto, 1917/1975, p. 100.

[36] Ibid. pp. 14–15.

[37] Freud, 1913/1961, p. 26.

[38] Ibid. pp. 26–27.

[39] Durkheim, 1912/1965, pp. 359–360.

[40] Ibid. p. 360.

[41] Ibid. p. 358.

[42] Ibid. p. 358.

[43] Otto, 1917/1975, p. 4.

[44] Ibid. p. 64.

[45] The date for Weber's *Economy and Society* is for the original manuscript. See Ephraim Fischoff's appendix in Weber's *The Sociology of Religion*, Boston: Beacon Press, 1964, p. 277. (Original work published 1922, after Weber's death).

[46] For a discussion of some of the interpretive controversies, see Structure and Infrastructure in Primitive Society: Levi-Strauss and Radcliffe-Brown by Neville Dyson-Hudson in Macksey and Donato, 1970/1972, pp. 218–246.

[47] Macksey & Donato, 1970/1972.

[48] Howard Gardner, 1973/1981, p. 135.

[49] *Totemism*, p. 98.

[50] Some of the very same issues are addressed in mystical theology. See for instance Ewert Cousins' *Bonaventure and the Coincidence of Opposites* (1978).

[51] Gardner, 1973/1981, p. 113.

[52] Ashley, 1988, p. 105.

[53] Leach, *The Structural Study of Myth and Totemism*, 1967, p. xvii.

[54] In his discussion of bricolage in *The Savage Mind* (1962/1966, p. 17), Levi-Strauss gave four brief examples, one involved Georges Melies and another Charles Dickens. Both were magic performers, a fact probably unknown to Levi-Strauss.

[55] Leach, *Claude Levi-Strauss*, 1970, p. 28.

[56] One cannot divorce the ideas from the man, and Levi-Strauss' comments on his own personality give insight into his theories. He admitted that "I never had, and still do not have, the perception of feeling my personal identity. I appear to myself as the place where something is going on, but there is no 'I', no 'me.'" (1978/1979, p. 3–4). He also acknowledged that "I don't have the feeling that I write my books. I have the feeling that my books get written through me" (1978/1979, p. 3). These statements are a bit reminiscent of mediumship. His comparisons and metaphors often require reflection but are frequently fruitful. The opening sentence of his book *Totemism* is intriguing: "Totemism is like hysteria..."

[57] Comparing the ideas of the two men is a difficult task, Ron Messer (1986), who has written on the trickster, has made an attempt to do so, with perhaps only limited success.

[58] James Boon, in an appendix appropriately entitled Trick*ster*ing in his book *Other Tribes, Other Scribes* (1982), remarks on these three anthropologists' interest in marginality and the supernatural.

Chapter 23—Literary Criticism, Meaning, and the Trickster

[1] King James Version

[2] For an idea of the range of structuralism, see Macksey and Donato (1970/1972), a collection of papers presented at a 1966 symposium at Johns Hopkins University.

[3] As mentioned in the chapter on reflexivity, ethnomethodology used the same strategy to accommodate itself to the establishment.

[4] For biographical material on Leach, see An Interview with Edmund Leach by Adam Kuper, *Current Anthropology*, Vol. 27, 1986, pp. 375–382; Glimpses of the Unmentionable in the History of British Social Anthropology by Edmund Leach, *Annual Review of Anthropology*, Vol. 13, 1984, pp. 1–23 (see pp. 9–10 for comments on the engineering influence). See also *Edmund Leach: A Bibliography*, London: Royal Anthropological Institute of Great Britain and Ireland, Occasional Paper no. 42, 1990.

[5] Lane, 1970, p. 14.

[6] Ibid. p. 17.

[7] Saussure, 1916/1959, p. 113.

[8] Saussure, 1916/1959, pp. 111–112.

[9] Saussure, 1916/1959, p. 112.

[10] Ibid. p. 113.

[11] Leach, 1964, p. 34.

[12] Ibid. p. 35.

[13] Ibid. p. 37.

[14] With semiotics being raised, a short digression on Charles Sanders Peirce is warranted because of his connections with psychical research. Peirce's father taught mathematics at Harvard, and Charles received a degree in chemistry from that university but worked as a physicist for 30 years for the U.S. Coast and Geodetic Survey. Peirce was an anti-structural character in many ways. He held few and brief academic positions. He did not ingratiate himself to administrators, colleagues, or students, often refusing to keep appointments. Peirce inherited a bit of money that allowed him to purchase a house, but he did not have enough for an easy existence, and he complained that he could not afford books. He died poor and forgotten in 1914, and Edward Moore tells us that "Only William James did what he could to make Peirce's final years easier." (See *American Pragmatism: Peirce, James, and Dewey* by Edward C. Moore, 1961, pp. 21–22.)

Peirce published only one book in his lifetime, and that was on astronomical observations, but his many papers were collected years after his death and released in a series of eight volumes (1931–1958). The Charles S. Peirce Society is now devoted to his work, and it has published a professional journal since 1965. Peirce was far ahead of his time, and he understood that academic bureaucracy is conducive to neither scientific creativity nor inventiveness. He commented that "Wherever there is a large class of academic professors who are provided with good incomes and looked up to as gentlemen, scientific inquiry must languish." (See *Collected Papers of Charles Sanders Peirce: Volume 1: Principles of Philosophy* edited by Charles Hartshorne and Paul Weiss, Cambridge, MA: Harvard University Press, 1931, p. 22.) Peirce recognized something about the anti-structure required for innovation, and sociologist C. Wright Mills and others have since made similar observations (see Mills, 1959/1967, pp. 103–106.).

Peirce is most famous for the philosophical school of pragmatism, which he founded along with William James. Pragmatists had some impact on psychical research. In England, F. C. S. Schiller was pragmatism's leading proponent, and both James and Schiller served as president of the Society for Psychical Research. Peirce contributed skeptical pieces to the *Proceedings of the American Society for Psychical Research* and his brother, Harvard professor and dean, James M. Peirce, was a member of the ASPR committee on thought-transference. (See Criticism on 'Phantasms of the Living.': An Examination of an Argument of Messrs. Gurney, Myers, and Podmore by C. S. Peirce, *Proceedings of the American Society for Psychical Research*, Vol. 1, No. 3, 1887, pp. 150–157; Mr. Peirce's Rejoinder, *Proceedings of the American Society for Psychical Research*, Vol. 1, No. 3, 1887, pp. 180–215. The reports of the ASPR committee on thought-transference, which J. M. Peirce signed, are found in *Proceedings of the American Society for Psychical Research*, Vol. 1, No. 1, 1885, pp. 6–9, Vol. 1, No. 2, 1886, pp. 106–112.)

[15] This was Saussure's and Barthes' usage which is not shared by everyone in semiotics, a field with some confusion in its terminology.

[16] Eco, 1967/1976/1979, p. 7.

[17] Eco's *Limits of Interpretation* opens with a discussion of John Wilkins' *Mercury; or, The Secret and Swift Messenger* (1641) which was one of the very first to discuss mentalist methods (though this was not mentioned by Eco); Wilkins also favorably discussed communication with angels and spirits. He was no marginal figure but rather one of the original members of the British Royal Society.

[18] De Man, 1971/1983, p. 11.

[19] Barthes, 1967/1970, p. 410.

[20] Smith, 1990, p. 279.

[21] For a brief discussion of some of the scandals, see Postmodernism, Theory, and the End of the Humanities by E. Christian Kopff, *Chronicles*, January 1996, pp. 16–19.

[22] Lehman, 1991, p. 187.

[23] Telepathy by Jacques Derrida, translated by Nicholas Royle, *Oxford Literary Review*, Vol. 10, Nos. 1–2, 1988, pp. 3–41.

[24] Royle, 1991, p. 10.
[25] Ibid. p. 11.
[26] Derrida, 1993/1994, p. 11.
[27] Royle, 1991, p. 15.
[28] Ibid. p. 25.
[29] Babcock and Cox, 1994, p. 103.
[30] Blaeser, 1996, p. 98.
[31] Ibid. p. 155.
[32] Ibid. p. 17.
[33] Ibid. p. 146.
[34] Kroeber, 1979, p. 76.
[35] Ibid. p. 81.
[36] Ibid. p. 79.
[37] There are variant spellings, versions, and combinations of Eshu-Elegba. For consistency with earlier chapters, I will continue with the combination and spelling here.
[38] Gates cannot be considered an advocate of deconstructionism, but he understands and utilizes its ideas. Gates was not the only African American scholar to recognize the importance of liminality in relation to the trickster figure. He specifically thanked Houston A. Baker, Jr., author of *Blues, Ideology, and Afro-American Literature: A Vernacular Theory* (Chicago: University of Chicago Press, 1984) for his writings on that. Baker is one of few who appreciated Barbara Babcock's work not only on liminality and the trickster, but also her writings on reflexivity.
[39] Gates, 1988, p. 6.
[40] Ibid. p. 21.
[41] Ibid. p. 25.
[42] Levi-Strauss, 1950/1987, pp. 55–56.
[43] Kurzweil, 1980, p. 136.
[44] Turkle studied with Victor Turner at the University of Chicago. For a profile of her, see An Ethnologist in Cyberspace by Marguerite Holloway, *Scientific American*, April 1998, pp. 29–30.
[45] Schneiderman, 1983, p. 161.
[46] Schneiderman, 1983, p. 14.
[47] Roudinesco, 1993/1997, p. 211.
[48] "Lacan died of postoperative complications after a tumor was removed from his *intestines*" (emphasis added, Schneiderman, 1983, p. 23). The connection of the trickster and intestines has been previously mentioned. In light of this ex-

ample, one might recall that Harry Houdini, another trickster figure, died of appendicitis.

[49] Roudinesco, 1993/1997, p. xv.
[50] Ibid. p. 8.
[51] Roudinesco, 1986/1990, pp. 104–105.
[52] Schneiderman, 1983, p. 11.
[53] Ibid. p. 119.
[54] Turkle, 1978/1992, p. 99.
[55] Schneiderman, 1983, p. 109.
[56] Schneiderman, 1983, p. 57.
[57] Schneiderman, 1983, p. 76.
[58] Ibid. pp. 60–61.
[59] This might be extended with the ideas of Jungian psychologist Rafael Lopez-Pedraza (1977/1989, p. 61) who pointed out in *Hermes and His Children* that Hermes' sacrifice was a true one whereas Prometheus' was a fraud.
[60] Schneiderman, 1983, p. 58.
[61] Kurzweil, 1980, p. 147.

Chapter 24—The Imagination

[1] Galton, 1883/1973, p. 58, 59.
[2] Singer, 1975, p. 61–63.
[3] Mills, 1959/1967, p. 5.
[4] Ibid. p. 14.
[5] Macionis, 1989, p. 8.
[6] Durkheim, 1912/1965, p. 490.
[7] Macionis, 1989, p. 431.
[8] On the Psychology of Parapsychology by James Hillman, In *A Century of Psychical Research: The Continuing Doubts and Affirmations: Proceedings of an International Conference Held at Le Piol, St. Paul De Vence, France September 2, 3, 4, 1970.* Edited by Allan Angoff and Betty Shapin, pp. 177–187, New York: Parapsychology Foundation, 1971.
[9] Hillman, 1985/1986.
[10] E.g., see Sass, 1988/1992.
[11] For further comparisons of Hillman and Lacan, see Adams (1985/1992).
[12] Hillman, 1975, p. 2.
[13] Hillman, 1975, p. 8.

[14] Hillman, 1975, p. 17.

[15] Stephen, 1989, p. 212.

[16] Hillman, 1975, p. 12.

[17] Ibid, p. 11.

[18] See George and Krippner (1984) for a review article on imagery as a component of psychic experiences.

[19] See Ring 1989, 1992.

[20] Rojcewicz, 1989, 1991, 1993.

[21] Ring, Rojcewicz, and Stillings were all involved with the New York Fortean Society (NYFS), which was organized by John Keel. Wolf acknowledged his intellectual indebtedness to Rojcewicz and Michael Grosso, another member of the NYFS.

[22] In passing, it should be mentioned that Corbin's ideas have been adopted by a few in psychology. Notable is the book *Invisible Guests: The Development of Imaginal Dialogues* (1986/1990) by Mary Watkins. Mary Gergen, another psychologist, presented a paper at the 1987 American Psychological Convention entitled "Social Ghosts: Opening Inquiry on Imaginal Relationships." Mary Gergen is wife of Kenneth J. Gergen, author of *The Saturated Self: Dilemmas of Identity in Contemporary Life* (BasicBooks A Division of HarperCollinsPublishers, 1991), which is one of the best books discussing postmodernity. Religious scholar Daniel C. Noel has also utilized the concept of the imaginal in his *The Soul of Shamanism* (1997).

[23] Hansen, 1992b.

[24] For a discussion of some imaginal creatures, in a couple of relatively reputable looking books, the reader may wish to examine Hilary Evans' *Visions, Apparitions, Alien Visitors* (1984) and *Gods, Spirits, Cosmic Guardians* (1987).

[25] Ring, 1992, p. 239.

[26] For some comments on Ring's *The Omega Project*, see the review by Karlis Osis, *Journal of the American Society for Psychical Research*, Vol. 88, 1994, pp. 71–76.

[27] Literature has the capacity to address matters that science cannot yet reach. Among others, this point was made by psychologist Lawrence LeShan in his *The Dilemma of Psychology* (1990). He frankly admitted that he found more insight into people in great literature than in professional psychology.

[28] Clements, 1987, p. 39.

[29] King, 1981, p. 40.

[30] This is also sometimes cited to explain the enjoyment of magic tricks, and there too it is of little value.

[31] Noel Carroll, 1990, p. 74.

[32] Ibid. p. 81.

[33] Fundraising letter from CSICOP entitled "Your Generous Help is Vitally Needed!" February 23, 1996. For articles see Paranormal and Paranoia Intermingle on Fox TV's 'X-Files' by C. Eugene Emery, Jr., *Skeptical Inquirer*, March/April 1995, pp. 18–19; The *X-Files* Meets the Skeptics, *Skeptical Inquirer*, January/February 1997, pp. 24–30.

[34] Mitchell, 1993, p. 73.

[35] Mitchell, 1993, p. 82.

[36] See Mitchell, 1993, which cited A Group of Young Chimpanzees in a One-Acre Field by E. W. Menzel, Jr., In *Behavior of Nonhuman Primates: Modern Research Trends* edited by Allan M. Schrier and Fred Stollnitz, New York: Academic Press, 1974, pp. 83–153, see pp. 133–135.

[37] Mitchell, 1993, p. 72.

[38] Ibid. p. 83.

[39] Mitchell's work on primates led him to address the broader issues of representation, simulation, communication, and the development of self-awareness. For some of Mitchell's other work see *Deception: Perspectives on Human and Nonhuman Deceit* in 1986 (edited by Robert W. Mitchell and Nicholas S. Thompson, Albany, NY: State University of New York Press) and *Anthropomorphism, Anecdotes, and Animals* in 1997 (edited by Robert W. Mitchell, Nicholas S. Thompson, and H. Lyn Miles, Albany, NY: State University of New York Press). The academic establishment has long denigrated anthropomorphism, but it is slowly regaining some respectability.

Chapter 25—Paranoia

[1] Derived from a conversation reported in *Helter Skelter: The True Story of the Manson Murders* by Vincent Bugliosi with Curt Gentry, New York: W. W. Norton & Company, 1974, p. 238.

[2] *Webster's Ninth New Collegiate Dictionary*, Springfield, Mass: Merriam-Webster Inc., 1985, p. 854.

[3] For a discussion of aggression and nightmares, see *Nightmares & Human Conflict* by John E. Mack, Boston: Houghton Mifflin, 1974 (Originally published 1970).

[4] Babcock-Abrahams, 1975a, pp. 177–178. Babcock-Abrahams' wording in quotes is slightly different than Radin, 1956/1972, p. 134.

[5] Berman, 1981/1984, p. 301.

[6] Lacan, 1948/1977, p. 15.

[7] Hartmann, 1991, p. 101.

[8] Douglas, 1963, p. 141.

[9] Kottmeyer's article emphasized pathological aspects and used some weak case material. Nevertheless, Kottmeyer deserves credit for recognizing a fundamental aspect of the UFO phenomenon. He understood that status loss was an important factor.

[10] Jung's opinion about UFOs has been a source of speculation among ufologists. For a discussion of the controversies see "What Did Carl Gustav Jung Believe About Flying Saucers?" by Dennis Stillings, in Stillings, 1989 (pp. 33–49).

[11] Epstein, 1989, p. 92.

[12] Ibid. p. 103.

[13] Epstein, 1989, p. 45.

[14] Perot-noia by Laurence I. Barrett and Richard Woodbury, *Time*, November 9, 1992, p. 28.

[15] Emery, 1994.

[16] Toch, 1965, p. 62.

[17] Ehrenwald is another immigrant (boundary crosser) who did innovative work in parapsychology. For some brief biographical material on him see Pilkington, 1987.

[18] Ehrenwald, 1948, p. 123.

[19] Ibid. p. 147.

[20] Palmer, 1992.

[21] See Eisenbud, 1946/1953; Irwin, 1989; LeShan, 1966; Tart 1982, 1984, 1986; Tart and Labore, 1986; Wren-Lewis, 1974.

[22] Both social masking theory and primal conflict repression theory involve blocking awareness of deception, deception that is generally healthy and adaptive. Here again a linkage is seen between deception and psi.

[23] For a more in-depth psychoanalytic discussion, see Mother-Child Symbiosis: Cradle of ESP by Jan Ehrenwald (1971).

Chapter 26—Conclusions

[1] Telepathy, clairvoyance, precognition, and micro-PK do not seem to degrade as distance increases. Macro-PK does appear to be attenuated by distance. Very few macro-PK events occur more than a few meters from the PK agent.

REFERENCES

Abbott, David P. (1908). *The History of a Strange Case.* Chicago, IL: Open Court Publishing Company.

Ackerman, Robert. (1987). *J. G. Frazer: His Life and Work.* Cambridge, England: Cambridge University Press.

Adams, Michael Vannoy. (1992). Deconstructive Philosophy and Imaginal Psychology: Comparative Perspectives on Jacques Derrida and James Hillman. In Richard P. Sugg (Ed.), *Jungian Literary Criticism,* (pp. 231–248, 408–410). Evanston, IL: Northwestern University Press. (Original work published 1985)

Adler, Margot. (1986). *Drawing Down the Moon: Witches, Druids, Goddess-Worshippers, and Other Pagans in America Today.* (Revised and Expanded Edition). Boston, MA: Beacon Press. (Original work published 1979)

Ady, Thomas. (1655). *A Candle in the Dark: Shewing The Divine Cause of the Distractions of the Whole Nation of England, and of the Christian World.* London: Printed for Robert Ibbitson.

Alvarado, Carlos S. (1993). Gifted Subjects' Contributions to Psychical Research: The Case of Eusapia Palladino. *Journal of the Society for Psychical Research,* 59: 269–292.

Ammons, Elizabeth, & White-Parks, Annette. (Eds.). (1994). *Tricksterism in Turn-of-the-Century American Literature: A Multicultural Perspective.* Hanover, NH: University Press of New England.

Anderson, Rodger I. (1985). The Life and Work of James H. Hyslop. *Journal of the American Society for Psychical Research,* 79: 167–204.

Annemann, [Theodore]. (1938). Was Prof. J. B. Rhine Hoodwinked? *Jinx,* No. 47, August, pp. 329, 333.

Aron, Raymond. (1970). *Main Currents in Sociological Thought: Volume II: Durkheim, Pareto, Weber.* (Translated from the French by Richard Howard and Helen Weaver). Garden City, NY: Doubleday & Company, Inc. (Earlier published 1967.)

Ashley, Kathleen M. (1982). The Guiler Beguiled: Christ and Satan as Theological Tricksters in Medieval Religious Literature. *Criticism: A Quarterly for Literature and the Arts.* 24: 126–137.

Ashley, Kathleen M. (1988). Interrogating Biblical Deception and Trickster Theories: Narratives of Patriarchy or Possibility. *Semeia,* 42: 103–116.

Ashmore, Malcolm. (1989). *The Reflexive Thesis: Wrighting Sociology of Scientific Knowledge*. Chicago: University of Chicago Press.

Ashworth, C. E. (1980). Flying Saucers, Spoon-Bending and Atlantis: A Structural Analysis of New Mythologies. *Sociological Review*, 28: 353–376.

Associated Investigators Group. (1993). Associated Investigators Report AIR #1 The Fund for CIA Research? or Who's Disinforming Whom? *Third Eyes Only*, No. 14, July, pp. 1–14.

Atwater, P.[hyllis] M. H. (1994). *Beyond the Light: What Isn't Being Said About Near-Death Experience*. New York: A Birch Lane Press Book.

Aziz, Robert. (1990). *C. G. Jung's Psychology of Religion and Synchronicity*. Albany, NY: State University of New York Press.

Babcock-Abrahams, Barbara. (1975a). "A Tolerated Margin of Mess": The Trickster and His Tales Reconsidered. *Journal of the Folklore Institute*. 11: 147–186.

Babcock-Abrahams, Barbara. (1975b). Why Frogs Are Good to Think and Dirt is Good to Reflect on. *Soundings*, 58: 167–181.

Babcock, Barbara A. (1978). Introduction. In Barbara A. Babcock (Ed.) *The Reversible World: Symbolic Inversion in Art and Society* (pp. 13–36). Ithaca, NY: Cornell University Press.

Babcock, Barbara A. (1980). Reflexivity: Definitions and Discriminations. *Semiotica*, 30(1/2): 1–14.

Babcock, Barbara A. (1982). Ritual Undress and the Comedy of Self and Other: Bandelier's *The Delight Makers*. In *A Crack in the Mirror: Reflexive Perspectives in Anthropology* edited by Jay Ruby, pp. 187–203. Philadelphia, PA: University of Pennsylvania Press.

Babcock, Barbara A. (1984). Arrange Me into Disorder: Fragments and Reflections on Ritual Clowning. In *Rite, Drama, Festival, Spectacle: Rehersals Toward a Theory of Cultural Performance* edited by John J. MacAloon, pp. 102–128. Philadelphia, PA: Institute for the Study of Human Issues.

Babcock, Barbara A. (1987). Reflexivity. In Mircea Eliade (Ed.). *The Encyclopedia of Religion*, Vol. 16 (pp. 234–238). New York: Macmillan Publishing Company.

Babcock, Barbara A. (1990). Mud, Mirrors, and Making Up: Liminality and Reflexivity in Between the Acts. In Kathleen M. Ashley (Ed.). *Victor Turner and the Construction of Cultural Criticism: Between Literature and Anthropology* (pp. 86–116). Bloomington, IN: Indiana University Press.

Babcock, Barbara; & Cox, Jay. (1994). The Native American Trickster. In Andrew Wiget (Ed.). *Dictionary of Native American Literature* (pp. 99–105). New York: Garland Publishing, Inc.

Bainbridge, William Sims. (1989). Wandering Souls: Mobility and Unorthodoxy. In George K. Zollschan, John F. Schumaker, and Greg F. Walsh (Eds.), *Exploring the Paranormal: Perspectives on Belief and Experience* (pp. 237–249). Bridport, Dorset, U.K.: Prism Unity.

Bainbridge, William Sims. (1995). Review of *Wondrous Events: Foundations of Religious Belief* by James McClenon in *Journal for the Scientific Study of Religion*, 34(4): 533.

Baker, Robert A. (1990). *They Call it Hypnosis*. Buffalo, NY: Prometheus Books.

Baldwin, Samri S. (1895). *The Secrets of Mahatma Land Explained*. Brooklyn, NY: T. J. Dyson & Son.

Ballinger, Franchot. (1989). Living Sideways: Social Themes and Social Relationships in Native American Trickster Tales. *American Indian Quarterly*, 13(1): 15–30.

Bandelier, Adolf F. (1971). *The Delight Makers*. New York: Harcourt Brace Jovanovich. (Originally published 1890.)

Barber, Theodore Xenophon. (1993). *The Human Nature of Birds: A Scientific Discovery with Startling Implications*. New York: St. Martin's Press.

Barber, Theodore Xenophon, & Silver, Maurice J. (1968). Fact, Fiction, and the Experimenter Effect. *Psychological Bulletin* Monograph Supplement, Vol. 70, No. 6, Part 2, December, 1–29.

Barcellos, Anthony. (1979). A Conversation with Martin Gardner. *Two-Year College Mathematical Journal*, 10(4): 233–244.

Barnouw, Erik. (1981). *The Magician and the Cinema*. New York: Oxford University Press.

Barrow, Logie. (1986). *Independent Spirits: Spiritualism and English Plebians, 1850–1910*. London: Routledge & Kegan Paul.

Barthes, Roland. (1970). Science Versus Literature. In *Introduction to Structuralism* (Edited by Michael Lane), pp. 410–416. New York: Basic Books. (Originally published 1967.)

Barthes, Roland. (1979). *Mythologies*. (Translated by Annette Lavers). New York: Hill and Wang a Division of Farrar, Straus & Giroux. (Originally published 1957.)

Barthes, Roland (1983). *Elements of Semiology*. (Translated by Annette Lavers and Colin Smith). New York: Hill and Wang A Division of Farrar, Straus and Giroux. (Originally published 1964.)

Basso, Ellen B. (1987). *In Favor of Deceit: A Study of Tricksters in an Amazonian Society*. Tucson, AZ: The University of Arizona Press.

Batcheldor, K. J. (1979). PK in Sitter Groups. *Psychoenergetic Systems*. 3: 77–92.

Batcheldor, Kenneth J. (1984). Contributions to the Theory of PK Induction From Sitter-Group Work. *Journal of the American Society for Psychical Research*, 78: 105–122.

Batcheldor, Kenneth J. (1994). Notes on the Elusiveness Problem in Relation to a Radical View of Paranormality. (Compiled, edited and with a preface and notes by Patric V. Giesler). *Journal of the American Society for Psychical Research*, 88: 90–116.

Belmont, Nicole. (1979). *Arnold Van Gennep: The Creator of French Ethnography*. (Translated by Derek Coltman). Chicago: University of Chicago Press. (First published in French in 1974)

Ben-Yehuda, Nachman. (1985). *Deviance and Moral Boundaries: Witchcraft, the Occult, Science Fiction, Deviant Sciences and Scientists*. Chicago, IL: The University of Chicago Press.

Berger, Arthur S. (1985a). The Early History of the ASPR: Origins to 1907. *Journal of the American Society for Psychical Research*, 79: 39–60.

Berger, Arthur S. (1985b). Problems of the ASPR under J. H. Hyslop. *Journal of the American Society for Psychical Research*, 79: 205–219.

Berger, Arthur S. (1988). *Lives and Letters in American Parapsychology: A Biographical History, 1850–1987*. Jefferson, NC: McFarland & Company.

Berger, Arthur S., and Berger, Joyce. (1991). *The Encyclopedia of Parapsychology and Psychical Research*. New York: Paragon House.

Berger, Peter L. (1990). *A Rumor of Angels: Modern Society and the Rediscovery of the Supernatural*. (Expanded edition). New York: Anchor Books Doubleday. (First edition published 1969.)

Berman, Morris. (1984). *The Reenchantment of the World*. New York: Bantam Books. (Originally published 1981)

Bernstein, Morey. (1956). *The Search for Bridey Murphy*. Garden City, NY: Doubleday & Company.

Besterman, Theodore (Compiler). (1934). *A Bibliography of Sir James George Frazer O.M.* London: Macmillan and Co.

Beyerstein, Dale. (Editor). (1992). *Sai Baba's Miracles: An Overview*. Vancouver, B.C.: Dale Beyerstein.

Bharati, Agehananda. (1976). *The Light at the Center: Context and Pretext of Modern Mysticism.* Santa Barbara, CA: Ross-Erikson.

Bierman, D[ick]. J. (1979). A Methodological Hint for Research in RSPK Cases. *European Journal of Parapsychology,* 3(1): 111.

Birdsell, Polly Griffin. (1989). *How Magicians Relate the Occult to Modern Magic: An Investigation and Study.* Simi Valley, CA: Silver Dawn Media.

Bishop, Morris. (1974). *Saint Francis of Assisi.* Boston, MA: Little, Brown and Company.

Blaeser, Kimberly M. (1996). *Gerald Vizenor: Writing in the Oral Tradition.* Norman, OK: University of Oklahoma Press.

Bluemle, Bob. (1994). Marcello Truzzi: Vibrations Interview, Part 2. *Vibrations* (Psychic Entertainers Association newsletter), July, pp. 7–8.

Bolen, Jean Shinoda. (1982). *The Tao of Psychology: Synchronicity and the Self.* HarperSanFrancisco. (Originally published 1979.)

Bolen, Jean Shinoda. (1989). *Gods in Everyman: A New Psychology of Men's Lives and Loves.* New York: Harper & Row.

Boles, Jacqueline; Davis, Phillip; & Tatro, Charlotte. (1983). False Pretense and Deviant Exploitation: Fortunetelling as a Con. *Deviant Behavior,* 4: 375–394.

Boon, James A. (1972). *From Symbolism to Structuralism: Levi-Strauss in a Literary Tradition.* New York: Harper & Row.

Boon, James A. (1982). *Other Tribes, Other Scribes: Symbolic Anthropology in the Comparative Study of Cultures, Histories, Religions, and Texts.* Cambridge, England: Cambridge University Press.

Booth, John. (1988). *Dramatic Magic: The Art of Hidden Secrets.* Los Alamitos, CA: Ridgeway Press.

Borges, Jorge Luis. (1968). *Other Inquisitions 1937–1952.* (Translated by Ruth L. C. Simms). New York: Simon and Schuster. (Book originally published 1952)

Bourguignon, Erika. (Editor). (1973). *Religion, Altered States of Consciousness, and Social Change.* Columbus, OH: Ohio State University Press.

Bourke, John G. (1891). *Scatalogic Rites of All Nations. A Dissertation upon the Employment of Excrementitious Remedial Agents in Religion, Therapeutics, Divination, Witchcraft, Love-Philters, etc., in all Parts of the Globe.* Washington, DC: W. H. Lowdermilk & Co.

Bowen, Nancy Ruth. (1994). *The Role of YHWH as Deceiver in True and False Prophecy*. Ph.D. Dissertation, Princeton Theological Seminary. Princeton, NJ.

Brady, Ernest W. (1966). Mercury: Messenger of the Gods and Magician. *Linking Ring*, 46(4), April, pp. 25–27, 57–58.

Braud, William G. (1980). Lability and Inertia in Conformance Behavior. *Journal of the American Society for Psychical Research*, 74: 297–318.

Braud, William. (1981). Lability and Inertia in Psychic Functioning. In Betty Shapin and Lisette Coly (Eds.), *Concepts and Theories of Parapsychology: Proceedings of an International Conference Held in New York, New York December 6, 1980*, (pp. 1–28). New York: Parapsychology Foundation.

Braud, William. (1985). The Two Faces of Psi: Psi Revealed and Psi Obscured. In Betty Shapin and Lisette Coly (Eds.), *The Repeatability Problem in Parapsychology: Proceedings of an International Conference Held in San Antonio, Texas October 28–29, 1983*. New York: Parapsychology Foundation.

Braud, William. (1993). On the Use of Living Target Systems in Distant Mental Influence Research. In Lisette Coly and Joanne D. S. McMahon (Eds.), *Psi Research Methodology: A Re-examination. Proceedings of an International Conference Held in Chapel Hill, North Carolina October 29–30, 1988*, (pp. 149–181). New York: Parapsychology Foundation, Inc.

Braude, Ann. (1989). *Radical Spirits: Spiritualism and Women's Rights in Nineteenth-Century America*. Boston, MA: Beacon Press.

Brinton, Daniel G. (1885). The Chief God of the Algonkins, in His Character as a Cheat and Liar. *American Antiquarian and Oriental Journal*, 7: 137-139.

Broad, C.[harlie] D.[unbar] (1976). The Relevance of Psychical Research to Philosophy. In James M. O. Wheatley and Hoyt L. Edge (Eds.), *Philosophical Dimensions of Parapsychology*, (pp. 10–29). Springfield, IL: Charles C Thomas Publisher. (Original work published 1949)

Brooke, Tal. (1990). *Lord of the Air*. Eugene, OR: Harvest House Publishers. (Original work published 1976)

Broughton, Richard S. (1991). *Parapsychology: The Controversial Science*. New York: Ballantine Books.

Brown, Norman O. (1947). *Hermes the Thief: The Evolution of a Myth*. The University of Wisconsin Press.

Brown, Paula, & Tuzin, Donald. (Eds.). (1983). *The Ethnography of Cannibalism*. Washington, DC: Society for Psychological Anthropology.

Bugliosi, Vincent; with Gentry, Curt. (1974). *Helter Skelter: The True Story of the Manson Murders*. New York: W. W. Norton & Company.

Burger, Eugene; and Neale, Robert E. (1995). *Magic & Meaning*. Seattle, WA: Hermetic Press.

Butler's Lives of the Saints. (1981). Edited, revised and supplemented by Herbert J. Thurston, S.J., and Donald Attwater. (4 Volumes). Westminster, MD: Christian Classics. (Original work published 1756–59, revised 1926–38.)

Cameron, Grant, and Crain, Jr., T. Scott. (1991). *UFOs, MJ-12 and the Government: A Report on Government Involvement in UFO Crash Retrievals*. Seguin, TX: Mutual UFO Network.

Camp, Claudia V. (1988). Wise and Strange: An Interpretation of the Female Imagery in Proverbs in Light of Trickster Mythology. *Semeia*, 42: 14–36.

Campbell, Bruce F. (1980). *Ancient Wisdom Revived: A History of the Theosophical Movement*. Berkeley, CA: University of California Press.

Campbell, Jeremy. (1982). *Grammatical Man: Information, Entropy, Language, and Life*. New York: Simon & Schuster.

Campbell, Joseph. (1987). *The Masks of God: Primitive Mythology*. New York: Penguin Books. (Originally published 1959.)

Carrington, Hereward. (1909). *Eusapia Palladino and Her Phenomena*. New York: B. W. Dodge & Company.

Carrington, Hereward. (1920). *Mind Reading (Telepathy) (How To Do It)*. New York: Dodd, Mead.

Carroll, Michael P. (1977). Leach, Genesis, and Structural Analysis: A Critical Evaluation. *American Ethnologist*, 4: 663–677.

Carroll, Michael P. (1981). Levi-Strauss, Freud, and the Trickster: A New Perspective Upon an Old Problem. *American Ethnologist*, 8: 301–313.

Carroll, Michael P. (1984). The Trickster as Selfish-Buffoon and Culture Hero. *Ethos*, 12: 105–131.

Carroll, Michael P. (1986). The Trickster-Father Feigns Death and Commits Incest: Some Methodological Contributions to the Study of Myth. *Behavioral Science Research*, 19: 24–57.

Carroll, Noel. (1990). *The Philosophy of Horror or Paradoxes of the Heart*. New York: Routledge.

Casti, John L. (1990). *Searching for Certainty: What Scientists Can Know About the Future.* New York: William Morrow and Company.

Charles, Lucile Hoerr. (1945). The Clown's Function. *Journal of American Folklore*, 58: 25–34.

Child, Irvin L. (1985). Psychology and Anomalous Observations: The Question of ESP in Dreams. *American Psychologist*, 40: 1219–1230.

Christensen, Andrew; and Jacobson, Neil S. (1994). Who (Or What) Can Do Psychotherapy: The Status and Challenge of Nonprofessional Therapies. *Psychological Science*, 5(1): 8–14.

Christopher, Milbourne. (1962). *Panorama of Magic.* New York: Dover Publications.

Christopher, Milbourne. (1973). *The Illustrated History of Magic.* New York: Thomas Y. Crowell Company.

Christopher, Milbourne. (1975). *Mediums, Mystics & the Occult.* New York: Thomas Y. Crowell Company.

Clegg, III, Claude Andrew. (1997). *An Original Man: The Life and Times of Elijah Muhammad.* New York: St. Martin's Press.

Clements, William M. (1987). The Interstitial Ogre: The Structure of Horror in Expressive Culture. *South Atlantic Quarterly*, 86(1): 34–43.

Clements, William M. (1991). Interstitiality in Contemporary Legends. *Contemporary Legend*, 1, 81–91.

Coleman, Kate. (1979). Elisabeth Kübler-Ross in the Afterworld of Entities. *New West*, July 30, pp. 43–50.

Coleman, Loren. (1989). *Tom Slick and the Search for the Yeti.* Boston: Faber and Faber.

Colie, Rosalie L. (1966). *Paradoxia Epidemica: The Renaissance Tradition of Paradox.* Princeton, NJ: Princeton University Press.

Collins, H.[arry] M. (1985). *Changing Order: Replication and Induction in Scientific Practice.* London: Sage Publications.

Collins, H. M. (1989). Scientific Knowledge and Scientific Criticism. In *Parapsychology and Human Nature: Proceedings of an International Conference Held in Washington, D.C. November 1–2, 1986*, Edited by Betty Shapin and Lisette Coly (pp. 36–52). New York: Parapsychology Foundation, Inc.

Collins, H. M.; and Pinch, T. J. (1982). *Frames of Meaning: The Social Construction of Extraordinary Science.* London: Routledge & Kegan Paul Limited.

Collins, Harry; & Pinch, Trevor. (1993). *The Golem: What Everyone Should Know About Science*. Cambridge, England: Cambridge University Press.

Combs, Allan; & Holland, Mark. (1990). *Synchronicity: Science, Myth, and the Trickster*. New York: Paragon House.

Corbin, Henry. (1976). *Mundus Imaginalis or the Imaginary and the Imaginal*. Ipswich: Golgonooza Press. (Original work published 1972)

Cousins, Ewert H. (1978). *Bonaventure and the Coincidence of Opposites*. Chicago: Franciscan Herald Press.

Cox, Jay. (1989). *Dangerous Definitions: Female Tricksters in Contemporary Native American Literature*. Wicazo Sa Review, 5(2): 17–21.

Crossan, John Dominic. (1976). *Raid on the Articulate: Comic Eschatology in Jesus and Borges*. New York: Harper & Row.

Crumrine, N. Ross. (1969). Capakoba, The Mayo Easter Ceremonial Impersonator: Explanations of Ritual Clowning. *Journal for the Scientific Study of Religion*, 8: 1–22.

Crumrine, N. Ross; and Halpin, Marjorie. (Editors.) (1983). *The Power of Symbols: Masks and Masquerade in the Americas*. Vancouver, BC: University of British Columbia Press.

Davis, Winston. (1980). *Dojo: Magic and Exorcism in Modern Japan*. Stanford, CA: Stanford University Press.

Dawes, Edwin A. (1979). *The Great Illusionists*. Secaucus, NJ: Chartwell Books.

Dawes, Robyn M. (1994). *House of Cards: Psychology and Psychotherapy Built on Myth*. New York: The Free Press A Division of Macmillan, Inc.

Dawson, Jr., John W. (1997). *Logical Dilemmas: The Life and Work of Kurt Gödel*. Wellesley, MA: A K Peters.

Dean, E. Douglas. (1966). Plethysmograph Recordings as ESP Responses. *International Journal of Neuropsychiatry*, 2(5): 439–446.

Dean, Jodi. (1998). *Aliens in America: Conspiracy Cultures from Outerspace to Cyberspace*. Ithaca, NY: Cornell University Press.

Decremps, Henri. (1784). *La Magie Blanche Dévoilée ou Explication*. Paris: Langlois Libraire et Chez L'Auteur.

Degh, Linda; & Vazsonyi, Andrew. (1973). *The Dialectics of the Legend*. Folklore Preprint Series, Vol. 1, No. 6. Bloomington, IN: Folklore Publications Group, Folklore Institute.

de Man, Paul. (1983). *Blindness and Insight: Essays in the Rhetoric of Contemporary Criticism.* (Second edition). Minneapolis, MN: University of Minnesota Press. (Originally published 1971)

de Mille, Richard. (1977). *Castaneda's Journey: The Power and the Allegory.* Santa Barbara, CA: Capra Press. (First published 1976.)

de Mille, Richard. (Editor). (1980). *The Don Juan Papers: Further Castaneda Controversies.* Santa Barbara, CA: Ross-Erikson Publishers.

Derrida, Jacques. (1988). Telepathy. (Translated by Nicholas Royle). *Oxford Literary Review,* 10(1–2), 3–41. (First published 1981.)

Derrida, Jacques. (1994). *Specters of Marx: The State of the Debt, the Work of Mourning, and the New International.* (Translated by Peggy Kamuf). London: Routledge. (Earlier published 1993.)

Diamond, Stanley. (1969). Plato and the Primitive. In Stanley Diamond (Ed.). *Primitive Views of the World* (pp. 170–193). New York: Columbia University Press. (Original work published 1960)

Diamond, Stanley. (1972). Introductory essay: Job and the Trickster. In The *Trickster: A Study in American Indian Mythology* by Paul Radin (pp. xi–xxii). New York: Schocken Books.

Dingwall, Eric John. (1962). *Some Human Oddities: Studies in the Queer, the Uncanny and the Fanatical.* New Hyde Park, NY: University Books. (Originally published 1947).

Dingwall, Eric John. (1962). *Very Peculiar People: Portrait Studies in the Queer, the Abnormal and the Uncanny.* New Hyde Park, NY: University Books. (Originally published 1950)

Dingwall, Eric J. (Editor). (1967–1968). *Abnormal Hypnotic Phenomena: A Survey of Nineteenth-Century Cases.* (4 volumes). London: J. & A. Churchill Ltd.

Dingwall, E. J. (1971). Responsibility in Parapsychology. In *A Century of Psychical Research: The Continuing Doubts and Affirmations: Proceedings of an International Conference Held at Le Piol, St. Paul De Vence, France September 2, 3, 4, 1970* (Edited by Allan Angoff and Betty Shapin), pp. 37–52. New York: Parapsychology Foundation.

Dingwall, [E. J.]. (1974). Discussion. In *Parapsychology and Anthropology: Proceedings of an International Conference Held in London, England August 29–31, 1973,* (Edited by Allan Angoff and Diana Barth), p. 284. New York: Parapsychology Foundation.

Dingwall, Eric J.; Goldney, Kathleen M.; & Hall, Trevor H. (1956). *The Haunting of Borley Rectory.* London: Gerald Duckworth & Co.

Dingwall, Eric J.; & Hall, Trevor H. (1958). *Four Modern Ghosts.* London: Gerald Duckworth & Co.

Dodds, E.[ric] R.[obertson]. (1971). *The Greeks and the Irrational.* Berkeley, CA: University of California Press. (Original work published 1951)

Dossey, Larry. (1996). The Trickster: Medicine's Forgotten Character. *Alternative Therapies,* 2(2): 6–14.

Doty, William G. (1986). *Mythography: The Study of Myths and Rituals.* Tuscaloosa, AL: University of Alabama Press.

Doty, William G. (1995). Everything You Never Wanted to Know About the Dark, Lunar Side of the Trickster. *Spring: A Journal of Archetype and Culture,* No. 57: 19–38.

Douglas, Mary. (1963). Techniques of Sorcery Control in Central Africa. In John Middleton and E. H. Winter (Eds.) *Witchcraft and Sorcery in East Africa* (pp. 123–141). London: Routledge & Kegan Paul.

Douglas, Mary. (1966). *Purity and Danger: An Analysis of Concepts of Pollution and Taboo.* New York: Frederick A. Praeger, Publishers.

Douglas, Mary. (1973). *Natural Symbols: Explorations in Cosmology.* New York: Vintage Books a Division of Random House. (Originally published 1970.)

Douglas, Mary. (1987). *How Institutions Think.* London: Routledge & Kegan Paul.

Downing, Christine. (1993). *Gods in Our Midst: Mythological Images of the Masculine: A Woman's View.* New York: Crossroad.

Drewes, Athena A.; & Drucker, Sally Ann. (1991). *Parapsychological Research With Children: An Annotated Bibliography.* Metuchen, NJ: Scarecrow Press.

Ducasse, C.[urt] J.[ohn] (1960). How the Case of The Search for Bridey Murphy Stands Today. *Journal of the American Society for Psychical Research,* 44: 3–22.

Duff-Cooper, Andrew. (1994). Part I: Commentary in *Andrew Lang on Totemism,* CSAC Monographs 8, pp. 1–115. Canterbury: Centre for Social Anthropology and Computing The University of Kent at Canterbury.

Duke, Gail; & Hansen, George P. (1991). Bibliography on the SORRAT Phenomena and Experiments. *Artifex,* 9: 45–49.

Durant, Robert J. [& Hansen, George P.]. (1992). Will the *Real* Scott Jones Please Stand Up? *Third Eyes Only*, No. 1: 26–51.

Durkheim, Emile. (1965). *The Elementary Forms of the Religious Life.* (Translated from the French by Joseph Ward Swain.). New York: The Free Press A Division of Macmillan Publishing Co., Inc. (Original work published 1912)

Durkheim, Emile; & Mauss, Marcel. (1975). *Primitive Classification.* (Translated from the French by Rodney Needham). Chicago: University of Chicago Press. (Original work published 1903.)

Durkheim, Emile; et al. (1964). *Essays on Sociology and Philosophy* (Edited by Kurt H. Wolff). New York: Harper Torchbooks The Academy Library Harper & Row, Publishers. (Book originally published 1960 under the title *Emile Durkheim, 1858–1917.*)

Dutch, Steven. (1986). Four Decades of Fringe Literature. *Skeptical Inquirer*, Vol. 10, No. 4, Summer, pp. 342–351.

Eco, Umberto. (1979). *A Theory of Semiotics.* Bloomington, IN: Indiana University Press. (Earlier versions published 1967 and 1976).

Eco, Umberto. (1990). *Foucault's Pendulum.* (Translated by William Weaver). New York: Ballantine Books. (Originally published 1988.)

Eco, Umberto. (1994). *The Limits of Interpretation.* Bloomington, IN: Indiana University Press. (Originally published 1990.)

Edmundson, Mark. (1995). *Literature Against Philosophy, Plato to Derrida: A Defence of Poetry.* Cambridge, England: Cambridge University Press.

Edwards, Jay D. (1978). *The Afro-American Trickster Tale: A Structural Analysis.* Monograph Series of the Folklore Publications Group. Vol. 4. Bloomington, IN: Folklore Institute of the University of Indiana.

Ehrenwald, Jan. (1948). *Telepathy and Medical Psychology.* New York: W. W. Norton & Company.

Ehrenwald, Jan. (1971). Mother-Child Symbiosis: Cradle of ESP. *The Psychoanalytic Review*, 58: 455–466.

Eisenbud, Jule. (1953). Telepathy and the Problems of Psychoanalysis. In George Devereux (Ed.). *Psychoanalysis and the Occult*, (pp. 223–261). New York: International Universities Press. (Originally published in 1946 in *The Psychoanalytic Quarterly*)

Eisenstadt, S. N. (1968). Introduction. In S. N. Eisenstadt (Ed.). *Max Weber on Charisma and Institution Building.* Chicago, IL: University of Chicago Press.

Eliade, Mircea. (1967). *Myths, Dreams and Mysteries: The Encounter Between Contemporary Paths and Archaic Realities* (Translated by Philip Mairet.). New York: Harper Torchbooks. (Originally published 1957.)

Eliade, Mircea. (1964). *Shamanism: Archaic Techniques of Ecstasy* (Translated by Willard R. Trask). Princeton, NJ: Princeton University Press. (Original work published 1951.)

Ellenberger, Henri F. (1968). The Concept of Creative Illness. (Translated by Henri F. Brugmans). *Psychoanalytic Review*, 55(3): 442–456. (Originally published 1964.)

Ellenberger, Henri F. (1970). *The Discovery of the Unconscious: The History and Evolution of Dynamic Psychiatry*. New York: Basic Books.

Ellis, Bill. (1982–83). Legend-Tripping in Ohio: A Behavioral Survey. In Daniel R. Barnes, Rosemary O. Joyce, & Steven Swann Jones (Eds.), *Papers in Comparative Studies*, Volume II (pp. 61–73). Columbus, OH: The Ohio State University Center for Comparative Studies in the Humanities.

Ellis, Bill. (1988). The Fast-Food Ghost: A Study in the Supernatural's Capacity to Survive Secularization. In Gillian Bennett & Paul Smith (Eds.). *Monsters with Iron Teeth*, pp. 37–77. Sheffield, England: Sheffield Academic Press.

Ellis, Bill. (1991). Cattle Mutilation: Contemporary Legends and Contemporary Mythologies. *Contemporary Legend*, 1: 39–80.

Ellis, Larry. (1993). Trickster: Shaman of the Liminal. *Studies in American Indian Literatures*, Series 2, 5(4): 55–68.

Ellwood, Jr., Robert S. (1979). *Alternative Altars: Unconventional and Eastern Spirituality in America*. Chicago: University of Chicago Press.

Ellwood, Jr., Robert S. (1973). *Religious and Spiritual Groups in Modern America*. Englewood Cliffs, NJ: Prentice-Hall.

Emery, Jr., C. Eugene. (1987). Catching Geller in the Act. *Skeptical Inquirer*, 12(1), Fall, pp. 75–80.

Emery, Jr., C. Eugene. (1994). New Age Believers Favor Third-Party Conservatives. *Skeptical Inquirer*, 18, Fall, pp. 458, 460.

Engar, Ann W. (1990). Old Testament Women as Tricksters. In Vincent L. Tollers & John Maier (Eds.) *Mappings of the Biblical Terrain: The Bible as Text*. Lewisburg, PA: Bucknell University Press.

Epstein, Edward Jay. (1989). *Deception: The Invisible War Between the KGB and the CIA*. New York: Simon and Schuster.

Evans, Henry Ridgely. (1897). *Hours With the Ghosts or Nineteenth Century Witchcraft*. Chicago, IL: Laird & Lee.

Evans, Hilary. (1984). *Visions * Apparitions * Alien Visitors*. Wellingborough, Northamptonshire: The Aquarian Press.

Evans, Hilary. (1987). *Gods * Spirits * Cosmic Guardians: A Comparative Study of the Encounter Experience*. Wellingborough, Northamptonshire: The Aquarian Press.

Evans-Pritchard, E[dward]. E[van]. (1950). *Witchcraft, Oracles and Magic Among the Azande*. Oxford: At the Clarendon Press. (First pubished 1937.)

Evans-Pritchard, E. E. (1964). *Social Anthropology and Other Essays*. New York: The Free Press of Glencoe. (Published earlier in 1962.)

Evans-Pritchard, E. E. (1972). *Theories of Primitive Religion*. Oxford: At The Clarendon Press. (Original work published 1965.)

Evans-Pritchard, E. E. (Editor). (1967). *The Zande Trickster*. Oxford: At the Clarendon Press. Copyright Oxford University Press.

Evans-Pritchard, Edward. (1981). *A History of Anthropological Thought* (Edited by Andre Singer). New York: Basic Books.

Fawcett, Lawrence, & Greenwood, Barry J. (1984). *Clear Intent: The Government Coverup of the UFO Experience*. Englewood Cliffs, NJ: Prentice-Hall.

Feilding, Everard; Baggally, W. W.; and Carrington, Hereward. (1909). Report on a Series of Sittings with Eusapia Palladino. *Proceedings of the Society for Psychical Research*, 23: 309–569.

Ferguson, Marilyn. (1980). *The Aquarian Conspiracy: Personal and Social Transformation in the 1980s*. Los Angeles, CA: J. P. Tarcher, Inc.

Feuerstein, Georg. (1991). *Holy Madness: The Shock Tactics and Radical Teachings of Crazy-Wisdom Adepts, Holy Fools, and Rascal Gurus*. New York: Paragon House.

Fine, Gary Alan. (1983). *Shared Fantasy: Role-Playing Games as Social Worlds*. Chicago: University of Chicago Press.

Flaherty, Gloria. (1992). *Shamanism and the Eighteenth Century*. Princeton, NJ: Princeton University Press.

Fornell, Earl Wesley. (1964). *The Unhappy Medium: Spiritualism and the Life of Margaret Fox*. Austin, TX: University of Texas Press.

Foster, A. A. (1940). Is ESP Diametric? *Journal of Parapsychology*, 4(2): 325–328.

Francesco, Grete de. (1939). *The Power of the Charlatan*. (Translated from the German by Miriam Beard). New Haven, CT: Yale University Press.

Fraser, Angus. (1992). *The Gypsies.* Oxford, U.K.: Blackwell.
Fraser, Robert. (1990). *The Making of The Golden Bough: The Origins and Growth of an Argument.* New York: St. Martin's Press.
Frazer, J.[ames] G.[eorge]. (1910). *Totemism and Exogamy: A Treatise on Certain Early Forms of Superstition and Society.* (4 volumes). London: Macmillan and Co.
Frazer, James George. (1937). *Totemica: A Supplement to Totemism and Exogamy.* London: Macmillan and Co.
Frazier, Kendrick. (1998). A Mind at Play: An Interview with Martin Gardner. *Skeptical Inquirer*, March/April, pp. 34–39.
Freud, Sigmund. (1961). *Totem and Taboo: Resemblances Between the Psychic Lives of Savages and Neurotics.* (Translated by A. A. Brill). New York: Vintage Books. (Original work published 1913)
Fromm, Erika; and Shor, Ronald E. (Eds.). (1972). *Hypnosis: Research Developments and Perspectives.* Chicago: Aldine Atherton.
Gallup, Jr., George H.; & Jones, Timothy. (1992). *The Saints Among Us.* Ridgefield, CT: Morehouse Publishing.
Galton, Francis. (1973). *Inquiries Into Human Faculty and Its Development.* New York: AMS Press. (Original work published 1883)
Gardner, Howard. (1981). *The Quest for Mind: Piaget, Levi-Strauss, and the Structuralist Movement.* (Second edition). Chicago: University of Chicago Press. (First published 1973.)
Gardner, Howard. (1993). *Creating Minds: An Anatomy of Creativity Seen Through the Lives of Freud, Einstein, Picasso, Stravinsky, Eliot, Graham, and Gandhi.* New York: BasicBooks.
Gardner, Martin. (1952). *In the Name of Science.* New York: G. P. Putnam's Sons.
Gardner, Martin. (1957). *Fads and Fallacies in the Name of Science.* New York: Dover Publications.
[Gardner, Martin]. (1979). Martin Gardner: Defending the Honor of the Human Mind by Irving Joshua Matrix. *Two-Year College Mathematical Journal*, 10(4): 227–232.
Gardner, Martin. (1981a). Parapsychology and Quantum Mechanics. In *Science and the Paranormal: Probing the Existence of the Supernatural* edited by George O. Abell and Barry Singer, pp. 56–69, 366–370. New York: Charles Scribner's Sons.
Gardner, Martin. (1981b). *Science: Good, Bad and Bogus.* Buffalo, NY: Prometheus Books.
Gardner, Martin (1983). *The Whys of a Philosophical Scrivener.* New York: Quill.

Gardner, Martin. (1988). *The New Age: Notes of a Fringe Watcher*. Buffalo, NY: Prometheus Books.

Gardner, Martin. (1989). *How Not to Test a Psychic: Ten Years of Remarkable Experiments With Renowned Clairvoyant Pavel Stepanek*. Buffalo, NY: Prometheus Books.

Gardner, Martin. (1992). *On the Wild Side*. Buffalo, NY: Prometheus Books.

Gardner, Martin. (1994). *The Flight of Peter Fromm*. Amherst, NY: Prometheus Books. (Originally published by William Kaufmann, Inc., 1973.)

Gardner, Martin. (1996). *The Night Is Large: Collected Essays 1938–1995*. New York: St. Martin's Press.

Garfinkel, Harold. (1967). *Studies in Ethnomethodology*. Englewood Cliffs, NJ: Prentice-Hall.

Gates, Jr., Henry Louis. (1988). *The Signifying Monkey: A Theory of Afro-American Literary Criticism*. New York: Oxford University Press.

Gatling, William; and Rhine, J. B. (1946). Two Groups of PK Subjects Compared. *Journal of Parapsychology*, 10: 120–125.

Gauld, Alan. (1968). *The Founders of Psychical Research*. New York: Schocken Books.

Gauld, Alan. (1987). Recollections of E. J. Dingwall. *Journal of the Society for Psychical Research*, 54: 230–237.

Gauld, Alan. (1992). *A History of Hypnotism*. Cambridge, England: Cambridge University Press.

Gay, Volney P. (1983a). Ritual and Self-Esteem in Victor Turner and Heinz Kohut. *Zygon*, 18(3): 271–282.

Gay, Volney P. (1983b). Winnicott's Contribution to Religious Studies: The Resurrection of the Culture Hero. *Journal of the American Academy of Religion*, 51: 371–395.

Geller, Uri. (1975). *My Story*. New York: Praeger.

George, Leonard; and Krippner, Stanley. (1984). Mental Imagery and Psi Phenomena: A Review. In Stanley Krippner (Ed.), *Advances in Parapsychological Research 4*, (pp. 64–82). Jefferson, NC: McFarland & Company, Inc., Publishers.

Gergen, Mary. (1987). *Social Ghosts: Opening Inquiry on Imaginal Relationships*. Paper presented at the 95th Annual Convention of the American Psychological Association, New York City. August.

Gibbs, Nancy. (1993). Angels Among Us. *Time*, December 27, pp. 56–65.

Gibson, Litzka R.; and Gibson, Walter B. (1969). *The Mystic and Occult Arts: A Guide to Their Use in Daily Living*. West Nyack, NY: Parker Publishing Co.

Gill, Sam D.; and Sullivan, Irene F. (1992). *Dictionary of Native American Mythology*. Santa Barbara, CA: ABC-CLIO.

Girard, Rene. (1977). *Violence and the Sacred*. (Translated by Patrick Gregory). Baltimore, MD: The Johns Hopkins University Press. (Originally published 1972)

Glasberg, Ronald. (1990). Eulenspiegel's Rebellion Against the Civilizing Process: A Psychohistorical Perspective. *Psychoanalytic Review*, 77(3): 423–445.

Glassman, Ronald M.; & Swatos, Jr., William H. (Eds.). (1986). *Charisma, History and Social Structure*. Westport, CT: Greenwood Press.

Goldstein, Steven. (1994). Watch What You're Thinking! The Skeptic's Toolbox II Conference. *Skeptical Inquirer*, Vol. 18, Summer, pp. 345–350.

Goldston, Will. [1906]. *Crystal Gazing. Astrology, Palmistry, Planchette, and Spiritualism*. London: A. W. Gamage.

Goldston, Will. (1933). *Secrets of Famous Illusionists*. London: John Long.

Goleman, Daniel. (1988). *The Meditative Mind: The Varieties of Meditative Experience*. Los Angeles, CA: Jeremy P. Tarcher, Inc. (Most of book originally published 1977.)

Gregory, Anita. (1985). *The Strange Case of Rudi Schneider*. Metuchen, NJ: Scarecrow Press.

Greenwood, Susan F. (1990). Emile Durkheim and C. G. Jung: Structuring a Transpersonal Sociology of Religion. *Journal for the Scientific Study of Religion*, 29: 482–495.

Grof, Stanislav; & Grof, Christina. (Eds.). (1989). *Spiritual Emergency: When Personal Transformation Becomes a Crisis*. Los Angeles, CA: Jeremy P. Tarcher, Inc.

Grottanelli, Cristiano. (1983). Tricksters, Scapegoats, Champions, Saviors. *History of Religions*, 23(2): 117–139.

Gruber, Elmar R. (1979). Conformance Behavior Involving Animal and Human Subjects. *European Journal of Parapsychology*, 3(1): 36–50.

Gruber, Elmar R. (1980). PK Effects on Pre-Recorded Group Behavior of Living Systems. *European Journal of Parapsychology*, 3(2): 167–175.

Guiley, Rosemary Ellen. (1989). *The Encyclopedia of Witches and Witchcraft*. New York: Facts On File.

Hacking, Ian. (1988). Telepathy: Origins of Randomization in Experimental Design. *Isis*, 79: 427–451.

Haines, Gerald K. (1997). A Die-Hard Issue: CIA's Role in the Study of UFOs, 1947–90. *Studies in Intelligence*. Unclassified Edition, 1(1): 67–84.

Hall, Trevor H. (1978). *Search for Harry Price*. London: Gerald Duckworth & Company.

Halpin, Marjorie M.; and Ames, Michael M. (Editors) (1980). *Manlike Monsters on Trial: Early Records and Modern Evidence*. Vancouver, BC: University of British Columbia Press.

Hansen, George P. (1990a). Deception by Subjects in Psi Research. *Journal of the American Society for Psychical Research*, 84: 25–80.

Hansen, George P. (1990b). Magicians Who Endorsed Psychic Phenomena. *The Linking Ring*, Vol. 70; No. 8, August, pp. 52–54; No. 9, September, pp. 63–65, 109.

Hansen, George P. (1991). The Elusive Agenda: Dissuading as Debunking in Ray Hyman's *The Elusive Quarry*. *Journal of the American Society for Psychical Research*, 85: 193–203.

Hansen, George P. (1992a). CSICOP and the Skeptics: An Overview. *Journal of the American Society for Psychical Research*, 86: 19–63.

Hansen, George P. (1992b). Demons, ETs, Bigfoot, and Elvis: A Fortean View of Ghosts. In Linda A. Henkel & Gertrude R. Schmeidler (Eds.). *Research in Parapsychology 1990* (pp. 140–141). Metuchen, NJ: The Scarecrow Press.

Hansen, George P. (1992c). Magicians on the Paranormal: An Essay with a Review of Three Books. *Journal of the American Society for Psychical Research*, 86: 151–185.

Hansen, George P. (1992d). The Research With B.D. and the Legacy of Magical Ignorance. *Journal of Parapsychology*, 56: 307–333.

Hansen, George P., & Broughton, Richard S. (1991). Card-Sorting Tests With SORRAT. *Artifex*, 9, pp. 19–26, 30.

Hansen, George P.; Utts, Jessica; & Markwick, Betty. (1992). Critique of the PEAR Remote-Viewing Experiments. *Journal of Parapsychology*, 56: 97–113.

Haraldsson, Erlendur. (1987). *'Miracles Are My Visiting Cards': An Investigative Report on the Psychic Phenomena Associated with Sathya Sai Baba*. London: Century.

Haraldsson, Erlendur; & Houtkooper, Joop M. (1991). Psychic Experiences in the Multinational Human Values Study: Who Reports Them? *Journal of the American Society for Psychical Research*, 85: 145–165.

Haraldsson, Erlendur; Houtkooper, Joop M.; & Hoeltje, Claudia. (1987). The Defense Mechanism Test as a Predictor of ESP Performance: Icelandic Study VII and Meta-Analysis of 13 Experiments. *Journal of Parapsychology*, 51: 75–90.

Haraldsson, Erlendur, & Wiseman, Richard. (1994). Investigating Macro-PK in India. In Dick J. Bierman (Ed.). *The Parapsychological Association 37th Annual Convention Proceedings of Presented Papers* (pp. 147–160). Parapsychological Association.

Harary, Keith. (1992). Spontaneous Psi in Mass Mythology, Media and Western Culture. In Betty Shapin & Lisette Coly (Eds.). *Spontaneous Psi, Depth Psychology and Parapsychology: Proceedings of an International Conference Held in Berkeley, California October 31–November 1, 1987*, (pp. 200–212). New York: Parapsychology Foundation, Inc.

Harary, Keith. (1993). Memories of Charles Honorton and the Politics of Psi Research. *Journal of the American Society for Psychical Research*, 87: 343–351.

Harding, M. Esther. (1973). *The 'I' and the 'Not-I': A Study in the Development of Consciousness*. Princeton, NJ: Princeton University Press. (Original work published 1965)

Harpur, Patrick. (1994). *Daimonic Reality: A Field Guide to the Otherworld*. London: Viking Arkana.

Hartmann, Ernest. (1991). *Boundaries in the Mind: A New Psychology of Personality*. BasicBooks A Division of HaperCollins Publishers. (No city listed)

Hastings, Arthur. (1991). *With the Tongues of Men and Angels: A Study in Channeling*. Fort Worth, TX: Holt, Rinehart and Winston, Inc.

Hastings, Robert. (1989). The MJ-12 Affair: Facts, Questions, Comments. *MUFON UFO Journal*, No. 254, June, pp. 3–11.

Hatengdi, M. U. (1984). *Nityananda: The Divine Presence*. Cambridge, Mass.: Rudra Press.

Hawkes, Terence. (1977). *Structuralism & Semiotics*. Berkeley, CA: University of California Press.

Herdt, Gilbert; & Stephen, Michele. (Eds.). (1989). *The Religious Imagination in New Guinea*. New Brunswick, NJ: Rutgers University Press.

Hero of Alexandria. (1971). *The Pneumatics of Hero of Alexandria*. (Translated and edited by Bennet Woodcroft). London: MacDonald. (Original work published circa 62(?) though there is much dispute regarding the date. Woodcroft edition published 1851.)

Hertz, Robert. (1960). *Death & The Right Hand* (Translated by Rodney and Claudia Needham). Glencoe, IL: The Free Press. (Original work published 1907 and 1909.)

Heschel, Abraham J. (1969). *The Prophets*. Volume I. New York: Harper Torchbooks, Harper & Row. (Original work published 1962).

Heschel, Abraham J. (1975). *The Prophets. Part II*. New York: Harper Colophon Books, Harper & Row. (Original work published 1962).

Heseltine, G. L. (1985). PK Success During Structured and Nonstructured RNG Operation. *Journal of Parapsychology*, 49: 155–163.

Hess, David J. (1988). Gender, Hierarchy, and the Psychic: An Interpretation of the Culture of Parapsychology. In *The Parapsychological Association 31st Annual Convention Proceedings of Presented Papers*. pp. 341–353.

Hess, David J. (1992). Disciplining Heterodoxy, Circumventing Discipline: Parapsychology, Anthropologically. In David Hess & Linda Layne (Eds.). *Knowledge and Society: The Anthropology of Science and Technology*, Volume 9. (pp. 223–252). Greenwich, CT: JAI Press.

Hess, David J. (1993). *Science in the New Age: The Paranormal, Its Defenders and Debunkers, and American Culture*. Madison, WI: The University of Wisconsin Press.

Hicks, David. (1976). *Tetum Ghosts and Kin: Fieldwork in an Indonesian Community*. Palo Alto, CA: Mayfield Publishing Company.

Higgins, Howard. (1985). An Anthropologist Looks at Magic. *Linking Ring*, Vol. 65; No. 9, September, pp. 46–47, 56; No. 10, October, pp. 57–58; No. 11, November, pp. 48–50, 65.

Hillman, James. (1972). An Essay on Pan. In *Pan and the Nightmare*, pp. i–lxiii. Zurich: Spring Publications.

Hillman, James. (1975). *Re-Visioning Psychology*. New York: Harper & Row, Publishers.

Hillman, James. (1979). *The Dream and the Underworld*. New York: Harper & Row, Publishers.

Hillman, James. (1986). *On Paranoia*. Dallas, TX: Spring Publications, Inc. (Originally published 1985)

Hinkle, Jr., Roscoe C. (1964). Durkheim in American Sociology. In Kurt H. Wolff (Ed.). *Essays on Sociology and Philosophy*, pp. 267–295. New York: Harper Torchbooks. (Original work published 1960)

Hocus Pocus Junior. The Anatomie of Legerdemain. Or, The Art of Jugling Set Forth in His Proper Colours, Fully, Plainely, and Exactly, So That an Ignorant Person May Thereby Learne the Full Perfection of the Same, After a Little Practice. (1634). London: Printed by T. H. for R. M.

Hofstadter, Douglas R. (1979). *Gödel, Escher, Bach: an Eternal Golden Braid*. New York: Basic Books, Inc., Publishers.

Honorton, Charles. (1977). Psi and Internal Attention States. In *Handbook of Parapsychology* edited by Benjamin B. Wolman, pp. 435–472. New York: Van Nostrand Reinhold Company.

Hopkins, Budd. (1996). *Witnessed: The True Story of the Brooklyn Bridge UFO Abductions*. New York: Pocket Books.

Howe, Linda Moulton. (1993). *An Alien Harvest: Further Evidence Linking Animal Mutilations And Human Abductions to Alien Life Forms*. Huntingdon Valley, PA: Linda Moulton Howe Productions. (First published 1989.)

Huysmans, J.[oris]-K.[arl] (1979). *Saint Lydwine of Schiedam*. Translated from the French by Agnes Hastings. Rockford, IL: Tan Books and Publishers, Inc. (Originally published in 1901)

Hyde, Lewis. (1998). *Trickster Makes This World: Mischief, Myth, and Art*. New York: Farrar, Straus and Giroux.

Hyman, Ray. (1977). "Cold Reading": How to Convince Strangers That You Know All About Them. *The Zetetic*, 1(2), Spring/Summer, pp. 18–37.

Hyman, Ray. (1989). The Psychology of Deception. *Annual Review of Psychology*, 40: 133–154.

Hynes, William J., & Doty, William G. (Eds.). (1993). *Mythical Trickster Figures: Contours, Contexts, and Criticisms*. Tuscaloosa, AL: The University of Alabama Press.

Hyslop, James H.; Guthrie, L. V.; Abbott, David P.; Clawson, G. W.; and Clawson, Mrs. G. W. (1913). The Case of Mrs. Blake. *Proceedings of the American Society for Psychical Research*, 7: 570–788.

Iaccino, James F. (1994). *Psychological Reflections on Cinematic Terror: Jungian Archetypes in Horror Films*. Westport, CT: Praeger.

Irwin, H.[arvey] J. (1987). Charles Bailey: A Biographical Study of the Austalian Apport Medium. *Journal of the Society for Psychical Research*, 54: 97–118.

Irwin, Harvey J. (1989). On Paranormal Disbelief: The Psychology of the Sceptic. In George K. Zollschan, John F. Schumaker, and Greg F. Walsh (Eds.). *Exploring the Paranormal: Perspectives on Belief and Experience*, (pp. 305–312). Bridport, Dorset: Prism Unity.

Isherwood, Christopher. (1965). *Ramakrishna and His Disciples*. New York: Simon and Schuster.

Jensen, Adolf E. (1973). *Myth and Cult Among Primitive Peoples*. (Translated by Marianna Tax Choldin and Wolfgang Weissleder). Chicago: University of Chicago Press. (Originally published 1951.)

Johnson, George. (1983). *Architects of Fear: Conspiracy Theories and Paranoia in American Politics*. Los Angeles, CA: Jeremy P. Tarcher, Inc.

Johnson, Martin. (1973). A New Technique of Testing ESP in a Real-Life, High-Motivational Context. *Journal of Parapsychology*, 37: 210–217.

Jones, Ernest. (1957). *The Life and Work of Sigmund Freud* (3 volumes). New York: Basic Books, Inc.

Jung, C.[arl] G.[ustav]. (1967). The Spirit Mercurius. In his *Alchemical Studies* (pp. 191–250) (Volume 13 of the Collected Works. Translated by R. F. C. Hull.). Princeton, NJ: Princeton University Press. (Original work published 1943.)

Jung, C. G. (1972). On the Psychology of the Trickster Figure. In Paul Radin, *The Trickster: A Study in American Indian Mythology*, (pp. 195–211). New York: Schocken Books. (Originally published 1956.)

Jung, C. G. (1978). *Flying Saucers*. (Translated by R. F. C. Hull). New York: MJF Books. (Originally published 1958. 1978 is copyright date given in book.)

Jung, C. G. (1963). *Memories, Dreams, Reflections*. Recorded and edited by Aniela Jaffe. Translated by Richard and Clara Winston. New York: Pantheon Books. (Originally published 1962)

Jung, C. G. (1973). *Answer to Job*. (Translated by R. F. C. Hull). Princeton, NJ: Princeton University Press. (Originally published 1952.)

Kalweit, Holger. (1988). *Dreamtime & Inner Space: The World of the Shaman*. Translated from the German by Werner Wunsche. Boston, MA: Shambhala. (Original work published 1984)
Kapitza, Sergei. (1991). Antiscience Trends in the U.S.S.R. *Scientific American*, 265, August, pp. 32–38.
Katlyn. [Katlyn Miller]. (1982). *Charms and Enchantments*. (No publisher listed)
Katlyn. [Katlyn Miller]. (1989). *The Art of Scrying and the Magick Mirror*. Long Beach, CA: Mermade Magickal Arts.
Keel, John A. [Alva John Kiehle]. (1957). *Jadoo*. New York: Messner.
Keel, John A. (1975a). *The Eighth Tower*. New York: Saturday Review Press, E. P. Dutton & Co.
Keel, John A. (1975b). *The Mothman Prophecies*. New York: Saturday Review Press, E. P. Dutton & Co.
Keene, M. Lamar; as told to Spraggett, Allen. (1977). *The Psychic Mafia*. New York: A Dell Book. (Originally published 1976.)
Kellehear, Allan. (1996). *Experiences Near Death: Beyond Medicine and Religion*. New York: Oxford University Press.
Kelly, Aidan A. (1991). *Crafting the Art of Magic, Book I: A History of Modern Witchcraft, 1939–1964*. St. Paul, MN: Llewellyn Publications.
Kennedy, J. E. (1978). The Role of Task Complexity in PK: A Review. *Journal of Parapsychology*, 42: 89–122.
Kennedy, J. E. (1979). Redundancy in Psi Information: Implications for the Goal-Oriented Hypothesis and for the Application of Psi. *Journal of Parapsychology*, 43: 290–314.
Kennedy, J. E., & Taddonio, Judith L. (1976). Experimenter Effects in Parapsychological Research. *Journal of Parapsychology*, 40: 1–33.
Kermode, Frank. (1979). *The Genesis of Secrecy: On the Interpretation of Narrative*. Cambridge, MA: Harvard University Press.
Kerr, Howard. (1972). *Mediums, and Spirit-Rappers, and Roaring Radicals: Spiritualism in American Literature, 1850–1900*. Urbana, IL: University of Illinois Press.
King, Stephen. (1981). *Stephen King's Danse Macabre*. New York: Everest House Publishers.
Kirby, E[rnest]. T[heodore]. (1974). The Shamanistic Origins of Popular Entertainments. *The Drama Review*, 18(1): 5–15.
Kirby, E. T. (1975). *Ur-Drama: The Origins of Theatre*. New York: New York University Press.

Klimo, Jon. (1987). *Channeling: Investigations on Receiving Information From Paranormal Sources.* Los Angeles, CA: Jeremy P. Tarcher, Inc.

Kodimela, Venu K. (1992). Doordarshan Tape Unveils Baba "Magic". *Deccan Chronicle.* November 24, pp. 1, 4.

Koepping, Klaus-Peter. (1985). Absurdity and Hidden Truth: Cunning Intelligence and Grotesque Body Images as Manifestations of the Trickster. *History of Religions,* 24: 191–214.

Koestler, Arthur. (1972). *The Roots of Coincidence.* London: Hutchinson & Co.

Kopff, E. Christian. (1996). Postmodernism, Theory, and the End of the Humanities. *Chronicles,* January, pp. 16–19.

Kottmeyer, Martin. (1988). Abduction: The Boundary Deficit Hypothesis. *Magonia,* No. 32, March, pp. 3–7.

Kottmeyer, Martin S. (1989). Ufology Considered as an Evolving System of Paranoia. *Archaeus,* 5: 51–60.

Kottmeyer, Martin. (1994). Testing the Boundaries. *Bulletin of Anomalous Experience,* 5(4), August, p. 15.

Kottmeyer, Martin. (1995–96). UFO Flaps. *The Anomalist.* No. 3: 64–89.

Kreisel, G. (1980). Kurt Gödel 28 April 1906—14 January 1978. *Biographical Memoirs of Fellows of the Royal Society,* Vol. 26, pp. 149–224. London: The Royal Society.

Kreiser, B. Robert. (1978). *Miracles, Convulsions, and Ecclesiastical Politics in Early Eighteenth-Century Paris.* Princeton, NJ: Princeton University Press.

Kress, Kenneth A. (1977). Parapsychology In Intelligence: A Personal Review and Conclusions. *Studies in Intelligence,* 21, Winter, pp. 7–17.

Kress, Kenneth A. (1999). Parapsychology In Intelligence: A Personal Review and Conclusions. *Journal of Scientific Exploration,* 13: 69–85.

Krippner, Stanley. (1975). *Song of the Siren: A Parapsychological Odyssey.* New York: Harper & Row.

Krippner, Stanley. (Editor). (1994). *Advances in Parapsychological Research 7.* Jefferson, NC: McFarland & Company, Inc., Publishers.

Kroeber, Karl. (1979). Deconstructionist Criticism and American Indian Literature. *Boundary 2,* 7(3): 73–89.

Krueger, Derek. (1996). *Symeon the Holy Fool: Leontius's Life and the Late Antique City.* Berkeley, CA: University of California Press.

Kübler-Ross, Elisabeth. (1997). *The Wheel of Life: A Memoir of Living and Dying.* New York: Scribner.

Kurtz, Paul. (1976). Committee To Scientifically Investigate Claims of Paranormal and Other Phenomena. *The Humanist*, 36(3), May–June, p. 28.

Kurtz, Paul. (1986). *The Transcendental Temptation: A Critique of Religion and the Paranormal.* Buffalo, NY: Prometheus Books.

Kurtz, Paul. (1994). *Toward A New Enlightenment: The Philosophy of Paul Kurtz.* (Edited by Vern L. Bullough and Timothy J. Madigan). New Brunswick, NJ: Transaction Publishers.

Kurzweil, Edith. (1980). *The Age of Structuralism: Levi-Strauss to Foucault.* New York: Columbia University Press.

La Barre, Weston. (1972). *The Ghost Dance: Origins of Religion.* New York: A Delta Book. (Originally published 1970.)

Lacan, Jacques. (1977). *Ecrits: A Selection* (Translated from the French by Alan Sheridan). New York: W. W. Norton & Company. (Work quoted originally dated 1948 and 1949)

Lancaster, Kurt. (1994). Do Role-Playing Games Promote Crime, Satanism and Suicide Among Players as Critics Claim? *Journal of Popular Culture*, 28(2): 67–79.

Lane, Michael. (Editor). (1970). *Introduction to Structuralism.* New York: Basic Books.

Lang, Andrew. (1903). *Social Origins.* New York: Longmans, Green, and Co.

Lang, Andrew. (1905). *The Secret of the Totem.* London: Longmans, Green, and Co.

Lantis, Margaret. (1971). *Alaskan Eskimo Ceremonialism.* Seattle, WA: University of Washington Press. (Original work published 1947)

Latour, Bruno. (1988). The Politics of Explanation: An Alternative. In *Knowledge and Reflexivity: New Frontiers in the Sociology of Knowledge* edited by Steve Woolgar (pp. 155–176). London: Sage Publications.

Lawson, Hilary. (1985). *Reflexivity: The Post-Modern Predicament.* La Salle, IL: Open Court.

Leach, Edmund R. (1961). Golden Bough or Gilded Twig? *Daedalus: Journal of the Academy of Arts and Sciences*, 90(2): 371–387.

Leach, Edmund. (1964). Anthropological Aspects of Language: Animal Categories and Verbal Abuse. In *New Directions in the Study of Language* (Edited by Eric H. Lennenberg), pp. 23–63. Cambridge, MA: The M.I.T. Press.

Leach, Edmund R. (1967). Magical Hair. In *Myth and Cosmos: Readings in Mythology and Symbolism* edited by John Middleton, pp. 77–108. Garden City, NY: Natural History Press. (Originally published in *The Journal of the Royal Anthropological Institute*, 1958, 88(2): 147–64.)

Leach, Edmund. (Editor). (1967). *The Structural Study of Myth and Totemism*. (A.S.A. Monographs 5). London: Tavistock Publications.

Leach, Edmund. (1969). Genesis as Myth. In his *Genesis as Myth, and Other Essays*, (pp. 7–23). London: Jonathan Cape. (Original work published 1962)

Leach, Edmund. (1969). High School [Review of *The Teachings of Don Juan: A Yaqui Way of Knowledge* by Carlos Castaneda]. *New York Review of Books*, Vol. 12, No. 11, June 5, pp. 12–13.

Leach, Edmund. (1970a). *Claude Levi-Strauss*. New York: The Viking Press.

Leach, Edmund. (1970b). The Legitimacy of Solomon: Some Structural Aspects of Old Testament History. In Michael Lane (Ed.). *Introduction to Structuralism* (pp. 248–292). New York: Basic Books, Inc., Publishers. (Essay originally published 1966.)

Leach, Edmund. (1974). Anthropology Upside Down [Review of *Reinventing Anthropology* by Dell Hymes]. *New York Review of Books*, Vol. 21, No. 5, April 4, pp. 33–35.

Leach, Edmund. (1976). *Culture & Communication: The Logic by Which Symbols Are Connected: An Introduction to the Use of Structuralist Analysis in Social Anthropology*. Cambridge, England: Cambridge University Press.

Leach, Edmund. (1984). Glimpses of the Unmentionable in the History of British Social Anthropology. *Annual Review of Anthropology*, 13: 1–23.

Lee, Edwin. (1866). *Animal Magnetism and Magnetic Lucid Somnambulism*. London: Longmans, Green, and Co.

Lefebvre, Vladimir A. (1992). *A Psychological Theory of Bipolarity and Reflexivity*. Lampeter, Dyfed, Wales: Edwin Mellen Press.

Lehman, David. (1991). *Signs of the Times: Deconstruction and the Fall of Paul de Man*. New York: Poseidon Press.

LeShan, Lawrence. (1966). Some Psychological Hypotheses on the Non-Acceptance of Parapsychology as a Science. *International Journal of Parapsychology*, 8(3): 367–385.

LeShan, Lawrence. (1990). *The Dilemma of Psychology: A Psychologist Looks at His Troubled Profession*. New York: Dutton.

Levine, Donald N. (1985). *The Flight from Ambiguity: Essays in Social and Cultural Theory*. Chicago: University of Chicago Press.

Levi-Strass, Claude. (1963). *Structural Anthropology*. (Translated by Claire Jacobson & Brooke Grundfest Schoepf). New York: Basic Books. (Original work published 1958.)

Levi-Strauss, Claude. (1963). *Totemism*. (Translated by Rodney Needham). Boston, Mass.: Beacon Press. (Original work published 1962.)

Levi-Strauss, Claude. (1966). *The Savage Mind*. (Translated from the French). Chicago, Ill.: The University of Chicago Press. (Original work published 1962.)

Levi-Strauss, Claude. (1975). *The Raw and the Cooked: Introduction to a Science of Mythology: I* (Translated by John and Doreen Weightman). New York: Harper Colophon Books. (Originally published 1964.)

Levi-Strauss, Claude. (1979). *Myth and Meaning*. New York: Schocken Books. (Original work published 1978)

Levi-Strauss, Claude. (1987). *Introduction to the Work of Marcel Mauss*. (Translated by Felicity Baker). London: Routledge & Kegan Paul. (Originally published 1950.)

Levy-Bruhl, Lucien. (1923). *Primitive Mentality* (Translated by Lilian A. Clare). New York: The Macmillan Company. (Original work published 1922)

Levy-Bruhl, Lucien. (1985). *How Natives Think* (Translated by Lilian A. Clare). Princeton, NJ: Princeton University Press. (Originally published 1910.)

Lewis, Angelo J. (1886). How and What to Observe in Relation to Slate-Writing Phenomena. *Journal of the Society for Psychical Research*, 2: 362–375.

Lewis, I[oan]. M. (1971). *Ecstatic Religion: An Anthropological Study of Spirit Possession and Shamanism*. Harmondsworth, England: Penguin Books. (Second edition was published 1989.)

Lindahl, Carl. (1986). Psychic Ambiguity at the Legend Core. *Journal of Folklore Research*, 23(1): 1–21.

Littleton, C. Scott. (1976). An Emic Account of Sorcery: Carlos Castaneda and the Rise of a New Anthropology. *Journal of Latin American Lore*, 2(2): 145–155.

Littleton, C. Scott. (1985). Introduction (1985) Lucien Levy-Bruhl and the Concept of Cognitive Relativity. In *How Natives Think* by Lucien Levy-Bruhl, pp. v–lviii. Princeton, NJ: Princeton University Press.

Littleton, Scott. (1997). I Went to School with Castaneda . . . [Letter]. *The Excluded Middle*, No. 7, p. 6.
Lommel, Andreas. (1967). *Shamanism: The Beginnings of Art* [Translated from the German by Michael Bullock]. New York: McGraw-Hill Book Company.
Lopez-Pedraza, Rafael. (1989). *Hermes and His Children*. (New expanded edition). Einsiedeln, Switzerland: Daimon Verlag. (Earlier version published 1977)
Luhrmann, T.[anya] M. (1989a). The Magic of Secrecy. *Ethos*, 17: 131–165.
Luhrmann, T. M. (1989b). *Persuasions of the Witch's Craft: Ritual Magic in Contemporary England*. Cambridge, Mass.: Harvard University Press.
Lurie, Nancy Oestreich. (1953). Winnebago Berdache. *American Anthropologist*, 55: 708–712.
Maccabee, Bruce. (1991). Hiding the Hardware. *International UFO Reporter*, September/October, pp. 4–10, 23.
Macionis, John J. (1989). *Sociology*. (Second edition). Englewood Cliffs, NJ: Prentice Hall.
Mack, John E. (1993). Stirring Our Deepest Fears. *International UFO Reporter*, 18(2), March/April, pp. 17, 21.
Mackenzie, Brian, & Mackenzie, S. Lynne. (1980). Whence the Enchanted Boundary? Sources and Significance of the Parapsychological Tradition. *Journal of Parapsychology*, 44: 125–166.
Macksey, Richard; and Donato, Eugenio. (Editors). (1972). *The Structuralist Controversy: The Languages of Criticism and the Sciences of Man*. Baltimore, MD: The Johns Hopkins University Press. (Originally published 1970.)
Makarius, Laura. (1970). Ritual Clowns and Symbolical Behaviour. *Diogenes*, No. 69: 44–73.
Makarius, Laura. (1973). The Crime of Manabozo. *American Anthropologist*. 75: 663–675.
Makarius, Laura. (1974). The Magic of Transgression. *Anthropos*, 69: 537–552.
Makarius, Laura. (1983). The Mask and the Violation of Taboo. In *The Power of Symbols: Masks and Masquerade in the Americas* (Edited by N. Ross Crumrine & Marjorie Halpin). pp. 195–203. Vancouver: University of British Columbia Press.
Makarius, Laura. (1993). The Myth of the Trickster: The Necessary Breaker of Taboos. In *Mythical Trickster Figures: Contours,*

Contexts, and Criticisms (Edited by William J. Hynes & William G. Doty) pp. 66–86. Tuscaloosa, AL: The University of Alabama Press. (Work originally published in French in 1969. This translation by Christopher G. Nichols and revised by William G. Doty.)

Malinowski, Bronislaw. (1944). *A Scientific Theory of Culture and Other Essays*. Chapel Hill, NC: University of North Carolina Press.

Marks, David; & Kammann, Richard. (1980). *The Psychology of the Psychic*. Buffalo, NY: Prometheus Books.

Marks, John. (1979). *The Search for the "Manchurian Candidate": The CIA and Mind Control*. New York: Times Books.

Martinez-Taboas, Alfonso, & Francia, Margarita. (1993). The Feilding Report, Wiseman's Critique and Scientific Reporting. *Journal of the Society for Psychical Research*, 59: 120–129.

Maskelyne, J. [ohn] N.[evil]. (1885). Mr. Maskelyne and the Spiritualists. *Pall Mall Gazette*, April 23, p. 2.

Maskelyne, John Nevil. (1910). "My Reminiscences". *The Strand Magazine*. 39, January, 17–24.

Mattuck, R. D. (1977). Random Fluctuation Theory of Psychokinesis: Thermal Noise Model. In *Research in Parapsychology 1976: Abstracts and Papers from the Nineteenth Annual Convention of the Parapsychological Association, 1976* edited by J. D. Morris, W. G. Roll & R. L. Morris, pp. 191–195. Metuchen, NJ: Scarecrow Press.

Mattuck, R. D. (1979). Thermal Noise Theory of Psychokinesis: Modified Walker Model With Pulsed Information Rate. *Psychoenergetic Systems*, 3: 301–325.

Mattuck, Richard D.; and Walker, Evan Harris. (1979). The Action of Consciousness on Matter: A Quantum Mechanical Theory of Psychokinesis. In *The Iceland Papers: Select Papers on Experimental and Theoretical Research on the Physics of Consciousness: Frontiers of Physics Conference Reykjavik, Iceland November 1977* edited by Andrija Puharich, pp. 111–159. Amherst, WI: Essentia Research Associates.

Mauskopf, Seymour H.; and McVaugh, Michael R. (1977). Parapsychology and the American Psychologists: A Study of Scientific Ambivalence. In *The Philosophy of Parapsychology: Proceedings of an International Conference Held in Copenhagen, Denmark August 25–27, 1976*, edited by Betty Shapin and Lisette Coly, pp. 216–233. New York: Parapsychology Foundation.

Mauskopf, Seymour H.; & McVaugh, Michael R. (1980). *The Elusive Science: Origins of Experimental Psychical Research*. Baltimore, MD: The Johns Hopkins University Press.

May, Edwin C. (1996). The American Institutes for Research Review of the Department of Defense's Star Gate Program: A Commentary. *Journal of Parapsychology*, 60: 3–23.

McBeath, Michael K. (1985). Psi and Sexuality. *Journal of the Society for Psychical Research*, 53: 65–77.

McClelland, David C. (1964). *The Roots of Consciousness*. Princeton, NJ: D. Van Nostrand Company.

McClenon, James. (1982). A Survey of Elite Scientists: Their Attitudes Toward ESP and Parapsychology. *Journal of Parapsychology*, 46: 127–152.

McClenon, James. (1984). *Deviant Science: The Case of Parapsychology*. Philadelphia, PA: University of Pennsylvania Press.

McClenon, James. (1994). *Wondrous Events: Foundations of Religious Belief*. Philadelphia, PA: University of Pennsylvania Press.

McDougall, William. (1967). The Case of Margery. In Raymond Van Over and Laura Oteri (Compilers and Editors). *William McDougall: Explorer of the Mind: Studies in Psychical Research*. (pp. 180–209). New York: Helix Press Garrett Publications. (Original work published 1925, 1926)

McGill, [Ormond]. (1938). The Psychic Circle. *The Tops*, 3(12), December, pp. 34–37.

McGill, Ormond. (n.d.). *Psychic Magic* (6 vols.). Colon, MI: Abbott's Magic Novelty Co.

McGill, Ormond. (1977). *The Mysticism and Magic of India*. South Brunswick, NJ: A. S. Barnes and Company.

McIntosh, Donald. (1970). Weber and Freud: On the Nature and Sources of Authority. *American Sociological Review*, 35: 901–911.

McKean, Philip Frick. (1971). The Mouse-deer (*Kantjil*) in Malayo-Indonesian Folklore: Alternative Analyses and Significance of a Trickster Figure in South-East Asia. *Asian Folklore Studies*, 30(1): 71–84.

Mead, George H. (1934). *Mind, Self & Society: From the Standpoint of a Social Behaviorist* (Edited by Charles W. Morris.). Chicago: University of Chicago Press.

Meade, Marion. (1980). *Madame Blavatsky: The Woman Behind the Myth*. New York: G. P. Putnam's Sons.

Meeker, William B; and Barber, Theodore X. (1971). Toward an Explanation of Stage Hypnosis. *Journal of Abnormal Psychology*, 77(1): 61–70.

Mehan, Hugh; and Wood, Houston. (1975). *The Reality of Ethnomethodology*. New York: John Wiley & Sons.

Melton, J. Gordon. (Editor). (1996). *Encyclopedia of Occultism & Parapsychology* (Fourth Edition). Detroit, MI: Gale.

Melton, J. Gordon; Clark, Jerome; & Kelly, Aidan A. (1991). *New Age Almanac*. New York: Visible Ink Press.

[Merrifield, F.]. (1903). A Sitting With D. D. Home. *Journal of the Society for Psychical Research*, 11: 76–80.

Messer, Ron. (1982). A Jungian Interpretation of the Relationship of Culture: Hero and Trickster Figure Within Chippewa Mythology. *Studies in Religion/Sciences Religieuses*, 11: 309–320.

Messer, Ron. (1983). Nanabozho: History and Mythology. *Bulletin of Bibliography*, 40: 242–251.

Messer, Ron. (1986). The Unconscious Mind: Do Jung and Levi-Strauss Agree? *Journal of the Anthropological Society of Oxford*, 17(1): 1–26.

Middleton, John. (1973). Some Categories of Dual Classification Among the Lugbara of Uganda. In Rodney Needham (Ed.). *Right & Left: Essays on Dual Symbolic Classification* (pp. 369–390). Chicago, IL: The University of Chicago Press. (Original work published 1968)

Middleton, John; and Winter, E. H. (Eds.). (1963). *Witchcraft and Sorcery in East Africa*. London: Routledge & Kegan Paul.

Mills, C. Wright. (1967). *The Sociological Imagination*. New York: Oxford University Press. (Originally published 1959)

Minch, Stephen. (1991). Evolution of the Bizarre. *The New Invocation*, No. 61, February, pp. 732–734.

Minch, Stephen. (1992). Apocalypse Later. *Genii*, 55(6), April, pp. 386–388.

Miska, Maxine. (1995). Aftermath of a Failed Seance: The Functions of Skepticism in a Traditional Society. In *Out of the Ordinary: Folklore and the Supernatural*, edited by Barbara Walker, pp. 90–106. Logan, UT: Utah State University Press.

Mitchell, Robert W. (1993). Animals as Liars: The Human Face of Nonhuman Duplicity. In Michael Lewis and Carolyn Saarni (Eds.). *Lying and Deception in Everyday Life* (pp. 59–89). New York: The Guilford Press.

Mitchell, Robert W. (1993). Mental Models of Mirror-Self-Recognition: Two Theories. *New Ideas in Psychology*, 11(3): 295–325.

Mitchell, Robert W. (1994). The Evolution of Primate Cognition: Simulation, Self-Knowledge, and Knowledge of Other Minds. In *Hominid Culture in Primate Perspective* edited by Duane Quiatt and Junichiro Itani, (pp. 177–232). University Press of Colorado.

Moore, Edward C. (1961). *American Pragmatism: Peirce, James, and Dewey.* New York: Columbia University Press.

Moore, R. Laurence. (1977). *In Search of White Crows: Spiritualism, Parapsychology, and American Culture.* New York: Oxford University Press.

Moore, William D. (1997). "To Hold Communion with Nature and the Spirit-World": New England's Spiritualist Camp Meetings, 1865–1910. In *Exploring Everyday Landscapes: Perspectives in Vernacular Architecture, VII* edited by Annmarie Adams and Sally McMurry, pp. 230–248. Knoxville, TN: University of Tennessee Press.

Moritz, Charles. (Editor). (1988). Randi, James. *Current Biography Yearbook 1987* (pp. 454–458). New York: The H. W. Wilson Company.

Moseley, James W. (1991). The Lawsuits Against James Randi. *Saucer Smear*, 38(8), October 10, pp. 1–3; 38(9), November 5, pp. 2–4.

Moseley, James W. (1993). Magician Defamed Scientist, Jury Rules. *Saucer Smear*, 40(6), August 5, p. 1.

Moseley, James W. (1994). Left to Right. *Saucer Smear*, 41(9), December 5, p. 6.

Müller, Lutz. (1991). Psi and the Archetype of the Trickster. (Translated by Wolfgang Taraba.) *Artifex*, 9: 31–41. (Original work published 1981).

Murphy, Michael. (1992). *The Future of the Body: Explorations Into the Further Evolution of Human Nature.* Los Angeles, CA: Jeremy P. Tarcher, Inc.

Nardi, Peter M. (1988). The Social World of Magicians: Gender and Conjuring. *Sex Roles*, 19: 759–770.

Needham, Rodney. (1967). Introduction. In *The Semi-Scholars* by Arnold van Gennep, pp. ix–xx. London: Routledge & Kegan Paul.

Needham, Rodney. (Editor). (1973). *Right & Left: Essays on Dual Symbolic Classification*. Chicago, IL: The University of Chicago Press.

Needham, Rodney. (1974). *Remarks and Inventions: Skeptical Essays About Kinship*. London: Tavistock Publications.

Needham, Rodney. (1975). Introduction. In *Primitive Classification* by Emile Durkheim and Marcel Mauss, pp. vii–xlviii. Chicago: University of Chicago Press. (Introduction first published 1963.)

Needham, Rodney. (1979). *Symbolic Classification*. Santa Monica, CA: Goodyear Publishing Company.

Needham, Rodney. (1985). *Exemplars*. Berkeley, CA: University of California Press.

Nelson, Donald F. (1971). *Portrait of the Artist as Hermes: A Study of Myth and Psychology in Thomas Mann's Felix Krull*. Chapel Hill, NC: University of North Carolina Press.

Nelson, Geoffrey K. (1969). *Spiritualism and Society*. New York: Schocken Books.

Newmann, C. A. G. [Christian Andrew George Naeseth]. (1923). Experimental Telepathy With Cards. In. J. W. Elliott, *Elliott's Last Legacy: Secrets of the King of All Kard Kings* (Houdini, Ed.; C. Burgess, Comp.) (pp. 274–292). New York: Adams Press.

Niditch, Susan. (1987). *Underdogs and Tricksters: A Prelude to Biblical Folklore*. San Francisco, CA: Harper & Row.

Noel, Daniel C. (Editor). (1976). *Seeing Castaneda: Reactions to the "Don Juan" Writings of Carlos Castaneda*. New York: G. P. Putnam's Sons

Noel, Daniel C. (1997). *The Soul of Shamanism: Western Fantasies, Imaginal Realities*. New York: Continuum.

Norris, Christopher. (1991). *Deconstruction Theory and Practice*. (Revised edition.). London: Routledge. (Originally published 1982.)

Oberg, Jim. (1997). Skeptic Jim Oberg Makes a Very Important Statement. *Saucer Smear*, Vol. 44, No. 6, June 20th, pp. 2–3.

O'Dea, Thomas F. (1966). *The Sociology of Religion*. Englewood Cliffs, NJ: Prentice-Hall, Inc.

Oetgen, Jerome. (1976). *An American Abbot: Boniface Wimmer, O.S.B. 1809–1887*. Latrobe, PA: The Archabbey Press.

O'Keefe, Daniel Lawrence. (1983). *Stolen Lightning: The Social Theory of Magic*. New York: Vintage Books A Division of Random House. (Orginally published 1982.)

Ong, Walter J. (1977). *Interfaces of the Word: Studies in the Evolution of Consciousness and Culture.* Ithaca, NY: Cornell University Press.

Oppenheim, Janet. (1985). *The Other World: Spiritualism and Psychical Research in England, 1850–1914.* Cambridge, England: Cambridge University Press.

Osis, Karlis. (1953). A Test of the Relationship Between ESP and PK. *Journal of Parapsychology,* 17: 298–309.

Osis, Karlis. (1985). The American Society for Psychical Research 1941–1985: A Personal View. *Journal of the American Society for Psychical Research,* 79: 501–529.

Osty, Eugene. (1935). Alexis Didier: Clairvoyant Extraordinary. *Journal of the American Society for Psychical Research,* 29: 323–338.

Otto, Rudolf. (1975). *The Idea of the Holy: An Inquiry into the Non-rational Factor in the Idea of the Divine and its Relation to the Rational.* (Translated by John W. Harvey), London: Oxford University Press. (Original work published 1917.)

Otto, Rudolf. (1987). *Mysticism East and West: A Comparative Analysis of The Nature of Mysticism.* Wheaton, IL: Theosophical Publishing House. (Original work published 1926.)

Oursler, Fulton. (1964). *Behold This Dreamer!* (Edited and with Commentary by Fulton Ourlser, Jr.). Boston, MA: Little, Brown and Company.

Owen, Alex. (1990). *The Darkened Room: Women, Power and Spiritualism in Late Victorian England.* Philadelphia, PA: University of Pennsylvania Press.

Pallikari-Viras, Fotini. (1997). Further Evidence for a Statistical Balancing in Probabilistic Systems Influenced by the Anomalous Effect of Conscious Intention. *Journal of the Society for Psychical Research,* 62: 114–137.

Palmer, Helen. (1992). The Psychic Factor in Neurotic Style. In Betty Shapin & Lisette Coly (Eds.). *Spontaneous Psi, Depth Psychology and Parapsychology: Proceedings of an International Conference Held in Berkeley, California October 31–November 1, 1987* (pp. 181–192), New York: Parapsychology Foundation, Inc.

Palmer, John. (1977). Extrasensory Perception: Research Findings. In Stanley Krippner (Ed.). *Advances in Parapsychological Research: 2 Extrasensory Perception,* (pp. 59–243). New York: Plenum Press.

Palmer, John A.; Honorton, Charles; and Utts, Jessica. (1989). Reply to the National Research Council Study on Parapsychology. *Journal of the American Society for Psychical Research,* 83: 31–49.

Parapsychological Association. (1988). Terms and Methods in Parapsychological Research. *Journal of the American Society for Psychical Research*, 82: 353–357.

Parsons, Talcott. (1964). Introduction. In *The Sociology of Religion* by Max Weber, (pp. xix–lxvii). Boston, MA: Beacon Press. (Introduction originally published 1963.)

Peacock, James L. (1969). Mystics and Merchants in Fourteenth Century Germany: A Speculative Reconstruction of Their Psychological Bond and Its Implications for Social Change. *Journal for the Scientific Study of Religion*, 8(1): 47–59.

Peacock, James L. (1975). *Consciousness and Change: Symbolic Anthropology in Evolutionary Perspective*. New York: John Wiley & Sons.

Peebles, Curtis. (1994). *Watch the Skies! A Chronicle of the Flying Saucer Myth*. Washington, DC: Smithsonian Institution Press.

Pekala, Ronald J.; Kumar, V. K.; & Cummings, James. (1992). Types of High Hypnotically-Susceptible Individuals and Reported Attitudes and Experiences of the Paranormal and the Anomalous. *Journal of the American Society for Psychical Research*, 86: 135–150.

Pelton, Robert D. (1980). *The Trickster in West Africa: A Study of Mythic Irony and Sacred Delight*. Berkeley, CA: University of California Press.

Perovsky-Petrovo-Solovovo, Count. (1912). On the Alleged Exposure of D. D. Home in France. *Journal of the Society for Psychical Research*, 15: 274–288.

Perovsky-Petrovo-Solovovo, Count. (1930). Some Thoughts on D. D. Home. *Proceedings of the Society for Psychical Research*, 39: 247–265.

Peters, Larry G. (1982). Trance, Initiation, and Psychotherapy in Tamang Shamanism. *American Ethnologist*, 9(1): 21–46.

Peters, Larry G. (1994). Rites of Passage and the Borderline Syndrome: Perspectives in Transpersonal Anthropology. *Anthropology of Consciousness*, 5(1): 1–15.

Pilkington, Rosemarie. (Editor). (1987). *Men and Women of Parapsychology: Personal Reflections*. Jefferson, NC: McFarland & Company.

Pinch, T.[revor] J.; and Collins, H.[arry] M. (1984). Private Science and Public Knowledge: The Committee for the Scientific Investigation of the (*sic*) Claims of the Paranormal and Its Use of the Literature. *Social Studies of Science*, 14: 521–546.

Pinchbeck, William Frederick. (1805). *The Expositor; or Many Mysteries Unravelled.* Boston, MA: Printed for the Author.

Podmore, Frank. (1902). *Modern Spiritualism: A History and a Criticism* (2 vols.). London: Methuen & Co.

Polan, Dana. (1986). *Power and Paranoia: History, Narrative, and the American Cinema, 1940–1950.* New York: Columbia University Press.

Popper, Karl R. (1984). *Conjectures and Refutations: The Growth of Scientific Knowledge* (Fourth edition). London: Routledge and Kegan Paul. (First edition published 1963)

Potter, Jack (Comp.); and Hades, Micky. (Editors). (1967–1975). *The Master Index to Magic in Print: Covering Books and Magazines in the English Language Published Up to and Including December 1964.* (14 volumes). Calgary, Alberta: Micky Hades Enterprises.

Poundstone, William. (1985). *The Recursive Universe: Cosmic Complexity and the Limits of Scientific Knowledge.* New York: William Morrow and Company.

Poundstone, William. (1988). *Labyrinths of Reason: Paradox, Puzzles, and the Frailty of Knowledge.* New York: Anchor Press Doubleday.

Pratt, J. G.; Rhine, J. B.; Smith, Burke M.; Stuart, Charles E.; & Greenwood, Joseph A. (1940). *Extra-Sensory Perception After Sixty Years: A Critical Appraisal of the Research in Extra-Sensory Perception.* New York: Henry Holt and Company.

Price, David. (1983). Has Magicdom Reached Maturity? *Genii*, May, pp. 337–338.

Price, David. (1985). *Magic: A Pictorial History of Conjurers in the Theater.* New York: Cornwall Books.

Price, Harry. (1925). *Stella C: An Account of Some Original Experiments in Psychical Research.* London: Hurst & Blackett Ltd.

Prince, Walter Franklin. (1928). *Noted Witnesses for Psychic Occurrences.* Boston, MA: Boston Society for Psychic Research.

Prince, Walter Franklin. (1930). *The Enchanted Boundary: Being A Survey of Negative Reactions to Claims of Psychic Phenomena 1820–1930.* Boston, MA: Boston Society for Psychic Research.

Radin, Paul. (1957). *Primitive Man as Philosopher* (Second revised edition). New York: Dover Publications. (Original work published 1927.)

Radin, Paul. (1972). *The Trickster: A Study in American Indian Mythology.* New York: Schocken Books. (Originally published in 1956).

Randi, The Amazing [Randall James Hamilton Zwinge]. (1975). *The Magic of Uri Geller*. New York: Ballantine Books.

Randi, James. (1982). *The Truth About Uri Geller* (Revised edition of *The Magic of Uri Geller*). Buffalo, NY: Prometheus Books.

Randi, James. (1987). *The Faith Healers*. Buffalo, NY: Prometheus Books.

Rao, K. Ramakrishna. (1965). The Bidirectionality of Psi. *Journal of Parapsychology*, 29: 230–250.

Rao, K. Ramakrishna. (1968). Spontaneous ESP in Laboratory Tests: The Error Phenomenon. *Journal of the American Society for Psychical Research*, 62: 63–72.

Raschke, Carl. (1989). UFOs: Ultraterrestrial Agents of Cultural Deconstruction. In Dennis Stillings, (Ed.), *Cyberbiological Studies of the Imaginal Component in the UFO Contact Experience*, (pp. 21–32). *Archaeus*, Volume 5. [Minneapolis, MN]: Archaeus Project. (Essay originally published 1981.)

Rauscher, William V. (1983). *The Wand: In Story and Symbol*. (Woodbury, N.J.: Author)

Rauscher, William V. (1984). *E.S.P. or Trickery?: The Problem of Mentalism Within the Art of Magic*. (Woodbury, N.J.: Author)

Rauscher, William V. (1998). *ESP or Trickery?: The Problem of Mentalism Within the World of Magic*. (Second edition). Woodbury, NJ: Author.

Rauscher, William V. (2000). *The Houdini Code Mystery: A Spirit Secret Solved*. Pasadena, CA: Mike Caveney's Magic Words.

Rauscher, William V., with Spraggett, Allen. (1975). *The Spiritual Frontier*. Garden City, NY: Doubleday & Company.

Rawlins, Dennis. (1981). sTARBABY. *Fate*, 34(10), October, pp. 67–98.

Reichbart, Richard. (1978). Magic and Psi: Some Speculations on Their Relationship. *Journal of the American Society for Psychical Research*, 72: 153–175.

Reidhead, Van A. (1993). Structure and Anti-Structure in Monasticism and Anthropology: Epistemological Parallels and Adaptive Models. *Anthropology of Consciousness*, 4(2): 9–22.

Report of the Committee Appointed to Investigate Phenomena Connected With The Theosophical Society. (1885). *Proceedings of the Society for Psychical Research*, 3: 201–400. (Often referred to as The Hodgson Report)

Rhine, J. B. (1934). *Extra-Sensory Perception*. Boston, MA: Boston Society for Psychic Research.

R.[hine], J. B. (1944). The Practice of Fake Telepathy. *Journal of Parapsychology*, 8: 251–253.

R.[hine], J. B. (1945). Parapsychology and Religion. *Journal of Parapsychology*, 9: 1–4.

Rhine, Joseph Banks. (1953). *New World of the Mind.* New York: William Sloane Associates.

Rhine, J. B.; and Pratt, J. G. (1957). *Parapsychology: Frontier Science of the Mind.* Springfield, IL: Charles C Thomas.

Rhine, J. B.; and Rhine, Louisa E. (1927). One Evening's Observation on the Margery Mediumship. *Journal of Abnormal and Social Psychology*, 21(4): 401–421.

Richards, Douglas G. (1996). Boundaries in the Mind and Subjective Interpersonal Psi. *Journal of Parapsychology*, 60: 227–240.

Richards, John Thomas. (1982). *SORRAT: A History of the Neihardt Psychokinesis Experiments, 1961–1981.* Metuchen, NJ: Scarecrow Press.

Richards, John Thomas. (1992). *The Year of the Sorrats Volume 1.* Ashland, OH: BookMasters, Inc.

Ricketts, Mac Linscott. (1966). The North American Indian Trickster. *History of Religions*, 5: 327–350.

Ricketts, Mac Linscott. (1987). North American Tricksters. In Mircea Eliade (Ed.), *The Encyclopedia of Religion*, Vol. 15, pp. 48–51. New York: Macmillan Publishing Company.

Ricketts, Mac Linscott. (1993). The Shaman and the Trickster. In *Mythical Trickster Figures: Contours, Contexts, and Criticisms* edited by William J. Hynes and William G. Doty, pp. 87–105. Tuscaloosa, AL: University of Alabama Press.

Ring, Kenneth. (1989). Toward an Imaginal Interpretation of "UFO Abductions". *ReVision*, 11(4), Spring, pp. 17–24.

Ring, Kenneth. (1992). *The Omega Project: Near-Death Experiences, UFO Encounters, and Mind at Large.* New York: William Morrow and Company.

Rinn, Joseph F. (1950). *Sixty Years of Psychical Research: Houdini and I Among the Spiritualists.* New York: Truth Seeker.

Roberts, J. J. M. (1988). Does God Lie? Divine Deceit as a Theological Problem in Israelite Prophetic Literature. *Supplements to Vetus Testamentum*, Vol. 40, Congress Volume Jerusalem 1986 edited by J. A. Emerton, pp. 211–220. Leiden: E. J. Brill.

Roberts, John W. (1989). *From Trickster to Badman: The Black Folk Hero in Slavery and Freedom.* Philadelphia, PA: University of Pennsylvania Press.

Rogerson, Peter. (1986). Taken to the Limits. *Magonia*, No. 23, July, pp. 3–12.

Rojcewicz, Peter M. (1986). The Extraordinary Encounter Continuum Hypothesis and Its Implications for the Study of Belief Materials. *Folklore Forum*, 19(2): 131–152.

Rojcewicz, Peter M. (1987). The "Men In Black" Experience and Tradition: Analogues with the Traditional Devil Hypothesis. *Journal of American Folklore*, 100(396): 148–160.

Rojcewicz, Peter M. (1989). The Folklore of the "Men In Black": A Challenge to the Prevailing Paradigm. *ReVision*, 11(4): 5–16.

Rojcewicz, Peter M. (1991). Between One Eye Blink and the Next: Fairies, UFOs, and Problems of Knowledge. In Peter Narváez (Ed.), *The Good People: New Fairylore Essays* (pp. 479–514). New York: Garland Publishing.

Rojecwicz, Peter M. (1993). Enchanting the Unfamiliar: History and Storytelling [Essay review of *Angels and Aliens* by Keith Thompson]. *Artifex*, 11: 24–31.

Rooth, Anna Birgitta. (1961). *Loki in Scandinavian Mythology*. Lund: C. W. K. Gleerups Forlag.

Rose, Ronald. (1952). Psi and Australian Aborigines. *Journal of the American Society for Psychical Research*, 46: 17–28.

Rosenthal, Robert. (1966). *Experimenter Effects in Behavioral Research*. New York: Appleton-Century-Crofts Division of Meredith Publishing Company.

Rosenthal, Robert. (1994). On Being One's Own Case Study: Experimeter Effects in Behavioral Research—30 Years Later. In *The Social Psychology of Science* edited by William R. Shadish and Steve Fuller, pp. 214–229. New York: The Guilford Press.

Rossman, Michael. (1979). *New Age Blues: On the Politics of Consciousness*. New York: E. P. Dutton.

Roudinesco, Elisabeth. (1990). *Jacques Lacan & Co.: A History of Psychoanalysis in France, 1925–1985* (Translated by Jeffrey Mehlman). Chicago: University of Chicago Press. (Original work published 1986.)

Roudinesco, Elisabeth. (1997). *Jacques Lacan* (Translated by Barbara Bray). New York: Columbia University Press. (Original work published 1993.)

Royle, Nicholas. (1991). *Telepathy and Literature: Essays on the Reading Mind*. Cambridge, MA: Basil Blackwell.

Rucker, Rudy. (1983). *Infinity and the Mind: The Science and Philosphy of the Infinite.* New York: Bantam Books. (First published 1982.)

Rucker, Rudy. (1984). *The Fourth Dimension: Toward a Geometry of Higher Reality.* Boston, MA: Houghton Mifflin Company.

Ruthchild, Myriam. (1983). Cold Reading: The Reality and the Illusion. *The New Invocation.* No. 17, October, p. 195.

Saler, Benson; Ziegler, Charles A.; & Moore, Charles B. (1997). *UFO Crash at Roswell: The Genesis of a Modern Myth.* Washington, DC: Smithsonian Institution Press.

Sampson, Geoffrey. (1980). *Schools of Linguistics.* Stanford, CA: Stanford University Press.

Sass, Louis A. (1992). The Self and Its Vicissitudes in the Psychoanalytic Avant-Garde. In George A. Levine (Ed.). *Constructions of the Self* (pp. 17–58). New Brunswick, NJ: Rutgers University Press. (Essay originally published 1988.)

Saussure, Ferdinand de. (1959). *Course in General Linguistics.* (Edited by Charles Bally and Albert Sechehaye. Translated by Wade Baskin). New York: Philosophical Library. (Originally published 1916.)

Saward, John. (1980). *Perfect Fools: Folly for Christ's Sake in Catholic and Orthodox Spirituality.* Oxford: Oxford University Press.

Schechner, Richard. (1990). Magnitudes of Performance. In Richard Schechner and Willa Appel (Eds.). *By Means of Performance: Intercultural Studies of Theatre and Ritual* (pp. 19–49). Cambridge, England: Cambridge University Press.

Schechner, Richard; & Appel, Willa. (Eds.). (1990). *By Means of Performance: Intercultural Studies of Theatre and Ritual.* Cambridge, England: Cambridge University Press.

Schechter, Ephraim I. (1993a). Honorton's Credentials. *Journal of the American Society for Psychical Research*, 87: 360.

Schechter, Ephraim I. (1993b). Psychophysical Research Laboratories. *Journal of Parapsychology*, 57: 67–82.

Schick, Lawrence. (1991). *Heroic Worlds: A History and Guide to Role-Playing Games.* Buffalo, NY: Prometheus Books.

Schieffelin, Edward L. (1976). *The Sorrow of the Lonely and the Burning of the Dancers.* New York: St. Martin's Press.

Schieffelin, Edward L. (1980). Reciprocity and the Construction of Reality. *Man: The Journal of the Royal Anthropological Institute*, 15(3): 502–517.

Schiffman, Richard. (1989). *Sri Ramakrishna: A Prophet for the New Age*. New York: Paragon House.

Schlitz, Marilyn; and Braud, William. (1997). Distant Intentionality and Healing: Assessing the Evidence. *Alternative Therapies*, 3(6), November, 62–73.

Schmerler, Henrietta. (1931). Trickster Marries His Daughter. *Journal of American Folk-Lore*, 44: 196–207.

Schmidt, Helmut. (1969). Precognition of a Quantum Process. *Journal of Parapsychology*, 33: 99–108.

Schmidt, Helmut. (1974a). Comparison of PK Action on Two Different Random Number Generators. *Journal of Parapsychology*, 38: 47–55.

Schmidt, Helmut. (1974b). Psychokinesis. In Edgar D. Mitchell & John White (Eds.) *Psychic Exploration: A Challenge for Science* (pp. 178–193). New York: G. P. Putnam's Sons.

Schmidt, Helmut. (1975). Toward a Mathematical Theory of Psi. *Journal of the American Society for Psychical Research*, 69: 301–319.

Schmidt, Helmut. (1976). PK Effect on Pre-Recorded Targets. *Journal of the American Society for Psychical Research*, 70: 267–291.

Schmidt, Helmut. (1978). A Remark on the "Divergence Problem". *European Journal of Parapsychology*, 2(2): 163–166.

Schmidt, Helmut. (1982). Collapse of the State Vector and Psychokinetic Effect. *Foundations of Physics*, 12(6): 565–581.

Schmidt, Helmut. (1984). Comparison of a Teleological Model With a Quantum Collapse Model of Psi. *Journal of Parapsychology*, 48: 261–276.

Schmidt, Helmut. (1993). Observation of a Psychokinetic Effect Under Highly Controlled Conditions. *Journal of Parapsychology*, 57: 351–372.

Schmidt, H.; Morris, R.; and Rudolph, L. (1986). Channeling Evidence for a PK Effect to Independent Observers. *Journal of Parapsychology*, 50: 1–15.

Schmidt, Helmut; and Stapp, Henry. (1993). PK With Prerecorded Random Events and the Effects of Preobservation. *Journal of Parapsychology*, 57: 331–349.

Schmidt, Mary. (1987). Crazy Wisdom: The Shaman as Mediator of Realities. In *Shamanism: An Expanded View of Reality* compiled by Shirley Nicholson, pp. 62–75. Wheaton, IL: Theosophical Publishing House.

Schnabel, Jim. (1993). *Round in Circles: Physicists, Poltergeists, Pranksters and the Secret History of the Cropwatchers.* London: Hamish Hamilton.

Schnabel, Jim. (1994). Puck in the Laboratory: The Construction and Deconstruction of Hoaxlike Deception in Science. *Science, Technology, & Human Values,* 19(4): 459–492.

Schnabel, Jim. (1994). *Dark White: Aliens, Abductions, and the UFO Obsession.* London: Hamish Hamilton.

Schnabel, Jim. (1996). *An American Hero: The Truth About Dave Morehouse and Psychic Warrior.* 7 November. 18 pages. Posted on Internet.

Schnabel, Jim. (1997). *Remote Viewers: The Secret History of America's Psychic Spies.* New York: Dell Publishing.

Schneiderman, Stuart. (1983). *Jacques Lacan: The Death of an Intellectual Hero.* Cambridge, MA: Harvard University Press.

Schneiderman, Stuart. (1988). *An Angel Passes: How the Sexes Became Undivided.* New York: New York University Press.

Schouten, Sybo A. (1993). Are We Making Progress? In *Psi Research Methodology: A Re-examinination Proceedings of an International Conference Held in Chapel Hill, North Carolina October 29–30, 1988* edited by Lisette Coly and Joanne D. S. McMahon, pp. 295–322. New York: Parapsychology Foundation.

Schuessler, John F. (1982). Radiation Sickness Caused by UFOs. *UFO's... Canada: A Global Perspective, Thirteenth Annual MUFON UFO Symposium Proceedings.* pp. 50–64.

Schuessler, John F., & O'Herin, Edward F. (1993). Truck Driver Injured by UFO: The Eddie Doyle Webb Case. *MUFON 1993 International UFO Symposium Proceedings, Ufology: The Emergence of a New Science.* pp. 59–84.

Schumaker, John F. (1990). *Wings of Illusion: The Origin, Nature and Future of Paranormal Belief.* Buffalo, NY: Prometheus Books.

Schwartz-Salant, Nathan; & Stein, Murray. (1991). *Liminality and Transitional Phenomena.* Wilmette, IL: Chiron Publications.

Scot, Reginald. (1584). *The Discoverie of Witchcraft.* Imprinted at London by William Brome.

Shah, Dhwani. (1996). *UFOs and the Experience of the Sacred: Discovering Living Myths in Post-Modernity.* Undergraduate thesis submitted to Rutgers College, New Brunswick, NJ.

Sharp, Henry S. (1988). *The Transformation of Bigfoot: Maleness, Power, and Belief Among the Chipewyan.* Washington, DC: Smithsonian Institution Press.

References

Sheler, Jeffery L. (1994). Spiritual America. *U.S. News & World Report*, April 4, pp. 48–59.
Shiels, Tony `Doc'. (1989). *The Cantrip Codex*. (Chicago, IL): Tony Andruzzi.
Shiels, Tony `Doc'. (1990). *Monstrum! A Wizard's Tale*. London: Fortean Tomes.
Siegel, Lee. (1991). *Net of Magic: Wonders and Deceptions in India*. Chicago, IL: University of Chicago Press.
Silverman, Kenneth. (1996). *Houdini!!! The Career of Ehrich Weiss*. New York: HarperCollins.
Singer, Jerome L. (1975). *The Inner World of Daydreaming*. New York: Harper & Row, Publishers.
Singer, Philip. (1990). "Psychic Surgery": Close Observation of a Popular Healing Practice. *Medical Anthropology Quarterly*, 4(4), New Series, 443–451.
Singer, Philip; and Ankenbrandt, Kate W. (1980). The Ethnography of the Paranormal. *Phoenix: New Directions in the Study of Man*, 4(1): 19–34.
Singer, Philip; and Ankenbrandt, Kate (1983). "Hungry for a Miracle:" Psi, Science, and Faith in Psychic Surgery and Parapsychological Anthropology. *Phoenix Journal of Transpersonal Anthropology*, 7(1 & 2): 81–118.
Smith, Jeanne Rosier. (1997). *Writing Tricksters: Mythic Gambols in American Ethnic Literature*. Berkeley: University of California Press.
Smith, Michael F. (1993). Memories of Charles Honorton in Relation to the "Set and Setting" in the Dream Lab 1973–1978. *Journal of the American Society for Psychical Research*, 87: 362–366.
Smith, Morton. (1968). Historical Method in the Study of Religion. In James S. Helfer (Ed.), *On Method in the History of Religions* (pp. 8–16). Middletown, CT: Wesleyan University Press.
Smith, Page. (1990). *Killing the Spirit: Higher Education in America*. New York: Viking.
Smullyan, Raymond. (1992). *Satan, Cantor, and Infinity And Other Mind-Boggling Puzzles*. New York: Alfred A. Knopf.
Soloman, Jack. (1988). *The Signs of Our Time: Semiotics: The Hidden Messages of Environments, Objects, and Cultural Images*. Los Angeles, CA: Jeremy P. Tarcher, Inc.
Solovyoff, Vsevolod Sergeyevich. (1976). *A Modern Priestess of Isis* (Translated by Walter Leaf). New York: Arno Press. (Original work published 1892.)

Spanos, Nicholas P. (1986). Hypnotic Behavior: A Social-Psychological Interpretation of Amnesia, Analgesia, and "Trance Logic". *Behavioral and Brain Sciences*, 9: 449–502.
Spanos, Nicholas P.; and Gottlieb, Jack. (1979). Demonic Possession, Mesmerism, and Hysteria: A Social Psychological Perspective on Their Historical Interrelations. *Journal of Abnormal Psychology*, 88(5): 527–546.
Spencer-Brown, G.[eorge]. (1979). *Laws of Form*. New York: E. P. Dutton. (First published 1969)
Spinks, Jr., C. W. (1991). *Semiosis, Marginal Signs and Trickster: A Dagger of the Mind*. London: Macmillan.
A Spiritualistic Expose–II. (1885). *Pall Mall Gazette*, April 20, pp. 4–5.
Spraggett, Allen, with Rauscher, William V. (1973). *Arthur Ford: The Man Who Talked With the Dead*. New York: New American Library.
Stanford, Rex G. (1974). An Experimentally Testable Model for Spontaneous Psi Events II. Psychokinetic Events. *Journal of the American Society for Psychical Research*, 68: 321–356.
Stanford, Rex G. (1977). Are Parapsychologists Paradigmless in Psiland? In *The Philosophy of Parapsychology Proceedings of an International Conference Held in Copenhagen, Denmark August 25–27, 1976* edited by Betty Shapin and Lisette Coly, pp. 1–16. New York: Parapsychology Foundation.
Stanford, Rex G. (1978). Toward Reinterpreting Psi Events. *Journal of the American Society for Psychical Research*, 72: 197–214.
Stanford, Rex G. (1981). Are We Shamans or Scientists? *Journal of the American Society for Psychical Research*, 75: 61–70.
Stanford, Rex G.; Zenhausern, Robert; Taylor, Adelle; and Dwyer, Mary Ann. (1975). Psychokinesis as Psi-Mediated Instrumental Response. *Journal of the American Society for Psychical Research*, 69: 127–133.
Starhawk. [Miriam Simos]. (1979). *The Spiral Dance: A Rebirth of the Ancient Religion of the Great Goddess*. San Francisco, CA: Harper & Row, Publishers.
Stassinopoulos, Arianna; and Beny, Roloff. (1983). *The Gods of Greece*. New York: Harry N. Abrams Inc. Publishers.
Stebbins, Robert A. (1984). *The Magician: Career, Culture, and Social Psychology in a Variety Art*. Toronto: Clarke Irwin. (Copyright 1983.)

Stefula, Joseph J.; Butler, Richard D.; & Hansen, George P. (1993). A Critique of Budd Hopkins' Case of the UFO Abduction of Linda Napolitano. *Third Eyes Only*, No. 8, January, pp. 10–34.

Steiner, Ralph. (1993). Unmasking The 'Disinformers'. *UFO*, 8(2): 28–36.

Stephen, Michele. (1989). Constructing Sacred Worlds and Autonomous Imagining in New Guinea. In Gilbert Herdt & Michele Stephen (Eds.), *The Religious Imagination in New Guinea*, pp. 211–236. New Brunswick, NJ: Rutgers University Press.

S[tillings], D[ennis]. (1983). Horror in the PK Lab. *Newsletter* [of the] *Archaeus Project*, 2(6), October, pp. 7–8.

Stillings, Dennis. (1984). The Darker Side of Psi: Letters to Dr. Charles T. Tart. *Newsletter* [of the] *Archaeus Project*, 3(6), December, pp. 12–15.

Stillings, Dennis. (1988). Helicopters, UFOs, and the Psyche. *Artifex*, 7(3), Fall, pp. 2–14.

Stillings, Dennis. (Editor). (1989). *Cyberbiological Studies of the Imaginal Component in the UFO Contact Experience*. (*Archaeus*, Vol. 5). (Minneapolis, MN): Archaeus Project.

Stillings, Dennis. (1991). The Society for Research on Rapport and Telekinesis: Experiences and Experiments. *Artifex*, 9: 4–18.

Tabori, Paul. (1950). *Harry Price: The Biography of a Ghosthunter*. London: Athenaeum Press.

Tabori, Paul. (1972). *Pioneers of the Unseen*. New York: Taplinger Publishing Company.

Targ, Russell; & Puthoff, Harold. (1974). Information Transmission Under Conditions of Sensory Shielding. *Nature*, 251: 602–607.

Tart, Charles T. (Editor). (1969). *Altered States of Consciousness: A Book of Readings*. New York: John Wiley & Sons.

Tart, Charles T. (1979). A Survey of Expert Opinion on Potentially Negative Uses of Psi, United States Government Interest in Psi, and the Level of Research Funding of the Field. In *Research in Parapsychology 1978 Abstracts and Papers from the Twenty-first Annual Convention of the Parapsychological Association, 1978* edited by William G. Roll, pp. 54–55. Metuchen, NJ: Scarecrow Press.

Tart, Charles T. (1982). The Controversy About Psi: Two Psychological Theories. *Journal of Parapsychology*, 46: 313–320.

Tart, Charles T. (1984). Acknowledging and Dealing With the Fear of Psi. *Journal of the American Society for Psychical Research*, 78: 133–143.

Tart, Charles T. (1986). Psychic's Fears of Psychic Powers. *Journal of the American Society for Psychical Research*, 80: 279–292.

Tart, Charles T., and Labore, Catherine M. (1986). Attitudes Toward Strongly Functioning Psi: A Preliminary Survey. *Journal of the American Society for Psychical Research*, 80: 163–173.

Tatro, Charlotte R. (1974). Cross My Palm With Silver: Fortunetelling as an Occupational Way of Life. In Clifton D. Bryant (Ed.), *Deviant Behavior: Occupational and Organizational Bases*, (pp. 286–299). Chicago, IL: Rand McNally College Publishing Company.

Taylor, Rogan P. (1985). *The Death and Resurrection Show: From Shaman to Superstar*. London: Anthony Blond.

Thalbourne, Michael A. (1995). Science Versus Showmanship: A History of the Randi Hoax. *Journal of the American Society for Psychical Research*, 89: 344–366.

Theoharis, Athan. (1993). Review of The Secret File on J. Edgar Hoover. *The Journal of American History*, 80: 1201–1203.

Thomas, Alexander [pseudonym]. (1989). *Initiations: A Viewpoint on the Art of Cold Reading*. Albuquerque, NM: Flora & Company.

Thomas, Gordon. (1988). *Journey Into Madness: Medical Torture and the Mind Controllers*. London: Bantam Press.

Thurston, Herbert. (1952). *The Physical Phenomena of Mysticism*. London: Burns Oates.

Thurston, Howard. (1910). Believes In Palladino: Magician Thurston Offers $1,000 If It Be Shown She Depends on Fraud. *New York Times*, May 14, p. 2.

Tierney, Patrick. (1989). *The Highest Altar: The Story of Human Sacrifice*. New York: Viking.

Tietze, Thomas R. (1973). *Margery*. New York: Harper & Row.

Tietze, Thomas R. (1985). The "Margery" Affair. *Journal of the American Society for Psychical Research*, 79: 339–379.

Toch, Hans. (1965). *The Social Psychology of Social Movements*. Indianapolis, IN: The Bobbs-Merrill Company, Inc.

Toelken, Barre. (1987). Life and Death in the Navajo Coyote Tales. In *Recovering the Word: Essays on Native American Literature* edited by Brian Swann and Arnold Krupat, pp. 388–401. Berkeley, CA: University of California Press.

Toelken, Barre. (1995a). Fieldwork Enlightenment. *Parabola*. Summer, pp. 28–35.

Toelken, Barre. (1995b). The Moccasin Telegraph and Other Improbabilities: A Personal Essay. In *Out of the Ordinary: Folklore and the Supernatural* edited by Barbara Walker, pp. 46–58. Logan, UT: Utah State University Press.

Toelken, Barre. (1996). From Entertainment to Realization in Navajo Fieldwork. In *The World Observed: Reflections on the Fieldwork Process* edited by Bruce Jackson and Edward D. Ives, pp. 1–17. Urbana, IL: University of Illinois Press.

Toelken, Barre; and Scott, Tacheeni. (1981). Poetic Retranslation and the "Pretty Languages" of Yellowman. In *Traditional Literatures of the American Indian: Texts and Interpretations* edited by Karl Kroeber, pp. 65–116. Lincoln, NE: University of Nebraska Press.

Tournier, Paul. (1965). *Secrets*. (Translated by Joe Embry). Richmond, VA: John Knox Press. (Originally published 1963.)

Truzzi, Marcello. (1987). Reflections on "Project Alpha": Scientific Experiment or Conjuror's Illusion? *Zetetic Scholar*, Nos. 12/13: 73–98.

Truzzi, Marcello. (1997). Reflections on the Sociology and Social Psychology of Conjurors and Their Relations with Psychical Research. In *Advances in Parapsychological Research 8*, edited by Stanley Krippner, pp. 221–271. Jefferson, NC: McFarland & Company.

Turkle, Sherry. (1992). *Psychoanalytic Politics: Jacques Lacan and Freud's French Revolution* (Second edition). New York: Guilford Press. (Originally published 1978.)

Turnbull, Colin. (1990). Liminality: A Synthesis of Subjective and Objective Experience. In Richard Schechner and Willa Appel (Eds.). *By Means of Performance: Intercultural Studies of Theatre and Ritual* (pp. 50–81). Cambridge, England: Cambridge University Press.

Turner, Edith. (1993). The Reality of Spirits: A Tabooed or Permitted Field of Study? *Anthropology of Consciousness*, 4(1): 9–12.

Turner, Edith; with Blodgett, William; Kahona, Singleton; & Benwa, Fideli. (1992). *Experiencing Ritual: A New Interpretation of African Healing*. Philadephia, PA: University of Pennsylvania Press.

Turner, Victor. (1967). Betwixt and Between: The Liminal Period in Rites de Passage. In his *The Forest of Symbols: Aspects of Ndembu Ritual*. (pp. 93–111). Ithaca, NY: Cornell University Press. (Originally published in the *Proceedings of the American Ethnological Society*, 1964).

Turner, Victor W. (1968). Myth and Symbol. In David L. Sills (Ed.), *International Encyclopedia of the Social Sciences*, Vol. 10, (pp. 576–582). New York: The Macmillan Company & The Free Press.

Turner, Victor W. (1969). *The Ritual Process: Structure and Anti-Structure*. Chicago, IL: Aldine Publishing Company.

Turner, Victor. (1974). Passages, Margins, and Poverty: Religious Symbols of Communitas. In his *Dramas, Fields, and Metaphors: Symbolic Action in Human Society* (pp. 231–271). Ithaca, NY: Cornell University Press. (Original essay published 1972.)

Turner, Victor. (1974). Metaphors of Anti-structure in Religious Culture. In his *Dramas, Fields, and Metaphors: Symbolic Action in Human Society* (pp. 272–299). Ithaca, NY: Cornell University Press. (Original work published 1974.)

Turner, Victor. (1975). *Revelation and Divination in Ndembu Ritual*. Ithaca, NY: Cornell University Press.

Turner, Victor. (1978). Comments and Conclusions. In Barbara A. Babcock (Ed.). *The Reversible World: Symbolic Inversion in Art and Society* (pp. 276–296). Ithaca, NY: Cornell University Press.

Turner, Victor. (1982). *From Ritual to Theatre: The Human Seriousness of Play*. New York City: Performing Arts Journal Publications.

Turner, Victor. (1985). *On the Edge of the Bush: Anthropology as Experience* (Edited by Edith L. B. Turner). Tucson, AZ: University of Arizona Press.

Turner, Victor. (1992). *Blazing the Trail: Way Marks in the Exploration of Symbols* (Edited by Edith Turner). Tucson, AZ: University of Arizona Press.

Ullman, Montague; and Krippner, Stanley. (1970). *Dream Studies and Telepathy: An Experimental Approach. Parapsychological Monographs No. 12.* New York: Parapsychology Foundation.

Ullman, Montague; Krippner, Stanley; with Vaughan, Alan. (1973). *Dream Telepathy*. New York: Macmillan Publishing Co.

Unusual Personal Experiences: An Analysis of the Data From Three National Surveys. (1992). Las Vegas, NV: Bigelow Holding Corporation.

Vallee, Jacques. (1975). *Passport to Magonia: From Folklore to Flying Saucers*. London: Tandem. (First published 1969.)

Vallee, Jacques. (1979). *Messengers of Deception: UFO Contacts and Cults*. Berkeley, CA: And/Or Press.

Vallee, Jacques. (1991). *Revelations: Alien Contact and Human Deception*. New York: Ballantine Books.

van Gennep, Arnold. (1960). *The Rites of Passage.* Translated by Monika B. Vizedom and Gabrielle L. Caffee. Chicago, IL: The University of Chicago Press. (Original work first published 1909.)

Varvoglis, Mario P. (1993). Ganzfeld and RNG Research. *Journal of Parapsychology,* 57: 55–65.

Vecsey, Christopher. (1981). The Exception Who Proves the Rules: Ananse the Akan Trickster. *Journal of Religion in Africa,* 12: 161–177.

Vizenor, Gerald. (Editor). (1989). *Narrative Chance: Postmodern Discourse on Native American Indian Literatures.* Albuquerque, NM: University of New Mexico Press.

Vizenor, Gerald. (1990). Trickster Discourse. *American Indian Quarterly,* 14: 277–287.

Walker, Evan Harris. (1970). The Nature of Consciousness. *Mathematical Biosciences,* 7: 131–178.

Walker, Evan Harris. (1971). Consciousness as a Hidden Variable. *Physics Today,* 24(4), April, p. 39.

Walker, Evan Harris. (1973). Application of the Quantum Theory of Consciousness to the Problem of Psi Phenomena. In *Research in Parapsychology 1972: Abstracts and Papers from the Fifteenth Annual Convention of the Parapsychological Association, 1972,* edited by W. G. Roll, R. L. Morris, and J. D. Morris, pp. 51–53. Metuchen, NJ: Scarecrow Press.

Walker, Evan Harris. (1975). Foundations of Paraphysical and Parapsychological Phenomena. In *Quantum Physics and Parapsychology Proceedings of an International Conference Held in Geneva, Switzerland August 26–27, 1974,* edited by Laura Oteri, pp. 1–44. New York: Parapsychology Foundation.

Walker, Evan Harris. (1977a). Comparison of Some Theoretical Predictions of Schmidt's Mathematical Theory and Walker's Quantum Mechanical Theory of Psi. *Journal of Research in Psi Phenomena,* 2(1): 54–70.

Walker, Evan Harris. (1977b). Quantum Mechanical Tunneling in Synaptic and Ephaptic Transmission. *International Journal of Quantum Chemistry,* 11: 103–127.

Walker, Evan Harris. (1984). A Review of Criticisms of the Quantum Mechanical Theory of Psi Phenomena. *Journal of Parapsychology,* 48: 277–332.

Walker, Mark. (1991). *Ghostmasters.* Copyright by Mark Walker.

Wallace, Anthony F. C. (1956). Revitaliztion Movements. *American Anthropologist,* 58: 264–281.

Wallace, Anthony F. C. (1968). Review of *Studies in Ethnomethodology* by Harold Garfinkel. *American Sociological Review*, 33(1): 124–126.

Walsh, Roger N. (1990). *The Spirit of Shamanism*. Los Angeles, CA: Jeremy P. Tarcher, Inc.

Wang, Hao. (1988). *Reflections on Kurt Gödel*. Cambridge, MA: A Bradford Book The MIT Press. (Copyright 1987.)

Warner, Richard. (1980). Deception and Self-Deception in Shamanism and Psychiatry. *The International Journal of Social Psychiatry*, 26: 41–52.

Warner, W. Lloyd. (1959). *The Living and the Dead: A Study of the Symbolic Life of Americans*. New Haven, CT: Yale University Press.

Warren, Donald I. (1970). Status Inconsistency Theory and Flying Saucer Sightings. *Science*, 170: 599–603.

Washington, Peter. (1995). *Madame Blavatsky's Baboon: A History of the Mystics, Mediums, and Misfits Who Brought Spiritualism to America (sic)*. New York: Schocken Books. (Originally published 1993.)

Waters, T. A. (1988). *The Encyclopedia of Magic and Magicians*. New York: Facts on File Pubications.

Watkins, Mary. (1990). *Invisible Guests: The Development of Imaginal Dialogues*. Boston, MA: Sigo Press. (Original work published 1986.)

Watzlawick, Paul. (1990). *Münchhausen's Pigtail: or Psychotherapy & "Reality" Essays and Lectures*. New York: W. W. Norton & Company.

Webb, James. (1976). *The Occult Establishment*. La Salle, IL: Open Court Publishing Company.

Weber, Max. (1958). *The Protestant Ethic and the Spirit of Capitalism*. Traslated by Talcott Parsons. New York: Charles Scribner's Sons. (Originally published 1904–1905).

Weber, Max. (1964). *The Sociology of Religion*. Boston, MA: Beacon Press. (Original work published 1922.)

Weber, Max. (1968). *Max Weber on Charisma and Institution Building* (Edited by S. N. Eisenstadt). Chicago: University of Chicago Press.

Weber, Max. (1978). *Economy and Society: An Outline of Interpretive Sociology*. (2 vols.). Edited by Guenther Roth and Claus Wittich, translated by a number of scholars. Berkeley, CA: University of California Press.

Weber, W. C. (1953a). Exposing the Crystal Racket. *M-U-M*. March, pp. 288–291.

Weber, W. C. (1953b). More on the Crystal Racket. *M-U-M*. June, pp. 16–18.

Webster, Hutton. (1973). *Magic: A Sociological Study*. New York: Octagon Books. (Original work published 1948)

Weiner, Debra H.; and Geller, Jeffery. (1984). Motivation as the Universal Container: Conceptual Problems in Parapsychology. *Journal of Parapsychology*, 48: 27–37.

Wells, Wesley R. (1946). A Basic Deception in Exhibitions of Hypnosis. *The Journal of Abnormal and Social Psychology*, 41(2): 145–153.

Welsford, Enid. (1935). *The Fool: His Social and Literary History*. London: Faber and Faber.

Wescott, Joan. (1962). The Sculpture and Myths of Eshu-Elegba, The Yoruba Trickster. *Africa: Journal of the International African Institute*, 32: 336–354.

West, D.[onald] J.[ames]. (1987). Obituary [of Eric J. Dingwall]. *Journal of the Society for Psychical Research*, 54: 92–95.

West, D. J.; and Fisk, G. W. (1953). A Dual ESP Experiment with Clock Cards. *Journal of the Society for Psychical Research*, 37: 185–197.

Weyer, Edward Moffat. (1969). *The Eskimos: Their Environment and Folkways*. Hamden, CT: Archon Books. (Original work published 1932)

Whaley, Bart. (1990). *Who's Who in Magic: An International Biographical Guide From Past to Present*, Standard Edition. Oakland, CA: Jeff Busby Magic.

White, Rhea A. (1976). The Limits of Experimenter Influence on Psi Test Results: Can Any be Set? *Journal of the American Society for Psychical Research*, 70: 333–369.

Wickramasekera, Ian. (1991). Model of the Relationship Between Hypnotic Ability, Psi, and Sexuality. *Journal of Parapsychology*, 55: 159–174.

Wigner, Eugene P. (1962). Remarks on the Mind-Body Question. In *The Scientist Speculates: An Anthology of Partly-Baked Ideas* edited by Irving John Good, Alan James Mayne, and John Maynard Smith, pp. 284–302. New York: Basic Books.

Wilkins, John. (1641). *Mercury, Or the Secret and Swift Messenger: Showing, How a Man May With Privacy and Speed Communicate*

His Thoughts to a Friend at Any Distance. London: Printed by I. Norton for John Maynard, and Timothy Wilkins.
Willeford, William. (1969). *The Fool and His Scepter: A Study in Clowns and Jesters and Their Audience.* [Evanston, IL?]: Northwestern University Press.
Williams, Walter L. (1986). *The Spirit and the Flesh: Sexual Diversity in American Indian Culture.* Boston, MA: Beacon Press.
Wilson, Ian. (1989). *Stigmata: An Investigation into the Mysterious Appearance of Christ's Wounds in Hundreds of People from Medieval Italy to Modern America.* San Francisco, CA: Harper & Row, Publishers.
Winkelman, Michael. (1982). Magic: A Theoretical Reassessment. *Current Anthropology,* 23(1): 37–66.
Winkelman, Michael James. (1992). *Shamans, Priests and Witches: A Cross-Cultural Study of Magico-Religious Practitioners.* Arizona State University Anthropological Research Papers No. 44. Tempe, AZ: Arizona State University.
Winter, E. H. (1963). The Enemy Within: Amba Witchcraft and Sociological Theory. In John Middleton and E. H. Winter (Eds.). *Witchcraft and Sorcery in East Africa* (pp. 277–299). London: Routledge & Kegan Paul.
Wiseman, Richard. (1992). The Feilding Report: A Reconsideration. *Journal of the Society for Psychical Research,* 58: 129–152.
Wiseman, Richard. (1993). Martinez-Taboas, Francia and Palladino: Nine Major Errors. *Journal of the Society for Psychical Research,* 59: 130–140.
Wolf, Fred Alan. (1994). *The Dreaming Universe: A Mind-Expanding Journey Into the Realm Where Psyche and Physics Meet.* New York: Simon & Schuster.
Wolman, Benjamin B. (Editor). (1977). *Handbook of Parapsychology.* New York: Van Nostrand Reinhold Company.
Woolgar, Steve. (Editor). (1988). *Knowledge and Reflexivity: New Frontiers in the Sociology of Knowledge.* London: Sage Publications.
Woolgar, Steve. (1988). Reflexivity is the Ethnographer of the Text. In his *Knowledge and Reflexivity: New Frontiers in the Sociology of Knowledge,* pp. 14–36.
Woolgar, Steve. (1996). Sociology of Science. In *The Social Science Encyclopedia* (Second edition), edited by Adam Kuper and Jessica Kuper, pp. 828–830. London: Routledge.
Wren-Lewis, John. (1974). Resistance to the Study of the Paranormal. *Journal of Humanistic Psychology,* 14(2): 41–48.

Young, Dudley. (1991). *Origins of the Sacred: The Ecstasies of Love and War*. New York: St. Martin's Press.

Zeidman, Jennie. (1979). *A Helicopter-UFO Encounter Over Ohio*. Evanston, IL: Center for UFO Studies.

Zha, Leping, & McConnell, Tron. (1991). Parapsychology in the People's Republic of China: 1979–1989. *Journal of the American Society for Psychical Research*, 85: 119–143.

Zijderveld, Anton C. (1970). *The Abstract Society: A Cultural Analysis of Our Time*. Garden City, NY: Anchor Books Doubleday & Company, Inc.

Zijderveld, Anton C. (1982). *Reality in a Looking-Glass: Rationality Through an Analysis of Traditional Folly*. London: Routledge & Kegan Paul.

Zingrone, Nancy L. (1994). Images of Woman as Medium: Power, Pathology and Passivity in the Writings of Frederic Marvin and Cesare Lombroso. In Lisette Coly and Rhea A. White (Eds.). *Women and Parapsychology: Proceedings of an International Conference Held in Dublin, Ireland September 21–22, 1991*. (pp. 90–121). New York: Parapsychology Foundation, Inc.

Zöllner, Johann Carl Friedrich. (1881). *Transcendental Physics. An Account of Experimental Investigations from the Scientific Treatises*. (Translated by Charles Carleton Massey). Boston, MA: Colby & Rich Publishers.

Zolotow, Maurice. (1952). *It Takes All Kinds*. New York: Random House.

Zorka, Artur. (1976). Official Report: Society of American Magicians, Assembly 30, Atlanta Chapter. In *The Geller Papers: Scientific Observations on the Paranormal Powers of Uri Geller*, edited by Charles Panati, pp. 157–167. Boston, MA: Houghton Mifflin Company.

Zumwalt, Rosemary. (1982). Arnold van Gennep: The Hermit of Bourg-la-Reine. *American Anthropologist*, 84: 299–313.

Index

Abbott, David P., 132
Abbott, Jay, 125
Abbott's Magic Novelty Company, 141
Aberdeen Proving Grounds, 321, 331
Abimelech, 43
Abnormal Hypnotic Phenomena, 139
Abram, 43
abstraction, 78, 83, 147, 281, 282
   classification and, 354
   communitas and, 83
   conjurors and, 135, 146
   deception and, 146, 147, 247
   primitive mind and, 354
   rationalization and, 105
   totemism and, 362
   trickster and, 105
academe
   CSICOP's presence in, 148, 160
   disenchantment and, 106
   magic, aversion to, 106, 107, 355, 365, 366
   paranormal and, 20, 176, 185–88, 405, 406, 424
   parapsychology's failure to be integrated into, 187, 193
   personification, hostility to, 400
   rationalization and, 27, 155, 429
   reflexivity, aversion to, 277, 307
Academy of Humanism, 154
Act of Creation, The, 60
Adler, Margot, 174, 355
Advances in Parapsychological Research, 15, 330, 418
Ady, Thomas, 131

Aerial Phenomena Research Organization, 222, 227
Afro-American Trickster Tale, The, 61
Age of Structuralism, The, 385
agriculture, 98, 100
Air Force
   disinformation, 223, 224
   Office of Special Investigations (AFOSI), 226–35, 243
Akarama, 283
alchemy, 30, 41, 42, 44, 130, 364, 401, 426
Alcock, James, 151, 153
Alexander II, Czar, 122, 172
Alexander, John B., 169, 170, 237–40, 243, 244
Alien Harvest, An, 226, 228
altered states of consciousness, 79
   charisma and, 104
   hypnosis, 139
   legend-trips and, 164
   liminality and, 56
   magico-religious practitioners and, 99–101, 429
   meditation, 288–89
   mediums and, 100, 172
   New Age movement, 174
   psi and, 317, 330, 340, 342, 425
   shamanism and, 98
   Spiritualism, 172
   witchcraft, modern-day, 175
Altered States of Consciousness, 289
Alternative Altars, 123, 173, 355
Amatenstein, Sherry, 181
ambiguity, 308
   benefits, 269
   Blavatsky, H. P., and, 122

deconstructionism and, 364, 376, 390
divination and, 383
Esu and, 383
hoaxes and, 270
Home, D. D., and, 122
hypnosis, 139
initiations and, 55
interstitiality and, 183
Levi-Strauss', Claude, innate, 361, 364
magical power and, 65
meaning and, 369, 375, 390
mysticism and, 75
paranormal and, 215
psi and, 22
psychics and, 119
reflexivity and, 278, 303
sexual, 76, 282
structuralism and, 363
trickster and, 31, 46, 369
ufology and, 219, 246, 260
Vizenor, Gerald, and, 381
American Anthropological Association, 97, 127
American Association for the Advancement of Science (AAAS), 200, 316
American Atheist, 154
American Humanist Association, 148
American Indian Quarterly, 380
American Institutes for Research (AIR), 199
American Physical Society, 142, 151
American Psychological Association (APA), 201, 318
American Psychologist, 318
American Rationalist, 154
American Society for Psychical Research (ASPR), 60, 125, 168, 196–97, 202, 240, 326. *See* also *Journal of the American Society for Psychical Research*

expenditures, 197
number of members, 196
American Woman, The, 144
Ames, Aldrich, 199
analytic psychology, 400
Anaximander, 62
Anderson, John Henry, 121
Anderson, Philip, 205
Andrus, Walter, 253, 254, 255, 258, 264
Angel Passes, An, 385
angels, 19, 64, 130, 248, 270, 385, 402, 426
belief in, 156
Angleton, James Jesus, 416, 417
Annemann, Theodore, 295
Answer to Job, 84
anti-structure, 22, 24, 25, 27, 31, 117, 309. *See* also liminality; communitas; interstitiality; betwixt and between
advantages of term, 59
charisma and, 27, 112
classification, 343
danger and, 65–69
defined, 59
institutions and, 178
lability and, 341
mysticism and, 73, 81–83
paranoia and, 417–18, 421
paranormal and, 69–71, 118, 424
parapsychology and, 191–209
randomness, 343
revitalization and, 110, 113, 115
status and, 26
trickster and, 28, 59
Apollo, 39, 170
apparitions, 14, 425
Marian, 114
Apple II computers, 206
Aquarian Conspiracy, The, 174
Aquarian Guide to the New Age, The, 265

Aquinas. *See* Thomas Aquinas, Saint
archetype
  Blavatsky, H. P., as exemplar of trickster, 123
  conjuror-trickster exemplars, 142
  de Man, Paul, as exemplar of trickster, 379
  defined, 28, 35
  Vizenor, Gerald, as exemplar of trickster, 380
Aristotelian logic, 31, 62, 274, 306, 429
Arizona State University, 97
Arneson, David L., 263
Aron, Raymond, 351
Ashley, Kathleen, 36, 363
Ashmore, Malcolm, 278, 279, 284, 286, 288, 307, 375
Asimov, Isaac, 148
Associated Investigators Group (AIG), 237, 239, 243
Association for Research and Enlightenment, 179, 189
Atwater, P. M. H., 84
Babcock, Barbara, 25, 34, 36, 44, 46, 59–60, 78, 92, 278, 346, 381, 414
Bainbridge, William Sims, 70, 186–87
Baldwin, Samri, 121, 132
Balfour, Arthur, 192
Bandelier, Adolf, 44
Barham, Jay, 164
Barker, Patricia, 206
Barrett, William F., 196
Barthes, Roland, 374, 376, 377, 378, 391
basic limiting principles, 311
Basso, Ellen, 36, 60–61
Batcheldor, Kenneth, 335
BDM International, 242
Bechterev, Vladimir, 139
Behind the Flying Saucers, 224

Belief, Language, and Experience
  dedicated to Levy-Bruhl, 353
Bell Laboratories, 312
Bellachini, Samuel, 132
Benedictines, 82
Bennewitz, Paul, 227, 228, 230, 233, 237, 244
Bentley, William Perry, 197
Ben-Yehuda, Nachman, 156, 178
berdache, 64, 93, 426
Berger, Peter, 155, 156
Berger, Rick, 206
Bergson, Henri, 60, 139, 192, 361, 362, 373
Berlitz, Charles, 224
Berman, Morris, 414
Bernstein, Morey, 139
Besant, Annie, 123
Bessent, Malcolm, 203
betwixt and between, 31, 55, 62, 64, 65, 71. *See also* liminality; interstitiality; anti-structure
  birds, 79
  CSICOP's status as, 151
  Hermes and, 38, 39
  imaginal realm and, 402
  Mercurius, 42
  mysticism and, 75
  psi and, 426
  semiotics and, 374, 382
  UFOs and, 248, 270
Biblical tricksters, 43–44
Bigelow, Robert, 197
Bigfoot, 19, 23, 117, 210, 404, 407
  paranoia and, 415
binary arithmetic, 370
binary opposition, 274, 346, 347, 369
  child-adult, 31
  dream-reality, 414
  fact-fiction, 146
  fantasy-reality, 30, 421
  food-excrement, 30, 55, 59, 64, 77, 81. *See also* intestines

God-human, 31, 64, 75, 304, 426
God-man, 65
heaven-earth, 31, 79, 426
imagination-reality, 30, 270, 389, 393, 409
internal-external, 30, 393, 401, 421
life-death, 31, 55, 59, 64, 426
male-female, 30, 55, 59, 84, 352, 387, 426
mind-matter, 426
representation-object, 393
self-other, 414, 421, 426
signifier-signified, 374, 383
subjective-objective, 30, 426
binary oppositions, 62–64, 395–97, 402, 414, 421, 422, 426. *See also* opposites
  boundaries inherent to, 30, 426
  initiations and, 55
  law of the excluded middle and, 429
  liminality and, 347
  paranormal and, 383
  reversals, 64
  status and, 62, 426
  trickster as mediator, 59
birds, 56, 78, 87
Bisaha, John, 202
bizarre magic, 135–37, 143
Black Elk Speaks, 166
Blackburn, Douglas, 295
Blackmore, Susan, 153, 185
Blaeser, Kimberly, 36, 381
Blake, William, 83
Blavatsky, Helena, 122–24, 179, 189
Blindness and Insight, 376
Blowsnake, Sam, 37
Boeing Scientific Research Laboratories, 318
Bogoras, Waldemar, 93
Bolen, Jean Shinoda, 24, 36, 38, 39, 40, 48–51

Bolton, Frances, 197
Bonaventure, Saint, 78
Books in Print, 133, 344
Booth, John, 294
borderline personality disorder, 57
Boston Society for Psychic Research, 196
boundaries, 30–31
  binary oppositions and, 30, 426–27
  classification and, 346
  hypnosis and, 140
  liminality and, 59
  logic and, 274
  magic and, 367
  mazeway and, 111
  mental, 48–51, 56
  methods of designating, 427
  mysticism and, 75
  paranormal and supernatural, 275
  psi and, 309, 311
  rationalization and, 358
  unbounded conditions and, 210–18
Boundaries in the Mind, 48
Boundary Questionnaire, 49
Bourke, John, 44
Bowen, Nancy, 43
Br'er Rabbit, 62
Braud, Lendell, 202, 205
Braud, William, 25, 107, 205, 310, 321, 331, 339–41, 425
Braude, Ann, 172
Breen, Ed, 230
Brennan, J. H., 265
bricolage, 29, 363
bricoleur, 363, 385
Brinton, Daniel G., 35
British Intelligence, 239
Broad, C. D., 311
Brooke, Tal, 129
Brooksher, William, 230

Broughton, Richard, 15, 167, 206
Brown, Norman, 38, 39, 40, 61, 388
Browning, Elizabeth Barrett, 122
Browning, Robert, 122
Bryan, Joseph, 222
Buddha, 358
Bush, George, 133
Butler, Richard, 252, 255, 261
Butler's Lives of the Saints, 76
Byrd, Eldon, 142
California Institute of Technology, 222
Cambridge University, 311, 347
Camp, Claudia, 36
Campbell, Eileen, 265
Campbell, Jeremy, 291
Campbell, Joseph, 87, 204
cannibalism, 67
Cannon, Martin, 216, 238, 244
Carlson, Chester F., 197
Carnap, Rudolf, 293
Carnegie-Mellon University, 91
Carrington, Hereward, 120, 138
Carroll, Lewis, 192
Carroll, Michael, 134
Carroll, Noel, 408
Carter, Chris, 183
Cash-Landrum UFO case, 115, 238
Castaneda, Carlos, 127, 128, 282, 283, 307
Castaneda's Journey, 127
Casti, John, 291
Catechism of the Catholic Church, 23
Catholicism, 24, 80, 83, 84
 rationalization and, 105, 302
Catholics Anonymous, 154
cattle mutilations, 210, 228, 229, 241–43, 245
cause and effect, 35, 328, 332, 370
Cayce, Edgar, 129, 174, 179, 189

celibacy, 84
Center for UFO Studies. *See* CUFOS
Changing Order, 286
channeling, 174, 204
Charcot, Jean-Martin, 389
Chari, C. T. K., 332
charisma, 26, 96, 112, 153, 161, 172, 377
 altered states of consciousness and, 104
 anti-structure and, 112
 defined, 102
 instability of, 103
 liminality and, 27, 103
 miracles and, 104, 107, 429
 shamanism and, 98
 telepathy and, 27, 104, 106
 weather control, 104
Child, Irvin, 202, 205, 318
Chipewyan, 415
Christianity, 67, 110, 145, 349, 354. *See* also Catholicism, Protestantism
Christopher, Milbourne, 90, 145, 146
Chukchee, The, 93
Church, George W., Jr., 197, 206
Church's Fried Chicken, 206
CIA (Central Intelligence Agency), 169, 198, 199, 202, 211, 221–23, 233, 237–40, 242–43, 249, 318, 416, 417
Citizens Against UFO Secrecy (CAUS), 221, 223, 229
City College of New York, 168, 202
Civilian Flying Saucer Investigators, 222
clairvoyance, 14, 19, 29, 49, 70, 139, 179, 300, 309, 389, 393. *See* also ESP; psi; remote viewing
 Catholic Church's prohibition against, 23

distinguishing from other types of psi, 319, 425
experiments, 314
saints and, 79, 80, 84
Clark, Jerry, 253, 254, 255, 258
classification, 30, 274, 343. *See also* binary oppositions
abstraction and, 354
binary oppositions and, 362
high-strangeness and, 404
imaginal realm and, 404
interstitiality and, 183, 407
liminality and, 343, 346
paranormal and, 404, 407
psi, problems with, 22, 319
structuralism and, 427
totemism and, 274, 345–47, 350, 361
trickster and, 46
Claude Levi-Strauss, 361
Clear Intent: The Government Coverup of the UFO Experience, 221, 223
Clements, William, 66, 183, 407
Clinton, William Jefferson, 219
Clodd, Edward, 349
clowns, 30, 44, 45, 46, 64, 428
coincidence of opposites, 30, 43, 78
Collins, Harry, 150, 286, 298, 307
Collins, James, 124
Collins, Robert, 230, 233, 236, 237
Columbia University, 89, 196, 381
Committee for the Scientific Investigation of Claims of the Paranormal. *See* CSICOP
Communication Studies Laboratory, 204
communitas, 57–58, 61, 83. *See also* liminality, anti-structure
charisma and, 103, 104
conjuring and, 133

trickster and, 59, 84
comparative methods, 53
conformance behavior, 203, 321, 331, 338–39, 340
conjuring, 29
bizarre magic, 135–37
communitas and, 133
definition confusion, 19, 130
hypnosis and, 138–41
institutions and, 132–33
liminality and, 135
marginality and, 132, 147
paranormal and, 23, 130–47
conjurors, 117
CSICOP and, 158, 160
Gardner, Martin, 295
liminality and, 117
paranormal and, 117, 119, 121, 124, 126
sexuality and, 143, 144
trickster exemplars, 141–46
trickster qualities of, 134
Conjuror's Magazine, The, 131
Controllers, The, 216, 238
Corbin, Henry, 389, 402–4
Cornell University, 52
Cortile, Linda (pseudonym). *See* Napolitano, Linda
Council for Democratic and Secular Humanism (CODESH), 154, 304
Course in General Linguistics, 371
Course in Miracles, A, 174
coven, 174
Cox, Jay, 46
Cox, W. E., 166
Coyne helicopter UFO case, 115
coyote, 35, 67, 68, 413
Crafting the Art of Magic, 174
Crandall, James, 205
Crandon, Le Roi, 124
Crandon, Mina. *See* Margery
Creating Minds, 60
creative illness, 57, 102, 112, 290
creativity, 56, 57, 59, 60

Creevy, Vincent, 253
Crick, Francis, 148
Crookes, William, 122, 192
Crowley, Aleister, 67
Cseh, Thomas A., 230
CSICOP, 79, 89, 117, 121, 128, 142, 143, 145, 148–61, 177, 183, 184, 202, 203, 219, 232, 245, 286, 293, 294, 296, 298, 301, 303, 304, 409, 424
  anti-religious sentiment, 154–55
  astrology study, 150
  magicians, 158
  Manual for Local, Regional and National Groups, 150
  office facilities, 148
  policy against research, 149–50, 151
CUFOS, 225, 250, 253, 255, 258, 260, 267
Culture & Communication, 370
Curie, Marie, 192
Current Anthropology, 97
Cyberbiological Studies of the Imaginal Component of the UFO Contact Experience, 403
Dakota Sioux, 112
Dames, Edward A., 168–70, 237, 243, 244
Danse Macabre, 407
Dark White, 250
Darwin, Charles, 397
Darwinism, 349, 360
Davenport brothers, 119, 120, 121
Davis, Winston, 106, 107
Dawes, Edwin, 146
Dawes, Robyn, 91
Dawkins, Richard, 148
Dawson, John, 290
de Camp, L. Sprague, 185
de Graef, Ortwin, 379
de Man, Paul, 376, 379, 391

de Mille, Richard, 120, 127, 128, 283
Dean, Douglas, 202, 316, 320
Death and Resurrection Show, The, 135
deception, 30, 117, 393. *See also* disinformation; hoaxes; pretense; conjuring; sham of shamanism; psychics, trickery, allegations of
  abstraction and, 146, 147, 247
  benefits, 267–69
  divine, 43
  Hermes and, 39
  hypnosis and, 140
  liminality and, 61, 73
  paranormal and, 422
  primates, 410–11
  psi and, 40
  semiotics and, 374
  Wakdjunkaga and, 37
  YHWH and, 44
Deception: The Invisible War Between the KGB and the CIA, 416
deconstructionism, 27, 30, 41, 46, 59, 64, 108, 273, 274, 289, 345, 362, 364, 368, 369, 374, 375–83, 385, 390, 406
  psi and, 27
  trickster and, 27, 380–83
Decremps, Henri, 131
Defense Intelligence Agency (DIA), 198, 223
Defense Investigative Service (DIS), 226
Degh, Linda, 66
Delight Makers, The, 44
Delmore, Bill, 194, 203
Derrida, Jacques, 376, 378–80, 383
Devery, Betty, 126
Deviance and Moral Boundaries, 156, 178
Diamond, Stanley, 37, 84, 356

dice
  experiments, 314, 316, 326, 340
  Hermes and, 39, 343
Dickson, Abb, 132
Dingwall, Eric, 79, 81, 82, 122, 139, 144–45, 146
Dionysus, 39, 94, 170
Discoverie of Witchcraft, The, 130, 131
disenchantment, 95, 117, 161, 189, 215, 302, 345, 358, 364–66, 377, 400, 428, 429. *See also* rationalization
  defined, 105
disinformation, 117, 219–46
  trickster and, 220, 221, 245
divergence problem, 321, 336–37
divination, 44, 98, 99, 100, 130, 174
  charisma and, 104
  classification and, 354
  Eshu-Elegba and, 40
  Hermes and, 39
  Ifa, 40, 382, 383
divine, 66, 75, 84, 302, 426
  charisma and the, 103
  deceit, 43
diviners, 65, 112, 113
divorce, 49, 84, 164, 165, 170, 173
Dixon, Jeane, 129
Dobyns, York H., 206
Dodds, E. R., 78
Dodgson, Charles Lutwidge. *See* Carroll, Lewis
Don Juan Matus, 120, 127
Don Juan Papers, The, 127, 283
Don, Norman S., 205
Doty, Richard C., 226–36, 237, 241, 243, 244
Douglas, Mary, 66, 364, 415
Downing, Christine, 36, 38
Doyle, Sir Arthur Conan, 172

Drawing Down the Moon, 174, 355
dread, 66, 136, 351, 356, 366
Dream Telepathy, 318
Dreaming Universe, The, 403
dreams, 26, 56, 60, 66, 175, 386, 401, 402
  ESP and, 317, 318, 340
  lucid, 48
  nightmares, 48, 51
  precognition and, 130, 316
  sexual, 41
Duff-Cooper, Andrew, 345, 350
Duke of Brunswick, 80
Duke University, 193, 194, 204, 295, 304, 313, 325, 424
Dungeons & Dragons, 263, 264, 265, 266
Dunne, Brenda J., 206
Dunninger, Joseph, 119, 120, 126, 127
Durant, Robert, 228, 239, 240
Durkheim, Emile, 25, 64, 337, 344, 346, 350, 351, 355, 357, 359, 360, 366, 371, 399
  problems in comprehending, 351
dyadic relationships, 84
Eastern Kentucky University, 410
Eater of Ordure, 81
Ecker, Don, 228
Eco, Umberto, 246, 373–75
Economy and Society, 102
Edwards, Ernest, 227, 230
Edwards, Jay, 61
Edwards, Michael, 142
Ehrenwald, Jan, 418, 419
Eighth Tower, The, 85
Einstein, Albert, 60
Eisenbud, Jule, 420
Eisenstadt, S. N., 105
Elegba. *See* Eshu-Elegba
Elementary Forms of the Religious Life, The, 350, 399
Eliade, Mircea, 78, 86, 89

Eliot, T. S., 60
Elizabeth City State University, 187
Ellenberger, Henri, 57, 112, 290
Ellis, Bill, 163, 164
Ellsworth Air Force Base, 229, 230, 232
Ellwood, Gracia Fay, 123
Ellwood, Robert, 123, 173, 355
Elusive Science, The, 193, 304
Emenegger, Robert, 233
enchanted boundary, 300
  equivalence to limen, 157
Enchanted Boundary, The, 157
Encyclopedia of Impromptu Magic, 295
Encyclopedia of Magic and Magicians, The, 120, 132
Encyclopedia of Stage Hypnotism, The, 141
entertainment. *See also* fiction
  paranormal and, 182–85, 191
Epimenides' paradox, 277
Epstein, Edward Jay, 416
Eshu-Elegba, 35, 40–41, 46, 62, 382–83
ESP, 29, 273, 424. *See also* psi; telepathy; clairvoyance; precognition; remote viewing
  defined, 14
  factors enhancing, 25, 26, 51, 289, 330, 340. *See* altered states of consciousness
  forced-choice tests, 317, 318
  free-response tests, 317–18
ESP: A Scientific Evaluation, 293
Esu. *See* Eshu-Elegba
Eternity Science Fiction magazine, 242
ethnomethodology, 83, 277, 278, 279–83, 289, 306, 324
  breaching experiments, 280, 308
Evans, Henry Ridgely, 132
Evans-Pritchard, E. E., 360–61

excluded middle, law of the, 31, 62, 429
excrement. *See also* binary opposition, food-excrement
  Eater of Ordure, 81
  intestines, 79
  Mercurius and, 42
  Scatalogic Rites of All Nations, 45
  Wakdjunkaga and, 37
  witchcraft and, 45
exogamy, 348, 351, 352
Exorcist, The, 201, 408
experimenter effects, 287–88, 321
  parapsychology, 322–24
extrasensory perception. *See* ESP
Extra-Sensory Perception, 193
Extra-sensory Perception After Sixty Years, 314
extraterrestrial aliens, 20, 426. *See also* UFOs
extraterrestrial hypothesis
  misnamed, 261
Fads and Fallacies in the Name of Science, 292
fantasy role-playing games (FRPGs), 263
  cheating in, 265
  liminality, 264–66
  ufology compared with, 266
Farrakhan, Louis, 113
Fate magazine, 150, 184, 185, 202, 213, 242
Fawcett, Lawrence, 221, 222, 223, 227
FBI (Federal Bureau of Investigation), 242
Ferguson, Marilyn, 174
Fetzer, John E., 197
Feuerstein, Georg, 76, 81
Few, William Preston, 193
fiction, 30, 117, 182–84, 395, 406–9, 424. *See also* entertainment
Fine, Gary Alan, 263–65

Fisk, George W., 322–23, 324
Flaherty, Gloria, 90
Flammarion, Camille, 192
Flight of Peter Fromm, The, 293, 301, 302, 303
Flying Saucers: A Modern Myth of Things Seen in the Skies, 114, 416
Folk Lore Society, 349
Fool and His Scepter, The, 44
Fool: His Social and Literary History, The, 44
Ford, Arthur, 120, 125, 126
Fornell, Earl Wesley, 120
Fort Meade, 199
Fort, Charles Hoy, 213
Fortean groups
  anti-structure and, 213
Fortean Times magazine, 143
Forwald, Haakon, 333, 334
Foucault, Michel, 378, 391
Foucault's Pendulum, 246, 375
Foundation for Research on the Nature of Man (FRNM), 193, 194, 202, 206. *See also* Rhine Research Center; Institute for Parapsychology
Fourth Dimension, The, 291
Fox sisters, 120, 171
Fox, John, 120
Frames of Meaning, 286
Francesco, Grete de, 44
Francis of Assisi, Saint, 23, 27, 77, 78, 83, 104, 302
Francois de Paris, 81
Franklin, Benjamin, 140
Franklin, Penelope, 254
Frazer, James George, 106, 348–50, 355, 359, 360, 361, 366
Frazier, Kendrick, 153, 185
Free Inquiry magazine, 154
Freedom of Information Act (FOIA), 221, 226, 227, 229, 239

Freud, Sigmund, 25, 57, 60, 139, 192, 344, 351–53, 355, 356, 357, 360, 361, 366, 379, 380, 385, 386, 388, 389
  Jung, Carl, conversation with, 352
From Trickster to Badman, 61
Fromm, Erika, 139
FUFOR, 236, 242
Fuller, Curtis, 185
Fund for UFO Research. *See* FUFOR
Future of the Body, The, 15
Gallup, George H., Jr., 70
Galton, Francis, 397
Gandhi, Mahatma, 60
ganzfeld, 203, 206
  Braud, William, 339
Gardner, Howard, 60, 362, 363
Gardner, Martin, 153, 158, 159, 160, 185, 278, 291–308, 334, 335
  critic of paranormal, 294–300
  paradox vs. ambiguity, 303
  paranoia, 300
  religion, 293–94, 300–305
Garfinkel, Harold, 278, 279, 280, 282, 285, 289, 303, 307
Garrett, Eileen, 129
Garrison, Jim, 238
Gates, Henry Louis, Jr., 25, 27, 41, 62, 382–83, 384
Gatling, William, 304
Gauld, Alan, 139, 145
Gauquelin, Michel, 150
GeBauer, Leo, 224, 225
Geller, Uri, 120, 128, 142, 194, 202, 203, 269
Gell-Mann, Murray, 148
General Accounting Office (GAO), 225, 230, 231
Genii magazine, 136
George, Leonard, 206
Gersten, Peter, 229, 231
Ghost (movie), 191

Ghost Dance, The, 87, 112
Ghostbusters (movie), 191
ghosts, 14, 23, 29, 55, 64, 66, 69, 156, 358, 388, 402, 407, 426
  academic aversion to, 379
  fiction, 183
Gibbons, John, 237
Gibson, Walter, 126, 132
Giesler, Patric, 335
Gladstone, William, 193
Gödel, Escher, Bach, 288, 291
Gödel, Kurt, 57, 277, 289–91, 302, 307
Gods in Everyman, 38
Gods in Our Midst, 38
Golden Bough, The, 348
Goldschmidt, Walter, 127
Goldston, Will, 132, 141
Golem, The, 286
Goleman, Daniel, 288, 289
Goriely, Georges, 379
Goslin, David, 199
Gould, Stephen Jay, 148
Graham, Lee, 226, 228
Graham, Martha, 60
Grammatical Man, 291
Great Illusionists, The, 146
Greeks and the Irrational, The, 79
Greeley, Horace, 120, 172
Greenwood, Barry, 221, 222, 223, 227
group marriage, 84
group mind, 351
Gruber, Elmar, 329, 339
Guillotin, Joseph Ignace, 140
Gulf Breeze Sightings, The, 237
Gygax, E. Gary, 263
gypsies, 19, 70
Hacking, Ian, 315
Hades, Micky, 133
Haines, Gerald, 222–23
hair, 41, 352
Hammid, Hella, 203
Handbook of Parapsychology, 159
Hansel, C. E. M., 292

Hansen, George P.
  Budd Hopkins' opinion of, 255
Hanuman, 80
Harary, Keith, 182, 195, 203, 207
Harding, M. Esther, 351
Harlequin, 44
Harribance, Lalsingh, 203
Hartmann, Ernest, 24, 33, 48–51, 83, 111, 114, 415
Harvard University, 25, 41, 62, 199, 250, 382
Hastings, Robert, 226, 227
Hatengdi, M. U., 77
Hawkes, Terence, 374
Hegel, Georg Wilhelm F., 291
helicopters, 210, 211, 212
Helms, Richard, 417
Hennessey, Barry, 233
hermaphrodites, 65
hermeneutics, 31, 41, 246, 368
Hermes, 24, 31, 35, 38–40, 41, 42, 46, 49, 59, 61, 158, 246, 368, 379, 380
  dice and, 39, 343
  divination and, 39
  liminality and, 38
  midwife to birth of Dionysus, 39, 94, 170
  prophecy and, 39
Hermes and His Children, 38, 158
Hermes the Thief, 38, 61, 388
Hero of Alexandria, 135
Heroic Worlds: A History and Guide to Role-Playing Games, 263
Hertz, Heinrich, 192
Hertz, Robert, 64, 347, 360
Heschel, Abraham, 70
Heseltine, Gary, 206
Hess, David, 182, 187
Hicks, David, 65
Higbee, Marie, 197
Higgins, Howard, 93
high-strangeness, 404–6

Hillenkoetter, Roscoe, 221, 222
Hillman, James, 400–401
   Lacan, Jacques, compared with, 400
Hinduism, 77, 80
Hinkle, Roscoe, 351
History of Anthropological Thought, A, 359
History of Hypnotism, A, 139
History of the Incas, 350
hoaxes
   benefits, 267–69
   case study (Napolitano), 249–67
   Castaneda, 127, 282
   MJ-12, 224–26
   Steiner case, 211–12
Hocus Pocus Junior, 130, 131
Hodgson, Richard, 123
Hofstadter, Douglas, 288, 291, 292
Holloman Air Force Base, 233
Hollywood, 182
Holy Madness, 76, 81
Home, Daniel Dunglas, 120, 122, 172
Honorton, Charles, 195, 196, 206, 298
Hook, Sidney, 148
Hoover, J. Edgar, 238
Hopkins, Budd, 249–62, 266–67
   Hansen, George, opinion on, 255
Houdini, 121, 124, 125, 126, 130, 133
Houdini, Bess, 125
House of Cards, 91
How Natives Think, 281, 353
How Not to Test a Psychic, 295–98
Howe, Linda Moulton, 226, 228–30, 231, 233, 241, 242, 243
Hubbard, G. Scott, 207
Hubbell, Webb, 219

Huey, Frank M., 230
Humanist, The, 89, 150
Humphrey, Beverly S., 207
hunter-gatherers, 86, 98, 428
Husserl, Edmund, 279
Huxley, Aldous, 60
Huyghe, Patrick, 250
Hyde, Lewis, 36
Hyman, Ray, 138, 153, 158, 159, 293, 296
Hynek Center for UFO Studies. *See* CUFOS
hypnosis, 48, 51, 117, 138–41, 250, 389, 402
Hyslop, George H., 197
Hyslop, James H., 196
hysteria, 389
   Lacan as hysteric, 386
I and the Not-I, The, 351
Idea of the Holy, The, 65, 156, 355
Ifa, 40, 382–83, 384
Illustrated History of Magic, The, 146
imaginal realm, 389, 402–6
   marginality of theorists, 403
imagination, 393, 394–412
   anti-structure and, 401
   marginality and, 398
   paranormal and, 402
   religious, 399
   sexual, 411
   sociological, 398, 399, 401
   status and, 397, 398, 399, 412
   trickster and, 411
impostors, 40, 61
In Favor of Deceit, 60
In Search of White Crows, 172
In the Name of Science, 292
incest, 67, 144, 348, 351
Independence Day (movie), 224, 248
Infinity and the Mind, 291

initiations, 54, 55, 57, 62, 87, 105, 357, 405. *See* also rites of passage
  binary oppositions and, 55
  similarity to cultural revitalizations, 111
Inphomation Communications Inc., 181
Inquisition, Office of the, 80, 82
Institute for Advanced Study, 290
Institute for Parapsychology, 15, 16, 318, 321. *See* also Foundation for Research on the Nature of Man (FRNM); Rhine Research Center (RRC)
institutions
  conjuring and, 132–33
  modern-day witchcraft and, 423
  paranormal and, 22, 23, 118, 178–90, 423
  psychics and, 180, 189
  Spiritualism and, 423
International Association for Near-Death Studies, 238
International Brotherhood of Magicians, 131, 134
International Journal of Parapsychology, 332
International Psychoanalytic Association, 386
International UFO Reporter, 250, 255
Interstitial Ogre, 183, 407
interstitiality, 31, 65. *See* also liminality; betwixt and between
  creatures, 66
  trickster and, 67
intestines, 79
Introduction to Structuralism, 362
Introduction to the Work of Marcel Mauss, 384
iron cage of modernity, 26
Irwin, Harvey, 420
Isaac, 43

Isherwood, Christopher, 80
Islam, 110
It Takes All Kinds, 126
J. Allen Hynek Center for UFO Studies. *See* CUFOS
Jacobs, David, 250, 254, 255, 258
Jadoo, 213
Jahn, Robert G., 204, 206, 209
Jakobson, Roman, 361
Jaks, Stanley, 306
James S. McDonnell Foundation, 195, 206
James, Christine L., 207
James, William, 60, 139, 192, 348
Janet, Pierre, 139
Jansen, Cornelius, 80
Jansen, Harry, 132
Jansenism, 80, 81
Jerome, Lawrence, 185
jesters, 46, 55, 59
Jesus, 84, 106, 151, 301, 422
  resurrection, 293, 303
Jinx, The, 295
Job, Book of, 37, 84, 302, 356
John F. Kennedy University, 202, 205
Johns Hopkins University, 361
Johnson, Martin, 325
Joint Chiefs of Staff, 236
Jones, C. B. Scott, 228, 239–41, 243, 244
Jones, Ernest, 353
Jones, Timothy, 70
Jordan, Pascual, 332
Joseph of Copertino, Saint, 79, 80
Journal for the Scientific Study of Religion, 186, 293
Journal of Abnormal and Social Psychology, 140
Journal of Humanistic Psychology, 157

Journal of Parapsychology, 15, 51, 97, 194, 195, 198, 207, 208, 313, 323, 327, 329, 332, 334
  circulation, 148
Journal of Popular Culture, 265
Journal of Recreational Mathematics, 292
Journal of Research in Psi Phenomena, 336
Journal of the American Society for Psychical Research, 15, 84, 127, 138, 195, 197, 323
Journal of the Folklore Institute, 59
Journal of the Society for Psychical Research, 124, 322
Journey to Ixtlan, 127
Jung, Carl, 28, 29, 30, 37, 41, 42, 44, 57, 84, 87, 114, 352, 403, 416, 426
  Freud, Sigmund, conversation with, 352
  Levi-Strauss, Claude and, 364
Just Cause, 221, 232
Kaempffert, Waldemar, 193
Kagan, Dan, 242
Kalweit, Holgar, 94
Kammann, Richard, 120
Kanthamani, H., 206
Kapitza, Sergei, 113
Keane, Patrice, 197, 240
Keck, Paul, 82, 83
Keel, John, 25, 85, 212–15
Keene, M. Lamar, 125, 179
Keep the River on Your Right, 283
Kellar, Harry, 121, 132
Kelly, Aidan, 174, 175
Kelly, Edward F., 204
Kennedy assassination, 217, 219, 238
Kennedy, J. E., 321, 323, 327
Kerr, Howard, 173
Keyhoe, Donald, 222
KGB, 222
Kidd, James, 197
Killing the Spirit, 378

Kimball, Janet (pseudonym), 251, 252, 257
King, Stephen, 182, 407
Kirby, E. T., 90, 94
Kirtland Air Force Base, 227, 229, 241, 243
Klass, Philip J., 159, 185, 219, 226, 231, 236
Knowledge and Reflexivity, 284, 285
Kodimela, Venu K., 120
Koestler, Arthur, 60, 197, 332
Kottmeyer, Martin, 51, 114, 416
Kreizer, B. Robert, 81
Kreskin, 119, 120, 126, 139, 194
Krippner, Stanley, 15, 195, 203, 205, 317, 318, 330
Krishna, Shanti, 206
Kristeva, Julia, 183
Kroeber, Karl, 381, 382, 383
Kubler-Ross, Elisabeth, 164–66, 170, 326
Kurtz, Paul, 149–54, 156, 158, 160, 294, 303
Kurzweil, Edith, 385, 389
Kusche, Larry, 185
La Barre, Weston, 87, 112
lability and inertia, 25, 203, 310, 321, 331, 339–41, 425
laboratory
  role in parapsychology, 312–13
Labyrinths of Reason, 291
Lacan, Jacques, 385–89, 391, 414
  Hillman, James, compared with, 400
Lamport, Joe R., 230
Lancaster, Kurt, 265
Lane, Michael, 362, 370
Lang, Andrew, 192, 344, 349–50, 355
Lantis, Margaret, 90
Lantz, Nevin D., 207
Lasky, Michael, 181
Latour, Bruno, 278, 284, 285, 303, 306, 307

Lavoisier, Antoine, 140
law of the excluded middle. *See* excluded middle, law of the
Laws of Form, 274
Lazarus, 151
Leach, Edmund, 25, 43, 65, 281, 341, 347, 352, 361, 363, 364, 370, 372, 373, 387, 391
Leadbeater, C. W., 123
Lederman, Leon, 148
Legba. *See* Eshu-Elegba
legend-trip, 163–64
Lehman, David, 379
Lehman, Dr., 230
Leibnitz, 80
LeShan, Lawrence, 420
Levi-Strauss, Claude, 25, 30, 43, 64, 346, 347, 361–64, 368, 373, 384
 Jung, Carl and, 363
levitation, 78, 80
Levy, Walter J., 194, 323
Levy-Bruhl, Lucien, 25, 281, 285, 324, 351, 353–55, 359, 360, 361
Lewis, Angelo, 132
Libertarian Review, 242
Liechtenstein, Prince Hans-Adam, 240, 257
liminality, 22, 25, 26, 31, 54–57, 117, 395. *See also* anti-structure; communitas; interstitiality; betwixt and between
 charisma and, 27, 103
 classification and, 346
 conjuring and, 135
 deception and, 73
 fantasy role-playing games, 264
 fiction and, 409
 Hermes and, 38
 hypnosis and, 138
 imaginal realm and, 403, 405
 institutionalization of, 75, 82, 83

 meditation, 289
 mysticism and, 73, 75, 77, 79
 participation and, 282
 permanent state, 78
 reflexivity and, 278, 282, 285, 308
 revitalization movements and, 110, 112, 115
 shamanism and, 86–87
 sociological imagination and, 399
 taboo and, 378
 trickster and, 28, 38, 59
 UFOs and, 248
liminoid, 104
Limits of Interpretation, The, 374
Lincoln, Abraham, 172
Linking Ring, The, 93, 131
literary theory, 27, 273, 309, 343, 368–91
 telepathy and, 27, 380
Littleton, C. Scott, 353, 355
Llewellyn Publications, 185
Locke, W., 131
Lodge, Sir Oliver, 192
Loki, 35
Lopez-Pedraza, Rafael, 38, 39, 158
Los Alamos National Laboratory, 169, 238, 239
Lugbara, 65
Luhrmann, Tanya M., 175–76
Luke, Wanda L. W., 207
Lund University, 325
Luther, Martin, 358
Lydwine of Schiedam, Saint, 79, 84
MacArthur Foundation, 142
Maccabee, Bruce, 236, 239, 242, 243, 244
Macionis, John, 398, 399
Mack, John E., 250, 255, 258
Madame Blavatsky: The Woman Behind the Myth, 122
Madigan, Tim, 154

magic. *See* conjuring for legerdemain, etc.
  Catholic Church's prohibition of, 24
  charisma and, 106
  definition confusion, 19, 130
  irrationality and, 106
  Levi-Strauss, Claude, on, 384
  meaning and, 27, 108, 383–84
  psi and, 176, 309, 347, 366, 383–84
  rationalization and, 105, 358, 359, 361, 364–66
  taboo and, 31, 67, 348
  totemism and, 345
Magic Circle, 145
Magic: A Pictorial History of Conjurers in the Theater, 146
magical thinking, 420
Magonia magazine, 51
Maia, 38
Maimonides Medical Center (Brooklyn), 195, 203, 317, 318
Makarius, Laura, 36, 67
Malcolm X, 113
Male Infibulation, 144
Manson, Charles, 413
Manzano Weapons Storage Area, 227
Mao, 113
Margery, 120
Margery (Mina Crandon), 124, 125
marginality, 22, 26, 422
  anti-structure and, 70
  communitas and, 57, 58
  conjuror's role and, 132
  creative illness and, 57
  creativity and, 60
  Fate magazine and, 184
  hypnosis and, 139, 140
  imagination and, 398
  liminality and, 55, 60
  New Age movement and, 173
  paranoia and, 262, 417

  paranormal and, 71, 107, 182, 184, 189, 365
  personification and, 400, 401
  sociological imagination and, 398
  Spiritualism and, 173
  trickster and, 46, 61
  UFOs and, 214, 217, 220, 246, 248
  Victor Turner and, 70
Marine Corps boot camp, 58
Marks, David, 120, 185
Martinek, Mary E.
  wife of Pflock, Karl, 242
Marx, Karl, 361
Mary, Blessed Virgin, 19, 84, 114
Maskelyne, John Nevil, 120, 121, 132
Masks of God: Primitive Mythology, The, 87
Master Index to Magic in Print, 133
Mathematical Association of America, 294
Mathematical Biosciences, 332
Mathematical Gardner, The, 292
mathematical logic, 289–91
Matlock, James, 197
Mattuck, Richard, 335
Matus, Don Juan, 127
Mauskopf, Seymour, 193, 304
Mauss, Marcel, 25, 344, 346, 350, 360, 361
May, Edwin C., 198, 199, 207, 208
mazeway, 110, 111, 115
  defined, 110
McCarthy, Joseph, 418
McClenon, James, 24, 90, 153, 162, 186–87
McDonnell Laboratory for Psychical Research, 204
McDonnell, James S., 195, 197, 206. *See also* James S. McDonnell Foundation

McDonough, Bruce, 205
McDougall, William, 120, 125, 139, 192, 193, 196
McGill, Ormond, 132, 141
McLennan, John Ferguson, 347
McVaugh, Michael, 193, 304
Mead, George Herbert, 351
Meade, Marion, 122
meaning, 27, 108, 368, 369, 374, 375, 377
  ethnomethodology and, 281
  magic and, 27, 383–84, 391
  psi and, 384, 391
meditation, 277, 288–89
  liminality and, 289
Meditative Mind, The, 288
mediums, 14, 29, 69, 97, 100, 101, 121, 122, 124, 125, 171–73, 402, 426. *See* also Spiritualism; Fox sisters; Davenport Brothers; Margery; Palladino, Eusapia; Home, D.D.
  altered states of consciousness, 172
  Catholic Church's prohibition against, 23
  ESP of, 313
  mediators of binary oppositions, 121, 172
  New Age and, 174
  shamans as, 31
  trickery of, 422
Mediums, and Spirit-Rappers, and Roaring Radicals, 173
Mediums, Mystics & the Occult, 145
Medjugorje, 114
Mehan, Hugh, 278, 280–83, 308
memory
  primitive mentality and, 354
Mencken, H. L., 299
Mendez, Simone, 232
Menken, Adah Isaacs, 121
mentalism, 135, 137–38, 295

merchants, 61
Mercurius, 30, 41–43
Mercury, 38, 134. *See* also Hermes
Mercury: Or the Secret and Swift Messenger, 130
Merrell, Floyd, 291
Mesmer, Franz Anton, 139, 140
Messengers of Deception, 216
meta-analysis, 207
Middleton, John, 65
Miller, Jerald D., 227, 229, 230, 233
Miller, Katlyn, 132
Mills, C. Wright, 153, 398
Mims, Forrest, 304
mind over matter. *See* PK
Mind Science Foundation, 203, 205, 208, 318, 329, 339
Mind, Self & Society, 351
miracles, 19, 20, 23, 106, 422. *See* also mysticism, paranormal phenomena
  charisma and, 104, 429
  Francis of Assisi, St., 78
  Gardner's, Martin, opinion on, 293, 301, 302
  Jansenists and, 81
  Joseph of Copertino, St., 80
  Lydwine of Shiedam, St., 79
  numinous and, 65, 358
  Protestant attack on, 106, 302
  Sai Baba and, 128
Miracles, Convulsions, and Ecclesiastical Politics in Early Eighteenth-Century Paris, 81
Mitchell, Robert W., 410
MJ-12, 224–26, 228, 234
Mogul balloon, 224, 234
Mohammed, 106, 358, 422
Mondo 2000: A User's Guide to The New Edge, 291
Montgomery, Ruth, 174
Moody, Raymond, 326
Moore, R. Laurence, 172

Moore, William L., 223–31, 243, 244
Morehouse, David A., 168, 170
Morris, Robert L., 202, 204, 329
Moseley, James, 143
Moses, 106, 422
Mothman Prophecies, The, 213
MUFON, 20, 21, 227, 250, 253, 258, 260, 267
  expenditures, 248
  number of members, 264
MUFON UFO Journal, 226
Mundelein College, 202
Murphy, Bridey, 139
Murphy, Gardner, 197, 209
Murphy, Michael, 15
Murray, Gilbert, 60, 192
Mute Evidence, 242
Mutual UFO Network. *See* MUFON
Myers, Frederic, 139
Mysterium Coniunctionis, 42
mysterium tremendum, 66, 302
mysticism, 20, 21, 70, 73, 74–85
  anti-structure and, 81–83
  conjuring and, 135, 146
  deception and, 76, 79, 82
  definition problem, 75
  imaginal realm and, 402, 403
  liminality and, 73, 75, 77, 79
  paranormal phenomena, 76–81, 82, 426
  Protestant rejection of, 105, 302, 429
  reflexivity and, 282, 289
  sexuality and, 76, 80, 82, 84
  trickster and, 73, 76, 77, 78, 79, 81–83
Mythical Trickster Figures, 88
Mythologies, 374
Myths of the New World, 35
Napolean III, 122, 172
Napolitano, Linda, 249–59, 260, 261, 266–67
Nash, Carroll, 202, 205

Nation of Islam, 113
National Academy of Sciences, 238, 288
National Investigations Committee on Aerial Phenomena. *See* NICAP
National Reconnaissance Office, 222
National Research Council (NRC), 199, 238, 288
National Science Foundation, 186, 187
National Security Agency (NSA), 223, 229
National Security Council, 222
Nature, 128, 296
Navajo, 67–69
Ndembu, 52
near-death experiences (NDEs), 14, 64, 84, 238, 326, 403, 404, 405, 426
Nebel, Long John, 213
Needham, Rodney, 346, 347, 349, 353, 387
Neihardt, John, 166
Nelson, Roger D., 206
neo-paganism. *See* witchcraft, modern-day
Neoplatonism, 30, 43, 78, 401
New Age Almanac, 173
New Age movement, 117, 171, 173–74, 240
New Age: Notes of a Fringe Watcher, The, 294
New Realities magazine, 204
New York Area Skeptics, 142
New York Fortean Society, 213
New York Post, 253
New York Review of Books, 292
New York Times, 124, 193, 252, 288
New York Times Magazine, 206
Newark College of Engineering, 202
Newmann, George, 138

Newton, Silas, 224, 225
NICAP, 221, 240
Nickell, Joe, 121, 153, 185
Niditch, Susan, 36, 43, 61, 70
Nietzsche, Friedrich, 57
Night Is Large, The, 292
Nighteyes, 253, 257
Nightmare, The, 51
Nisbet, Lee, 149
Nityananda of Ganeshpuri, 76
Nityananda: The Divine Presence, 77
Norse, 35
Norton Air Force Base, 233
Nosenko, Yuri, 416
Novel, Gordon, 238
numinous, 65, 88, 156, 157, 291, 308, 356, 366, 367
  defined, 356
  obliviousness to, 357
  paranormal and the, 356
O'Dea, Thomas, 156
O'Hair, Madalyn Murray, 154
Oberg, James, 185, 219, 232, 245
observational theories, 331
Occult Establishment, The, 173
Oetgen, Jerome, 82
Olcott, Henry Steel, 123
Omega Project, The, 406
Omni magazine, 250, 252
On Death and Dying, 164
On the Wild Side, 294
Operation Right to Know, 241
opposites, 30–31, 42. *See also* binary oppositions
Oprah (TV show), 236
Expositor, 132
Ortiz, Gilbert, 239
Osis, Karlis, 197, 213, 325, 326, 327
Otto, Rudolf, 25, 65, 88, 156, 302, 355–56, 357, 358, 360
Oursler, Fulton, 132
Oxford University, 347, 359
Ozanne, Charles, 197

Palladino, Eusapia, 120, 124
Palmer, Helen, 419
Palmer, John, 202, 205, 206, 299, 330
Palmer, Ray, 185
paradox, 30, 277, 306, 308
  deconstructionism and, 375
  Epimenides', 277
  initiations and, 55
  numinous and, 356
  psi and, 278, 309
  reflexivity and, 277, 278
  trickster and, 88
paranoia, 216, 244, 246, 262, 269, 278, 280, 300, 393, 413–21
  anti-structure and, 415, 416, 417–18, 421
  defined, 413
  intelligence agencies, 220, 416
  Lacan on, 389
  psi and, 418–19
  trickster and, 414, 417, 421
  UFOs and, 214, 217, 219, 222, 241, 242, 260, 262, 266
  witchcraft accusations and, 413, 415, 418
paranormal
  academe and, 185–88
  alternative religions and, 171–77
  anti-structure and, 69–71, 424
  classification and, 404
  conjuring and, 130–47, 130–47
  CSICOP and, 148–61
  cultural change and, 110–16
  entertainment and, 182–85
  hoaxes and, 247–71
  imagination and, 394–412, 402
  institutions and, 22, 178–90, 178–90, 423
  laboratory research and, 191–209, 309–43
  mysticism and, 74–85
  paranoia and, 413–21
  shamanism and, 86–94

small groups and, 162–70
synonym of supernatural, 21
Parapsychological Association
 (PA), 200, 201, 208, 311, 316,
 317, 333
 number of members, 201
 survey of presidents, 159
parapsychology, 117, 191–209,
 273, 309–43. *See also* psi
 1970s, 201
 1980s, 203
 anti-structure and, 191–209
 CIA and, 223
 defined, 192
 DIA and, 223
 expenditures, 202, 205–7
 failure to be integrated into
  academe, 19, 23, 187, 193,
  423
 funding, 20, 197, 200, 417
 Gardner, Martin, critic of, 294–
  300
 laboratory role in, 312–13
 NSA and, 223
 size of research effort, 201
 sociology of scientific
  knowledge and, 286
 UFOs and, 220, 223, 228, 240,
  243, 403
Parapsychology Foundation, 213,
 316, 326, 333
Parapsychology Laboratory, 194
Parapsychology Review, 203, 208
*Parapsychology: The Controversial
 Science*, 15
Paris Match magazine, 252
Parise, Felicia, 203
Parks, Loren, 167
Parsons, E. A., 132
Parsons, Talcott, 105
participation, 281, 282, 283, 285,
 286, 287, 307, 353, 354, 365,
 405
 psi and, 324, 342
Pascal, Blaise, 80

Passport to Magonia, 262
Peacock, James, 61
Peebles, Curtis, 231, 235, 416
Peirce, Charles Sanders, 374
Pell, Claiborne, 239, 240
Pelton, Robert, 40
Pennsylvania State University,
 163
People's Republic of China, 113
Perez de Cuellar, Javier, 250, 251,
 256, 257, 260
Perfect Fools, 76
Perlstrom, James R., 206
Perot, Ross, 417
Perovsky-Petrovo-Solovovo,
 Count, 120
personification, 399–402
 marginality and, 400
 trickster as a, 36, 45, 427
Persuasions of the Witch's Craft,
 175
Peters, Kurt (pseudonym). *See*
 Pflock, Karl
Peters, Larry, 56, 57
Pflock, Karl, 242–43
Phillips, Peter, 204
Philosophy of Horror, The, 408
*Physical Phenomena of Mysticism,
 The*, 76
Physical Society of the U.S.S.R.,
 113
Physics Today magazine, 332
Picasso, Pablo, 60
Pierce, John, 312
Pike, James, 125
Pinch, Trevor, 150, 279, 286,
 298, 307
Pinchbeck, W. F., 131
Piper, Leonora, 295
PK, 19, 25, 29, 273, 393, 426.
 See also psi; poltergeist;
 levitation
 defined, 14
 experiments, 314, 318, 319,
  324, 326, 328, 333, 341

macro-, 335
macro-, defined, 14
micro-, distinguishing from other types of psi, 425
mirco-, defined, 14
retroactive, 203, 321, 328–29, 332, 336, 425
Plato, 130
plethysmograph
  psi testing with, 316, 320
Polan, Dana, 183
poltergeist, 214, 268, 425
Popper, Karl, 215
postmodernism, 27, 108, 284, 291, 406
post-structuralism, 108, 246, 273, 345, 362, 368, 369, 376, 390, 426
Potter, Jack, 133
Poundstone, William, 291
Power and Paranoia, 183
Power of the Charlatan, The, 44
Pratt, J. G., 202, 314
Pratt, Robert, 230
prayer, 19, 20, 300, 301, 303, 304, 358
precognition, 328, 332, 336. *See also* psi; ESP; PK
  distinguishing from other types of psi, 319, 425
  dreams, 130, 316
  experiments, 314, 315, 317, 323
pretense, 30, 393, 409–11
Price, David, 120, 137, 146
Price, Harry, 132
Price, Pat, 203
priests, 31, 64, 84, 97, 100, 101, 105, 165, 302, 358, 426, 429
  rationalization and, 106
primal conflict repression theory, 420
primal horde, 352
Primitive Classification, 346, 350
Primitive Man as Philosopher, 93

Primitive Mentality, 353
primitive mind, 309, 324, 344–67
  memory and, 354
Prince, Walter Franklin, 125, 157, 196, 300
Princeton Engineering Anomalies Research (PEAR), 204, 206, 208
Princeton Theological Seminary, 43
Princeton University, 183, 204, 206
probability
  psi testing and, 315
Proceedings of the IEEE, 128
Project Alpha, 142, 204
Project Blue Book, 227, 229
projection, 277, 413, 414, 415, 416, 418, 419
Prometheus, 148, 157, 158, 160, 388
Prometheus Books, 89, 126, 155, 158, 160, 294
prophecy, 19, 70
  false, 44
  fools and, 44
  Hermes and, 39
Prophetic Books, 83
prophets, 23, 65, 70, 86, 112, 174
  charisma and, 104
Prophets, The, 70
Protestant Ethic and the Spirit of Capitalism, The, 102
Protestantism, 20, 293, 302, 358, 366, 429
  rationalization and, 105, 302
psi, 309–43. *See also* parapsychology; ESP; PK; telepathy; clairvoyance; precognition; synchronicity; remote viewing
  boundaries and, 311
  classification and, 32

deconstructionism and, 27
defined, 14
fear of, 420–21
goal oriented, as, 327, 339, 425
informational models, 310, 333, 335, 341, 343
liminality and, 426
limits, 424
magic and, 176, 309, 347, 366, 383–84
meaning and, 383–84
negative definition of, 311, 312, 391
non-intentional, 324–25
paradox and, 278
paranoia and, 418–19
redundancy, 321
response bias avoidance, 340
source problem, 321
task complexity and, 203, 321, 325–28, 338, 425
Psi Tech, 168–70, 237, 240–42
psi-mediated instrumental response (PMIR), 321
Psychic Discoveries Behind the Iron Curtain, 202
Psychic Entertainers Association, 137
Psychic Entertainers News & Information Service, 137
Psychic Friends Network, 180
psychic hot lines, 180–82, 423
Psychic Mafia, The, 125, 179
Psychic magazine, 49, 202, 204
psychic phenomena. *See* psi
psychic spies, 20. *See also* Psi Tech; remote viewing
psychic surgeons, 90
Psychical Research Foundation (PRF), 202
psychics, 117
   institutions and, 180, 189
   trickery, allegations of, 119–29
Psychoanalytic Politics, 385
Psychoenergetic Systems, 203, 208

Psychoenergetics, 208
psychoid, 403
psychokinesis. *See* PK
Psychophysical Research Laboratories (PRL), 16, 195–96, 206, 208
psychotherapy, 56
   ineffectiveness of, 91, 192
Publishers Weekly magazine, 127
Pueblo, 44
Puharich, Andrija, 128
Purity and Danger, 66
Puthoff, Harold, 128, 168, 207, 238, 318
Quant, Marta, 206
quantum mechanics, 310, 321, 331–38
Radical Spirits, 172
Radin, Dean, 207
Radin, Paul, 37, 78, 84, 87, 93, 356, 414
Ramakrishna, Sri, 80
Randi, James, 128, 137, 142–43, 146, 153, 158, 160, 204, 269, 293
Randle, Kevin, 225
random number generator, 32, 205, 206, 207, 318–19, 324, 328, 329, 332, 343
randomization
   psi testing, 315, 317
randomness
   theories of psi and, 338, 339, 340
Rao, K. Ramakrishna, 206, 299
Raschke, Carl, 114
Rationalist Press Association (RPA), 79, 145, 154, 155, 349
   Watts & Co., 155
rationalization, 22, 24, 26, 27, 45, 95, 117, 153, 155, 161, 189, 215, 302, 345, 358, 364–66, 377, 400, 422, 428, 429. *See also* disenchantment
   defined, 104

magic and, 27, 105, 358, 361, 364, 365, 377, 428
Rauscher, William V., 120, 125, 137
Rawlins, Dennis, 150, 185
Rayleigh, Lord, 192
Reality of Ethnomethodology, The, 280, 283
Reason magazine, 242
Rebekah, 43
Recursive Universe, The, 291
Reeves-Stevens, Garfield, 253
Reflexive Thesis, The, 278, 284
reflexivity, 22, 25, 30, 274, 277–91, 306–8, 309, 368, 375, 376
  ambiguity and, 278, 303, 308
  avoidance of, 278, 279, 285, 307
  defined, 277
  experimenter effects, 324
  Lacanian analysis, 386
  paradox and, 277, 278, 279, 308
  synonyms for problems of, 278, 288
Reichbart, Richard, 90, 138
Reidhead, Van A., 82, 83
reincarnation, 14, 29, 64, 139, 156, 426
Remarks and Inventions dedicated to Andrew Lang, 349
remote viewing, 168, 169, 199, 203, 207, 238, 241, 244, 318
  cattle mutilations and, 220
  UFOs and, 169, 220, 237, 239, 240, 245
replication, 286, 287, 307
  parapsychology, 324, 342
representation, 284, 303, 337, 365, 370, 376, 397, 410
  collective, 337, 346, 371, 399, 427
  Walker's theory and, 337

Resources for the Scientific Evaluation of the Paranormal (RSEP), 158, 293
Revelations, 229, 235
Re-Visioning Psychology, 400
revitalization movements, 23, 96, 110–16
Reynard the Fox, 61
Rhine Research Center, 206, 208. *See also* Foundation for Research on the Nature of Man (FRNM); Institute for Parapsychology
Rhine, J. B., 60, 125, 137, 166, 175, 193, 194, 203, 206, 209, 288, 295, 304, 313–15, 318, 320, 323, 324, 325, 424
Richards, Douglas, 51
Richards, Elaine, 166
Richards, John Thomas, 166, 167
Richet, Charles, 139, 192, 315
Ricketts, Mac Linscott, 88–89, 93
Right & Left, 347
Ring, Kenneth, 403, 404, 405, 406
rites of passage, 26, 57. *See also* initiations
  legend-trips and, 164
  similarity to cultural revitalizations, 112
Rites of Passage, The, 52, 54, 92, 96, 110
Ritual Process, The, 52, 55, 59, 78, 92
Robert-Houdin, Jean Eugene, 132
Roberts, J. J. M., 43
Roberts, Jane, 174
Roberts, John, 61
Robertson, H. P., 222
Robin, Henri, 121
Rockefeller, Laurence, 240
Rogo, D. Scott, 182
Rojcewicz, Peter, 403
Roots of Coincidence, The, 332

Roper survey, 113
Rose, Ronald, 90
Rosenthal, Robert, 199, 287–88, 307, 323
Rosicrucianism, 401
Roswell Incident, The, 224, 226
Roswell UFO case, 224–35, 242
Roudinesco, Elizabeth, 386
Royle, Nicholas, 379, 380, 383
Rucker, Rudy, 291, 307
Rudolph, Luther, 329
Rumor of Angels, A, 156
Ruskin, William, 192
Sagan, Carl, 143, 148
Sai Baba, Sathya, 120, 128, 129
Saint-Medard cemetery, 81
Saints Among Us, The, 70
Sampson, Geoffrey, 371
Sandler, Alan, 233
Sandow, Greg, 250
Sarai, 43
Satan, Cantor, and Infinity, 291
Saussure, Ferdinand de, 25, 108, 360, 361, 362, 371–72, 374, 375, 383
Savage Mind, The, 361
Saward, John, 76
Saybrook Institute, 205, 317
Scatalogic Rites of All Nations, 44
Schechter, Ephraim, 195, 206
Schick, Lawrence, 263
Schiff, Steven, 225, 230, 242
Schiller, F. C. S., 192
Schlitz, Marilyn, 205, 206
Schmeidler, Gertrude, 168, 202, 205
Schmidt, Helmut, 205, 298, 318–19, 321, 327–29, 332, 336
Schmitt, Donald R., 225
Schnabel, Jim, 250
Schneebaum, Tobias, 283
Schneiderman, Stuart, 385–89
Schools of Linguistics, 371
Schouten, Sybo, 201
Schucman, Helen, 174

Schumaker, John F., 157
Schwarz, Berthold E., 126
Schwarzkopf, Norman, 133
Science Applications International Corporation (SAIC), 198, 199, 208
Science in the New Age, 182
Science magazine, 148
Science Unlimited Research Foundation, 206, 208
Science: Good, Bad and Bogus, 294, 299
Scientific American, 113, 124, 292, 299, 304, 305
Scientific American Committee for the Investigation of Psychic Phenomena, 126
Scientology, 304
Scot, Reginald, 130, 131
Scully, Frank, 224
Seaborg, Glenn, 148
Search for Bridey Murphy, The, 139
Searching for Certainty, 291
Secret Life of Plants, The, 202
Secret of the Totem, The, 350
Secret Service, 255
Secular Humanist Bulletin, 154
self-awareness, 37, 393, 411, 414
self-reference, 30, 277, 290, 291
semiotics, 22, 41, 279, 290, 309, 343, 373, 374, 390
  trickster's domain, 374
  Walker's theory and, 337
Senate Appropriations Committee, 199
sexuality. *See also* exogamy; incest
  ambiguity, 283
  Biblical tricksters and, 43
  conjurors and, 134, 143, 144
  deconstructionists and, 378
  Eshu-Elegba and, 41
  Freud on, 352
  Hermes and, 39
  hypnosis and, 140

Kubler-Ross, Elisabeth, and, 165
legend-trips and, 164
mediumship and, 122, 124, 126
Mercurius and, 42
mysticism and, 76, 80, 82, 84
perversion, 67
Prometheus Books and, 158
Psi Tech and, 170
shamanism and, 93, 404
Spiritualism and, 173
Wakdjunkaga and, 37
witchcraft, modern-day, and, 175
Shah, Dhwani, 259
sham of shamanism, 73, 89–92
shamanism, 31, 56, 57, 69, 73, 86–94, 97, 98, 406, 428
altered states of consciousness, 98, 172
anti-structure and, 73
clowns and, 44
liminality and, 73, 86–87
New Age and, 174
sexuality and, 93, 404
skepticism, 92–93
trickery. *See* sham of shamanism
trickster and, 31, 87–89, 93–94, 123
Shamanism: Archaic Techniques of Ecstasy, 78, 86, 89
Shamans, Priests and Witches, 95, 97
Shandera, Jaime, 224
Shanti Nilaya, 164, 165
Shared Fantasy: Role-Playing Games as Social Worlds, 263
Sharp, Henry, 415
Shaw, Steve, 142
Sheaffer, Robert, 185, 219
Sheppard, Jack W., 230
Shiels, Tony, 143–44, 146
Shor, Ronald, 139
Signifying Monkey, The, 382

Signs of the Times, 379
Simeon Salus, Saint, 77
Simmons, Thomas, 230
Singer, Jerome, 398
Skeptical Inquirer, 153, 160, 184, 185, 219, 301, 409
circulation, 148
readership, educational level of, 148
Skinner, B. F., 148
Slick, Thomas Baker, Jr., 197, 205
Smith, Michael, 195
Smith, Morton, 89
Smith, Page, 378
Smithsonian Institution Press, 231
Smullyan, Raymond, 291
Social Anthropology and Other Essays, 359
social masking theory, 420
Social Origins, 350
social structure
defined, 53
Social Studies of Science, 283
Society for Psychical Research (SPR), 60, 76, 123, 139, 144, 145, 192, 193, 196, 311, 313, 315, 322, 349, 362
eminent members of, 192
Society for Research on Rapport and Telekinesis. *See* SORRAT
Society for the Anthropology of Consciousness, 97
Society of American Magicians, 134
Sociological Imagination, The, 153, 398
Sociology of Scientific Knowledge, 286
sociology of scientific knowledge (SSK), 279, 283–87, 289, 298, 306
Solovyoff, Vselovod S., 123

Solovyoff, Vsevolod Sergyeevich, 120
Some Human Oddities, 79, 81, 82
Sophia of Holland, Queen, 122, 172
SORRAT, 166–68, 170
Specters of Marx, 379
Spencer, Chrystal, 126
Spencer, Herbert, 344
Spencer-Brown, George, 274
Spirit and the Flesh, The, 93
Spirit Mercurius. *See* Mercurius
Spirit of Shamanism, The, 91
spirits, 112
  ESP and PK subsume phenomena of, 15, 314
  Gödel, Kurt and, 290
  Kubler-Ross, Elisabeth, and, 164
  liminality of, 64
  mediums and, 100
  priests and, 100
  shamanism and, 87, 94, 98
  similarity to social statuses, 54
  Turner, Edith, and, 188
  unconscious, the, and, 215, 314, 335
  Wilkins, John, 130
  Xosa and, 112
Spiritual Frontiers Fellowship (SFF), 126
Spiritualism, 23, 117, 120, 121, 125, 164, 171–73, 180, 355, 423. *See* also Davenport brothers; Fox sisters; Margery; Palladino, Eusapia; Home, D.D.; mediums
Spiritualist camps, 179, 189, 423
  liminality of, 172
Spottiswoode, James P., 207
Spraggett, Allen, 120, 125
SRI International, 168, 198, 207, 208
Srikanth, Meenakshi, 129

St. John's University (New York), 202, 324
St. Joseph's University (Philadelphia), 202
Standard Cross-Cultural Sample, 97
Stanford Research Institute, 168, 203, 207, 295, 304, 318
Stanford, Ray, 324
Stanford, Rex, 202, 205, 321, 324, 331, 338–39, 340, 341
Stanford, Thomas Welton, 197
Starhawk, 175
State University of New York at Buffalo, 148
Stefula, Joseph, 252, 254, 255, 261
Stein, Gordon, 154, 185
Stein, Murray, 38
Steiner, Ralph, 211–12
Stepanek, Pavel, 295–98
Stephen, Michele, 401
Stevenson, Ian, 202, 324
Stevenson, Robert Louis, 193
stigmata, 78, 79, 80, 83
Stigmata, 82
Stillings, Dennis, 212, 403
Stone, W. Clement, 197
Strange Harvest, A (film), 229
Stravinsky, Igor, 60
structuralism, 22, 25, 41, 43, 46, 59, 64, 96, 274, 279, 309, 310, 341, 343, 361–62, 368–76, 385, 390, 395, 426, 427
  as anti-causal, 370
Structuralism & Semiotics, 374
Structuralist Controversy, The, 361
Stubblebine, General Albert N., III, 168, 169, 170, 238, 242
Studies in Ethnomethodology, 279, 282
Studies In Intelligence, 222
Summers, Ian, 242
supernatural
  synonym of paranormal, 21

surrealism, 143, 385
Swann, Ingo, 129, 168, 169, 203, 318
Swedenborg, Emanuel, 169, 401, 403
Symbolic Classification, 347
Symbols, Signals and Noise, 312
synchronicity, 39, 41, 49, 68, 107, 216, 339, 384
synesthesia, 49, 56
Syracuse University, 204, 329
tabloids, 20, 21, 184
taboo, 21, 31, 37, 54, 65, 66, 67, 155, 161, 289, 305, 346, 348, 351–53, 357, 359, 366, 373, 378, 387, 388, 390, 391, 430
Taddonio, Judith, 323
Tahltan Indians, 93
Tanous, Alexander, 203
Tao of Psychology, 49
Targ, Russell, 168, 207, 318
Tart, Charles, 200, 202, 205, 289, 420
Taylor, Rogan, 135
Teachings of Don Juan, The, 127
telepathy, 29, 108, 127, 141, 162, 211, 214, 215, 310, 325, 383, 393, 420, 425, 426. *See also* ESP; psi
   charisma and, 27, 104, 106
   Derrida essay, 379, 380
   distinguishing from other types of psi, 319, 425
   experiments, 314, 316, 318
   fake, 137
   literary theory and, 27
   mystics and, 77, 80
   paranoia and, 278, 300, 419
   reflexivity and, 278
Temple University, 250
Tennyson, Alfred, 193
Tetum Ghosts and Kin, 65
Texas Southern University, 202
Theoretical Parapsychology, 208
Theories of Primitive Religion, 359

Theory of Semiotics, A, 374
Theosophical Society, 122, 123, 179, 189
Thomas Aquinas, Saint, 78
Thompson, Angela, 206
Thompson, J. J., 192
Thurston, Herbert, 76
Thurston, Howard, 124, 132
Tighe, Virginia. *See* Murphy, Bridey
Time magazine, 156, 417
Todd, Robert, 224, 234
Toelken, Barre, 67–69
Tops, The, magazine, 141
Totem and Taboo, 351, 356
Totemica, 348
totemism, 273, 344–67
   classification and, 274, 345, 350
Totemism, 347, 361
Totemism and Exogamy, 348
Transcendental Meditation, 289
Transcendental Temptation, The, 151
Transformation of Bigfoot, The, 415
transitional space, 31
transubstantiation, 105, 302, 429
travelers, 55, 59, 70
Treatment and Research of Experienced Anomalous Trauma (TREAT), 169, 237
trickster, 117
   anti-structure and, 59–62
   archetype defined, 36
   Biblical, 43–44
   breaching experiments and, 280
   characteristics, 427
   communitas and, 84
   conjuror exemplars, 141–46
   conjurors as, 134
   deconstruction and, 114
   deconstructionism and, 28, 380–83
   defined, 28

ethnomethodology and, 282, 283
Gardner, Martin, and, 294, 306
gender and, 36
hypnosis and, 138–41
imaginal realm, 406
liminality and, 112
overview, 35–47
paranoia and, 413, 417
personification, 399, 402
reflexivity and, 306, 308
revitalization movements and, 110, 112, 116
shamanism and, 87–89, 93–94
solitariness of, 134
summary of characteristics, 45
Trickster in West Africa, The, 40
Trickster Makes This World, 36
Trickster, The, 37, 78, 84, 87, 356
Trinity College, 193
Truzzi, Marcello, 137, 158, 185, 203, 208, 293
Tufts University, 48
Tunguska explosion, 240
Turkle, Sherry, 385
Turnbull, Colin, 56
Turner, Cathy (pseudonym), 256
Turner, Edith, 52, 90, 188, 189
Turner, Victor, 22, 25, 26, 27, 34, 52–60, 62, 65, 69, 70, 75, 78, 81, 82, 83, 84, 86, 88, 92, 103, 107, 113, 115, 123, 157, 164, 173, 175, 188, 339, 341, 346, 354, 364, 403, 427
gypsies and, 70
Twilight Zone Magazine, 143
Twitchell, Arthur C., Jr., 197
Tyson, Neil deGrasse, 183
U.S. Army Intelligence and Security Command, 168
U.S. News & World Report magazine, 155
U.S.S.R., 243
paranormal surge at dissolution, 22, 113, 425

UFO magazine, 228
ufology, 117, 247–49, 262, 267. *See also* MUFON; CUFOS; FUFOR
fantasy role-playing games compared with, 266
marginality of, 220, 245, 248
trickster and, 220
UFOs, 19, 20, 117, 210–18, 219–46, 393
abductions, 23, 51, 140, 169, 211, 229, 230, 237, 238, 249–67
cultural stress and, 114
Farrakhan, Louis, and, 113
hoaxes, 422
liminality of, 64, 248
loss of national pride and, 114
marginality and, 214, 217
paranoia and, 114, 416
parapsychology and, 243
trickster and, 114
UFOs and the Experience of the Sacred, 259
Ullman, Montague, 195, 318
unbounded conditions, 81, 210–18
Underdogs and Tricksters, 43, 70
University of Arizona, 59
University of California at Davis, 202
University of California at Irvine, 202
University of California at Los Angeles, 279
University of California at San Francisco, 49
University of California at Santa Barbara, 202
University of California Press, 127
University of Chicago, 52, 88, 293, 304
University of Connecticut, 403
University of Copenhagen, 335

University of Denver, 114
University of Edinburgh, 60
University of Idaho, 205
University of Illinois at Chicago, 205
University of Missouri, 166
University of Missouri-St. Louis, 82
University of Pennsylvania, 110
University of Pennsylvania Press, 187
University of Southern California, 123
University of Vienna, 289
University of Virginia, 52, 188, 202, 324
University of Wisconsin, 408
Ur-Drama, 94
Utah State University, 67
Vallee, Jacques, 25, 216, 229, 235, 262
van Gennep, Arnold, 25, 34, 52–53, 54–55, 58, 59, 92, 96, 110, 115, 157, 164, 344, 350, 360
Vanderbilt, Cornelius, 172
Variety magazine, 224
Varvoglis, Mario, 206
Vaughan, Alan, 318
Vazsonyi, Andrew, 66
Vega, Garcilaso de la, 350
Venn, J., 192
Very Peculiar People, 82
Victorian, Armen, 239
Vienna Circle, 289, 290, 293
Vilenskaya, Larissa, 207
Vivekananda, 80
Vizenor, Gerald, 27, 62, 380–81
von Neumann, John, 290
Wakdjunkaga, 30, 37–38, 42
Walker, Evan Harris, 310, 321, 331–38, 340, 341
Walker-Mattuck model of PK, 335
Wall Street Journal, 240, 252
Wallace, Alfred Russel, 193

Wallace, Anthony F. C., 24, 96, 110–12, 115, 279, 406
Walsh, Roger N., 90, 91
Walter Reed Army Medical Center, 170
Walters, Ed, 236
Wang, Hao, 290
War of the Worlds, 409
Warner, Richard, 90, 91
Warren, Charles, 205
Warwick, Dionne, 180
Washington University (St. Louis), 204
Watch the Skies!, 231, 416
Waters, T. A., 120, 132
Watts & Co., 349
Weaver, Richard L., 231, 233–35
Webb, Eddie Doyle, 115
Weber, Max, 22, 25, 26, 27, 45, 57, 95, 96, 102–9, 117, 153, 155, 160, 161, 172, 215, 302, 345, 355, 358, 360, 361, 364, 377, 400, 428, 429
  error on magic, 27, 107
  types of authority, 26, 102, 103, 109
Webster, Hutton, 90
Weinberg, Steven, 148
Weinbrenner, George, 233
Weiner, Debra H., 206
Welles, Orson, 409
Wells, Wesley, 140
Welsford, Enid, 36, 44
Weschcke, Carl Llewellyn, 185
Wescott, Joan, 36, 40, 41
West, Donald J., 144, 322–23, 324
Weyer, Edward Moffat, 90
Whaley, Bart, 120
Wheel of Life, The, 164
Wheeler, John, 200, 201
White, Rhea, 323
Who's Who in Magic, 120, 213
Whys of a Philosophical Scrivener, The, 300, 301, 302

Wigner, Eugene, 334
Wilkins, John, 130, 131
Willeford, William, 44
William James Award, 91
Williams, Walter L., 93
Wilson, Colin, 144
Wilson, Ian, 82, 83
Wimmer, Boniface, 82
Winkelman, Michael, 24, 94, 95, 96, 97–101, 105, 424
Winnebago, 37
Wiseman, Richard, 153
witchcraft, 68, 415
 accusations, 393, 415, 418
 excrement and, 45
 modern-day, 23, 117, 171, 174–76, 355, 423
Witnessed: The True Story of the Brooklyn Bridge UFO Abductions, 249
Wittgenstein, Ludwig Josef Johann, 278
Wolf, Fred Alan, 403
Wolman, Benjamin, 159
Wondrous Events, 162, 186–87
Wood, Houston, 278, 280–83, 308
Wood, Ryan, 170
Woolgar, Steve, 284, 285, 286
Worrall, Olga, 203
Wren-Lewis, John, 157, 420
Wright-Patterson Air Force Base, 233
Wundt, Wilhelm, 344
X-Files (TV show), *The*, 183, 409
Xosa, 112
Yale University, 202, 318, 376, 382, 398
Yearley, Steven, 279
Yoruba, 40, 382
Zen, 289
Zener cards, 317
Zener, Karl, 314
Zetetic Scholar, 203, 208
Zeus, 38, 39, 158

Zingrone, Nancy L., 206
Zöllner, Johann, 295
Zolotow, Maurice, 126

Printed in Great Britain
by Amazon.co.uk, Ltd.,
Marston Gate.